CRIME, CRIMINOLOGY AND PUBLIC POLICY

Frontispiece by Lotte Meitner-Graf

Crime, Criminology
and
Public Policy

Essays in Honour of
Sir Leon Radzinowicz

Edited by Roger Hood

HEINEMANN
LONDON

Heinemann Educational Books Ltd

LONDON EDINBURGH MELBOURNE AUCKLAND TORONTO
HONG KONG SINGAPORE KUALA LUMPUR
IBADAN NAIROBI JOHANNESBURG
LUSAKA NEW DELHI

ISBN o 435 82422 8
Introduction and Selection © Heinemann Educational Books 1974
First published 1974

259582

Published by Heinemann Educational Books Ltd
48 Charles Street, London W1X 8AH

Printed in Great Britain by
Morrison and Gibb Ltd, London and Edinburgh

CONTENTS

CONTRIBUTORS

Marc Ancel
Presiding Judge of the Supreme Court of France, Member of the
Institut de France, President, Centre Français de Droit Comparé,
University of Paris.

Inkeri Anttila
Professor and Director of the Institute of Criminology,
Ministry of Justice, Helsinki.

A. E. Bottoms
Senior Lecturer in Criminology, University of Sheffield.

The Rt. Hon. Lord Butler of Saffron Walden, K.G., P.C., C.H.
Master of Trinity College, Cambridge.

W. G. Carson
Lecturer in Criminology, University of Edinburgh.

Karl O. Christiansen
Professor of Criminology, Institute of Criminal Science,
University of Copenhagen.

Nils Christie
Professor of Criminology, Institute of Criminology and
Criminal Law, University of Oslo.

Donald R. Cressey
Professor of Sociology, University of California at
Santa Barbara.

Kent Greenawalt
Professor of Law, Columbia University School of Law.

Keith O. Hawkins
Research Fellow, Centre for Socio-Legal Studies and Fellow of
Wolfson College, Oxford.

The Rt. Hon. Lord Justice James
Lord Justice of Appeal.

Professor Dr. Hans-Heinrich Jescheck
Director of the Max Planck Instituts für
auslandisches und internationales Straftrecht,
Freiburg-im-Breisgau.

T. S. Lodge, C.B.E.
Formerly, Director of Research and Statistics, Home Office
Research and Scientific Department.

Manuel López-Rey
Professor, U.N. Adviser on Social Defence Planning,
Visiting Fellow at the Institute of Criminology, Cambridge.
Formerly, Chief of the United Nations Section of Social Defence.

J. P. Martin
Professor of Social Administration, University of Southampton.

F. H. McClintock
Professor of Criminology, University of Edinburgh.

Allison Morris
Assistant Director of Research, Institute of Criminology
and Fellow of Newnham College, Cambridge.

Adam Podgorecki
Professor of Sociology, University of Warsaw.

Thorsten Sellin
Professor Emeritus, University of Pennsylvania.

Peter H. Solomon, Jr.
Assistant Professor of Political Science, University
of Toronto.

The Hon. Mr. Justice J. H. Steyn
Judge of the Supreme Court of South Africa,
Cape Provincial Division.

D. A. Thomas
Assistant Director of Research, Institute of Criminology and
Fellow of Trinity Hall, Cambridge.

Giuliano Vassalli
Advocate and Professor of Penal Law, University of Rome.

Nigel D. Walker
Wolfson Professor of Criminology and Director of the
Institute of Criminology, University of Cambridge.

Herbert Wechsler
Harlan Fiske Stone Professor of Constitutional Law,
University of Columbia Law School; Director of the
American Law Institute.

D. J. West
University Reader in Clinical Criminology, Institute of
Criminology, and Fellow of Darwin College, Cambridge.

David G. T. Williams
University Lecturer in Law and Fellow of Emmanuel College, Cambridge.

Marvin E. Wolfgang
Professor of Sociology and Director, Center for Studies in
Criminology and Criminal Law, University of Pennsylvania.

ACKNOWLEDGEMENTS

I have been greatly helped by my editorial advisers Professor F. H. McClintock and Professor Marvin Wolfgang, particularly in drawing up the list of contributors to this volume. Professor McClintock also advised me in relation to a number of the papers while he was Acting Director of the Institute of Criminology, but I must take full responsibility for all the editorial decisions. I am also grateful to Miss Allison Finch and Mr. Leslie Hill for their translation of Marc Ancel's paper and to Judith Heward and Joanna Shapland for a great deal of assistance in the preparation of the papers for publication.

To thank Mr. Alan Hill, Chairman of Heinemann Educational Books seems almost superfluous since he has given that enthusiastic support for this venture which has been such a feature of his long and friendly collaboration with Sir Leon in the production of so many volumes of the *Cambridge Studies in Criminology*. He and I have been greatly helped by Paul Richardson and Philippa Stratton.

Finally, as someone who has been associated with Professor Radzinowicz for many years, first as a student, later as a colleague and now as a collaborator, I acknowledge my own indebtedness to him.

ROGER HOOD

INTRODUCTION

On the 30th of September 1973 Sir Leon Radzinowicz retired from his post as the first Wolfson Professor of Criminology at Cambridge, a post he had held since the foundation of the Institute of Criminology in 1959. He had also been Director of the Institute until 1972 when, with characteristic decisiveness, he handed over the administrative reins in order to concentrate on the next stage of his remarkable career. For although he has left the Institute, his work is far from complete. He has now embarked with vigour on further volumes of his massive and renowned *History of the English Criminal Law and Administration*; he is engaged on an extensive programme of teaching in major American Law Schools; he is travelling, still at great speed by plane and always by taxi, as an eminent consultant all over the world. Indeed it is impossible to imagine him in a state of leisurely retirement.

He has already been honoured at home and abroad—knighted in 1970; elected a Fellow of the British Academy, the first criminologist to gain this distinction; made an Honorary Foreign Member of the American Academy of Arts and Sciences, so joining a small band of outstanding British scholars; and distinguished in many other ways. Our intention in embarking upon this book was to provide an opportunity for some of Sir Leon's colleagues and friends to pay their personal tribute in appreciation of his extraordinary range of scholarship and of his exceptional contribution to the firm foundation and vigorous development of criminological studies not only at Cambridge but at many other universities in England and abroad.

It has not been easy to draw up a list of contributors to a *Festschrift* for a man with such an extensive and many-faceted career, and we are conscious that there are many who would have liked to join us in this tribute. My editorial advisers and I decided that we should try to draw representatives from the wide range of people who have been associated with Leon Radzinowicz through the various activities he promoted at the Cambridge Institute and through his international pursuits. Thus, the collection includes essays by his former colleagues in the Institute and Law Faculty of Cambridge, former students now holding university posts, distinguished scholars who have been Visiting Fellows at Cambridge, some of those in government and public life who have been closely associated with Cambridge, as well as a few of his very many friends in so many parts of the world, particularly in Western Europe, the Scandinavian countries, the Council of Europe, the United Nations, South Africa and the United States. I know that those who were not invited to join us will appreciate the need to keep this large volume within manageable proportions.

I shall not be so presumptuous as to attempt to write here a short biography of Leon Radzinowicz. He personally is, and his career has been, far too complex for an assessment in a few pages by someone who has known him in only one of the many sectors of his life. Nevertheless, I shall point to some of the most important features of his career, particularly at Cambridge, and relate them to the contributors and to the subjects chosen by them. They have each dealt with a theme which reflects his interests and concerns. But that was hardly difficult to arrange for he is renowned for his exceptional diversity of scholarship, his extensive experience in public life, his unrivalled international knowledge and his catholic interests ranging, as they do, through penal philosophy, criminological theory and the history of ideas, the history of criminal law and penal developments, the empirical study of the phenomenon of crime, the implications of ideas and research findings for public policy as well as the wider international and historical assessments and comparisons of crime and punishments in their varying political and social settings. He has always insisted that matters of penal policy, 'the systematic study of all the measures to be taken in the spheres of prevention (direct and indirect), of legislation, of the enforcement of the criminal law, of punishments and other methods of treatment, constitute an indisputable and integral part of criminology' and that 'to rob it of this practical function is to divorce criminology from reality and render it sterile'. On the other hand he has never been one of those heady social 'scientists' who believe that knowledge of crime and the effects of penalties will alone determine the shape of public policy. In his *In Search of Criminology* he warned 'criminologists must be aware that the specific solution of many legal and penal problems cannot be determined exclusively, or even predominantly by the factual criminological evidence which they can provide. There are deep rooted and far reaching issues of public morality, of social expediency, of the subtle and vital balance between the rights of the individual and the protection of the community, which underlie decisions of penal policy, and must often override the conclusions of the experts'. And it is for this reason that I have chosen the title *Crime, Criminology and Public Policy* for these essays written in his honour.

No one should underestimate the persistence and effort which went into creating in Cambridge a climate in which criminology could germinate and flourish. Dr. Radzinowicz's involvement began soon after he had arrived in

England on behalf of the Polish government in 1938. By 1940 Volume One of *English Studies in Criminal Science* had been edited by Radzinowicz and his close friend J. W. Cecil Turner and published under the auspices of a Committee set up by the Cambridge Law Faculty to consider the promotion of research and teaching in Criminal Science under the Chairmanship of Professor Winfield. In 1945, when the small Department of Criminal Science had been established, the fourth volume in the series *The Modern Approach to Criminal Law* contained a masterly outline of the scope of criminological studies by Radzinowicz and Turner as well as a series of articles by Radzinowicz on various aspects of the English penal scene which illustrated his unique blending of the historical with the contemporary, the theoretical with the empirical, the pragmatic with a humanitarian concern. But despite the presence in their midst of someone so obviously gifted in a subject so far undeveloped by the British (and only with continental footholds established by Mannheim in London and Grünhut in Oxford) Cambridge remained sceptical. Sir Leon is fond of recalling that in these days it was hardly an exaggeration to say that Cambridge 'was more frightened of criminologists than of criminals'. But in 1946 he was appointed an A.D.R. and in 1949 made Director of the Department of Criminal Science. During the next ten years, besides working upon his *History*, he directed the research of the Department towards the collection of basic data on crime and the operation of the penal system, the lack of which he had already complained of in his essays. The most notable of these studies was *Sexual Offences* which combined the empirical element (largely carried out by F. H. McClintock whom he had brought as a young man into his team) with a consideration of problems in the administration and interpretation of the Criminal Law. I am confident that this was an angle not then considered at all relevant to criminology even in the widest sense, but now, of course, the subject is spreading to include attempts to understand legal norms and their interpretation. This growing interest is marked in this volume by Dr. West's perceptive remarks on the case for sexual law reform.

It was this concern for solid empirical research together with an unrivalled knowledge of criminology and criminal policy in its historical and contemporary frameworks which, as Lord Butler points out, made Leon Radzinowicz the outstanding candidate to be head of an Institute of Criminology when, as Home Secretary, he made his approach to the Universities in 1958. Lord Butler's account of the establishment of the Institute will, no doubt, dispel much of the ill-informed gossip which surrounds that subject. But more important, it emphasizes the weight he attached to Professor Radzinowicz's other major attributes—his energy, determination and a personal vivacity combining great persuasiveness, charm, wit and remarkable foresight—characteristics which would be needed if the Institute newly-founded were to survive in a sceptical world. Conscious as he was that all eyes were on the new venture (which at the time attracted enormous publicity) Professor Radzinowicz's major priority throughout his Directorship was to ensure the success of its programme in all its aspects—teaching, research, as a national centre for meetings and exchange of information, in its contacts with and service for practitioners, in building up an unrivalled specialist library and in fostering international connections. His own enthusiasm, drive and political acumen were concentrated on maintaining unimpeded progress and avoiding the set-backs which occur when goods are not delivered. He saw his task as Director to *direct*, and while he never made decisions without wide consultations, once he had decided a course of action he moved ahead with an absolute determination, not characteristic of most academics, and with a will that was respected and in some quarters even feared. He was not a man to court popularity or put personal friendship before what he saw to be the interests of the Institute and undoubtedly the exacting standards he set for himself and others did not make him the easiest of bosses. But it did ensure that we owe to him the fact that the Cambridge Institute of Criminology was firmly established with a world wide reputation.

The research programme of the Institute was, from the start, diverse, reflecting the different academic backgrounds and interests of the senior staff in charge of the projects. Of particular prominence were the enquiries on various aspects of the state of crime in England undertaken by F. H. McClintock. His contribution to this volume on facts and myths about the state of crime reviews some of the major advantages and pitfalls of these fundamental studies which continue to provide the only detailed data available about reported crime and known criminals. Other projects included Professor Martin's on the cost of crime, a major element of which was the attempt to assess the use of police resources: he has brought us up to date with the problems of this approach in his essay. A further area was the longitudinal study of delinquent development undertaken by Dr. West, and this approach is reflected in Professor Marvin Wolfgang's account of the career of a cohort of young men in Philadelphia and in the final reassessment by Professor Christiansen of his famous Danish twin studies. It is true, as Nigel Walker once pointed out, that the Cambridge tradition had been largely empirical rather than theoretical, and certainly Leon Radzinowicz had on a number of occasions made sceptical remarks about the futility of searching for the causes of crime. It is therefore refreshing that Professor Walker, the new Wolfson Professor, has chosen to contribute a critique of two contrasting types of causal explanation.

Despite the tremendous drain on time and energy devoted to the Institute, Leon Radzinowicz continued with his own academic work. The publication of the first volume of his History in 1948 was marked by exceptional praise, by his election to a Fellowship at Trinity College (to which he is deeply attached) and by the James Barr Ames Prize and Medal awarded by the Harvard Law School in 1950. The second and third volumes appeared in 1956 and the fourth in 1968. Altogether they mark an extraordinary achievement, yet in retrospect it might even be thought a strange topic for a foreign-trained criminologist to choose, particularly at a time when the academic fashion was for studies of the contemporary penal scene or for social surveys or field work of various kinds. While, perhaps, history was not regarded necessarily as 'bunk', it was considered hardly relevant to criminology. Indeed when it was announced that Leon Radzinowicz was to be the first Professor of Criminology, one leading newspaper noted that although he was a distinguished legal historian 'it is unlikely that his researches will have practical consequences'—a sentiment that was echoed more or less quietly by some academic criminologists. How times have changed! And how he has been proved right in seeking to understand the more complex relationships of crime, public attitudes and official reaction to it, by using the historical and comparative method. At the very least the historical perspective shows how few of the problems of public policy are new and at its best it aids our understanding of the shifting patterns of ideas and practice in the penal field. Indeed, historical studies are now almost *de rigueur* among modern sociologists of law and deviance. Naturally, the historical approach is represented here. Professor Sellin, an old friend and the first Visiting Fellow from the United States to the Institute writes on Slavery and Crime and W. G. Carson, a former member of the Cambridge postgraduate course, has chosen to explore the social and political factors underlying the emergence of the Factory Acts.

Professor Radzinowicz has chosen a number of occasions to deliver public lectures and contribute incisive articles to the Press on controversial issues of policy. He has in his History and in recent years, been particularly concerned with the rôle of the police at times when there is public pressure to grapple more effectively with crime. His experience, particularly of Europe in the thirties, has made him especially wary of measures for the control of crime which can become distorted and instruments of repression. He raised this subject recently in his lecture *Them and Us* and the theme is developed in two contributions, one on the accountability of the police by his Cambridge Law Faculty colleague, David Williams, and the other on the right to silence written by his Columbia Law School colleague, Kent Greenawalt during his recent visit to the Institute in Cambridge in 1973. Professor

Cressey, sometime a Visiting Fellow at the Institute, has illustrated yet another facet of discretion in criminal justice in his analysis of the police rôle in relation to motoring offenders. The wider issues surrounding control over the exercise of judicial and administrative discretion in the penal system are discussed by David Thomas, whose *Principles of Sentencing* was brought into the Cambridge Series by Leon Radzinowicz.

He has also had a very active public life. He was a member of the Royal Commission on Capital Punishment; of the Advisory Council on the Treatment of Offenders; of the Royal Commission on the Penal System, where his resignation was a decisive factor in causing this ineffective enquiry to be dissolved; of the Advisory Council on the Penal System, being particularly influential as Chairman of the sub-committee which rejected Lord Mountbatten's plans for a British 'Alcatraz' in favour of a more humane environment for long-term dangerous prisoners. In my own essay I have tried to reflect on some of the assumptions about crime and punishment made by British government enquiries and on the part that criminological knowledge has played in the formulation of policy. A. E. Bottoms and Allison Morris have contributed case studies of the background to the recent reforms of the English and Scottish Juvenile Justice systems. Their essays provide fascinating examples of the benefits to be gained from the study of how penal change occurs.

To some extent the grants and facilities for research that the Home Office has given the Institute, have led to speculation in some quarters about the independence of the Institute from those who control penal affairs. It is therefore very valuable to read the account by Mr. Tom Lodge, who built up the Home Office Research Unit, of the work carried out there, and his frank assessment of the relationship between the Home Office and outside bodies. While Leon Radzinowicz was obviously delighted to be able to count on the financial support of the Home Office he has always emphasized that the Institute's strength, unlike many other organizations, lay in having a permanent senior staff paid out of University central funds. As his attitude to the Royal Commission on the Penal System showed, the support of the Home Office did not deter him from taking an independent line on a number of important controversial issues.

Among his most important accomplishments at the Institute was the establishment of the post-graduate course leading to the Diploma in Criminology. He was anxious as he put it 'to give a chance to young people in this country to start to specialize in criminology', and the course undoubtedly did so. It not only attracted many good students but eventually provided a substantial number of those who are now teaching or carrying out research in British Universities as well as several overseas. Four of the contributors were former members of the course, Tony Bottoms, Kit Carson, Allison Morris and Keith Hawkins (who went on to complete a doctorate under Professor Radzinowicz's supervision).

In addition to this course, the Professor also set about ensuring that the Institute would be a centre for criminological discussion. Biennial National Conferences were organized around a variety of themes, some of them strictly criminological but others appealing to broader issues of policy such as the sessions on the Codification of Criminal Law held in 1970. Anyone who considers that such a subject is of no concern to criminologists or sociologists of law should read Professor Herbert Wechsler's paper which is an expanded version of his notable address to that conference. In addition his paper marks the very warm and close collaboration he has had with Leon Radzinowicz for nearly three decades. Contacts and exchanges were fostered on a wide front. At home the Senior Course in Criminology was established as a biennial seminar for senior practitioners in various areas concerned with the administration of justice and the penal system. They and post-graduate students received the stimulation of sentencing seminars conducted originally with the strong support of Lord Parker, by a number of distinguished High Court judges among whom was Lord Justice James who has marked the contribution of the judiciary to the Institute by his commentary on David Thomas's essay on discretion in the criminal process. On the international plane the highly successful Cambridge–Columbia exchange scheme, involving a two-way traffic of both staff and students, was established entirely on the basis of Professor Radzinowicz's outstanding reputation in the United States. In 1962 he had been Walter Meyer Visiting Professor at Yale and later, when others would have been contemplating a quiet run-in to retirement, he launched on a vigorous new career. After the highly praised Carpentier Lectures delivered at Columbia Law School in 1965, which were subsequently published as the little masterpiece *Ideology and Crime*, he became in 1968 Adjunct Professor at Columbia, travelling there twice a year to introduce criminology to an enthusiastic audience at his seminars. Not content with this he accepted invitations to lecture at the Law Schools of Virginia and Rutgers and in the Centre for Criminology at Pennsylvania directed by his friend Marvin Wolfgang who had collaborated with him in co-editing the three-volume *Crime and Justice* when he had been Visiting Fellow in Cambridge. Sir Leon's concern to see criminology become part of the curriculum of the great Law Schools and to have an independent status in an Institute is reflected in his important concise report for the Bar Association of the City of New York and the Ford Foundation, published as *The Need for Criminology*. It was indeed a great tribute to him personally and to the reputation of Cambridge that a foreigner should have been invited to advise the Americans on a subject where they already had the resources of what Leon Radzinowicz himself had called, in *In Search of Criminology*, 'a vast laboratory'. Obviously what had impressed the Americans was the success of the concentrated effort embodied in the Cambridge model under its dynamic leader. At a later stage he was involved in yet another capacity in American public life as an active consultant to President Johnson's Commission on the Causes and Prevention of Violence.

Of course Leon Radzinowicz's links with the continent of Europe have remained strong. When he came to England in 1938 he already had an established career behind him. In the old tradition he had travelled with remarkable precocity and intensity between the great centres of learning. At an extraordinarily young age he gained degrees in Paris and Rome where he was an outstanding student of Enrico Ferri, completing a thesis on the indeterminate sentence. He then went to Geneva, where at the age of 23 he became Assistant Professor. On returning to Poland he added a further doctorate from Cracow, became Assistant Professor at the Free University of Warsaw and undertook empirical enquiries into a number of important topics, most notably the relationship between economic conditions and crime, the results of which were published in the *Sociological Review* and are still regarded as one of the major contributions to the subject. He was active in Belgium where as a young man he was awarded the Chevalier de l'ordre de Leopold in 1930 for his critical study of the Belgian penal reform. But it is not only the richness of this experience or his command of all the major European languages which makes him unique among criminologists. He had been steeped in the great debates on penal philosophy which have resounded around Europe. These debates are elegantly recalled and put in their contemporary context in this volume by President Marc Ancel whose collaboration with Leon Radzinowicz goes back to their jointly edited *Introduction au droit Criminel de l'Angleterre* published in France in 1959, and since then continually expressing itself in so many other valuable ways. They are also given a rather novel twist by Professor Nils Christie whose analysis of research findings leads him back towards a twentieth-century version of the Classical School. Other European developments are also discussed in this volume. The problems of Italian society and its penal machinery are vividly portrayed in Professor Vassalli's review of the Parliamentary Commission on the Mafia. Professor Vassalli was also a student of Rome's criminological school, which was so greatly influenced by Enrico Ferri. The contrasting penal ideologies and crime problems of the two Germanies are discussed in Professor Jescheck's insightful analysis. Peter Solomon has contributed an account of the politics of criminology in the Soviet Union to add to the valuable bibliography on Russian Criminology which he prepared for the

Cambridge Institute at Professor Radzinowicz's invitation a few years ago. Professor Podgorecki, writing from Sir Leon's native Poland, not only reflects the latter's own impatience with mere speculation about the effects of laws, but provides the kind of cross-cultural perspective of which both most heartily approve.

This concern for Europe was nowhere more apparent than in the time and effort he gave to the Council of Europe. As his friend from Finland, Professor Anttila, recalls, he was the first Chairman of the Scientific Council of the Division on Crime Problems, shaping its programme and giving it a practical direction. In particular he gave the younger criminologists of Europe an opportunity to present their views at the Annual Conference of Directors of Criminological Research Institutes. He was also the instigator of the recent successful collaboration between Scandinavian and English criminologists, which is marked in this volume by Tony Bottom's paper, presented to the first Conference held in Norway in 1971.

Leon Radzinowicz has also had a long standing involvement with the United Nations. In 1945 he was in charge of the Section for Social Defence in New York, where he recruited to his staff Karl Otto Christiansen from Denmark, a contributor to this volume. His tenure was marked by the important publications on Probation and on International Collaboration in Criminal Science. Sir Leon's international standing and his reputation as an outspoken frank commentator was acknowledged when he was invited to be the first General Rapporteur of a United Nation's Congress to come from outside governmental circles. His address to the Kyoto Conference in 1971 was a brilliant assessment of the basic problems which still have to be tackled to ensure even a minimum of decent standards in the administration of justice and the treatment of offenders throughout the member nations. The rôle of the United Nations in the field of crime problems is a topic of great importance and it is discussed in this volume by the leading expert Professor Manuel López-Rey, a regular Visiting Fellow to the Institute, with his characteristic frankness and freshness.

In recent years Professor Radzinowicz has undertaken more work all over the world—visiting South America, the Far East, Yugoslavia, Australia, where he is an Honorary Foreign Member of the Australian Academy of Forensic Sciences and South Africa. This last journey he made as a bold attempt to lend support, in a totally uncompromising way, to those in South Africa who are attempting to establish an independent Institute of Criminology at the University of Cape Town and promote change in the South African penal system. One of his main sponsors on that trip was Judge Steyn of the Supreme Court in Cape Town, the President of the newly formed National Institute for the Crime Prevention and Rehabilitation of

Offenders. It is a fine tribute to the importance of that visit that he should have written such an enlightening and frank assessment of the present state of affairs in his country.

All of us who have contributed to this volume hope that in our essays some of the qualities and perspectives which Sir Leon Radzinowicz has brought to the study of criminology and penal policy have emerged. It is in admiration of his extraordinary talent and in gratitude for the service he has done in promoting our subject and establishing its academic reputation that we pay him this tribute.

ROGER HOOD

THE FOUNDATION OF
THE INSTITUTE OF CRIMINOLOGY
IN CAMBRIDGE

Lord Butler

When I became Home Secretary early in 1957 the mood of Parliament and the country favoured a radical reappraisal of the penal system. There was a strong case for a thorough review of the prisons; to improve archaic conditions, to make the concept of training a reality and to remove as many from prison as could be dealt with safely by non-custodial alternatives. The slow pace of change in the prisons combined with agitation and even alarm at the continuing rise in crime, particularly by the young, had led to a call from all sides for more effective action.

I was determined that there should be a long-term plan: a course of action that would lay a path for an enlightened penal policy. In particular I believed that changes should not be based on swings in emotion and opinion, prone as they are to the influence of dramatic events and bizarre cases, but upon reliable information about the phenomenon of crime, its social and personal roots and the effectiveness of the preventive and penal measures available. My review of the evidence at hand to the Home Office and of the expenditure on research was the biggest single shock which came to me in the whole area of penal policy. Two months later in a Supply debate on the Supplementary Estimates for the Prison Commissioners I told the House that such was the paucity of information at my disposal that planning ahead was virtually impossible. I had ascertained that since 1948, when the Home Secretary was given power to spend money on research into criminological and penal matters, only £12,000 had been allocated—a hopelessly inadequate sum. Although some useful work had begun in the Universities on studies of borstal, approved schools and probation, this was only scratching the surface. A handful of research workers were attempting to undertake investigations into one of the most intractable problems on shoe-string budgets. It is no wonder, looking back, that their methods were often rudimentary. I therefore pledged as my first priority the expansion of the research programme. But how was it to be achieved? How was the work to be organized? What would be the respective roles of the Government and independent organizations?

The Criminal Justice Bill of 1948, as presented to Parliament, had not contained any power for the Government to undertake research itself or to provide funds to Universities or other independent bodies. In this respect it differed from both the Education Act of 1944 and the National Health Service Act of 1946. A memorandum drawing attention to this omission and stating a strong case for Government support of research was circulated to the Standing Committee by Major Vernon, M.P., and later incorporated into an amendment by Mr. Victor Collins (later Lord Stonham). The paper drew attention not only to the vast social cost of crime and law enforcement but also to the types of research which it was considered might lead to a reduction in these costs in the future. Major Vernon concluded that investigation into the origins, causes and treatment of recidivism might open the door to methods of social and psychological intervention at an early stage in delinquent careers and so cut off at source the supply of habitual prisoners. The money spent on research, he claimed, could be expected to earn 'enormous dividends'. Such enquiries, he recognized, would have to be undertaken by teams of research workers with varying backgrounds—sociologists, statisticians, psychologists and psychiatrists—some of it within the Government service and some by independent bodies. A sum of about £50,000 a year was suggested, to be apportioned equally between these two interests. Wisely he noted that the beginning might have to be slow because of the small number of trained research workers but he recognized that unless the Government committed itself to establishing expanding opportunities for research no one would train for it. Thus the proposals were optimistic in their belief that expenditure on research could bring tangible results in the form of decreasing crime and ambitious in their intent to establish a flourishing programme of criminological studies. The Home Secretary agreed to insert a new clause at the Report stage of the Bill, and section 77 (b) empowered the Secretary of State to incur expenses 'in the conduct of research into the causes of delinquency and the treatment of offenders, and matters connected therewith . . . to such amount as may be sanctioned by the Treasury'.

The first provisions for contributing to criminological research were made in the estimates for 1951/52 when £1,500 was allocated. It was devoted mainly to the first stages of the now famous borstal prediction study by Dr. Hermann Mannheim and Mr. Leslie Wilkins who was then at the Government Social Survey. Small amounts were also given to Dr. Grünhut at Oxford and Dr. Radzinowicz at Cambridge to begin empirical research. The grants were welcomed by Mr. (later Sir) George Benson of the Howard League who congratulated the Home Office on realizing 'the futility of groping in the twilight of surmise and conjecture'. Yet, as he said, 'In relation to our ignorance £1,500 is a pitiful sum'. But the growth from then on was much slower than Mr. Vernon and others could ever have expected in 1948. By 1955/56 the annual expenditure was still only £2,500. The borstal prediction study had been completed and so had Dr. Grünhut's book on variations in the disposal of juvenile offenders before courts in different parts of the country. At Cambridge work proceeded on the follow-up study of the results of probation and attendance centres and on a valuable study of sexual offenders: in addition a new large-scale enquiry on violence had begun. In London two studies on the use of short-term imprisonment were underway. At the Home Office, Mr. Wilkins had been appointed during 1956 as a research officer to undertake enquiries which otherwise would have been passed to the Social Survey. Thus, at the beginning of 1957 there was only a very modest programme of research in the Universities. In the main research workers were employed on short-term contracts with limited opportunities before them for a career in research or teaching in criminology. There was no strong organization either within the Home Office or outside to give an impetus to research nor, despite the pioneering teaching in London, Oxford and Cambridge, was there anywhere where a student could gain any training at the graduate level other than through the rigours of the Ph.D. Furthermore there was no meeting ground in an academic setting between research workers and teachers and those with responsibility for formulating and executing penal policy. Before the end of 1957 the prospect for the future had changed remarkably.

In May 1957 I was able to announce the formation of the Home Office Research Unit consisting then of two research workers and four civil servants, and in June—prompted I was told by my undertaking to promote research—I received a letter from Mr. Klare, the Secretary of the Howard League for Penal Reform, asking me to give my support to a proposal to establish an Institute of Criminology by approaching the Vice-Chancellors of the Universities. I discussed the tentative proposals in the letter with Lord Drogheda, Chairman of the Advisory Council on the Treatment of Offenders, and Miss Margery Fry, representing the Howard League, a month later. The case for an independent Institute was clearly a strong one. As Mr. Klare and Miss Fry pointed out, there was not a single chair of criminology in England whereas on the continent most countries had one or more Institutes. Furthermore, the impending retirement of Dr. Mannheim in London and Dr. Grünhut in Oxford 'involved the risk that the subject might disappear altogether from two of the three universities where it was at present established'. The scope of the work of the Institute appeared to present no problems—it would, in particular, establish post-graduate teaching to stimulate the development of criminology through the training of teachers and research workers of high competence and act as a central meeting place for all those concerned with both the academic and practical side as well as being a leading centre for research. However, the questions relating to its organization to achieve these objectives and its location were much more difficult issues. The Howard League had in mind an Institute with a director (possibly part-time) and full-time secretary but drawing its lecturers and researchers from the various relevant faculties within the University. Thus it would be more like a Centre or 'confederation' of experts with a common interest whose appointments were in general made on the basis of their contribution to their parent faculties. Miss Fry estimated that it would need no more than one lecture room, an office and a good library. Partly because this was the structure envisaged, the University of London with its well-developed faculties of social science and psychiatric medicine was seen as the appropriate base. It is possible that in these early proposals the League had not dared hope for an autonomous organization with the funds to appoint its own staff representing the necessary discipline. For this reason Miss Fry did not think that it would be so useful to build upon the Department of Criminal Science in Cambridge. While recognizing the valuable work being carried out by Dr. Radzinowicz and his collaborators she felt that an Institute in Cambridge was likely to continue too closely the close links with criminal law. Cambridge had no well-developed departments of sociology, social psychology or psychiatry nor was it within reach of so many penal and medical institutions or of areas which might be the subject of field work as a London Institute would be. While I recognized the force of these arguments I wanted to give the matter further consideration for I felt that the department at Cambridge would provide the best nucleus. In addition to all the other arguments it was necessary to find a suitable man to be the Director of this new venture. If the Institute were to be a success it had to be launched by a person of outstanding academic reputation and powerful personality. Yet in the end the choice was not made between two competing Universities as many have since supposed—London remained barely luke-warm while Cambridge was enthusiastic and vital in its negotiations.

I was convinced that I should do everything possible to promote an Institute which would be independent of the Home Office. In November 1957 at the Annual General Meeting of the Howard League I said, 'I intend through various contacts to see that this proposal will be seriously considered, not just by the Government, because it is not primarily our business, but by the Universities. Crime and its treatment seem to me to be no less suitable as a subject for study and teaching by the universities than a number of other social phenomena; and this is a field in which we particularly need the help and urge of the informed but detached public opinion which the universities are so well able to produce.' Indeed there was a great deal of support in Parliament and in the press—the London evening paper *The Star* ran a campaign on its leading pages—for an Institute which would be such an educational force in the community.

It seems that at first the Howard League had merely sought my approval to act as a stimulus to the universities. But it was soon clear that, as I believed the impetus should come from the Government and not from private trusts, the University Grants Committee would need to make a special grant. With a financial climate as dismal as it was at that time the new venture needed the strongest push from the Home Secretary. Once the financial basis was provided by the Government I hoped that outside sources would be encouraged to make their contributions.

In March 1958 I wrote to Lord Adrian, the Vice-Chancellor of Cambridge University, and Mr. John Lockwood, the Vice-Chancellor of London, outlining the case for an Institute and asking whether their University would be willing to give this impetus to criminological studies. Within three weeks of my informal enquiry a meeting had taken place between the authorities in Cambridge and my senior officials. They were most sympathetic to the proposal especially because it was felt that Cambridge, with its substantial current commitment to the Department of Criminal Science, could establish a fully-fledged Institute more easily than any other university. If they could be assured that the new Institute would not be in competition for existing funds with other departments there would be a good prospect of a favourable decision.

It was in June that my officials had a meeting with the representatives of London University who made it quite clear that there was no prospect of a new Institute being established there in the foreseeable future. This was partly, it seems, because of doubts about its functions, partly because there was a feeling that there were already enough Institutes of various kinds in the University, but very largely because they took the view that an Institute which cut across different faculties had no prospect of success unless a really outstanding man could be found as its first director and they were unable to find a suitable candidate in London. It was in this respect, in particular, that Cambridge was in a far stronger position. Two of the three leading figures in British criminology, Dr. Mannheim at the L.S.E. and Dr. Grünhut at Oxford, were at the end of their academic careers. Both had nurtured some promising students but they were all still in junior academic posts. By contrast, Cambridge had as its Director of the Department of Criminal Science the third leading British criminologist, Dr. Leon Radzinowicz who combined both academic distinction and remarkable personal drive. His *History of the English Criminal Law* had been widely acclaimed for its extraordinary illumination of the nexus of crime and punishment in their social and political contexts of the nation's life. The intended organization there would also overcome some of the difficulties feared at London and to some extent neutralize the criticism that a Cambridge Institute would be dominated by lawyers. The specialists in the various disciplines necessary for a comprehensive study of criminology—sociology, statistics, penology, psychiatry and criminal law—were to be appointed to work solely in the Institute on the same basis as the existing appointments in the Department of Criminal Science. There would be no question of divided loyalties, competition for staff time, reliance on sometimes ephemeral interests and the necessity of attempting to persuade factions to co-operate. The Director would thus be in a position to develop with his colleagues a specific programme, and there would be the continuity of staff to see it successfully completed. Although the Institute would be within the Faculty of Law it would have the guidance of a Committee of Management representing other faculties with relevant concerns. On 31 July 1958, just over four months after my initial letter to Lord Adrian, I announced to Parliament that Cambridge would establish the Institute if sufficient funds could be made available.

As far as money for research was concerned I had raised the estimate for grants, to the Universities and other outside bodies, from just over £3,000 in 1956/57 to £10,000 in 1957/58. However, funds were needed towards premises and the library and for the appointment of permanent staff whose employment would not always be subject to the vagaries of research budgets. At first the financial situation looked intractable because the U.G.C. neither had the money to provide for the remaining three years of the quinquennium nor could commit itself to anything in the following period. The Nuffield Foundation generously offered £25,000 for these first three years on the understanding that support would be forthcoming in the following quinquennium, but as it turned out a slight easing of the situation made it possible for the U.G.C. to give a capital grant of £15,000 towards the building and library and a reasonable sum for current expenditure (an average of £7,000 a year) together with an indication that the University could look to the U.G.C. for at least an equal sum in the next quinquennium. But to put the Institute on a firm financial base it was necessary to raise more, particularly if the size of staff was to be expanded to include the Chair and four senior posts. While the University would not have objected in principle to a direct grant from the Home Office vote it was our view that it would be far better if this could be avoided and funds secured from an independent source. It was most important in my view that the Institute should be seen to be entirely separate from the Home Office, although of course the two bodies would need to work in close association. I therefore wrote to Lord Nathan, the Chairman of the newly-founded Isaac Wolfson Trust, and this resulted in a handsome sum of £150,000 to endow the Wolfson Chair and another senior post (originally intended as a Readership but established as the Deputy Directorship) with any remaining funds to be used perhaps for an appropriate building. In the event there was not enough to house the Institute properly and it is my one regret that we did not press ahead at that time to secure the funds to make this possible. But this is a relatively minor matter. What is important is that we had managed, with the aid of the Wolfson Trust, to establish an Institute whose resources in terms of permanent appointments at a senior level would be the envy of other institutions throughout the world; and all within one year of beginning negotiations. It was particularly gratifying to me that this remarkable development should have taken place in my own university, to which I had just had the honour of being appointed High Steward.

The scope of the work of the Institute was outlined in the White Paper *Penal Practice in a Changing Society*, in which I gave prominence to the great importance the Home Office attached to research. Paragraph 22 stated:

The institute would be broadly based; and it would be closely linked with all the faculties concerned in any aspect of the study of delinquency. It would necessarily have to keep itself informed of all that is being done in the furtherance of that study, both at home and abroad. Its purposes would be various. It would teach criminology, especially on the post-graduate level; and it would undertake and encourage research on the highest academic standard. It would therefore not only itself contribute to our knowledge of criminology; it would help to produce the teachers of that subject, and the highly qualified research workers, who are at present so scarce. It would also, it may be hoped, be able from time to time to bring together groups of those concerned with the administration of justice and the treatment of offenders. By doing so it would help to keep them abreast of current thought and the findings of research; and it would at the same time strengthen its own contacts with those doing the practical work of which it would study the results. Finally, the institute should be able, as no existing agency is in a position to do, to survey with academic impartiality—in the light of the results of the research effort as a whole—the general problem of the criminal in society, its causes and its solution.

The more detailed programme on which this statement was based was formulated by Dr. Radzinowicz who became the first Wolfson Professor and Director in the summer of 1959. In addition to the post-graduate course of intensive seminars and practical placements, teaching was extended to undergraduates reading for the law tripos, for here were a group of young people, many of whose future careers might be enriched and shaped by the study of the characteristics of those with whom they would deal in the criminal process. On the other side the commitment to teaching non-university courses to those engaged in administrative and executive positions of the various agencies dealing with offenders was more restricted than perhaps originally conceived and put into an academic context at a higher level. Every two years short courses of about four weeks were to be held for senior police, prison, probation and children's officers, magistrates, and magistrates' clerks. This would provide for the exchange of views so necessary both for the practitioner and the academic, while at the same time not overburdening the Institute's staff with general training functions and leaving them free for their research. On the research side the programme was to be essentially pragmatic. As Professor Radzinowicz's report stated:

> The Institute would aim to provide an environment in which systematically planned research on problems of limited scope would in time build up a body of objective information and lead eventually to the solution of more fundamental issues. It would be concerned with such problems as trends in crime, the treatment of offenders, the medical and social aspects of criminal behaviour, the administration and enforcement of the criminal law and the reform both of the substantive criminal law and of criminal procedure.

Through its library, publication of research, distribution of bulletins, organization of conferences and international activities, the Institute was to be a true centre for the interchange of information on criminological matters.

It was certainly an ambitious programme for a small staff of a Director and four other permanent senior members. In general the announcement of the Institute's establishment was well received with feature and leading articles in the major newspapers, but in some quarters the response was lukewarm. On the one hand there were those who considered the solutions to the problem of crime to be self-evident, and on the other there were still doubts whether Cambridge was the right place for the Institute to be. Typical of the first category was a leading article in the *Daily Telegraph* doubting whether Professor Radzinowicz's researchers would achieve any practical results. 'His department may well make illuminating contributions to the philosophy of law. It may also provide agreeable summer schools, in which magistrates, youth workers and the police can exchange experiences. But the causes of crime are always so much what they always have been that they are unlikely to be removed by giving them a different name'. Apparently the *Daily Telegraph* thought it more important that the Government should take the right attitude: 'All need to inspire a detestation spreading from the very top throughout society of the shoddiness of mind from which crime springs.' Perhaps such views, and others favouring heavier deterrents as a more speedy remedy than research, were to be expected for, of course, it was precisely this approach which I hoped in the long run would be counteracted by the educative impact of the Institute.

On the academic side the coolness was perhaps best reflected by the formal announcement without comment in the London-based *British Journal of Delinquency*. A long comment on the section devoted to research in the White Paper ended tartly 'In the same section there follows a paragraph on the Institute of Criminology to be established at Cambridge and on the advantages expected from it'. Some criminologists who had criticized the research carried out in the Department of Criminal Science still waited to be convinced that the new organization would set a standard of excellence expected of a national institution.

This is not the place to review the progress of the Institute over thirteen years but it is necessary to say that it has achieved, with a staff that has hardly expanded at all, remarkable success in nearly all the fields originally envisaged by its proposers. First, the post-graduate course has been a major source of supply of teachers and research workers in this country and overseas—I am told that nearly fifty former graduates hold such posts. The other developments in teaching, especially the senior course and the recently founded Cropwood scheme of Round Table Conferences and Visiting Fellowships for those involved in penal matters have kept the Institute to the forefront in educating those facing the practical problems of the criminal justice and penal systems. It has not been insular. An active part has been played in the United Nations, in the Council of Europe and in many international gatherings of experts. Throughout, the Institute has kept in close liaison with the Home Office, has been practical in its outlook and energetic in its research activities. The magnificent library of the Institute is one of the best in the world as a specialist collection—its renaming recently as the Radzinowicz Library is a tribute to Sir Leon's energy and resourcefulness in establishing it as a major centre not only for the Institute's own teaching and research but for many other scholars. On the publishing side the Cambridge series consisting of works by members of the Institute and many distinguished criminologists from other Universities and overseas has now reached thirty volumes. The Series is unique and still going strong. But it is now increasingly recognized that it is a painfully slow business to produce conclusive findings of direct practical importance. The dream of Major Vernon in 1948 is as far away as ever and, perhaps paradoxically, it has been one of the strengths of the Institute and its Director that from the start it has recognized the elusiveness of finding the causes of crime or effective measures to combat it.

Undoubtedly it is to the credit of the Institute in Cambridge that criminology has now been firmly established as a subject of vital academic importance in so many universities. I count my involvement in its foundation as one of the most significant acts of my term as Home Secretary: perhaps in the long run it will prove the one I shall be remembered for.

It has given me great pleasure to have the opportunity to write this article as a tribute to Professor Sir Leon Radzinowicz. He was chosen, as I have noted, as the first Wolfson Professor because of his drive and imagination. That drive and imagination ensured a national and international reputation for the Institute of Criminology within only a few years of its establishment. The Institute will continue to prosper as a result of the initiative which he inspired.

THE FOUNDING OF
THE HOME OFFICE RESEARCH UNIT

T. S. Lodge

At first sight it might seem strange to offer, for publication in a volume dedicated to the founder of the Institute of Criminology, an article about another research organization. But this would be to ignore the close links between the Institute and the Research Unit and also their common origin in the forces that for many years had been building up to make inevitable the development in Great Britain of scientific criminological research. Still less is it inappropriate to present such an article in a volume honouring Sir Leon Radzinowicz personally. He did much to stimulate the interest in criminology that grew rapidly from the 1930s onwards, himself undertook research in England in the 1940s, and from 1949 onwards helped to advise the Home Office on criminology and criminal statistics—subjects more closely related to each other than has even yet been fully appreciated.

Time and space do not, fortunately, permit yet another review of criminological thought in this country over the last century or more. Ideas were centred mainly on penal reform and, especially from the 1920s (Sir Cyril Burt published his classical work *The Young Delinquent* in 1925) on the prevention and treatment of juvenile delinquency. Following work done for the Medical Research Council by Dr. Grace Pailthorpe, the Association for the Scientific Treatment of Criminals (later to become the Institute for the Study and Treatment of Delinquency) was set up in 1931. The Howard League for Penal Reform had, even under that name, by then been in existence for more than ten years; and one of the milestones, as far as the Home Office is concerned, in the progress towards research is a paper sent in March 1936 by Miss Margery Fry to Mr. Maxwell (later Sir Alexander Maxwell) at the Home Office, which makes a case, in a remarkably topical way, for action to start criminological research. Mr. Maxwell did indeed take action by approaching All Souls College, which later gave Dr. Grünhut some financial support. But for the next year or two Home Office attention was turned more to the new Criminal Justice Bill than to the need for research, though Dr. Mannheim, Dr. Grünhut and Dr. Radzinowicz

C.C.P.P.—2

were already conducting research, and the Home Office approached the London School of Economics in 1938 with a view to the undertaking of the study later described in *Young Offenders* by Carr-Saunders, Mannheim and Rhodes, published in 1942.

Though the 1939 war stopped the Criminal Justice Bill in its tracks and prevented the Government from spending much time on worrying about research, a good deal of criminological activity continued in the universities and, in particular, Cambridge University set up in August 1940 a 'Committee to consider the promotion of research and teaching in Criminal Science' consisting of Professor Winfield and Drs. L. Radzinowicz, R. M. Jackson and J. W. C. Turner. The subsequent story of this committee needs no narration here, though it may be mentioned that the first volume of *English Studies in Criminal Science* was published late in 1940. In June 1942 Professor Harold Laski suggested to the Home Office that a Royal Commission on crime should be set up, in order 'to create the atmosphere of large-scale change', and this may have led, or helped to lead, to the setting up in September 1944 of the Advisory Council on the Treatment of Offenders under the Chairmanship of Mr. Justice Birkett. Earlier in the same year an official committee on the treatment of offenders was set up to be a counterpart for the Advisory Council (though it lasted only two years because all official effort was needed to revive the Criminal Justice Bill). This committee may well be seen as the precursor of the present Home Office Research Committee.

Another milestone was passed when in 1948, at the Committee and Report stages of the Criminal Justice Bill, a clause was inserted enabling the Home Secretary to spend money on grants for criminological research. As far as is shown by any records now available, this clause slipped into the Bill in the most casual way. In the Second Reading Debate, Major Wilfrid Vernon made a short speech about resources for research which produced no Governmental or other response at all: he also circulated a memorandum on the subject to the members of the Standing Committee and sent a copy to the Home Office. In Committee, on 4 March 1948, five Members, Major Vernon, Mr. Victor Collins, Dr. Barnett Stross, Mr. Anthony Greenwood and Mrs. Nichol had put forward in their names an amendment (which was proposed by Mr. Collins, later to be Lord Stonham and a Home Office Minister) giving the Home Secretary this power. The official Home Office comment to the Secretary of State was broadly to the effect that, though there was not much of a case for it at that time, it might come in handy sooner or later and in any case could do no harm. The amendment was warmly endorsed in advance by Mr. George Benson. Mr. Chuter Ede accepted it in principle without hesitation, and at the Report Stage incorporated a suitably revised subsection in what became Section 77 of the Criminal Justice Act, which received the Royal Assent on 30 July 1948.

Major Vernon has very kindly provided, from what must be a capacious memory, some elaboration of this bald (though one would not add unconvincing) narrative. With a background of research and development in engineering going back many years he was, it seems, almost alone among Members of Parliament at that time in realizing not only that research must be done but that proper arrangements were needed to provide money for it. Consequently he made his Second Reading speech—which was severely cramped for time by the time-table of the Debate—and circulated the memorandum mentioned above. It is interesting that in these actions he received enthusiastic support (as well as assistance in getting the memorandum duplicated) from Dr. John Bowlby of the Tavistock Clinic, whose influence in encouraging criminological research and in pressing for proper research methods was of great importance in the ten years and more following the end of the War. The precise way in which the amendment was prepared remains obscure, but the probability seems to be that it was Mr. Collins who took the baton from Major Vernon and made the rest of the running. Major Vernon's initiative in this matter may perhaps be seen as the earliest example in this country, in the criminological field, of the benefits of cross-fertilization between the social and the physical sciences.

The importance of the inclusion of Section 77 (3) (f) in the Act, in relation to the founding of the Home Office Research Unit, is that it was much the widest breach made so far in a general attitude to criminological research that had persisted theretofore—and still persists in many countries, though one can fairly say much less now in Great Britain. This was that such research was an activity to be carried out in universities or by voluntary bodies, with only such time and interest as could be spared for it, without the need for any particular training in research methods and, as a matter of course, at the expense of either private funds or such part of their general resources as universities could spare for the purpose. The breach was about to widen rapidly; and one of the implements that widened it was the association soon to be formed between research and statistics.

The Statistical Approach

This association came about, as most things seem to, without being clearly, if at all, foreseen. Its history, from such documents as a rapid search has been able to unearth, makes curious reading. As early as 1944 the Home Office invited the Central Statistical Office to review the criminal statistics, and a report was presented by Dr. (now Professor) John Cohen in December 1944. Its statistical recommendations were fairly modest, but it included a far-sighted proposal that better liaison was needed between the Statistical Branch and administrative departments of the Home Office. And, what would have been startling if anyone, including Dr. Cohen, had realized what was implied, it recommended the study of the effectiveness of penal treatment, recidivism, the value of approved school training, the personality of offenders, the criteria used by the police in recording crime, and the efficiency of probation officers. For reasons that would now be difficult to discover, this report was laid aside for nearly four years; then in 1948 two kettles came simultaneously to the boil. During that year it happened to become necessary to replace the Statistical Branch's 40-column Powers-Samas machines by new machines processing cards with the staggering capacity of 65 columns. This led to consideration of what to do with the extra 25 columns and the discovery that the Home Office departments concerned were not on the whole very well satisfied with the criminal statistics. At much the same time, Mr. Benson complained to the Home Secretary that the criminal statistics were inadequate: this caused the Cohen Report of 1944 to be uncovered, and there followed some rapid activity within the Home Office, further stimulated, no doubt, by an interest taken in Home Office statistics by the recently formed Interdepartmental Committee on Social and Economic Research under the chairmanship of Dr. North, the Registrar General. In a month or two, in February 1949, the Secretary of State appointed an official committee, the Working Party on Home Office Statistics, to consider the Cohen Report on the organization of statistics in the Home Office. It would be difficult to say which of Sir George Benson's activities had most effect on criminology—he was, after all, Chairman of the Howard League for nearly a quarter of a century—but a case could be made for putting near the top of the list his complaint that led to the creation of this Working Party.

The Working Party certainly considered the Cohen Report, but the report's statistical proposals were not very exciting and as it turned out the Working Party did more in the short run for research than for statistics. It began by seeking advice about the criminal statistics from those three eminent criminologists, Drs. Grünhut, Mannheim and Radzinowicz. From them, from Mr. Benson, and from within the Home Office came the observation, among others, that a great deal of research, as opposed to the collection of statistics, seemed to be necessary, and from some of them that, to use an all too modern expression, there should be a better pay-off from preventing crime than from trying to prevent recidivism (the Home Office has been worrying about the rights and wrongs of this last question ever since). The

Working Party was also closely connected with the decision, taken in 1949, to appoint a Home Office Statistical Adviser. To the present writer this last decision is naturally one that appears singularly important.

By taking the actions referred to in the preceding paragraph, the Home Office was not only exposing itself to yet more proposals about research and inviting professional examination of the criminal statistics: it was, though no one knew it, opening the door to mathematical, as well as administrative, statistics, the use of advanced methods for obtaining and analysing sample data, and the serious consideration of research design in criminology. By doing so it influenced both its own research methods and those of many universities for twenty and more years to come.

The Juvenile Delinquency Approach

At the same time as Home Office research was being approached from the direction of the criminal statistics, pressure towards it was building up through the concern felt, not only in the Home Office, about juvenile delinquency. The number of juveniles appearing before the courts had slowly increased during the 1930s and leapt up during the 1939–45 war. After the war the figures did not, as had been hoped, fall back materially. Since the end of the war—and as far as was practicable during it—the Home Office Children's Branch had adopted a generally helpful attitude when asked for facilities for research on juvenile delinquency, and in December 1948 approached the Carnegie United Kingdom Trust with a view to the consolidation of research efforts towards the prevention of juvenile delinquency and the co-ordination of the research grants which the Carnegie and other Trusts had already begun to make. This approach was warmly welcomed by the Carnegie Trust. Also, in the latter part of 1948, the Home Secretary became justifiably alarmed by a projected increase of some 25 per cent in the juvenile court statistics from 1947 to 1948 and, together with the Minister of Education, convened a national conference, held on 2 March 1949, to review juvenile delinquency from all points of view and consider what action could be taken to reduce it. As a result of the conference the Home Office asked all local authorities to set up juvenile delinquency committees and the Ministry of Education asked H.M. Inspectors of Schools to encourage various measures, including co-operation between teachers and parents, in schools. The Archbishop of Canterbury proposed research on the cost of crime (a subject that still stands as a challenge to criminologists) and there were pleas for more research from such distinguished medical psychologists as Dr. Denis Carroll and Dr. John Bowlby.

In March 1949 the Home Office was invited by the Carnegie Trust to prepare a comprehensive research programme on juvenile delinquency. Mr. C. P. Hill of the Children's Department pursued discussions with many universities and other organizations and later in 1949 presented a masterly research plan involving at least ten universities. The plan included survey work on the aetiology of juvenile delinquency and research on juvenile courts and methods of treatment of delinquents. The cost was to be in the neighbourhood of £50,000 a year, an enormous sum by 1949 standards for expenditure on social research. The Department of Criminal Science at Cambridge was to undertake the largest slice of research on juvenile courts and methods of treatment. It was envisaged that charitable trusts should provide the funds and that the 'experiment', which was to take five years, would prove itself to an extent that would justify public expenditure under the Criminal Justice Act 1948 on further research. The plan was approved by the Home Secretary, and in internal discussions the question of setting up a research organization within the Home Office was also raised, but not pursued.

Unfortunately—or so, at any rate, it seemed at the time—towards the end of 1949 the Carnegie Trustees decided against supporting the research plan and instead appointed Mr. John Mack[1] to carry out a general survey of juvenile delinquency. One of the reasons given by the Trust for withholding financial support was that the Government had been enabled by the 1948 Act to pay for such research itself. The plan remained in being for some time as an ideal to aim at, and two further important conferences on juvenile delinquency research were held; the first at the Royal Institution on 1 October 1949, convened by six social, psychological and medical organizations,[2] and the second on 13–15 January 1950, convened by the Home Office and held at Nottingham University. No other Foundation was willing however, to replace the Carnegie Trust, and because of restrictions on Government expenditure criminological research in the United Kingdom could in the event be built up only very slowly. If things had happened as had been planned, research at Cambridge and other universities would probably have expanded much more rapidly than it did and it is possible to speculate with interest, though little profit, on whether there would ever have been a Home Office Research Unit and what the consequences of its

[1] His report, submitted to the Carnegie Trust in June 1953, still makes worthwhile reading, and includes a penetrating remark to the effect that people find research on the prevention of delinquency so difficult that they thankfully fall back on research on the treatment of offenders.

[2] An interesting report on this conference entitled: 'Why Delinquency? The Case for Operational Research' was published in pamphlet form by the National Association for Mental Health.

absence would have been. What can hardly be doubted is that, if the planned programme had been undertaken, research in the 1950s would have been directed more than it was towards the study of the prevention and cure of delinquency amongst juveniles. Whether the available research capacity and techniques would have been equal to carrying out such investigations successfully is far from certain; nor can it be assumed that co-operation between the different Government Departments would have been close enough to implement adequately any research findings.

The First Research Grants

In 1950, then, the Home Office badly wanted research done on juveniles, and on various other subjects arising out of the examination of the criminal statistics, and the Prison Commission was more than sympathetic to the idea of research. Mr. George Benson had just discovered the work of Sheldon and Eleanor Glueck on the prediction of reconviction among discharged prisoners and was pressing the Home Office to make a grant for similar work. The Department of Criminal Science at Cambridge was finishing its study of detention in remand homes (in connection with which the present writer had the first of a 20-year series of debates on research logic with Dr. Radzinowicz and Mr. McClintock) and proceeding with its study of sexual offences; and a few other criminological research studies were in progress, in particular one by Dr. Grünhut on probation and one by Mr. Gordon Rose on borstal boys. The Home Office decided it must use its power to make research grants. Because of the severe limitation placed on Government expenditure only £1,500 could be spared for the 1951/2 estimates, but the allocation of this money marked a vitally important stage in the progress of criminological research.

It was decided to offer a token sum of £250 to Oxford University and the same amount to Cambridge, in each case for research on young offenders, and the remaining £1,000 to the Government Social Survey, which would assist Dr. Mannheim to carry out a pilot prediction study of borstal boys. These events set the Home Office on a course, to which it kept, more or less, for many years, involving:

(i) an emphasis on the study of offenders and their treatment rather than the study in society of the social and socio-psychological origins of delinquency or the effect of different methods of law enforcement or delinquency prevention;

(ii) the study of delinquents under the age of 21, with a preference for those between 17 and 21, rather than, say, research on the organization of adult prisons.

Also, the link between research and statistics led to an emphasis on methodology and to a preoccupation, though ideas were still far from clear, with the logic of research design. For the last tendency, at least, no apology is needed: still, today, there is often great difficulty in getting the logic of a piece of research clear before the study is begun or a grant is offered, and an appalling amount of time is wasted in considering what valid conclusions can be drawn from the results of research that was badly designed in the first place; worse, the Press and others not infrequently accept invalid conclusions as proved.

To assist Dr. Mannheim in the borstal research referred to above, the Social Survey took the important step of assigning Mr. (now Professor) Leslie Wilkins to the project, and Mr. Wilkins's enthusiasm and ability had far-reaching consequences for this study and eventually for criminological research as a whole. Instead of using a system like the Gluecks' of assigning points in order to give an offender a 'failure score' in accordance with various of his characteristics, Mannheim and Wilkins used multiple regression analysis on a large number of variables, reduced in the end to about half a dozen, grappling on the way with a number of problems of scaling, dichotomization, and choice of variables. They obtained a system of scoring which gave a very reasonable prediction of the chance of reconviction within three years of discharge and, what is more surprising, did not lose power when validated on a different sample. The research report, containing not only the research results but an important account of the history of prediction, was effectively completed in 1954, though it was 1955 before it was published as Volume 1 of the Home Office series: 'Studies in the Causes of Delinquency and the Treatment of Offenders'.

The Home Office Research Committee and its Policy

By 1954, research was losing its amateur status in Home Office eyes, and on 17 March a committee of officials called the Research Committee on Delinquency was set up to co-ordinate research with which the Department was concerned and to formulate research policy (later, after some vicissitudes, this committee was reconstituted as the Home Office Research Committee, which still exists). The Committee got seriously off the ground in October 1955 when, having been presented with a strong case for internal research on the prediction of reconviction rates, it recommended that Mr. Wilkins should be offered a post in the Home Office as a research expert and Deputy Statistical Adviser. He was appointed on 1 September 1956, and in practice, though not yet formally, this was the beginning of the Home Office Research Unit.

It was not then, however, and never has been since, contemplated that the Home Office should itself undertake all or even most of the criminological research it wanted done. It became possible gradually to make available slightly larger sums of money by way of grants to universities, and Home Office policy was to encourage universities to build up criminological research strength in one or another of their faculties. This was not only because a great deal of research was needed and it was proposed that universities should do most of it, but also because it was hoped that some thriving criminological research organizations would be absorbed into the universities concerned and have their future research expenses paid by the university. In general, this proved too optimistic. Moreover, while the possible number of research studies that might usefully be done was virtually infinite, the Home Office was tempted, by its policy of encouragement, into financing a few projects that were handled less than competently: and in any case the need for a system of priorities was evident. In fact, the Department was becoming more businesslike and knowledgeable and wanted to be able to implement a programme of research according to its own ideas. It also continued to spend a large proportion of its research funds on grants to universities and other outside bodies, and within reason to support such research as universities wished to do.

The Research Unit

The need for more, and more systematic, research on the work of the courts and the treatment of offenders came specially to the notice of the Home Secretary, Mr. Butler, when he was preparing for the Supply Debate on Prisons (England and Wales) which took place on 13 March 1957. Mr. Butler had been Home Secretary for only two months and was struck by the lack of information to enable him to justify the expenditure on prisons and penal policy in general. In his speech opening the debate he said he intended to give first priority to expanding the research programme. After mentioning an analysis by the Statistical Adviser of the reasons for the increase in the prison population, and referring to the sciences of statistics and sociology, he went on to say:

C.C.P.P.—2*

We need, therefore, to find out by systematic research much more than we know now about the results of the various methods of treatment which are available to the courts, and to place that knowledge at their disposal. We need also to put ourselves in a position to furnish the courts with the fullest possible information about the offenders before them so that in all proper cases they may be able to select the treatment appropriate to each individual on the basis of an expert diagnosis of his history and personality. If we are to do this, which is exploration work, we need proper tools.

The very next day, on 14 March 1957, Sir Frank Newsam, the Permanent Under-Secretary of State, told the Treasury that the Secretary of State said the Home Office must have a research unit. The justification given was the need to study the treatment of offenders, and it is this sequence of events that largely explains why for so long the Research Unit's own work, at least until the passing of the Children and Young Persons Act 1963, was confined to that subject. The date of the Treasury reply, 21 March 1957, may perhaps be taken as that on which the Research Unit was formally founded.

Any adequate account of the development of the Research Unit and of Home Office criminological research policy (for it can be said that, thanks to continuity of research management and to the existence, except for a short period, of a strong official Research Committee, a research policy has at any given time existed) would require a book rather than a short article for its exposition. Immediately the Research Unit was founded, a plan of classifying research dating back to 1952 was re-examined and presented to the Research Committee together with a barrage of proposals about the policy and organization of research and the parts that might be played by the Research Unit itself and by universities. At the same time, a serious attempt was made to bring about an examination of the criminal statistics. If the Secretary of State lacked the information he needed for forward planning, this was as much the fault of inadequate criminal statistics as of insufficient research. As early as June 1958 it was pointed out in Home Office papers that the Statistical Adviser's proposals implied that a Departmental Committee was needed: and, though it took another six years, the Perks Committee was set up in 1964 and in 1967 made proposals which, if they had been implemented, would by now have provided a really informative picture of crimes recorded by the police and laid a proper foundation for the study of the 'dark figure' of unrecorded crime. Unfortunately, it was considered impracticable to implement the recommendations at the time of the presentation of the report: in 1971, however, the Secretary of State approved them in principle and preparations are now being made to implement them for offences of violence against the person. The great criminological importance of having Perks-type statistics for all types of serious offence has not been understood.

Amid a frenzy of arguments about the theory and practice of research, and in the face of acute staff and management problems, the Home Office Research Unit managed to survive and grow. By 1968, grants to universities and other outside bodies were in the neighbourhood of £120,000 a year and the professional staff of the Unit numbered 23. The demands on the Unit and the difficulties it faced were then such that a Working Party on the Home Office Research Unit was set up to consider the scope of its future duties and the staff it would need. Its research responsibilities were thereby considerably extended and it was planned that, even after concessions to manpower restrictions, the professional complement should increase to at least 88 by 1973. Since then there have been organizational changes within the Home Office and the Research Unit's problems of management and supervision, which the Working Party assumed would be dealt with, have grown worse rather than better. Nevertheless, in 1973 the staff numbered 82, of whom 53 were professionally qualified, and the 1973/74 estimate for research grants dealt with by the Unit was over £250,000, notwithstanding that some of the research on children was transferred in 1971, along with the Home Office Children's Department, to the Department of Health and Social Security.

The original object of setting up the Research Unit was mainly to enable a coherent long-term programme of research on the treatment of offenders to be carried out. From the start, however, it was correctly foreseen that it might be hard, and perhaps undesirable, to stick closely to the original concept, which in fact meant at the time the development and elaboration of prediction studies of convicted offenders. The Unit has, it is true, specialized in research involving what it is by now rather out of date to call prediction studies of offenders, and can claim to know a great deal about their uses and limitations. But this work has led not only to the further study of ways of allocating different offenders to different types of treatment, but to wider questions such as the fundamental reappraisal of methods of evaluating the treatment of offenders; whether any present form of treatment is, taken as a whole, sufficiently reformative and if not, what might be done about it; what the real purposes of sentencing are; whether the formidable paraphernalia of trial and punishment are correctly applied as between different kinds of offence and offender; the relationship between crime and mental abnormality, the possibility of conducting experiments in penal treatment in order to get over the so far unsolved difficulty of interpreting the results of *posthoc* research; and, it has to be admitted even though this leads outside the Home Office's present responsibilities, the relationship between crime and social, economic and educational conditions. The emphasis of Home Office research is accordingly changing and is tending (though these things develop slowly) to cover more of the whole span of criminology.

Throughout its life the Research Unit has tried to complement the work of universities. If a university, or other outside body, was willing, and seemed able, to undertake a research study the Home Office thought desirable, the Research Unit and the Research Committee would almost always provide finance for it rather than have it done by the Home Office itself. A very high proportion of the time of the senior staff of the Unit—regrettably, sometimes to the detriment of internal management—has been spent in discussion and negotiation with universities and other outside research organizations. The point, and the value, of having a Home Office Research Unit is that it can organize these complementary activities with a complete technical appreciation of all that is involved; that it can undertake large and continuing programmes of research which outside bodies could only exceptionally be relied on to do; that it has an obligation to undertake a certain amount of dry and tedious research that universities would not always be willing to carry out; and that it can give the Home Office day-to-day criminological advice which, while scientifically detached, is based on a commitment to Home Office interests and an understanding of the Home Office point of view that could hardly be expected of any outside organization.

The Official Attitude to Criminological Research

The scientific detachment of Home Office research has sometimes been looked at with dubiety by members of universities. It is true that to preserve scientific integrity while acting as a servant of the Secretary of State has never been easy; it is claimed, however, that it has been done. The Home Office has recognized that its research organization must be able to preserve its scientific self-respect. The Research Unit, for its part, has appreciated that it would be inappropriate to express its findings and conclusions in immoderate terms. No conclusion reasonably drawn from research data by the Research Unit has ever been suppressed and the only restriction placed on Research Unit staff (whose reports are normally published under their names) has been that they were not usually allowed to add to research reports expositions of their personal views, as distinct from conclusions derived from the research being reported combined with earlier authentic research. It may well be claimed that this has positive advantages, for it is not always easy, in reading academic publications to which this restriction does not apply, to see precisely where reasonable deductions from the data stop and the personal views of the author begin.

Since outside research supported by Home Office funds preceded research carried out within the Home Office, the official attitude to internal research was modelled on the attitude to outside research rather than the other way about. The basic attitude has changed very little over the last 23 years: within the limits of its resources and with due regard to its views from time to time on priorities, the Home Office has been willing to give financial support to research if satisfied about the competence and integrity of the person or organization who would be responsible, and if there seemed to be a reasonable chance that the research would produce a worthwhile result. Similar arguments, and the same conditions, applied if facilities for access to records or institutions were given. The cost of granting facilities can often, if properly assessed, be very considerable, and the trouble caused to staff employed by the Home Office, or for whom the Home Office has some responsibility, can be even more important: if offenders are to be interviewed their point of view must equally be taken into account. It has also to be carefully considered whether confidential information about offenders can properly be given to an applicant for research facilities. With all these points in mind, it usually happens that facilities are refused to post-graduate students whose object is only to complete a higher degree: at all events, applications that might come in this category are especially scrutinized and if facilities are given at all they are given to the supervisor. The offer of research grants for educational purposes only is in any case not within the province of the Home Office.

The conditions on which research grants or facilities are offered were laid down in 1954, and have since undergone little essential change. They include certain safeguards about publication, mainly so as to protect confidential information about individuals, and these could be tiresome, not to say unduly restrictive, if interpreted unreasonably. In practice, however, reasonableness has almost always prevailed, and the close liaison maintained by periodical meetings to discuss the research has generally disposed of any difficulties without friction. Provided that individual people are not pilloried, the Home Office does not mind—indeed, welcomes—constructive criticism of systems, however radical it may be. The most difficult problems occur when staff in institutions or in the field, who have put themselves out to help research workers, are strongly attacked or criticized in a research report: too much of this would make it impossible to obtain co-operation and would bring research to a standstill. The only solution, considering that few existing systems can be altered immediately on the basis of a single research report, seems to be to make the people concerned quite unidentifiable; and it is only when this is exceptionally difficult that a real dilemma emerges.

For one reason or another any social research organization has a hard life to lead: and though an official research unit's problems are different from those of a university department or a privately financed research body it would be rash to say that they were on the whole any more severe, at any rate in Great Britain. The Home Office Research Unit is now well established and, besides making a special contribution towards the provision of information for policy-making, fills a useful place in the network of research bodies concerned with criminological problems.

THE FOUNDATION OF CO-OPERATION IN EUROPEAN CRIMINOLOGICAL RESEARCH: Sir Leon Radzinowicz and the Criminological Scientific Council at the Council of Europe

Inkeri Anttila

Introduction

It is of course well known that Sir Leon Radzinowicz is a very active member of many international organizations. He has participated in numerous seminars, symposia and congresses not only as a delegate but also as chairman or rapporteur to the conference. He also made his Institute an international meeting-place for criminologists, who came to attend international courses in criminology or otherwise engage in co-operation with colleagues from abroad.

This short survey only attempts to cover one sector of Sir Leon's international work, namely, his important contribution to the European Committee on Crime Problems (E.C.C.P.) of the Council of Europe. My observations are, I am afraid, haphazard and fragmentary as my experience is limited to the annual meetings of the Directors of Criminological Research Institutes in which I have taken part as an observer since 1965. While I cannot give a complete account of all the work involved in his activities connected with the E.C.C.P., I shall underline the most significant aspects of his contribution to this arena of European co-operation on criminological matters. According to official documents involvement with the Council began in 1962. In that year a very important step was taken when, as a new body, the Criminological Scientific Council was founded. The Council was set up by the decision of the Committee of Ministers, and its function was defined as

giving technical advice to the Council of Europe about putting into practice a scientific programme in the field of crime problems.

The Council held its first meeting on 30 May 1963. Sir Leon was nominated the first Chairman and he served until 1967. To set up a new body always takes a lot of time and energy. The first years are the most important, because then the goals and methods of a new organization are determined. It is not easy to estimate the degree of success of an international organization. Many variables would need to be considered such as the continuity of the activities, the number and quality of people willing to participate and the volume of publications. One could also try to assess more subtle achievements, such as the possible influence on policy planning and decision-making, or the fertility of the ideas produced. It would take extensive 'research on research' to elucidate all these dimensions. But there could hardly be any dissenting views as to the usefulness of the work of the Criminological Scientific Council.

First Phase : Let us Co-ordinate our Efforts

Looking at the working-papers and other written documents it is easy to discern the fact that the first priority of the directors' meetings was the need for information. These were the subjects chosen for the discussions of the first meeting:

— problems of administration and organization of criminological research
— programmes and methods of fundamental research
— means of co-operation between institutes and the Council of Europe.

Thus much interest was directed towards problems which had been thoroughly dealt with in Professor Radzinowicz's *In Search of Criminology*. Written only two years before the meeting it provided excellent background material for the discussion. These and similar questions were put forward: What kind of institutes are there in different countries? What, actually, is a proper Institute of Criminology like? Should it be directed by a sociologist, a psychologist or by a criminal law professor? Professor Radzinowicz was the rapporteur of that meeting and in presenting his paper made the following statement:

> When a professor of criminal law with a genuine interest in criminology or penology, with two or three rooms in a University building, an assistant, a part-time typist and a small annual grant for the building up of a library—even if this is called an institute in criminology or criminal law and criminal science—it is in fact something which should more properly be called a seminar.[1]

[1] *First European Conference of Directors of Criminological Research Institutes*, Strasbourg, 1964, p. 6.

This realistic observation was, I suppose, received with approval by many participants who at that time struggled with 'hopeful beginnings' of criminological institutes. There was also, I think, general agreement with the rapporteur's view of the interdisciplinary nature of criminology. But there were other, more difficult, problems. Should research be concentrated in universities or could it be carried out also by groups connected with governmental bodies? Professor Radzinowicz mentioned in his report that the traditional framework of an Institute was that provided by a university, but he thought that this was not the only possible solution: there were university centres, inter-state institutes, regional institutes of the United Nations, and governmental research units. In the course of the discussion he made an attempt to analyse the benefits and the drawbacks of different types of institutes. His comments, now ten years old, still retain their accuracy and relevance:

> In criminological institutes there are many dangers and disadvantages. It is easy for an initial enthusiasm to pass and be succeeded by slackness. After thirty or forty years even great science departments lose their impetus. It is easy for great objectives to be lost in petty rivalries. Yet full mobilisation of resources does help to achieve the break-down which criminal science needs. This is the advantage of the large institute.
>
> With official research units too the advantages and disadvantages are obvious. Clearly it is of the highest importance that there should be the right to pursue enquiry with no fettering of freedom of thought. For this there must be a liberal climate of opinion in which they can work. In the absence of this liberal climate then it is possible for the State through its control of the unit's money to exercise an influence which could only be regarded as bad. The advantage of course is that once a ministry has set up such a project there is a natural desire to believe that it has value. This gives it a permanence and stability which may be lacking in a University institute where there are so many conflicting claims for money.[2]

As some participants of the first conference rightly pointed out, this is ultimately a question of power; who is to decide the topics to be studied and who is to have the power to apply the results obtained? Professor Nils Christie, a typical representative of the university approach from Norway, introduced a new perspective into the discussion. He spoke about the difficulties which arise because research workers and administrators are trained in fundamentally different ways; it is not possible for the administrator to direct the research worker because he simply does not know enough about empirical research. Professor Christie also spoke about the importance to criminologists of their academic reference group. Isolation

---

[2] *First European Conference of Directors of Criminological Research Institutes,* Strasbourg, 1964, pp. 12–13.

from other social scientists would, he warned, easily lead to a lack of scientific control.

In the next meeting, held in 1964, the ideas expressed a year before were further discussed and developed. It was now possible on the basis of the conclusions reached by the first conference, to state precisely how information would be exchanged and how co-operation between research workers would be fostered. The scheme was as follows:

1. Exchange of information on criminological research conducted in member countries: information supplied on themes and methods would be published in the two official languages in the form of a less official but fairly frequent publication, with a more elaborate bulletin appearing every 3–4 years. Information on research institutes, and on total direct costs of crime suppression and criminological research would be needed.

2. Co-ordination of criminological research in Europe would be needed to avoid duplication and to stimulate research.

3. Exchange of information would also cover collection and documentation, study of methods of selection and classification of projects, contact with the National Research and Information Centre (New York), UNESCO, I.P.P.F., International Association of Penal Law, the International Society of Criminology and the International Society for Social Defence, with regional bodies like the Scandinavian Council for Criminology and the Benelux Prison Commission, and with national centres and institutes.

4. Special attention was given to the possibilities of exchanging research workers.

It is not always easy to discover who first introduced some new idea, afterwards approved and accepted by a meeting. However, it seems to be common knowledge that at least the idea to create a bulletin on current research in Europe, as well as the idea to set up criminological research fellowships (first mooted as early as 1963) were suggested by Professor Radzinowicz. Both projects were clear successes. The first bulletin of current criminological research which was published in 1966, contained material from eight member countries and information about 110 projects. The second bulletin was also published in 1966, and the third in 1967. The Committee of Ministers approved the regulations for the criminological research fellowships in 1966. These fellowships were partly 'individual fellowships', intended to give research workers an opportunity to improve their knowledge of both research objectives and methods in member countries of the Council of Europe by travelling and staying for varying periods (1–6 months) and partly 'co-ordinated fellowships', to give research workers an opportunity to participate in criminological studies and research of common European interest, in collaboration with two or three other research workers and a director of studies. Still another of Professor Radzinowicz's initiatives was to urge the setting up of small committees of research workers. These were originally intended to be rather informal groups which were expected to focus on topics of special interest to sub-committees of the Committee on Crime Problems. For example, the sub-committee on short-term methods of treatment for young offenders was assisted by a small committee of specialists, the task of which was to consider the effectiveness of short-term treatment measures applied to young offenders.

Second Phase : From Organizational Problems to Topics of Research—from Methods to Results

As mentioned above, the first two meetings of Directors of Criminological Institutes were mostly devoted to the needs of mutual exchange of information. In addition, the second meeting also dealt with two important research topics, namely 'Research into methods of crime prevention', with a paper presented by Professor Nils Christie, and 'Research into effectiveness of punishment and treatment', with a paper presented by Dr. Roger Hood. In the discussion, the ineffectiveness of many ill-planned large-scale crime prevention programmes was stressed, and the results of various treatment methods were strongly criticized. In his summary report, Professor Radzinowicz observed that 'great beliefs in great solutions and rapid formulas had now disappeared'. He also pointed out that 'it was dangerous for criminology to be identified too closely with preventive programmes which linked it with the vast fields of social policy, social hygiene and social work. These were not crime prevention programmes but were concerned with social amelioration and readjustment. They were a support to the social conscience and an attempt to build social services when the Welfare State had not yet been developed. They should be re-named.'

Naturally, the great topic of the sixties, the prison community, appeared on the agenda of the directors' meetings. In the conference of 1965 the prison as an institution was discussed on the basis of a paper presented by a Norwegian sociologist, Dr. Thomas Mathiesen, the author of the book *The Defences of the Weak*. In particular much interest was aroused by the description of the vested interests of the prison personnel in the status quo, and of the methods by which the application of reforms was neutralized in the everyday life of the prison. In his summing up, Chairman Radzinowicz weighed against each other the negative and positive qualities of penal institution and stated that the usefulness of prisons seemed very doubtful.

The next meetings, in the years 1966–67, concentrated more than earlier ones on the results of some crucial criminological research. The main topics were:

— relationship between types of offender and types of treatment
— forecasting criminality
— road traffic offences.

In his last year as Chairman of the Criminological Scientific Council, Professor Radzinowicz presented a report in 1967 which included a frank and penetrating evaluation of the activities of the European Committee on Crime Problems:

> International activities were of course fraught with difficulties and disappointments:
> — The working tempo was inevitably sluggish.
> — Considerable circumspection was necessary.
> — Only limited projects could be tackled, while more important issues had to be shelved.
> — There was no immediate visible result.
> — There were very frequent difficulties stemming from the differing approach of research workers and administrators.
> Nonetheless, the work merited encouragement and expansion. Good headway had already been made in international co-operation in the study of crime problems. Patience was called for in those concerned, but at the same time enthusiasm.[3]

He also called for further action and emphasized that the following questions merited particular attention:

(a) Contacts with East European countries.
(b) Collaboration with the United Nations Social Defence Research Institute in Rome.
(c) Collaboration with non-governmental organizations.
(d) Organization of enlarged conferences.
(e) Conferences of Directors of Criminological Research Institutes at the national level.
(f) Co-ordination of research.
(g) Increased resources for criminological research fellowships.
(h) Triennial assessment of criminological research.

[3] *Fifth European Conference of Directors of Criminological Research Institutes,* Strasbourg, 1968, p. 16.

(i) Membership of the Criminological Scientific Council for the younger generation of research workers together with the older experts.[4]

These observations and suggestions of the first Chairman of the Criminological Scientific Council obviously have not lost their relevance today; they still serve as guidelines for those whose task it is to continue the work which he started.

Some Problems for the Future

My review so far has put the emphasis on the obvious value of the work of the Scientific Council. But as an outside observer, I hope it will be useful if I make some comments on the advantages and disadvantages of the present organization, as far as it is possible in the light of my very limited experience.

It is not my intention to consider technical problems. Everyone knows that they are numerous; many of them, like difficulties caused by the slow tempo of meetings and by the necessity to ensure early preparation of the working papers, were mentioned by Sir Leon himself in his general surveys. I shall try to turn to questions of a more general nature.

Obviously, there are many advantages gained by the fact that the member states of the Scientific Council and participants at meetings arranged by the Council belong to the same 'culture' as to their societal views, scientific traditions and financial opportunities. But this advantage may very well turn into a disadvantage in the field of criminal policy discussions. The more the interest is shifting from traditional issues to general topics such as societal trends and community planning, the more new ideas are needed. A club of well-known criminologists is perhaps not the best breeding-ground for innovations. It will be crucial to expand the range of participants and try to seek more contact with research workers and administrators from countries with other types of criminality, other forms of crime control, divergent socio-economic systems and different cultural settings.

There are also other, perhaps more difficult problems. Looking back to the early years of the activities of the Scientific Council it is very easy to recognize that the significance of criminological research was at that time greatly over-estimated. It was believed that once the area of research was covered and the results obtained, the rationality of the consequent policy-making was guaranteed. Now we know that this was just wishful thinking. Research plays a very modest part in actual decision-making; it is symptomatic that many pieces of research in the last few years have been related to

[4] *Fifth European Conference of Directors of Criminological Research Institutes,* Strasbourg, 1968, p. 15.

the problem of assessing to what extent research has actually influenced policy-making in a given society.

I believe that the whole research atmosphere has undergone some vital changes. Even ten years ago it was often thought that criminological research was, and should be, mainly a fact-finding process, while decision-making was, and should be, just the application of the results obtained. Since then, the value-consciousness of criminological research has considerably increased. This development seems to be a necessity in a field like ours, with many divergent societal goals, beliefs, and traditions.

Can other new trends be discerned? It appears safe to predict a continuing change from narrow criminological studies to research concerned with social control in a wide sense; the merging of crime problems with the general problems of societal policy.

Of course, many of these ideas were already discussed during Sir Leon's Chairmanship of the Scientific Council. The scientific discussion, then started, will continue in the coming years: research will test the scientific significance of new ideas, and their usefulness will be reflected in the field of crime control policy. Further comments on this subject would, however, fall outside the scope of this short review.

FACTS AND MYTHS ABOUT THE STATE OF CRIME

F. H. McClintock

Introduction

Academic criminology has its roots in late eighteenth and early nineteenth century European thought.[1] Few would doubt that the twin sources of its growth have been the study of environmental influences on the social behaviour of man, and the study of the development of the human personality in its biological and psychological aspects.[2] No attempt will be made here to assess the relative contribution of these two sources and their influence on current thinking about crime problems. This paper is in fact concerned with a rather restricted view of the former of these sources, namely, some of the problems arising from studying crime as a social phenomenon. Central to such a study has been a critical concern with the realistic application and uses of official criminal statistics.

Some of the earliest attempts to lay the foundations of a sociology of crime can be found in the writings of Quetelet and Guerry who were publishing simultaneously, in Belgium and France respectively, during the first half of the nineteenth century.[3] Their studies were largely based upon the raw material contained in official criminal statistics, and to some extent they could be regarded as trying to realise the aim formulated by Bentham in the late eighteenth century, when he suggested that there should be official returns on crime, or 'bills of delinquency', comparable to the 'bills of

[1] Precursors to the sociological school of crime are, of course, to be found in the seventeenth century among the writers on political arithmetic, for example, William Petty and John Graunt.

[2] The writings dealing with the individualistic approach to the study of crime are probably less diffuse than those of the sociological school. See Hermann Mannheim, *Comparative Criminology*, London, Routledge and Kegan Paul, 1965, especially Part Three, pp. 201 et seq.; and Leon Radzinowicz, *Ideology and Crime*, London, Heinemann Educational Books, 1966.

[3] See, for example, 'Recherches sur le Penchant au Crime aux Différents Ages', by L. A. J. Quetelet, in *Nouveaux Mémoires de l'Académie* (1831), Vol. VII and 'Essai sur la Statistique Morale de la France' (1833), by A.-M. Guerry.

mortality published annually in London; indicating the moral health of the country . . . as these latter do the physical'.[4]

Bentham was aware of the difficulties in obtaining reliable statistical returns from official sources, but in putting forward his proposals for criminal statistics he was perhaps rather optimistic in his hope that they would be 'a little more accurate' than the bills of mortality.[5] Quetelet and Guerry were also far from being unaware of some of the shortcomings and defects of such data. At the same time Rawson, in England, stressed the extent to which crime returns depended 'in a great measure, upon the disposition of the injured parties or the public to prosecute, and the efficiency of the system of police'.[6] The earliest reference to the value of checking official crime returns by keeping a register of crimes committed on the basis of interviews with a random selection of victims is found in some reports in 1840, while the actual existence of such a register for vagrancy in certain parts of Scotland is referred to in a study published in 1853 by Frederic Hill.[7]

The earlier writers who advocated the need for official criminal statistics did so on two grounds: first, they would indicate the *moral* state of the nation and secondly they would be a way of testing the effectiveness of legislation and the penal remedies applied.[8] To quote Bentham again: 'The ordering of these returns is a measure of excellent use in furnishing *data* for the legislator to go to work upon. They will form altogether a kind of *political barometer,* by which the effect of every legislative operation relative to the subject may be indicated and made palpable.'[9]

By the middle of the nineteenth century several of the main European countries had established annual series of official statistics on crime. Leading commentators related these data to demographic and other social information, and one had the beginnings of a critical assessment of the state of crime, or the moral health of the nation; further progress followed attempts to estimate the effectiveness of the processes of law-enforcement, of the criminal justice system, including sentencing, and the results of the application of penal measures. Subsequent writings based partly on criminological

[4] 'A view of the Hard-Labour Bill', by Jeremy Bentham, in *Works* (Bowring's ed., 1838–43), Vol. 4, p. 29.

[5] Ibid.

[6] Rawson W. Rawson, 'An Inquiry into the Statistics of Crime in England and Wales', in *Journal of the Royal Statistical Society*, Vol. II, 1839, p. 320.

[7] Frederic Hill, *Crime: its amount, causes and remedies* (1853), pp. 19–25.

[8] Although formulated in a slightly different way these aims tend to be the basis of current studies of Criminal Statistics, see: F. H. McClintock, *Crimes of Violence* (London, Macmillan, 1963); T. Sellin and M. E. Wolfgang, *The Measurement of Delinquency* (New York, Wiley, 1964); and *Report of the Departmental Committee on Criminal Statistics* (London, HMSO, 1967).

[9] Bentham, op. cit.

research have been devoted to the development of methods of study and of techniques for the elucidation of these problems.

Criminal Statistics and the 'Dark Figure'

The early advocates of official returns on crime showed an awareness of the incomplete state of Criminal Statistics which tended to be overlooked by many subsequent writers and the fashion developed in which trends in crimes *recorded* in the official returns were interpreted as if they gave an accurate account of the amount of crime actually *committed*. The realization of deficiencies and inaccuracies in the number of incidents reported to the police as crimes, and accepted by them as the basis of their official returns, led to the recognition of the 'dark figures' in crime: those criminal incidents *not* known to or recorded by the police. For some time discussions were focused upon whether 'police statistics' or 'Court statistics' were the most suitable for the measurement of criminality in the community. Eventually, 'police statistics' were accepted as the more accurate data for indicating the amount of crime committed. But their value as giving the true facts about crime was criticized on two main grounds: (a) the doubtful accuracy of the police in recording some of the criminal events reported to them, and (b) the great number of situations in which the victims, losers or members of the public omitted to report breaches of the law. These criticisms, as they have become more fully explored, have shaken the earlier faith in the absolute value of police returns in attempting to assess the amount of crime committed, or to judge the impact of penal measures when assessments are based upon reconviction rates alone.

Hermann Mannheim, in a pioneer study published in 1940 on the social aspects of crime, used official crime data to throw light on a number of problems, but prefaced this with an important chapter on the difficulties and pitfalls in the interpretation of official Criminal Statistics.[10] In an insightful article published as early as 1945, Leon Radzinowicz pointed out the many drawbacks of unreliability in the use of Criminal Statistics as providing a true picture of the state of crime. The problems of reporting, recording and classifying crimes are all considered by him in some detail. The issues are also advantageously put in their historical context: 'It is, for instance, a known fact that the number of certain crimes reported depends on the attitude to them of public opinion, on the methods of punishment, and on

[10] See Hermann Mannheim, *Social Aspects of Crime in England between the Wars* (London, George Allen and Unwin, 1940), Chapter 3, and *Comparative Criminology* (London, Routledge and Kegan Paul, 1965), Chapter 5.

the degree of confidence which the prevailing system of criminal justice inspires. In the course of England's social and penal evolution, these factors have changed, bringing in their turn a change in the percentage of crimes which the public thought worth reporting to the police.'[11] This article— written initially over thirty years ago—clearly indicates the complex interaction between public opinion, legislative changes and the recording of crime.[12] It contains optimism as to the improvements that can be made in these statistics for their use in formulating criminal policy; but in terms of assessing the true nature of the state of crime Leon Radzinowicz gives an explicit warning: 'The crimes actually committed and the crimes legally recorded are two fundamentally different phenomena.'[13] During the same period Max Grünhut saw the difficulty of ascertaining the true nature of the state of crime and discussed the various meanings that could be ascribed to the concept of the 'dark figure'.[14] These arguments served to keep statistical returns in their proper perspective and encouraged an interpretation of what lies behind the apparent facts about crime, rather than a mere acceptance of criminal statistics at their face value as accurately portraying the state of crime in the community.[15] Criminal statistics were, however, generally considered as giving some indication of the shape of trends in crime: but T. S. Lodge anticipated later critics by suggesting that the 'interpretation of criminal statistics is not unlike attempting to draw a man's picture . . . from his shadow on wire-netting'.[16]

The recognition of the 'dark figure' has led to an examination of the circumstances in which crimes are not reported to the police and a useful

[11] 'English Criminal Statistics: a critical analysis', by Leon Radzinowicz, in *The Modern Approach to Criminal Law* (London, Macmillan, 1945). Edited by L. Radzinowicz and J. W. C. Turner, p. 174, at p. 176.

[12] Its relevance for contemporary discussion is unfortunately often ignored by the new criminologists.

[13] Op. cit. at p. 193. This statement goes as far as those made by the more extreme contemporary critics of Criminal Statistics. My own view is that, although these numerical totals are different, they are nevertheless interrelated and that official crime statistics are not merely a reflection of action in law enforcement. This is clearly a view shared by Leon Radzinowicz: see his Peter le Neve Foster Lecture: 'The Criminal in Society', in *Journal of the Royal Society of Arts*, Vol. 62, (1964), pp. 916 et seq.

[14] See 'Statistics on Criminology', by M. Grünhut, in *Journal of the Royal Statistical Society*, Series A (General), Vol. CXIV, Part II, (1951), pp. 149 et seq.

[15] The Cambridge report on Sexual Offences analysed the trends in sexual crime on the basis of official statistics, but the report also contained a critical commentary on the limitations of such figures. See: *Sexual Offences* (London, Macmillan, 1957), a report of the Department of Criminal Science, prepared by F. J. Odgers and F. H. McClintock under the direction of Leon Radzinowicz.

[16] 'Criminal Statistics', by T. S. Lodge, in the *Journal of the Royal Statistical Society*, Series A (General), Vol. CXVI, Part III, (1953), p. 283, at p. 290.

impression has been gained of the probable magnitude of the 'dark figure' phenomenon.[17] Attempts to make a fairly accurate assessment of the quantity and quality of the 'dark figure' began in the 1930s supplemented by a spate of criminological research which first of all concentrated on 'self-reporting' studies of 'hidden delinquency' and more recently on the results of 'self-reporting' studies of 'victimization'.[18] These studies have been important in developing a more critical appraisal of the statistical data contained in official returns which purport to give the facts about crime; but the researchers' methods and essential definitions themselves suffer from a number of weaknesses, so that the unreliability of official figures as a true record, due to lacunae, may be only replaced by a different kind of unreliability due to methods of *ad hoc* empirical research.[19] Certainly, these studies have indicated that there is a very much larger volume of crime in the community than is generally assumed and that a very much wider sector of the community is involved than is indicated by the data on persons apprehended. This has led to a reassessment as to whether the main part of total crime is committed by members of the lower socio-economic groups who live in the materially and socially deprived areas, or whether such findings—based on official data—are not the result of a bias in law-enforcement and criminal justice. Martin Gold and others have suggested, however, that if duration and seriousness of criminal activities are taken into account, the facts as indicated by official data are not so distorted as some of the authors of hidden delinquency studies have indicated.[20] However, as a result of hidden delinquency research, the view that the majority of crime is committed by a relatively small proportion of the population, who can be clearly distinguished from the main body of law-abiding citizens, is now open to considerable doubt, although the precise differences as to the circumstances of the unreported offences, and the backgrounds of the persons involved, from those in recorded crime, has not as yet been made clear.

[17] On reasons why some crimes are not reported see *Sexual Offences* (1957), Appendix I; F. H. McClintock, 'The Dark Figure', in *Collected Studies in Criminological Research* (Vol. V, Council of Europe, Strasbourg, 1970), pp. 14 and 15; and Nigel Walker, *Crimes, Courts and Figures* (London, Penguin Books, 1971), Ch. 1. On suggestions as to the dark figure, see *Sexual Offences* (1957), Introduction by L. Radzinowicz; and 'The Criminal in Society', by L. Radzinowicz, *Journal of the Royal Society of Arts*, Vol. 62 (1964). For comments on the estimates of the dark figures of crime, see F. H. McClintock, 'The Dark Figure', cited above, and Bernard Wehner, *Die Latenz der Straftaten* (1957).
[18] For a critical review of some of the research studies on hidden delinquency and victimization, see R. Hood and R. Sparks, *Key Issues in Criminology* (London, Weidenfeld and Nicolson, 1970), chs. 1 and 2.
[19] See F. H. McClintock, 'The Dark Figure', op. cit.
[20] See, for example, Martin Gold, 'Undetected delinquent behaviour', *Journal of Research in Crime and Delinquency*, Vol. 3, (1966), pp. 27–46.

The Classification of Recorded Crime

While a considerable amount of attention has been directed to the phenomenon of the 'dark figure' in relation to the difficulties of assessing the true nature of the state of crime, a problem of no less importance—which has received much less attention—is the extent to which there is adequate information about the crimes which have been reported and subsequently recorded in official criminal statistics. The recorded crime relates primarily to anti-social behaviour of sufficient gravity to have led to an official complaint which the police have accepted as constituting an offence and in respect of which some decisions have to be made in relation to law-enforcement and the criminal justice system. Very little as to the social significance of such behaviour can be gained from the pages of *Criminal Statistics*. As a result, speculative interpretations as to the various trends in crime abound in the popular press, the mass media and not infrequently in more learned publications.

The limitations of such methods of recording solely on the basis of a legal classification has been clearly recognized for some considerable time among criminologists. This shortsighted simplicity was condemned by Leon Radzinowicz in the article published in 1945: 'This complete subordination of the classification in the criminal statistics to the dogmatic classification of criminal law renders investigations on the state of criminality particularly difficult. The best dogmatic classification of crime must always be somewhat artificial and schematic, because it does not sufficiently take into account the peculiar social, psychological and moral aspects of particular offences, aspects which are most important from the point of view of criminal policy and criminology. . . . The anti-social act which we call a crime becomes to a great extent distorted when expressed in statistical terms.'[21] Some twenty years later, when a government committee was reporting on the need for changes in official criminal statistics, its first recommendation was: 'The statistics should include a considerable amount of factual information about offences (relating to victims, types and values of property stolen, scene of crime and so on) to supplement the present purely legal classification system and should also include fuller information about offenders.'[22]

The formal and basically legalistic way in which official criminal statistics have been published has had a considerable influence on both public discussion about the state of crime and upon the work of many of those engaged

---

[21] 'English Criminal Statistics: a critical analysis', by Leon Radzinowicz, op. cit. (1945), pp. 183 and 193.

[22] *Report of the Departmental Committee on Criminal Statistics* (London, HMSO, 1967), p. 39.

in criminological research. There has been a tendency to regard crime as if it were some homogeneous entity capable of straightforward general explanations as to causes. Questions about reasons for the increase of crime are regarded as meaningful without any detailed consideration being given to the nature of the different social behaviour that makes up the complicated volume of recorded crime. Again, a great deal of criminological research has been concentrated almost entirely upon the study of personality and other characteristics of those who are labelled criminals, with scant regard for the variety of circumstances and qualities of their crimes. As stated in an earlier paper, this 'comparative neglect of a detailed and systematic study of the crimes as such, is one of the principal sources of the lack of precision in the results of research which not only affects the practical application of such results but also the formulation and validation of clearly defined and significant hypotheses'.[23] Baroness Wootton, in reviewing criminological research in Great Britain, stated the point very succinctly: 'Faith in the overwhelming importance of criminality as a thing-in-itself has certainly had a stultifying effect upon the trend of research in this field.'[24] Robert Merton can also be cited as taking up the same attitude when he denounced the mistake of hypothesizing the homogeneity of criminal conduct: 'The decision to encompass a wide array of behaviour in the one rubric of crime or delinquency tends to lead to the assumption that a single theory will account for the entire range of behaviour placed in this category . . . [like the assumption] that there must be *a* theory of disease rather than distinct theories of disease—of tuberculosis and arthritis. . . . Just as classifying enormously varied conditions and processes under the one heading of disease led some zealous medical systematists to believe that it was their task to evolve a single over-arching theory of disease, so, it seems, the established idiom, both vernacular and scientific, of referring to "juvenile delinquency" as though it were a single entity, leads some to believe that there must be *a* basic theory of "its" causation. Perhaps this is enough to suggest what is meant by referring to crime or juvenile delinquency as a blanket-concept which may get in the way of theoretical formulations of the problems.'[25] The new criminologists—the interactionists and the phenomenologists—have stressed the need to understand criminal behaviour as a social entity comprehending the specific nature of the conduct and its

[23] 'Ways of classifying offences for criminological research', by F. H. McClintock and N. H. Avison (a paper delivered to the National Conference on Research and Teaching in Criminology, Cambridge, 1964).

[24] Barbara Wootton, *Social Science and Social Pathology* (London, George Allen and Unwin, 1959), p. 306.

[25] R. K. Merton, *Social Theory and Social Structure* (USA, The Free Press, revised edition, 1957), p. 231.

meaning to the individual deviant in relation to the context in which it occurs and to the life-styles of those involved. Failure to do this and to formulate views on the basis of abstract data from criminal statistics is likely to lead to a situation in which stereotypes are mistaken for social facts.[26] The central myth about the state of crime is that crime *per se* exists as a meaningful social entity.

Criminological research which was focused on descriptive and classificatory analysis of criminal behaviour has given proof that even within the more restricted legal groups of crime, such as sex offences, robbery, violent crime, fraud or burglary, there are variations of such substantially different behaviour that, as regards both theory and criminal policy, it is very dubious whether such legal categories have any meaning or use as descriptions of social reality.[27] In various research studies attempts have been made to evolve descriptive classifications for robbery and other forms of criminal violence, based primarily upon the circumstances in which such crimes occurred. These situational classifications have been used to indicate the prevalence of different kinds of violent crimes, the differences in the process of law-enforcement, in trial and sentencing of offenders, as well as in the heterogeneity of crime among violent recidivists.[28] In a more recent discussion of the problem a somewhat different five-fold classification has been put forward as a basis for the study of criminal violence and for considering the practical aspects of prevention and control.[29]

[26] See, for example, Stanley Cohen (ed.), *Images of Deviance* (London, Penguin Books Ltd., 1971), esp. Chapter 1; and Denis Chapman, *Sociology and the Stereotype of the Criminal* (London, Tavistock Publications, 1968).

[27] See: *Sexual Offences* (London, Macmillan, 1957), a report of the Department of Criminal Science, prepared by F. J. Odgers and F. H. McClintock under the direction of Leon Radzinowicz; F. H. McClintock and Evelyn Gibson, *Robbery in London* (London, Macmillan, 1961); F. H. McClintock *et al.*, *Crimes of Violence* (London, Macmillan, 1963); T. Hadden, 'The development and administration of the English law of criminal fraud' (University of Cambridge, unpublished PhD. thesis, 1967); D. Chappell, 'The development and administration of the English law relating to breaking and entering' (University of Cambridge, unpublished PhD. thesis, 1965). For a more general discussion of this problem in relation to the subject of offences against the person and crimes of violence, see: F. H. McClintock, *Crimes against the Person* (Manchester Statistical Society pamphlet, 1963) and F. H. McClintock, 'The phenomenological and contextual analysis of criminal violence', in *Violence in Society* (Council of Europe, Strasbourg, 1973).

[28] See literature referred to in previous footnote. See also F. H. McClintock and N. H. Avison, *Crime in England and Wales* (London, Heinemann Educational Books, 1968), esp. Ch. 8, 'The Recidivist', and F. H. McClintock, *Aspects of Criminal Violence in England* (forthcoming, 1974).

[29] T. B. Hadden and F. H. McClintock, 'Social and legal definitions of criminal violence' in Proceedings of the Fourth National Conference on Research and Teaching in Criminology (1970, mimeograph), and F. H. McClintock, 'Phenomenological and contextual analysis of criminal violence', op. cit.

I. Instrumental violence:
  (a) Violence in furtherance of property crime (robbery, etc.).
  (b) Violence in furtherance of some forms of sexual coercion (rape, and indecent assault).
  (c) Violence to avoid individual arrest.
II. Interpersonal violence:
  (a) Prior personal relationship of permanence or of some duration.
  (b) Prior personal relationship of a casual or transitory nature.
III. Destructive and sensational violence:
  (a) Local community level.
  (b) National and international levels.
IV. Ideological and political violence:
  (a) Local community level.
  (b) National and international levels.
V. Community disturbance and disorderly conduct.

There is, of course, overlap between these classes and, on a practical level, information will not always be available or even obtainable so as to enable one to place every criminal event in its appropriate sub-class. In this classification it is suggested that the aim should be to isolate the main situational clusters of violence, rather than to obtain a unidimensional and exhaustive classification. The fifth class, dealing with disorderly conduct we have described as a 'threshold' class in that the elements of social behaviour are not ignored but are mainly minor in character. Not to include this class would unduly limit a discussion on the phenomenon of criminal violence. In addition it has to be taken into account in considering the legal and other control systems. It can also be regarded as the 'grey' area between recorded criminal violence and the 'dark figure'.

In a classification of this sort, where the emphasis is placed primarily on the context in which violence occurs, a stock-taking and static perspective which merely tries to ascertain how much violence has taken place can be extended so as to see both the *occurrence* of criminal violence and the *recording* of criminal violence as interactive processes where the criminal justice system is seen as one of the systems of control of deviant behaviour within society.[30]

[30] Other control systems include the educational system, the medical and social services, economic organizations and religious institutions, ibid. F. H. McClintock and T. B. Hadden, 'Law in social control systems: a functional analysis', in *The Division and classification of the Law* (London, Butterworths, 1970), ed. by J. A. Jolowicz. On the question of regarding criminal statistics as part of an interactive process see: Stanton Wheeler, 'Criminal Statistics: a reformulation of the problem', in *Journal of Criminal Law, Criminology, and Police Science* (1967), Vol. 58, pp. 317–24.

Apart from developing situational classifications of crime, various other techniques have been devised in an attempt to distinguish between the kinds of offences and the degrees of seriousness of the various incidents that make up the volume of recorded crime.[31] The one that has received the most attention from criminologists in recent years has been the various attempts to construct crime indexes.[32] The most comprehensive and systematic venture is that of Sellin and Wolfgang in which the weighting of the recorded crime incident, or event, is related to an assessment of the gravity of that event based upon the attitudes of samples of the population in the community in which the crime occurs.[33] These developments have introduced a great deal more sophistication unto the assessments made as to the state of crime. They have clearly indicated the falsification underlying a great deal of public discussion in which the implication is that all crimes can be regarded as of equal importance. The methods and techniques utilized in the construction of indexes have not only raised a large number of questions as to the validity of the results obtained but have also cast some doubt as to the specific aims for which these indexes have been constructed.[34] A great deal of the discussion has been focused on the techniques of measuring attitudes to crime and to the seriousness of criminal acts; but if questions are raised as to the basic assumption that the general concept of 'crime' refers to a meaningful category of social behaviour, then it could be argued that the whole process is merely lending technological support to the maintenance of a myth.

[31] 'Social variations in crime and the construction of a criminotype', in *Crime in England and Wales* (London, Heinemann Educational Books Ltd., 1968), by F. H. McClintock and N. Howard Avison; 'Crime problems in Great Britain Today', by N. Howard Avison and F. H. McClintock, *Sixth International Congress in Criminology* (Madrid, 1970, mimeograph); and 'The role of information and research', by F. H. McClintock and P. Wiles, in *The Security Industry in the United Kingdom* (Cambridge Institute publication, 1972), ed. by Paul Wiles and F. H. McClintock.

[32] See *The Index of Crime: Some Further Studies* (Strasbourg, Collected Studies in criminological research, Vol. VIII, Council of Europe, 1970).

For a more general discussion see 'Indexes of delinquency and crime', in *Criminology*, by Sutherland and Cressey (New York, Lippincott, 8th ed. 1970 by D. Cressey), and 'Indexing Crime', in *Crimes, Courts and Figures* (London, Penguin Books, 1971), by Nigel Walker.

[33] T. Sellin and M. E. Wolfgang, *The Measurement of Delinquency* (New York, Wiley, 1964).

[34] See: G. N. G. Rose, 'Concerning the measurement of delinquency', in *British Journal of Criminology*, 1966, **6** (4); Nigel Walker, op. cit.; *Report of the Departmental Committee on Criminal Statistics* (London, HMSO, 1967); A Keith Bottomley, *Decisions in the penal process* (London, Martin Robertson, 1973), esp. Ch. I, 'Criminal Statistics and Social Attitudes'.

Criminal Statistics and Criminal Justice

It is generally claimed that criminal statistics are the most unreliable as well as being the most difficult of all official statistics to interpret.[35] A close study of other sets of official statistics, e.g. public health, education, or social welfare, and the uses to which they can be put, would lead to a serious questioning of the validity of this view. All official statistics have their 'dark figure' as well as problems of meaningful classifications. The major difficulty in the discussions on crime is that official statistics are assumed to be—or criticized for not being—an accurate assessment of the amount of crime committed in a given place over a given period of time. In that sense criminal statistics are still regarded as contributing to what Durkheim would describe as the social morphology of criminality. The current discussions on criminal statistics are at two levels. First, with the recognition of the inadequacy of the official data for assessing the state of crime as a result of the 'dark figure' phenomenon and the paucity of relevant social facts on the crimes that are reported and recorded by the police, a whole series of discussions focus on suggestions as to the ways in which official criminal statistics can be improved and augmented. Secondly, a series of discussions which question the validity of attempting to create a static abstract assessment of what is termed the state of crime, when, in fact, both criminal behaviour and criminal justice should both be recognized as interactive processes.

Some method of periodic assessment of criminality seems to be essential for those responsible for penal policy and for those responsible for law-enforcement, criminal law administration and the correctional system. More informative data of the static kind can therefore be seen as a way of introducing greater rationality in decision-making among those responsible for social control under the system of criminal justice. Such an approach also involves building up data on recidivism, as well as follow-up studies to assess results of different penal measures.[36] It could, however, be argued that attempting to solve such problems—and providing the required data for such a purpose—is primarily the concern of those responsible for criminal policy and the administration of the various parts of the criminal justice system. It might be thought that it is a healthy development to have criminologists involved in this way, and in particular that it indicates the recognition of the practical relevance of modern criminology but in so far as the criminologist undertakes the rôle of the technological research worker in the social sphere

[35] See, for example, Cressey, op. cit.
[36] On this see L. Wilkins, *Social Policy, Action, and Research* (London, Tavistock Publications, 1967).

C.C.P.P.—3

he may neglect—or even be expected to abandon—his more fundamental rôle of being an independent and informed critic of the basic issues of the social and penal processes in contemporary society. As a result of this some contemporary criminologists have become less like their academic counter-parts of the nineteenth century and more like the research technologists of industrial and governmental organizations. In this sense, some criminol-ogists are seen to be working primarily in the *applied* aspects of criminal policy and would seem to be basically committed to working *within* the existing criminal justice system: by them the facts on the state of crime and penal process are seen mainly from the perspective of the system of control.[37] We have suggested elsewhere that perhaps criminologists can assist in bringing about more effective control and yet also remain independent critics of the social and penal system but clearly these two rôles are inevitably to some extent in conflict and they are difficult to fulfil by the same in-dividual.[38] Nils Christie, among others, throws some doubt on the rôle of the criminologist as a 'problem solver' and suggests that perhaps his main task is that of a 'problem raiser'.[39] However, even as a 'problem raiser' he needs to be an informed critic and an adequate fund of basic data on crime and the control system is a prerequisite for public accountability of those with direct duties and responsibilities for criminal justice within a parlia-mentary democracy.[40]

The academic criminologist, as an informed critic, has an important rôle in the public discussions of crime problems and the criminal justice system. He can introduce both cautionary and rational elements into public discussion through his awareness of the inadequacies of criminal statistics and the false images and stereotypes of crime and criminals that can consequently so easily develop. In a recent study—the question of public opinion and criminal violence was discussed and it was noted that a considerable number of references are made to 'public opinion' by politicians, judges, penal

[37] It is of some significance that criminologists committed in this way tend to be in much demand to speak at meetings and conferences comprising such groups as judges and magistrates, police and probation officers, prison and other correctional staff.

[38] See further, 'Crime Problems in Great Britain Today', by N. Howard Avison and F. H. McClintock, *Sixth International Congress in Criminology* (1970, mimeograph).

[39] Scandinavian Criminology facing the '1970s', by Nils Christie, in *Scandinavian Studies in Criminology*, Vol. 3 (Oslo, Scandinavian University Books, 1971).

[40] See further, 'The role of information and research', by F. H. McClintock and P. Wiles, in *The Security Industry in the United Kingdom*, op. cit. Almost two decades ago Donald R. Cressey pointed out that the inadequacy of criminal statistics had been well-known for many years, so that the lack of improvement needed to be accounted for. He suggested that one reason might be a desire by administrators to avoid meaningful public discussions about the control system of criminal justice. See Donald R. Cressey, 'The State of Criminal Statistics', in *National Probation and Parole Association Journal* (1957).

administrators and other prominent persons in public life, as if there were a considerable body of knowledge on the subject and acceptable techniques for ascertaining precisely what that opinion is, at a particular time on a particular topic. Yet as the research worker knows full well it is no easy task to ascertain public attitudes to specific crimes; moreover, the relationship between the findings on social attitudes and the notion of 'public opinion' is by no means clear.[41]

Obviously, the concept of public opinion is a highly abstract and very general term and it has to be recognized that it contains a complex pattern of many shades and must be studied for differences between various social groups. Also it may be important to distinguish between sporadic, or perhaps superficial attitudes, relating to specific violent crimes that have been highlighted or extensively reported and attitudes on violence which may possibly be of a more permanent and fundamental nature and which are perhaps facets of an individual's personality or of his more enduring 'reference' groups.[42]

At the second level of discussion on crime problems, the criminologists question the usefulness of criminal statistics other than that of reflecting the activities of the law-enforcement and criminal justice process. Criminal statistics are seen primarily as a part of the control system and not in any way as indicating changes in patterns of social deviance. In an attempt to understand the significance of deviance and the interaction between the deviant and those responsible for social control, a great deal of recent criminological research has taken the official statistics on crime and criminals as a starting point in a process of going behind these data in order to study the law in action. This has led to a greater emphasis being placed on the study of the rôle of the victim or loser in the crime situation and to focusing attention on the question of styles of policing in relation to knowledge about crime, as well as the processes in decision-making in the context of criminal law administration and sentencing. The criminal law, procedure and criminal administration are all seen as undergoing change. Criminal statistics reveal little or nothing about these dynamic processes: they are rather like the photograph taken at a picnic which indicates something about who was there but give no indication as to the drama that took place.[43]

---

[41] Stanley Cohen (ed.), *Images of Deviance* (London, Penguin, 1971); Stanley Cohen, *Folk devils and moral panics: the creation of mods and rockers* (London, MacGibbons & Kee, 1972); and Stanley Cohen and Jock Young (eds.), *The manufacture of news: social problems, deviance and the mass media* (London, Constable, 1973).

[42] F. H. McClintock, 'The phenomenological and contextual analysis of criminal violence', op. cit.

[43] On crime as 'entertainment' and 'drama' see Laurie Taylor, *Deviance and Society* (London, Michael Joseph, 1971).

Conclusion

Over the last two centuries attempts have been made to ascertain the state of crime on the basis of statistics derived from governmental sources. In the earlier period the emphasis was placed upon the need for developing statistics for that purpose. In the middle period criminologists were critical as to the use of criminal statistics for the purposes of ascertaining the state of crime. Research has contributed to delineating the 'dark figure' phenomenon as well as bringing to notice the paucity of relevant social information on crimes that are recorded. In the more recent period, some criminologists have contributed to attempting to make improvements in the kind of data available, while other criminologists have seen criminal statistics as primarily a method of approaching a study of the various control agencies concerned with criminality and criminal justice of which the official criminal statistics form an integral part. During this process the idea of attempting to ascertain the state of crime *per se* has largely been abandoned and, in fact, the reality behind the idea of a state of crime has been widely questioned. Many myths about different kinds of crime and criminals have also been exposed and the rôle of criminal statistics have come to have a more limited—and yet in many ways more significant—rôle in research and in discussions on crime and the criminal justice process.

Criminal statistics have been mainly developed as part of a system of public accountability in democratic societies; attempts to use them for different purposes by criminologists is perhaps not unconnected with the greater awareness and sophistication that has been developing in studies of crime as a social phenomenon. In recent years criminologists have called in question the adequacy of criminal statistics as public documents of accountability from those who have duties and responsibilities directly connected with law-enforcement, criminal justice administration and the penal system. In this new development criminological research is much nearer to assessing criminal statistics for the purposes for which they are required by parliament and the community.

LOST CAUSES IN CRIMINOLOGY

Nigel D. Walker

Criminologists say some very strange things about causation and explanation. Some of these things are said by positivists in an attempt to give their explanations the status of those in the natural sciences; some by anti-positivists in their efforts to discourage the search for scientific explanations. I shall take an example from each school: one of them I call 'the criminologists' stone', the other 'Aristotle rides again'.

The Criminologists' Stone

The criminologists' stone is the rallying point of those positivist sociologists who have for the last century been at war with what is sometimes called 'the multifactorial approach' and sometimes simply 'multiple causation'. On the one side in this guerilla war are the field-workers who patiently glean data about the multiplicity of variables associated with different kinds of mis-behaviour, bent over their calculating machines like peasants over their ploughs. Sniping at them from the heights are the glamorous partisans of unitary theory, believing either in some general explanation of all crime (and sometimes deviance to boot), or at least in the ultimate victory of such an explanation. For this is to some extent an ideological feud, in which the partisans are sustained by faith rather than by facts, the peasants by common sense rather than by success.

The feud seems to have been started by Durkheim when, in *The Rules of Sociological Method*[1] he attacked J. S. Mill's common sense assumption that the same effect could be due sometimes to one cause, sometimes to another.

'This supposed axiom of the plurality of causes is, in fact, a negation of the principle of causality,' he wrote: a sentiment which was to be echoed by Cohen and Wilkins more than half a century later. The principle which

[1] Emile Durkheim, *The Rules of Sociological Method*, Paris, 1895; (tr. S. A. Solovay and J. H. Mueller, (ed.) G. E. G. Catlin, Gleneve, Free Press, 1950).

Durkheim laid down was 'one effect, one cause'.[2] In his case no great harm was done, because he reasoned that if, say, suicide was attributable to more than one cause, it was because there was more than one kind of suicide. 'The same is true of crime'. The trouble was partly that the principle itself was hopelessly perfectionist, but chiefly that not all criminologists have reasoned from it to the common sense and harmless conclusion that there must be more than one kind of crime. Instead, they have arrived at the incredible inference that there must be a single explanation of crime, if only it could be found and formulated.

It is worth noting that those who have reasoned in this way have all been sociologists. 'Grand theory' has the sort of prestige among sociologists of deviance which Grand Opera has in the world of singers. Durkheim's followers have included such well-known sociologists as Sutherland, Albert Cohen, Matza and Wilkins. Most, if not all, of them have been concerned to protect their own more or less monolithic object of worship, whether this was differential association, delinquent value-systems, drift, or 'a general theory of deviance'.[3]

[2] '*A un même effet correspond toujours une même cause.*' Note how the use of the word 'effet' makes it sound like an analytically true proposition. In fact it is merely what Toulmin would call 'a principle of inference' (S. Toulmin, *The Philosophy of Science: an Introduction*, London, Hutchinson's University Library, 1953), and by no means a necessary one. In more exact language what is said is that the explicandum must be so defined that it is susceptible of a single explanation. This is sometimes possible: we can distinguish between sheet lightning and earth-striking lightning and offer a somewhat different explanation for each. On the other hand, we are sometimes in the position of knowing that different instances of what is called by the same name have different explanations, and yet being unable to point to observable differences between them (as we could in the case of the two kinds of lightning). In such cases we can adhere to the principle only by defining circularly one set of instances as those which are explicable by explanation A and the other as those which are explicable by explanation B. What Durkheim should have said was, 'It would be much better if we could so define social explicanda that each class was susceptible of a single explanation'.

[3] See E. H. Sutherland and D. R. Cressey, *Criminology*, 8th ed., Philadelphia, Lippincott, 1970, Chapter 4, entitled 'A sociological theory of criminal behavior'.

It is not quite clear how general Cohen or Matza intend their application of their own theories to be. Both were writing about young male delinquents, although Cohen does say, 'If the explanation is sound, then the general theory should provide a key to the understanding of other subcultures as well. If the general theory does not fit other subcultures as well then the explanation of this particular subculture is thrown into question.' (A. K. Cohen, *Delinquent Boys*, Glencoe Free Press, New York, 1955, p. 50). Matza's *Delinquency and Drift* (New York, John Wiley & Sons, 1964) was written with young male delinquents in mind, and it is not entirely clear whether 'drift' is offered as a universal explanation. His later book, *Becoming Deviant* (New Jersey, Prentice-Hall, 1969), adds two other explanatory concepts, 'affiliation' and 'signification'. On the other hand, there is no doubt about Wilkins' intentions, for he calls his type of explanation 'A General Theory of Deviance' (see *Social Deviance: Social Policy, Action and Research*, London, Tavistock, 1964, Ch. 4).

The targets of this guerilla warfare have usually been psychologists, such as Healy and Burt.[4] Very few sociologists have dared to question the mono-lithic approach, although Merton is an exception:

> . . . the assumption that a single theory will account for the entire range of behavior placed in this category [sc. 'crime or delinquency'] . . . is not too remote, in logical structure, from the assumption of a Benjamin Rush . . . that there must be *a* theory of disease, rather than distinct theories of disease . . . Just as classifying enormously varied conditions and processes under the one heading of disease led some zealous medical systematists to believe that it was their task to evolve a single over-arching theory of disease, so, it seems, the established idiom, both vernacular and scientific, of referring to 'juvenile delinquency' as though it were a single entity, leads some to believe that there must be *a* basic theory of 'its' causation . . .[5]

But this was a cry in the wilderness. Even the Gluecks, who were so often the targets in this guerilla war, hesitated to renounce the idea of a single theory completely, although at first they questioned whether it was attainable:

> We regret that we are as yet not able to emerge with a single theory that will 'explain' all delinquency and crime: and there is of course the question whether this will ever be possible in view of the 'multitude of sins' and the varieties of acts . . . We are searching for the relevant facts and will continue to do so, unimpeded, we hope, by the strangle-hold of a vague, thin and cloudy unilateral 'theory' of crime causation . . .[6]

Two years later, however, when they wrote the introduction to *Ventures in Criminology*, they seem to have succumbed to intimidation, or perhaps convinced themselves that at last they were within sight of the criminologists' stone:

> We hope that by a systematic, widely embracing process it will be possible to arrive at a unifying theory which will integrate relevant information from both a constitutional and a socio-cultural matrix. This may well provide a break-through in the quest for definitive explanations of the delinquency phenomenon.[7]

The search for the stone may seem a little passé nowadays: so many megaliths have risen and fallen and so varied are the types of conduct which

---

[4] William Healy, *The Individual Delinquent*, Boston, Little, Brown & Co., 1915; and Cyril Burt, *The Young Delinquent*, London, University of London Press, 1925 (4th ed., London, University of London Press, 1944).

[5] R. K. Merton, *Social Theory and Social Structure*, New York, The Free Press, 1968 edition, p. 231.

[6] 'Family environment and delinquency in the perspective of etiologic research.' Paper presented at the XII International Course in Criminology, Hebrew University, Sept. 1962. Reproduced in their *Ventures in Criminology*, London, Tavistock, 1964, p. 79.

[7] *Ventures in Criminology*, ibid., p. 9.

they have purported to explain. There is however nothing actually illogical about this optimism. Indeed, as Matza points out:

> theories should be elegant and parsimonious, and not simply for reasons of aesthetic sensibility . . . When many factors matter rather than few, and no one can pretend to know how many is too many, this may be a signal that our model is not a truthful simplifying of reality but instead a complicated falsehood.[8]

This is a slightly arabesque version of Occam's razor, but none the less sharp for that.

Wolfgang and Ferracuti seem to regard heuristic considerations as paramount:

> . . . the basic issue is: which approach provides for greater efficiency in the pursuit of adequate applicable knowledge *and which is more consonant with a sound philosophy of science* . . .[9]

Perhaps the most interesting part of this quotation, however, is the clause which I have italicized. This implies that whichever of the two approaches— multiple causation or unitary theory—is heuristically the more useful will also be more consonant with a sound philosophy of science. It would have been interesting if the authors had followed up this remark by a logical analysis of the case for and against multiple-factor approaches; but they did not, probably because they were intent on patching up a sort of peace treaty between the two sides.[10]

[8] *Delinquency and Drift*, op. cit., p. 23.

[9] M. Wolfgang and F. Ferracuti, *The Subculture of Violence: Towards an Integrated Theory in Criminology*, London, Tavistock, 1967, p. 61.

[10] 'The two positions, when viewed in this perspective, are not, in fact, so far removed from one another that resolution of differences is impossible. Multiple-factor adherents should:

1. state more explicitly the reasons for their 'choice' of particular items for analysis;
2. attempt to arrange these reasons for delimited factor choice within an integrated and meaningful relationship of factors, for factors that remain outside the framework of the rationale for selection are meaningless even if correlated with the dependent variable;
3. seek to link previous unintegrated but highly correlated data to existing theory; and
4. produce new theory which their integrated efforts may provide.

'The generalizing theorists should:

1. examine and make more extensive use of analysis of data already collected by the multiple-factor approach in order to produce theory more closely linked to existing research;
2. specify more explicitly the range and parameters of their conceptualizations;
3. employ wherever possible the full complement of operational concepts in the theories so that data may be gathered to support the theories directly;
4. provide wherever possible operational hypotheses that flow directly from the general theory;
5. suggest the best sources and levels of quantitative and qualitative data that could be used to examine the specific components of the theory' (ibid., p. 62).

It is difficult to resist the impression, however, that the peacemakers are really monolith-seekers who are trying to practise the charitable maxim of *parcere subjectis*. Wolfgang and Ferracuti are by their own admission working towards an integrated theory. Hirschi and Selvin[11]—who have done a great deal to clarify the notion of causation[12] in criminology—have contributed a most judicial and acute summing-up, which has to be read with great care before it is apparent that they are at heart monolith-preservers:

> Now if researchers have erred in thinking that multiple causation makes an overall theory of delinquency untenable, theorists have erred in thinking that the idea of a single theory makes multiple causation untenable. The researcher who finds that there are 'more than 170 distinct conditions . . . conducive to childish misconduct', is mistaken if he concludes that this number cannot be reduced by theoretical abstraction. The theorist who concludes that his two or three theoretical variables cannot be expanded to hundreds of distinct measures is also mistaken . . .[13]

There are some excellent points here. Many of the 'variables' which are listed by Healey, Burt and the Gluecks are really *indices*; that is, they are attempts to measure something which *may* contribute to delinquency, but which cannot be assessed directly. Thus Burt's 'mother deserted, separated or divorced' and his 'mother at work' were not so much independent variables as two indirect and crude measures of the adequacy of maternal supervision. In any case, even if they are regarded as variables in their own right, they can be 'abstracted' into 'adequacy of maternal supervision', which by a further abstraction can be combined with similar information about the father into 'quality of parental care', etc.

Eclecticism

It seems to me, however, that an important distinction is being overlooked. It is true

(i) that a *variable* can be measured by more than one *index*;
(ii) that a single explanatory statement can include more than one *variable* (as it does, for example, whenever it describes a set of sufficient conditions for the occurrence of an event).

[11] *Delinquency Research: An Appraisal of Analytic Methods*, New York, Free Press, 1967.

[12] Although they continue to talk, like Mill and Durkheim, in terms of 'causes'. Philosophers of science such as Harré would say that while it is scientific to talk about 'causation' it is only colloquially correct to talk about 'causes'.

[13] Wolfgang and Ferracuti, op. cit., p. 181. The reference is to Sir Cyril Burt, *The Young Delinquent*, op. cit.

But it is equally undeniable

   (iii) that—to use the language of sufficient conditions[14]—there may be more than one set[15] of sufficient conditions for the occurrence of an event.

And it is perfectly reasonable—and consistent with (i) and (ii)—to hold

   (iv) that not all sets of sufficient conditions can be linked to the event by the same scientific theory.

Thus in criminology there are common-sense peasants who will persist in assertions which take the following logical form:

   (1) the explanation of some crimes is to be found in congenital defects, leading to difficulty in cognitive learning or socialization;
   (2) the explanations of others are to be found in faulty upbringing;
   (3) there are some crimes which cannot plausibly be explained in ways (1) or (2), but must be attributed to the influence of reference-groups;
   (4) there are some crimes which cannot be explained in ways (1), (2) or (3), but must be attributed to sheer pressure of circumstances, such as hunger, fear or the absence of legitimate car-parking space.

No conceivable process of abstraction could produce out of these a statement or set of statements that could plausibly be called a 'single' or 'integrated' theory. It would be possible, of course, to produce a *summary* of sorts, on the following lines: 'the incidence of crime is a function of congenital traits, upbringing, reference-group values, opportunities and rational motivation'. But this is not a theory. It is what Homans rightly dismisses as a mere 'orienting statement'[16] which tells us in what directions to look for relevant variables.

In short, it is when multifactorial approaches take what can be called an 'eclectic' form that the conflict with the integrated theory school becomes irreconcilable. Eclectism in this context means involving whatever body of theory seems to offer the most plausible explanation of a particular sub-group of 'crime'. It is really eclecticism which worries—or ought to worry—the monolith-seekers. So much so that the out-and-out monolith-seeker is not content with Occam's razor or weak heuristic arguments, but tries to discredit the eclectic by arguing that there is something logically or methodologically unsound about his position. This argument has not so far been

---

[14] Because it is the simplest though not the only terminology in which the point can be made.

[15] Different sets may, of course, have some but not all conditions in common.

[16] G. C. Homans, *The Nature of Social Science,* New York, Harcourt, Brace & World, 1967, p. 14.

clearly and fully stated, and it is therefore worthwhile to piece it together from the main sources.

Cohen's statement of it is to be found in his doctoral thesis.

> A multiple factor approach is not a theory; it is an abdication of the quest for a theory. It simply asserts that this particular event is 'caused' by this particular combination of circumstances and that particular event by another combination of circumstances. [Cohen uses the term 'factor' to mean 'a particular concrete circumstance'.] This delinquency is caused by 'bad neighbourhood', 'feeble-mindedness' and 'drunken mother'; that delinquency is caused by 'poverty', 'broken home', 'bad health' and 'premature puberty' . . .[17]

He makes it clear, however, that this does not exclude theories which involve a multiplicity of *variables*. A variable he describes as 'a logical universal . . . a characteristic or aspect with respect to which an object or event may vary, such as "velocity" . . . Values of the variable are logical particulars; they are the logically possible different concrete circumstances which meet the criterion defining the variable, such as "30 miles per hour".' This makes a 'factor' in Cohen's sense sound rather like a particular value of a variable: but he is intent on distinguishing the two terms and does not discuss this. For he has to concede, of course, that there is nothing wrong with a theory which involves more than one variable. What he does insist upon is that:

> Explanation calls not for a *single factor* but for a *single theory* or system of theory applicable to all cases. It is not the attendant circumstances but the demonstration that the event and the attendant circumstances are a special case of generalised theory which constitutes an explanation.[18] (his italics).

What would constitute a 'single theory' in Cohen's eyes? As we have seen, it cannot be the use of not more than one 'variable'. But must it link together in one statement all the variables which it uses? The point can be illustrated by considering what sort of explanation can be offered of cases in which vehicles overturn on roads. The ordinary motorist would probably be prepared to say that this happens *either* because they are knocked sideways by another vehicle *or* because they were struck by a strong wind *or* because

---

[17] 'Multiple Factor Approaches.' Extracted from *Juvenile Delinquency and the Social Structure*, unpublished Ph.D. thesis, Harvard University, 1951. Reproduced in *The Sociology of Crime and Delinquency*, ed. Wolfgang, Savitz and Johnson, New York, John Wiley & Sons, 1962 (2nd edition, 1970).

[18] Ibid. Genuine *single-factor* theories are quite rare. Henry VIII believed that idleness was 'mother and root of all vices . . . thefts, murders and other heinous offences and great enormities' (see the preamble to the statute 22, Henry VIII, c. 12). In modern times the late Edward Glover believed that 'the unconscious need for punishment' was 'the key to all problems of delinquency' (*The Roots of Crime: Selected Papers on Psycho-Analysis*, Vol. II, New York, International Universities Press, 1964, p. 302).

they changed direction too quickly *or* because an axle or some other part gave way.

Any single statement which would embrace all these possibilities would obviously be a very complex one. To explain collisions one would have to describe the traffic system; to explain overturning in high winds one would need a bit of meteorology; to explain capsizing on bends one would have to talk about Newton's first law of motion: to explain the failure of an axle one might have to drag in metallurgy and chemistry. This may be why Cohen is careful to say 'single theory or *system of theory*' (my italics), a phrase which would certainly allow of more than one statement using more than one set of concepts.

But what would then give it a claim to *unity*? What distinguishes a system from a collection? Cohen does not tell us; so that we may speculate. The minimum requirement is obviously *consistency*; no pair of theoretical statements could be regarded as part of the same system if they contradicted each other. This would allow a system to consist of two or more non-contradictory explanations even if one were drawn from, say, physics and the other from chemistry. This sort of eclecticism would be quite satisfactory for the common-sense criminologist, who would like to invoke psychiatry to explain some crimes, and learning theory, economics and perhaps culture-conflict to explain others.

But Cohen is certainly not preaching eclecticism: so what is he demanding? Probably that all the general statements should come from the same science. Just as one could conceivably ask that all the explanations of overturned vehicles should be drawn from physics, so might he be asking that all the explanations of crime should be drawn from, say, psychology (or even from a branch of it, such as learning theory). After all, this is what some of the major theorists—Sutherland and Eysenck being examples—have attempted.[19] Nor are such attempts confined to criminology. Skinner and Homans, for example, offer general theories to explain all forms of social behaviour.[20]

But Cohen does not carry his argument further than the passages I have quoted, so that we are already within the realm of speculation. Are Wilkins or Matza more explicit?

Wilkins, writing in the middle sixties, is clearly a spiritual descendant of Durkheim, through Cohen. Durkheim regarded 'the supposed axiom of the plurality of causes' as a 'negation of the principle of causality'. Cohen labelled it 'an abdication of the quest for a theory'. Wilkins outdoes both

[19] See Sutherland and Cressey, op. cit., and H. J. Eysenck, *Crime and Personality*, London, Routledge, 1964.

[20] Homans, op. cit.; B. F. Skinner, *Beyond Freedom and Dignity*, London, Jonathan Cape, 1971.

when he says that it can hardly 'be dignified by the term "theory" . . . At best it must be considered an anti-theory which proposes that no theory can be formed regarding crime.'[21]

A logician, however, could fairly point out that the multiple causation approach is neither a theory nor an anti-theory. It might conceivably be called a 'meta-theory', if it involved a categorical statement *about* theories. It is doubtful, however, whether it even does that. It would be more precise to call it (as Matza does) a 'principle': that is, a prescription for an approach to the problem of explanation. The principle could be stated in either a strong or a weak form. In the strong form it would be 'Plan your research on the assumption that there is no monolith to be found'. In a more moderate form it would be 'Plan it so that *if there is no monolith* to be found your work will not be wasted'.

It is this logical error which leads Wilkins to take up the extreme view that the multiple causation approach is in some way unscientific:

> Proponents of the theory would claim that since research has found no single factor as the cause of crime, but rather that many different factors appear together associated with greater or lesser frequency of criminal activity, this is evidence for multiple causation. But the theory does not facilitate the deduction of any hypotheses or practical consequences that are of any help whatsoever. If it is claimed that the theory applies to all factors which are operationally found to be related to criminal tendencies as they become known, it is apparent that the theory lacks the major and essential feature of any scientific theory—it is framed in such a way that it is impossible to find any test whereby it could be proved wrong.[22]

This is a very odd argument. Of course it is impossible to think of any test by which the principle could be proved wrong. To prove it wrong would be to prove the opposite: that is, that a 'single factor' is responsible for crime. Leaving aside any views one may have about the likelihood of this, what sort of 'test' would prove this? Only, I suggest, the actual discovery of some single 'factor' which could be shown to be a 'cause' of all crime; or at least could not be shown to be. The alternative would be to devise some sort of proof in advance of any such discovery that there must be such a factor, which is hardly conceivable.

Matza's reasoning is more satisfactory (and incidentally leads to a less extreme view about the acceptability of what he calls 'multi-causation'). I have already quoted his sensible reminder about Occam's razor. He also has an interesting distinction to make, this time between *factors* and *contingencies*:

[21] Op. cit., pp. 36–7.
[22] Ibid., p. 37.

When factors become too numerous, there is a tendency for them to be not factors at all, but rather contingencies. The term factor after all means something. A factor is a condition that is applicable to a given universe. It has an effect on everyone, not equally to be sure but according to degree. Factors may matter to varying extents, but every factor must by definition matter to some extent. Is the way in which a policeman responded to a child on their first meeting a factor? Does it matter or not? Is American foreign policy a factor? Does it matter or not? . . . And so on, endlessly. Common sense tells us that these occurrences may matter, or not, depending on many other things that may more legitimately be called factors. Some occurrences may or may not matter. Thus, they are contingencies and not factors . . .[23]

The point is worth making. But it will not reduce Burt's list very substantially; and hardly any of the Gluecks' list can be dismissed as 'contingencies'. I doubt whether Matza himself regards this as a conclusive argument against the principle of multiple causation.

Where I think he does carry Cohen's argument a stage further is where he says:

Whenever objections are raised about a specific viewpoint or more fundamental objections about the preconceptions of positive criminology, serious discussion and scrutiny is evaded by the seemingly frank and humble admission that 'other factors are operative'. The principle of multi-causation may be an honorable heuristic device. But it may also become a powerful force for intellectual inertia. It may point the way to new discoveries. Or it may allow discussants to dodge the necessity of a serious reappraisal of the nature of their object of study. Whether the principle of multi-causation is a legitimate heuristic device or *a way of avoiding the implications of negative evidence* depends, partially, on the number of factors invoked.[24]

The crucial clause in this passage is the one in which he points out that the notion of multiple causation may be 'a way of avoiding the implications of negative evidence'. This seems to me the clearest and most logical statement of the case against eclecticism, although Matza can hardly be said to have stated it in full in nine words. For the eclectic position, in its simplest form, is this:

Some crimes are ascribable to cause A, some to cause B, some to cause C . . . (and so on).

Thus, if evidence is produced to show that a particular crime is not ascribable to A, or that not all crimes of a certain category are ascribable to A, the eclectic can always say, 'Ah well, it (or some, as the case may be) must be ascribable to B or C.' It is this which gives the eclectic position the appearance

[23] *Delinquency and Drift*, op. cit., pp. 22–3.
[24] Ibid., p. 22, my italics.

of being incapable of falsification; and if Wilkins' objection had taken this form, rather than the more sweeping form which it did take, it would have been less easy to dispose of.

There does seem, however, to be a valid answer even to this formidable objection. So long as two conditions are fulfilled, it can be maintained that eclectic approaches are *not* unfalsifiable. The conditions are:

1. that the eclectic's list of possible causes is a finite one: that is, that having named those which he can name he does not end up by saying, 'and so on' or words to that effect;
2. that every one of his named possibilities is capable of being falsified empirically.

If these conditions are both fulfilled, then any given eclectic set of explanations is falsifiable.

At first sight, of course, these conditions appear to set an impossibly high standard. Must the eclectic show how each possible explanation could be falsified, given our present techniques of research? Or is it sufficient that it should be possible to imagine how each might be falsified? In short, is he being asked for practical or theoretical falsifiability? Karl Popper, to whom we owe the falsifiability criterion, would clearly answer 'theoretical falsifiability'.[25]

By the same token, the eclectic can argue that so long as the list of causes which he has in mind is finite in nature, his position can be regarded as scientific (in Popper's sense) even if he cannot confidently say at this stage 'and that is the end of the list'. It might be reasonable, however, to ask of him that he should reach a point on his list at which he is prepared to say, 'and there are some other causes, but the crimes attributable to them are negligible in number'. This would give his opponent the chance of pointing to a category of crimes which was *not* negligible in number, and could not be explained by anything on the eclectic's list. That particular list would then be shown to be defective, although the eclectic peasant could then get down to work in the hope of unearthing the missing explanations.

In this discussion I have had to include a rather tedious collection of quotations in order to show that not only Durkheim but also several contemporary sociologists with high and deserved reputations really have expressed the views which I have been dissecting. But here is one final quotation—this time from a philosopher—which I include for the sheer love of it:

[25] See K. R. Popper, *Conjectures and Refutations*, London, Routledge and Kegan Paul, 1963: 'The criterion to falsifiability . . . says that statements, or systems of statements, in order to be regarded as scientific, must be capable of conflicting with possible, or *conceivable*, observations' (p. 39, my italics).

There was once a man who aspired to be the author of the general theory of holes. When asked 'What kind of hole—holes dug by children in the sand . . . holes dug by gardeners . . . tank traps, holes made by roadmakers?' he would reply indignantly that he wished for a *general* theory that would explain all of these. He rejected *ab initio* the . . . pathetically common-sense view that of the digging of different holes there are quite different kinds of explanation to be given; why then, he would ask, do we have the concept of a hole? . . .[26]

MacIntyre was in fact writing about political science, but he could well have been thinking of general theories of deviance.

Aristotle Rides Again

But it is time to turn to the anti-positivists and a new logical muddle.

'By definition, a major cause of crime is the criminal law itself': the quotation is from a broadcast talk by Stanley Cohen.[27] To do him justice, he was simply echoing the authors of *The New Criminology*,[28] who refer to the legal prohibition of certain acts as the 'formal cause' of crime. They in turn acknowledge their debt to Professor Sarbin and Dr. Miller,[29] who were in their turn exhuming an Aristotelian view of causation.

Aristotle distinguished four kinds of cause: material, efficient, final and formal. In his well-known example, the making of a statue, the material cause is the stone from which it is sculpted; the efficient cause is the sculpting, and the final cause is the sculptor's purpose. All this is fairly clear, although it belongs to long out-moded metaphysics. It is undeniable that the statue could not come into existence without stone or some other material, or without sculpting, and that the sculptor would not shape it as he does without some fairly definite objective.[30] All these things could therefore be called in more modern language 'necessary conditions' of the statue's coming into existence.

The notion of *formal* cause needs a little more explanation. It is the essence of a statue that it is a representation of something; this is what makes it a statue instead of a mere piece of irregularly shaped stone. If it

[26] A. MacIntyre, *Against the Self-images of the Age*, London, Duckworth, 1971, p. 260.

[27] In the BBC programme *Controversy* on 23 August 1973. Reprinted as 'The Failures of Criminology', *The Listener*, **90**, 622, 8 Nov. 1973.

[28] Ian Taylor, Paul Walton and Jock Young, *The New Criminology*, London, Routledge, 1973, pp. 46, 65.

[29] See T. R. Sarbin and J. E. Miller, 'Demonism revisited: the XYY chromosome analogy', *Issues in Criminology*, 1970, **5**, pp. 195 et seq.

[30] Much more than this, of course, was implied in the notion of final causes and still survives in teleological forms of functional explanation; but that is not the subject of this article.

were not a representation it would not be a statue: being a representation is its formal cause. The authors of *The New Criminology* would argue that in the same way a crime is by definition conduct which is prohibited by the criminal law: unless it were prohibited it would not be a crime. Similarly, to be deviant an action must be regarded as such. So the criminal law or the disapproval of others are the formal causes of crimes or deviance, as the case may be.

At first sight there is little wrong with talking in this mediaeval way. If one wants to emphasize that a necessary condition of an action's being a crime is that it should fulfil the definition of a crime—that is, be prohibited by the criminal law in the jurisdiction within which it takes place—and if one feels that this tautology is made more impressive by using the language of Aristotle and Aquinas, is any harm done?

But it is more serious if the aim of doing so is to imply, without actually saying so, that we should not have the misbehaviour in question—or at least not so much of it—if we had not been so ill-advised as to prohibit it. The logical fallacy is obvious. Granted that breaking into other people's premises without their permission would not be a crime if it had not been prohibited by the criminal law, that does not entail that people would not do it, or would do it less often. An old-fashioned criminologist might even suggest that more people would do it, and that people who had already done it would do it more often.

On the other hand, there are some valid points which Cohen and his colleagues sometimes link with this fallacy. First, there is John Stuart Mill's point that we use, or try to use, the criminal law to discourage quite a number of sorts of behaviour which *ought* not to be penalized because they harm only the doer. Mill's point was a moral one; but latter-day utilitarians have added the more forceful points that there are also types of criminal behaviour of which the harm may be imaginary, or which, though undeniably harmful, are not really influenced by the criminal law. To point this out, however, is not to answer the question 'Why do people behave in these ways?'. Instead, it suggests the entirely separate questions: 'Why do societies (i) disapprove so much of these forms of behaviour and (ii) resort to the criminal law rather than other ways of discouraging them?'

Secondly, there is Lemert's point about 'secondary deviance': that some people break the law because they have been labelled as law-breakers.[31] The mechanism underlying this generalization may be the simple reluctance of employers to give legitimate employment to people with criminal records, so that the latter see illegitimate acquisition as their only opportunity.

[31] E. M. Lemert, *Human Deviance, Social Problems and Social Control*, Englewood Cliffs, N.J., Prentice-Hall, 1969, Ch. 3.

Sometimes ostracism compels the convicted person to seek companionship amongst people ostracized for similar reasons, so that he becomes a member of a group whose rules of conduct permit or even encourage law-breaking. Sometimes the labelling process changes his own view of himself, so that he believes himself to be the sort of person who is bound to behave as the label says he does. To tell someone that he is an alcoholic may well destroy any confidence he had in his ability to control his drinking. These and other mechanisms have been suggested and described by 'labelling theorists', and in particular by one of the authors of *The New Criminology*.[32] It is fair to say that they have been credibly described rather than demonstrated, and it is worth noting that although two social psychologists—Freedman and Doob —have carried out experiments which give limited support to labelling theory, their book[33] is not cited by the sociologists who are most in need of such evidence. In any case the question which labelling theorists are trying to answer is not 'Why has this or that society resorted to making this or that form of conduct criminal?' nor 'Why do people indulge in it at all?' but the question 'Why are people who have indulged in it likely to go on doing so?'[34]

There is yet another question, however, which it is sensible to ask. Given that a certain kind of behaviour is an infringement of the criminal law, given that some people nevertheless infringe the law in this way, and given that their behaviour is observed by others whose values are law-abiding, why are some of the infringements seen as such, others not? Why is a fight between football players seen as a matter for the referee rather than the police, when there is no law that excuses assaults on the football field? Again, a man who offers a tentative sexual caress to a woman who knows him will at worst have it rejected; but if he is a stranger the same gesture may lead to his being charged with indecent assault. There are subtler determinants than these, of course; the conventions governing the perception of thefts as thefts or as mere taking of perquisites are complex and vary from organization to organization. (Some organizations tacitly allow employees of certain ranks to claim first-class travelling expenses if they choose to travel second-class: others treat this as fraud.) There is a profitable

[32] See Jock Young, *The Drugtakers*, London, MacGibbon and Kee, 1971, and his essay 'The Role of the Police as Amplifiers of Deviancy, Negotiators of Reality and Translators of Fantasy', in S. Cohen (ed.), *Images of Deviance*, Harmondsworth, Penguin Books, 1971.

[33] J. L. Freedman and A. N. Doob, *Deviancy: The Psychology of Being Different*, New York, Academic Press, 1968.

[34] The bigoted labelling theorist seems to believe that his is the only answer to this question: the broad-minded one admits that people sometimes repeat their misbehaviour because they enjoy it, or get into the same sort of situations, or for other obvious reasons. But that is a side-issue.

field of study here which has been barely entered; but my object is simply to demonstrate that those who do enter it are trying to answer a *third* sort of question.

Fourthly, it is undoubtedly the case that some infringements of the law would not be committed if they were not infringements of the law. Adolescents and even older people will steal because of the excitement which they get out of risking arrest. Some people break the law as a protest, either against the irrationality—real or supposed—of the prohibition itself, or against the legitimacy of the prohibiting authority. If one believes that it is irrational to prohibit the use of cannabis while countenancing the use of nicotine, alcohol and tranquillizers, one may smoke pot as a protest. If one believes that the King of England has no right to tax one's tea, one may empty it into Boston harbour. These situations come nearer than any other to justifying the assertion that 'if it weren't a crime they would not do it'. But they are, of course, rather special situations, and are far from being all that is meant by the authors of *The New Criminology*.

It is possible that they are really trying to make a fifth point: that crime is so serious a problem because there are a lot of things which people inevitably do, but which societies—or the power-wielding elites in societies, to be more precise—are ill-advised enough to discourage by means of the criminal law. I am tempted to nickname this 'Eden-ideology' because one of the implications of Genesis, Chapter 3, is that Adam and Eve were happy and harmless nudists until they were 'criminalized' by the knowledge of good and evil and the punishment of Jehovah.

Eden-ideology is again based on something that happens occasionally but not nearly often enough to be made the basis of an ideology. There are situations in which people are happily and harmlessly doing something when they are suddenly told that it is wicked or illegal. The missionaries' imposition of cloths on South Sea islanders was a latter-day enactment of Adam and Eve's criminalization. In present-day Britain the Ministry of Transport has decided that for their own good people must be discouraged by the criminal law from riding motor-cycles without crash-helmets. But Eden-ideology is quite inapplicable to the crimes such as murder, rape, robbery or burglary, which have been serious crimes in every civilized culture—and most uncivilized ones too—for many generations. If asked why a young man illegally rides his motor-cycle without a crash-helmet one may reasonably explain that he was in the habit of doing so before it was made a crime, and either forgot or felt that nobody had the right to force him to wear a helmet. But this sort of answer will not satisfy anyone in his senses where long-established crimes are concerned. In this case the question must be 'Why, in a society in which such actions are widely known to be criminal and severely punishable, are they committed?' For the purpose of the present argument it does not matter whether the answer is in terms of constitutional weakness of self-control, faulty upbringing, delinquent subcultures, or lower-class value systems, so long as it is a genuine attempt to answer *this* question.

To call the criminal law the 'formal cause' of crime, however, is an intellectual card-trick by which the answers to other questions are forced on us as if they were the answer to *this* question. Those other questions are also fascinating, but this fascination is apt to conceal the fact that they are completely distinct. The purpose of this sleight of hand is also very worthy: to emphasize the part which 'society'—to use that inexact but popular term—plays in generating criminal behaviour. But there are more straightforward and convincing ways of doing so which do not need to be dressed up in scholastic metaphysics.

What the two fallacies which I have been discussing have in common is that both originate from a failure to think about what is being explained. In the case of the criminologists' stone it was simply assumed by Durkheim and his successors[35] that because we have a general concept called 'crime' we ought to have a general theory to account for it: '*à un même effet correspond toujours une même cause*'. The same reasoning could be, and has been, applied to 'disease', 'deviance' and 'holes'. In the case of formal causes several quite distinct *explicanda*—the reasons for prohibitions, secondary deviance, the selective perception of behaviour as criminal, and the Eden-situation— are thoroughly mixed and given a fancy name which suggests a new sociological insight. Criminological explanation will not make much progress until we analyse more precisely than this what it is that we want explained.

[35] But *not* Merton this time.

SERIOUSNESS OF CRIMINALITY AND CONCORDANCE AMONG DANISH TWINS

Karl O. Christiansen

The Nature-Nurture Problem

Most of the previous criminological twin studies have aimed at elucidating the problem of heredity and environment. Among the older students of twins there has, with a few exceptions, not been much doubt as to the interpretation of the results. It is, however, worthy of note that Francis Galton, the founder of the twin method, was much more conservative in his conclusions than were many of his successors. Through his studies of 35 twin sets 'of close similarity' and 20 sets of 'unlike' twins he discovered, as early as 1875, that similar twins were alike and dissimilar twins unlike with respect to a large spectrum of characteristics; that is, he discovered the existence of two kinds of radically different twins, monozygotic (MZ) and dizygotic (DZ) pairs. When a pair was closely similar in some traits, this would most probably also be true of other traits (mental, physical and pathological) even when life had carried the twins into different environments. There is no doubt that he emphasized, or over-emphasized, the importance of inheritance, but he still maintained that the problem of the relative effect of *nature* and *nurture* has to be answered this way: 'There is no escape from the conclusion that nature prevails enormously over nurture *when the differences of nurture do not exceed what is commonly to be found among persons of the same rank of society in the same country*' [my italics].[1] The emphasized reservation is an example of his genius.

In the first criminological twin study *Verbrechen als Schicksal* (1929), Johannes Lange compared 13 monozygotic twin pairs and 17 dizygotic pairs. He found 10 and 2 pairs, respectively, which were concordant with respect

---

[1] F. Galton, 'History of Twins, as a Criterion of the Relative Powers of Nature and Nurture', *Journal of the Anthropological Institute*, 1875, pp. 391 ff, quoted from Karl Pearson, *The Life, Letters and Labours of Francis Galton*, Vol. I, Cambridge University Press, 1914, p. 8, see also Vol. II, 1924, pp. 126 ff.

to criminality. Lange's conclusion ran without any reservations as follows: 'As far as crime is concerned, monozygotic twins react on the whole in a definitely similar manner, dizygotic twins behave quite differently. In accordance with the significance of the twin method we must conclude that heredity plays a quite preponderant part among the causes of crime.'[2] He seems to be the most faithful geneticist among the criminologists, but he was not the last of the Mohicans. As late as 1959 his view was accepted and repeated by Freiherr von Verschuer in his *Genetik des Menschen*: 'Discordance with monozygotic twins may as a rule be attributed to peristaltical influences'.[3] In respect of criminality particularly, he wrote: 'Discordance with mono-zygotic twins, however, merely appears when only one of the pair has . . . [become] . . . mentally ill or abnormal through a demonstrable (shown) external injury, or in cases of minor or isolated offences on which external conditions more frequently exert a concurrent influence'.[4] He added, further, that it was the abnormal, heritable character of recidivists that was the most important cause of their recidivism.

A. M. Legras, writing in 1933, admitted that his 4 concordant monozygotic twins may have influenced each other, because they had not been reared apart, but as the 5 dizygotic pairs were all discordant he concluded that heredity was the decisive factor.[5]

Rosanoff and his collaborators published in 1934 results from 33 probably monozygotic and 23 probably dizygotic adult twins, and 42 probably monozygotic and 25 dizygotic juveniles. Their conclusion came, as far as adult criminality was concerned, close to that of Lange and Legras, but juvenile delinquency was considered a predominantly socially conditioned phenomenon. They particularly discussed the possible explanations of the existence of discordant monozygotic twins, but did not touch upon the problem of greater environmental similarities in MZ pairs than in DZ pairs.[6]

Friedrich Stumpfl, seven years after Lange's book, made a more prudent assessment on the basis of his investigation of 18 MZ pairs and 19 DZ pairs which showed concordance rates of 61 and 37 per cent, respectively: 'From our insight into the greater environmental similarity of monozygotic twins compared to the dizygotic it becomes evident that if the twin method is

[2] *Verbrechen als Schicksal*, Leipzig, Georg Thieme, 1929, p. 14.

[3] Otmar Freiherr von Verschver, *Genetik des Menschen*. Lehrbuch der Humangenetik. München-Berlin: Urban & Schwarzenberg, 1959, p. 20.

[4] Ibid., p. 344.

[5] *Z. ges. Neurol. Psychiat.*, 1933, **144**, pp. 198–222; and *Psychosen en criminaliteit bij tweelingen*, Utrecht, 1932.

[6] A. J. Rosanoff, L. M. Hardy and I. A. Rosanoff, *J. Crim. Law Criminol.*, 1934, **24**, p. 932.

used as a method of studying the causes of crime then the generally more frequent concordant behaviour of the partner in monozygotic pairs (among those showing signs of early recidivism) compared to the considerable differences of dizygotic twins who have exhibited the same type of behaviour, ought not to be used exclusively in favour of heredity.'[7]

Heinrich Kranz in 1936 dealt with the problem of identification ('Sich-Eins-Fühlen') in some detail,[8] but he did not regard it as a factor which could influence considerably the conclusions drawn from twin studies. Consequently in his summary he stated, on the basis of his study of 32 monozygotic and 43 dizygotic twins with 66 and 53 per cent concordant pairs, respectively, that Lange's conclusion was confirmed—although the difference is far from being statistically significant. Kranz maintained that heredity played a greater rôle as a cause of crime than was generally assumed, but he admitted that the existence of only a relatively small proportion of concordant, and the existence of discordant, monozygotic pairs demonstrated that in a few cases other factors were also of some importance.[9]

C. A. Borgström in 1939 defined the problem in the same way as Lange, but did not discuss the interpretation of his results at great length.[10]

In his first publication in 1941 Shûfu Yoshimasu by and large followed in the footsteps of Lange and Kranz. He considered psychopathy to be the main factor in crime. Concordant monozygotic pairs, he claimed, are similar with respect to frequency of offence, type of offence and form of psychopathy. Here, too, we observe 'the preponderant influence of heredity' on the occurrence of socially harmful acts.[11]

In his later works (1961 and 1965) Yoshimasu also interpreted his results in the same way as Lange, without any discussion of the intra-pair differences in environment between monozygotic and dizygotic pairs. He simply stated that 'there is no special difference in regard to their [MZ's and DZ's] environment, especially their earlier family backgrounds'. The different concordance rates in monozygotic and dizygotic pairs were 'mainly due to hereditary factors'. In 1965, however, he abandoned the concept of psychopathy as a crime factor and concentrated on studies of the 'life curves' of the twins, i.e. the distribution of offences and punishments in the criminal career. He found that the really late beginners among the monozygotic twins were

[7] *Die Ursprünge des Verbrechens. Dargestellt am Lebenslauf von Zwillingen*, Leipzig, Georg Thieme, 1936, p. 131. There is, however, no doubt about Stumpfl's final conclusion, see pp. 67–8 below.

[8] *Lebensschicksale krimineller Zwillinge*, Springer, Berlin, 1936, p. 246.

[9] Ibid., p. 250.

[10] *Arch. Rass.-u. Ges. Biol.*, 1939, **33**, pp. 334–43.

[11] *Psychiatr. Neurol. Jap.*, **45**, pp. 455–531.

'either first offenders or had undoubtedly mild curves'. The fact that 70 per cent of the brothers of a criminal DZ twin remained non-criminal may, he thought be explained to some extent by interpersonal relations in the family, but a more complete understanding would be impossible 'without assuming the extent of the difference in hereditary factors'.[12]

The fundamental assumption which underlies such conclusions about nature and nurture as have been drawn from most of the criminological twin studies is that the two twins in each pair, *regardless of zygocity*, live and have lived in closely similar environments, especially during childhood. In other words: intrapair environmental variations must be the same for MZ twins as it is for DZ twins. It is open to serious doubt whether this condition was ever fulfilled.

On the contrary, among most social psychologists and a number of psychiatrists, it seems generally accepted that the environment experienced by MZ twins is more similar than that of DZ twins. Since von Bracken (1934) a number of studies have confirmed this assumption.[13] Among factors which have been considered to be of importance a few will be mentioned. Monozygotic pairs tend on the whole to establish much more similar environments than do dizygotics; they spend a considerably longer time together, follow each other to school, do their lessons together, and choose the same friends more often than do dizygotics. Lehtovaara's conclusion is that: 'In any case it can be considered as proved that in psychological twin studies MZ and DZ twins reared together can, under no circumstances, be called equally similar with respect to environment.'[14] In another study[15] the MZs were, according to their parents, more closely attached to and dependent on each other than DZs. Their level of education and their choice of occupation were also more similar. They were more happy to be twins, and their 'index

---

[12] *Acta Crim. Med. Leg. Jap.*, 1961, **27**, pp. 117–41, and 1965, **31**, pp. 144–53 and 190–97,

[13] See among others: A. Lehtovaara, *Psychologische Zwillingsuntersuchungen*, Helsinki· Suomalainen Tiedeakatemia, 1938; E. Østlyngen. *Psykologisk tvillingforskning og dens problemer*, Oslo, Norsk Gyldendal, 1946; D. Burlingham, *Twins: A Study of Three Pairs of Identical Twins*, London, Imago, 1952; T. Husén, *Psychological Twin Research*, I. A. Methodological Study, Uppsala, Almquist & Wiksell, 1959 (Stockholm studies in educational psychology); R. Zazzo, *La méthode des jumeaux*, Paris, University of France Press, 1960; and *Les jumeaux. Le Couple et la personne*, Paris, University of France Press, 1960; S. J. Dencker, *Acta Psychiatr. Scand.*, 1963, **40**, Suppl. **180**, pp. 317–21; D. H. Stott, *Brit. J. Psychol.*, 1966, **57**, pp. 423–9; Tom Nilsson, *Om den sociala miljøns inverkan på intrapardifferenser hos monozygota tvillingpar*, Stencil, Stockholm, 1966 (mimeo.); L. Mosher and D. Feinsilver, *Special Report: Schizophrenia*, (Publ. No. (HSM) 72–9007), NIMH, Rockville, Md., 1971.

[14] Op. cit., pp. 299 ff.

[15] Husén, op. cit., pp. 189 ff.

of devotion to each other' was greater than among DZs. MZ-twins co-operate, DZ-twins compete: von Bracken spoke of a 'tendency towards differentiation in dizygotic twins'.[16]

Opponents of this view refer to the existence of particular organic conditions in the pre-natal phase, to damage at birth, and to later cerebral disturbances and illnesses which are supposed to veil the basic, inheritable likeness of MZ twins. By this they claim not only to have accounted for a number of cases of discordant MZ pairs, but also to have found a set of factors which will, in some way, counterbalance the increasing environmental similarities of MZ pairs which occur later. As far as the present author can see, however, it is not possible to weigh, for instance, the relative impact of factors which make for greater disparity against those which lead to greater similarity in MZ twins.

On the basis of our present limited knowledge the following would be a conservative statement: In the behavioural sciences the twin method can throw light on the question of the interaction of environment and personality, which in itself is a product of inheritance and environment, but twin studies cannot solve the problem of nature and nurture.

Before conclusions can be drawn about the hereditary and environmental factors which play a part in the breaching of social norms, other factors have to be taken into account. Inspired by Gottesman and Shield's recent book *Schizophrenia and Genetics* (1972), the present author would define these as follows: If genes are important in the manifestation of criminality, MZ twins should be affected more often than DZ twins. Such a result would prove the importance of the genotype if the following two conditions are observed: firstly that the MZ twins *as such* are *not* especially predisposed to criminality, and secondly that the environments of MZ twins are *not* systematically more alike than those of DZ twins in respects which can be shown to be of ætiological significance for criminality.[17] It must, however, be stated that it will be extremely difficult to demonstrate that the latter of these two necessary, *negative*, conditions is fulfilled.

Behind the general interpretation of the findings in criminological twin studies, other similarities than those expressed in simple rates of concordance are invoked. Stumpfl, who notes various degrees of concordance, maintains that monozygotic male twin pairs characterized by early and

[16] *Character and Personality*, **2**, 1933–4, p. 306.

[17] I. Gottesman and J. Shields (*Schizophrenia and Genetics*, New York and London, Academic Press, 1972, p. 25) express the sequence as: 'Such a result proves the importance of genotype *unless it can be shown* that the MZ twins as such . . .' [My italics]. This wording *might* be read to mean that the authors want to place the burden of proof on the opponents, if any, not on the originator of new findings—but this can hardly be their opinion.

persistent criminality will show an 'almost one hundred per cent concordance' as one moves up to the groups of offenders with the highest levels of concordance.

Kranz analysed his sample with regard to number of convictions, length of sentence, type of offence, and age at the commencement of the criminal career. He found a far-reaching similarity in monozygotic concordant pairs and only a rather limited similarity in dizygotic concordant pairs, decreasing as more indices of crime were taken into consideration.

The validity of such results as a basis for conclusions regarding the influence of inheritable factors will be discussed later. First we shall look at some results concerning type of offence, number of sanctions for offences against the Criminal Code, and severity of such sanctions.

A DANISH STUDY

The Sample

The basic material of the present study is drawn from the Danish Twin Register.[18] It comprises 3,586 twin pairs born on the Danish Islands (i.e. Denmark excluding Jutland) between 1881 and 1910 where both twins were alive at least until the age of 15. In 799 pairs one or both twins were convicted of crime, delinquency or minor offences. It can be regarded as an almost complete, unselected sample, and so far it comes closer to the ideals of Siemens and Luxenburger[19] than any of the previous criminological twin studies.

Before discussing the results it will be necessary to consider the definitions used in the study.

The Concept and Classification of Offences

In this enquiry criminality includes (a) 'crime proper', i.e. acts which have been punished by some kind of conditional or unconditional deprivation of liberty; it includes juvenile delinquency, but not acts committed by persons below the age of criminal responsibility which in Denmark is 15 years. Such acts are as a rule offences against the Criminal Code. In the following this is

[18] M. Hauge, B. Harvald, M. Fischer, K. G. Jensen, N. J. Nielsen, I. Raehild, R. Shapiro, T. Videbech, 'The Danish Twin Register', *Acta Geneticae Medicae et Gemellogiae*, 17, pp. 313–31.

[19] H. W. Siemens, *Die Zwillingspathologie*, München: Springer Verlag, 1924, p. 61; H. Luxenburger, *Zentralblatt für die gesamte Neurologie und Psychiatrie*, 1930, 56, pp. 146 ff., 153 ff., and particularly pp. 164 ff.

called 'crime'. Criminality also includes (b) 'minor offences', i.e. acts which have been punished only by fines or even less serious penalties, such as warnings. Such acts are as a rule offences against Special Laws.

Type of offence. The offences are classified into three types: (a) Violence and sexual offences (VS), occurring either alone (about three-fifths of these cases) or together with other offences; (b) Other offences against the Criminal Code (P+), which are almost exclusively property offences; and (c) Offences against Special Laws (SL), among which 8 per cent are cases of drunkenness. Concordance means that the two co-twins in a pair are registered for the same *type* of offence.

Number of sanctions. The number of sanctions for offences against the Criminal Code are counted, and combined into three classes: 0; 1; 2 and more sanctions. Twins are called concordant when both belong to the same *class*. Concordance with respect to the class '2 and more sanctions' may include twins with rather different criminal careers, e.g. one with 4 and one with 10 sanctions, but the size of the sample prohibits more detailed subdivisions.

Seriousness. Because of the limited size of the sample and the distribution of the sanctions, they are divided into three categories according to their seriousness: (a) No sanctions for offences against the Criminal Code; (b) Warnings, fines, various forms of lenient imprisonment of short duration, child welfare disposals (probation or removal to an approved school), and conditional sentences; (c) Prison sentences and special measures (Youth Prison, Work House, Mental Hospital, etc.). It goes without saying that this categorization has required some more or less expedient compromises.

In the following analysis seriousness is graduated as: Firstly, concordance in respect of the most severe sanctions (i.e. 'c' above) which is called *Concordance of the Second Degree*: CII. Secondly, other types of concordance for example between the most severe sanctions imposed on one of the co-twins and only moderately severe or mild sanctions on the other is called *Concordance of the First Degree*: CI. The last concept of concordance (i.e. CI) is the widest, and the first (CII) the most narrow.

Measures of Concordance

In criminological twin investigations the degree of concordance has been expressed by *the pairwise concordance rate,* which is defined as the ratio of concordant pairs to all criminal pairs, i.e.

$$\frac{C}{C+D}$$

where C means the number of concordant pairs, and D the number of discordant pairs.

The similarity with respect to crime may also be expressed by *the proband concordance rate,* which is the conditional frequency of one twin being criminal when it is known that the other *is* criminal. It is defined as

$$\frac{C+x}{C+x+D}$$

where C means the number of concordant pairs, D the number of discordant pairs, and x the number of pairs in the sample represented by two cases checked independently against the penal register.

In the present study, where every twin is checked separately in the penal register, x is identical with the number of concordant pairs. (This is because in such pairs both twins will be found independently of each other.) The conditional frequency can therefore be expressed as

$$\frac{2\,C}{2\,C+D}$$

The Twin Coefficient

To evaluate the influence of background factors on the concordance rates in various sub-groups of twins it is necessary to compare the concordant pairs with the total twin population. This is of particular importance when the frequency of the phenomenon is relatively high, as in the case of criminality. Here the most expedient procedure is probably to relate the proband concordance rate to the expected crime rate in the same population.

The expected frequency of criminality in a group of concordant and discordant twins, ECrR, is

$$\frac{2C+D}{2\,S}$$

where C and D have the same meaning as above, and S is the total number of criminal and non-criminal pairs in the sample. The ratio between the proband concordance rate (PRCR) and the expected crime frequency of a group of twin pairs, *the twin coefficient* (TW.Coef.)

$$\frac{PRCR}{ECrR}$$

is a measure of specific, but largely unknown properties attached to the twin situation, e.g. similarities with respect to inheritance, the general and specific social background, and situational factors. It answers the question:

how much does the probability of criminality increase for a twin (as compared to the general crime rate of the group) provided the other twin is registered for criminality.

Some Results

According to the basic assumptions of the classical twin method and some of the earlier criminological twin studies[20] it should be expected that those offenders who are registered for the most serious offences, or sentenced most often, or given the most severe sanctions will constitute a group in which the similarities between the twins as characterized by the twin coefficient will be strong.

Type of Offence
Table 1 shows the distribution of the above-mentioned kinds of offences in male monozygotic and male dizygotic twin pairs.

TABLE I

325 Male MZ Pairs and 611 Male DZ Pairs, according to Type of Offence: Violence and/or Sexual Offences (VS), Other Criminal Code Offences [mostly property offences (P+)], Special Law Offences (SL), and Zero Offences, in the Twins.

MZ Pairs

		TWIN I				
		VS	P+	SL	Zero Offences	Total
TWIN II	VS	5	2	0	6	13
	P+	2	15	8	7	32
	SL	1	5	12	33	51
	Zero Offences	2	11	23	0	36
	Total	10	33	43	46	132

DZ Pairs

		TWIN I				
		VS	P+	SL	Zero Offences	Total
TWIN II	VS	3	1	2	5	11
	P+	3	9	6	33	51
	SL	2	7	5	39	53
	Zero Offences	11	29	36	0	76
	Total	19	46	49	77	191

[20] Especially the above-mentioned works of Kranz, Stumpfl, and Yoshimasu.

It appears from the table that among 18 MZ pairs registered for violence or sex offences 5 are concordant. This gives a pairwise concordance rate of 28 per cent, and a proband concordance rate of 44 per cent. Among 27 DZ pairs 3 are concordant, corresponding to pairwise and proband concordance rates of 11 and 20 per cent respectively.

A summary of the results is presented in Table 2 which also includes data on the expected offence rates and the twin coefficients.

TABLE 2

Number of Criminal and Concordant Pairs, Pairwise Concordance Rates (PWCR), Proband Concordance Rates (PRCR), and Twin Coefficients (TWCoef), according to Type of Offence among 325 Male MZ and 611 Male DZ Twin Pairs.

	MZ Pairs			DZ Pairs		
	VS	P+	SL	VS	P+	SL
No. Criminal	18	50	82	27	88	97
No. Concordant	5	15	12	3	9	5
PWCR	0·278	0·300	0·146	0·111	0·102	0·052
PRCR	0·435	0·463	0·255	0·200	0·186	0·098
Expected	0·035	0·100	0·145	0·025	0·079	0·083
TW Coef.	12·43	4·62	1·77	8·00	2·35	1·17

PW and PR concordance rates are higher in MZ than in DZ pairs for all types of offences. In both MZ and DZ pairs they are higher for VS and P+ offences (which are at the same level) and lower for SL offences. It would, therefore, now seem possible to conclude that hereditary or environmental factors exert a certain influence on all three types of offences, although apparently a somewhat greater one on offences against the Criminal Code than on offences against special laws.

If, however, one looks at the twin coefficient, which tells how much the proband concordance rate increases in relation to the probability of one of the twins becoming a criminal, the picture changes. It then becomes obvious that both MZ and DZ pairs registered for crimes against the person show higher coefficients than pairs registered for other crimes against the Criminal Code; the lowest coefficient is for pairs with special law offences. Furthermore, the twin coefficient is higher for MZ than for DZ pairs for all three types of offences.

Thus, so far the general hypothesis on the importance of the seriousness of the offence is confirmed.

Number of Sanctions

Table 3 shows the distribution of number of sanctions for offences against the Criminal Code. It should be read in the same way as Table 1.

TABLE 3

325 Male MZ Pairs and 611 Male DZ Pairs, according to Number of Criminal Code Sanctions: 0, 1, 2 and more, for the Twins.

		MZ Pairs						*DZ Pairs*			
		TWIN I						TWIN I			
		0	1	2+	Total			0	1	2+	Total
TWIN II	0	65	16	4	85	TWIN II	0	80	30	19	129
	1	15	8	5	28		1	34	2	5	41
	2+	8	5	6	19		2+	13	0	8	21
	Total	88	29	15	132		Total	127	32	32	191

In Table 4 a summary of the results is presented.

TABLE 4

Number of Criminal and Concordant Pairs, Pairwise (PWCR) and Proband (PRCR) Concordance Rates, and Twin Coefficients (TWCoef), according to Number of Criminal Code Sanctions in 325 Male MZ and 611 Male DZ Pairs.

	MZ Pairs			*DZ Pairs*		
	0	1	2+	0	1	2+
No. Criminal	108	49	28	176	71	45
No. Concordant	65	8	6	80	2	8
PWCR	0·602	0·163	0·214	0·455	0·028	0·178
PRCR	0·751	0·281	0·353	0·625	0·055	0·302
Expected	0·266	0·088	0·052	0·209	0·060	0·043
TW Coef.	2·82	3·19	6·79	2·99	0·92	7·02

Here again the PW and PR concordance rates are higher in MZ than in DZ pairs in all sub-groups, but the rates do not increase regularly with the number of sanctions: the rates are highest for no sanction, and lowest for 1 sanction, 2 and more sanctions being placed in between. But again *the twin coefficients* change the picture. Contrary to expectation DZ pairs show slightly higher coefficients in two of the sub-groups than do MZ pairs, namely for 'no sanction' (2·99 in DZs compared to 2·82 in MZs) and for '2 sanctions or more' (7·02 in DZs compared to 6·75 in MZs). However, for 1 sanction the coefficient is as expected, according to the hypothesis: namely, 0·98 in DZ twins, and 3·19 in MZ twins.

The increase of the twin coefficient with increasing number of sanctions in MZs and partly in DZ pairs gives some support to the hypothesis about the significance of the number of offences. The irregularity in DZ twins may be due to the small absolute numbers of concordant DZ twins with 1 sanction.

Severity of Sanction

The distribution of the twins according to severity of sanctions for offences against the Criminal Code is shown in Table 5.

TABLE 5

325 Male MZ Pairs and 611 Male DZ Pairs, according to Severity of Sanctions: No Sanctions for Offences against the Criminal Code (a), Lenient Sanctions (b), Severe Sanctions (c), for the Twins.

		MZ Pairs							DZ Pairs			
		TWIN I							TWIN I			
		a	b	c	Total				a	b	c	Total
TWIN II	a	65	13	7	85		TWIN II	a	80	25	24	129
	b	14	7	3	24			b	28	3	8	39
	c	9	4	10	23			c	19	1	3	23
	Total	88	24	20	132			Total	127	29	35	191

The results are summarized in Table 6.

TABLE 6

Number of Criminal and Concordant Pairs, Pairwise (PWCR) and Proband (PRCR) Concordance Rates, and Twin Coefficients (TWCoef) according to Degree of Concordance in 325 Male MZ and 611 Male DZ Twin Pairs.

	MZ Pairs		DZ Pairs	
	CI	CII	CI	CII
No. Criminal	67	33	111	55
No. Concordant	24	10	15	3
PWCR	0·358	0·303	0·135	0·055
PRCR	0·527	0·465	0·238	0·103
Expected	0·140	0·066	0·103	0·048
TW Coef.	3·76	7·05	2·31	2·15

Both the PW and PR first and second degree concordance rates are higher in MZ than in DZ pairs, but the rates in both zygocity groups are higher for first degree than for second degree concordance.

If we look at the twin coefficient the picture once again changes. MZ pairs still show higher coefficients than do DZ pairs. However, in MZ pairs the twin coefficient is higher for concordance of the second degree (CII) than for concordance of the first degree which agrees with the general hypothesis; in DZ pairs the difference between the twin coefficients for first and second degree concordance is negligible. Again we must conclude that the results partly support the hypothesis tested here.

Discussion

It is evident from the above analysis of the Danish material that the general hypothesis gains some support from the results obtained. The most serious types of offenders and recidivists, or those who have received the most severe sentences show on the whole higher twin coefficients than other groups, i.e. they are more strongly influenced by the similarities of the twins and their environment, than are offenders against Special Laws and other petty offenders, or one-timers, or those who have got only fines or short-term sentences.

The question is whether this proves or renders it probable that heredity plays a more predominant rôle in the more serious criminal cases than in the less serious ones. Although it may seem obvious, it is not as simple as that.

The twin coefficient is not a measure of heredity. It is, as mentioned on page 70 above, an index which expresses something about the impact of the similarities of the twins, whether these are determined by environmental factors or factors in the personality, which is itself a product of heredity and environment. Consequently a greater frequency of concordance among MZ than among DZ twins means only that similar hereditary factors and/or similar prenatal, natal or postnatal environment conditions result in a greater probability of similarities in social behaviour than do disparate hereditary factors and/or disparate environmental conditions.

What has been demonstrated through the analysis of the Danish material, then, is that the more serious the crime and the criminal career, the greater the similarities as expressed in the twin coefficient. This result may seem of little consequence to a criminologist. However, seen in the light of Thorsten Sellin's theory of the significance of 'group resistance to crime'[21] it becomes more meaningful.

According to this theory the criminal code is in no way the only factor which influences social behaviour. Conduct norms also come from institu-

---

[21] *Culture, Conflict and Crime*, New York, Social Science Research Council, 1938, pp. 33 ff.

tions such as the family, the church, colleagues, etc. and are effective through the actual attitude of the community to the individuals, through ridicule, estrangement, ostracism, etc.

The group resistance against criminality is determined by the strength of the sanctions connected with conduct norms. They raise a barrier against violations. If the barrier is weak it may be because the group does not offer much resistance to violations. If, however, violations against the norm imply severe sanctions, especially of the kind which deprive the non-conformist of rights and benefits highly treasured by the group, the group resistance must be strong.[22]

Group resistance as defined by the severity of the sanction is, however, experienced differently by different people, depending on the internalization of the norm and on the definition of the act within the groups to which the actor belongs. The psychological experience of group resistance will very often be reduced in a community with a heterogeneous population and a correspondingly strongly differentiated culture including many opposing elements.[23] This means that strong group resistance involves—all other things being equal—only a small number of criminal acts, and weak group resistance involves a greater number of criminal acts.

Group resistance also seems to have an influence on the selection of persons who become criminals. Sellin recommends that criminological research concentrate on persons who have violated norms of the following characteristic nature: (a) the norms must be connected with severe sanctions; (b) the norms should have a hold on the personality of the violator; and (c) experience of the norms should be strongly emotional:

'Offenders who have overcome the greatest and most comprehensive group resistance probably disclose more clearly than others the types of personalities which are important to our aims of research'.[24]

This implies that a strong group resistance is more easily overcome by persons who, because of mental deviations, feel the resistance less strongly, or by persons who, due to unfortunate social conditions, are living under particular pressure.[25] And here the twin coefficient again enters the picture. When the twin coefficient for more serious manifestations of criminality is high, it follows that twin offenders are more often alike (i.e. MZ twins) than

---

[22] Ibid., p. 34.
[23] Ibid., pp. 42 ff.
[24] Ibid., p. 44.
[25] See, for instance, G. Inghe, *Acta Psychiatr. Neurol.,* 1941, **16,** pp. 421–58; G. Dahlberg *J. Crim. Law Criminol.,* 1948–9, **39,** pp. 327–41; Karl O. Christiansen, 'Recidivism among Collaborators. A follow-up study of 2,946 Danish men convicted of collaboration with the Germans during World War II', in M. E. Wolfgang (ed.), *Crime and Culture. Essays in Honor of Thorsten Sellin.,* New York, John Wiley, 1968.

twins who have only committed few or less serious offences. This is true, not only with respect to their criminal behaviour, but also with respect to background factors. They have acted against a greater group resistance, and greater group resistance is more easily overcome by socially or psychologically deviating persons.

The deviations which are effective in this respect are more closely connected with the personalities of the twins and their environment than are factors which lead to more milder forms of criminality. As they are common to both twins, deviations connected with the more serious forms of crime and criminal careers must be deep-rooted in common genes or common environmental factors, or both, but it is hardly possible to separate them.

The first condition for discriminating between what Galton called nature and nurture is that MZ twins are *not* especially predisposed to criminality. It is definitely not fulfilled. In MZs the frequency of persons sentenced to deprivation of liberty is 6·6 per cent, and of persons with more lenient punishments 7·4 per cent; in DZs the numbers are 4·8 and 5·6 per cent respectively. This source of error, however, is eliminated by comparing MZs and DZs in respect of the twin coefficient which is, as defined above, the ratio of the proband concordance rate and the expected frequency of persons with the same characteristics in the corresponding group of twins.

The second condition, that the environments of MZ twins are not systematically more alike than those of DZ twins is probably not fulfilled. At least, it is not possible to demonstrate that it is. Galton's conclusion still holds true, but as far as crime is concerned it may be that the differences of nurture do exceed what is commonly to be found among persons of the same rank of society in the same country.

Conclusion

The general hypothesis, that the most serious manifestations of criminality are more strongly influenced by similarities in the twins and their environment than are petty offences and minor breaches of norms, has gained support from the results of the analysis of the present sample of monozygotic and dizygotic twins. Nothing in these results, however, can be interpreted as indicating that a higher twin coefficient in MZ than in DZ twins, or in pairs with more serious than in pairs with less serious forms of criminality, is due to what Lange called the quite preponderant part played by heredity in the causation of crime.

CRIME IN A BIRTH COHORT*

Marvin E. Wolfgang

In 1964 the National Institute of Mental Health began sponsoring a unique study of delinquency in the United States. Under the direction of Professor Thorsten Sellin and myself, the Center for Studies in Criminology and Criminal Law—at the University of Pennsylvania—launched a programme to capture and analyse a group of boys born in 1945 who lived in a given locale (Philadelphia) at least from their tenth up to their eighteenth birthday. This group constitutes a birth cohort. Our main interest was to determine a fact thus far unknown, namely, the probability of becoming officially recorded as a delinquent. Only in Norway[1] and England[2] had efforts been made to discover this datum; and nowhere had a study been so elaborately designed and executed. All previous criminological research had been retrospective, i.e. looking backward on a group of known and recorded delinquents of varying ages to determine their age of onset of delinquency (as the Gluecks[3] at Harvard have so often done), or prospective, i.e. looking forward from a group of delinquents of varying ages to describe their adult patterns of criminality. Neither of these types of studies, known as cross-sectional, validly provides proper probability statements of the chances of

* First presented at the meeting of the American Philosophical Society, Friday 20 April 1973, Philadelphia, Pennsylvania.

[1] Nils Christie, *Unge norske lorovertredere*, Oslo, Universitetsforlaget, 1960.
[2] Glenn Mulligan, J. W. B. Douglas, W. A. Hammond, and J. Tizard, 'Delinquency and Symptoms of Maladjustment: The Findings of a Longitudinal Study', *Proceedings of the Royal Society of Medicine*, December 1963, **56**, no. 12, pp. 1083–6.

J. W. B. Douglas, J. M. Ross, W. A. Hammond and D. G. Mulligan, 'Delinquency and Social Class', *British Journal of Criminology*, July 1966, **6**, pp. 294–302.

[3] Sheldon and Eleanor T. Glueck, *Five Hundred Criminal Careers*, Millwood, New York, Kraus Reprint Co., 1930; *Later Criminal Careers*, Millwood, New York, Kraus Reprint Co., 1937; *Criminal Careers in Retrospect*, Millwood, New York, Kraus Reprint Co., 1943; *One Thousand Juvenile Delinquents*, Millwood, New York, Kraus Reprint Co., 1934; *Juvenile Delinquents Grown Up*, Millwood, New York, Kraus Reprint Co., 1940; *Unraveling Juvenile Delinquency*, Cambridge, Mass., Harvard University Press, 1950; *Delinquents and Non-delinquents in Perspective*, Cambridge, Mass., Harvard University Press, 1968; *Toward a Typology of Juvenile Offenders*, New York, Grune and Stratton, 1970.

ever becoming a delinquent or an adult criminal. Neither can offer valid
assertions about patterns of delinquent behaviour by specific ages, about the
onset of criminality, desistance (or stopping delinquency), nor about relative
degrees of seriousness of the offences committed.

Delinquency in a Birth Cohort (University of Chicago Press, 1972[4]) is the
title of the study which I published with my associates, Robert Figlio and
Thorsten Sellin. Through school, police and Selective Service files we
traced 9,945 boys, or all those born in 1945 who lived in Philadelphia at
least from age 10 to 18. From this total birth cohort universe, 35 per cent
became delinquent, that is, had at least one contact with the police for
something other than a traffic violation. These 3,475 boys committed 10,214
offences up to the end of the juvenile court statute age of 17.

Our figure of 35 per cent delinquent needs further clarification. Firstly, it
has commonly been said that in any given calendar year only about 2 per cent
of juveniles are arrested, and that probably no more than 10 per cent are
ever arrested. Hence, the probability figure of 35 per cent of urban males
being arrested before their eighteenth birthday seems comparatively high.
Secondly, race is one of the most significant variables in this analysis. Non-
whites make up 29 per cent of the birth cohort but 50·2 per cent are recorded
delinquents; whites form 71 per cent of the cohort, 29 per cent of whom are
delinquent. The 50 per cent and 29 per cent delinquent populations may be
used as probability statements because we have the entire universe traced
longitudinally through their juvenile years, thus indicating significant racial
differential probabilities of becoming labelled delinquent. Major differences
in the proportions of non-whites and whites in other cities, assuming
relative constancy to the delinquent probabilities, could make for lower or
higher general probabilities of delinquency.

Thirdly, it should be clearly understood that the offence histories we have
analysed are derived from police arrest records. We are aware of the concept
and studies of 'hidden delinquency',[5] or the 'dark numbers'[6] of crime, which
refer to illegal acts unknown or unrecorded by official agencies. For certain
types of offences, usually the less serious, racial and socio-economic disparities
found in official police records are often reduced among self-reporting
studies from anonymous questionnaires or interviews. There may also be
race differentials in police arrests. Therefore, we generally use the phrase
'having a police record' or a 'police contact'. When the term 'delinquent' or
'delinquency' is used, officially recorded person and acts are described. Yet, if

[4] Marvin E. Wolfgang, Robert Figlio, Thorsten Sellin, *Delinquency in a Birth Cohort*,
Chicago, University of Chicago Press, 1972.
[5] There are many studies of hidden delinquency. See notes 32 and 34, ibid., pp. 15–16.
[6] S. Oba, *Unverbesserliche Verbrecher und ihre Behandlung*, Berlin, 1908.

society is concerned about the process of labelling persons as offenders and providing dispositions through our justice systems, it is important that we know who these persons are, and what their probabilities are of being so processed.

Finally, among these preliminary considerations, there is the issue of the generalizability of a birth cohort. Each cohort is in a sense unique, time-bound, as the demographer, Norman Ryder,[7] has clearly remarked. How representative a single cohort may be for other communities, for different birth cohorts, for females, can only be conjectured. Cohort subset comparisons as, for example, delinquents with non-delinquents, on the basis of social, economic and personality variables, may be representatively valid and reliable beyond the single cohort itself. Moreover, the career patterns of the delinquent group, the character of their delinquency, a probability model that forms a dynamic typology of movement from one stage to another—all of these empirical findings may be converted to conclusions for other cohorts. Minimally, every finding from this cohort has the posture of an hypothesis for testing on other cohorts elsewhere and at other times.

After examining the relationship between such background variables as race, socio-economic status (SES), types of schools attended, residential and school moves, highest grade completed, I.Q., achievement level, we concluded that the variables of race and SES were most strongly related to the offender-non-offender classification. The remaining variables in the school records had little or no relationship to delinquency status. For example, although high achievers are much less likely to be classified as offenders than are low achievers, the relationship between race and achievement is such that most of the variance between achievement and delinquency status is explained by race, for being a poor achiever is highly related to being non-white. This relationship also exists between race and the remaining background variables.

The 3,475 boys in the cohort who are recorded delinquents were responsible for 10,214 known delinquent acts up to the age of 17. Whites were involved in 4,458, or 44 per cent, and non-whites in 5,756, or 56 per cent of these offences. The offence rate, of course, is different from the offender rate. When the rate of delinquency is computed on the basis of the number of boys ever recorded as having had a delinquency contact with the police, the offender rate is 349·4 per 1,000 cohort subjects. But this kind of computation ignores the number of offences committed and statistically treats each boy alike, regardless of the number or types of acts committed. An offence rate, computed for the birth cohort by using the number of

[7] N. B. Ryder, 'The Influence of Declining Mortality on Swedish Reproductivity', *Current Research in Human Fertility*, New York, Milbank Memorial Fund, 1955, pp. 65–81.

events as numerator and the 9,945 boys as denominator, times the constant, 1,000, yields a cohort rate of 1,027. The non-whites' rate is three times as high as the whites' rate (1983·5 to 633·0).

Besides crude rates of delinquency per population unit, the birth cohort study employs seriousness scores. Derived from an earlier study of psychological scaling by Sellin and Wolfgang, *The Measurement of Delinquency* (Wiley and Sons, 1964),[8] these scores denote relative mathematical weights of the gravity of different crimes. The scores represent a ratio scale such that a murder is generally over twice as serious as a rape; an aggravated assault, depending on the medical treatment necessary, may be two or three times more serious than a car theft, etc. The scale has been replicated[9] in over a dozen cities and countries and proved useful in the cohort analysis. Each offence against the penal code committed by members of the cohort was scored. This process permitted us to assign cumulative scores to the biography of each offender, to average seriousness by race, SES, age and other variables.

These scores were also applied to index and non-index offences. Index offences are those used by the Federal Bureau of Investigation and students in criminology to refer to serious acts of highest utility in constructing a crime index, similar to a price, wage or productivity index. Index offences are those involving bodily injury, theft or damage to property, or a combination of any of these. Non-index offences are all other acts, like truancy, disorderly conduct, and other minor violations.

The non-white crude rate (1983·5) is 3·1 times as great as the white crude rate (633·0), but the rate when seriousness scores are considered is 4·4 times as great for non-whites (2585·9) as for whites (587·8). Among index offences, the non-white crude rate is 2·4 times as great as the white rate, but the weighted rate is 4·6 times as great. Among non-index offences, non-whites have a crude rate 2·6 times and a weighted rate 3·7 times as great as the respective white rates. These figures reveal that, among these known offenders, non-whites proportionately commit not only more offences but more serious offences than do whites.

Among the 5,756 offences committed by non-white cohort boys, 2,413 were index offences with a mean seriousness score of 265·0. Among the 4,458 offences committed by white cohort boys, only 1,400 were index offences, with a mean score of 243·3. Incidence and average seriousness make

[8] Thorsten Sellin and Marvin E. Wolfgang, *The Measurement of Delinquency*, New York, John Wiley and Sons, 1964. This study was based on the work of S. S. Stevens, of Harvard University, who is the modern developer of psychophysical scaling.

[9] For the many replications of this study, see Thorsten Sellin and Marvin E. Wolfgang, *Delinquency: Selected Studies*, New York, John Wiley and Sons, 1969, pp. 8–9, note 3.

for the considerable difference in the computed rates for whites and non-whites. Non-whites committed 3,343 non-index offences, with a mean seriousness score of 33·2; whites had 3,058 non-index offences and a mean score of 24·0.

Another way to view the weighted rates is in terms of cumulative scores for the offences and the total amount of social harm inflicted on the community. For example, non-whites inflicted on the city 750,433 units of social harm or seriousness points—639,455 of which were from index offences and 110,988 from non-index offences. If a 10 per cent reduction, not of all non-white offences but of index offences, were shifted to a 10 per cent increase in non-index offences, the corresponding reduction in seriousness units would amount to 72,777. That is, index gravity units would dip to 565,501, and non-index gravity units would increase to 122,087—a socially favourable trade-off. The overall crude rate of 1983 would remain the same, but the reduction of 72,777 seriousness units (or a weighted rate reduction from 2585·91 to 2403·81) would be equivalent to the elimination of 28 homicides, or 104 assaults that send victims to hospitals for treatment, or 181 assaults treated by physicians without hospitalization.

In short, if juveniles must be delinquent, a major thrust of social action programmes might be toward a change in the character rather than in the absolute reduction of delinquent behaviour. It could also be argued that concentration of social action programmes on a 10 per cent reduction of white index offences ($N = 1400$; $WR = 483·63$) would have a greater social payoff than a 10 per cent reduction of non-white non-index offences ($N = 3343$; $WR = 382·45$). To inculate values against harm to the body or property of others is obviously the major means to reduce the seriousness of delinquency, both among whites and non-whites. We are simply faced with the fact that more social harm is committed by non-whites, so that the resources and efforts of social harm reduction should be employed among non-white youth, especially the very young.

Although delinquency in a birth cohort has been analysed in many other ways, including juvenile justice dispositions that reveal significantly more severe sentences for non-white offenders, even holding constant seriousness of offences and number of prior offences, perhaps the most important and new analysis is of the dynamic flow of delinquency.

By benefit of a birth cohort, we have been able to consider offences as a stochastic process, or more specifically, whether the commission of delinquency and the types of delinquent acts are a function of frequency and the preceding history of delinquency. If the commission of an offence is independent of time and not a function of prior offence types, the result may be designated, mathematically, as a Markov chain. Essentially, we compared the instant, or last offence (kth offence), with the immediately preceding one (k-1st offence), and then the empirical transitions between offence types for the first through the kth (in our case, the 15th) offence. Five offence types were clustered and classified as Injury, Theft, Damage, Combination, or Non-index. A sixth opportunity was Desistance. Assessing the k-1st and kth offence as well as all k-1st and kth offences presented problems of distributions and trend analysis. Later we were able to examine shifts from one type of offence to another as the cohort passed from the first to their fifteenth offence.

We visualized the progression from birth to the first offence, then to the second, to the third, and so on as pathways along the branch of a tree with six alternative paths of offences or desisting at each juncture (see Fig. I). Each point of departure becomes the probability of arriving at a given location, having come from the offence type at the origin point along the path. After any offence, or from birth, one may desist from delinquency and thus become 'absorbed' into the state of desistance. We call this analysis a branching probability model of offence diversity.

We have noted that the probability of committing a first offence of any type is ·3511. The likelihood of a second offence is ·5358, but if a second offence is committed, the probability of a third of any type is greater, ·6509. Beyond the third offence the likelihood of further offences ranges from ·70 to ·80.

Besides these probabilities are those concerned with moving from one type of offence to another. Does the type of offence that a cohort member committed at the k-1st offence number have any bearing on the probability that he will commit a certain type of offence at the kth number? Analysing our data for offence switching generated a set of matrices, or transition configurations, that provided an answer.

The typical offender is most likely to commit a non-index offence next (·47 probability), regardless of what he did in the past. He is next most likely to desist (·35), commit a theft (·13), an injury (·07) or combination (·05). With the exception of the moderate tendency to repeat the same type of offence, this pattern obtains regardless of the type of previous offence (see Table 1).

Knowledge of the immediate prior offence type (k-1st) does aid slightly in the prediction of the kth type, for there is some tendency to repeat the same type of offence. But this inclination is not strong. It is clear, however, that the offence history up to the immediately previous offence, or prior to the k-1st offence, has no bearing on the observed probabilities of committing the kth offence. That is, knowledge of the number and type of offences prior to the k-1st gives us no aid in predicting the type of the next offence. Because the same process operates at each offence number, we suggest than an offender 'starts over', in a sense, each time he commits an offence and that there is no specialization in offence types. Thus the transition probabilities associated with commission of juvenile offences may be modelled by a homogeneous Markov chain.

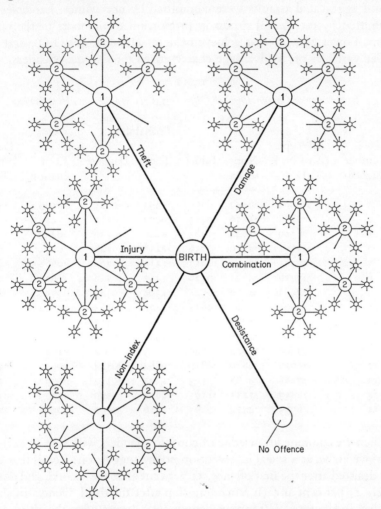

FIGURE I   *Branch Probability Model of Offence Diversity*

Chronic recidivists represent a special group for analysis. Of the entire cohort, 627 boys were recorded as having committed five or more offences before age 18. They represented 6 per cent of the cohort and 18 per cent of the delinquent subset. Yet they were responsible for 52 per cent of all offences, and about two-thirds of all violent crimes. Race differences are particularly striking among chronic offenders: 417, or 10 per cent, of non-whites but only 210, or 3 per cent, of whites are chronic offenders. Non-whites committed 71 per cent of all offences committed by this group. All the murders, 91 per cent of the rapes, 93 per cent of the robberies and 88 per cent of aggravated assaults were committed by non-whites. Larcenies were committed by each racial group in proportion to numbers in the chronic group. Lower SES, lowest achievement in school, lowest I.Q., and other similar variables of disadvantage characterized the chronic offenders.

TABLE I

Probability of Committing kth Offence by Type of Offence, All Offenders

k (Number of Offence)	All Types (Σ of N, I, T, D, C)	Probability					Desisted (after kth offence)
		Non-index	Injury	Theft	Damage	Combination	
1	1·0000	·6547	·0760	·1393	·0725	·0576	·4641
2	·5358	·3430	·0455	·0794	·0222	·0458	·3492
3	·6509	·4044	·0483	·1246	·0236	·0499	·2838
4	·7161	·4439	·0736	·1238	·0248	·0503	·2778
5	·7223	·4320	·0657	·1313	·0264	·0668	·2584
6	·7416	·4705	·0526	·1435	·0128	·0622	·2085
7	·7913	·4409	·0925	·1398	·0387	·0796	·2337
8	·7663	·4511	·0815	·1440	·0163	·0734	·2021
9	·7978	·4787	·0887	·1241	·0177	·0887	·1733
10	·8266	·4489	·1111	·1956	·0089	·0622	·2096
11	·7903	·4624	·0645	·1559	·0054	·1022	·1974
12	·8027	·4830	·0816	·0884	·0544	·0952	·2712
13	·7288	·4068	·0593	·1441	·0254	·0932	·1162
14	·8837	·5233	·1163	·0814	·0349	·1279	·3026
15	·6973	·4474	·0263	·1316	·0000	·0921	·2453

When we combine knowledge of chronic offenders with that of desistance rates, we arrive at a social intervention policy suggestion: Recall that 46 per cent desisted after the first offence, 35 per cent after the second, and approximately 25 per cent at each remaining step after the third offence. In short, a stability in the rate of stopping delinquency occurs after the third act. At what point, then, in a delinquent boy's career should an intervention programme occur? Our answer would be that the best time is that point beyond which the natural loss rate, or probability of desistance, begins to level off. Because 46 per cent of delinquents stop after the first offence, a major and expensive treatment programme at this point would be wasteful.

Intervention could be held in abeyance until the commission of the third offence. We would thus reduce the number of boys requiring attention in this cohort from 3,475 after the first offence, to 1,862 after the second offence, to 1,212 after the third offence, rather than concentrating on all 9,945 or some large sub-group under a blanket community action programme.

Since 1968 the Center has been engaged in a follow-up of the original birth cohort. A systematic 10 per cent random sample yielded 974 subjects. An effort was made to locate and to interview as many as possible. Despite nearly three years of diligent searching—with the use of the Selective Service address file, motor vehicle registrations, post office assistance, Social Service Exchange, and other agencies—more than a few of our cohort sample remained unlocated. We were taught a lesson about the high rate of mobility of young urban males, despite the fact that most of it is intra-urban migration. Approximately 12 per cent were known to have left Philadelphia, although they scattered wide, from suburbs to Vietnam and prisons.

An important difference should be noted between our sample subjects and social surveys that seek to interview one or more members of national representative samples of household units, a common target for attitude studies. In the latter, geographic, or area samples are taken, and interviewers are assigned to given addresses on predesignated blocks. Should no one be present, or should a member of the household refuse to be interviewed, a systematic scheme provides alternates, such as the next household, or an address across the street, etc. In our case, no substitutes were possible; we had to locate a specific person. Upon location, however, no persons refused to be interviewed.

Our interviews were between one and two hours long, covering many details concerned with the personal history of these young men whom we were tracing up to their 26th birthday; educational, occupational and military background, marital and family history, juvenile gang activity, detailed situational aspects of their first and last contacts with the police and other agencies of the juvenile and adult justice systems. We asked about 'hidden delinquency', or the amount and kinds of violations of the law for which they were not arrested, including an unusually wide range of acts from murder and serious drug offences to petty larceny. We have applied our scale of seriousness scores to the unreported offences as well as to the offences known to the police, and shall be able to make comparisons for the first time.

The follow-up study is in the data processing, data analysis stage.[10] By

---

[10] The Center has produced a special study on the history of drug offence among our cohort members for the National Commission on Marihuana and Drug Abuse: Joseph Jacoby, Neil Weiner, Terence Thornberry, Marvin E. Wolfgang, 'Drug Use and Criminality in a Birth Cohort', 1973.

August 1974 we expect to have a manuscript for publication. But I can report a few basic statistical findings about the birth cohort in adulthood, from ages 18 to 26. For the first time in criminology it is possible to offer probability statements about the likelihood of being arrested up to the mid-twenties. We shall later, of course, be able to speak about the types of offences, convictions, sentencing and recidivism in more detail.

There is another interesting methodological note to be mentioned about the follow-up. The 10 per cent sample drawn produced 974 subjects who were representative of such subsets as white and black delinquents and non-delinquents. We have collected official arrest and dispositional documentary data on all of them up to age 26. But other life history material is available only for the 567 young men who were interviewed. A fundamental issue is the extent to which the interviewed sample is statistically representative of (a) the drawn sample (974) and (b) the total universe of the birth cohort (9,945).

Research methodologists commonly refer to the problems of non-respondents in large-scale studies, but rarely resolve those problems by specific and generally acceptable techniques. Our interviewed sample, we know, is slightly over-representative of white non-delinquents and under-representative of black former delinquents. Our chief concern has been to determine the degree of concordance or discordance, on variables about which we have background information from the total cohort, between the interview sample, the drawn sample and the whole cohort. From this analysis, we shall then be able to determine the appropriateness or validity of making inferences from the interviewed sample to the larger populations about variables known only from the drawn sample. Generalizability is the issue. Where known, statistically significant differences exist between the interviewed sample and the cohort, we intend to provide a statistical correction that will permit probability inferences to be made on variables known only from the interviews. We are currently content, however, that for most variables no standardized correction need be performed; in short, our interviewed sample adequately reflects the larger universe along most dimensions.

What are the chances of ever having an official arrest record before reaching age 27? The answer is ·4308 (see Table 2). This 43 per cent probability is based on juvenile as well as adult police data and is considerably higher than most of us suspected. Having previously reported that there is a ·35 probability of having a police record prior to age 18, we may now note that an additional 8 per cent of the cohort, who had no previous juvenile arrest record, became adult offenders.

Yet another way to question the data is to ask about the probability of becoming an adult offender from among those members of the cohort who escaped being arrested up to age 18. That probability is ·1218. The chances of being an adult offender, regardless of juvenile record, is ·2320. Calculation of this last probability is based on the number of previously known juvenile offenders plus new offenders in adulthood ($\geq$18), divided by the total cohort. But most of the contribution to this relatively high rate of adult offence

TABLE 2

Age of Offenders and Non-offenders, before age 18, age 18 and over

		Age 18 and over		
		Offender	Non-offender	
Under age 18	Offender	149 (A)	193 (B)	342 (A+B)
	Non-offender	77 (C)	555 (D)	632 (C+D)
		226 (A+C)	748 (B+D)	974 (E)

Probabilities of being a:

(1) Juvenile offender ($<$18) $= \cdot 3511 \left(\dfrac{A+B}{E}\right)$

(2) Offender ($\leq$26) $= \cdot 4308 \left(\dfrac{A+B+C}{E}\right)$

(3) Adult offender only ($>$18 to $\leq$26) $= \cdot 2320 \left(\dfrac{A+C}{E}\right)$

(4) Adult offender, having been a juvenile offender $= \cdot 4357 \left(\dfrac{A}{A+B}\right)$

(5) Adult offender, *not* having been a juvenile offender $= \cdot 1218 \left(\dfrac{C}{C+D}\right)$

commission comes from persons who also had a juvenile delinquency record. Of the total adult offenders (226), 66 per cent (149) had also been arrested under age 18, whereas only 34 per cent (77) were new recruits into the arrest file after age 18.

Perhaps the most disquieting, albeit not unexpected, finding is that the chances of becoming an adult offender are much higher for persons who had a delinquency record than for those who did not. The probability of being arrested between 18 and 26 years of age, having had at least one arrest under age 18, is ·4357, which is three-and-one-half times higher than the probability (·1218) of being arrested as an adult, having had no record as a juvenile. This is another way of saying, with new precision, that the chances of recidivating from a juvenile to an adult status are higher than commencing an adult arrest record—at least up to age 26. These observed data conform very closely to the curvilinear probability expectations we projected from our earlier Phase 1 study of the birth cohort.[11] It should be no surprise, therefore, if we find in later projections that half of the entire cohort had an offence record by age 35.

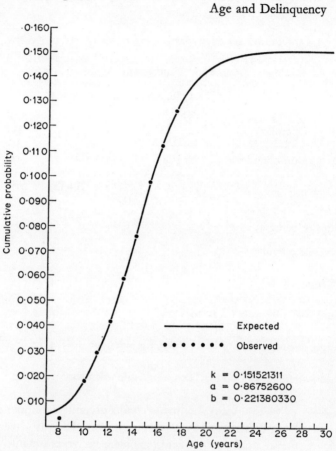

Age and Delinquency

FIGURE 2
Cumulative Probability of at Least One Index Offence by Age

[11] See Fig. 2. *Cumulative Probability of at Least One Index Offense by Age.* From this earlier analysis in Phase 1 of the cohort study we have calculated and extrapolated as follows:

$$·127 = \text{Probability of Index offences, ages 7–17.}$$
$$·3511 = \text{Probability of any record, ages 7–17.}$$
$$·1520 = \text{Probability of Index offences, ages 18–30.}$$
$$∴ \quad ·4202 = \text{Probability of any record, ages 18–30.}$$

By examining age-specific probabilities of ever being arrested, or of having a first offence, some interestingly new information can be reported (see Table 3). Age 17 has the peak probability of having a first arrest (·007). Up to age 17, the probabilities increase monotonically from age 8 (·0020), for example, to age 12 (·0284) and age 16 (·0801). They also decrease from

TABLE 3

Age, Probability of Arrest by Age, Proportion Arrested by Age, and
Cumulative Probability of Arrest

Age (x_i)	N	Frequency (x_i)	(a) $(P_i = x_i)$ $\overline{N_i - 1}$	(b) $(P\, x_i/N)$	(c) $(2P\, x_i/N)$
7	974	0	0	0	0
8	973	1	·0010	·0010	·0010
9	971	2	·0020	·0020	·0030
10	966	5	·0051	·0051	·0081
11	952	14	·0145	·0144	·0225
12	925	27	·0284	·0277	·0502
13	896	29	·0314	·0298	·0800
14	857	39	·0435	·0400	·1200
15	799	58	·0677	·0595	·1795
16	735	64	·0801	·0657	·2452
17	661	74	·1007	·0760	·3212
18	631	30	·0454	·0308	·3520
19	614	17	·0269	·0174	·3694
20	596	18	·0293	·0185	·3819
21	581	15	·0252	·0154	·4033
22	572	9	·0155	·0092	·4125
23	569	3	·0052	·0031	·4156
24	563	6	·0105	·0062	·4218
25	556	7	·0124	·0072	·4290
26	555	1	·0018	·0010	·4300

(a) Probability of first arrest by given age.
(b) Proportion arrested by given age.
(c) Cumulative probabability of arrest by given age.

age 17 in a nearly monotonic fashion through age 18 (·0454), age 20 (·0293), age 22 (·0155) and age 26 (·0018). However, the cumulative probabilities of ever being arrested rise much more rapidly and dramatically up to age 17 than they do after that age. For example, the probability of at least one arrest jumps from ·0502 at age 12 to ·3511 at age 17, which is an absolute 30 per cent increase, or seven-and-one-half times greater. However, this probability of ever being arrested climbs much more slowly after age 17 and reaches, as we have observed, ·4300 by age 26, and absolute 8 per cent increase, or only one-and-one-half times as great. Thus, based on these and other data, we know that the probability of ever being arrested, as well as committing offences generally, declines with age, beginning with the 18th year.

There are many other kinds of data by racial and socio-economic groups, by transition matrices from one type of offence to another over frequency of offences, by family, work and educational history, and by varied contacts with the criminal justice system that we are currently analysing. Among all of these data there are three major questions we hope to answer:

(1) What is the desistance rate after one offence? two? three? n number of offences? Buried in this question are others concerned with explanations about status shifts and status stabilities. For example, some multiple juvenile offenders become adult non-offenders; juvenile non-offenders become adult criminals; juvenile offenders remain adult criminals; and juvenile non-offenders are also adult non-offenders. Criminological literature is peculiarly devoid of information about why delinquents cease to commit offences and become law-abiding citizens without arrest records. Much of this desistance is what may be called 'spontaneous remission', due less, perhaps, to ineffectual treatment programmes than to other factors in the life history of delinquents as yet unknown to analysts. It is our hope to capture some of these variables so as to provide further insights for a concerted, purposeful social policy that might promote and encourage the development of those factors.

(2) Is there a continuation of the same Markovian chain for adult offenders as was noted for juveniles? Or is there a form of offence specialization that occurs among adults which was absent for juveniles?

(3) Is there an optimal point in adult offenders' lives when strong intervention should be taken to maximize efficiency and effectiveness of such intervention to reduce their further criminality and protect society better? This last question raises further ones about being able to predict future dangerousness, an omnipresent but usually unanswered question. By applying the research methods embraced by this unique longitudinal cohort study, we may come closer than our scientific pursuits have done thus far to answering these and other socially significant questions.

SLAVERY AND THE PUNISHMENT OF CRIME

Thorsten Sellin

When Pollock casually mentioned that among the Anglo-Saxons 'slaves were liable to capital and other corporal punishments, and generally without redemption', he added that 'the details have no material bearing on the general history of the law and may be left to students of semi-barbarous manners.'[1] Some students of early Germanic law have not dismissed these 'details' so cavalierly. Indeed, they maintain that slavery has had a crucial influence on the history of penal law. This was noted in 1882 by von Bar,[2] among others; but the outstanding advocate of the idea was Gustav Radbruch, who elaborated it in a remarkable essay originally published in 1938.[3] Contrary to the views of some earlier historians, who believed that punishments gradually introduced into the public penal law of the Germanic peoples during the Middle Ages were offshoots of ancient rituals of human sacrifice or of outlawry, Radbruch held that they were originally private domestic punishments applied to slaves and over the centuries made applicable to all offenders. He saw this transformation as a product of changes in

[1] Sir Frederick Pollock and Frederic William Maitland, *The History of English Law Before the Time of Edward I*, 2nd ed., 2 vols. (Cambridge, Cambridge U.P., 1968) Vol. I, p. 49. After the appearance of the first edition in 1895, Pollock wrote to his American friend, Justice Oliver Wendell Holmes, that his only contribution to this monumental work was most of the Introduction, the chapter on Anglo-Saxon Law, and the bulk of the chapter on Contract. See C. H. S. Fifoot, *Frederic William Maitland: A Life* (Cambridge, Mass., Harvard U.P., 1971), pp. 139–40.

[2] L. von Bar, *Geschichte des deutschen Strafrechts und Straftheorien* (Berlin, 1882); English translation in Carl Ludwig von Bar *et al.*, *A History of Continental Criminal Law* (London, John Murray, 1916), pp. 74–5.

[3] 'Der Ursprung des Strafrechts aus dem Stande der Unfreien.' In his *Elegantiae Juris Criminalis*, 2nd ed., (Basel, Verlag für Recht und Gesellschaft AG, 1950), pp. 1–12. Another version in Gustav Radbruch and Heinrich Gwinner, *Geschichte des Verbrechens* (Stuttgart, K. F. Koehler Verlag, 1951), chs. 1–2. The same view was later expounded by Eberhardt Schmidt in his *Einführung in die Geschichte der deutschen Strafrechtspflege* (Göttingen, Vanderhoek–Ruprecht, 1947) without mention of Radbruch, an oversight corrected in the second edition of 1951, p. 26. Arthur Wenger, in his *Strafrecht: Allgemeiner Teil* (Göttingen, 1951), p. 42, praises Radbruch and Schmidt for having 'sharpened our view of slave punishments as the root of corporal punishments'.

the structure of Germanic society and rooted in that primitive community which Tacitus, most eminent of Roman historians, described in A.D. 98 in his *Germania*, a very slim monograph, which is still the chief source of information about the political, economic and social life of the many independent tribes—he names half a hundred of them—who occupied central and northern Europe in his day.

Slavery was firmly established among the Germans.[4] It must have been widespread and the slaves numerous, for manual labour was considered beneath the dignity of free men, who preferred hunting, feasting, gambling, and especially fighting, to drudgery. Most slaves were the spoils of war. They lived in huts assigned to them by their masters on plots of land which they cultivated and on which they raised cereal crops and livestock. Of these products a part had to be delivered to their masters. Although this makes them appear like share-croppers, they were in fact chattels without personal rights and could be traded like the oxen and horses which constituted the chief wealth of their owners. Their lowly status set them apart from the society of free men, tainted them even when freed, and subjected them to a justice peculiar to chattel slavery.

According to Tacitus, the chief punishment found in the unwritten law of a tribe was death. It was imposed for crimes committed during warfare. The offences were adjudicated by the tribal assembly of freemen authorized to bear arms and convened, on specific days or when an emergency arose, to deliberate and decide matters of public policy and to function as a court of justice. They were acts threatening the safety of the tribe and odious to the gods, whose standards were carried into battle and whose invisible presence on the field inspired the warriors. The importance of the cult may be seen from the fact that only priests were authorized to execute death sentences imposed by the assembly, as well as punishments of fetters or flogging for minor offences during warfare and unspecified punishment of those disturbing the peace of the assembly.

Death sentences were promptly and publicly executed and the two methods used were adapted to the nature of the crime. 'Traitors and deserters are hanged on trees; cowards, shirkers and sodomites[5] are pressed down under a wicker hurdle in the slimy mud of a bog.[6] This distinction in the punishments is based on the idea that offenders against the state should be made

---

[4] E. A. Thompson, 'Slavery in Early Germany'. Reprinted in M. I. Finley, ed., *Slavery in Classical Antiquity* (Cambridge, Heffer, 1960), pp. 191–203.

[5] The meaning of 'corpore infames', which learned translators have assumed to denote homosexuals, has been disputed. See Dieter Feucht, *Grube und Pfahl* (Tübingen, 1967), pp. 90–2, 125–7.

[6] Evidence of this practice in Tacitus' time has been unearthed, especially in northwest Germany and Denmark. See P. V. Glob, *The Bog People* (London, Faber & Faber, 1969).

a public example of, whereas deeds of shame should be buried out of men's sight.'[7] Soldiers, who threw away their shields, were punished by being barred from the assembly and sacred rites, which was such a disgrace that they often committed suicide.

In such manner the assembly, acting as a kind of collective court-martial, dealt with serious offences against the tribal community. Historians who have claimed that conduct such as harmful sorcery or murder were public crimes in times immemorial have found no support from Tacitus. Nor did the assembly, if its criminal jurisdiction is completely described, declare any man an outlaw, expelling him from the community and expecting him to be killed by his pursuers or any one encountering him. This practice appeared later in history, when public vengeance began to supplant the private vengeance which a primitive community regarded as the proper means of exacting retribution for private wrongs.

In Tacitus' time, homicides, woundings, robberies, thefts, and the like were the private concern of the kinship groups of which a tribe was composed. We are not specifically told how such events were dealt with when they occurred within a given kinship group, but if a member of such group killed or injured a member of another group a kind of private war would break out. It might last some time since heirs were obligated to take up the feud of a father or kinsman. Ultimately a feast of reconciliation would be held after reaching an inter-group agreement by which a stated number of livestock were transferred by the offender, aided by his kin, to the victim or his kin as compensation for the wrong done. If a private settlement could not be reached, the injured party could bring the matter before the assembly. If the plaintiff's cause was decided in his favour, the assembly would order his adversary to indemnify him and his kindred in an amount proportioned to the injury and consisting of horses and cattle and similarly pay the tribe an amount proportioned to the indemnity.[8] Tacitus did not mention what action the assembly would take if its order were not obeyed, nor did he mention the rôle that the social rank of the victim might have played in fixing the size of these amounts. Radbruch noted that 'the prerogative of

---

[7] Tacitus, ch. 12. I have used Mattingly's translation, as revised by Handford and published in *The Agricola and Germania*, by Penguin Books, 1970. The notes are mine. Historians generally believe that those executed were not killed merely because they had compromised success in war or discipline in the army, but that they were primarily sacrificial offerings to the gods. According to Tacitus, the Germans did sacrifice humans to their chief god, the god of tempests, but to the gods of war and thunder they made animal sacrifices 'in accordance with ordinary civilized custom'. Tacitus did not identify the human victims. Were they criminals, captured enemies, or slaves?

[8] Minor wrongful acts were adjudicated by magistrates elected by the assembly. With the aid of a panel of a hundred assessors, they administered justice in districts and villages.

feud and indemnity, which is central to the arrangements antedating the criminal law, was a prerogative of those only who could demand satisfaction and could pay'.[9] Since enslavement could result from inability to pay a gambling debt, an insolvent defendant perhaps became the slave of the victim or his family and was delivered to their mercy.

The disciplinary power of the head of a household was unlimited and of no concern to the tribal state. If his wife misbehaved sexually, he could cut off her hair, strip her naked and flog her through the village in the presence of kinsmen. We are told that after this experience she would find it difficult to get another husband. As for slaves, their masters could deal with such chattels at will. They could be flogged, fettered and put to hard labour or even killed. These were the domestic punishments specifically mentioned by Tacitus, but since external official restraints on the slave-owner were absent, other painful devices were probably also used, then as later, in the disciplining of offensive slaves.

The report by Tacitus on the public administration of criminal justice among the primitive Germans and on their custom of settling private feuds leaves many gaps, which, in the absence of documentary evidence, modern historians have tried to fill by retrojecting beliefs and customs current in much later times, because four centuries were to pass before information about Germanic legal customs became available again. They were the centuries of the great westward migrations of the tribes into Italy, Gaul and Spain in the fourth and fifth centuries.[10] Rome accepted them as confederates and granted them large shares of land, livestock and slaves at the expense of the native populations. As the Roman empire crumbled in the West, the barbarian kings established sovereignty over their territories of settlement or conquest—the Ostrogoths in northern Italy, the Visigoths in south-west Gaul and the Iberian peninsula, the Burgundians in eastern Gaul and western Switzerland, and the Franks in northern Gaul. We do not know exactly when they began to put their legal customs in writing. The Goths had been given an alphabet by Bishop Ulfila a century earlier than the first known fragments of law—in Latin—appeared about the year A.D. 480, issued by the Visigothic king Euric.[11] They marked the end of the first dark age of German legal history and foreshadowed the many written 'barbarian codes' or folk-laws of later centuries.[12]

[9] Op. cit., p. 8.

[10] Graphically described by Edward Gibbon, *The Decline and Fall of the Roman Empire*, Chicago, *Encyclopaedia Britannica*, 1955, chs. 30–1, 38.

[11] 'Under this king the Goths began to have the ordinances of the laws in writing, for before this they were bound only by customs and habit.' Isidore of Seville's *History of the Goths, Vandals, and Suevi*, trans. G. Donini and G. B. Ford (Leiden, E. J. Brill, 1970), p. 17.

[12] See Katherine Fischer Drew, 'The Barbarian Kings as Legislators and Judges', in

The barbarian codes were mostly concerned with penal justice. They evidence a growing effort by the state to limit the practice of private vengeance and feuding. Indeed, the Visigoths prohibited it, as did the Bavarians much later—neither with conspicuous success. Chief reliance was instead placed on fixed or agreed indemnities (composition) imposed or approved by order of a court and paid by an offender to his victim or his victim's kin, in default of which he could be delivered to his adversary for retaliation or enslavement. Indemnities were of two kinds: specific amounts, called wergeld, for killing, wounding or assaulting a person; and others which basically corresponded to the value of property stolen, damaged or destroyed. They were usually expressed in units of Constantine's gold *solidus*, even though payments were more often made in kind than in coin. In all but a few exceptional cases, an offender also had to pay a fine to the state treasury; it often exceeded by far the size of the indemnity and tended to grow in proportion to it as the administration of justice was found to be a most lucrative source of revenue. Prosecutions were initiated by the aggrieved party and centuries were to pass before public prosecution was haltingly begun. Cases were adjudicated in the courts of counts or village justices except for capital cases, which were usually dealt with in the king's high court.

The barbarian codes mirrored societies where social class differences rendered even freemen unequal before the law. The Burgundian code,[13] for instance, subdivided them into noble, middle and lower classes. Below these were the half-free freedmen and serfs, whose legal status was often barely distinguishable from that of the lowest class—the slaves. The position of these classes on the social scale may be seen, in part, in the basic value—the wergeld—placed on their lives. For a noble, this sum was 300 solidi, for a middle-class man 200 and for one of the lower class 150. If a master killed his own slave no punishment awaited him, but if he killed another's slave, the indemnity he had to pay depended on the slave's occupation, i.e., his market value. An ordinary slave—unskilled, ploughman, swineherd—was worth 30 solidi, a carpenter 40, a blacksmith 50, and a trained house servant or messenger 60 solidi; but a silversmith or steward cost 100 solidi, a royal steward as much as lower-class freeman, and a goldsmith as much as middle-class one. If someone knocked out the tooth of a slave, he had to

Robert S. Hoyt (ed.), *Life and Thought in the Early Middle Ages*, 165 pp. (Minneapolis, University of Minnesota Press, 1967), pp. 7–29. A brief but richly documented history of German medieval penal law is found in Robert von Hippel's *Deutsches Strafrecht*, 2 vols. (Berlin, J. Springer, 1925, 1930), Vol. I, pp. 100–58.

[13] Katherine Fischer Drew (transl.), *The Burgundian Code*, xiii, 106 pp. (Philadelphia, University of Pennsylvania Press, 1949). This code was compiled by King Gundobad about 500 A.D.

pay his owner two solidi; if the victim was a freedman he owed three solidi to the victim, and a lower-class man's tooth would cost him five solidi.

When a freeman was charged with a crime, he could clear himself by oath and the oaths of his sons or parents and twelve relatives; but if this procedure, fraught with the risk of perjury, was invalidated,[14] the judge would order him to engage in a trial by combat,[15] i.e., a duel with his accuser, permitting a judgement—*Urtheil*, ordeal—of God to decide the issue. Although this may seem to us a novel way of settling a dispute, it must have appeared quite natural to a people who were known in Tacitus' time to have used the outcome of a duel by champions as an omen of the result of an impending battle.

The Burgundians threatened with death any freeman who murdered a freeman or royal servant of barbarian origin or was privy to such murder by his slave. Assaulting a Christian priest was a capital offence, if committed by a Jew. A freeman could be executed for plundering houses or treasure chests and for stealing oxen, horses, mares, or cows. If he committed adultery, he and his partner could be killed. A freeman's daughter, who voluntarily united with a slave, could be executed but might instead be made the king's slave. The ancient punishment of burial alive in a bog threatened the wife who deserted her husband. Otherwise the method of execution was not referred to in the Burgundian code. The judge would 'hand over' the offender to be publicly killed by the accuser and his kin.

Most offences by freemen against persons or property were liquidated by payment of indemnities, often without official intervention. In some cases, these indemnities were punitive and amounted to treble or even ninefold the basic values involved. If the defendant could not raise the amount, in money or in kind, he was doomed to enslavement by his accuser. This must have been the common fate of poor defendants, when one considers that a wergeld of 150 solidi to satisfy the kin of a slain lower-class freeman, for instance, was equivalent to 75 oxen, 150 sheep or 30 draft horses. Enslavement by the parents of an abducted girl definitely faced an indigent abductor, and if a horse thief was executed his wife and children over fourteen years of age became the slaves of the horse's owner.

A mutilating punishment was found in Burgundian law. A freeman might

[14] In the earliest Anglo-Saxon laws we find kinsmen being replaced as oath helpers by men 'of the same class' as the accused. Even this was judged as likely to tip the scale of justice in favour of the accused. Before the end of the seventh century, the principle had been well established that at least one man of high social rank should be among the oath helpers. See F. E. Stenton, *Anglo-Saxon England*, 3rd ed., xli, 730 pp. (Oxford, Clarendon Press, 1971), pp. 316–17.

[15] For a history of this custom, see George Neilson, *Trial by Combat*, xvi, 348 pp. (Glasgow, William Hodge, 1890).

suffer the amputation of a hand if he aided a fugitive to escape or removed or destroyed boundary markers. In the latter case, at least, he could avert the punishment by paying an indemnity and this was probably also possible in the former instance. If a Jew struck a Christian he had to pay ten solidi to save his hand.

In Tacitus' time slave-owners were held responsible for the misdeeds of their living chattels as if they themselves had committed them. Since then the notion had developed that the slave had a will of his own and should share responsibility for his crime and suffer public punishment for it.[16] The choice of appropriate punishments had posed a problem for the barbarian legislator, however. Some punishments suitable for freemen could not be imposed on a slave. Outlawing him would give him freedom, however precarious. Since he had no possessions he could call his own, he could not pay fines and indemnities, and if he was a suspect he could not exercise a freeman's prerogative of calling on oath helpers to support his plea of innocence. Substitutes for these expedients had to be devised, and they were at hand. The legislator simply converted into public punishments and judicial procedure the practices that slave-owners were using within the domestic establishment—flogging, castration, cutting off the hand, blinding, death,[17] and physical force to elicit confessions. These devices were hallowed by tradition, and since slaves were, in the sight of man, inferior to other humans they were appropriate for slaves. They seemed equally proper for serfs and freedman and, in time, even for the humblest of the free, whose poverty prevented them from purchasing immunity from physical punishments. Eventually they were to place an indelible stamp on the penal law of the Middle Ages and be made applicable to most everybody, free or unfree, until the end of the eighteenth century. Some of them have survived until today in the penal laws of some countries and in the disciplinary practices or regulations of 'correctional' institutions.

Under Burgundian law flogging was the paramount punishment for slaves and serfs. No freeman was subjected to this treatment, which was to be regarded throughout history as the most degrading of punishments. It was

[16] Georg Meyer, 'Die Gerichtsbarkeit über Unfreie und Hintersassen nach ältestem Recht', *Zeits. der Savigny-Stiftung f. Rechtsgeschichte* (German. Abt.), 1881, 2:83-114, p. 92.

[17] von Bar, op. cit. (English ed.), p. 74, no. 4. As previously noted, death was not an official punishment in Tacitus' time for offences against the life or property of private persons. As such it was imposed only for certain crimes, which during warfare threatened the security of the state or the success of a war enterprise—treason and desertion. Tacitus did mention that minor military offences were punished by flogging, and Heinrich Brunner (*Deutsche Rechtsgeschichte*, 2 vols. (Leipzig, Duncker and Humblot, 1887, 1892); Vol. II, p. 607) believed that freemen were thus punished. Since even the earliest folk-laws did not permit the flogging of freemen, it is not unlikely that the offenders thus treated were not freemen soldiers, but unfree servants, alien camp followers, and the like.

prescribed for a long list of offences committed by slaves. The number of blows allowed ranged from 75 to 300 depending on the offence. Theft of livestock, grain standing in sheaves, or a beehive earned the maximum penalties. In most instances, the owner of the culprit also had to indemnify the victim of the crime according to a fixed tariff, varying from a third of a solidus for a stolen goat to ten solidi for a fine horse. An ox was worth two solidi and a cow, pig or sheep one solidus each. A slave who voluntarily knocked out the tooth of a freeman was not only flogged but also might lose a hand.

Murder, theft and robbery were capital offences for freemen and slaves alike, but slaves could also be condemned to death for manslaughter, assaults on freewomen, sexual relations with free girls, aiding a fugitive to escape and removing or destroying boundary markers, for instance, when freemen only paid indemnities.

When a slave or serf was accused of crime, the court could order him to be tortured for the purpose of establishing his guilt or innocence. Strangers were not exempt, because they were generally believed to be fugitive slaves or serfs. If a stranger entered a community, any one learning of it was in duty bound to bring him before a judge, who might order him to be tortured in order to discover to whom he belonged.

Freemen were not subjected to judicial torture. The use of oath helpers and ordeals was more compatible with their status. Generally speaking this held true for all Germanic folk-laws with one exception. Visigothic law did not only permit the flogging of freemen for most offences but also allowed the torture of even nobles and dignitaries charged with capital crimes and of lower-class freemen accused of crimes carrying indemnities of 300 or more solidi. The Visigothic code was a mixture of Germanic and Roman elements in which the latter strongly dominated; its penal provisions showed this influence most clearly.[18] A few exceptions have also been noted in other codes. An Alamanic law of the late sixth century permitted the torture of suspected witches, slave or free, and the Council of Reisbach in Bavaria, circa A.D. 800 prescribed torture of suspected sorcerers. But, as the use of ordeals everywhere increased during the feudal period, judicial torture seems to have disappeared until it was to fill the void caused by the firm stand against ordeals by the Lateran Council in A.D. 1215.[19]

[18] 'The Visigothic compilation [Breviary of Alaric] became the standard source of Roman law throughout Western Europe during the first half of the Middle Ages . . .', Paul Vinogradoff, *Roman Law in Medieval Europe* (Oxford, 1968), p. 16.

[19] Piero Fiorelli, *La tortura giudiziaria nel diritto comune*, 2 vols. (Milano, Giuffré, 1953), Vol. I, pp. 56, 68 n.4, 69. A. Esmein, *A History of Continental Criminal Procedure* (Boston, Little, Brown & Co., 1913), pp. 107–14.

Judging from its provision of capital punishments and its adoption of judicial torture in proceedings against the unfree, the Burgundian code was contaminated by Roman law to some degree. Its more famous contemporary, the law of the Salian Franks,[20] was more representative of early medieval Germanic law. It was compiled under King Clovis about A.D. 500. Before his death in 511 he had subjugated Burgundy and most of Gaul. The Merovingian Dynasty of which he was the most eminent head was succeeded in the late seventh century by the Carolingians, whose greatest ruler, Charlemagne (768–814), extended Frankish dominion over most of Italy and central and western Europe from the Pyrenees to the Baltic and was crowned emperor of the Roman empire in A.D. 800. Soon after his death the empire disintegrated and by the end of the ninth century the Frankish era had ended.

The sources of data needed for an examination of Radbruch's hypothesis belong mainly to that era. They are quite meagre considering that the history of four centuries is involved—a period equal to the time from the landing of Columbus in the West Indies in 1492 to the beginning of the present century—but they dry up completely during the next three hundred years— the second dark age or 'silent centuries' of Germanic legal history[21]—before they begin to flow again in the early thirteenth century.

During the Frankish era the stigma of slavery destined the slave and his near social kin, the freedman and the serf, to suffer discriminatory treatment in the administration of justice. Salic law did not permit the torture of freemen, but it authorized the torture of a slave accused of theft sufficiently large to cost a freeman thief an indemnity and fine of 15 solidi. The suspect was stretched on a bench and given up to 120 blows with switches the thickness of the little finger. If he did not confess, his accuser could demand that the torture be continued; but if he still maintained his innocence, his accuser must buy him from his owner who thus placed him at the mercy of his new proprietor. If he confessed to a theft which a freeman thief could settle by a payment of 35 solidi he was castrated, the only mutilating punishment known to Salic Law.[22] However, his original owner could save him from the lashes by a payment of 3 solidi and from the castration by paying 6 solidi.[23]

In early Frankish times, mutilating punishments, such as blinding or the amputation of a hand, the nose or an ear, were legally defined slave punish-

---

[20] Joseph Balon, *Traité de droit salique*, 4 vols. (Namur, 1965).

[21] von Hippel, op. cit., p. 122. Fiorelli, op. cit., p. 65, n. 52, observed that among 614 known French and German court records before 1000 A.D. and 1063 Italian records before 1150 A.D. criminal cases are almost non-existent.

[22] Fiorelli, op. cit., p. 53, notes 9–11.

[23] Paul Leseur, 'Des conséquences du délit de l'esclave', *Nouv. Revue histor. de droit français et étranger*, 1888, **2**: 576–631, 657–728, p. 660.

ments. Occasionally, a freeman's death sentence might be commuted to mutilation, but after the sixth century freemen could be directly sentenced to such punishment 'for offences disclosing a slavish and base mind'.[24] It was always redeemable in accord with a minutely detailed tariff of values. A Lombard law of the same century threatened counterfeiters with a loss of a hand.

The use of mutilating punishments increased during the Carolingian period, partly for crimes like theft which previously had been capitally punished and partly for crimes like perjury, which had been redeemable. A law of Charlemagne threatened a conspirator with the loss of his nose and the recidivist thief with the loss of eye and nose. Similar provisions were found in contemporary Lombard law. Slaves found guilty of sex crimes were occasionally castrated. Blinding was considered the most serious mutilation and was sometimes substituted for capital punishment.[25] Bavarian folk-law punished a slave, who set fire to church property at night, with the loss of a hand and his eyes. Cutting off an ear became a common punishment for thieves during the Middle Ages and far into modern times. In addition to being painful, it served to identify them in the future.

Punishments 'to hide and hair' were slave punishments during the Frankish era and exclusively so in the early laws except the Visigothic. Under the Carolingians, thieving freemen could be flogged, theft being regarded as a most shameful crime evidencing a slavish mentality; but usually freemen were fined and slaves beaten.[26] The Merovingians whipped low-class persons but fined the well-to-do for disrespecting Sunday, and a west Frankish law of the ninth century punished slaves and serfs with flogging for falsifying measures; freemen were fined. If a freeman was flogged his head was shorn. Short hair was the mark of a slave; freemen wore their hair long.

Branding does not seem to have been a frequent punishment in the Frankish kingdom. A Lombard law of the eighth century ordered thieves to be branded, and after the ninth century counterfeiters were branded in France.

The early folk-laws were sparing in the execution of the death penalty, partly because the Church opposed it but mostly because the ancient custom

[24] Rudolf His, *Geschichte des deutschen Strafrechts bis zur Karolina* (Berlin, R. Oldenbourg, 1928), p. 84. I have relied heavily on this work and von Hippel's for data relating to the Frankish period.

[25] Influence of Frankish law may be seen in William the Conqueror's abolition of the death penalty and substituting for it castration and exoculation. See Pollock and Maitland, op. cit., Vol. II, p. 461. A gruesome illustration is found in William Renwick Riddell's 'A Glimpse of Law in the Early Thirteenth Century', *Journal of Criminal Law and Criminology*, 20: 568–571, Feb. 1930.

[26] Leseur, op. cit., p. 716.

of resolving inter-family conflicts by a financial settlement dominated even after the state gradually assumed authority to regulate and enforce such proceedings. Freemen were sentenced to death more as a threat to compel the payment of fines and indemnities than to achieve their extinction. Thieves caught in the act could be killed on the spot with impunity, but failing this, Salic law provided that they could be sentenced to death by the court. The punishment, however, was redeemable by payment of the offender's wergeld, the size of which depended on his social status. The reluctance to put freemen to death is clearly shown in the Bavarian law, which actually forbade their execution except for treason, an offence broadly defined to include lese-majesty.

The execution of corporal or capital sentences was at first the duty or prerogative of the accuser and his kin. Salic law, for instance, provided that if a slave was found to have had sexual relations with his free mistress, he was to be handed over to her kin to be 'broken', a method of inflicting death that was to become popular in the French and German laws of the Middle Ages and in common use until the late eighteenth century. A Lombard law of the eighth century (A.D. 724) specified that a slave found guilty of theft and not redeemed should be killed by his master or, if he refused, by the victim of the crime. If he, too, refused, the thief was to be executed by the court.[27] As time passed and the state assumed more direct control of penal justice, officers of the court executed the penalties publicly. Professional hangmen did not appear before the thirteenth century.

Judging from the data then, the punishment actually suffered by an offender during the Frankish era depended less on the kind of crime he committed than on his caste or social status. The unfree person—slave, freedman, serf—was subject to judicial torture, from which freemen were exempt. He was liable to corporal punishment prescribed by law. Flogging and mutilation were at first reserved for him, and his only avenue of escape from these punishments or from torture lay in his master's or patron's willingness to purchase his exemption when the law allowed it. In later centuries of the era, when these slave punishments first came to be used on freemen, it was not mainly crimes of violence openly committed that were thus sanctioned but shameful clandestine theft revealing the base and slavish nature of the offender.

If a freeman was unable to clear himself of a criminal charge by oath or ordeal, he could usually buy his exemption from punishment; but if he was unable to pay the often ruinous indemnities and fines, his poverty exposed him to mutilation or death, or to enslavement by the victim or his heirs,

---

[27] *The Lombard Laws.* Translated with an Introduction by Katherine Fischer Drew, xx, 280 pp., Philadelphia, Univ. of Penn. Press, 1973; p. 171; Leseur, op. cit., p. 589.

which lost him the rights belonging to freemen. These rights could also be lost if he was declared an outlaw by the court because he had escaped justice or had refused to face his accuser in court. If he persisted in his contumacy, his house was razed, his goods forfeited to the state, 'his wife became widow, his children orphans, his kin strangers'.[28] None could with impunity give him shelter or aid. Like the wolf of the forest, he was any man's legitimate prey.

During the 'silent centuries' that followed the collapse of the Carolingian empire, the political and economic debasement of the common people by a military aristocracy of great landowners reached its lowest point. By 'the tenth and eleventh centuries most of the peasants tended to be serfs who were bound to the soil and whose lives were virtually at the mercy of their lord . . . a very few held their land just as the lord held his—from the king or another great lord. Others were in varying degrees of servitude.'[29]

No longer did the emperor's travelling judges supervise the administration of justice by the counts and dukes who were kinglings in their domains. The old folk-laws and royal capitularies were forgotten and old tribal customs revived. Among the landed gentry feuding, which had never been completely eliminated, flourished again and was no longer limited to the blood feud. Constant disorders and the oppression of the peasantry by the magnates increased the number of fugitive slaves and serfs, who joined the outlaws who made the highways insecure.[30]

The repression of crime became more and more savage. The powerful and the wealthy settled their conflicts in their own way by payments;[31] but the poor were doomed to corporal and capital punishments made increasingly cruel, partly in the belief that this would counterbalance the glaring

[28] His, op. cit., p. 49.

[29] John B. Wolf, *The Emergence of European Civilization* (New York, 1962), p. 40. Interesting observations are also found in Friedrich Heer's *The Medieval World* (London, Wiedenfeld & Nicolson, 1961), Ch. 2, 'Aristocracy and Peasantry'.

[30] The general demoralization of the age was seen by Fulcher of Chartres as the reason why Pope Urban II called for the first crusade in 1095 A.D. 'He saw that the faith of Christianity was being destroyed to excess by everybody, by the clergy as well as by the laity. He saw that peace was altogether discarded by the princes of the world, who were engaged in incessant warlike contention and quarrelling among themselves. He saw the wealth of the land being pillaged continuously. He saw many of the vanquished, wrongfully taken prisoner and very cruelly thrown into foulest dungeons, either ransomed for a high price or tortured by the simple torments of hunger, thirst, and cold, blotted out by a death hidden from the world. He saw holy places violated, monasteries and villas burned. He saw that no one was spared of any human suffering and things divine and human alike were held in derision.' *Chronicle of the First Crusade*, transl. by Martha Evelyn McGinty (Philadelphia, University of Pennsylvania Press, 1941), p. 11.

[31] Louis Halphen, 'La justice en France au XIe siècle', in his *A travers l'histoire du Moyen Age* (Paris, Presses universitaires de France, 1950), pp. 176–202.

inefficiency of law enforcement. It was easy to evade justice by flight. The effect was noted by Maitland in describing the visit of the justices in eyre to Gloucester in A.D. 1221. They 'listened to an appalling tale of crime, which comprised some 330 acts of homicide. The result was that one man was mutilated and about 14 men were hanged, while about 100 orders for outlawry were given. . . . In 1256, the justices in Northumberland heard of 77 murders; 4 murderers were hanged, 72 were outlawed. They heard of 78 other felonies, for which 14 people were hanged and 54 outlawed. In 1279 their successors in the same county received reports of 68 cases of murder, which resulted in the hanging of two murderers and the outlawing of 65, while for 110 burglaries and so forth, twenty malefactors went to the gallows and 75 were left "lawless" but at large.'[32] Similar conditions prevailed on the continent.

Exemplary punishment of the few who were caught was believed to be a salutary deterrent to crime, but it was a self-defeating policy. 'Public executions of capital, mutilating, corporal and dishonouring punishments, often aggravated by horrible methods of inflicting them, dulled the aim of deterrence and harmed general deterrence by brutalizing the conscience of people. Equally disastrous was the effect of this penal law from the point of view of individual prevention. The outlawed, the banished, the mutilated, the branded, the shamed, the bereft of honour or stripped of power it expelled from the community of decent people and thus drove them out on the highway. Therefore the penal law itself recruited the habitual and professional criminals who flourished in those days.[33]

By the end of the twelfth century, the slave punishments of earlier days had been enshrined in public penal law and made applicable to free and unfree alike.[34] Political and economic changes connected with maturing feudal institutions had fostered this process by reducing most of the peasantry to a state of praedial servitude, which largely eliminated the need for chattel slaves except in domestic service. The punishment inflicted on a criminal no longer depended on his being a slave or a freeman, but on his being a noble or a commoner, a burgher or an outsider, a wealthy man or a poor man. The system of criminal justice was dominated and managed by aristo-

[32] Pollock and Maitland, op. cit., Vol. II, p. 557. Comparable data for Lincolnshire in 1202 are cited in Ralph Arnold's *A Social History of England 55 B.C. to A.D. 1215* (London, Constable Young, 1967), p. 328; and for Northumberland in 1279 by G. G. Coulton, *Medieval Panorama* (Cambridge, Cambridge U.P., 1938), pp. 337–8.

[33] von Hippel, op. cit., p. 158.

[34] No mention of punishments applicable only to unfree persons is found in the numerous source documents from the 13th and later centuries reproduced in Hans Planitz's *Handhaft und Blutrache und andere Formen des mittelalterischen Rechtsganges in anschaulichen Darstellungen* (Leipzig).

crats—kings and ecclesiastical or laic manorial lords or wealthy burghers, who were gaining control over town government.[35] To these noble or upper-class people, manual workers and more or less unfree peasants generally living near or on the brink of poverty and lacking political power, although they constituted the vast majority of the population, were an inferior breed providentially created to serve the economic needs of their betters. In such a society equality before the law was an illusion, as is well illustrated by Maitland. Writing of the English law of the twelfth century, he observed that 'a *wité* [fine] of £5 was of frequent occurrence and to the ordinary tiller of the soil this must have meant ruin. Indeed there is good reason to believe that for a long time past the system of *bót* [indemnity] and *wité* had been delusive, if not hypocritical. It outwardly reconciled the stern facts of a rough justice with a Christian reluctance to shed blood; it demanded money instead of life, but so much money that few were likely to pay it. Those who could not pay were outlawed or sold as slaves. From the very first it was an aristocratic system; not only did it make a distinction between those "dearly born" and those who were cheaply born, but it widened the gulf by impoverishing the poor folk. One unlucky blow resulting in the death of a thegn [noble] may have been enough to reduce a whole family of ceorls [serfs] to economic dependence or even to legal slavery. When we reckon up the causes which made the bulk of the nation into tillers of the lands of lords, *bót* and *wité* should not be forgotten. . . . The debasement of the great bulk of the peasants under a law of villeinage . . . gave their lords a claim upon those chattels that might otherwise have paid for their misdeeds.'[36]

In such a society, a noble sentenced to die was honourably beheaded and thus spared the infamy of hanging which the poor thief could not escape. And, because in such a society the chief determinant of the penal consequence of a crime to the offender was his lack or possession of wealth, a man of means could buy his freedom from physical punishment, while the poor man went into slavery or the life of an outlaw or to the wheel, the gallows, the mutilation block or the whipping post to suffer a capital or corporal punishment prescribed by law but originally reserved for slaves, a 'detail' which, as Radbruch demonstrated, does have a 'material bearing on the general history of the law' and should not 'be left to students of semi-barbarous manners.'

[35] Commenting on an Augsburg ordinance of 1276 A.D., von Bar, op. cit., p. 108, observed that it was administered by a 'hard-hearted citizen-body, proud of their wealth, caring everything for property and little or nothing for the life or misery of a poor man [and] willing to inflict the loss of a hand for merely entering an orchard or grass plot with intent to steal.'

[36] Pollock and Maitland, op. cit., Vol. II, pp. 460, 462.

SYMBOLIC AND INSTRUMENTAL DIMENSIONS OF EARLY FACTORY LEGISLATION: A Case Study in the Social Origins of Criminal Law

W. G. Carson

Introduction

The importance of studying the social basis and genesis of criminal laws as part of a specifically criminological enterprise has been acknowledged by many well-known authorities. Edwin Sutherland, for example, saw one of criminology's three principal divisions as 'the sociology of law, which is an attempt at scientific analysis of the conditions under which criminal laws develop . . .'—although he subsequently developed a remarkable blind spot in this respect when he turned his attention to white-collar crime.[1] Jerome Hall likewise regarded the sociology of criminal law and the concomitant investigation of legislative origins as synonymous with criminology.[2] More recently, writers such as C. R. Jeffery and Edwin Schur have argued cogently for the formal value of criminological theories which do not focus so exclusively upon offenders that the study of the criminal law, including its social basis as well as its enforcement, is neglected.[3] The point is put forcefully by Schur when he writes: 'once we recognise that crime is defined by the criminal law and is therefore variable in content, we see quite clearly that no explanation of crime that limits itself to the motivation and behaviour of individual offenders can ever be a complete one'.[4] At least by implication,

---

[1] E. Sutherland, *Principles of Criminology*, New York, Lippincott, 1960, p. 3.

[2] J. Hall, *General Principles of Criminal Law*, Indianapolis, Bobbs-Merrill Co., 1947, p. 559.

[3] C. R. Jeffrey, 'The Historical Development of Criminology', in H. Mannheim (ed.), *Pioneers in Criminology*, London, Stevens & Sons, 1960, pp. 364–94; E. M. Schur, *Our Criminal Society*, Englewood Cliffs, Prentice-Hall, 1969.

[4] E. M. Schur, op. cit., p. 10.

a similar concern with law is encouraged by the broader theoretical perspective on deviance which adopts the enjoinder that 'social control must be taken as an independent variable rather than as a constant or merely reciprocal, societal reaction to deviation' as one of its basic premises.[5]

Against this background, it is perhaps surprising that for many decades leading criminological textbooks both in Britain and overseas so often regarded the sociology of law, particularly the study of the conditions under which criminal laws develop, as outside the scope of criminology.[6] The subject was similarly excluded from university courses in criminology—and to a large extent still is.

The neglect of these issues is, for example, apparent in Nigel Walker's *Crime and Punishment in Britain*.[7] Here, a comparatively simple distinction is made between questions which cannot be answered without making moral judgements, and 'questions which are less ambitious, and to which the answers can be more factual'. To the self-posed question 'What is Criminal', these more factual answers turn out to comprise a descriptive inventory of the content of English criminal law and of 'the functions which are served by our present list of prohibitions'.[8] The whole socio-historical background to such law is dealt with cursorily in a single paragraph which takes pluralism almost to the point of *reductio ad personam*:

> The assembly of prohibitions which constitutes the substantive part of the English criminal law is the result of additions made over a long period of development and in response to demands from very different bodies of opinion, of which the churches, the police, and government departments are only the most obvious examples. Some of these additions undoubtedly reflected a widespread feeling: for example those dealing with cruelty to children. Others were inserted in the statute book by well organised or tactically skilful minorities or even individuals. The Litter Act of 1958, which made it an offence to drop litter in a public place, was the result of a Private Member's Bill.[9]

Such an approach is perhaps fair enough as a prelude to a description of crime and its control in contemporary Britain. But Walker goes on to devote

[5] E. M. Lemert, *Human Deviance, Social Problems and Social Control,* Englewood Cliffs Prentice-Hall, 1967, p. 18.

[6] Even where the subject was included it was seen as a related but separate area of study. Thus, although Hermann Mannheim in his *Comparative Criminology* (London, Routledge and Kegan Paul, 1967) included a lengthy chapter on the meaning of crime in relation to law, religion, custom and morals, he still felt compelled to warn that 'we are concerned with the behaviour of actual or potential offenders more than with that of the law giver', p. 67.

[7] N. Walker, *Crime and Punishment in Britain,* Edinburgh, Edinburgh University Press, 1965.

[8] Ibid., pp. 3 ff.

[9] Ibid., p. 10.

a substantial portion of his book to explanations of crime, and here, as so often happens, the sociology of criminal law becomes submerged. He fails to appreciate the relevance of the historical aggregation of value-choices to contemporary criminological explanation; in short, that without a theory of criminal law there can be no theory of crime. And in this he is not alone. In *Key Issues in Criminology*, Hood and Sparks not only omit systematic analysis of the criminal law's emergence as a key issue, but also welcome, at least in principle, general explanations of crime which would make no reference to the one feature that all crimes have in common:

> . . . it is different when our purpose is scientific explanation, since for this purpose we are interested in *generalisations*—preferably ones as wide as possible— and we seek as causes things which apply to all instances of the thing or event we are trying to explain, and not just to one particular case. Now, there is no absurdity or inconsistency in searching for a single theoretical explanation of all criminal, delinquent or deviant behaviour. Such a theory—which would consist of a number of logically connected and empirically verified statements specifying the conditions in which crime occurs—should aim to integrate all the different factors which are shown to distinguish offenders from non-offenders, and should aim to explain *how* these factors 'produce' delinquent behaviour.[10]

The allocation of such low priority to questions about the social basis and genesis of criminal law is not, however, an invariable feature of British criminology. Within what may be referred to, for brevity's sake, as the mainstream of the subject, Sir Leon Radzinowicz's *History of the English Criminal Law* stands out as one major exception, even if its empirical orientation precludes any elaboration upon the significance of such questions for the development of a theory of crime.[11] Indeed, it has been described by one writer—not otherwise notably uncritical of the developments in which Sir Leon has played such a leading part—as a 'massive contribution' and a 'firm base' upon which to start building a sociology of the criminal law in this country.[12] Similarly, among those who would identify themselves with a sociological rather than specifically criminological tradition, the criminal law's socio-historical basis has become a crucial, if not paramount concern. The various renditions of consensus and conflict theories of law have, for example, become the subject of relatively heated debate in works whose theoretical focus is upon crime, either in its own right or as a special form of deviance. Thus, in the somewhat self-conscious *New Criminology*, the authors include a lengthy discussion of the 'new conflict theorists' such as Turk and

[10] R. Hood and R. Sparks, *Key Issues in Criminology*, London, Weidenfeld and Nicolson, 1970, p. 111.
[11] L. Radzinowicz, *A History of English Criminal Law*, London, Stevens & Sons, 1948–56.
[12] S. Cohen, 'Criminology and the Sociology of Deviance in Britain'. Paper delivered before the *British Sociological Association*, London, 1971, p. 25.

Quinney, and while roundly castigating them in some respects, extend a guarded welcome to them for both reawakening our sense of history, and for fostering a climate in which legal institutions might be regarded as criminologically problematic.[13] Looking to the future, Taylor, Walton and Young can see some cause for optimism. 'In particular', they say, 'we can hope to see studies of law and crime which are informed, not by a static conception of pathological and/or anomic individuals colliding with a simple and taken-for-granted set of institutional orders, but rather by a conception of the complex interaction between developments in institutional structures and the consciousness of men living within such structures.'[14]

An equal concern with the generation of legal rules and with the complexity of the issues involved, is apparent in Paul Rock's recent book, *Deviant Behaviour*.[15] In an extremely sensitive examination of what he terms 'authoritative definitions of deviancy', Rock both stresses the need for further work in this area and sets out the broad contours within which such work might be carried out. While making only the most modest claims for his own generalizations about law, he nonetheless expresses his dissatisfaction with the intellectual tone which all too frequently pervades the debate. In a passage which would appear out of place in any discussion less sophisticated than his own, he writes:

> I believe that much existing sociology of law can be dichotomised into naive conspiracy theory and naive consensus theory. The one poses an image of society which is dominated by an intellectualised version of International Freemasonry; a knowing, self-interested and capable elite. The other acknowledges virtually no structural or moral differentiation within society. Societal norms attain legal expression without mediation. There is, as it were, a magical transition from consensus to legal code.[16]

From even these brief examples it is apparent that the issue of how and why laws are made, as well as broken, remains a live one in current criminological discussion. Having said this, however, I do not intend to embark upon any protected *tour d'horizon* of the positions advanced by different writers, usually reflecting with varying degrees of sophistication and explicitness, the broader social theories to which they adhere. Rather, by way of tribute to a career that has so often emphasized the importance of both law and history, I wish to focus upon one theoretical aspect of law-making and upon its application to one historical case.

---

[13] I. Taylor, P. Walton and J. Young, *The New Criminology*, London, Routledge and Kegan Paul, 1973.

[14] Ibid., p. 267.

[15] P. Rock, *Deviant Behaviour*, London, Hutchison & Co., 1973.

[16] Ibid., p. 144.

The Idea of 'Symbolic Crusades'

In recent years a number of writers have stimulated a renewed interest in the symbolic nature of rules and of the social processes involved in their creation.[17] Among these, probably the best known to students of deviance is Joseph Gusfield whose detailed investigation of the American Temperance Movement has, in some measure, informed the efforts of such familiar figures as Howard Becker, Troy Duster, Anthony Platt, and more recently, Stanley Cohen.[18] The major thrust of the argument advanced by Gusfield in *Symbolic Crusade*, a term now firmly entrenched in the standard repertory of literature in this field, can be discerned in his own summary of the social forces which underpinned the emergence of anti-drinking legislation in the United States:

> . . . the issue of drinking and abstinence became a politically significant focus for the conflicts between Protestant and Catholic, rural and urban, native and immigrant, middle class and lower class in American society. The political conflict lay in the efforts of an abstinent Protestant middle class to control the public affirmation of morality in drinking. Victory or defeat were consequently symbolic of the status and power of the cultures opposing each other. Legal affirmation or rejection is thus important in what it symbolizes as well or instead of what it controls. Even if the law was broken, it was clear whose law it was.[19]

In arriving at this succinct conclusion, Gusfield had already progressed—somewhat uneasily—through a series of relatively complex steps which can only be summarized. At the heart of the matter lay his dissatisfaction with what he saw as a predominant tendency to interpret American politics in terms of economic and class conflicts. For a society so characterized by 'consensus about fundamentals',[20] the overweening centrality of such interpretations was inappropriate. Thus, he argued, the vacuum created by such underlying agreement was partially filled by moral issues contested, not along class or economic lines, but along lines drawn by broader social formations which were concerned with their status and prestige. Borrowing the distinction between the politics of class and of status, he went on to contend that the two are analytically distinguishable in terms of their orientation and objectives. Class politics involve conflicts over the allocation

---

[17] See, for example, M. Douglas, *Purity and Danger*, Harmondsworth, Pelican, 1966; T. W. Arnold, *The Symbols of Government*, New York, Harcourt Brace and World, 1962.

[18] J. Gusfield, *Symbolic Crusade*, Urbana, University of Illinois Press, 1963.

[19] J. Gusfield, 'Moral Passage: The Symbolic Process in Public Designations of Deviance', in C. A. Bersani (ed.), *Crime and Delinquency*, London, Macmillan, 1970, p. 67.

[20] *Symbolic Crusade*, p. 2.

of material resources; they are oriented towards the 'interests' of particular groups in the economic system; and their goals are 'instrumental' in the sense that they comprise 'alterations in the system of behaviour characterizing the society'.[21] In contrast, status movements involve conflicts over the allocation of prestige, and while they may in that sense be described as 'interest-oriented', they seek their ends in symbolic rather than instrumental goals. Comprising groups which may well transcend economic and class divisions, they vie with one another for the enhanced prestige which stems from public endorsement:

> The fact of political victory against the 'enemy' shows where social and political dominance lie. The legislative victory, whatever its factual consequences, confers respect and approval on its supporters. It is at once an act of deference to the victors and of degradation to the losers. It is a symbolic rather than an instrumental act.[22]

In drawing attention to the symbolic significance which projected legal norms may hold for their instigators, Gusfield has underlined an important and often neglected aspect of legislative processes. But his tortuous and indeed, sometimes tortured attempt to rehabilitate much American political conflict from the baser forms of class conflict 'so salient in European history'[23] is not without its defects. In particular, it is important to note for purposes of the present argument that although Gusfield takes care to enter the heuristic caveat that most movements contain both symbolic and instrumental elements in varying degrees, the nature and dynamics of this empirical connection remain largely unexplored in his analysis. More specifically, while conceding that the instrumental and the symbolic are frequently yoked, he appears to neglect the possibility that there is no necessary congruence between a group's disposition towards the symbolic character of projected norms, and its stance in relation to their instrumental potential. Once the possibility of such divergence is admitted, there then arises the question of whether one element, by becoming the more salient feature of a mooted enactment, may not vitiate a favourable or unfavourable disposition based upon the other. As I shall shortly argue, for example, instrumentally oriented acquiescence in a measure may be undercut when the movement for its enactment begins to take on symbolic overtones which are unpalatable to some of the parties involved.

Such sequential possibilities highlight another feature of Gusfield's analysis. Throughout *Symbolic Crusade* we encounter groups ranging from

---

[21] Ibid., p. 20.
[22] Ibid., p. 23.
[23] Ibid., p. 1.

Mugwumps to teetotallers, campaigning on issues as diverse as fluoridation, domestic Communism and school desegregation, and seeking public affirmation or reaffirmation of their social status through the symbolic potentialities of law. Thus we are told, for example, that the men who founded the Temperance Movement in the eighteen-twenties, 'reasoned' that 'if they could not control the politics of the country . . . they might at least control its morals'.[24] Gusfield's crusaders are invested with an almost instinctive appreciation of how their self-respect may be salvaged through the public spectacle of law. Sad counterparts of Rock's knowing and capable élites, they achieve their goals through conquest of government's representational function. Shrewdly, they settle for the compromise of symbolic victory, and often—with even greater astuteness—avoid making the best the enemy of the good by declining to press home their legislative victory with demands for effective enforcement.[25]

The objection to this description, which I have admittedly caricatured, is that the symbolic end-product becomes too easily equated with the whole process of which it is the culmination. True, Gusfield is careful to specify that these 'significant meanings are not given in the intrinsic properties of the action but in what it *has come* to signify for the participants'[26] [my emphasis]. At the same time, however, he tarries little over how such meanings as cultural degradation and prestige enhancement are built up between the protagonists in a legislative struggle. In short, and despite his theoretical caution, he fails to portray symbolic meaning as an *emergent property* of the interactional sequences occurring in connection with particular pieces or types of legislation. Indeed, the whole characterization of crusades as 'symbolic' runs the risk of confusing ends with processes, and of adopting the stance of a historian who, in the words of Schutz, 'knows perfectly well what the actor intended to do because he knows what he did in fact do'.[27] In the brief discussion which follows, I shall attempt to show how one legislative issue assumed symbolic significance in the course of an interactional sequence, part of it historically specific, and other parts perhaps more typical of law-making as a whole.

[24] Ibid., p. 5.
[25] Ibid., p. 120
[26] Ibid., p. 21.
[27] *The Phenomenology of the Social World,* London, Heinemann Educational Books, 1972, p. 213.

Some Instrumental and Symbolic Dimensions of the 1833 Factories Act

1. *The Act and Instrumental Concerns*

In 1833 a statute entitled 'An Act to regulate the Labour of Children and Young Persons in the Mills and Factories of the United Kingdom' was passed.[28] Applying to a range of textile industries where steam, water or other mechanical power were used, this enactment prohibited the employment of children under nine years of age, limited the labour of those between nine and thirteen to nine hours per day (up to a limit of forty-eight hours per week), and restricted the employment of young people between thirteen and eighteen to twelve hours daily (up to a total of sixty-nine per week). For all under the age of eighteen, a ban was imposed—with some special exceptions —on their employment between 8.30 at night and 5.30 a.m. Children in the younger age group were to receive some elementary education, vouchers to that effect being made a prerequisite of their employment each week. A complex system of age certificates was also established in order to facilitate enforcement of the various provisions, and in the same context, four full-time Inspectors of Factories were to be appointed.

Although the very necessity for such regulations may seem somewhat staggering to the contemporary eye, this enactment was, in some ways, an unremarkable stage in the development of factory legislation.[29] Even if we discount the Health and Morals of Apprentices Act of 1802[30]—aimed at controlling the grosser abuses practised against pauper apprentices and therefore more in the tradition of the Elizabethan Poor Law than of modern factory legislation—intervention in relation to the employment of 'free' children was no innovation in 1833. This had already been established, at least for the cotton industry, as a result of the enthusiastic efforts of Robert Owen and the rather less fervent parliamentary sponsorship of Peel in 1819.[31] The minimum age for employment in cotton mills and factories had also been fixed at nine in the latter year, and a start had been made on limiting the hours to be worked by young people of employable age. Subsequent enactments, in 1825 and 1831, had retained the same minimum age and had made further though largely nugatory efforts to deal with problems such as night-working and enforcement.[32] Thus, although the Act of 1833 imposed

---

[28] 3 & 4 Wm. IV, c.103.
[29] Though not perhaps in the development of education.
[30] 42 Geo. III. c.73.
[31] 59 Geo. III. c.66.
[32] 6 Geo. IV. c.63 and 1 & 2 Wm. IV. c.39.

further restrictions and extended their application beyond cotton, it did not establish the principle of intervention itself. Nor indeed, did its terms represent any particularly dramatic and immediate victory for the bourgeoning cause of factory reform. Those who in the preceding months had campaigned vigorously for the hours of all under eighteen to be restricted to ten per day, could derive little comfort from the statute, and would have to wait for more than another decade before achieving their goal.

And yet the Act of 1833 is frequently regarded as an extremely important piece of legislation. In part, this is because it basks in the reflected glory of the Royal Commission which preceded it, one of the famous Blue Books of the early nineteenth century which are so often hailed as testaments to the informed humanitarianism of the age.[33] Apart from the detailed, though not necessarily unimpeachable investigations and arguments upon which the Report of this Commission was based, it is a significant document on account of the proposals that it made with regard to enforcement. According to M. W. Thomas' chronologically definitive, if uncritical, end-to-end history of the subject, the Royal Commission 'made possible a new and effective approach'.[34] This new approach was, of course, the appointment of inspectors, and in taking this step the Act of 1833 fully earned its prominent position in the history of factory legislation. Even if its efficacy sometimes seems no less questionable today than it was at the time of its inception,[35] the Factory Inspectorate still survives as the agency charged with enforcing the now voluminous regulations contained in the Factories Acts.

Within the present framework, however, Althorpe's Act as it is usually called, holds additional significance; for in the events leading up to the enactment, we can see an increasingly complex interplay between instrumental and symbolic elements, a process which resulted in the debate becoming infused with a new degree of symbolic meaning that would remain one of its characteristic features for many years after 1833. By attempting to analyse this progressive intermeshing, we can perhaps bring more theoretical order and even possibly greater dignity to the controversy which raged in those years.

There is little doubt that the various groups which pressed for further legislation between 1830 and 1833 were indeed interested in possible instrumental effects. In Gusfield's terms, this means that they *were* oriented towards the actual impact of legislation upon people's actions, towards 'influencing

[33] Parl. Papers (1833) XX.

[34] M. W. Thomas, *The Early Factory Legislation*, London, Thames Bank Publishing Co., 1948, p. 60.

[35] See, for example, my paper 'White-collar Crime and the Enforcement of Factory Legislation', *British Journal of Criminology*, 10, Oct. 1970, pp. 383–98.

behaviour through enforcement'.[36] Indeed, it was the vigour with which some of them pursued such objectives, combined with the particular fashion in which circumstances obliged them to engage their genuine concern, that forced the controversy into an increasingly symbolic mould.

In the process of mutual denigration which increasingly pervaded the debate during these years, the attribution of ulterior motives was by no means uncommon. This was particularly true with regard to the popular movement which, from 1830 onwards, began to gain ground among the operatives themselves, usually in the form of short-time committees. Thus, for example, Kirkman Finlay—a Scottish cotton manufacturer—was able to assure Lord Ashley that the 'demagogues' who travelled the country stirring up feelings on the subject of factory reform, existed 'upon the earnings of their more laborious brethren' and devoted themselves, profitably, to persuading the latter that through the Ten Hour Bill 'something will be done to give them more wages and less work'.[37] In scarcely less moderate vein, the Commission of 1833 itself disparaged the operatives' motives. Their real objectives, the Commissioners argued, were a reduction in the hours of adult labour to those of young people—a result which would necessarily ensue from a Ten Hour Act—and the improved wages and employment possibilities which they wrongly assumed would follow from such a reduction in hours.[38] 'We should not feel ourselves warranted', they concluded, 'in suppressing our conviction that the interests of the children, which alone supply materials for popular excitement on the subject of the proposed measure, are, of all other considerations, that (sic) which appears to enter least into the councils of the operative agitators . . .'[39] A more sophisticated (though not therefore necessarily correct) interpretation of the operatives' 'true' objectives has subsequently been advanced by Smelser, whose analysis places similar stress upon the desire to limit adult hours and to 'spread the total employment over greater numbers'.[40] Above all, he argues, the operative movement had in mind the protection of the traditional family structure:

> This complex of attitudes, which reappeared explicitly and implicitly in the agitation, shows that the ten hour movement, in the operatives' minds, would have achieved *much the same results* as the strikes against improved machinery—

[36] C. Bersani (ed.), op. cit., p. 65.

[37] K. Finlay, *Letter to the Right Hon. Lord Ashley on the Cotton Factory System*, Glasgow, E. Khull, 1833, p. 19.

[38] Op. cit., pp. 34–5.

[39] Ibid., p. 45.

[40] Smelser, *Social Change in the Industrial Revolution*, London, Routledge and Kegan Paul, 1959, p. 239.

to halt the flood of children and to protect the traditional economic relationships between parent and child by linking their hours and consequently maintaining the existing conditions of work.[41]

Thus, whether we take the aspersive comments of the day, or the views of someone less immediately involved, like Smelser, there is no suggestion that the operatives' goals were anything other than instrumental in the sense that this term is deployed by Gusfield. Their motives may or may not have been 'ulterior', their assumptions may have been mistaken, but their orientation was towards the actual effects that a Ten Hour Act might have. Moreover, whatever the true nature of such desired effects, it is clear that they could not be realized if the law, when passed, were to remain un-enforced like so many of its predecessors.

A similar instrumental 'integrity' must also be allowed to the men of higher estate who came forward to support the operatives' demands in these years. No reading of Richard Oastler's famous 'Yorkshire Slavery' letters which, from October 1830 onwards, constantly raised the temperature of the debate, can leave any doubt that he sincerely wished to see the conditions of child-labour improved. 'Would that I had Brougham's eloquence,' he lamented, 'that I might rouse the hearts of the nation, and make every Briton swear, "These innocents shall be free".'[42] Similarly, Michael Sadler—the High Tory who took over leadership of the parliamentary campaign after the debacle of Hobhouse's 1831 Act—had long devoted himself to 'the study of the condition, wants and miseries, of the labouring poor', and to devising 'means for the removal of these miseries'.[43] Indeed, according to Engels it was his 'noble enthusiasm' that in the end betrayed him in his efforts on behalf of the factory children.[44] As for Lord Ashley, there were certainly those who saw him as quixotic, but even they did not entirely deny his wish 'to carry into effect these benevolent designs'.[45] To all of these men their critics, while deploring the consequences which might follow from a Ten Hour Act, while showing little scruple over endowing them with additional, sinister motives, nonetheless allowed an 'amiable eagerness to suppress what they are persuaded is wrong'.[46] Even if their failure to light upon the idea of full-time factory inspectors as a solution to the problem of enforcement might seem to betoken a relative lack of concern for the

[41] Ibid., p. 240.
[42] C. Driver, *Tory Radical*, New York, Oxford University Press, 1946, p. 43.
[43] *Memoirs of the Life and Writings of Michael Thomas Sadler*, London, Seeley & Burnside, 1842, p. 280.
[44] Engels, *The Condition of the Working-class in England in 1844*, London, S. Sonnenschein, 1892, p. 170.
[45] *Hansard* (1833) XIX, 244.
[46] K. Finlay, op. cit., p. 19.

instrumental, such was not the case. For, as we shall see, their ideas about enforcement may have lacked imagination but not vigour. Indeed, it was partially the energy and form of their proposals in this respect that helped to infuse the issue with a high degree of symbolic meaning.

Still within the context of instrumentality, however, there is one last point which must be at somewhat greater length, namely that the possible effects of further legislation were by no means necessarily an anathema to at least some of the manufacturers themselves. A number, for example, could claim that they had already of their own accord introduced considerable improvements in the conditions of employment in their factories. The Act of 1833 was not passed for such people as the Gregs, Ashworths or Ashtons, one of the first inspectors was later to recall; 'had all factories been conducted as theirs are, and as many others I could name are, there would probably have been no legislative interference at any time'.[47] Similarly, the Commission of 1833 alluded, albeit not without qualification, to the improvements which had already taken place in the 'larger branches' of manufacturing, 'not by means of any legislation, but mostly by the voluntary care of more intelligent manufacturers . . .'[48]

This is not the place for any attempt to assess the nature and degree of such improvements. Nor is it necessary at this juncture to linger over the vexed question of the extent to which they may or may not have resulted from a spontaneous upsurge of social compassion on the part of the employer: many of the manufacturers and their supporters were themselves content to rest their case in this respect on other grounds, avowedly less purely altruistic. As one flax-spinner put it, in his somewhat piqued response to a questionnaire administered by the Commission, 'the proprietors and manager of these works have sufficient penetration to discover that the interests of masters and servants are too closely interwoven to require penal regulations to stimulate them to treat their hands well . . .'[49] A similar and growing convergence of interests was categorically asserted by Edward Baines, editor of the *Leeds Mercury* and ardent supporter of the manufacturers' cause:

> . . . nearly all [mill-owners], from their very habits of business, are accustomed to those extended views and calculations, which enable them to look forward with confidence to a distant advantage from an immediate outlay. Some from benevolence, some from emulation, some from shame, and more, perhaps, than all from a conviction that it would actually tend to profit, may follow the

[47] Letter from L. Horner to N. W. Senior in: N. W. Senior, *Letters on the Factory Act*, London, B. Fellowes, 1837, p. 33.

[48] Op. cit., p. 59.

[49] W. Jameson, Parl. Papers (1834) XX, 121.

examples set . . . I believe the conviction is strengthening and spreading that it is eminently the INTEREST [sic] of a manufacturer to have a moral, sober, well-informed, healthy and comfortable body of workmen.[50]

There is a big step, however, from recognizing the personal advantages to be derived from voluntary restraint, to advocating or acquiescing in legislative regulation for the trade as a whole. Yet some manufacturers, probably more than is frequently recognized, managed to take this step. And once again, the unalloyed altruism of moral entrepreneurship, while undoubtedly present in some cases,[51] need not be uncritically accepted as the only driving force. Without reducing the factory controversy of these years to a monopolistic conspiracy on the part of some employers—an interpretation which according to one historian appealed only to smaller masters at the time and to uncritical historians since[52]—there is strong evidence to suggest that reconcilement to the instrumental facets of further legislation may have been greatly facilitated by the competitive advantages which might ensue therefrom.

In a period when large profits were no longer so easily extracted as they had been in the early days, some larger manufacturers were prone to attribute their slightly straitened circumstances to the chronic malaise of over-production. Coupled with the incentive provided by the prototypical fortunes of the earlier period, they argued, the comparative ease with which production could be started on some small scale had created a situation in which, as John Marshall, the Leeds flax-spinner, put it, 'the trade has been overdone by many new adventurers entering into it'.[53] Thus, a link was perceived between their present troubles and the competition being encountered from the smaller and frequently isolated concerns in which, most observers seem to have been agreed, conditions were worst.[54]

Reports such as those from the Select Committee on Manufacturers[55] and, to an extent, from the Factory Commission itself, provide a catalogue of the stratagems to which various employers resorted in order to meet this situation.[56] What concerns us here, however, is not so much the nature of

[50] E. Baines, *History of the Cotton Manufacture in Gt. Britain*, London, Frank Cass & Co. 1966, p. 483–4; first published in 1835.

[51] E.g. John Fielden, author of *The Curse of the Factory System*, London, A. Cobbett, 1836.

[52] J. Butt (ed.), *Robert Owen: Prince of Cotton Spinners*, Newton Abbot, David & Charles, 1971, p. 106.

[53] W. G. Rimmer, *Marshall's of Leeds*, London, Cambridge University Press, 1960, p. 174.

[54] See, for example, Finlay, op. cit., pp. 10 ff.

[55] Parl. Papers (1833) VI.

[56] For some details of these and for an elaboration of the argument contained in this section, see my forthcoming book with Bernice Martin, *The Social Origins of Factory Legislation*, London, Martin Robertson & Co.

these manoeuvres as the fact that they were frequently unsuccessful. In consequence, throughout the period there runs a thin and sometimes almost indiscernible thread of acquiescence in effective legislation as a means, perhaps the only remaining one, of reducing competition. Thus, in the aftermath of the 1825 Act, a number of leading manufacturers in Manchester attempted to enforce the law themselves, and set up a committee for that purpose. 'They felt an interest', said the 1833 Commission, 'in carrying the act into execution as against the evasion practised by the small mill-owners'.[57] Similarly, a recurrent theme in the numerous petitions presented by manufacturers during the fraught days of the early thirties, as in their evidence before committees, was the request that any enactment, whatever its precise terms, should be made effective. 'To be just', said one petition from Manchester, not only should any restrictive Bill require nothing impracticable or unnecessary, it also 'ought to be efficient'.[58] Speaking of the likely consequences of a Ten Hour Bill, one employer could only envisage disaster resulting from such a drastic reduction; but this did not mean that he would oppose a limit of eleven hours per day. Such a restriction, he suggested, 'would place the selfish and the generous, the unfeeling and the compassionate, the considerate and the inconsiderate, among the masters, upon an equal footing'.[59] To another witness before the 1833 Commission, the attractions of an effective enactment were as great as they were freely admissible:

> The present Factory Bill is a very inefficient one; and the masters in the neighbourhood of Manchester openly boast that they have never regarded it. I should hope that, if another bill were passed, it would be an efficient one. If Lord Ashley's bill were passed, it would be almost equal to a moving power bill; but a restriction on the moving power would be better. The country masters produce cheaper than we can do, by working longer hours.[60]

Such expressions of positive interest in the instrumental effects of further legislation must not be obscured by the vehemence with which many masters greeted the reformers' concrete proposals for a Ten Hours Act. What Marx was later to call 'the cry of the capitalists for equality in the conditions of competition'[61] constantly added a discordant note to the rhetoric of laissez faire. But before such instrumental concerns could be

---

[57] Op. cit., p. 32.

[58] Parl. Papers (1833) XX, 856.

[59] Parl. Papers (1834) XX, 60.

[60] Mr. J. Bell Clarke, Parl. Papers (1833) XX, 769. A restriction on moving power would simply have made it illegal to run machinery between certain hours and would therefore have prevented firms in disadvantaged positions from making up lost time.

[61] Marx, *Capital,* Chicago, ed. publ. by Charles Kerr & Co., 1926, p. 537.

allowed their rein, the manufacturing class had to fight another and more subtle battle which arose out of the symbolic rather than instrumental connotations which the controversy assumed in the years following 1830.

2. *Symbolism as an Emergent Property*

With the gradual erosion of the social arrangements which had characterized the pre-industrial order, the raw materials out of which the factory controversy might be refashioned as a symbolic issue had been accumulating for many years before 1830. In factory labour, an emerging working class had increasingly encountered a form of discipline which was not only incompatible with a traditional family structure,[62] but also with a traditional style of life. 'Traditionalism in economic life', writes Bendix, 'was an obstacle to the new economic undertakings, not because it was more humane, but because its rhythm of work and leisure, the inviolability of an accustomed life routine, interfered at every point with the "new discipline" of the factory'.[63] Moreover, the decades preceding 1830 had witnessed a growing separation between the employer and the employed. Increased use of steam-power had enabled many manufacturers to move away from country areas into the towns, and as a consequence, had freed them from reliance upon a scarce but substantially dependent workforce. Equally, new styles of systematic management instituted by a new generation of wealthy mill-owners—born to the trade and far removed from the frequently humble antecedents of those who had founded their family fortunes—increasingly jeopardized the surviving vestiges of a personalized relationship between master and servant. As early as 1818, an astute operative was able to assert that there was now 'a greater distance observed between the master . . . and the spinner, than there is between the first merchant in London and his lowest servant or the lowest artisan'.[64]

On the ideological level, the old order had also been steadily losing ground before 1830. In particular, the ideal of paternalistic responsibility had been outflanked on two fronts: by the administration of theoretical absolution to the ruling establishment, at the hands of men like Burke; and by the deployment of arguments purporting to equate the enlightened self-interest of entrepreneurs with the best interests of their employees—as of the nation as a whole. Indeed, at a time when it was accepted that 'the best test of social institutions is the condition of the community subjected to their

---

[62] See above, p. 17.

[63] R. Bendix, *Work and Authority in Industry*, New York, John Wiley, 1956, p. 58.

[64] *Black Dwarf*, 30 September 1818, quoted in E. P. Thompson, *The Making of the English Working Class*, Harmondsworth, Penguin, 1968, p. 218,

influence',[65] the practice of paternalistic government was not only questioned but often openly indicted. By interfering with the freely competitive operation of capital in the hands of men who were enterprising, industrious and thrifty, it was argued, the ill-conceived restrictions and regulations of paternalism actually militated against the best interests of those whom it sought to protect.

If the ideology of traditionalism was suspect, then it followed that the political and economic hegemony which it had served to legitimate must be equally so. Thus, as the thirties approached, there was not only an increased and surprisingly successful demand for the removal of barriers against freedom of enterprise, but also a more and more vociferous insistence that the political structure itself should be altered in favour of the emergent middle class. In both cases there was an implicit assertion of a new right to legitimate authority. And in both too, there were recurrent strains of hostility to land, the institution which had lain at the very heart of the old order. It was the Corn Laws which provided propagandists and others with their most blatant example of the irresponsible exercise of power to the advantage of one sectional interest. Equally, it was by drawing an invidious contrast with the indolence of a caricatured landlord that men like Henry Ashworth most eloquently exalted the virtues of their own class, a class of men 'who may justly claim, more than any other, credit for the exhibition of that persevering industry and enterprise which, with the aid of science, has secured for our manufacturing and mercantile interests the prosperity which distinguished this beyond all other nations'.[66] Nor was the 'science' which had thus facilitated the successful exercise of virtue, to be confused with other and older traditions of learning:

> Grandees, as the spoiled children of the state, may be indulged in their learned play-things, as in the ribbon and the star, to mark their exclusive caste, and they may be allowed freely to waste their early years in the pastime of scanning Greek and Roman metres, provided they do not fancy themselves thereby, albeit ignorant of the principles of Science, Art, and Trade, qualified to scan the measures and to regulate the affairs of empires at their will.[67]

Against this background, it is significant that the men who came to the fore in the public agitation for further legislation in the third decade of the century were unrepentant traditionalists. Michael Sadler, for example, had entered parliament in 1829 with the express intention of opposing Catholic emancipation which he saw as an attack both on the constitution and on the

---

[65] 'The Condition of the Working Classes', *Westminster Review*, No. XXXVI, April 1833, p. 1.
[66] Parl. Papers (1840) XVI, p. 357.
[67] A Ure, *Philosophy of Manufactures*, London, Charles Knight, 1835, p. 404.

establishment.[68] Indeed, he felt so strongly on this issue that, when the Tory government persisted in passing the measure, he joined forces with the 'country party' to bring down 'those recreant friends whom they considered to have betrayed the Commonwealth'.[69] Paradoxically, the immediate consequence was a Whig government wedded to the idea of reforming the franchise, a step which Sadler regarded with scarcely less horror. The proposed measure would give, he argued, 'an injurious monopoly of power to one division of society' and would fatally undermine 'the influence which the crown exercises in this House, and the connexion of this House with the aristocracy'.[70]

A similar attachment to the ways of tradition can also be discerned in the other leaders. Thus Ashley, Hodder tells us, voted against the Reform Bill as a matter of course, having pledged himself to defend 'those great principles which inspirit and regulate our glorious Constitution in Church and State'.[71] Some years later, when he had long been the most prominent parliamentary advocate of further factory reform, he was to reject an offer of office in Peel's administration, counselling himself to wait for happier circumstances in which he might deploy his influence in 'the cause of paternal and constitutional government'.[72] Similarly, Bendix and others have stressed how heavily the rhetoric of working-class leaders in this period relied upon the idealised images of traditionalism.[73] The stance adopted by one of the greatest of them, though not himself working-class, has been nicely captured by his biographer:

> Oastler must be reckoned as a symbol as well as a personal force, and much of the influence he was able to exert is to be charted in terms of the effectiveness of that symbol . . . What was it then that he symbolized? Perhaps we cannot get any nearer to it than to say 'the good old days'; and if those days are but a myth, we just have to admit that for a while Oastler was the embodiment of a folk-dream which had an especial cogency in the days of transition to an industrial economy.[74]

Viewed in this light, it is tempting to cast these men as leaders in a straightforward 'symbolic crusade', activated by a sense of imperilled prestige and aimed at the salvage of some self-esteem through the act of legislating. Nor would it be difficult to marshall some superficial evidence in

[68] M. T. Sadler, *Memoirs*, op. cit., p. 116.
[69] Ibid., p. 221.
[70] Ibid., p. 252.
[71] E. Hodder, *The Life and Work of the Seventh Earl of Shaftesbury*, London, Cassell & Co., 1886, Vol. I, p. 125.
[72] Ibid., p. 357.
[73] R. Bendix, op. cit., p. 46.
[74] Driver, op. cit., p. 128.

support of the contention that the movement for factory reform in these years exhibited many of the features which one might expect to encounter in such a crusade. As E. P. Thompson has pointed out, for example, the utterances of men like Oastler, Sadler and Ashley did indeed reveal 'deep sources of resentment and insecurity among traditionalists before the innovations and the growing power of the moneyed middle-class'.[75] Similarly, and even after allowances are made for the rhetorical excesses of partisanship, there is an element of truth in Ure's claim that the agitation was generously laced with 'the ancient feeling of contempt entertained by the country gentlemen towards the burghers'.[76] Echoes of a no less crude concern over prestige can be heard in histories such as Von Plener's which describes how Tories rallied round the factory issue after 1832, 'still smarting under their defeat in the Reform question, and endeavouring with delight to bring to the surface everything likely to damage in the eyes of the public the industrial middle-classes, who had become more influential and attained a much higher position than heretofore in public esteem'.[77] While Ashley may well have believed that as 'the representative of a southern and agricultural county' he could not 'justly be suspected of studying herein his own political interests',[78] he was nonetheless fervent in his belief that 'Corn is God's coin'.[79] Likewise, his fears that any ultimate success over the Ten Hour Bill might rebound to his own personal credit rather than to that of 'Conservative rule and Conservative principle', may seem to betray as much concern for the prestige of his precepts as for the state of his own soul.[80] Such personal modesty would surely befit the archetypal symbolic crusader.

While many of these elements did indeed pervade the controversy by the time that Althorpe's Act was passed in 1833, this does not mean that in these early years, the movement for factory reform can be summarily characterized as a 'symbolic crusade'. To do so would be to elide both the historical and theoretical complexity of the issue. On the first count, as we have already seen, there is little doubt about the reformers' desire to effect real changes through the passage of legislation, an orientation which scarcely fits a crusade whose objectives are primarily to be realized on a symbolic rather than instrumental plane. Moreover, such a characterization which would rely so heavily on divisions between Tories and Whigs, landed gentry and middle-classes, traditionalists and innovators, would attribute undue structural clarity to the social genesis of the controversy. Although the period was

[75] Op. cit., p. 377.
[76] Op. cit., p. 277.
[77] E. Von Plener, *The English Factory Legislation*, London, Chapman & Hall, 1873, p. 10.
[78] Hodder, op. cit., p. 152.
[79] Ibid., p. 58.
[80] Ibid., p. 357.

indeed rife with disagreement and resentment, the structural referents of these conflicts were by no means clear-cut at the beginning of the thirties. Indeed, so frequently did men deviate from the positions which a simple structural determination of interest would predict for them, that one historian has been driven to the desperate expedient of inventing a category of 'social cranks' in order to force their actions into an ostensibly coherent framework.[81] Men like Oastler and Sadler, for example, were no more typical landed Tories than the radical John Fielden was a typical Whig mill-owner. The alignments of an earlier age had certainly been undermined by 1830, but the structural lines along which the battles of the new era would be fought, were still in the making and therefore remained blurred even to the eyes of many contemporaries. Hence, to represent the early campaign as having been *mounted* in defence of a position with easy structural concomitants, would be to confuse what the controversy had been about at its inception, with what it subsequently and to a substantial extent became.

Translated into theoretical terms, this historical complexity requires that the symbolic overtones which dominated the factory question by 1833, must be treated as an emergent rather than intrinsic property. The issue did indeed come to be seen as the inseparable counterpart to other social and political divisions; it did indeed become a symbolic focus for a broader contest between competing conceptions of social order; for a time too, the most likely outcome seemed to be a signal legislative victory for the diffuse forces of resistance, and a public affirmation of the cultural and moral inferiority of the manufacturing class. But these additional meanings grew out of the way in which the reformers pursued their instrumental objectives, and, no less important, out of the way in which their activities in this respect were interpreted by others. Moreover, once construed in symbolic terms, their efforts attracted a new order of resistance in which the instrumental acquiescence of some manufacturers became temporarily submerged.

Conditions conducive to reinterpretation of the issue in symbolic terms were fostered, first of all, by the movement's own political strategy and timing, both of which contributed significantly to a process of convergence between the factory controversy and the other questions of the day. An early portent of this approaching fusion was evident in Oastler's decision to couch his initial attack on the worsted mills of Bradford in terms of an analogy with colonial slavery. For slavery was already the subject of heated debate, and indeed, as he pointed out in his letter of 29 September 1830, Yorkshire itself was represented in Parliament by 'the giant of anti-slavery principles'.[82]

[81] H. Perkin, *The Origins of Modern English Society 1780–1880*, London, Routledge & Kegan Paul, 1969, pp. 220 ff. and p. 241.

[82] C. Driver, op. cit., p. 42.

Had the matter rested there however, the use of this trenchant comparison might be dismissed as evidencing nothing more than Oastler's undoubted rhetorical skill. But the matter did not rest, and in ensuing months, the continued determination of Oastler and others drove the controversy further and further along a path which led towards its symbolic association with the wider disagreements currently reshaping the political contours of the nation.

One important step in this direction was taken in 1831 when both Oastler and Sadler formed uneasy alliances with the operatives' own Short Time Committees. Born of the dilemma which confronted any traditionalist Tory who 'passed beyond reflective argument about the factory system, and attempted to give vent to his feelings in action',[83] this coalition was charged with immense interpretive possibilities. For it not only brought together those with a common cause in the Ten Hours Bill, but also forged an uneasy link between the rear guard of High Toryism and the vanguard of Radicalism within the working class itself. In doing so, the compact was to earn a significant place in the later development of Tory Democracy; but in the short term, it substantially extended the range of meaning which observers could attach to the factory agitation in terms of what is signified about emerging realignments and possible patterns of political legitimacy.[84]

The process of convergence was further accelerated by the decision to contest the Leeds election of 1832. After the emasculation of Hobhouse's Bill by a Whig Parliament in October 1831, Oastler appears to have realized that the intrinsic merits of his case would not, on their own, automatically ensure success. Recognizing that petitions to Parliament might fare better 'when we have secured good members', he opted to turn the Ten Hours Bill into an election issue, Sadler being chosen to run against a formidable Whig combination of Marshall and Macauley. But the Whig programme thus to be opposed was one which already embodied a forthright statement of middle-class principles on questions quite other than the regulation of childlabour in factories: abolition of slavery, Corn Laws and all monopolies; above all, passage of the Reform Bill which had been delayed in successive Parliaments, thus creating a situation of near insurrection in many parts of the country. Thus, in the Leeds election campaign which dragged on for over a year and attracted considerable attention throughout the country, the factory question was, in a sense, 'put up against' the Whig position on other burning issues. Added to the Tory/Radical alliance which underpinned Sadler's campaign, this juxtaposition was once again an open invitation to drastic reinterpretation.

[83] E. P. Thompson, op. cit., p. 379.

[84] For an excellent discussion of this alliance and its potential significance, see C. Driver, op. cit., pp. 106 ff.

Before the election actually took place in December 1832, however, other events transpired which were to provide further impetus towards convergence between the Ten Hours controversy and other political issues. Sadler was already sitting in the unreformed Commons and, in that same autumn of 1831, he undertook to introduce a new and categorical Ten Hours Bill. But once again, the theatre in which the attempt was to be staged was already given over to another drama—reform of the franchise. Hence, as in Leeds, so too in London there was a fateful contiguity between the factory question and other political disputes. To make matters worse, it was at precisely this same juncture that, according to Sadler's memoirists, he began to lose interest in the issue of parliamentary reform. Having been in the 'very front rank' of the debate, they tell us, his involvement declined rapidly from the autumn of 1831 onwards:

> . . . Mr. Sadler's interest in the question visibly abated, and his mind reverted to its accustomed course of thought. To his party, in skirmishing debate, he proved of little advantage; not that his talents were unable to be turned to such a purpose; but because his whole soul was absorbed in other pursuits. Rapidly therefore, his position in the house changed. A degree of disappointment naturally arose in some quarters; the mere politicians, or political economists or men of fashion, voted him more than ever 'a bore'; but the country at large soon began to comprehend his motives . . .[85]

Subsequent developments did little to stem the course of this seemingly inexorable process of political convergence. Early in 1832 Sadler duly introduced his Bill in the Commons, and on 16th March, only a few weeks before the ultimate passage of the Reform Bill,[86] the matter was referred to a Select Committee under his own chairmanship. We shall return to the significance of this enquiry at a later point; here, it is sufficient to recount that the Parliamentary session ended before the hearing of evidence was complete, and in particular, before the manufacturers had been given an opportunity to state their case. But in August of the same year, just as the election campaign under the reformed franchise was at last entering its closing stages, the incomplete evidence was published.[87] Some six months later—Sadler having in the end failed to gain either of the Leeds seats in the Reformed Parliament—Ashley took up the cause and attempted to push through a revised version of the Ten Hours Bill without any further enquiry.

Thus, through their own activities the reformers helped to create a situation in which the projected enactment could be interpreted as standing for much more than the straightforward imposition of further restrictions

[85] M. T. Sadler, *Memoirs,* p. 280.
[86] The measure was finally passed in June, 1832.
[87] Parl. Papers (1831–2) XV.

upon the labour of children in factories. Nor were their critics slow to read such additional significance into the mounting controversy. In Leeds, Sadler was openly accused of 'convenient philanthropy' and of 'contemptible trickery . . . to wheedle the working classes out of their principles'.[88] His efforts in Parliament hardly fared any better. 'Scarcely had the second bill of Sir J. Hobhouse been in operation twelve months', the manufacturer, R. H. Greg subsequently recalled, 'when the late Mr. Sadler, emerging as if from a long entombment, with all the political and religious prejudices of the olden times, comes forward with a new proposition . . .'[89] Echoing complaints from an earlier era,[90] many manufacturers viewed Ashley's attempt to proceed on the basis of the information already gathered, as nothing short of suspicious. According to George Wood, one of their parliamentary supporters, it was very surprising 'to hear from the noble Lord the argument that the manufacturers ought to be indifferent to the preservation of their characters everywhere else but in their own districts'.[91] In a vitriolic contribution to the *Westminster Review*, the motives of both Sadler and his successor were openly impugned:

> The direct and visible object of the inventor and mover of the Factory Bill was to run his Bill against Parliamentary Reform, Slave Emancipation and the removal of the Corn Laws . . . What have the opponents of retrenchment, reform and free trade to do with the interests of the working classes? Yet the manufacturing population run headlong into the snare and support the schemes of their oppressors for the beggarly boon of being directed how many hours their children may work to escape the artificial famine the same men are making for them . . . When the two nuisances have been abated which the Factory Bill was brought forward as a stalking horse to cover and protect—the Corn Laws and West Indian slavery—then and not till then, the Government should take the factory question in hand . . .[92]

Over and above the inevitable element of strategic innuendo pervading reactions such as these, we can see in their content, how during these years, the movement for further restriction became open to interpretations which transcended its immediate and overt objectives. On one level, we can see factory legislation being transformed into a political reciprocal for other issues, a process which was to continue relentlessly through the ensuing decade and the period of what Dicey saw as the 'accidental' coincidence of

[88] C. Driver, op. cit., pp. 115 and 201.

[89] R. H. Greg, *The Factory Question*, 1837, p. 7.

[90] Similar complaints had been made in 1818. See, for example, *Hansard* (1818) XXXVIII, p. 344 ff.

[91] *Hansard* (1833) XVII, p. 101.

[92] 'The Conditions of the Working Classes and the Factory Bill', *Westminster Review*, No. XXXVI, April 1833, pp. 17 and 24.

the movements to abolish the Corn Laws and to secure a Ten Hours Act.[93] On another, we are witnessing a more subtle transformation in which factory legislation is seen as standing for an attempt to reassert a revitalized establishment's entitlement to legitimate political authority, and more particularly, to the allegiance of an emergent working class.

In themselves, such interpretations might have been sufficient both to stiffen resistance on the part of those who were already opposed to further legislation, and to vitiate the acquiescence of some who might otherwise have stood to make substantial gains from a new enactment. As it turned out however, both also discerned an additional meaning in the projected Ten Hours Act, and this supplied an even sharper spur to resistance. To many manufacturers, the passage of such an enactment in the particular circumstances of 1833 would have been a degradation of much more humiliating potential than the public demonstration of someone else's social dominance and political legitimacy. But once again, this additional meaning emerged as much from what transpired in the course of an abortive attempt to make law, as from the unelaborated possibility of legislation itself.

In this context, two points may be made briefly about the Ten Hours agitation which preceded the Act of 1833. In the first place, and contrary to the views of those who simply dismiss the movement's successive proposals on enforcement as 'bankrupt',[94] the proponents of the measure *were* very determined to make any enactment effective. Inevitably, however, the form taken by this concern was traditional and, in particular, involved stiffer penalties rather than any dramatic alteration in the system of enforcement as such. Moreover, their suggestions in this respect were of such a kind as to foster a public identity of unambiguous criminality for the delinquent mill-owner. Thus, for example, Ashley's Bill not only provided for fines of up to £200, but also for three to twelve months' imprisonment in cases of persistent violation. Where a coroner's jury found that a death had been caused by an employer's negligence over the fencing of machinery, he was to be committed for trial on a charge of manslaughter.[95] In typically robust vein, Oastler would have gone even further and subjected offenders to flogging and the pillory, as well as to imprisonment.[96] Whatever their effectiveness as a deterrent, such penalties would have denied the existence of any significant moral distinction between the offending mill-owner and the common criminal. Indeed, the reformers sometimes made their objection to such distinctions quite explicit:

[93] A. V. Dicey, *Law and Public Opinion in England during the Nineteenth Century*, London, Macmillan (1962 ed.), p. 232.

[94] M. W. Thomas, op. cit., p. 39.

[95] Parl. Papers (1833) II, p. 263.

[96] Parl. Papers (1831–32) XV, p. 460.

Considering the disparity between the moral culpability perhaps of getting, we will say, an ounce of tobacco or a gill of ale contrary to some excise laws, when it is visited with a ruinous penalty on some individuals not able to pay it, would it not be just and desirable to annex an adequate penalty to those who possess thousands and disregard small fines.[97]

If the thrust of the movement's suggestions for more effective enforcement of the law tended towards the allocation of an unequivocal criminal status to some employers, other aspects of its campaign implied a second and broader moral indictment. At a time when it was commonly held that, as Sadler himself said, 'all legislation upon whatever subject, is an evil only to be tolerated for the purpose of preventing some greater evil',[98] the terms in which the relevant 'evil' was portrayed, and indeed, the evidence which was offered in proof of its very existence, often imputed moral inferiority to the manufacturer, his ideas and his entire factory system. Thus, for example, one propagandist could almost feel compassion for the political economists, even though they might have 'no idea of people save and except as tax-producing and money-gathering animals of the unplumed biped species'; but what, he asked, could possibly be said of the manufacturer, 'him whose heart is corrupted by the present profit he is making from the suffering and destruction of hundreds of little children; and who is able, with an untroubled face . . . to demand these infant hecatombs as a necessary sacrifice to the spirit of manufacturing avarice?'[99] A similar heartlessness was attributed to the system by Geoffrey Crabtree. The mill-owner, he declared, might have had a specious right to be heard on the question of factory legislation if he had been a slave-owner. But as regards the welfare of people 'with whom he has not one minute's sympathy, nor even a seeming mutuality of interest before or after the period during which he enjoys profit from their labour', he could not be said to have even the semblance of such a right.[100]

Statements like these cut deep at the roots of entrepreneurial claims to be both guardians of universalistic interests and practitioners of a benevolence no less real for being self-interested. So too did the evidence which was adduced by Sadler's Committee in the summer of 1832 and subsequently deployed as the justification for a further enactment. From witness after witness before this body came tales of the most appalling hardship, of children debilitated and permanently deformed, of systematic cruelty, and

[97] Ibid., p. 436.

[98] *Hansard* (1832) XI, p. 342.

[99] 'The Commission for Perpetuating Factory Infanticide', *Fraser's Magazine*, June 1833, p. 4.

[100] G. Crabtree, *The Factory Commission: The Legality of its Appointment Questioned, and the Illegality of its Proceedings Proved*, London, L. B. Seeley & Sons, 1833, p. 6.

of intimidation by masters. As it stood, without any embellishment by way of official report, the published evidence amounted to a massive indictment of the system as a whole. For many years to come, it would provide both reformers and historians with their most eloquent examples of the suffering endured by the operative class.

It is not possible here to enter into the continuing debate about the accuracy of the picture painted before Sadler's Committee which, as stated earlier, did not receive any evidence from the manufacturers. In any event, its significance in the present context does not hinge upon the veracity or otherwise of its contents, but on its contribution to the reconstruction of the issue in symbolic terms. And in this respect, the enquiry played a crucial rôle. Along with the 'criminalizing' thrust of their proposals and the derogatory tone of their rhetoric, the reformers' evidence for the existence of an evil justifying further legislative intervention facilitated reinterpretation of the movement as an attempt at cultural denigration.

This is certainly how many manufacturers and their supporters began to view the agitation from 1832 onwards. The punishments specified in Ashley's Bill were, according to one woollen-manufacturer, 'such as no free subject would consent to in a commercial and free country'. More than that, its stipulations in relation to such matters as manslaughter were 'of so severe and unusual a description as to be revolting to the best feelings of honourable men'.[101] Some employers were so sensitive on this issue that they even refused to answer questions subsequently put to them by the Commissioners of 1833 on the subject of prosecutions under earlier enactments. If such queries referred to the proprietors of his own works, complained William Jameson, 'we conceive the questions cannot be answered without compromising the high and honourable station they fill in society'.[102] Some four years later, long after Ashley's Bill had been supplanted by the much more modestly punitive measure of 1833, R. H. Greg was still smarting from the sting of even the mildest criminal sanctions:

> Does the Inspector suppose that it is no punishment to a man, we will say nothing of *a gentleman of education in society* equal to himself, to be dragged into a court of justice, tried and condemned, and to have his name entered on a register of convicts?[103]

Unquestionably however, the main force of the manufacturers' recrimination was reserved for the evidence produced by Sadler's Committee in proof of the need for further legislation. Not only, it was asserted, had the proceedings before the Committee been 'ex parte', but also the testimony itself

[101] Edward Sheppard, Parl. Papers (1833) XX, p. 951.
[102] Parl. Papers (1834) XX, p. 121.
[103] R. H. Greg, op. cit., p. 135.

had quite simply been untrue. Nor were the motives of those responsible treated as being above reproach. 'Atrocious falsehoods and calumnies . . . so insidiously managed, as to bear some semblance of truth', was one objector's verdict.[104] For others, the whole episode had been an exercise in calculated vilification, an attempt to 'abuse the public mind' with misrepresentations.[105] Significantly also, many employers saw the reformers' allegations as a reprehensible attack upon manufacturers as a group, and upon the factory system as a whole. Henry Ashworth—always proud to sign himself as 'cotton spinner' or 'manufacturer'[106]—inevitably took marked offence, not just on his own account. 'They have endeavoured, with singular ingenuity and audacity,' he grumbled, 'to fasten upon us, as a body, in the eyes of the public, the most unjust imputations of avarice and cruelty.'[107] Joseph Birley was even more caustic in his insistence that 'tales of sorrow, got up for a Parliamentary Committee, cannot establish the justness of a sweeping accusation'.[108] Similarly, when faced with what he saw as astonishingly pro-tracted attempts to claim credibility for Sadler's evidence, Greg devoted himself at length to showing how the alleged malpractices, even if true in some cases, were neither a function of, nor unique to the 'Factory System'.[109] One final extract from a speech in the Commons is as revealing on this subject as it is on the prevailing state of thinking about crime in general:

> . . . every sort of evil had been laid at the door of the 'factory system'; in truth, the 'factory system' had been used to express and designate every sort of abuse. He knew, as well as anyone, that there were abuses in the factory system as well as in any other; but it was as unfair to use the phrase of the factory system in this sense as it would be to designate all the atrocious crimes committed in this country by the name of the social system.[110]

Once again then, we can see the meaning of the proposed enactment being transformed in the making. Just as in broader terms the issue became a symbolic focus for emerging ideological and political divergences, so in this narrower context it came to stand—in the minds of manufacturers— for their own moral debasement. For a time indeed, the battle became one, not so much over 'whose law this would be', as over whose 'knowledge' and whose moral interpretation of the whole system would be publicly endorsed in the act of legislating. As the issue stood where we left it in

[104] *Exposition of the Factory Question*, London, 1832, p. 10.

[105] K. Finlay, op. cit., p. 3.

[106] R. Boyson, *The Ashworth Cotton Enterprise*, London, Oxford University Press, 1970, p. 88.

[107] Parl. Papers (1833) XX, p. 1105.

[108] J. Birley, *Sadler's Bill*, Manchester, T. Sowler, 1832, p. 6.

[109] R. H. Greg, op. cit., pp. 30 ff.

[110] Mr. Hyett, 5 July 1833, *Hansard* (1833) XIX, p. 243.

March 1833, when Ashley proposed the enactment of a measure without any further investigation, there were few manufacturers who accepted Lord Morpeth's tortuous argument that the 'vindication of the masters was . . . perfectly distinct from the Bill of his noble friend'.[111] A much more common attitude was the one expressed by Wilson Patten when he demanded the appointment of a Commission 'for the purpose of clearing the characters of the masters from those imputations which seemed to be cast upon them by the friends of this measure . . .'.[112] In April of the same year, a motion in favour of such a Commission was narrowly carried, and one of the most famous social investigations of the century was duly set in train.

The early Blue Books of which the report from this Commission was one, have sometimes been uncritically accepted as evidence of a profound awakening of social conscience during the first half of the nineteenth century. More sceptically, they have also been characterized as 'a battleground in which reformers and obstructionists fought . . . and in which humanitarian causes, as often as not, were buried'.[113] In the present case, the latter interpretation seems closer to the truth, though the 'battle' was perhaps more subtle than the sceptics sometimes appreciate. For the establishment of this enquiry marked a victory for the manufacturers in a war now being waged on a symbolic level as much as on any other. Conversely, it signalled a resounding defeat for the Ten Hours Movement which proceeded to ignore the Commissioners' investigations and to castigate them in terms no less vituperative than those levelled against Sadler's Committee.

If the setting up of the Commission was the first victory for the manufacturers, its report, when published, proved to be the second. For although it did come out in favour of some further intervention and of more adequate provision for enforcement, it also went a long way towards vindicating the system and the manufacturers as a body. Endorsing the view that the worst abuses were confined to small mills,[114] the Commissioners made a point of noting the paternal, considerate, gentle and beneficent approach adopted by the proprietors of many large factories.[115] In England, it appeared that corporal punishment was not only unpractised by most employers, but even prohibited by them on their premises.[116] Moreover, apart from a tendency to prolong the hours worked by children in order to match those of adults[117]— a tendency which, anyway, could be obviated by the use of relays—the

---

[111] *Hansard* (1833) XVII, p. 100.

[112] *Hansard* (1833) XVI, p. 640.

[113] E. P. Thompson, op. cit., p. 376.

[114] Parl. Papers (1833) XX, pp. 20 and 24.

[115] Ibid., p. 21.

[116] Ibid., p. 24.

[117] Ibid., p. 53.

system as such was to be exonerated. Not only would 'the natural course of commercial operations' lead to the smaller mills giving way before the competitive superiority of the larger ones,[118] but also, with increased size would come a self-interested necessity for conditions in which injurious 'filth and disorder' could have no place.[119] Similarly, far from there being any inherent impetus towards longer and longer hours in the factory system, 'there appears to be a general tendency in all manufacturers to settle down the extent of the labour in their operatives to about twelve hours daily'.[120] Indeed, to exceed the 'ordinary hours of the trade' was likely to be economically counter-productive.[121] As for the employment of children, while there was certainly a need for further restriction, factory labour was still 'amongst the least laborious' work performed by them, and of indoor employments, 'amongst the least unwholesome'.[122]

In the matter of penalties, the Commission was equally at odds with the proponents of the Ten Hour Bill. Ashley's proposals were roundly dismissed as 'vexatious and arbitrary',[123] and in preparing the Report, it was deemed appropriate to include a verbatim extract from the Greenock enquiry questioning the propriety of applying either his phraseology or penalties 'to individuals who have acted . . . in this most liberal, disinterested, and benevolent manner'.[124] Nor did the reformers themselves emerge unscathed. Exhibiting a kind of dismissive tolerance for the part played by 'benevolent individuals in a higher sphere',[125] the Commissioners resorted to the expedient, honoured by time and establishments the world over, of attributing popular unrest to the activities of professional malcontents, living by the trade of agitation.[126]

The Report from the 1833 Commission was then, in many respects, a great triumph for the influential segment of the manufacturing interest. For some of them, as indeed for many historians, it was to become the embodiment of truth in much the same way as Sadler's Committee did for the reform movement.[127] For some too, it helped to resolve the dissonance between desirable competitive effects and unpalatable symbolic connotations, since legislation on the basis of this information need not carry the same derogatory overtones which had come to be associated with the Ten Hours proposal. On the assumption that this latter dimension of meaning was not to be successfully neutralized, the way was open for the renewed pursuit of instrumental objectives through an effective enactment. Thus, for example,

---

[118] Ibid., p. 60.   [119] Ibid., p. 59.   [120] Ibid., p. 59.
[121] Ibid., p. 59.   [122] Ibid., p. 51.   [123] Ibid., p. 44.
[124] Ibid., p. 24.   [125] Ibid., p. 47.   [126] Ibid., p. 47.
[127] Greg, for example, was still referring to the Commission's findings in 1837, as 'an official and authenticated mass of evidence to which all must bow', op. cit., p. 8.

it was 'some of the most considerable manufacturers' who now suggested a plan for working 'double sets' of children and thereby maintaining prolonged production while still adhering to a restriction on hours;[128] and this despite the objections of country proprietors who argued that such a scheme would be unfeasible in rural areas.[129] Similarly, according to the Commissioners themselves, the need for inspectors was urged upon them by 'several eminent manufacturers', and most pressingly of all by those 'who have had chiefly in mind the restriction of the hours of labour in other factories to the level of their own'.[130]

Following the publication of the Commission's report, the only task remaining for those who still perceived a broader and distasteful import in the passage of an enactment at the hands of the reformers, was its removal from the parliamentary guardianship of Tory traditionalists altogether. And this was precisely what the Whigs, returned under the reformed franchise, succeeded in doing. Faced with the report and with the government's professed willingness to proceed with legislation on the basis of its recommendations, Ashley was forced to surrender his measure into the care of Lord Althorpe. Having taken up the subject fairly and conscientiously he said, he now found himself completely defeated and must therefore yield: 'but having taken it up with a view to do good to the classes interested, he would only say into whatever hands it might pass, God prosper it.'[131]

The statute which resulted was the Factories Regulation Act of 1833. While going further in some respects than the reformers themselves had envisaged,[132] its passage in no way impeached the legitimacy of the manufacturing system and its attendant ideology. Nor, while the Act indeed imposed further restrictions and controls, did it mark any imminent shift towards a more plainly 'criminal' status for the offending employer. Except for issuing or giving currency to false certificates—an offence to which people other than the millowner were anyway more likely to be prone—imprisonment was restricted to such secondary matters as default over payment of fines. Even the preamble was amended on the grounds that, as originally phrased, it was of a 'criminative character'.[133] It was in this same atmosphere of accommodation that the Factory Inspectorate was established.

If the Act of 1833 marked a great victory for at least a segment of the manufacturing interest, it also constituted a considerable setback for the

[128] Parl. Papers (1833) XX, 53.

[129] Ibid., p. 780.

[130] Ibid., p. 68.

[131] *Hansard* (1833) XIX, p. 913.

[132] For example, by reducing the hours of those between nine and thirteen years to nine per day.

[133] *Hansard* (1833) XX, p. 586.

factory reformers. Denying their basic demand for a Ten Hours Bill, it did not affix the seal of public approval to the cause which had come to stand for resistance to the new order and, more positively, for fusion between the ideals of revitalized traditionalism and nascent radicalism. Rather, the Act publicly endorsed the disparagement of the ideology, the 'legislative knowledge', the motives and the methods which had been the hallmark of such a compact. More than that, having campaigned under a banner which brooked no compromise—'A Ten Hour Bill Is Our Bill', the placards had proclaimed[134]—the reformers had been forced to endure the final indignity of seeing their measure pass into the protective care of their enemies. Eye-witnesses to the spectacle, they now faced the task of deciding what such a reverse signified in broader terms. Thus, the chronicle of how successive layers of meaning became embedded in the factory controversy does not end in 1833; for the events which have been described in this paper were to have an ineluctable effect upon the way in which the reformers would interpret both their present failure and their future enterprise.

Summary and Conclusion

In this paper I have attempted to describe and analyse the passage of one legislative enactment. By taking one theoretical scheme and applying it to a specific case, I have tried to demonstrate the importance of the symbolic dimension in law-making, and also to point up some of the deficiencies in the way that this dimension has previously been approached. More specifically, it has been suggested that although the distinction between the instrumental and symbolic import of legal norms is an important one, analysis in terms of an exclusive empirical dichotomy between the two is likely to be misleading. Such an approach not only glosses over the fact that, in practice, most attempts to make law probably contain elements of both, but also neglects the vital possibility of a dynamic interplay between them. Instrumental objectives may be recosted when their realization comes to entail an inflated symbolic price, and vice versa; there is no a priori reason to assume that attitudes towards the instrumental and symbolic ramifications of projected legislation will always run in the same direction.

Stress has also been placed upon the need to elucidate the way in which legislative issues actually 'take on' an additional range of symbolic significance. In this context, it is suggested that the glib characterization of law-making movements as 'symbolic crusades' substantially neglects this problem. Symbolic meanings are not an intrinsic property of the attempt to

[134] C. Driver, op. cit., p. 151.

make law, but an emergent property of the interaction which occurs along the way. They are constructed in the course of the reciprocal processes of interpretation which constitute an ongoing feature of legislative, as of any other interaction.

As far as the Factories Regulation Act of 1833 is concerned, this paper has been an attempt to trace out the empirical contours of these processes in one concrete setting. Particular emphasis was placed upon the fact that in the early thirties, instrumentally oriented support for further legislation existed, not only among the most vociferous advocates of factory-reform, but also among some of the manufacturers themselves. For the latter, however, the issue became increasingly infused with a symbolic significance which temporarily vitiated their instrumentally based acquiescence. This trans-formation was largely the result of interpretive possibilities opened up by the specific methods which the movement for reform chose to (or was forced to) adopt. Thus, the symbolic meaning of the struggle only emerged as the battle progressed.

Once invested with this additional significance, however, the symbolic dimensions of the issue became at least temporarily paramount. In neu-tralizing the distasteful connotations which the proposed enactment had assumed, an influential segment of the manufacturing interest scored a momentous victory. Stripped of its threatened import, the Act of 1833 publicly affirmed that the precepts of common humanity were not so alien to the logic of industrial capitalism that checks could only be imposed from without. In this way it facilitated public representation of the relationship between the state, capital and an emerging working-class as one of pre-eminent moral stature.

But the manufacturers' success did not stop there. Having reconstructed the symbolic significance of further legislation, some of them were able to give full rein, once again, to their instrumental aspirations. The extent to which these were realized can only be seen in the period following the enactment of 1833. In the present context, however, the salient point is that this important statute cannot be forced into any simple and arbitrary category which would characterize it as either instrumentally or symbolically under-pinned. Rather, it was in the complex interplay between the two that the shape and the ultimate fate of factory legislation in the early thirties was decided.

Finally, the events which have been related in this paper constitute one small fragment of a history which still impinges upon the contemporary criminologist. Today, we only rarely turn our attention to such peripheral areas of law-breaking as violation of the Factory Acts. Part of the nebulous phenomenon known as 'white-collar crime', such offences are subject to a criminological neglect which is the analogue of a broader social ambivalence about the criminality of the behaviour in question. Indeed, some writers have suggested that the controversy surrounding the criminality of white-collar crime should itself become the main focus for enquiry in that field.[135] If this view is correct, then reflection upon our own neglect of, and ambivalence towards factory offences should be informed by an appreciation of the legacy bequeathed by the legislators of 1833. A law was indeed passed in that year; but in the process, a tide which might have run much more strongly in the direction of the 'criminalization' of the offending employer was effectively stemmed. We also need to understand the social origins of an enforcement agency which, from its very inception, has not seen itself as being busy about the business of catching criminals. In adopting this historically explicable stance, the Factory Inspectorate has played its own inadvertent part in perpetuating a collective representation which portrays crime as being concentrated in circumscribed and morally peripheral segments of the community. By neglecting such areas of law-breaking, and their histories, criminology has tended to collude.

---

[135] V. Aubert, 'White-Collar Crime and Social Structure', *American Journal of Sociology*, 1952, **58**, pp. 263–71.

THE CONTROL OF DISCRETION IN THE ADMINISTRATION OF CRIMINAL JUSTICE

D. A. Thomas

Let us not oppose discretionary justice that is properly confined, structured, and checked; let us oppose discretionary justice that is improperly unconfined, unstructured and unchecked.—KENNETH DAVIS.

The principal focus of discussion of the issues posed by the existence of widespread discretion in the administration of criminal justice has shifted during the past decade from the *legitimacy* of discretion in legal systems professedly based on the concept of equality before the law to the more specific problem of *controlling the exercise of discretion* in an acceptable way. One of the more valuable contributions to this discussion is that of the American administrative laywer, Kenneth Culp Davis who in his essay, *Discretionary Justice: A Preliminary Enquiry*,[1] examines the actual and potential methods of controlling discretion within the American criminal justice system and other areas of decision-making. One useful insight which emerges from his work is the close analogy between decision-making in criminal justice and the much wider range of Governmental decision-making with which the administrative lawyer is more usually concerned, and the consequential possibility of applying to decision-making in the context of criminal justice the techniques of control developed in those other contexts. More valuable perhaps is his formulation of a theory of the proper rôle of discretion in the administration of justice. This can be stated in the following manner. First, discretion is indispensable to any legal system in which individualization plays a significant part; second, the first object of the legislator should be to eliminate unnecessary discretionary power, not to eliminate all discretionary power; third, that where discretionary power is conferred, it is the duty of the body exercising the discretionary power, as well as those bodies supervising the exercise of discretionary power, to

[1] K. C. Davis, *Discretionary Justice: A preliminary enquiry*, Baton Rouge, Louisiana State University Press, 1969.

C.C.P.P.—6

endeavour to structure the use of the power as far as is possible. The fourth principle is that discretionary power should generally be subject to a system of checks, either in the form of administrative appeals, or judicial review. My object in this essay is to consider the general trends in the development of English criminal law and procedure over the past decade in the light of Davis's theory of the proper rôle of discretionary power; to consider how far English criminal law is progressing towards a point which represents a proper balance between discretionary decision-making and rule-based decision-making; to examine the success of those attempts which have been made to structure particular discretionary powers within the English criminal justice system, and to consider the potential for the applications of these and other techniques of structuring to those parts of our system which are inadequately controlled at present. In attempting this analysis, I would not dispute that the distinction between a discretionary decision and a rule-based decision is one of degree rather than kind, that the interpretation of a rule may have most, if not all, of the characteristics of a frankly discretionary decision, and it is possible to regard an ostensibly interpretive decision as merely a highly structured discretionary decision.

Confining Discretion

The first principle of Davis's theory for the control of discretion is that unnecessary discretion should be eliminated; the first step towards controlling discretion is to confine it within appropriate limits. The scope for discretionary decision-making at most points within a criminal justice system is directly dependent on the substantive criminal law; it is a commonplace that the major source of discretion is the overreach of the law arising from the inevitable imperfection of the legal definitions of offences. Responsibility for confining discretion within proper limits thus lies primarily with the draftsmen of substantive criminal statutes, and the authoritative interpreters of those statutes, the appellate judiciary.

Despite the growth of concern over excessive scope for discretionary decision-making, the general tendency in criminal legislation in this country during the last ten years has been to emphasize discretion at the expense of particularity of definition, and the same tendency can be seen in judicial attitudes. The type of legislative technique which is likely to be increasingly employed in English criminal legislation as the process of codification develops is exemplified by the Theft Act 1968 and the Criminal Damage Act 1971. Both statutes, which together constitute a self-contained code of law dealing with property offences, employ broad and frequently overlapping definitions to which high maximum penalties are attached. They thus maximize discretion both in prosecuting and sentencing, with no serious attempt to establish a meaningful gradation of offences for either purpose. The Law Commission in its Report on the Law of Damage to Property, which led to the Criminal Damage Act 1971, showed that less than 1 per cent of property damage cases are tried on indictment in the Crown Court; the overwhelming majority are tried summarily in the Magistrate's Court, where the maximum penalty is six months' imprisonment. Despite this fact, the Law Commission proposed that it should be possible for the basic offence of intentionally or recklessly damaging the property of another person to be able to be tried on indictment in all cases, subject to a maximum sentence of seven years' imprisonment. It was not considered necessary to define the circumstances which should lead to trial in the Crown Court and the possibility of a long sentence of imprisonment, although the Law Commission did propose certain aggravated forms of the offence for which even longer maximum sentences were possible. A similar process is seen in the Theft Act 1968 in which eleven varieties of larceny, with different maximum penalties, were consolidated under the one definition of theft with a maximum penalty of ten years' imprisonment, as opposed to the maximum of five years formerly applicable to simple larceny. This legislative style indicates a parliamentary confidence in the workings of discretionary decision-making both by prosecutors and sentencers which is seen equally in judicial decisions on the definition of offences, during recent years. A significant, and to the lawyer accustomed to codified systems of criminal law, startling characteristic of recent developments in English criminal law has been the discovery of ancient common law offences which were not previously known to exist, and the resurrection of early statutes long since fallen into disuse. Despite the controversy which surrounded the case of *Shaw* v. *D.P.P.*[2] in 1961, English judges have continued to legislate extensively in one form or another. The offence of conspiracy to corrupt public morals which emerged in Shaw's case, has been the basis of frequent prosecutions in the decade since that decision, and its existence has recently been confirmed by the House of Lords,[3] despite a change in that Court's policy towards precedent which would have permitted it to reverse its earlier decision. In response to the growth of squatting and sit-ins, the Courts have acquiesced in the revival of the ancient statutory offences of forcible entry and forcible detainer, long since discarded in practice; while it would not have been open to the Courts to declare these offences to have disappeared from the law, there was no obvious reason why the Courts should not have narrowed their definitions.

[2] (1961) 45 Cr. App. R. 113.
[3] *Knuller Ltd.* v. *D.P.P.* (1972) 56 Cr. App. R. 633.

On the contrary, in a series of cases the Court of Appeal has adopted an extremely broad interpretation of these offences so that, for instance, it is now established that it is an indictable offence for persons to enter premises forcibly, even if there is no intention to remain, and no intention to commit an offence, and equally, it is an offence for persons who have entered premises in a peaceable manner, to maintain their possession by force; in each case, the requirement of force is satisfied by a show of force sufficient to deter the rightful owner to resume his own possession, or indeed, by the tacit threat implicit in the presence of a multitude of people.[4] These decisions, which have the effect of penalizing the typical student sit-in with the possibility of unlimited imprisonment, have produced a rule which it would have been impossible for a Government to have achieved by legislation without enormous political difficulty. It is significant that, although an element of violence was in fact present in all of the cases with which a Court was concerned, the Court did not include violence as a constituent element in the offence. In doing so, it was clearly relying on the assumption that prosecutions would not be brought in cases without a violent element, as is made clear in the latest of these cases, in which the Court declared that, quite apart from the provisions of the ancient statutes, there exists at common law an offence of conspiracy to trespass. In deciding so, the Court of Appeal declined the invitation of counsel for the prosecution to set limitations to this newly-discovered ancient offence, observing, however, that 'perhaps as a matter of practice, prosecutions should not be brought unless a combination of persons to trespass is likely to cause a breach of the peace, or to affect the public interest in some other way, or to be an outrageous interference with the right of others'.[5] The House of Lords subsequently incorporated the last two requirements as part of the definition.[6] This approach to the function of judicial interpretation, in which the Court adopts an extremely broad definition of the offence on the assumption that prosecutors will in practice adopt a narrow one, is seen in a wide range of other decisions dealing with the issue of strict responsibility. It is clear that Courts have frequently refused to find that a particular offence requires an element of fault on the part of the offender, assuming that the absence of fault will be a criterion in relation to prosecution or sentencing.[7]

These developments indicate that confining discretion has not been a major object either of legislators or of judges in recent developments in the

---

[4] *Mountford* (1971) 55 Cr. App. R. 266; *Robinson* (1970) 54 Cr. App. R. 441; *Brittain* (1971) 56 Cr. App. R. 235.

[5] *Kamara* (1973) 57 Cr. App. R. 144 at 152, *per* Lawton, L. J.

[6] *Kamara* v. *D.P.P.* (1973) 57 Cr. App. R. 880.

[7] E.g., *Evans* [1962] 2 All E.R. 1086.

substantive law. The only major attempt to confine discretion by changes in the substantive law which is worth noticing is the Misuse of Drugs Act 1971. This statute modifies the strict liability principles applied by earlier drug legislation to offences of possessing prohibited substances by allowing an affirmative defence of ignorance that the substance possessed was a prohibited substance within the meaning of the Act. The Act also introduces a significant attempt to structure sentencing discretion by replacing the existing twofold structure of offences of supplying drugs and possessing drugs with a threefold structure consisting of offences of supply, possession with intent to supply, and simple possession. The effect of this change is that it will no longer be proper for a court to sentence a person convicted of possession on the basis that he was in possession as a supplier unless the prosecution have established to the jury his intention to supply. The question of intent to supply has thus been transferred from the discretionary sentencing process to the stage of formal adjudication.

Structuring Discretion

Davis distinguishes between confining and structuring discretion in these terms. 'The purpose of confining is to keep discretionary power within designated boundaries and this can be accomplished through statutory enactments, through administrative rules or by avoiding the development of discretionary power beyond the boundary. The purpose of structuring is to control the manner of the exercise of the discretionary power within the boundaries and this too can be accomplished through statutory enactments, through administrative rules and other means.'

In England and Wales, the use of statutory techniques for structuring discretion has been limited to sentencing. A number of vigorous attempts to control the discretion of sentencers by legislation have been made in the last fifteen years, with varying degrees of success. Three distinct legislative techniques can be identified. The first can be described as 'bald exhortation' —the use of a statutory formula indicating a legislative preference for a particular policy, but not including any effective mandatory element. An example of this type of legislative approach is found in section 17 of the Criminal Justice Act of 1948 which provides that 'no court shall impose imprisonment on a person under twenty-one years of age unless the court is of the opinion that no other method of dealing with him is appropriate; and for the purpose of determining whether any other method of dealing with any such person is appropriate the court shall obtain and consider information about the circumstances, and shall take into account any information before the court which is relevant to his character and to his physical and mental condition'. This section, while having an immediate impact,[8] has not in the long term achieved its object of influencing sentencers against the use of imprisonment for offenders under twenty-one; nor has a similar formula directed at the use by Magistrates' Courts of imprisonment for first offenders.[9] Despite this lack of impact, the same formula has been re-enacted in the Criminal Justice Act 1972 in an attempt to discourage courts from imprisoning offenders of over twenty-one who have not previously undergone a custodial sentence. It is clearly unwise to generalize too far from the experience of this formula to the question whether any merely exhortatory formula will be effective. The formula is itself so general that courts have found no difficulty in interpreting it to permit a sentence of imprisonment on purely deterrent grounds[10] and the second limb of the section has been held not to require a court to obtain information relevant to the offender's character and physical and mental condition, but merely to consider such information if it is before the court.[11]

The failure of these provisions to influence judicial sentencing policy led to the use of a technique of structuring which was entirely opposite—the imposition of legal restrictions on the powers of courts to use imprisonment in certain cases, and the introduction of mandatory suspension of sentences. The Criminal Justice Act 1961 imposed complex restrictions on the powers of courts to imprison offenders under the age of twenty-one. The Act prohibited courts from imposing sentences of imprisonment on persons in that age group for periods of more than six months and less than three years, unless the offender had previous experience of borstal training or imprisonment. The object of this legislation was to compel courts to make use of borstal training instead of imprisonment in cases which were not of the first order of gravity.[12] These restrictions have been very much resented by the judiciary and in a few cases in the early days of the act, courts imposed sentences of three years' imprisonment on young men guilty of offences for which a shorter sentence would normally have been considered appropriate, in order to avoid the restrictions.[13] This practice was condemned in the

---

[8] See Roger Hood, *Borstal Re-assessed*, London, Heinemann Educational Books, 1965, p. 73.

[9] See Roger Hood, *Sentencing in Magistrates' Courts*, London, Stevens, 1962, p. 136.

[10] See D. A. Thomas, *Principles of Sentencing*, London, Heinemann Educational Books, 1970, p. 247; E. Hall Williams and D. A. Thomas, 'The use of imprisonment and borstal training for young offenders under the Criminal Justice Act, 1961', *Crim. L.R.* [1965], 193.

[11] *Vassal* v. *Harris* [1964], *Crim. L.R.*, 322.

[12] See Home Office, *The Treatment of Young Offenders* (Report of the Advisory Council on the Treatment of Offenders), London, HMSO, 1959.

[13] *Lowe* (1964) 48 Cr. App. R., 165.

Appeal Court and has rarely been seen in subsequent years. It is impossible to discern the effect of this legislation against the enormous increase in the number of offenders in this age group passing through the courts, but the proportion sentenced to imprisonment relative to the number sentenced to borstal training appears to have increased and the effect of the legislation may well have been to produce a relative increase in the number of short sentences of imprisonment, rather than in the use of borstal training.

The attempt to inhibit Magistrates' Courts in particular from extensive use of imprisonment by means of a mandatory technique has equally met with limited success. In 1967 it was enacted that any sentence of imprisonment not exceeding six months for any one offence (the maximum sentence which Magistrates' Courts are permitted to impose in the vast majority of cases) must be suspended for a period not exceeding three years, unless the case fell within one of five excepted categories. It appears to have been assumed that this provision would lead to the suspension of sentences in such cases where before the Act the courts would have imposed imprisonment; in fact it seems clear that the suspended sentence has been used widely in cases where before the Act, a non-custodial sentence would have been chosen and it does not appear to have significantly contributed to restraint in the use of imprisonment or a reduction in the prison population.[14] Indeed, it has been suggested that in an oblique way these provisions have led to an increase in the use of imprisonment in that courts prohibited from imposing terms of one or two months' immediate imprisonment on an offender having instead imposed a suspended sentence of six months, which has then fallen to be enforced, and to be enforced consecutively to the sentence imposed for subsequent offence. The effect is a sentence considerably longer than the offender would have received before the change was made, if sentenced to imprisonment at all. Partly as a result of this effect the mandatory provisions have now been repealed, and a formula has been added to the legislation governing suspended sentences, to the effect that a court should not impose a suspended sentence of imprisonment unless it would have imposed a sentence of immediate imprisonment in the absence of a power to suspend. Whether any court will succeed in making sense out of this provision remains to be seen.

The failure of the mandatory suspended sentence provision as an exercise in structuring discretion can probably be attributed to two facts in particular. The first is the failure of the legislature in enacting these provisions to specify clearly its policy objectives. Magistrates have been widely criticized for making improper use of the suspended sentence in cases where prior to the

[14] See Leon Radzinowicz, 'A foreseeable failure', *Sunday Times*, 24 Jan. 1971, and his Foreword to Marc Ancel's *Suspended Sentence*, London, Heinemann Educational Books, 1971.

legislation a different non-custodial measure could have been used; but no attempt was made in the original legislation to indicate to magistrates the type of case where this measure was to be considered appropriate. Secondly, the failure of Parliament to spell out its assumptions was compounded by the inadequacy of the directions given by the appellate court. It is true that the Court of Appeal eventually laid down the principle that before imposing a suspended sentence the sentencing court should consider and reject all non-custodial alternatives, determine that a sentence of imprisonment was appropriate and then consider whether that sentence should be suspended or immediate; but it is regrettable that the judgement in what is still regarded as the leading case[15] on suspended sentences devotes only two brief paragraphs to his question of general principle.

Two attempts to use statutory methods of structuring discretion in the context of sentencing have been relatively successful. Both employ a similar technique of requiring a court in particular situations to use a particular measure unless certain reasonably clearly defined circumstances are present; if they are present the court has a discretion to use that measure or to use alternatives. The first use of this technique is seen in disqualification of driving offenders. For a considerable period of years legislation now consolidated as the Road Traffic Act 1972 has provided that a driver convicted of any one of a number of serious motoring offences must be disqualified from driving for a minimum period of twelve months unless 'the court for special reasons thinks fit to order him to be disqualified for a shorter period or not to order him to be disqualified'. The expression 'special reasons' has been held to refer only to the immediate circumstances of the offence and not to include the effect of disqualification on the offender. This type of provision appears to have been reasonably successful in achieving its object. There has been little evidence of motorists eligible for mandatory disqualification escaping on the basis of generous definitions of the meaning of 'special reasons' and the provision has not generated any noticeable resentment on the part of the judiciary or magistracy, who have not sought means of evading its operation. A major reason for the relatively high degree of success of this provision has been the accident that the question of whether in a given case special reasons exist has been treated as a matter of law, and thus appealable in the case of convictions in the Magistrate's Court to the Divisional Court of the Queens Bench Division at the instance of the prosecution—this is in effect the only situation where the prosecution can appeal from the trial court on an issue connected with sentence. The existence of a prosecution right of appeal has undoubtedly prevented magistrates from taking too lenient a view of what may constitute excepting circumstances,

[15] *O'Keefe* (1969), 53 Cr. App. R., 91.

as the relative frequency of successful prosecution appeals demonstrates.

The second example of a reasonably successful attempt at legislative structuring of sentencing discretion is seen in the context of the enforcement of suspended sentences. A technique broadly similar to that seen in the case of mandatory disqualifications is employed. The 1967 legislation on suspended sentences provided that where an offender who is subject to a suspended sentence is convicted of an offence, the court was empowered to make one of four orders: to enforce the sentence with its original length, to enforce the sentence with a reduced length, to extend the operational period of the sentence, or to take no action in relation to the suspended sentence. However, the statute provides that the court *must* make an order that the suspended sentence shall take effect with the original term unaltered unless 'it is of the opinion that it would be unjust to do so in view of all the circumstances which have arisen since suspended sentence was passed, including the fact of the subsequent offence'. The course of action to be taken is thus prescribed unless excepting circumstances are present, and these excepting circumstances have again been relatively narrowly defined by the Appeal Court in a series of decisions which hold that a suspended sentence should normally be enforced unless the subsequent offence is of a comparatively trivial nature and of a different kind from that for which the sentence was originally imposed.[16] It appears to be generally the case that courts have enforced suspended sentences in accordance with Parliament's intentions and again there has been little evidence of judicial resentment of this restraint on discretion. The fact that the definition of excepting circumstances in this case cannot be characterized easily as an issue of law has prevented the development of a prosecution right of appeal in this case and it may be that the obligation to enforce a suspended sentence has not been honoured so consistently as the obligation to disqualify.

An impressionistic survey of the effectiveness of various legislative techniques of structuring sentencing discretion in England and Wales suggests that the most effective device is that of the required disposition subject to excepting circumstances. This device will work best where the definition of the excepting circumstances is reasonably precise and the statutory system is reinforced by appellate review. Bland exhortations to a particular policy do not appear to be effective although it is possible that the failure of this technique in English experience is attributable more to the weakness of the particular formula used rather than the inadequacy of the technique generally. It is possible that a more precise formula again supported by appellate review, might be more effective. The method of structuring by prohibiting certain established sentencing alternatives altogether will inevitably achieve

---

[16] *Moylan* (1969) 53 Cr. App. R. 590 is the leading case.

its object of denying those particular measures but is likely to create sub-stantial unintended side-effects as is probably true both of suspended sentences and the restrictions imposed by the Criminal Justice Act 1961; certainly this technique can hardly fail to create a considerable degree of judicial frustration and hostility. Other methods of structuring, such as the specification of factors to be taken into account in the making of decisions have yet to be tried in the context of sentencing, although it is worth mentioning that this technique has recently been employed in the award of maintenance in matrimonial cases.[17] Other relevant areas of decision-making —prosecution and parole—have not been the subject of attempts at legislative structuring, despite the fact that parole, a newly established system with a relatively limited range of choices to make, appears to provide excellent ground for experimentation with these techniques.

The structuring device in which Davis places most faith is administrative rule-making—formulation of rules for decision-making not by the body conferring power on the decision-maker, as in the case of legislative structur-ing, but by the decision-maker himself. Even allowing for the breadth of Davis's definition of administrative rule-making, which clearly extends to include much of what might be more accurately regarded as a case law technique, it is not a method which has found great popularity within the English criminal justice system. There are possibly three reasons why this is so. First, decision-making power tends to be decentralized and dispersed among a very considerable number of authorities—prosecution decisions for instance are largely the responsibility of the chief officers of various police forces, and it would be constitutionally improper for a central government agency to issue policy directives except where there was a statutory basis for doing so, as in the case of offences for which the consent of the Director of Public Prosecutions is required before a prosecution may be commenced. Second, there is a tendency both on the part of law enforcement agencies and paroling agencies whose decision-making is not open to continuous public assessment, to conceal the criteria on which they operate, partly out of a natural defensiveness and partly because some case can be made out for preserving the confidentiality of such criteria. A third reason for the reluctance of the decision-makers to evolve articulate statements of the criteria on which they operate is the general principle of English public law that an authority entrusted with a discretion may not fetter that discretion by self-created rules of policy. This long-established principle would not necessarily preclude the evolution of any administrative rules, but it would require them to be formulated in a way which clearly permitted departures to be made in particular cases.

[17] Matrimonial Property Act, 1970.

Administrative rule-making has emerged in two areas both of which are related to road traffic offences. In the context of enforcement there have evolved in many police forces bodies of rules, formulated as force orders to low-ranking police officers, regulating the exercise of discretion in relation to minor motoring matters such as speeding and lighting offences. Typically, such an order would specify the tolerance levels permissible in speeding cases before the case should be reported for consideration of prosecution, or stipulate that a driver of a vehicle which is not carrying the proper lights during hours of darkness should not be reported for prosecution unless the lights are found on inspection not to be in working order. Very little is known about the extent of these rules and, so far as I am aware, no systematic attempt has been made to observe their working in practice. The other interesting experiment in what Davis would regard as administrative rule-making is the formulation by the Magistrates' Association of standard sentencing tariffs, again for motoring offences. Typically these suggest the level of fine that might be appropriate, at least as a starting point for discussion, in the case of various regulatory routine motoring offences. It is by no means clear how successfully these tariffs operate in practice;[18] there seems little reason to suppose that up to the present time they have had any substantial effect on the sentencing behaviour of magistrates. Again, it would seem that the area in which this type of structuring has the greatest potential is the context of parole; it may be that the Parole Board is beginning to identify recurring issues of principle and to develop policies concerning them, but these policies have not been revealed, apart from some general guidelines in the Annual Reports, either for public discussion or the enlightenment of applicants for release on licence. It would not seem too ambitious a task for the Parole Board, in default of legislative provision, at least to formulate general criteria, say in relation to the importance attached to previous record, the stability of marriage, or the prospects of employment. An example of what might be done is provided by the Board's pronouncements on what it calls 'heinous offences' including 'trafficking in drugs, the use of violence and firearms and some sexual behaviour, including corruption of or harm to children and young persons where public feeling, local or national, may still be sensitive', where they 'feel bound to give particular consideration to public opinion, quite apart from the element of risk, before deciding whether to recommend parole, even though there may be other factors favourable to the prisoners concerned'.[19] Similarly, in relation to the prosecution of certain offences the scope for administrative rule-making

[18] See Roger Hood, *Sentencing the motoring offender*, London, Heinemann Educational Books, 1972, pp. 66–70, 143–152.
[19] *Report of the Parole Board for 1971*, para 58, HMSO.

even in an informal sense is evident. In those offences where discretion is frequently exercised in favour of the offender the possibility of articulating criteria is a real one—as the experiment with road traffic offences shows. The widespread restraint in the prosecution of unlawful sexual intercourse where the offender is relatively young for instance, provides a suitable example, as does the case of a motorist causing the death of a close relative by dangerous driving. The major obstacle to such developments is the decentralization of the prosecuting system in this country and it may be that structural changes in the institutions of prosecution, such as the introduction of a Scottish-style system, in which the prosecutor is a member of a jurisdiction-wide agency, or at least the assumption by the Director of Public Prosecutions of an expanded rôle in the control of prosecution decision-making by police forces, are a necessary condition for the development of this type of structuring.

Davis refers to 'other means' of structuring discretion, and in the English system undoubtedly the most important of these is the case law technique. Historically, the common law evolved from a purely discretionary system of remedies, through the development of precedents to a system which the legal analyst can describe in terms of general principle. Generations later equity followed much the same pattern. Similar processes are well-established in the context of sentencing, although it may be they will not take so long to mature. I have endeavoured elsewhere[20] to describe the body of sentencing principle which has emerged in the decisions of the Court of Appeal Criminal Division relevant to sentencing in the higher courts. It is becoming increasingly common for that court to reflect consciously on its rôle as the formulator of principles and to apply to the sentencing decisions the formal techniques of the law of precedent. It is becoming uncommon to hear the assertion that sentencing is a matter of dealing with an infinite variety of individuals on an intuitive basis. One decision of particular relevance to the status and nature of appellate review of sentences in this country is the case of *Newsome* in 1970.[21] The appellant had been convicted of causing death by dangerous driving and sentenced to seven months' imprisonment, a sentence which clearly reflected the fact that he was under the influence of alcohol at the time of the offence. Some confusion had arisen at the trial because the judge had originally passed a sentence of six months' imprisonment, which under the mandatory suspended sentence legislation described earlier was required to be suspended; when it was realized that this was so the sentence was varied by the trial judge to seven months' imprisonment. The question which arose before the appellate court was whether this approach was a

[20] *Principles of Sentencing*, op. cit.
[21] (1970) 54 Cr. App. R. 485.

permissible one. On appeal the court was confronted with two earlier decisions in which it had held that it was improper for a trial judge to increase a sentence once imposed in order to avoid the mandatory suspension on the sentence. Distinguishing these cases the court held that the imposition of a sentence sufficient to evade the mandatory suspension requirement was appropriate so long as the sentence could not be considered excessive in relation to the facts of the offence. What is particularly interesting about the case for the present discussion is the fact that the court adopted the pro-cedures—in particular, sitting with five judges—which are normally con-sidered necessary to the over-ruling of an earlier decision on an issue of substantive or adjectival law. The fact that the court was prepared to afford to the earlier decisions the status of binding precedents and to refer to 'the well-known duty of this division [of the Court of Appeal] to lay down principles and guide-lines to assist sentencers of all grades in the application of the discretion which the imposition of sentence requires' indicates that the process of the transition from pure discretion to that regulated discretion which constitutes the common law is well under way. The empirical question is whether the principles evolved by the court are followed to any significant extent by the trial courts which are subject to its jurisdictions. No extensive research on this question has yet been attempted so far as I am aware, but it is reasonably clear that the courts' decisions have, at the very least, the effect of suppressing the level of sentencing to within the pattern of sentences, for various combinations of offences and circumstances, which has evolved over the years. One indication of the extent to which courts' policies are followed by the trial judges is the relatively low level of success in appeals against sentences when measured in terms of the relationship between the number of sentences varied on appeal to the number of sentences which were imposed in the Crown Court. It is interesting that this proportion holds reasonably constant despite fluctuations in the proportion of different kinds of offenders (i e. defined by their offences) to appeal, and variations in the proportion of all offenders who appeal over different periods of time. If it is reasonable to assume even a modest degree of consistency in the actions of the appellate court, it may be justifiable to make some cautious inferences of the transfer of the courts' principles to the level of the trial court.

The major weakness in the use of case law techniques of structuring sentencing discretion in the English system is that the jurisdiction of the Court of Appeal does not extend downwards to the Magistrates' Courts where the overwhelming majority of cases are tried. It may be that the solution to structuring sentencing decisions by magistrates is to be found in the thoughtful development of legislative techniques supported by a more centralized appeal system.

Case law techniques are by no means limited to formal judicial adjudication. Although they have not yet made an impact on any other context of discretionary decision-making in criminal justice, the potential for their application to prosecution and parole decision-making is exemplified by the use of case law methods in such administrative contexts as planning law, where the systematic reporting of selective decisions on planning appeals has been practised for some years. One of the best examples of a rapidly evolved system of structured administrative discretion, more directly associated with criminal justice, is the work of the Criminal Injuries Compensation Board. In a relatively short time the Board, using the case law method, has developed a system of general principles dealing with the entitlement of claimants in general terms and a reasonably consistent tariff governing the level of awards in relation to the more common injuries.[22] This board is exercising discretion in a narrower field than for instance a prosecutor, but the analogy with parole is a more obvious one.

A related but distinct technique of structuring discretion is judicial review—primarily a method of check, in Davis's terms, which indirectly serves as a means of structuring. The principles of the English law of judicial review are well established and may be stated with confidence in general terms, although it is not always easy to predict their precise application to a particular context. The High Court claims jurisdiction to review the exercise of any discretionary power by any agency of central or local government, unless the exercise of that power is expressly or implicitly excepted from the Court's jurisdiction, on the ground that the power has been exercised improperly—that is to say that irrelevant considerations have been taken into account or relevant considerations have been ignored. The incidental effect of this process is to identify the relevant criteria. Certain types of decisions are also reviewable on procedural grounds, and all decisions are reviewable where jurisdiction has been exceeded. The function of High Court is not to assume the decision-making power of the agency whose determination is in question; the court merely declares the agency's decision to be of no effect, and orders it to reconsider the matter on proper principles. In the fifteen years after the Second World War the Courts on the whole adopted a retreatist position in relation to judicial review and declined to interfere in many cases where their predecessors of earlier generations would have taken action. A more vigorous approach to judicial review in the general field of public administration has become apparent since the decision of the House of Lords in 1964 in the case of *Ridge* v. *Baldwin*,[23] where the dismissal of a Chief Constable without a hearing was held to be invalid.

[22] See A. Samuels, 'Criminal Injuries Compensation Board', *Crim. L.R.* [1973], 418.
[23] [1963]2 All E.R. 66.

Since this case the courts have expanded the area of judicial review to include the activities of a number of bodies who had traditionally considered themselves immune from this form of control. Universities have learned to proceed more cautiously in matters affecting students and the courts have exerted control over trade unions in their dealings with their members.

Judicial review in this sense has until recently played a very limited part in the control of the criminal justice system. The decision-making of Magistrates' Courts has frequently been called in question in this way but the most significant development for our purposes is the recognition that the decisions of law enforcement agencies may be challenged in the courts. This development is the result of the efforts of Mr. Raymond Blackburn, who in 1968 attempted to secure from the courts an order of *mandamus* directed to the Commissioner of the Metropolitan Police requiring him to withdraw an instruction placing restrictions on the investigation of alleged offences against gambling legislation which was said to imply a policy of refusal to enforce those statutes. Although the applicant was unsuccessful, the court recognized for the first time that the discretion of a chief officer of police in matters of operational policy was not unfettered and absolute; the court declared that it had power in appropriate cases to grant the relief sought.[24] Subsequently, Mr. Blackburn attempted to compel the Commissioner to enforce more vigorously the law prohibiting the publication of obscene matter, but the court, again recognizing that there was power to review the decision of the Commissioner, held that he had a discretion and was exercising it properly on the facts declared.[25] These two decisions provide a firm basis for judicial review of police enforcement policies in general terms—there can be little doubt that the famous declaration of the then Chief Constable of Southend that he would no longer prosecute people accused of stealing in supermarkets would not now survive challenge in the courts. The possibility of the development through a series of court decisions of a body of principles determining the outer limits of police discretion and specifying at least what factors may *not* be taken into account, is a real and valuable one. It remains to be seen whether the courts will go so far as to review prosecution decisions in individual cases. Traditionally the view has been that a court dealing with a criminal case will not receive evidence that other offenders have not been prosecuted for similar behaviour,[26] although occasionally there are adverse judicial comments on the institution of proceedings in a given case. The logic of the two Blackburn cases suggests that there is no reason in principle why a refusal to institute proceedings in a

[24] R. v. *Metropolitan Police Commissioner ex parte Blackburn* [1968] 1 All E.R. 763.
[25] R. v. *Metropolitan Police Commissioner ex parte Blackburn* [1973] 1 All E.R. 324.
[26] *Arrowsmith* v. *Jenkins* [1963] 2 All E.R. 210.

specific case should not be reviewable (although it is unlikely that a court would grant *mandamus* requiring a Chief Constable to lay an information as opposed to reconsidering a case on proper grounds); and if this is so there seems to be no reason why a positive decision to prosecute should not be equally reviewable in collateral proceedings.[27]

An equally fertile ground for the development of a structural discretion by the application of judicial review is that of parole. It cannot be long before a civil rights or prisoner's rights organization puts the question of the reviewability of parole decisions to the test. The procedure of the Parole Board does not conform to most of the accepted principles of administrative decision-making—the rules of natural justice—but is probably sufficiently firmly established in explicit legislation to be proof against attacks on this ground. There seems to be no barrier however to a legal challenge to a Parole Board decision on the ground that improper or irrelevant considerations have been taken into account and it would not be unreasonable to expect a court either to grant *mandamus* to the Parole Board to reconsider an application for parole on proper principles, or to quash in appropriate proceedings a positive recommendation for release, where it could be shown that the board had followed inapplicable criteria. The practical problem of establishing the fact that inapplicable criteria have been adopted has been very much eased by a series of decisions greatly restricting the doctrine of Crown privilege, under which the Government was formerly able to withhold any evidence from production on the ground that its disclosure would be injurious to the national interest. A few minor problems—such as that of *locus standi* in the review of positive recommendation—need not prevent the development of a series of decisions which would gradually have the wholesome effect of destroying the appearance of irresponsible (in the constitutional sense), inscrutable and arbitrary power and providing a series of articulated, publicly known principles for the guidance of the board and for applicants for parole.

Davis's final principle is that of check—that discretionary decisions should generally be subject to procedural requirements protecting the interest of the individuals affected by the decision and amenable to the intervention either of a higher administrative agency or the courts. As has been shown, sentencing is subject to a vigorous system of appellate control and current developments in the law of judicial review suggest that the latter of these requirements may soon be satisfied in relation to prosecution and parole decisions. There is room, as Hawkins has argued,[28] for the development of

[27] This issue is dealt with in detail in D. G. T. Williams's paper in this volume.

[28] Keith Hawkins, 'Parole procedure: an alternative approach', *British Journal of Criminology*, **13**, 1973, 6.

an internal appeal mechanism in parole, which may indeed emerge from the current devolution of greater authority to the local review committees, leaving the national board with an essentially appellate function. In procedural structuring there is much more to do, although some progress has been made recently in a series of decisions preventing a court in sentencing from making adverse inferences against the prisoner without a proper foundation of evidence.[29] The area where procedural reform seems both most necessary and most easily achievable without significant loss is that of parole: there appears to be no sound reason, penological or political, why parole procedure should not be reconstructed so as to conform with the normal minimum requirements for administrative decision-making—a fair informal hearing, disclosure to the applicant of adverse information tendered to the board by other interested parties, and the statement of reasons for decisions.

Without doubt, however, the *major* obstacle to the achievement of a reasonable balance between discretion and formal rules is the tendency of those responsible for the development of the substantive criminal law, both legislators and judiciary, to favour broad definitions of offences and the abolition of internal gradations in the structure of criminal offences. If the problem of controlling discretion is to be resolved, a new legislative style must be sought which, while avoiding the extravagance of detail of the great nineteenth-century consolidating acts, preserves a necessary degree of distinction between different versions of the same basic offence, and avoids unnecessary overreach into areas of behaviour which are not intended to attract the criminal sanction in practice.

[29] E.g. *Robinson* (1969) 53 Cr. App. R. 314; *Huchison* (1972) 56 Cr. App. R. 307.

A JUDICIAL NOTE ON THE CONTROL OF DISCRETION IN THE ADMINISTRATION OF CRIMINAL JUSTICE

Lord Justice James

By invitation I add this note to David Thomas's Essay on the Control of Discretion in the Administration of Criminal Justice. I expressly refrain from comment upon recent case law. To do otherwise in the context of this note would not be ethical. Thomas accepts the existence of 'a widespread discretion in the administration of criminal justice'. By implication he accepts the principle that, in a legal system in which regard is paid to the particular circumstances of the case, of the offence and of the offender, the existence of discretion is an essential factor. Individualization cannot be achieved without a discretion being exercised. English criminal law makes provision for individualization and few, if any, would now challenge the right of the Courts to the use of discretion in the conduct of criminal business. It is true that the difference between a decision based on the exercise of a discretion and a decision based on the interpretation of a rule may be one of fine distinction or, as Thomas says, one of degree. Nevertheless, to regard the 'ostensibly interpretive decision as merely a highly structured discretionary decision' is, I would suggest, a dangerous approach. It is an approach which serves to blur the fundamental distinction and which may lead to unreasonable confinement and over-structuring of the discretionary field. A complete and unfettered discretion can rarely be justified. Discretion which is exercised in such a haphazard manner as results in inequitable differentiation undermines the authority of the criminal law. Boundaries must be set, and within the boundaries some structuring must take place.

The exercise of discretion in the administration of the Criminal Law is firstly limited by the terms in which the law is expressed, whether it be Law as enacted by Parliament or deriving its force from the Common Law. The development of the criminal law by the creation of new offences is today solely entrusted to Parliament. There is no discretion in the Courts to extend the criminal law. Those offences recognized and based on the common law are confined within their long-established limits. But within the law as enacted in some modern Statutes there is required a wider use of discretion than was possible under earlier legislation. Thomas illustrates this with examples of the Theft Act 1968 and the Criminal Damage Act 1971. The Court cannot escape from the exercise of discretion in evaluating the particular offence within the general description of the offence in such Statutes. This method of legislation has the advantage of making the criminal law simple, readily understood and free from the technicalities which attend over-particularization. In contrast Parliament, in modern times, has sought both to limit and to structure the Courts' discretion. This has been almost entirely within the area of the sentencing process. As Thomas rightly points out the desired effect has not always been achieved.

It must be remembered that discretion in the administration of the criminal law has its place in many aspects other than the sentencing process. The decision as to severing the trial of different accused or different offences charged on one indictment is frequently made upon the basis of a discretion. The decision to admit, or to refuse to admit, evidence when probative value has to be balanced against prejudicial effect is a discretion-based decision. The exercise of a discretion determines the decision as to the admission of evidence of the accused's character at the instance of the prosecution. Within these important areas the Court has worked out the practice and laid down guide lines for the use of discretion within the framework of the law. It must be a matter for the exercise of the Court's discretion when a decision has to be made as to the procedure to be followed in the face of conduct deliberately disruptive of the proceedings. If differences in practice arise in such matters guidance (structuring) can be given by the Appellate Court. On important questions of practice the use of an Appellate Court constituted of five Judges is of especial value in establishing uniformity in the exercise of discretion. This self-imposed oversight is preferable to extrinsic structuring. The former is apt to preserve the maximum of flexibility while meeting the needs of a particular situation; the latter is apt to prescribe for all situations, and thus to be unnecessarily restrictive, when applied to a particular case.

The same self-imposed surveillance of the discretionary field is appropriate to the sentencing process. Within this field, legislation plays its proper part when a change is to be made in the criminal law. When a new method of disposal is required, legislation is necessary. This was the case for example when the Suspended Sentence of Imprisonment and the Community Service Order were made available to the Courts. Legislation was necessary to abolish the power to pass a sentence of Preventive Detention, to create the power to pass an Extended Sentence and to remove the mandatory requirement of suspending a sentence of imprisonment of not more than six months

These matters restrict, or enlarge, the power of the Court but I do not regard them as confining or structuring the Court's discretion in the true sense. They are changes in the Criminal Law. Such statutory requirements as those which introduced mandatory suspended sentences into the sentence of imprisonment, which prohibited the passing of a sentence of imprisonment on persons under the age of 21 years 'unless the Court is of the opinion that no other method of dealing with him is appropriate', the provisions of the Criminal Justice Act 1961 in relation to imprisonment of young offenders and the mandatory requirement to order disqualification for certain Road Traffic Act Offences are examples of legislative confinement and structuring of the Court's discretion. That imposed by section 17 of the Criminal Justice Act 1948 and the comparable provision in section 14 of the Criminal Justice Act 1972 are examples of the legislature putting into statutory form that which had been the self-imposed and established practice of the Courts. No dramatic change was to be expected to flow from the statutory recognition of an existing situation. It is suggested that, in a system in which individualization plays a prominent part, the greater the range of powers of sentence entrusted to the Courts the more likely it is that the justice of a particular case can be met. Further, that in respect of the sentencing process, while boundaries to the area of discretion must be set, and may properly be set by the legislature, the structuring of discretion, except in relation to sentences in which individualization plays little, if any, part, should be the function of the Court. Within the area of road traffic offences there is little room for the individualization of sentences and legislative structuring of the Court's discretion has proved to be acceptable and successful. In the area of suspended sentences the structured discretion prescribed by the legislature has been reasonably successful in relation to the activitation of the sentence because individualization was not substantially eroded, but it failed in relation to the mandatory sentence because that provision did cut across the need for individualization. There has been no serious criticism of the way in which the Court has discharged the function of structuring discretion in aspects other than sentencing. There is no reason to believe that in relation to the sentencing process the Court would fail properly to structure and control the use of discretion. Such criticism as has been made has been directed at situations which have arisen through lack of communication between the Appellate Court and the Trial Courts. This is a problem which, insofar as it still exists, can be readily solved. Should the Court fail properly to structure its discretion then Parliament can and should intervene. So long as the Court properly discharges this function, any additional structuring of the Court's discretion imposed by the legislature is attended by the risk of impairing the Court's ability to meet the needs of a particular case.

PROSECUTION, DISCRETION AND THE ACCOUNTABILITY OF THE POLICE

David G. T. Williams

Those concerned with the administration of criminal justice have been reminded in recent years that 'a wide discretion is exercised by the police as to what offences shall or shall not be prosecuted', that the 'day-to-day business of prosecuting offences up and down the country is ... shot through with discretion', and that it has never been the rule 'that suspected criminal offences must automatically be the subject of prosecution'.[1] Wide discretionary powers are entrusted to the police in many areas related to the enforcement of the law, but the special and critical importance of the decision whether or not to prosecute stands out in the criminal process. This has become increasingly recognized in legal writings in the United States, where concern about discretion in prosecution has been expressed in the more general context of informally exercised discretion in all areas of government and administration.[2] The part which discretion plays in police work in this country has been 'seldom acknowledged publicly',[3] and

[1] See respectively, 'Solicitor', *English Justice* (1932), London, George Routledge, 1932 at p. 92; Geoffrey Marshall, *Police and Government (The Status and Accountability of the English Constable)*, London, Methuen, 1965, at p. 116; Sir Hartley Shawcross, A.-G., H.C. *Debates*, Vol. 483, c. 681 (29 January 1951).

[2] See especially, K. C. Davis, *Discretionary Justice (A Preliminary Inquiry)*, Baton Rouge, Louisiana Univ. Press, 1969, and A. W. Bradley, 'Research and Reform in Administrative Law', *Journal of the S.P.T.L.*, 1974, **13**, 35. Articles published in North America relating to police discretion include Joseph Goldstein, 'Police Discretion Not to Invoke the Criminal Process: Low-Visibility Decisions in the Administration of Justice', *Yale L.J.*, 1960, **69**, 543; Norman Abrams, 'Internal Policy: Guiding the Exercise of Prosecutorial Discretion', *U.C.L.A. Law Rev.*, 1971, **19**, 1; James R. Silkenat, 'Limitations on Prosecutor's Discretionary Power to Initiate Criminal Suits: Movement Toward a New Era', *Ottawa L.R.*, 1971, **5**, 104; Symposium on Police Practices, *Law and Contemp. Problems*, 1971, **36**, 445–588; Joseph H. Tieger, 'Police Discretion and Discriminatory Enforcement', *Duke L.J.*, 1971, 717; Arthur Rosett, 'Discretion, Severity and Legality in Criminal Justice', *S. Cal. L.R.*, 1972, **46**, 12. See also Brian A. Grosman, *The Prosecutor*, Toronto, Univ. of Toronto Press, 1969.

[3] John Lambert, 'The Police Can Choose', *New Society*, 18 September 1969.

the 'shadowy' and 'virtually uncharted' territory[4] of prosecution is no exception. Controversy about individual prosecutions or prosecution policies has erupted from time to time, but the absence of sustained attention is perhaps attributable to a variety of factors: these include the difficulty of defining or assessing the range of discretion over the entire field of the criminal law, the fact that prosecutions are not exclusively the responsibility of the police, the problem of disentangling the processes of investigation and prosecution where the police are involved, the 'local' as opposed to 'national' organization of the police with resulting variations in attitudes and policies, the varying rôle and influence of the Home Office and the Law Officers and the Director of Public Prosecutions, uncertainty about the extent to which police functions are subject to political as well as judicial control, the need to examine police discretion from the standpoint of constitutional and administrative as well as criminal law, and an acceptance by many people of the inevitability of a substantial measure of such discretion combined with an understandable reluctance to interfere with or impede the police in the performance of their duties.

There are also the inhibitions derived from the laws of contempt of court, defamation and official secrets. The strict sanctions of contempt must necessarily limit the extent to which particular prosecutions may be discussed pending the actual trials, and comment upon a decision not to prosecute in a particular case might expose someone to an action for defamation of character. Policy decisions and the entire process of criminal investigation are protected by the official secrets laws. It was held in *Lewis* v. *Cattle*[5] that the police hold office under the Crown for the purposes of section 2 of the Official Secrets Act 1911, and several prosecutions relating to police information have been undertaken since that decision. The confidential nature of many police communications and documents has also been recognized in cases where disclosure in the course of litigation has been resisted on grounds of 'Crown privilege'; in *Conway* v. *Rimmer*, for instance, Lord Morris of Borth-y-Gest spoke of 'the weight of the consideration that the police in their work of fighting crime, which is work that is so much in the public interest, must in no way be impeded or frustrated'.[6] A considerable

---

[4] A. F. Wilcox, *The Decision to Prosecute*, London, Butterworth, 1972, at p. v. A recent book in which several aspects of police discretion are discussed is A. Keith Bottomley, *Decisions in the Penal Process*, London, Martin Robertson, 1973. On prosecution discretion in particular, see Glanville Williams, 'Discretion in Prosecuting', *Crim. L.R.* [1956], 222; Bernard M. Dickens, 'Control of Prosecutions in the United Kingdom', *L.C.L.Q.*, 1973, **22**, 1; Louis Blom-Cooper, 'To Prosecute or Not to Prosecute', in J. C. Alderson and P. J. Stead (eds.), *The Police We Deserve*, London, Wolfe, 1973, pp. 67–77.

[5] [1938] 2 K.B. 454.

[6] [1968] A.C. 910, 972. See also, R. v. *Lewes JJ., ex p. Home Secretary*, [1972] A.C. 388.

amount of material about police activities may qualify for exemption from public disclosure after the normal period of thirty years under the Public Records Acts 1958–67. During the parliamentary proceedings leading to the Public Records Act 1958, the Solicitor-General explained that there 'is a Home Office practice in relation to documents which are strictly criminal records not to let them loose in circumstances where they are likely to be emotionally disturbing to living relatives';[7] though the Advisory Council on Public Records, in concurring during 1971 in the closure for a hundred years of three classes of Metropolitan Police Records, recommended that a period of seventy-five years would in future suffice 'in cases of personal sensitivity' and where there are no 'exceptional' circumstances.[8]

The Franks Committee of 1971–2,[9] which was set up to consider the operation of section 2 of the Official Secrets Act, was well aware of the arguments for secrecy. In written submissions to the Committee, the Association of Chief Police Officers of England and Wales argued that there are certain areas where open disclosure of police plans and intentions would be 'entirely undesirable'[10] and the Police Federation regarded it as 'imperative' that documents used in the police service should continue to be protected from unauthorized publication.[11] The Committee recognized that the public have a legitimate interest in information about such matters as 'general police methods and procedures',[12] but the interests of the police themselves appear to be amply safeguarded in the Official Information Bill which the Committee proposed as a replacement for section 2.[13] The clause protecting the 'confidences of the citizen reposed in the Government' would apparently include information about prisoners and other criminals, or suspected criminals, and information about those seeking the prerogative of mercy or complaining against the police.[14] The clause relating to the 'maintenance of law and order' would apparently include 'information about police measures and equipment for the prevention and detection of crime, criminal intelligence, the identity of informers, information about police plans for dealing with a possible serious public disturbance, and information in the hands of the police or of prosecuting authorities which might enable

[7] *H.C. Debates*, Vol. 590, c. 1796 (4 July 1958).

[8] *Thirteenth Report of the Advisory Council on Public Records*, H.C. 218 (10 May 1972), Report for 1971, para. 10.

[9] *Report of the Departmental Committee on Section 2 of the Official Secrets Act 1911*, Cmd. 5104, London, HMSO, September 1972.

[10] Departmental Committee on Section 2 of the Official Secrets Act 1911, *Volume 2* (Written Evidence submitted to the Committee) (London, HMSO, 1972), p. 209 (para. 9).

[11] Ibid., at p. 308.

[12] Cmd. 5104, para. 172.

[13] Ibid., Part VI.

[14] Ibid., para. 193.

an offender to escape justice'.[15] It was also envisaged by the Franks Committee that the law would impose a duty of confidentiality not only upon the police themselves but upon members of private, statutory police forces (such as the British Airports Authority Police), civilian employees of the police, and members of the legal profession acting for the Crown or the police in bringing prosecutions.[16]

Few would dispute the desirability of protecting much of the information in the hands of the police, especially that which is directly concerned with criminal investigations or which, if publicized would prejudice the reputation or livelihood of private individuals. Whether or not section 2 of the Official Secrets Act is replaced, the public will have to rely for much of its information upon well-established channels such as the annual reports of the Chief Inspector of Constabulary, of the Metropolitan Police Commissioner, and of Chief Constables; formal statements made or interviews allowed by police officers; published statistical information; speeches and comments by the Home Secretary and the Law Officers; the reports of official inquiries (when published); accounts and reports of criminal proceedings in courts of law and occasionally of civil proceedings as well; the results of research work undertaken and published with the approval of the Home Office or the police; and material drawn incidentally from books, pamphlets, proceedings of Parliament and of local authorities, unofficial inquiries, articles or items in national and local newspapers, and documentary or other programmes on radio or television. The output of information often varies according to the interest or controversy surrounding a particular criminal trial or area of the criminal law or some national or local police policy in relation to law enforcement. The ill-assorted and unpredictable flow of information makes it peculiarly difficult to assess the nature, scope and control of police discretion in law enforcement; and the difficulty is enhanced in England and Wales by the intimate and overlapping relationship between the prosecuting and investigating functions of the police.

The absence of sufficient information is one reason why it would be unrealistic to expect the courts to investigate and control the discretionary powers of the police in law enforcement, especially those concerned with prosecutions, through the familiar process of judicial review of administrative action.[17] Over the years certain principles have been formulated by the courts to govern the exercise of discretionary powers. They have been summarized as follows in the leading work on administrative law:

[15] Ibid., para. 175.
[16] Ibid., Part IV.
[17] On the distinction between appeal and review, see H. W. R. Wade, *Administrative Law*, 3rd ed., Oxford, Clarendon Press, 1971, pp. 53–5.

The authority in which a discretion is vested can be compelled to exercise that discretion, but not to exercise it in any particular manner. In general, a discretion must be exercised only by the authority to which it is committed. That authority must genuinely address itself to the matter before it: it must not act under the dictation of another body or disable itself from exercising a discretion in each individual case. In the purported exercise of its discretion it must not do what it has been forbidden to do, nor must it do what it has not been authorised to do. It must act in good faith, must have regard to all relevant considerations and must not be swayed by irrelevant considerations, must not seek to promote purposes alien to the letter or to the spirit of the legislation that gives it power to act, and must not act arbitrarily or capriciously. These several principles can conveniently be grouped in two main categories: failure to exercise a discretion, and excess or abuse of discretionary power.[18]

These principles provide an invaluable guide for the exercise of police discretionary powers as much as for any discretionary power. In some areas of administrative discretion—such as local government expenditure, licensing, and town and country planning—they have had a pronounced impact through enforcement by the courts. Apart from two recent decisions of the Court of Appeal[19] concerned with policy decisions as to the enforcement of betting and gaming and obscenity laws respectively, prosecution discretion has been relatively immune from judicial review. Immunity from the formal process of judicial review does not, of course, mean that the police enjoy immunity from judicial scrutiny of their actions in the course of ordinary criminal and civil proceedings; but it does mean that the courts have had relatively little opportunity of influencing some important areas of prosecution discretion.

In this essay an attempt will be made to indicate why prosecution discretion in England and Wales requires different treatment from so many other discretionary powers. Since the chief responsibility for prosecutions rests in practice with the police, the question of regulating and controlling this area of discretion is bound up with the question of regulating and controlling the police in all their functions of law enforcement. It is proposed to deal in order with the people and bodies who act as prosecutors in England and Wales, the factors and criteria which affect the decision whether or not to prosecute, and the status and accountability of the police.

[18] S. A. de Smith, *Judicial Review of Administrative Action*, 3rd ed., London, Stevens, 1973, at pp. 252–3.
[19] R. v. *Metropolitan Police Commissioner, ex p. Blackburn*, [1968] 2 Q.B. 118; R. v. *Metropolitan Police Commissioner, ex p. Blackburn (No. 3)*, [1973] 1 All E.R. 324.

The Prosecutors of England and Wales

In its Report of 1962[20] the Royal Commission on the Police (under the chairmanship of Sir Henry Willink) stated that one of the main functions of the police in England and Wales is 'the responsibility of deciding whether or not to prosecute persons suspected of criminal offences'.[21] But the responsibility is not theirs alone. A former Home Secretary claimed less than twenty years ago that one of the four 'essential features of our police system which make it an effective guardian of our liberties and not an agent of oppression' is that the police have no sole right to prosecute.[22] More recently, during committee proceedings on the Cinematograph and Indecent Displays Bill 1973, the Minister of State at the Home Office described the right of private prosecution, despite the fact that it is seldom used, as 'a cherished right' in this country.[23] Indeed the right of private prosecution has been described at various times as 'a safety valve', 'a very important control over executive power', 'a fundamental principle of English criminal law'[24] and as 'a firmly entrenched principle of our constitution'.

Prosecution by private people was frequent and important before the advent of the modern police forces, in a period when it could be asserted that prosecuting for criminal offences was the patriotic duty of all citizens.[25] Nowadays the number of private prosecutions each year is extremely small, partly because of a growing acceptance of the rôle of the police as prosecutors and partly because of the prohibitive cost of instituting and conducting the proceedings.[26] The cost, of course, is a less serious obstacle when prosecutions are undertaken by commercial organizations or private bodies such as the Royal Society for the Prevention of Cruelty to Animals.[27] An

[20] *Final Report of the Royal Commission on the Police,* Cmd. 1728, London, HMSO, May 1962.

[21] Ibid., para. 59.

[22] Gwilym Lloyd-George, 'The Arm of the Law', in *Liberty in the Modern State* (pamphlet, Conservative Political Centre, 1957) at p. 21.

[23] H.C., Standing Committee B, Tenth Sitting, 17 January 1974, c. 472.

[24] See respectively, A. F. Wilcox, op. cit. at 4; H.C., Standing Committee A (Criminal Justice Bill 1967), 21 March 1967, c. 1023 (Sir John Hobson); *H.C. Debates,* Vol. 604, c. 840, 24 April 1959 (Sir Reginald Manningham-Buller, A.-G.); Sir Norman Skelhorn, the Director of Public Prosecutions, quoted in Charles Wegg-Prosser, *The Police and the Law,* London, Oyez Pubs., 1973, at p. 119.

[25] See Leon Radzinowicz, *A History of the English Criminal Law and its Administration from 1750,* Volume 3 (Cross-Currents in the Movement for the Reform of the Police), London, Stevens, 1956, at pp. 26–7.

[26] See generally, Delmar Karlen, *Anglo-American Criminal Justice,* Oxford, Clarendon Press, 1967, at pp. 21–2; A. F. Wilcox, op. cit., at pp. 3–6.

[27] See Bernard M. Dickens, 'Control of Prosecutions in the United Kingdom', *I.C.L.Q.,* 1973, **22**, 1, 2.

outstanding drawback of many private prosecutions is that, often after the police or other authorities have declined to proceed because of insufficient evidence or for some other reason, defendants are exposed to the possibility of considerable expense, worry and time-wasting.[28] They are given some element of protection by the exercise of discretion by magistrates on the issue of a summons, at the end of the prosecution's case, or, where appropriate, at the stage of committal. The Director of Public Prosecutions is entitled to take over any proceedings and, if he chooses, offer no evidence or invite an acquittal; and the Attorney-General could in exceptional circumstances enter a *nolle prosequi* to stop a trial on indictment.[29]

A judge of the Court of Appeal has said that the process of private prosecution 'is becoming regarded with increasing disfavour in this country',[30] but it is nonetheless a hardy survivor in our legal system. It is commonly associated with minor cases of assault, arising from family quarrels or disputes between neighbours, and with some cases of shoplifting or petty fraud; occasionally, however, a summons will be sought in the context of political controversy—as in the prosecution for assault arising from the events at Caerau in 1934,[31] the charges brought by two members of the League of Empire Loyalists after disturbances at the Conservative party conference at Blackpool in 1958,[32] and the conspiracy allegations against Mr. Peter Hain which led to a costly trial at the Central Criminal Court in 1972.[33] Supporters of the retention of the right of private prosecution see it as an effective and unique remedy against non-prosecution, 'as a necessary safeguard for the citizen against inaction on the part of the authorities'.[34] In the later nineteenth century, for instance, there was a case in which, after the Director of Public Prosecutions had declined to prosecute, a private

---

[28] See H.C., Standing Committee B, Tenth Sitting, note 23, *supra*, c. 464.

[29] See J. Ll. J. Edwards, *The Law Officers of the Crown*, London, Sweet & Maxwell, 1964, at ch. 16 and 17 on the office of Director of Public Prosecutions and ch. 12 on the *nolle prosequi* power of the Attorney-General. The D.P.P.'s power to take over proceedings is provided for in s. 2(3) of the Prosecution of Offences Act, 1908.

[30] R. v. *Metropolitan Police Commissioner, ex p. Blackburn*, [1968] 2 Q.B. 118, 149, *per* Edmund Davies L.J.

[31] *Thomas* v. *Sawkins*, [1935] 2 K.B. 249.

[32] *The Times*, 13 October 1958, p. 6; 18 October 1958, p. 4; 20 December 1958, p. 4; 11 April 1959, p. 4; 16 May 1959, p. 4; 2 June 1959, p. 6.

[33] See *The Times*, 2 September 1972, p. 2: in awarding costs to the private prosecutor the judge at the Central Criminal Court said that the 'right of a private person to have unrestrained access to the courts and magistrates is a centuries-old right. . . . It exists until and unless Parliament takes it away. It is not for the courts to encourage its erosion'. See also, the *N.C.C.L. Bulletin*, Sept. 1972, No. 5.

[34] JUSTICE, *False Witness (The Problem of Perjury)*, London, Stevens & Sons, 1973, para. 89.

person successfully prosecuted two blackmailers;[35] and the Sheffield Police Appeal Inquiry of 1963 brought out the circumstances in which a solicitor reluctantly felt obliged to proceed with a prosecution against two police officers.[36] It is questionable, however, whether the availability of private prosecutions should continue. Trials on indictment at the behest of private prosecutors ought to be barred, if only because there is no longer a grand jury (an institution which belongs to the fertile days of private prosecutions) to provide, in Viscount Alverstone's apt words, 'a great protection in certain classes of cases where persons are charged with criminal offences to which there attaches no real criminality'.[37] At summary level the recent tendency has been for decisions whether or not to prosecute in shoplifting cases to be entrusted more and more to the police:[38] this is a welcome development, for the consequences of ill-advised prosecutions could be serious and it is imperative that prosecution discretion should be exercised by those capable of taking a relatively detached view against a wide background of experience. It is tempting to suggest that private prosecutions should continue in relation to minor assaults, especially since the police themselves are often understandably reluctant to become involved; even so, the reputation of the judicial process is not enhanced when despairing magistrates are sometimes driven to resolve such proceedings by binding over the defendants and the prosecutors and even the witnesses.

Any abolition of or limitation upon the right of private prosecution need not affect those areas where prosecutions are entrusted to government departments, public authorities and local authorities.[39] These are frequently areas where technical, specialist knowledge is required. Prosecution policies vary dramatically: proceedings are readily undertaken for failure to take out licences for radio or television sets, whereas criminal proceedings against an allegedly fraudulent taxpayer are undertaken only after elaborate con-

[35] Sir Theobald Mathew, *The Office and Duties of the Director of Public Prosecutions* (pamphlet, 1950), at pp. 10–11; quoted in J. Ll. J. Edwards, op. cit., at p. 367.

[36] *Sheffield Police Appeal Inquiry*, Cmd. 2176, London, HMSO, November 1973, esp. paras. 16–17.

[37] Viscount Alverstone, *Recollections of Bar and Bench*, London, Edward Arnold, 1914, at p. 291.

[38] Shoplifting and Thefts by Shop Staff (Home Office working party), London HMSO, October 1973. See also, *The Times*, 30 October 1973, p. 17 (leading article on 'Temptation in the Shopper's Way'); Hilary M. Bennett, 'Shoplifting in Midtown', *Crim. L.R.* [1968] 413, 421–2; Bernard M. Dickens, 'Shoplifting and Prosecutions', *Crim. L.R.* [1969] 464.

[39] See Bernard M. Dickens, 'Discretion in Local Authority Prosecutions', *Crim. L.R.* [1970], 618; Bernard M. Dickens, 'Control of Prosecutions in the United Kingdom', *I.C.L.Q.*, 1973, **22**, 1, 4–7; J. Phillips, 'Cambridge Trade Descriptions: a Study in Enforcement', *Crim. L.R.* [1974], 25.

sideration.[40] The variations can largely be explained in the context of the particular area of administration. There are some difficult and troublesome areas (such as prosecutions over social security benefits), but in other areas the prosecution policy is benign and well-understood by those who are most directly affected. As opposed to private prosecutors, however, the prosecutors acting for public bodies are relatively confined in their operation within the criminal law, operate in accordance with administrative policies, owe some responsibility in varying degrees inside their organization, and do not 'compete' with the police in the enforcement of the law. If the responsibility for prosecutions generally were to be taken away from the police and entrusted to 'public prosecutors', it might be desirable in due course to treat prosecutions now handled by public bodies in the same way. Pending such a change these public bodies, whose prosecution discretion cumulatively extends over a wide range of activity, will continue to play an important rôle in the administration of the criminal law; and the manner in which each exercises its discretion should be regarded as relevant, in research studies or otherwise, in efforts to assess or regulate powers of prosecution.

In turning to prosecutions undertaken by the police, it should at once be recognized that, in Lord Devlin's words, 'every *police* prosecution is in theory a private prosecution; the information is laid by the police officer in charge of the case, but in so doing he is acting not by virtue of his office but as a private citizen interested in the maintenance of law and order'.[41] The practice has long ago departed from the theory however, and it would be unrealistic nowadays to equate police prosecutions with ordinary private prosecutions. The theory has lingered on because the effective assumption by the police of the rôle of public prosecutors in England and Wales has been a gradual and tentative process from the second quarter of the nineteenth century. By the nineteenth century the old reliance upon prosecutions by private people had become discredited: it was claimed 'that prosecutions were compounded, that prosecutions were instituted for vexatious purposes, that, when there was no private prosecutor with means, cases came to trial in an unprepared state'.[42] Over several decades there were numerous proposals for setting up a formal system of public prosecutions, but—with the exception of the institution of the office of Director of Public Prosecutions[43] —these came to nothing. The decline of the old system of prosecutions,

[40] A. F. Wilcox, op. cit., ch. 1; Sir Alexander Johnston, *The Inland Revenue*, London, Allen & Unwin, 1965, at pp. 66–7.
[41] Patrick Devlin, *The Criminal Prosecution in England*, London, Oxford Univ. Press, 1960, at p. 17.
[42] F. W. Maitland, *Justice and Police*, London, Macmillan, 1885, at p. 148.
[43] See J. Ll. J. Edwards, op. cit., note 29.

and the protracted failure to establish a clear alternative, coincided with the creation, extension and consolidation of statutory or professional police forces from 1829 onwards: and it was these who, by default and not by a deliberate political decision, filled the void. The system which has evolved—the primacy of the police in prosecutions—stands in stark contrast to the system in Scotland, under which 'the police are responsible only for the collection of information about offences, all subsequent action with regard to prosecution being undertaken by a solicitor in the public service'.[44]

The actual procedure observed by the police in the exercise of their prosecution powers varies from force to force. Professional legal help is obviously required in the conduct of many proceedings in court, and there has been a growing tendency to set up solicitors' departments as a source of readily available legal advice.[45] However, apart from those cases where the Attorney-General or the Director of Public Prosecutions are involved, the ultimate responsibility for the enforcement of the law rests with the chief officer of police. The fact that he is equally responsible for investigation and prosecution has caused many misgivings. The Justice committee which reported in 1970 on *The Prosecution Process in England and Wales* set out a list of the actual or potential defects and criticisms of the present system, and went on to emphasize two basic points: that the system confuses two 'quite distinct and disparate functions and responsibilities' (investigation and prosecution) and that it offends against 'the principle that the prosecution should be—and should be plainly seen to be—independent, impartial and fair: concerned only with the pursuit of truth and not with winning or losing'.[46] It was recommended that both the decision to prosecute and the conduct of prosecutions should in the main be entrusted to a separate body, organized centrally and regionally, which would be entirely independent of the police and subject to the overall control of the Attorney-General. Such a scheme is similar to those which it became 'a mark of enlightenment'[47] to

[44] *Report of the Advisory Committee on the Police in Northern Ireland*, Cmd. 535 (Belfast, HMSO, October 1969), para. 142. See generally Bernard M. Dickens, 'Control of Prosecutions in the United Kingdom', *I.C.L.Q.*, 1973, **22**, 1, on the Scottish system at pp. 19–28 and on the position in Northern Ireland, at pp. 28–34. See also, R. M. Jackson, *Enforcing the Law*, rev. ed., Harmondsworth, Penguin Books, 1972, at pp. 82–4.

[45] The Royal Commission on the Police agreed (at para. 380) that it was desirable that police in England and Wales should have more legal advice in deciding upon prosecutions and recommended the appointment of a prosecuting solicitor for every force. Several police forces apparently still do not have prosecuting solicitors. See in general, Andrew Boyle, *Trenchard*, London, 1962, at p. 660 (on the formation of a solicitors' department for the Metropolitan Police); Wegg-Prosser, op. cit., at p. 122; JUSTICE, *The Prosecution Process in England and Wales*, 1970, at pp. 4–5; Bow Group pamphlet, *Scales of Justice*, 1962, at pp. 37–8.

[46] JUSTICE, *The Prosecution Process in England and Wales*, 1970, at para. 9.

[47] Maitland, op. cit., at 148.

propose during the nineteenth century, and its adoption would certainly bring the administration of the criminal law in England and Wales more into line with that in most other countries. At the same time it would be wrong to assume that the choice is a simple one between police prosecutions and public prosecutions. The present system has evolved and changed, and today there are numerous checks and balances which the police have to take into account. A crucial independent element has been injected into the system by the functions which have been increasingly entrusted to the Attorney-General and the Director of Public Prosecutions.

The Director of Public Prosecutions, albeit equipped with a relatively small staff, brings considerable central direction into the exercise of prosecution discretion in important cases.[48] Information about a number of offences is collected and sifted in his department, he is available for a wide range of advice to chief officers of police and others, he is under a duty to prosecute in certain cases and in others where it *appears to him* that the matter is of importance or difficulty or which for any other reason requires his intervention, and he has the statutory right *if he thinks fit* to intervene in any summary or indictable proceedings.[49] The italicized phrases remind an administrative lawyer of the virtually unqualified discretion entrusted to the Director in some of his functions,[50] and it is difficult to envisage circumstances in which the exercise of these functions could be successfully challenged through the processes of judicial review. The control is political rather than through the courts, for the Director acts under the general direction of the Attorney-General who is in turn answerable to Parliament. The Attorney-General himself has a direct part to play in the criminal law in a number of ways: in the conduct of certain prosecutions, in directing that a prosecution should take place in a particular case, and in entering a *nolle prosequi* in trials on indictment.[51] The latter is a prerogative power and, despite recent developments,[52] the courts are unlikely to regard its exercise as justiciable—any more than they have been prepared to question the

---

[48] See J. Ll. J. Edwards, op. cit., ch. 16 and 17; R. M. Jackson, op. cit., at pp. 86–8; *The Guardian*, 27 November 1973, p. 18 (article on 'Public Prosecutor Number One').

[49] The italicized phrases appear respectively in the Prosecution of Offences Regulations 1946, reg. 1(c) and the Prosecution of Offences Act 1908, s. 2(3).

[50] See S. A. de Smith, *Judicial Review of Administrative Action*, op. cit., at pp. 253–62 ('Are There Unreviewable Discretionary Powers?').

[51] See J. Ll. J. Edwards, op. cit., esp. ch. 8, 10, 11, 12; Sir Elwyn Jones, 'The Office of Attorney-General', *C.L.J.*, 1969, 43. The *nolle prosequi* is discussed by Edwards at pp. 227–37.

[52] See S. A. de Smith, op. cit., at pp. 254 (esp. note 39) and 529; D. G. T. Williams in *C.L.J.*, 1971, 178 (case-note); B. S. Markesinis, 'The Royal Prerogative Re-visited' *C.L.J.*, 1973, 287. Some recent judicial developments suggest a possible departure from the rule that the exercise of a prerogative power cannot be questioned in the courts.

exercise by the Home Secretary of the prerogative of mercy.[53] Yet the political responsibility owed by the Attorney-General for his prerogative and statutory powers, direct and indirect, in the criminal law is bound in the nature of things to be patchy: detailed comment or explanation would often be either premature or inappropriate. The responsibility to Parliament is nonetheless valuable as an ultimate check, especially in matters of grave concern, upon the actions of the Law Officers or the Director of Public Prosecutions. Whether the responsibility should be extended, as proposed by the Justice committee, to encompass a nation-wide system of public prosecutions is doubtful. To make the Attorney-General answerable for important but essentially limited prosecution functions is one thing; to make him answerable for the vast majority of prosecutions could impose an intolerable burden upon the Law Officers' Department. The Attorney-General has, after all, extensive political and legal functions outside the administration of the criminal law. One of the constitutional consequences of adopting a system of public prosecution in England and Wales might well be the creation of a Ministry of Justice, with the public prosecutors organized in a semi-independent agency under overall departmental direction.

The complications of the tasks of the Attorney-General and the Director of Public Prosecutions are nowhere better illustrated than in those cases where formal consent has to be obtained before prosecutions can be brought in relation to certain statutory offences.[54] Consent requirements, which are mandatory in their effect,[55] have steadily grown in number since the mid-nineteenth century: they provide another example of the tendency since that time to curb private prosecutions and also reflect something of the movement in favour of a formal system of public prosecutions. They are to be found in one form or another in a surprising variety of statutes, including private or local acts of Parliament. There is no coherent policy to determine when restrictions should be imposed and in what manner they should be framed. It has been suggested—at least as far as public statutes are involved—that among the considerations which from time to time have led to the imposition of consent provisions are the need to secure consistency of practice in bringing prosecutions, to prevent trivial or vexatious private prosecutions, to enable account to be taken of mitigating factors, to provide some central control in sensitive or controversial areas, and to ensure that decisions on prosecution are taken in the light of major considerations of public policy.[56]

[53] *Hanratty* v. *Lord Butler* (1971), 115 S.J. 386.
[54] J. Ll. J. Edwards, op. cit., at pp. 237–46; A. F. Wilcox, op. cit., at pp. 17–20.
[55] E.g., *Secretary of State for Defence* v. *Warn*, [1968] 3 W.L.R. 609.
[56] See Minutes of Evidence, Volume 2, of the Franks Committee on Section 2 of the Official Secrets Act 1911, London HMSO, 1972, at pp. 149–50, esp. 124–6; the Report of the Franks Committee, Cmd. 5104, at pp. 90–95 and 138–40; *Information and the Public*

Many of the arguments for restriction are persuasive in particular contexts. Yet it is noticeable how readily they can be queried or rebutted in other, apparently equally appropriate contexts. In opposing formal restrictions on prosecution it has been asserted, for instance, that they are not justified simply because of the novelty or uncertain scope of a criminal offence, that the formal granting of consent could be unfair to a defendant by giving the appearance of prejudgement, and that encroachments upon the right of private prosecution should be allowed only upon strong grounds.[57] The least convincing of these arguments, though it is sometimes the most passionately advanced, is the claim that private prosecutions should be maintained. Advocates of consent provisions are perhaps equally to blame by over-speculation in many cases about unjustified and improper private prosecutions. One suspects that much of the impetus for consent provisions comes from an underlying wish to abolish private prosecutions altogether. If this is so, the process of piecemeal abolition has gone on long enough. The fundamental issue should be faced, if only because abolition would ironically make it more feasible to reduce or rationalize the enactment of consent provisions. The Director of Public Prosecutions would be free to use his existing powers to secure consistency of practice in the exercise of police powers of prosecution, while the Attorney-General could be entrusted with a statutory power of veto on prosecutions in those areas where account has to be taken 'of important considerations of public policy or of a political or international character, such as may arise, for instance, in relation to official secrets or hijacking'.[58]

At the present time the decision whether or not to authorize a prosecution can be highly controversial. The Attorney-General is particularly exposed because his is a political appointment in the Government of the day. Prosecutions under the Official Secrets Act, for example, pose numerous difficulties: the Attorney-General has been accused of persecuting the Press, harrying members of Parliament, departing from the original intentions of the legislators or ignoring undertakings given by his predecessors, acting

---

Interest, Cmd. 4089, June 1969, HMSO, para. 34; *Joint Committee on Censorship of the Theatre*, Report of June 1967, H.L. 255, H.C. 503, para. 48; Lord Shawcross, 'The Law and the Press', *Encounter*, March 1966, p. 87.

[57] See views expressed in the House of Commons in 1969 in the Second Reading debate on the Freedom of Publication (Protection) Bill (*H.C. Debates*, Vol. 776, cc. 1709 ff., 31 January 1969) and in the Tenth and Eleventh sittings of Standing Committee B on the Cinematograph and Indecent Displays Bill 1973, 17 and 22 January 1974; D. G. T. Williams, 'The Control of Obscenity', *Crim. L.R.*, [1965] 471, 473–76; and especially J. Ll. J. Edwards, op. cit., at pp. 237–46.

[58] Minutes of Evidence, Volume 2, Franks Committee on Section 2 of the Official Secrets Act 1911, at para. 7 on p. 126.

too selectively in authorizing prosecutions, granting his consent in cases of trivial infringements of the law (killing a fieldmouse with a field-gun), and taking decisions whether or not to prosecute 'when his party and his Government may have strong vested interests in the matters concerned'.[59] In comments regarding the *Sunday Telegraph* case of 1970–1 it was claimed that the Attorney-General was placed in an impossible or invidious, even unconstitutional, position in having to exercise a dispensing power as to official secrets offences.[60] The Franks Committee accepted that there was public unease but, in its proposed legislation, preferred to retain a provision requiring the Attorney-General's consent for most purposes: the 'point of central importance' is that these decisions are irremediably decisions of a political nature, in that they are concerned with questions of public policy although not partisan advantage.[61] Transfer of responsibility to the Director of Public Prosecutions was, save in one area, rejected, and the Committee rightly made the point that the Director is in any event under the control of the Attorney-General; though it might have added that their relationship is exceedingly obscure. The factors or criteria taken into account in the granting or withholding of consent are presumably the same as those which are taken into account in the normal process of undertaking prosecutions, except that Parliament can be assumed in areas affected by consent provisions to have implicitly accepted that prosecutions may be infrequent and instituted only if it is in the national interest to do so.

Prosecutions Decisions: Relevant Factors and Criteria

The decision to prosecute in a particular case is made after an assessment of the evidence by the police or by any other body or person which has the responsibility or has assumed the responsibility for the institution of proceedings. It is arguable that, once it has been determined that the evidence is sufficient for the presentation of a case, a prosecution should be undertaken: unless, as in the case of consent provisions, there is legislative sanction

[59] See the Franks Report, Cmd. 5104, and 3 volumes of evidence, London, HMSO, 1972; David Williams, *Not in the Public Interest* (*The Problem of Security in Democracy*), London, Hutchinson, 1965; Jonathan Aitken, *Officially Secret*, London, Weidenfeld & Nicolson, 1971. The quotation comes from the *Sunday Telegraph*, 7 February 1971, p. 12 ('Secrets Case that Never Was', by Brian Roberts) and the remark about using a field-gun to kill a fieldmouse comes from the *Manchester Guardian* of 1 June 1948, cited in *H.C. Debates*, Vol. 452, c. 1693–1702 (24 June 1948).

[60] See Jonathan Aitken, op. cit.; and leading articles in *The Times*, 18 March 1970, p. 11 ('The Secrets Act'), 21 March 1970, p. 9 ('The Attorney-General's Discretion') and 4 February 1971 ('The Secrets Act Must Be Reformed').

[61] Cmd. 5104, para. 255.

for a more selective approach. Both the theory and practice in this country, however, suggest that the selective principle does and should apply throughout the criminal law. The system of criminal trial and the flexibility of the criminal law make this inevitable. Apart from the initial decision whether to prosecute or not, it has to be considered whether one or more offenders should be charged, whether one or more offences should be alleged, and whether summary or indictable trial should be sought. At each stage of decision there are numerous factors which may be relevant, including the trivial or technical nature of the offence, the obscurity or antiquity of the law, and the current state of public feeling.[62] Because it is known that the discretion to prosecute is exercised after assessing any such factors which are deemed to be appropriate, the defendant in many cases is prone to feel that he has been unfairly picked upon or unjustly treated either in the bringing of the case or in the selection of offences with which he is charged. This may well occur, for instance, in prosecutions where some new and controversial legislation is being enforced, or an offence has been revived after a long period of virtual desuetude, or there is an atmosphere of public outrage, or the prosecutions have an overtly deterrent purpose, or there are issues of public morality, or the charges are alleged to be inspired by political rather than strictly legal considerations.[63] The criminal courts, while recognizing that a prosecutor has 'a very broad discretion' and that 'myriad factors'[64] can enter into his decision, are understandably reluctant to allow the determination of guilt or innocence to be confused by suggestions that the prosecution itself is arbitrary or unnecessary. The defendant's submission in *Arrowsmith* v. *Jenkins*[65] that she had been picked on by the police was met by the reply that that was nothing to do with the court. Yet it is clear that the exercise of prosecution discretion is by no means immune from judicial control. Disapproval of a particular prosecution can be seen or reflected in the strictures of the judges, in the sentences imposed, in the award of costs against the prosecution, and in advice offered for the future.

The rôle of the appellate courts is especially important. In some circum-

---

[62] See especially the invaluable discussion in A. F. Wilcox, op. cit., including the summary in Appendix A of reasons for not prosecuting although prima facie evidence of guilt is available.

[63] Controversy particularly arises in relation to such common law offences as conspiracy (see now the Law Commission's Working Paper, No. 50, on Conspiracy, Attempt and Incitement, 1973) and riot and unlawful assembly. Statutory offences causing difficulty include those in relation to illegal drugs: a Commission of Inquiry of the Canadian government noted that the 'problem of enforcement has generated legal responses that are relatively peculiar to the drug context' (*The Non-Medical Use of Drugs: Interim Report*, 1970, Penguin ed. 1971, at p. 256).

[64] *Newman* v. *United States* 382 F. 2d 479, 480–82 (1967).

[65] [1963] 2 Q.B. 561, 566.

stances, of course, they will urge prosecutors to be more severe and not to allow considerations of 'convenience and expedition'[66] alone to determine the choice between summary and indictable trial. But they are equally prepared to stress the need for a sense of proportion. The Court of Appeal in a recent case[67] criticized the bringing of riot and affray charges against seven youngsters for 'noisy and loutish' behaviour resulting in a lot of noise but little else; the trial had been lengthy and costly, and it was felt that such severe charges ought never to have been brought. Likewise in *Ambrose*[68] the addition of a trivial count to an indictment was disapproved of by the Court of Appeal: Lawton L.J. commented that the ordinary man was right in disliking 'the book being thrown at someone' or 'everything being thrown at an accused person except the kitchen sink'.[69] Sometimes it is the hypothetical ill-advised prosecution which the appellate courts have in mind, as in *Kamara* where the Court of Appeal saw no likelihood of a charge of theft when a clerk uses one of his employer's envelopes for a personal letter or of a prosecution for conspiracy to trespass where two or more people agree to take a short cut across a field.[70] Many ill-advised prosecutions do not reach the stage of appeal, however, for the incensed or adverse reaction of the judges can lead to the withdrawal of its case by an embarrassed prosecution, or a peremptory verdict of acquittal, or the imposition of a nominal penalty. In some recent trials on indictment, the prosecution for shoplifting of an elderly, invalid spinster of excellent character was described as 'a most shameful thing'; the prosecution of a retired minister, who was 'in a state of great distress and desolate in his loneliness and isolation', for causing the death of his wife by dangerous driving was deplored by the trial judge; and an enquiry was demanded as to the reasons for an 'outrageous' and 'absolutely dreadful' prosecution brought against a young married man for a minor housebreaking offence committed eight years earlier.[71]

Control of prosecution discretion in the context of individual cases is bound to be unpredictable and incomplete. Some kinds of prosecution have obviously been discouraged by the cumulative impact of judicial restiveness over the years; but it would be interesting to know the extent to which judicial advice on prosecutions is collated on an up-to-date basis in the Home

[66] R. v. *Coe* [1969] 1 All E.R. 65, 67.

[67] *Cambridge Evening News*, 6 February 1974, p. 14. The trial cost between £3,000 and £4,000.

[68] (1973) C.A.R. 538.

[69] At 541.

[70] (1973) C.A.R. 144, 153. The case subsequently went to the House of Lords: see (1973) C.A.R. 880.

[71] See respectively *The Times*, 17 November 1972, p. 3; *The Times*, 8 October 1970, p. 4; and the *Daily Telegraph*, 29 March 1969, p. 15.

Office or elsewhere in an effort to ensure that it will permeate through all the channels of prosecution. In any event, it is the judges on appeal or in trials on indictment (in the latter case, often stiffened by the presence of juries) who are most likely to take the exceptional course of questioning the background to a prosecution. The judges' views are possibly not sufficiently known in magistrates' courts, especially in relation to the handling of committal proceedings. Another and significant feature of most judicial comments is that they are directed to the police. The assumption once again is that the responsibility for prosecutions rests with the police, guided where necessary by the Director of Public Prosecutions. What, then, of the private prosecutor? In referring to a Law Officer's assurance about prosecutions for conspiracy to corrupt public morals, which one would expect to have much the same influence as judicial advice on prosecutions, Lord Diplock recently observed that, since every private citizen has the right to initiate a prosecution for criminal conspiracy 'and the executive government has no power to prevent his doing so', it was difficult to see how effect could be given to the assurance except by 'unprecedented' use by the Attorney-General of his *nolle prosequi* power.[72] There is also the power of the Director of Public Prosecutions to take over proceedings, but this too would only rarely be used to intervene in cases undertaken by private people. It is claimed, as we have seen, that the availability of private prosecutions is a valuable deterrent against inaction on the part of the police. Conversely it could be argued that private pressures and the threat of private prosecutions militate against the proper exercise of police discretion in circumstances where inaction may be, in the light of established criteria, the desirable course.

The discretionary decision not to prosecute clearly raises problems of a special kind. An actual prosecution directly affects one person and is exposed to a public trial, judicial scrutiny and possible publicity outside court. Failure to prosecute is seldom publicized, and those directly affected are unlikely to feel aggrieved—except in certain cases, of which riot is an example, where those who shared in the conduct for which the defendants are charged may choose to demonstrate their disapproval of the prosecution by petitioning for equality of treatment before the law. Among the best-known of individual instances of failure to prosecute are decisions of the Attorney-General to refuse his statutory consent to the institution of proceedings. These can be at least as controversial as decisions to grant his consent. In noting the very small number of prosecutions for incitement to racial hatred since 1965, the Select Committee on Race Relations and

[72] *Knuller (Publishing, Printing and Promotions) Ltd.* v. *Director of Public Prosecutions,* [1973] A.C. 435, 480.

Immigration suggested that neither the rule of law nor race relations are best served by treating such a recent provision as section 6 of the Race Relations Act as a dead letter. 'It should either be repealed,' the Committee declared, 'or occasionally brought to bear against publications and speeches manifestly seeking to stir up racial hatred.'[73] The Government's reply in 1973 rejected any immediate possibility of repeal and had this to say:

> Prosecutions under the section may be instituted in England and Wales only by or with the consent of the Attorney General. There have been prosecutions in only 7 cases, involving a total of 15 people, since the Act came into force. The small number of prosecutions may indicate that the section has a deterrent effect: the Attorney General would not hesitate to prosecute or give his consent to a prosecution if he believed that it would be in the public interest to do so.[74]

The operation of section 6 provides a good example of relative 'inaction' on the part of the Attorney-General, for the number of complaints addressed to him has certainly far exceeded the number of prosecutions undertaken.[75] When questioned in the House of Commons about the reasons for his decisions in this and in other fields where consent provisions operate, he has rarely gone beyond the explanation that he considers the sufficiency of the evidence, the gravity of the charge, and—perhaps above all—whether the public interest justifies the institution of proceedings.[76] Is there any supplementary legal remedy for his refusal of consent? In an article in 1972 Bernard Dickens advanced the interesting suggestion that in principle the order of *mandamus* might be sought as a means of compelling the Attorney-General to exercise his discretion properly in accordance with the policy and objects of the statute in question.[77] It is perhaps doubtful whether the courts would be prepared to question individual decisions: for, apart from anything else, disclosure of the Attorney-General's reasons may be resisted

[73] *Police/Immigrant Relations*, Report of the Select Committee on Race Relations and Immigration, Session 1971–72, H.C. 471–I (August 1972), para. 259.

[74] *Police/Immigrant Relations in England and Wales*, Cmd. 5438 (October 1973), observation (8) at p. 8. During the proceedings in Standing Committee B on the Race Relations Bill 1965, the Home Secretary (Sir Frank Soskice) said that the provision was intended 'to deal with the major malefactor and not with the tiny, unimportant man who uses offensive language' (Second Sitting, 27 May 1965, c. 56) and the Solicitor-General (Sir Dingle Foot) said that it would be 'very seldom invoked' and then only in 'the extreme and very bad case' (Third Sitting, 1 June 1965, c. 131).

[75] See, e.g., Anthony Dickey, 'Prosecutions under the Race Relations Act 1965, s. 6 (Incitement to Racial Hatred)', *Crim.L.R.* [1968], 489.

[76] See *The Times*, 9 February 1971, p. 13 (letter from Sir Dingle Foot, Q.C.). Sir Reginald Manningham-Buller, when Attorney-General, said: 'I authorise prosecutions for offences against the Official Secret Acts in those cases where, having regard to the relevant facts, I consider that it would be in the public interest to institute proceedings.' (*H.C. Debates*, Vol. 657, c. 611, 5 April 1962).

[77] 'The Attorney-General's Consent to Prosecutions', M.L.R., 1972, **35**, 347.

on the ground of confidentiality under a claim of 'Crown privilege'. Where the reasons are known—as, for example, where immunity from prosecution was granted to three witnesses appearing before the Tribunal of Inquiry into the cessation of trading by the Vehicle and General Insurance Company Limited[78]—the courts are still likely to be inhibited: both because they might not feel competent to assess the validity of the reasons and because, whatever their validity, they would recognize that prosecution is not an automatic process in English law. Private prosecutions in the areas of consent provisions were abolished by Parliament, and it is not for the courts to substitute the right of private complaint. If a pattern of decisions were to emerge in relation to one of these areas and the general prosecution policy of the Attorney-General was dubious, the courts might be more prepared to intervene. There would still obviously be difficulties, but tentative steps have been taken in recent years to establish judicial review of policy decisions made by the police.

In R. v. *Metropolitan Police Commissioner, ex parte Blackburn*[79] the Court of Appeal was concerned with a policy decision which amounted in effect to 'an instruction to take no proceedings against clubs for breach of the gaming laws unless there were complaints of cheating or they had become haunts of criminals'.[80] The applicant for *mandamus*, Mr. Raymond Blackburn, sought to compel the Commissioner to revoke the policy decision. He failed at first instance but, at the hearing of the appeal, counsel for the respondent undertook that the policy would be officially revoked and that the law would be enforced. Had this undertaking not been given the Court of Appeal would apparently, subject to technical arguments, have allowed the appeal. Edmund Davies L.J. said that the application for *mandamus* was 'designed simply and solely to ensure that the police do not abdicate, in consequence of a policy decision, their functions as law enforcement officers',[81] and he dismissed as 'repugnant' the suggestion that the police

---

[78] *Report of the Tribunal of Inquiry appointed to inquire into certain issues in relation to the circumstances leading up to the cessation of trading by the Vehicle and General Insurance Company Limited*, H.L. 80, H.C. 133 (February 1972), para. 260: the Attorney-General informed the Tribunal 'that it was in the public interest that we should hear the evidence . . . and that, as such evidence would tend to incriminate the witness, it was also in the public interest that the evidence should be given without fear of subsequent prosecution for offences admitted'. In its report on *The Law and the Press* (1965) a joint working party of Justice and the British Committee of the International Press Institute wished the Attorney-General, if a consent provision were to be introduced for contempt of court, to be able to take 'an unfettered view of any particular case' (para. 54).

[79] [1968] 2 Q.B. 118. See D. G. T. Williams, 'The Police and Law Enforcement', *Crim.L.R.* [1968], 351; Norman Abrams, 'Internal Policy: Guiding the Exercise of Prosecutorial Discretion', *U.C.L.A. Law Rev.,* 1971, 1.

[80] [1968] 2 Q.B. at 134, *per* Lord Denning M.R.

[81] Ibid., at p. 147.

are not answerable to the courts in the performance of their duties.[82] In R. v. *Metropolitan Police Commissioner, ex parte Blackburn (No. 3)*[83] the same applicant sought *mandamus* to compel proper enforcement of the Obscene Publications Act 1959. The Court of Appeal sympathized with his concern about the ineffectiveness of measures taken to combat pornography, but felt that the blame for this ineffectiveness should be attributed principally to the Act itself and to the framework in which the police have to operate. In dismissing the application, the three appellate judges nonetheless took the opportunity of critically examining some of the methods adopted by the police. The unusual caution and disclaimer procedure,[84] which enables search and seizure cases to be disposed of without reference to the magistrates' courts, attracted particular attention. Another matter considered was the practice of the police not to prosecute in any case until a report had been made to the Director of Public Prosecutions and his advice secured. On this Roskill L.J., while pointing out that the police are entitled to prosecute on their own initiative, said that there 'can be no objection to a prosecuting authority seeking to achieve so far as possible a uniform practice or standard by which to judge whether or not a particular prosecution should be launched. So to do is not to refuse to enforce the law but to judge as a matter of the exercise of a proper executive discretion whether or not a particular prosecution should be launched, an exercise of judgement oft fraught with great difficulty and only to be taken after very many different and often conflicting factors have been considered'.[85] Several years ago Sir Hartley Shawcross, when he was Attorney-General, made plain the immensely difficult balancing of interests and assessment of fact and degree which are required in deciding whether to prosecute in cases of obscenity;[86] and there is also the point, as a Home Secretary indicated in the nineteenth century, 'that prosecutions sometimes do more harm than good, by making obscene publications more widely known; and that it is desirable not to prosecute unless it is tolerably certain that a jury will convict'.[87] Recognition of such difficulties and factors goes some way to explain why the courts, in

---

[82] Ibid., at p. 148. Earlier in his judgement (at p. 145), Edmund Davies L.J. said: 'It would be difficult to exaggerate the importance of these proceedings. If there are grounds for suspecting that a grave social evil is being allowed to flourish unchecked because of a set policy of inaction decided upon by a pusillanimous police force, public confidence must inevitably be gravely undermined.'

[83] [1973] 1 All E.R. 324. The *Blackburn* case No. 2 occurred in 1968 ([1968] 2 Q.B. 150) and concerned criminal contempt of court. In this article *Blackburn (No. 3)* will be referred to as the second *Blackburn* case.

[84] See Paul O'Higgins, *Censorship in Britain*, London, Nelson, 1972, at pp. 50-1.

[85] [1973] 1 All E.R. at 338-39.

[86] H.C., Vol. 465, cc. 872-3 (23 May 1949).

[87] H.C., Vol. 330, c. 892 (12 November 1888).

dealing with alleged failures to enforce the law, are reluctant to intervene in individual cases.

Even in relation to policy decisions the courts have made only modest claims. It would certainly be premature to interpret the two *Blackburn* cases as representing a major advance in judicial review of executive action. Only in 'extreme cases'[88] will the courts be prepared to intervene, as, for example, if a chief constable were 'to issue a directive to his men that no person should be prosecuted for stealing any goods less than £100 in value'[89] or if he were 'to issue an instruction that as a matter of policy the police would take no steps to prosecute any housebreaker'.[90] Policy decisions have operated or continue to operate in relation to certain types of offences and certain types of offenders. They may vary in emphasis from police force to police force, and it is not difficult—for instance, with road traffic offences[91]—to identify glaring discrepancies in the enforcement of the law.[92] They may also vary with the passage of time, reflecting the views of the courts and the changing standards of society to such an extent that some branches of the criminal law have almost been totally eroded by consistent and sustained inaction. The courts would not in theory concede the complete abdication of a duty to exercise an independent discretion in each particular case. But in practice it is difficult to isolate the point at which prosecution discretion must be exercised: for there is the earlier stage of whether, when and how to investigate or pursue inquiries and the discretionary decisions there depend upon an overall appreciation of priorities. 'It is no part of the duty of this court,' said Roskill L.J. in the second *Blackburn* case, 'to presume to tell the respondent how to conduct the affairs of the Metropolitan police, nor how to deploy his all too limited resources at a time of ever-increasing crime, especially of crimes of violence in London.'[93] The courts for their part not only accept the inevitability of many policies but will not hesitate to urge their adoption. In the first *Blackburn* case Salmon L.J. saw nothing wrong, for instance, in a policy decision 'not to prosecute, save in exceptional circumstances, young teenage boys who have had sexual intercourse with girls just under the age of sixteen' and added that, if a prosecution does take

[88] [1973] 1 All E.R. at 331, *per* Lord Denning M.R.
[89] [1968] 2 Q.B. at 136, *per* Lord Denning M.R.
[90] Ibid., at 139, *per* Salmon L.J.
[91] See *Report of the Royal Commission on the Police, 1962*, Cmd. 1728, at pp. 114–17; Report of Her Majesty's Chief Inspector of Constabulary for 1964, H.C. 251 (July 1965) at p. 53; Report of Her Majesty's Chief Inspector of Constabulary for 1972, H.C. 289 (June 1973) at ch. V; *Drive* (the Automobile Association's magazine), New Year 1974, p. 74 ('Beware the County Crackdown').
[92] See generally, A. F. Wilcox, op. cit.
[93] [1973] 1 All E.R. at 338.

place in such circumstances, 'the courts usually take the humane and sensible course of imposing no penalty'.[94] Lording Denning M.R., in the civil case of *Buckoke* v. *Greater London Council*, speculated about a rule not to prosecute fire-engine drivers for crossing red traffic lights provided that they use all care and there is no danger to others. 'This would be,' he suggested, 'a justifiable policy decision so as to mitigate the strict rigour of the law. If any police officer, notwithstanding this direction, should prosecute for this technical offence, I would expect the justices to give the driver an absolute discharge. . . .'[95] Even overt abdication of discretion to prosecute will presumably be acceptable to the courts where it is for a limited time under an amnesty,[96] the ultimate effectiveness of which can in any event be safeguarded by the prerogative of mercy.

There are further reasons why the *Blackburn* cases should be approached with caution. In the first place, police policies may be only sketchily formulated and perhaps identifiable from inferences drawn from a long-term course of conduct. They are often confidential, and there is obviously an argument for maintaining confidentiality lest the exercise of prosecution discretion should be transformed into a formal dispensing power without legislative sanction. The policy decision in the first *Blackburn* case was unusually formal and all-embracing, and doubtless invited judicial disapproval because it was apparently based on a misinterpretation of the law and ran counter to recent legislation. Most policy decisions are less vulnerable. The very complexity of the situation in the second *Blackburn* case must have discouraged judicial intervention. It may be that there should be greater formality and even publicity in the formulation of policy decisions, but the courts have not asked for this nor are they likely to do so. A second reason for caution is that it is unclear as to who may seek a remedy for non-enforcement of the law. In the first *Blackburn* case the Court of Appeal regarded it as an 'open question' as to whether the applicant for *mandamus* had a sufficient interest in the performance of the duty to have standing, while in the second case it seems to have been assumed that Mr. Blackburn, together with his wife who joined in making the application, had a sufficient interest through concern for their five children.[97] The question of standing remains entirely uncertain: and this is illustrated by a recent case in Ontario

[94] [1968] 2 Q.B. at 139.

[95] [1971] 2 All E.R. 254, 258.

[96] See *The Control of Firearms in Great Britain* (Consultative Document), Cmd. 5297, May 1973, at p. 41: there have been seven amnesties on firearms since 1933. See also, Colin Greenwood, *Firearms Control*, London, Routledge and Kegan Paul, 1972, at pp. 235 ff.

[97] On the problem of *locus standi* in relation to *mandamus*, see S. A. de Smith, op. cit., at pp. 490–3.

where a Toronto solicitor sought *mandamus* to restrain the police 'from using audio surveillance in the course of their duties in those cases where the chief of police has given his approval after being of opinion that there is reasonable and probable cause to believe that a criminal offence has been or is about to be committed'.[98] An alternative method of proceeding through the courts would be to seek an appropriate remedy through a relator action, which would initially require the fiat of the Attorney-General in his capacity as guardian of the public interest.[99] Once the Attorney-General has granted his permission there are no problems of standing or *locus standi*, but since the decision whether or not to grant permission is a prerogative discretion it has been assumed until recently that its exercise could not be challenged in the courts.[100] There is nothing automatic about the formal approval of requests for relator proceedings: between 1965 and the beginning of 1973 it was granted in 63 cases out of 70, but a further 70 enquiries were not pursued.[101] Relator actions have had some impact upon the criminal law[102] but not hitherto in connection with prosecution discretion. It is uncertain both whether the Attorney-General would allow proceedings of the kind brought by Mr. Blackburn and whether, if he refused or delayed approval, his decision could be questioned in the manner suggested by the Court of Appeal in *Attorney-General (on the relation to McWhirter)* v. *Independent Broadcasting Authority*. In that case it was tentatively indicated, in the words of Lawton L.J., 'that if at any time in the future (and in my judgement it is not the foreseeable future) there was reason to think that an Attorney-General was refusing improperly to exercise his powers, the courts might have to intervene to ensure that the law was obeyed'.[103]

Two final points should be made. Firstly, the Court of Appeal in the first *Blackburn* case faced the argument that *mandamus* should be refused in accordance with well-established rules of judicial discretion in that the applicant had available an equally effective alternative remedy, namely the undertaking of a private prosecution. This was felt to be 'fantastically unrealistic',[104] and Edmund Davies L.J. was content with 'the simple observation that only the most sardonic could regard the launching of a private prosecution . . . as being equally convenient, beneficial and appro-

[98] *Re Copeland and Adamson* (1972), 28 D.L.R. (3d) 26, 31.

[99] See J. Ll. J. Edwards, op. cit., ch. 14; H. W. R. Wade, op. cit., at pp 124–7.

[100] *London County Council* v. *A.-G.*, [1902] A.C. 165.

[101] See *The Times*, 27 January 1973, p. 5 (law report for 26 January on proceedings in the *McWhirter* case, *infra*).

[102] E.g. *Attorney-General* v. *Harris*, [1961] 1 Q.B. 74.

[103] [1973] 1 All E.R. 689, 705. See S. A. de Smith, note 97 *supra*, at Appendix 3, pp. 527–9 ('Andy Warhol and Administrative Law').

[104] [1968] 2 Q.B. at 145, *per* Salmon L.J.

priate as the procedure in fact adopted by this appellant'.[105] So much, one might add, for many of the claims made in recent times about the right of private prosecution. Secondly, also in the first *Blackburn* case, the Court of Appeal assumed that the courts enjoyed exclusive control over the actions of the police. Lord Denning M.R. said:

> I hold it to be the duty of the Commissioner of Police, as it is of every chief constable, to enforce the law of the land. He must take steps so to post his men that crimes may be detected; and that honest citizens may go about their affairs in peace. He must decide whether or no suspected persons are to be prosecuted; and, if need be, bring the prosecution or see that it is brought. But in all these things he is not the servant of anyone, save of the law itself. No Minister of the Crown can tell him that he must, or must not, keep observation on this place or that; or that he must, or must not, prosecute this man or that one. Nor can any police authority tell him so. The responsibility for law enforcement lies on him. He is answerable to the law and to the law alone.[106]

But is he answerable only to the law?

The Accountability of the Police

There is undoubtedly authority for Lord Denning's assumptions about the constitutional status of the police. The evidence submitted to the Royal Commission on the Police included 'a wealth of judicial pronouncements, the effect of which has been to deny any relationship of master and servant as between the police authority and the constable or as between the Crown and the constable; and in thus denying that he is a servant of either a local or a central authority, the courts have been led to assert the independent character of the office'.[107] The judgement of McCardie J. in *Fisher* v. *Oldham Corporation*,[108] which was an action for false imprisonment, has been taken as the classic assertion of the independence of the police in enforcing the criminal law from any control or interference by a police authority. This denial of local supervision has been reflected outside court in the attitude adopted by the Home Office in relation to police authorities generally, as in the events surrounding the suspension of the Chief Constable of Nottingham in 1959,[109] and also in relation to the rôle of the Home Secretary as police

[105] Ibid., at 149.
[106] Ibid., at 136.
[107] Cmd. 1728, para. 61.
[108] [1930] 2 K.B. 364.
[109] See Geoffrey Marshall, *Police and Government*, London, Methuen, 1965, at ch. 1; T. A. Critchley, *A History of Police in England and Wales 1900–1966*, London, Constable, 1967, at pp. 270–2; B. Keith-Lucas and D. N. Chester, 'The Independence of Chief Constables', *Public Administration*, 1960, 1; *The Observer*, 23 August 1959.

authority for the Metropolitan Police.[110] Such cases as *Attorney-General for New South Wales* v. *Perpetual Trustee Company*,[111] which occurred in the narrow context of an action for loss of services, are taken as lending support to the view that the police throughout the country are equally free in the enforcement of the law from the directions of the central government through the Home Office or any other department. The underlying principle is that a police officer exercises an original as opposed to a delegated authority in the performance of his functions. He is answerable only to the law.

That is the orthodox theoretical position. It is patently open to objection, but efforts to unscramble and redefine the status of the police come up against further theoretical assumptions. For example, the Royal Commission on Police Powers and Procedure in 1929 stated its view, which was endorsed by the Royal Commission in 1962, that the police in this country 'have never been recognised, either in law or by tradition, as a force distinct from the general body of citizens'.[112] Yet in 1885 Maitland wrote that it 'may seem to us a matter of course that there is a large body of policemen, highly organised on a military plan, paid to maintain order, detect crime and arrest offenders'.[113] McCardie J. in *Fisher* v. *Oldham Corporation* may have been right in suggesting that to allow local authorities a full measure of control over arrest and prosecution would involve 'a grave and most dangerous constitutional change',[114] but he ignored 'an ill-defined degree of local supervision'[115] which emerged in the nineteenth century alongside the gradual extension of a professional police force and the eclipse of the old parish constabulary. In 1880, for instance, the Home Secretary refused to intervene in a dispute between the local Watch Committee and the Chief Constable over prosecution policy in Birmingham.[116] Another assumption is that a policeman is merely a citizen in uniform, possessing few powers beyond those enjoyed by the ordinary citizen. This view takes no proper account of the develop-

---

[110] See Lord Denning's Report, Cmd. 2152 (September 1963), para. 204 (on the attempts of Dr. Stephen Ward to stave off a prosecution).

[111] 1955 A.C. 477. On the police see Geoffrey Marshall, op. cit., note 109; T. A. Critchley, op. cit., note 109; J. C. Alderson and P. J. Stead (eds.), *The Police We Deserve*, op. cit. (a series of articles on the police by various authors); S. A. de Smith, *Constitutional and Administrative Law*, 2nd ed., Harmondsworth, Penguin Books, 1973, ch. 17; O. Hood Phillips, *Constitutional and Administrative Law*, 5th ed., London, Sweet & Maxwell, 1973, ch. 20; E. C. S. Wade and Godfrey Phillips, *Constitutional Law*, 8th ed., by Wade and A. W. Bradley, London, Longman, 1970, ch. 18; J. M. Hart, *The British Police*, London, Allen & Unwin, 1951.

[112] Cmd. 1728, paras. 30–1. The 1929 Report was Cmd. 3297.

[113] F. W. Maitland, *Justice and Police*, London, Macmillan, 1885, at p. 105.

[114] [1930] 2 K.B. 364, 378.

[115] Report of the Royal Commission, Cmd. 1728, para. 40.

[116] T. A. Critchley, op. cit., at pp. 131–2.

ments of well over a century, and it ignores not only massive legislation affecting the powers and status of the police but significant changes in the attitude of the courts. The law of arrest provides an excellent example of these changes.

In *Christie* v. *Leachinsky*,[117] a leading case in the field of arrest, Lord du Parcq referred to 'the reluctance of the courts to accord to the officer of the law any rights or privileges which are denied to private citizens'.[118] Parliament has long since overcome any feelings of reluctance, and very many statutory powers of arrest are now entrusted to the police alone. The courts have responded, even if slowly. An early response was the rule in *Walters* v. *W. H. Smith & Son*:[119] 'that a constable may arrest any person if he suspects with reasonable cause that a felony has been committed and that that person committed it, but that a private person may arrest only if the felony has in fact been committed and he suspects with reasonable cause that the person in question committed it'.[120] In tracing the origin of this rule Jerome Hall saw 'some conjunction of the lines of doctrinal development and those representing the growth of a modern professional police force'.[121] A more recent acceptance of an enlarged power for the police is to be seen in *Dallison* v. *Caffery*,[122] where the Court of Appeal was concerned with the 'reasonableness' of detention after arrest; Diplock L.J. expressly recognized that what 'was reasonable in connection with arrest and detention in the days of the parish constable, the stocks and lock-up, and the justice sitting in his justice room before there was an organised police force, prison system, or courts of summary jurisdiction, is not the same as what is reasonable today'.[123] A similar approach was adopted in a subsequent case on the law of search where due note was taken of the fact that, unlike the period of *Entick* v. *Carrington*,[124] 'there are throughout the country regular police forces whose officers are charged with the duty of preventing and detecting crime'.[125] In several recent cases involving charges of assaulting the police in the execution of their duty,[126] often in the context of arrest or detention short of arrest, the courts seem to be moving with obvious hesitation

[117] [1947] A.C. 573.

[118] Ibid., at 602.

[119] [1914] 1 K.B. 595.

[120] *Felonies and Misdemeanours*, 7th Report of the Criminal Law Revision Committee, Cmd. 2659 (May 1965), para. 7.

[121] 'Legal and Social Aspects of Arrest Without Warrant', *Harv.L.R.*, 566, 1936, **49,** 592.

[122] [1965] 1 Q.B. 348.

[123] Ibid., at 370.

[124] (1765) 19 St.Tr. 1029, 1066.

[125] *Chic Fashions (West Wales) Ltd.* v. *Jones* [1968] 2 Q.B. 299, 316, *per* Diplock L.J.

[126] E.g. *Donnelly* v. *Jackman*, [1970] 1 All E.R. 987; *Fennell,* [1971] 1 Q.B. 428; *Squires* v. *Botwright*, [1973] *Crim.L.R.* 106.

towards giving the police increased protection even when they have marginally exceeded their powers. This point has already been reached in some jurisdictions in the United States: in *New Jersey* v. *Koonce*[127] it was laid down that it is wrong for a private person to resist arrest by someone he knows or has reason to believe is an authorized police officer engaged in the performance of his duties, whether or not the arrest is illegal. Such a rule, if it were to be adopted in this country, would need to be qualified in several ways, but it is not entirely unrealistic to suggest that the special and difficult rôle of the police requires some modification of the right of self-defence allowed to private people.

The recognition of regular police forces and of special duties, powers and privileges assigned to policemen at common law and by statute is not confined to the law of arrest. It is to be found in the law relating to public order, the law of search, road traffic law, and much else. What is perhaps lacking is an overall recognition of the changed status of the police at the present day. One of the difficulties seems to be a nostalgic preoccupation with the days of the parish constable, perhaps even the fear of a police state. It is only a few decades ago that Sir John Moylan could write that the legal status of the policeman as prosecutor 'is only that of the common informer, a rôle which any citizen may fill but which, as a matter of custom and practice, is left to the police'.[128] The police are not simply filling a gap. Their rôle as prosecutors is one of the most important and distinctive features of the police forces of England and Wales; the existence by contrast of a system of public prosecutors in Scotland has been seen as altering the whole relationship of the police to other authorities and to the public.[129] Like many other functions previously performed by private people, the principal responsibility for prosecutions in England and Wales has been entrusted to the police irrevocably, unless and until Parliament rules otherwise. Acceptance of an irrevocable transfer of responsibility for these functions would help to clear the air in assessing the constitutional status of the police. It would also make it more feasible to examine realistically the accountability of the police. The

---

[127] 214 A.2d 428 (1965), Superior Ct. of New Jersey. Conford S.J.A.D. said (at 433): 'Force begets force, and escalation into bloodshed is a frequent possibility. The right or wrong of an arrest is often a matter of close debate as to which even lawyers and judges may differ. In this era of constantly expanding legal protections of the rights of the accused in criminal proceedings, one deeming himself illegally arrested can reasonably be asked to submit peaceably to arrest by a police officer, and to take recourse in his legal remedies for regaining his liberty and defending the ensuing prosecution against him.' See Paul G. Chevigny, 'The Right to Resist an Unlawful Arrest', *Yale L.J.*, 1969, **78**, 1128.

[128] Quoted in J. M. Hart, op. cit., at 89.

[129] J. D. B. Mitchell, 'The Constitutional Position of the Police in Scotland', *Juridical Rev.*, 1962, 1, 3.

Royal Commission of 1962 stated that policemen, like everybody else, are accountable to the law.[130] Their function as prosecutors suggests that in one area at least there are inevitable limitations in the rôle of the courts as a controlling mechanism.

The Royal Commission was fully aware of this problem. It drew a distinction, as the courts have done, between the enforcement of the criminal law in particular cases and the formulation and application of police policies.[131] In particular cases, where chief constables act in a 'quasi-judicial' manner in the pursuit of inquiries and decisions to arrest and to prosecute, the Commission felt that there should be no external control save through the Director of Public Prosecutions. Policy decisions did not in its view command such complete protection from 'the conventional processes of democratic control and influence', and certain proposals for supervision were put forward in the Report. Two suggestions which could have led to a dramatic change met with no success. The first of these, that there should be a national or unified police service,[132] was rejected by the Commission; though the point was made in a strong memorandum of dissent by Professor Goodhart that the system of local forces did not allow for adequate control of chief officers of police in the day-to-day enforcement of the law.[133] The second suggestion, that there should be a system of public prosecutors as in Scotland,[134] apparently fell outside the Commission's terms of reference. Advocates of this idea claimed that it would help good relations between the police and the public if the decision to prosecute were placed in other hands, that it would be in the public interest to relieve the police of their 'present unregulated discretion in this matter', and that it would make for greater uniformity in the enforcement of the criminal law. These arguments remain relevant, as the Juctice Report of 1970[135] made clear. At the same time it would be unwise to minimize some of the difficulties of adopting a system of public prosecutors, including that of finding sufficient and competent staff, the continuing if different problems of accountability, and sensitive issues of demarcation between the functions of prosecution and investigation.

The very nature of the power of prosecution, irrespective of the persons or body to whom it is entrusted, makes it unlikely that a single solution to the problem of responsibility or accountability can be found. From one angle the prosecutor can be expected to act impartially and without being subject

---

130 Cmd. 1728, para. 57.
131 Ibid., paras. 85–92.
132 Ibid., ch. V.
133 Ibid., Memorandum of Dissent, pp. 157 ff., para. 24.
134 Cmd. 1728, para. 379.
135 *The Prosecution Process in England and Wales* (1970).

to any external pressure; from another angle it can be argued with justification that unfettered discretion in the exercise of prosecution power is totally unacceptable. The fact that the chief responsibility for prosecutions in England and Wales has fallen into the hands of the police adds a further range of complications arising from traditional assumptions about the status and independence of the police. What is clear, however, is that the internal and external controls upon the exercise by the police of discretionary powers of prosecution are more numerous and varied than Lord Denning's statement in the first *Blackburn* case would suggest.

The hierarchical structure of each police force in itself is important. An inevitable consequence of the creation of disciplined, professional police forces in the nineteenth century, this hierarchy of authority is inconsistent with traditional views about the original and personal nature of a constable's responsibility in the enforcement of the law. There are many occasions when an individual policeman has to act on his own authority and initiative, but in general his theoretical status 'implies a degree of independence belied by his subordinate rank in the force'.[136] Policy decisions in matters of prosecution policy and decisions to prosecute in particular cases of an important or difficult kind would in practice directly involve the chief officer of police or those immediately below him in rank. The chief officer of police is in effect the beneficiary of the older constitutional assumptions, but even his freedom of action is curtailed by the structure and organization of his force. Much of his authority has of necessity to be delegated, especially since the formation of fewer and larger police forces, and the morale and efficiency of his force will depend to no small extent upon the quality and integrity of the decisions from above. In comparing the system of police prosecutions with the alternative of public prosecutors, it should not be forgotten that the distribution of authority in a large organization can in itself be a significant controlling factor in the exercise of discretion.

An uncertain measure of control over prosecutions is achieved by the process of public trial and possible avenues of judicial review. The attitude of the judges can be important in relation to all types of police discretion, including interrogation procedures, search procedures and the process of arrest. It is particularly important in relation to prosecution discretion as a means of securing some degree of uniformity and of providing a vital check upon oppressive and ill-considered proceedings. Judicial review of the kind sought in the two *Blackburn* cases is unlikely for a variety of reasons to be frequent, but the apparent readiness of trial judges to recognize the complex problems of discretionary power is encouraging. The unfavourable reaction to private prosecutions in the first *Blackburn* case is a reminder that the courts

---

[136] Cmd. 1728, para. 67.

now look to the police as the effective public prosecutors of England and Wales. Private prosecutors are largely irrelevant and of limited utility in the administration of the modern criminal law; and legislation to abolish the right of private prosecution, except arguably for trivial offences, might well be considered. Certain reputable private bodies, such as the Royal Society for the Prevention of Cruelty to Animals, could be allowed an express statutory power to prosecute in defined areas, and the prosecuting functions of public authorities including government departments need not be affected. So long as private prosecutions remain available, of course, they can in theory be regarded as a remedy against inaction on the part of the police: but it is a singularly inefficient and spasmodic method of control.

The rôle of the Director of Public Prosecutions in the regulation of police discretion is extremely important. He exerts a crucial unifying influence in the administration of the law and has the immense advantage of detachment. In the words of the Royal Commission, 'the institution and conduct of proceedings in the case of certain grave offences is statutorily reserved for the Director of Public Prosecutions; in a wider range of offences chief constables are obliged to report cases to the Director; and it is their practice to consult the Director and his officers freely on any case where they may be in doubt'.[137] Although responsible to the Attorney-General he is well-shielded from political pressures. The Attorney-General himself has a more limited part to play in the criminal process, but because of his direct responsibility to Parliament he is exposed to sometimes controversial scrutiny of his actions. His position is unusual, for the opportunity seldom arises of directly questioning someone involved in the exercise of prosecution discretion through normal democratic representative institutions.

Does this mean that the police are protected from political pressures? Every effort is rightly made to ensure that they are safeguarded from partisan political pressures, but accountability through 'the conventional processes of democratic control and influence'[138] is another matter. The composition of the police authority for each police area outside London allows for two-thirds of the members to be local councillors, the remaining one-third consisting of lay magistrates. It is the duty of each police authority to secure the maintenance of an adequate and efficient police force for its area and to exercise certain powers directly conferred upon it by statute.[139] The direction and control of a police force, however, is vested in the chief constable, though he is obliged to submit to the police authority an annual report on the policing of the area and, if required by the authority and subject

---

[137] Ibid., para. 86.

[138] Ibid., para. 87.

[139] See D. W. Pollard, 'The Police Act 1964', *Public Law*, 1966, **35**, 41–49.

to reservations about jurisdiction and confidentiality, reports on particular matters connected with the policing of the area. The Royal Commission, in discussing the relationship between chief constables and police authorities, was opposed to any interference in the enforcement of the law in particular cases, but was prepared to accept a measure of comment and enquiry about police policies of a general kind made by a chief constable 'in regard to law enforcement over the area covered by his force, the disposition of his force, the concentration of his resources on any particular type of crime or area, the manner in which he handles political demonstrations or processions and allocates and instructs his men when preventing breaches of the peace arising from industrial disputes, the methods he employs in dealing with an outbreak of violence or of passive resistance to authority, his policy in enforcing the traffic laws and in dealing with parked vehicles, and so on'.[140] Unfortunately the Police Act leaves a large element of uncertainty about the extent of influence which a police authority may bring to bear.[141] Moreover, although there is provision for the questioning of a nominated member of the police authority in a meeting of the relevant council,[142] the police authorities are closely associated with the Home Secretary in the performance of their functions. It is possible that the issues of formal accountability will become clearer under the new structure of administration provided for under the Local Government Act 1972.[143] The Royal Commission certainly envisaged a more effective supervision than arrangements up to 1962 appeared to recognize:

[140] Cmd. 1728, para. 89. In *Discretionary Justice (A Preliminary Inquiry)*, op. cit., K. C. Davis explains (at p. 81) that the police have many policy-making functions: 'Policy has to be made about what private disputes to mediate and how to do it, breaking up sidewalk gatherings, stopping undue noisiness during sleeping hours, legally or illegally tapping wires and using listening devices, helping drunks, deciding what to do with runaway boys who refuse to go home, breaking up fights and matrimonial disputes, deliberately destroying valuable property such as gambling devices even when admissible evidence that it has been used illegally is lacking, engaging in preventive detention in violation of the Constitution, stopping citizens on the street, entering and searching premises, and deciding which crimes not to investigate for lack of manpower. Policy has to be made for the enormous field of police control of juveniles. Policy has to be made on such huge and troublesome subjects as the relations between the police and various minority groups.' These examples, of course, arise in the American context. But (at p. 83) Davis regrets 'the continuing assumption' that the police do not make policy.

[141] See Geoffrey Marshall, 'The Government of the Police Since 1964', in J. C. Alderson and P. J. Stead (eds.), op. cit., at pp. 55–65.

[142] See *Hart's Local Government and Administration*, 9th ed. London, Butterworths, 1973, by W. O. Hart and J. F. Garner, at p. 679.

[143] See Richard Burton, *Local Government*, 2nd ed. Harmondsworth, Penguin Books, 1973, at pp. 58–60.

While the chief constable would continue to enjoy immunity from orders, he would nevertheless be exposed to advice and guidance of which he would be expected to take heed. If he persistently disregarded and flouted such advice his fitness for office would be in question. In this manner an element of supervision would be exercised over the chief constable's actions, but there would be no interference with law enforcement in particular cases.[144]

Under the Police Act 1964 a substantial measure of central control of the police is provided for by giving the Home Secretary important powers to be exercised 'in such manner and to such extent as appears to him to be best calculated to promote the efficiency of the police'.[145] These powers are concerned, for example, with the removal of chief constables, receiving reports from chief constables, holding local enquiries into the policing of any area, discipline and disciplinary appeals, and the appointment and direction of inspectors of constabulary. It is unnecessary to emphasize the very extensive influence which the Home Secretary can bring to bear over all police forces, both in the exercise of his express powers and by virtue of his central and co-ordinating rôle. In matters of law enforcement he is directly concerned where the Metropolitan Police are involved, and elsewhere effective guidance can be offered through the process of inspection and through the issue of circulars, meetings of chief constables, and a variety of formal and informal methods of approach.[146] A surprising number of general and specific issues on law enforcement throughout the country is raised in Parliament. Spokesmen for the Home Office will steadfastly remind members of Parliament that responsibility for prosecutions rests with chief officers of police and that it would be unconstitutional for the police to be instructed as to when and

[144] Cmd. 1728, para. 93. See Peter Moodie, 'The Use and Control of the Police', in Robert Benewick and Trevor Smith (eds.), *Direct Action and Democratic Politics* (London, Allen & Unwin, 1972), at pp. 231–47, esp. pp. 243–4.

[145] Police Act 1964, s. 28. See H. W. R. Wade, *Administrative Law*, op. cit., at pp. 31–2; J. A. G. Griffith, *Central Departments and Local Authorities*, London, Geo. Allen & Unwin, 1966, at pp. 59–61.

[146] Peter Moodie, op. cit., note 144, suggests (at p. 237) that 'the Home Office Circular "advising" Chief Constables has virtually the force of law'. The important rôle of the Home Office in the area of public order is indicated in D. G. T. Williams, 'Protest and Public Order', *C.L.J.*, 1970, **96**, 96–7, 115–16; and see also ch. 9 ('Problems relating to police and selective law enforcement') in the Report of the *Royal Commission in South Australia on the September Moratorium Demonstration* (Adelaide, 1971). The Home Office has a direct involvement in law enforcement in matters relating to the interception of communications (see Report of the Committee of Privy Councillors appointed to inquire into the Interception of Communications, Cmd. 283 of 1957) and in relation to the Security Service (see Lord Denning's Report, Cmd. 2152 of 1963, ch. xviii). It is perhaps arguable that the Home Office as much as local police authorities has inherited something of the supervisory powers over the police in law enforcement which were once exercised by justices of the peace (see Cmd. 1728, paras. 82–84).

when not to prosecute; but some of the explanations and answers are remarkably forthcoming on several matters of law enforcement.[147] The caveat about non-interference in particular decisions is, however, a firm indication as to where the line ought to be drawn. It is true that policy decisions affect particular decisions and that the two may overlap, but even in relation to the Metropolitan Police the practice of non-interference in actual cases is apparently observed. The Parliamentary Commissioner for Administration reported in 1967 that the Home Secretary had no administrative functions which he could investigate in relation to actions taken by the Metropolitan Police for the prevention and investigation of crime, 'nor has he power to give instructions to the members of that Force as to the manner in which they will carry out their duties as constables'.[148] In evidence before the Select Committee on the Parliamentary Commissioner, the Permanent Under-Secretary of State at the Home Office (Sir Philip Allen) amplified this by saying that the conduct of prosecutions had nothing to do with his department.[149]

Other forms of control which can serve as a check on discretionary powers include enquiries set up to investigate some matter involving the police. There have in the past been several important enquiries of different kinds, including Tribunals of Enquiry, but procedure is now provided under the Police Act.[150] There is also the procedure for the investigation of complaints by members of the public under section 49 of the Police Act.[151]

[147] Adjournment debates as well as parliamentary questions occur on specific issues of law enforcement: e.g. *H.C. Debates*, Vol. 852, cc. 1615 ff., 15 March 1973.

[148] First Report of the Parliamentary Commissioner for Administration, Session 1967–68, H.C. 6 (November 1967), para. 25.

[149] Second Report from the Select Committee on the Parliamentary Commissioner for Administration, Session 1967–68, H.C. 350 (July 1968), c. 520 of Minutes of Evidence. See also para. 35 of the Committee's Report.

[150] Section 32, providing that the Home Secretary may cause a local inquiry to be held into any matter connected with the policing of any area: an inquiry under s. 32 'would be justified only while there appear to be major defects of police organisation which are causing grave and widespread public concern and which have not been clearly identified by other methods of investigation' (Mr Elystan Morgan, Under-Secretary of State at the Home Office, *H.C. Debates*, Vol. 784, c. 1200, 9 June 1969). The Royal Commission on Tribunals of Inquiry, Cmd. 3121 (November 1966), suggested that several of the inquiries which had previously taken place under the Tribunals of Inquiry (Evidence) Act 1921 would now take place under s. 32 (see para. 25 of the Report): for accounts of Tribunals of Inquiry concerning the police, see George W. Keeton, *Trial by Tribunal*, London, Museum Press, 1960, esp. ch. 4, 5 and 9. The first inquiry under s. 32 arose from the Challenor case (Cmd. 2735 of 1965); see Report of the Commissioner of Police of the Metropolis for 1964, Cmd. 2710 (July 1965), pp. 14–16.

[151] See Cmd. 1728, ch. ix ('Complaints against the Police'); *H.C. Debates*, Vol. 851, cc. 934 ff. (23 February 1973), including an important speech by the Home Secretary at cc. 993 ff.; Dennis Paling, 'The Police Acts (Amendment) Bill 1973', *Crim.L.R.* [1973], 282.

This is an undoubtedly adaptable method of overall control of the police, but it is doubtful whether it will impinge greatly upon matters of prosecution discretion except where criminal proceedings against police officers are contemplated. Other areas of police discretion, such as the decision to arrest rather than issue a summons,[152] would seem to be more appropriate under section 49. The Local Commissioners (or local ombudsmen) under the Local Government Act 1974 are also unlikely to be able to deal with matters of prosecution discretion: among the functions not subject to enquiry by them are the commencement or conduct of criminal proceedings in the courts and action taken by any authority in connection with the investigation or prevention of crime.

The exercise of discretionary powers of prosecution is subject to controls which have evolved and varied over the years. Several of the forms of control are still uncertain in their extent. But their combined effect brings some measure of supervision into one of the most important areas of discretion in English law. If this supervision is to be maintained and improved, it will be necessary to ensure that the different methods of control are subject to detailed and regular examination. This can best be achieved if some of the traditional assumptions about the status of the police and their rôle as prosecutors are abandoned or modified. So long as the chief responsibility for prosecutions in England and Wales remains vested in the police, it should be recognized that the public are entitled to know as much as possible about police methods and policies in law enforcement and about the direction which comes from above through the Home Secretary, the Law Officers and the Director of Public Prosecutions. The confidentiality of many aspects of police work can be preserved so long as it is recognized that the police are accountable for their actions through democratic processes at central and local level as well as through the courts. The alternative to existing methods of control would be either the adoption of a separate system of public prosecutors or more precise regulation of the exercise of police discretion by the adoption of formal rules and standards. Few would deny the critical importance and immense difficulty of discretion in prosecution, but if the present system is to continue each police force must accept the desirability of a high degree of uniformity in the application of policies together with care and discrimination in deciding whether or not to prosecute in individual cases. The police do not and should not have an unfettered discretion. At the same time the critical responsibility for the day-to-day enforcement of the

---

[152] *Oxford Mail*, 14 Sept. 1967, p. 1 (report of chief constable's statement on an inquiry into why certain people involved in a small demonstration had been arrested). See generally on this problem, Martin L. Friedland, *Detention before Trial*, Toronto, Univ. of Toronto Press, 1965, ch. 1.

law must rest with the chief officer of police in each force. It is his duty to ensure that there is 'intelligent police administration'[153] and the law is administered with 'moderation, fairness, and discretion':[154] bearing in mind 'that the proper performance of the greater part of police work depends upon the skill, integrity, and general capacity of individual men . . .'.[155]

---

[153] The phrase was used by Frankfurter J. in *Niemotko* v. *Maryland* 340 U.S. 268, 289 (1950): 'It is true that breach-of-peace statutes, like most tools of government, may be misused. Enforcement of these statutes calls for public tolerance and intelligent police administration.'

[154] *Burton* v. *Power*, [1940] N.Z.L.R. 305, 307 (a case concerning the law of public order).

[155] *Report of the Royal Commission upon the Duties of the Metropolitan Police,* Cmd. 4156 of 1908, HMSO, p. 57.

THE SCOPE OF POLICE MANPOWER STUDIES

J. P. Martin

To study the cost of crime was attractive to Leon Radzinowicz because the subject was specific and relevant to policy—two of his major concerns in approving research to be done at the Institute in its early days. What he wanted was probably something rather like Abel-Smith and Titmuss' study of the Cost of the National Health Service.[1] The difficulty, however was that any analysis of costs would be complicated by the multiplicity of functions undertaken by most of the services dealing in some way with crime. This meant that a study of the cost of crime was inevitably more complex than one where the service had a relatively simple function, such as health or education.[2]

In the event it was decided to tackle the problem of allocating costs to different functions by instituting a survey of the use of police manpower—the police constituting by far the largest component of the total costs of relevant services. This was duly undertaken in 1965–6 and published in 1968.[3] It is still the only large-scale study of its kind attempted in England, although a number of other studies of a more local character have been conducted with varying amounts of concern for the recording and analysis of police time.[4] In the U.S.A. the major study appears to have been that of

[1] B. Abel-Smith and R. M. Titmuss, *The Cost of the National Health Service*, Cambridge University Press, 1956.
[2] J. P. Martin and J. Bradley, 'Design of a Study of the Cost of Crime', *British Journal of Criminology*, 1964, **4**, pp. 591–603.
[3] J. P. Martin and Gail Wilson, *The Police: A Study in Manpower*, London, Heinemann Educational Books, 1968.
[4] Col. T. E. St. Johnston, 'A Police Man Hours Enquiry conducted by the Durham County Constabulary', *The Police Journal*, 1951, **24**, Nos. 2–3, pp. 106–13 and 198–204. The Dixon Committee on *The Employment and Distribution of Strength: the Metropolitan Police*. Report, Part III, 1956 (unpublished). The survey conducted on behalf of the committee related to the employment of constables and sergeants during the second week of July 1950; M. L. Chambers, *Survey of Police Operations and Evaluation of Their Effectiveness*, University of Lancaster, Department of Operational Research, 1967 (unpublished); J. W. Bryant, M. L. Chambers and D. Falcon, *Patrol Effectiveness and Patrol*

Reiss which collected rather similar information but used different methods and adopted a more sophisticated sociological approach.[5]

As this first generation of academic studies of policing in Britain seems to be coming to an end this is probably a convenient opportunity to take stock of the fairly small number of police manpower studies that have been undertaken, and to consider what they may have to offer the police administrator and those concerned with the rôle of the police in society.

This paper will deal mainly with the practical problems of producing a quantitative description of police work, but this will be preceded by an *a priori* discussion of the possible significance of such surveys. An attempt will be made to see whether the various studies exhibit any consensus about the use of police time and what conclusions can be drawn from them. Finally I shall make a few comments on possibilities for future research.

The Potential Significance of Manpower Studies

In this paper the term *manpower studies* is used to refer to the analysis of the ways in which police manpower resources are used for various purposes. The groups of people whose work is thus studied may range from the whole of a large force to a subsection of a small one. I am, of course, aware of the ambiguities of the notion of purpose and shall discuss some of the problems arising from this later in the paper.

The significance of manpower studies is likely to be different for the police service and for those more interested in the wider rôle of the police in society. For the police service itself their significance should be obvious. Manpower is by far the largest single component of the cost of the service, it is also alleged to be in short supply, and people are *the* medium through which police work is done. Constant examination of whether this basic resource is being best used would seem to be essential. Research workers, however, tend to be disappointed in this respect; for example, in the U.S.A. Webster has commented: 'Police departments are about the most poorly managed organizations in our society.'[6] Similarly a recent unpublished English study remarked:

. . . that the police system seems to be managed with the help of only a very unsophisticated management control system. In fact, although a great deal of

Development, University of Lancaster, Department of Operational Research, 1968 (unpublished); Maureen Cain, *Society and the Policeman's Role*, London, Routledge and Kegan Paul, 1973.

[5] Albert J. Reiss Jr., *The Police and the Public*, New Haven, Yale University Press, 1971.

[6] John A. Webster, 'Police Task and Time Duty', *Journal of Criminal Law, Criminology and Police Science*, 1970, **61**, pp. 94–100. Quotation from p. 100.

information is recorded on individual incidents, only broad divisional data on crime rates, detection rates and accident rates seems to be used for monitoring performance.[7]

Without necessarily accepting these strictures at their face value we can hardly disagree with the general principle that manpower should be 'matched' with 'demand' as efficiently as possible, and this surely implies measurement of 'demand' and of the deployment of manpower in so far as this is possible. Unfortunately, however, 'demand' for policing is an ambiguous phenomenon, depending to a significant extent on the conceptions of policing held by all ranks of the service (which may well differ from level to level), the resources allotted to the police by the community, and social attitudes to all manner of forms of behaviour which might come to be treated as criminal. Even the police attitude is not necessarily in favour of a peaceful community. Police work in such areas may be unbelievably dull; as Maureen Cain found 'a good pitch to work was one in which crimes and fights were frequent'.[8]

While the sociologist may be less immediately concerned than the economist with the measurement of the relationship between 'demand' and 'supply' of police services, he or she cannot ignore the question because of its influence on the nature of the job. Cain's work illustrates very well the relationship between the characteristics of the area, the structure of the force and the pattern of police activity. Many of the main studies consider, amongst other things, the policing of holiday areas, differences in the work of men on foot and in vehicles, the separate identity of specialized units, the extent to which police officers actually meet members of the public, the nature of such interactions, etc.

Any of these questions might be illuminated in a manpower survey, though it is unlikely that all could be answered in a single operation. What, then, are the possibilities and the limitations of such surveys? In attempting to answer these questions I shall try to avoid being excessively technical, and shall not discuss the mechanics of organizing surveys except insofar as they are relevant to the sampling and classification of activities. A brief description of the procedures used for Martin and Wilson's survey is given on pp. 123–7 of their book.

Problems of Manpower Survey Design

1. Conceptual

Manpower surveys involve various levels of conceptual problems. The lesser ones will be considered under the heading of classification of activities, but

[7] Chambers, op. cit., p. 13.
[8] Cain, op. cit., p. 65.

we should first discuss the most difficult ones—the notion of 'work load' and the concept of 'prevention'.

Strictly speaking a manpower survey could be conducted without attempting to obtain independent measures of *work load*. Time would simply be recorded under whatever heading seemed appropriate, so that the 'load' of, say crime investigation, was estimated in terms of the time spent on it. This method suffers the grave limitation that as there are no units of work no real measurement of effort is possible.

One solution to this problem is to record the numbers of incidents and treat these as measures of work load, their seriousness sometimes being assessed by the average time involved. This may, however, be vitiated by the operation of Parkinson's Law—'work expands so as to fill the time available for its completion'[9]—while in any case the amount of time available is primarily controlled by the allocation of resources to the particular activity. An extreme example of this is the introduction of radar speed traps where the assigning of men to this task virtually guarantees the appearance of a 'work load', while other specialized units such as Drug or Fraud Squads are almost certain to unearth more examples of the particular behaviour they are concerned with.

Even detective work, concerned with crimes which are established facts, cannot adequately be measured on this basis simply because it is largely a matter of policy how long unsolved crimes continue to be investigated. This is a function of at least three factors—the manpower available, beliefs about how long it is worthwhile to investigate a crime without success, and the importance ascribed to this particular crime (and perhaps to this particular victim). Attempts have been made to classify crimes according to their 'importance' as measured by indices such as that devised by Sellin and Wolfgang,[10] and this has led to changes in the policy of Regional Crime Squads who are reported to concentrate on 'target criminals' responsible for major crimes.[11]

In short, the work load of the police, in spite of the existence of certain situations which have to be dealt with, can be substantially influenced by policy. The manpower survey therefore has to choose, somewhat uneasily, between the extremes of not trying to measure the work load at all or of becoming lost in the detailed work of trying to use measures sufficiently precise to satisfy the demands of theory.

[9] C. Northcote Parkinson, *Parkinson's Law*, London, John Murray, 1958.

[10] T. Sellin and M. Wolfgang, *The Measurement of Delinquency*, New York, Wiley, 1964.

[11] J. P. Martin, *The Application of Modern Techniques of Resource Allocation in the Field of Crime Problems*, Strasbourg, Council of Europe, European Committee on Crime Problems, DPC/CEPC XXIII (72)2, July 1972.

Even more difficult is the conceptual problem of *prevention*. Except in special situations, such as the guarding of, say, the homes of cabinet ministers, parliament or objects of unusual value, it is almost impossible to do more than record the claim that a particular activity is preventive. Some special patrolling, such as in the vicinity of notorious pubs on Saturday nights, may reasonably be claimed to be preventive, but such activity might just as well be classified as maintaining public order. The real difficulty arises over general patrolling, which may cover anything from touring an industrial estate, where there is a fairly high chance that break-ins will be attempted, to the man with a rural beat who spends much of his time travelling between the villages for which he is responsible.

It is well known that Unit Beat Policing was introduced following studies which, to say the least, cast considerable doubts on what was being achieved by conventional patrolling. Possibly the most important single element in Unit Beat Policing has been the introduction of the idea that an officer on patrol should, amongst other things, deliberately set out to gather 'criminal intelligence'. Indeed the effectiveness of the area constable was to be judged 'by the amount of information he feeds into the collator'.[12]

The use of this concept should make it possible to subdivide the rather large proportion of working time described as 'patrolling'. Unfortunately one suspects that, in a self-recording survey, officers (knowing that gathering criminal intelligence was regarded as a good thing by their supervisors) might be tempted to put more time into this category than was strictly justified. Nevertheless the prospect of improving the description of patrolling is so attractive that it would be worth going to considerable lengths to devise some sort of check to ensure that only genuine intelligence gathering was included.

Much as one would like to be able to characterize activity as preventive it is very difficult to avoid a situation in which *any* outdoor work which has no other specific purpose can be claimed to be preventive, and in practice this claim is very difficult to prove or disprove. It may be that further development of the thinking in Willmer's *Crime and Information Theory* will provide solutions to these problems,[13] but at present it is not clear how to do so in a survey. For the time being, therefore, we have little choice but to continue using the descriptive category of 'patrolling' with at least the presumption that for some of the time the activity is preventing some breaches of the law. (We also know, thanks to Maureen Cain and other

[12] Home Office, 'Police Manpower, Equipment and Efficiency'. *Working Party Report* (The Taverne Report), London, HMSO, 1967, p. 142.
[13] M. A. P. Willmer, *Crime and Information Theory*, Edinburgh University Press, 1970 (particularly chapter 5).

perceptive observers, that for some of the time the only form of police action consists of 'easing behaviour'.)[14]

2. *Data Collection*

Before going on to the problems of classifying activities we must consider the methods of collecting information, as these can have a major influence on both its accuracy and classification. 'Methods' must here be taken to include both the general nature of the data to be collected, and by whom the recording is to be done.

In principle the manpower survey is recording, usually by means of sampling, the work being done. There are two alternative ways of doing this: first, obtaining details of a sample of items of work, and second, sampling periods of time and recording the predominant type of work being undertaken in each period. Both methods have been used in police man-power surveys: most American studies, and part of the Lancaster University study have been based on items of work, while the Cambridge study, part of the Lancaster one, and Sir Eric St. Johnston's surveys summarized how certain periods of time were spent.

The choice between these two main methods of sampling police activity has to be made on a number of grounds, all of which relate to three under-lying considerations: accuracy, ease of handling, and relevance to the aim of the survey. Accuracy is a matter of recording events as soon as possible after they happen, using the appropriate classification, making sure events are not omitted and avoiding fabrication. Ease of handling is important not only for the economy of the research, but for accuracy. If recording is convenient it is more likely to be done quickly and without error. Relevance to the aims of the enquiry will influence such matters as whether the emphasis is to be on the work of departments, individuals or on particular types of incident.

On the basis of these criteria surveys using an 'items of work' approach have many advantages, particularly in being best able to relate the output of work done by officers to the input of requests for service and/or police-initiated activity. If this can be part of a computer-linked operation, as for example in Webster's 'Baywood' study,[15] the overall pattern of incidents can presumably be built up very easily. This has hardly been done in Britain, but the facilities of the Dorset and Bournemouth system or of the Birmingham computer could easily be used.[16] Such weaknesses as there may be probably lie in the difficulty of establishing officers' patterns of work, of describing incidents in terms of purpose, the risk of omitting minor events, and, if the

[14] Cain, *passim*.
[15] Webster, op. cit.
[16] Martin, op. cit.

officer has to record each event himself (as for example in the Lancaster study), the volume of paper may be difficult to control—with the consequent temptation to under-record.

Methods based on sampling activities over particular periods of time have disadvantages in terms of accuracy of recall, but if well designed may be fairly convenient to operate and do not require the individual to be linked to a communication network. Their results may be in a simpler form and require less elaborate data processing, though the importance of this advantage is decreasing with the spread of computerization. They also have some advantages in terms of showing the sequence of an individual's activities.

Data can be recorded either by independent observers, or by supervisors, or by the officer himself, or by some combination of these. Unless the research is founded on a massive scale, so far only achieved by Reiss, it is difficult for the number of observers to be large enough to record anything like a representative sample of incidents. Hence observers tend to have produced qualitative accounts, sometimes backed by general statistics.[17] Most American studies seem to have relied on analysing radio instructions to patrolmen, and also on their reports to their supervisors on what they had done on their own initiative. The Cambridge and Lancaster studies used self-recording, while St. Johnston used self-recording under the guidance of the supervising officer.

Each method has its own pros and cons, some of which were discussed by Miss Wilson and me as part of our account of the Cambridge study.[18] However the relatively undeveloped state of radio communication at that time precluded any attempt at sampling instructions so that our discussion was necessarily incomplete. It may now be useful to make some brief comments on the main methods used up to now, subject to the qualification that full details have not always been reported in the studies I have been able to see.

Observer studies. These appear to have the following *advantages*:
 (i) the observer can concentrate on the job without, normally, getting involved in the police work; potentially his observations should be more accurate than those of the man whose main attention is on his work as a policeman;
 (ii) the observer can be trained, or alerted to, a much more sophisticated awareness of what the research is trying to achieve than the person being observed;

[17] Cain, op. cit.
[18] Martin and Wilson, op. cit., pp. 123–27.

C.C.P.P.—8

(iii) he can not only observe but should have an understanding of what the police action is intended to achieve, whereas this might otherwise be lost in a more abstract statistic.

The *disadvantages* are very simple:
  (i) only a small-scale operation is possible, both on grounds of cost and possible disruption of police work;
  (ii) police are unlikely to allow observers to be present under all circumstances (Cumming *et al.*, for example, noted that 'the field worker could not go with the regular prowl car owing to a rule forbidding the officers to carry passengers. It is also *possible* that the captain did not want the field worker to see episodes that he did not himself monitor').[19] Maureen Cain also reported how her discretion was tested: 'After this I was allowed to see easing behaviour, though full acceptance in the sense of being allowed to witness legal infringements was never attained since it was impossible for me to share the associated risks';[20]
  (iii) there is a considerable risk that behaviour under the eye of an observer may not be typical.

On balance it would seem observers, while they may be able to gain considerable insight, are unlikely to be able to quantify their observations on any scale, so that their contribution to manpower studies is almost bound to be restricted to the pilot stage.

Supervisor studies, i.e. where observations are made at the point where the supervisor receives information.

Advantages:
  (i) recording can take place under relatively good conditions, often using automatic data processing so that the whole operation becomes a by-product of the normal system of command;
  (ii) timing is likely to be accurate;
  (iii) it is easy to relate incidents/complaints to the time spent dealing with them.

Disadvantages:
  (i) the method tends to be dependent on monitoring communications via one medium, and is likely to be limited to patrols. Large areas of police work cannot easily be covered by the system of sampling commands and reports;

---

[19] Elaine Cumming, Ian Cumming and Laura Edell, 'Policeman as Philosopher, Guide and Friend', *Social Problems*, 1964, **12**, pp. 276–86. From p. 283.
[20] Cain, op. cit., p. 199.

(ii) some sort of supervision bias would seem inevitable. One suspects that it would tend to understate action initiated by the individual officer and, generally speaking, his more 'informal' actions. The result might be a tendency to over-emphasize the fire-brigade (responding to calls) element of police work;

(iii) major activities may be relatively well recorded, but the residual time may be difficult to classify;

(iv) officers may be anxious to see that their work appears in a good light, and may therefore display the sort of zeal which they think their immediate supervisors expect of them. The supervisor himself is also likely to play down any activity which might be thought to be dis-approved of at a higher level. The duration of specific tasks might well be exaggerated;

(v) in some designs, for example the Lancashire Police survey, the information was only recorded in the official Record Book at the end of the shift and relied for its accuracy on a combination of the officer's memory and notebook. This survey could equally be regarded as a special form of self-recording survey.

Self-recording Studies, *Advantages*:

(i) the biggest advantage is that self-recording surveys can be conducted on a large scale so almost all members of a force can be included;

(ii) if done conscientiously information can be recorded with minimum delay.

Disadvantages:

(i) they are largely dependent on the interest and conscientiousness of the people taking part. Each individual is in a position to spoil his or her contribution. It is very easy for the uncooperative to delay recording events and to concoct a rough and ready account only at the end of the shift;

(ii) they depend on the system of classifying duties being understood by each person taking part. This either entails an extensive briefing system or means that the classification has to stick rather closely to the conventional terminology of the police service;

(iii) recording may have to be done under adverse conditions, for example by a motor-cycle patrol sheltering from the rain, and this means either that the record booklet gets rather tattered or the officer tries to keep the booklet clean and relies upon his memory when eventually he completes it under good conditions. Given the nature of police training—in England at any rate—he will find it hard not to keep the booklet clean at the expense of up-to-date recording;

(iv) timing may not be very accurate, and there is always a risk that minor events may be overlooked.

3. Classification of Activities

In this section I shall try to restrict myself to the general principles of devising classifications of activities—otherwise it would be all too easy to get lost in a mass of detail concerning such matters as how much of the time of an officer fetching a prisoner from the North of Scotland to Bournemouth should be regarded as overtime, and whether this should all be classified under crime enquiries; or how to classify the time of an officer required to be present while an oil tanker was unloading. In the last resort all such questions have to be matters of rulings depending on the purpose of the research.

The purpose of the research is indeed crucial for the design of a manpower survey. The range of possibilities is quite wide, at one extreme might be surveys conducted for purposes of police administration, as for example those devised by Sir Eric St. Johnston in Lancashire; at the other, the paper by Cumming *et al.* entitled 'Policeman as Philosopher, Guide and Friend' which attempted to reclassify police operations in terms of their social, indeed almost social *work*, functions.[21]

It is sometimes possible to convert classifications normally used for police purposes by grouping in a new way, and this has the advantage that it does not require policemen to adopt an unfamiliar terminology when describing their work.

The golden rule is unquestionably to think very carefully about the purpose of the research. This may seem a platitude, but it is surprisingly easy both to be tempted into unnecessary elaboration, and also to develop classifications which confuse different conceptual dimensions. The Cambridge study used a classification devised to fit the data into a larger framework relating to the cost of crime as a whole. It therefore had categories for activities, such as work involving convicted adult offenders, which were of negligible importance in police work. As the total number of categories was limited the price paid for adopting such a broad framework was that some categories were too general, e.g. crime enquiries, which had to cover everything from a murder case to the arresting of drunks and handling cases of causing death by dangerous driving.

Thinking carefully about the purpose of research may throw an entirely new light on the pattern of work. The paper by Cumming *et al.* is a good

[21] Cumming, *et al.,* op. cit.

example of trying a new classification, even though there are some methodological gaps in the article cited. They classified the calls received by a police department complaints desk in terms of the social problems underlying the request for help, with the result that they found almost exactly a half of all calls came into the category which they described as 'calls for support'. These in turn were divided into two main groups in a ratio of roughly 3 : 2, being 'persistent personal problems' (health, children, incapacitated persons, nuisances) and 'periodic personal problems' (disputes, violence, protection, missing persons, youths' behaviour).

This classification, and the research method, have obvious defects chiefly relating to the sample of cases on which the study was based, but the authors deserve credit for trying to get us to look at police work in a new light. They point out that . . .

> poor, uneducated people appear to use the police in the way that middle-class people use family doctors—that is, as the first port of call in time of trouble;

and that . . .

> there is reason to believe that most social workers, clergymen and doctors have no conception of the amount of support policemen give during a day's work. There is also reason to believe that they do not want the burden of the 'unmotivated' poor and ignorant whom they believe to be increasing in number.[22]

The first rule of classification is therefore to use a set of concepts which are all consistent with a particular aim. This may result in doing injustice to some aspect of the work, but at least it will place everything in a single perspective.

The second rule is the same as that which underlies all coding of information—categories must be mutually exclusive. This is not always easy in police studies—major crime, minor crime and traffic offences may all go hand in hand. Certain offences tend to occur in constellations, for example those grouped around the various forms of unauthorized driving. Is causing death by dangerous driving best seen as crime or traffic? How does one apportion the work of the Coroner's officer? When does attendance at a fire turn from a civil incident to a matter of maintaining public order? Should drunken driving be treated as crime or not? In practice such questions are almost innumerable, and there would seem to be two main solutions. The first is to anticipate the more obvious and frequently recurring problems, and lay down rules for their resolution. The second is to recognize that a set of rules covering all cases will never be devised, and problems will have to be resolved according to principles such as, 'if in doubt, classify as crime . . .'.

[22] Ibid, p. 286.

The third major problem of devising a classification is to decide on how many categories to use. Obviously if they are very few, recording and analysis will be easy but simple, and it will be impossible to answer many interesting questions. A more refined classification will be an improvement up to the point where diminishing returns set in. This may happen for one or both of two main reasons: the more categories there are the greater the risk that some of them will genuinely be almost empty, and, furthermore, the greater the risk that the recorder will make an arbitrary decision in order to save the time and thought needed to apply the rules fully and carefully.

Two examples of the problem of almost empty categories can be given. Sir Eric St. Johnston's Durham study involved 52 headings, 34 of which each occupied less than one per cent of time apiece. It is not until we come down to the seven categories of the University of Lancaster patrol study that all categories have a fairly sizeable proportion of cases in them.

At this point one should ask how much it matters. Research workers tend to be influenced by a statistical training which emphasizes the desirability of all cells of a table having a certain minimum 'expected' number of cases in them, but for purposes of mapping police activity it is surely just as important to know that things are *not* done as that they are. For example our figure for Public Order work was generally below one per cent, and this affords a useful perspective when it might be thought such matters involved substantially more time.[23] The same might be said for Webster's finding that crimes against persons consumed less than three per cent of patrolmen's time.[24] The most important consideration must be whether the figure itself is reasonably accurate, and the classification should therefore be made as straightforward as possible.

Much depends on who is to do the recording. The 1965 Lancaster Police Survey used no fewer than 69 categories, but this may not have been as confusing as might be expected because the categories were grouped according to the departmental structure of the force, so that in practice an officer's choice was limited to a very small proportion of the total. This amount of detail was presumably required for administrative purposes though one wonders how informative some of the very low figures were.

Probably the main general principle in this respect is that the research worker introduces non-police classifications at his peril (unless he is doing the recording himself). Furthermore, if he takes the risk he must deliberately use his own terminology which must not be liable to be confused with that

---

[23] Martin and Wilson, op. cit., p. 150. This figure related to provincial forces in 1965. The Metropolitan figure in April 1966 was slightly over 1 per cent. Presumably if there had been a big political demonstration the figure might have been a little higher.

[24] Webster, op. cit., p. 65.

normally used by the police. For example in the Cambridge study we incautiously used the short title of 'Administration' when we meant to refer only to those domestic operations required to keep the force running—pay, pensions, housing, leave, postings, etc. Administration in police terminology refers to virtually all paper work and we had some difficulty in explaining our restricted use of the term. After a time we got every man to change the phrase in his recording booklet and substitute 'Internal Organization' as this was what we really wanted, and it was then not so confusing to members of the service.

Above all, therefore, in a self-recording survey the classification must be completely intelligible to the recorder. Great efforts must be made to explain the object of the exercise and the survey will stand or fall by the effectiveness with which this is done.

It is difficult to produce sets of figures which allow comparison between the results of the various surveys because of differences in the classifications used. One thing however, is clear from Martin and Wilson, Reiss, and Cain, namely that all patrol officers spend a great deal of time waiting for something to happen. Reiss, for example, estimated that no less than 86 per cent of patrol officers' time was spent on routine patrol with only 14 per cent responding to a call. Maureen Cain's country beat men had less than ten crimes reported in their areas *per year*; even in the city area sergeants and p.c.'s averaged less than one arrest per month.

Value of Manpower Studies

The first merit is that, however inadequately they may have been done, they have thrown some light on the use of the most important single resource in police work. In England and Wales, at any rate, it is still claimed that there is a shortage of manpower; the Cambridge study showed, and more recent figures have confirmed, that in fact more *police* man hours are now being worked per thousand members of the population than at any time since 1891. If the contribution of civilians is taken into account the police *service* is vastly better off than it ever has been in the last 100 years.[25] The onus, therefore, is on the police service to examine its 'load' and its methods in order to make better use of the men it has got.

Second, the British studies have tended to show the extent to which the

[25] The basic statistics are given in Martin and Wilson, op. cit., Table IV.5, p. 78. It is not possible to update the figures to include recent years because of lack of information about overtime working. Recruiting, however, has improved since 1965, and the latest total for police officers in 1972 was 98,408, an increase of 13,983 on the 1965 total of 84,425.

departmental structure of the police has led to an almost tripartite service consisting of C.I.D., Traffic and the rest. They are not formally separate organizations, but they might almost as well be in terms of the work they do. The Cambridge study, for example, found that almost a quarter of police time went on traffic work, and that one traffic warden did as much traffic work as eight beat men. This in turn leads on to the question of specialization, which in my view is still the most neglected general issue facing police administrators. It is significant that Maureen Cain, conducting a very different kind of study, also laid considerable stress on its effects.

Third, and this is perhaps the chief contribution of the unpublished University of Lancaster study, is the evidence that the work 'load' of the police service is substantially influenced by the structure of the service itself. The extreme example of this is probably what the Lancaster team described as 'blitz' offences, i.e. when the police decide to set up radar speed traps, or to enforce, say, parking regulations strictly. It is absolutely clear that these form a substantial majority of all traffic 'offences' which come to the notice of the police.

Even where the 'load' is brought to the attention of the police the amount of work put in is largely influenced by departmental structure. Almost all detectives work very long hours and the total detective time is therefore a function of the number of men available which, in turn, is a matter of establishment.

Another minor example of the influence of departmental organization is the policing of holiday areas. The one thing in this respect which was quite clear from the Cambridge study was that traffic work increased significantly, and that traffic departments worked fewer hours, in summer than in winter, no doubt because their leave was better organized. All the extra work fell on beat patrols who, understandably, felt overworked.

Fourth, all the studies illustrate the problem of unoccupied time. Whatever the classification terminology employed—patrolling, general duties, administration, etc.—much of the policeman's time is spent waiting for something to happen. How to use this time to the best advantage is crucial for the use of manpower. Gathering 'criminal intelligence' is the best suggestion yet for doing so.

Fifth, those studies which have investigated the initiation of work (the University of Lancaster and the American studies) have shown the extent to which the police in fact play a fire-brigade rôle in relation to crime of all sorts and traffic accidents. The evidence suggests that about 80 per cent of this type of work—the hard core in fact—is brought to the attention of the police by others.

Future Prospects for Manpower Studies

1. There seems little scope for repeats of large-scale self-recording studies on the Cambridge model. They rely heavily on up-to-the-minute recording and, with the possibilities of computer-recorded command systems, are outdated for most purposes. At the time our study served a purpose of putting figures to some of the major functions of the police service, and indicated the influence of specialist groups. To go beyond this would demand more detailed studies of a limited range of activities.
2. The crucial problem is the analysis of the work load and this means that any study will have to consider,
    (a) how work comes to be undertaken,
    (b) how far the task is carried out.
It is quite possible to argue that, for example, it is only fruitful to investigate burglaries for 48 hours, and if they are cleared up after that it is likely to be due to chance. In practice all police work is likely to be limited by the consideration of whether further activity will pay off, and such questions will probably be affected by the general 'load'. Any worthwhile study must allow for the operation of Parkinson's Law; but how?

The University of Lancaster study made a start in this connection, but I imagine there might be scope for a procedure involving what intelligence officers call 'de-briefing', i.e. getting a description of what was actually done in handling a particular task.
3. Finally there is much to be said for those interested in social problems to attempt much more socially informative classifications of activities. The paper by Cumming *et al.* is an indication of some possibilities, but it could be carried much further. It might be very revealing to know not only about the incident, but about the *dramatis personae* as well. When is 'public order' a matter of political demonstrations as against displaying a police presence outside some pubs at closing time? What about helping the mentally ill? One of my greatest surprises in the Cambridge study was the small amount of time apparently devoted to civil incidents. Was this genuine? If so, the 'social work' rôle of the police has clearly been exaggerated; if not, a more specific study is obviously required.

LAW, ORDER AND THE MOTORIST

Donald R. Cressey

Police officials, experts, and research workers all have noted that a police department's policies with reference to motoring offences have serious consequences for police–public relations. Gardiner's study of traffic-law enforcement in several American cities uncovered numerous examples.[1] The police chief of a small town said that if he were to engage in an active ticket-writing campaign, his department would suffer at budget-allocation time. Other chiefs explained a 50 per cent rise in ticketing between 1963 and 1964 by pointing out that the first year was an election year and 'they did not want to make enemies'. Some officials said their city administrators tried to minimize unfavourable public reactions by refusing to provide the police with sufficient money and equipment for traffic-law enforcement.

My thesis, which must be presented more as hypothesis than as fact, is that three inter-related conditions are among the most significant events in the history of organized police. These are the arrival of the automobile and its affluent drivers, the correlated introduction of new methods for control of motorists, and assignment of the enforcement authority to police departments. Most important, interaction between police and automobile drivers seems to have contributed substantially to a blackening of the police image in motorized nations.[2]

---

[1] John A. Gardiner, *Traffic and the Police: Variations in Law-Enforcement Policy*, Cambridge, Massachusetts, Harvard University Press, 1969, pp. 116–17. See also O. W. Wilson, 'Police Authority in a Free Society', *Journal of Criminal Law, Criminology and Police Science*, June 1964, **54,** 175–7, Jerome H. Skolnick, *Justice without Trial: Law Enforcement in a Democratic Society*, New York, John Wiley, 1966, pp. 54–6; and T. C. Willett, *Criminal on the Road: A Study of Motoring Offences and Those Who Commit Them*, London, Tavistock, 1964, pp. 106–21.

[2] See Bruce Smith, *Police Systems in the United States*, 2nd rev. ed., New York, Harper, 1960, pp. 9–10; Christopher Williams, 'The Criminal Law and Public Opinion: Some Police Reactions', *Criminal Law Review*, 1961, 359–67; Christopher Williams, 'Traffic Law: Some Misgivings', *The Criminologist*, November 1969, **4,** 31–7; and James Q. Wilson, 'Police Morale, Reform and Citizen Respect: the Chicago Case', in David Bordua, (ed.), *The Police: Six Sociological Essays*, New York, John Wiley, 1967, p. 158.

The Car and its Driver

The most significant impact of the automobile's advent was the raising up of a different, and more powerful, population of offenders. The arrival of the motor car made it necessary for the police to deal with sections of the public only rarely encountered by them in the days of the horse and carriage and bicycle.[3] These were the upper- and middle-class adult males, who could afford the expensive costs of an automobile. Willett presents evidence that the social class distribution of serious motoring offenders in England now corresponds rather closely to that of offenders in general, and an American study also found that the class distribution of a sample of traffic offenders paralleled the class distribution of the community studied.[4] Yet there is no doubt that the early owners of automobiles and, hence, the early motoring offenders, were necessarily wealthy and powerful persons. Even today, automobile driving requires expensive equipment and insurance coverage which the least powerful persons of most communities—the poor and the young—cannot afford. Just as traditional criminal statutes, such as those outlawing burglary, placed a disproportionate number of working-class people under the jurisdiction of the police, the early motoring regulations placed a disproportionate number of wealthy persons under their jurisdiction.

One prerogative claimed by the rich and powerful is freedom from regulation. It has long been asserted, in many contexts, that powerful people's behaviour thought to be detrimental or hazardous to the community should not be brought into the domain of the criminal law. This point, frequently made with reference to business offences, occasionally appears when someone suggests that the private incomes of legislators and government executives be regulated by law. When applied to motoring offences the assertion takes a simple form: Motoring offences are not, or should not be, crimes at all.[5]

---

[3] Although I use the past tense here, it should be noted that the process exists in the present as well—in developing nations and in other nations where the number of automobiles per capita is still low. For example, a Nigerian criminologist recently wrote, 'Owing to the rapid increase in the number of motor vehicles on our roads and the consequent congestion of these roads, motoring offences, especially in large townships, have now become one of the main sources of friction between the police and the motoring public'. Cyprian O. Okonkwo, *The Police and the Public in Nigeria*, London, Sweet & Maxwell, 1966, p. 51.

[4] Willett, op. cit., p. 40; H. Lawrence Ross, 'Traffic Law Violation: A Folk Crime', *Social Problems*, Winter, 1960–1, **8**, 231–41.

[5] Much *malum prohibitum* legislation is enacted in response to the pleas of one group that is working for the betterment of a second. The first group often asks a third group to stop damaging the second. Since the legislation will criminalize behaviour which has

Resistance to regulation by law was the early motorists' first line of defence. Motor cars appeared on British roads at a time when, under the Locomotive Act of 1861 and 1865, all horseless vehicles were limited to speeds of four miles an hour outside towns and two miles an hour within them. Logically enough, motorists were asked to obey this law. But the new drivers both defied the law and worked for its repeal. In 1896 they managed to get the speed limit raised to fourteen miles an hour. Some profits were involved—the automobile clubs pressuring for non-regulation were closely allied with automobile manufacturers.

But the automobile's rôle as a symbol of the high status of the person who could own it, and of the group whose control was sought, seems to have more significance than direct profits in resistance to regulation. Generally speaking, a large part of the public was determined that the automobile should go faster than a carefully driven horse-drawn carriage only at risk of a criminal penalty for the driver. Another part of the public, the powerful citizens who could afford cars, insisted on their freedom to drive 'reasonably' without risk of criminal penalty. The motorists were even opposed to a clause in the Motor Car Act of 1903 that required motor vehicles to carry number plates, on the ground that this practice is 'degrading'. And in 1928 the motoring associations opposed legislation which would make it a separate offence to drive after one's driving licence has been suspended, just as they had opposed automobile registration, driving tests, traffic police, pedestrian crossings, and almost all other restrictions on drivers.[6]

Years ago, Thorsten Veblen argued that industrialized nations have high crime rates because the individualism of the criminal who takes what he wants is consistent with the economic individualism of the businessmen operating in such societies. Except for its reference to the conversion of goods and persons the following quotation could well have been written with the early businessman-motorist in mind. The early driver was a powerful citizen who well knew the advantages of manipulating the political process in such a way that government regulations criminalized the behaviour of

---

been profitable or personal among members of the third group, it is strenuously resisted. American pure food and drug laws, laws regulating fair employment practices, and, more recently, school desegregation laws, all have this kind of history. But this does not seem to be the history of the laws regulating the automobile. Here, a new pattern of behaviour, not a customary one, was criminalized. See Richard C. Fuller, 'Morals and the Criminal Law', *Journal of Criminal Law and Criminology*, March–April 1942, **32**, 624–30; Clarence Ray Jeffrey, 'Crime, Law and Social Structure', *Journal of Criminal Law, Criminology, and Police Science*, November–December 1956, **47**, 423–35, and Herbert L. Packer, *The Limits of the Criminal Sanction*, Stanford, Calif., Stanford University Press, 1969, pp. 251–6.
[6] Willett, op. cit., p. 79.

one's competitors, as well as the advantages of proclaiming the ideology of individualism whenever one's own conduct was in danger of being criminalized:

> The ideal pecuniary man is like the ideal delinquent in his unscrupulous conversion of goods and persons to his own ends, and in a callous disregard of the feelings and wishes of others and of the remoter effects of his actions, but he is unlike him in possessing a keener sense of status and in working more far-sightedly to a remoter end.[7]

It appears that this ideology continues to have an influence despite the fact that a wider cross-section of urbanized communities now drives cars. The conflict between motorists and others, including legislators, has been described by Willett as a 'cold war',[8] and Gardiner has concluded, 'Until a greater level of consensus and support is generated, the police are scarcely to be blamed for their varying responses to the problems of traffic policy and enforcement'.[9]

The ideology of individualism also seems to have a place in the motorists' second line of defence, the proposition that motoring offences are not 'really' crimes, even after they have been so designated by legislatures. There are numerous examples of this proposition and of the individualism involved in it.

England's Motor Car Act of 1903 raised the speed limit to 20 miles per hour and authorized the courts to suspend driving licences. The Act also made it an offence to 'drive dangerously' and established a fine of £20 for a first conviction of that offence, and a fine not exceeding £50 or three months' imprisonment for second and subsequent convictions. The motorists and their organizations strongly opposed these penalties, and their resistance continued even after their dangerous behaviour had been criminalized. A member of parliament set the style for years to come by saying, 'It is scandalous that these high penalties should be fixed . . . a wife beater was treated no worse than a motorist who exceeded the speed limit by half a mile an hour'.[10] Similarly, the Standing Joint Committee of the Automobile Association and the Royal Automobile Club in 1960 carefully distinguished between 'motorists' and 'persons who commit serious criminal offences', arguing that 'It is desirable that the manner in which the police deal with the

---

[7] Thorsten Veblen, *Theory of the Leisure Class,* New York, Macmillan, 1912, p. 237. See also Edward A. Duddy, 'The Moral Implications of Business as a Profession', *Journal of Business,* April 1945, **15,** 70–71; and David Matza and Gresham M. Sykes, 'Juvenile Delinquency and Subterranean Values', *American Sociological Review,* October 1961, **26,** 712–19.

[8] Willett, op. cit., p. 65.

[9] Gardiner, op. cit., p. 165.

[10] *The Times,* London, 8 August 1903. Cited by Willett, op. cit., p. 70.

motorists who commit minor offences should be very different from the attitude towards persons who commit serious criminal offences'.[11]

Motorists have managed to convince many authorities that drivers are, indeed, somewhat infallible. Among them is an American police expert, V. A. Leonard, whose treatise on police affairs has become something of a classic. Leonard supports recurring demands for a separate organization to control traffic with the argument that 'traffic violators are not criminals, and, obviously, do not fall into the same category as burglars, pickpockets, and other members of the criminal gentry'.[12]

Motorists also have convinced employers that there is a difference between traffic offenders and 'criminals'. John Martin asked ninety-seven English firms about known offenders' chances of employment with them. He summarized his findings about motoring offences as follows:

> Serious driving offences were regarded in a completely different light from all other criminal offences. It seems likely that they would only be regarded as a bar to employment if the job itself involved driving. So marked is this attitude that one may even wonder whether, in its way, it may not be just as irrational as the aversion towards sex offences. Among some who have studied traffic offences there is a school of thought that a man drives as he lives; if there is anything in this, then the bad driver may be more of an employment risk (even in non-driving) than is popularly supposed.[13]

Even many policemen and judges have been taught to take the 'soft view' of motoring offences. These officials consider previous convictions for traffic violations as irrelevant in the prosecution and sentencing of non-traffic cases, and to consider previous convictions for non-traffic offences as irrelevant in the course of prosecutions for traffic violations. This policy can be viewed as sensible only if one agrees that traffic offenders are not 'real criminals', despite legal definitions to the contrary.[14] Seventy English policemen interviewed by Willett accepted without question the practice of ignoring non-motoring offences when presenting evidence that a traffic offender had been previously convicted. Some thought they would be rebuked from the bench if they produced evidence of 'crime' as they called it, in motoring cases.[15] Willett described the general attitudes about motoring offenders and offences as follows:

[11] Standing Joint Committee, Automobile Association and Royal Automobile Club, *Memorandum to the Royal Commission on the Police* (1960). Cited by Willett, op. cit., p. 7.

[12] V. A. Leonard, *Police Organization and Management*, Brooklyn, Foundation Press, 1951, p. 301.

[13] John P. Martin, *Offenders as Employees*, London, Macmillan, 1962, p. 129.

[14] See Roger Hood, *Sentencing the Motoring Offender: A Study of Magistrates' Views and Practices*, London, Heinemann Educational Books, 1972, pp. 97–108.

[15] Willett, op. cit., p. 109.

It seems that there was little or no inclination among the police or the public to apply the term criminal or any social stigma to these motoring offenders. The police have a clear-cut but indefinable concept of a distinction between what they called crime—meaning usually offences handled by the C.I.D.—and motoring offences, a concept which was, generally speaking, shared by members of the public. It is also interesting that the offenders interviewed who had criminal records were careful to distinguish between motoring offences and what they called 'real crime' which they defined as 'breaking, burglary, and assault'.[16]

Fifteen years ago Barbara Wootton reported that essentially the same opinion prevailed among magistrates: 'Apparently on the Marxian principles that law is made and operated in the interests of the well-to-do, motoring offences in general, and infringements of the speed limits in particular, are not ordinarily thought to "count" as crimes at all.'[17]

Proactive Police Work

Opposition to laws regulating traffic and parking often becomes opposition to the police who enforce these laws. The distinguished Automobile Association began in 1905 as an organized group of motorists who employed bicycle patrols to warn drivers of the presence of policemen operating speed traps. From that time to this, as policemen well know, motor vehicle drivers all over the world are quick to say that the police spend so much time harrying motorists that they neglect their primary duty, that of catching 'real criminals'.

The controversy here is not about who is a criminal and who is not. It is concerned with the differences between police methods for dealing with outlawed motoring behaviour and police methods for dealing with outlawed violent behaviour and property offences. The differences seem to have their immediate roots in the way offences come to the attention of the police and their tap roots in the class status of the offenders.

With few exceptions, such as cases involving collisions, the police must discover motoring violations themselves, while more traditional crimes are reported to them by victims or witnesses. The old-fashioned foot patrolman might have himself discovered a few criminals in the process of committing a burglary or an assault, but most such discoveries were made by citizens, who then sought out the patrolman. Development of the telephone and radio car strengthened this arrangement whereby the citizen reported a crime and the

[16] Ibid., p. 302.
[17] Barbara Wootton, *Social Science and Social Pathology*, London, Allen and Unwin, 1959, pp. 25–6.

police reacted. But citizens do not report motoring offences. Accordingly, if the police are to issue traffic citations they must themselves seek out motoring offenders.

In Willett's study of six serious traffic offences (causing death by dangerous driving, drunken driving, driving while disqualified, failure to carry required third-party insurance, and failure to stop after an accident or report it), 60 per cent of 653 cases came to the attention of the police because there was a collision. Thirty-six per cent were noticed by the police or came to their attention when the driver was stopped 'on suspicion'. (Thirty-two per cent of those prosecuted for driving while disqualified and 69 per cent of the uninsured drivers were stopped 'on suspicion'.) Only 4 per cent of the cases were reported by members of the public.[18] In less serious cases, such as speeding, failure to heed stop signs, and illegal parking, the percentage of complaints registered with the police by citizen observers must be negligible.

Perhaps some citizens do not report traffic offences for the same reasons they commit them—they do not consider them 'real crime'. Others are not concerned about any given violation because they have not been damaged personally. Still others probably refrain from reporting observed offences because they believe that reporting them will not bring about any significant police action. In a sense, these last citizens are correct. Most traffic offences are misdemeanours, and the law of arrest is such that a policeman can hardly take significant action unless the offence is committed in his presence. But, whatever the reasons for non-reporting, the fact is that if action is to be taken in most traffic-violation cases it must be taken at the initiative of a policeman.

Most ordinary American and British citizens understand that the machinery of criminal justice is to be reactive rather than proactive.[19] But the modern policeman, especially when he is dealing with traffic, must in reality be a proactive rather than a reactive agent. One of the first controversies about Boston's newly-established nineteenth-century police department occurred because of a shift towards the proactive police rôle, and I suspect that other police departments may have had similar difficulties.

In 1838, Boston temperance advocates used their influence to implement passage of a law regulating liquor licensing and consumption, among other things. Because violations of this law necessarily occurred behind the closed

---

[18] Willett, op. cit., pp. 112, 181. See also D. J. Steer and R. A. Carr-Hill, 'The Motoring Offender—Who is he?', *The Criminal Law Review*, April 1967, 214–24.

[19] I have borrowed these terms from David Bordua and Albert Reiss, Jr., 'Environment and Organization: A Perspective on the Police', in Bordua, (ed.), *The Police*, op. cit., p. 40. Wilson uses a different terminology—'police-invoked action' and 'citizen-invoked action' —to indicate these two styles of law enforcement and order maintenance: James Q. Wilson, *Varieties of Police Behavior: The Management of Law and Order in Eight Communities*, Cambridge, Mass., Harvard University Press, 1968, pp. 83–89.

doors of shops and houses, and because evidence of violation could be obtained by eyesight alone, the law in effect called upon the police to act as detectives on their own initiative, to enter private places without a warrant, and to seize evidence. Boston police (later to be emulated by federal prohibition agents) answered the call, and the subsequent outcry and hostility towards them were enormous.[20] Similar poor relationships between police and public, stemming from assignment of similar proactive responsibilities to the police seem to have become the heritage of modern cities.[21]

In contemporary times, this heritage is constantly being reinforced on the streets and highways. The automobile has brought about a dramatic increase in the proportion of police work which is proactive. The effects have made the relationship between police and motor car drivers fundamentally different from the relationships between police and potential violators of more traditional laws. This unusual relationship between policeman and motorist has had a profound influence in producing hostility towards the police—with reference to police handling of motoring offences and civil disorders, and even with reference to the handling of traditional crimes like burglary and assault.

Use of proactive methods—often called 'police harassment'—in dealing with the crimes and potential crimes of slum dwellers, blacks, teenagers, organized criminals, and political radicals is a logical extension of the proactive methods developed to deal with motorists. Yet the use of these methods might not have produced significant resistance had they not also been used on the cross-section of the population represented by motorists. Stated in another way, the proactive 'doctrine of aggressive patrol', which figures prominently in modern police thinking and which is antithetical to the ancient idea that the legal system is merely reactive, probably would not be so harshly criticized had motorists not learned to empathize with the persons now being aggressively patrolled.

An alternative hypothesis is that the police were proactive all along, but no one paid any attention to their behaviour until they encountered the affluent motorist. Perhaps the doctrine of legal restraint did not restrain policemen when their most important duty was repression of crime among the working-class population. Early policemen were themselves mostly working-class men who were employed by more affluent persons to keep peace in their own social class and to protect 'respectable people' from 'them'. Consistently, upper- and middle-class citizens either were indifferent to police

[20] Roger Lane, *Policing the City: Boston, 1822–1885*, Cambridge, Mass., Harvard University Press, 1967, pp. 39–44.
[21] See Arthur Stinchcombe, 'Institutions of Privacy in the Determination of Police Administrative Practices', *American Sociological Review*, September 1963, **69**, 150–60.

methods or cheerfully supported the police, whatever the methods they used. As one standard American textbook for policemen puts it, 'Often, the general public was apathetic to police operations directed toward anti-social elements of the community, and, as long as these anti-social elements were kept under control, did not bother to scrutinize or evaluate police methods'.[22] We do know, however, that rudeness, arrogance, and repression—like certain, swift, and severe penalties—were the order of the day. When these methods and principles were applied to motorists they were deemed inappropriate, crude, unjust, and even 'brutal'.

Other difficult problems arose as police methods became proactive, and with reference to powerful middle- and upper-class persons. One was the clash of social status. A few years ago a retired Oslo policeman told me that when he was a young officer he and his colleagues wore out a half-dozen uniforms a year, most of them destroyed in fights with criminals and hooligans. Drunken sailors considered a fight with police as pretty much a regular part of shore leave, and the police thought that fighting with the sailors and other toughs was one of their routine duties. The combatants understood each other. One can imagine the strife occurring when these policemen—accustomed to participating in violence, to displaying an over-bearing demeanour, and to speaking the tough language of the slums—encountered the community's new automobile drivers: the mayor, judges, members of parliament, newspaper publishers, important businessmen and, perhaps, even the chief of police.

One American police public relations expert contends that current unfavourable stereotypes of policemen stem from the old days when the stereotype of him as an authoritarian brute was quite accurate.[23] Clearly, the automobile has been the principal vehicle for increased contacts between the police and the so-called law-abiding members of the community. Also, as suggested above, the proactive police rôle dominating these contacts seems to have established a public interest in police methods and, more recently, a widespread hostility towards them.

More specifically, it probably was the early motorists' attention which, more than any other condition, influenced police chiefs to introduce training programmes stressing courtesy, precise but not colourful language, non-violence and, generally, a demeanour consistent with middle-class values and behaviour patterns. In addition, policemen had to learn how to neutralize the differences between high-status motorists and low-status

[22] A. C. Germann, Frank D. Day, and Robert R. J. Gallati, *Introduction to Law Enforcement*, Springfield, Ill., Charles C. Thomas, 1966, p. 68.
[23] G. McManus, 'Human Relations Training for Police', *Journal of Criminal Law, Criminology, and Police Science*, May 1955, **46**, 105–11.

officers. So as to avoid arousing motorists' resentment at being stopped by a person regarded as his social inferior, policemen were taught to make the interaction highly impersonal, 'to convey the impression that he is acting purely as a policeman, and that he is not, as a citizen himself, passing judgement on the subject's statements'.[24] Not all such 'professionalization' programmes were introduced at the same time; in some parts of the world, police authorities are just getting around to them. Perhaps an historical study would show that such training programmes were introduced in various nations and cities shortly after the number of automobiles came to be a 'problem' in these areas.

That police training in courtesy has been effective is suggested in Willett's report on his recent study of 181 serious motoring offenders. Three-quarters said their treatment by the police had been courteous, a proportion that is surprisingly high when consideration is taken of the fact that 60 out of 153 offenders (39 per cent) whose attitudes could be assessed were 'undoubtedly hostile' to the police.[25] Similarly, of 163 non-offenders studied, 135 (85 per cent) thought the police treated the motoring public with courtesy and consideration.[26]

It is likely, also, that the early motor car drivers inaugurated the demand for educated policemen. Although I have made no compilation, there seems to be a positive correlation between the per capita number of automobiles and the educational level of the policemen in a community. It does not seem a mere coincidence that the urban areas of Southern California have the highest proportion of automobile drivers in the world and also the most highly educated policemen. Nowadays, this correlation might well be attributed to the general effects of urbanization and industrialization: as a nation or city becomes educated, so do its policemen. Further, the stress on the need for better educated police has accompanied technological developments which increased the demand for police experts. Yet the influence of the motorists' reaction to the policeman's proactive rôle seems to have been specifically, and overwhelmingly, important:

> Traffic enforcement responsibilities have brought the police into frequent contact with the law-abiding members of the community. These contacts have resulted in a public interest in police methods, for when police attitudes and habits usually extended to the anti-social members of the community, were extended to the law-abiding, the outcry was loud and clear. The resulting attention paid to selection and training had a great effect in eliminating ugly early practices.[27]

[24] Michael Banton, *The Policeman in the Community*, London, Tavistock, 1964, p. 183.
[25] T. C. Willett, *Drivers After Sentence*, London, Heinemann Educational Books, 1973, pp. 77–9.
[26] Ibid., p. 79.   [27] Germann, Day, and Gallati, op. cit., p. 69.

The Motorist and Police Discretion

As the number of automobiles in a city increases, the amount of police time and energy devoted to traffic matters increases, but no one knows in what ratio. While legislators might not regard motoring offences as 'real crimes', they nevertheless continue to place them within the domain of the criminal law, and to assign enforcement responsibilities to the police. Assignment of such responsibilities has not been accompanied by proportional increases in police department budgets. Policemen have, almost literally, been required to take on the regulation of the automobile as an extra burden.

In one sense, this situation is neither unusual nor deplorable. Police departments have been, and are, asked to assume many administrative tasks without expecting significant increases in budgetary allocations. These tasks range from the granting of permits for taxicabs to the licensing of amusement parks, dance halls, theatres, certain weapons, auctioneers, and places for storing explosives. Police leaders have a tendency to look lovingly at the money they spend on administrative affairs and to wish it could be spent on 'law enforcement'. But the police never have enough men and equipment to stamp out all crime. Like constitutional restrictions on police power, assignment of administrative tasks to police departments without increasing budgets proportionately is a way of asking the police to overlook some crimes and settle others out of court. Policemen are asked to 'combat' or 'fight' crime, as if we had declared war on criminals, but fortunately they are not given the money, manpower, equipment, or constitutional authority necessary to going to war.

Further, no amount of equipment, manpower or money will make the police of democratic societies into automatons that strictly follow the coercive directives of criminal laws, whether these refer to traditional crimes or to traffic crimes. This is true because justice demands that general rules of law not be uniformly applied to the wide variety of offenders and offences involved in specified outlawed acts.[28] Gross injustices would be done if the police were not given room for flexibility, diplomacy and discretion in enforcing the law.[29]

---

[28] Cf. Hood, op. cit., pp. 4–6, 137.

[29] See Joseph Goldstein, 'Police Discretion Not to Invoke the Criminal Process: Low-Visibility Decisions in the Administration of Justice', *Yale Law Journal*, March 1960, **69**, 543–94; Wayne R. LaFave, *Arrest: The Decision to Take a Suspect into Custody*, Boston, Little, Brown & Co., 1965, pp. 83–101; and Donald R. Cressey, 'Control of Crime and Consent of the Governed', in Gresham M. Sykes and Thomas E. Drabek (eds.), *Law and the Lawless*, New York, Random House, 1969, pp. 270–87.

But there is a fundamental difference between the exercise of police discretion in motoring cases and in more traditional criminal cases: discretion in traffic cases is openly demanded by persons with enough power to enforce their demands. The early cry of the driver for police courtesy, educated accents, utilization of common sense and treatment as something other than a 'common criminal' was not a request that the police temper enforcement of the criminal law with mercy and justice. It was a demand that police systematically overlook law violations by high-status offenders. Thus, calls for the exercise of police discretion in motoring cases were demands that began and ended with an order: 'Do not arrest *me*.' The demands continue, as in incidents where police are told to pay attention to 'real crime' or 'serious offences' and 'flagrant violations' but not to *my* violations.

Moreover, the same attitude is expressed indirectly in vigorous opposition, complete with budget cuts, when police try to move against motoring offenders as enthusiastically as they move against violators of other laws. Some contemporary American examples were given above. When, at the turn of the century, British policemen were granted the power to arrest motorists without a warrant, a Member of Parliament noted that the powerful automobile drivers had begun a campaign designed to make any policeman sorry he had used this law-enforcement tool. He berated the Minister for bowing to what he called the 'passive resistance' of the motorists:

> This is a government by the rich for the rich. When there is passive resistance against the Education Bill you will not give in, but when the motorists resist you give in at once. What's the use of power to arrest without a warrant if policemen are open to prosecution for false imprisonment or wrongful arrest by all the power and wealth of the motorists.[30]

Consistently, Gardiner recently found in an American city that *not* writing a traffic ticket usually will not get a policeman into trouble, but that writing tickets can do so:

> It seems that a Lynn (Massachusetts) policeman is more likely to get into trouble for a ticket wrongly written . . . than for a deserved ticket not written. The stories told of punishment arising from traffic matters were stories of excessive zeal rather than of laziness.[31]

The notion that motorists are a privileged class whose offences should be overlooked as a routine discretionary practice may also be seen in the recurring controversy about using unmarked police cars on the streets and highways. In a joint memorandum to England's 1960 Royal Commission on

[30] *The Times*, London, 5 August 1903. Cited by Willett, *Criminal on the Road*, op. cit., pp. 69–70.
[31] Gardiner, op. cit., p. 56.

Police, the Automobile Association and the Royal Automobile Club complained about the practice of 'plain-clothes officers patrolling in cars which are not identifiable as police cars . . . There is a marked distaste for this kind of offence'.[32] The 'distaste', I think, is the same acerbity experienced by a burglar or automobile thief who has been tracked down by a plain-clothesman.

When marked patrol cars are present, traffic violations diminish. Empty marked police cars parked by the roadway have a deterrent effect, and even cardboard cutouts of a police car or motorcycle officer (used on some American highways) cause motorists to obey the law. But marked patrol cars cannot be everywhere, and when cardboard cutouts become common they become commonly ineffective. Accordingly, motorists violate the law with impunity, as is known by any rush-hour driver who puts his speedometer exactly on the speed limit and keeps it there. A London lawyer did just this, and kept an account of the number of times he was passed during a sixty-day period in various speed zones. In 40 m.p.h. zones he was passed by 4,000 vehicles of all types, including two tricycles; in 30 m.p.h. zones he was passed by 3,700 vehicles, including three invalid chairs and a hearse. Because he was law-abiding, he was awarded a mixture of epithets, uncomplimentary names, and advice about where to go and what to do.[33]

The theory of deterrence, which underlies most contemporary criminal law, suggests that unmarked cars driven by plain clothesmen could do much to cut down this high violation rate. However, it is likely that utilizing deterrence theory to cut down the rate of traffic violations—in defiance of motorists' wishes—would further jeopardize police–community relations.[34] In Western societies, with their traditional bars against *ex post facto* legislation, punishments of criminals are accepted as legitimate, as fair and just, only if there is evidence that violators were given *advance notice* that deviation from prohibitory rules will have punishment as its consequence. The advance notice serves to maintain the consent of the governed.[35] Systematic non-reaction to motoring offences by police makes motorists wonder if the law has in fact warned them that infractions will be punished.

One common assumption in criminal justice circles is that carefully formulated and precisely stated criminal statutes, each stipulating a penalty, provide the advance notice necessary to both justice and docility. However, this is rarely the case. It is not correct to assume that criminal laws are

[32] Cited by Willett, *Criminal on the Road*, op. cit., p. 107.
[33] Ibid., p. 108.
[34] Cf. D. W. Elliott and Harry Street, *Road Accidents*, London, Allen Lane, The Penguin Press, 1968, pp. 65, 75.
[35] Cressey, op. cit., pp. 277–80.

perfectly clear, or that law-makers want them enforced with equal vigour. Citizens readily learn that they are not expected to obey all criminal laws, and they are likely to rebel if they are punished for violating obscure or little-used laws. As a corrective, so that punishments will not be imposed irrationally or capriciously, the police inform citizens as to just which of their behaviours are indeed 'punishable by law'. With reference to crimes such as murder the police try to do this by maintaining high clearance rates ('See what happens to murderers'). But with reference to other crimes, including most traffic offences, advance notice is given in the form of warnings that *further* violations of specified statutes will be followed by punishment.

When a policeman informs an offender that his observed conduct will *henceforth* be handled as crime he signifies both that the instant statutory offence will be overlooked and that the next offence will bring the wrath of society down on the offender's head. Plain-clothesmen rarely perform this warning function. Instead, they proactively 'enforce the law'. Because doing so reduces the degree of consent among citizens who believe they have not been given sufficient advance notice that their behaviour is in fact punishable by law, plain-clothesmen must be used sparingly, and in connection with rather powerless individuals, such as 'real criminals'.

Admonitions and warnings by uniformed policemen are not likely to be effective unless records are kept on who is warned about what. Nevertheless, the advance notice involved in them seems designed to maintain consent of the governed by insuring that punishments for law violations will be accepted as legitimate by those being punished, and by others. England's 'courtesy cop' plan, initiated in 1938 for the benefit of motorists, is a good example of this practice of decentralizing the warning function so as to pacify a powerful segment of the public. Under this scheme, the police were asked to use prosecution only as a last resort—when advice, admonition, and other means of 'educating' the traffic violator had failed.[36] Banton gives several examples of less general police policies, such as the directive that the driver of an illegally parked car should be persuaded to move the car or, at least, should be allowed to park illegally for fifteen to twenty minutes before a citation is issued.[37] Such tolerance policies order the police to overlook prosecution of crimes which a legislature has stipulated as 'strict responsibility', 'absolute liability', or (in American terms) 'strict liability' offences. In such offences, criminal intent is not to be considered—one who exceeds a speed limit is guilty, despite his intentions.[38] It is therefore inconsistent

[36] Willett, *Criminal on the Road*, op. cit., p. 108.
[37] Banton, op. cit., pp. 148–9.
[38] Cf. Hood, op. cit., pp. 2–3.

to try to educate him in such a way that he will have only good intentions. But advice and admonition can teach him that in practice his violations will be overlooked unless they are 'flagrant'.

This extension of judicial discretion to policemen in traffic cases has backfired. Because every motorist knows that most violations result in neither warning nor citation, he is likely to view either action as evidence of police inefficiency on the one hand, and as evidence of police prejudice on the other. With reference to the first issue, motorists argue that policemen inefficiently warn and cite motorists rather than arresting 'real criminals' because it is easier for them to do so. It is commonly assumed, perhaps correctly, that policemen win promotions and other rewards when they make 'good pinches'.[39] From this assumption it is erroneously concluded that issuing a traffic ticket is an easy but inefficient way to chalk up a good pinch. Indeed, this argument was made at the beginning. The clause in Britain's 1903 Motor Car Act that gave police the power to arrest speeders without a warrant was deemed highly objectionable because, according to one Member of Parliament, a policeman armed with the power 'would find it very easy to sally out from the police station, stop-watch in hand, and shortly find two stripes blossoming on his shoulder'.[40]

A variant of this theme, based on a more realistic conception of police departments as rank-oriented bureaucracies rather than as creative bureaucracies,[41] does not hold that the policeman will win a promotion if he issues citations. Instead, it holds that he will *not* win a promotion *unless* he issues a standard quota of citations. The difference here is a variation in the conception of the promotion system as one in which advancements are given to men who excel, in contrast to systems in which advancements are withheld from men who fail to attain an agreed-upon 'standard' level of performance.[42] Many police departments do in fact use the second system, which means that they expect policemen to 'produce' traffic tickets.[43]

The notion—whether based on fact or not—that a policeman is merely filling his quota when he issues a traffic citation enables motorists to bolster their contention that they are law-abiding conformists who are being discriminated against as a class. This belief, like a belief in police inefficiency,

[39] William A. Westley, 'Violence and the Police', *American Journal of Sociology*, July 1953, 56, 34–41.
[40] *The Times*, London, 8 August 1903. Cited by Willet, *Criminal on the Road*, op. cit., p. 69.
[41] See Donald R. Cressey, 'Prison Organizations', Chapter 24 in James G. March, (ed.), *Handbook of Organizations*, New York, Rand McNally, 1965, pp. 1023–70.
[42] See Donald R. Cressey, 'Contradictory Directives in Complex Organizations: The Case of the Prison', *Administrative Science Quarterly*, June 1959, 4, 1–19.
[43] See Wilson, *Varieties of Police Behavior*, op. cit., pp. 53, 96–7.

negates any effects of prior warnings. As McNamara has said, citizens who receive traffic tickets are 'likely to feel that the officer's action in serving a ticket is arbitrary and based on some criterion other than the traffic violation itself'.[44] When this attitude is present, 'advance notice' in the form of warnings has not functioned to maintain the consent of the governed. On the contrary, police freedom to choose between warning or citation has made citations seem illegitimate.

There is evidence that the motorists' view of police arbitrariness is correct in at least one respect; persons who are abusive to officers are more likely than others to receive a ticket.[45] Edelman's theory suggests that abusiveness changes the policeman's conception of the offence in such a way that he can no longer overlook the statutory violation and merely warn the offender that henceforth the police will treat the motorist's conduct as punishable by law. The situation becomes one of 'dogma' about the legislative definition of crime rather than of a 'game' played with reference to the policeman's and motorist's acknowledged mutual need for discretion and diplomacy:

> What happens psychologically when law is enforced as if it were a command rather than a virtuous generalization around which a game can be played? Instead of a trial of wits, it becomes a trial of force. Where law is treated as dogma, defiance becomes heresy and this formulation states exactly the change in social rôles and in symbolic interplay that takes place. Where enforcement is played as a game, none of those involved pretends that the offence is virtuous; but all recognize, through mutual rôle-taking, that there are temptations, that there is a shared interest in resisting them; and that, within the rules, offenders caught under specified conditions will pay the specified penalties.[46]

By and large, however, it is the policeman's rôle as a law-enforcement officer, not his rôle as a peace agent or as a servant of the public, that thrusts him into a relationship with motorists.[47] Accordingly, the offender is likely

[44] John McNamara, 'Uncertainties in Police Work', in Bordua, (ed.), *The Police*, op. cit., p. 175.

[45] Banton, op. cit., p. 137. See also Wayne R. LaFave, 'The Police and Nonenforcement of the Law', *Wisconsin Law Review*, 1962, 104–137 and 179–239.

[46] Murray Edelman, *The Symbolic Uses of Politics*, Urbana, Ill., University of Illinois Press, 1964, p. 47.

[47] In the last decade, much consideration has been given to the observation that the policeman is more a servant of the public and a peace officer than a law-enforcement officer. See, for example, Raymond I. Parnas, 'The Police Response to the Domestic Disturbance', *Wisconsin Law Review*, 1967, 914–60; Egon Bittner, 'The Police on Skid-Row: A Study of Peace Keeping', *American Sociological Review*, October 1967, **32,** 699–715; Donald R. Cressey and Elg Elgesem, 'The Police and the Administration of Justice', in Nils Christie, ed., *Scandinavian Studies in Criminology*, Vol. 2, Oslo, Universitetsforlaget, 1968, pp. 53–72; John R. Lambert, *Crime, Police and Race Relations*, London, University of London Press, 1970, pp. 138–43; and Maureen E. Cain, *Society and the Policeman's Role*, London, Routledge and Kegan Paul, 1973.

to believe from the start that the situation is one of dogma, in which the state is unjustly accusing him, 'a respectable citizen', of transgressing its sacred values. He knows his traffic-law violation does not signify withdrawal of allegiance to political authority. In view of the large number of traffic offences he has witnessed, he is also convinced that his detainment is arbitrary and capricious. He is therefore not prepared to 'pay the specified penalties'. Perhaps these conditions are what make him abusive. Thirty-four per cent of the 181 serious motoring offenders recently studied by Willett 'thought the evidence of the police in court had been . . . unscrupulous; most were dangerous drivers who thought they had been singled out for blame when others were equally at fault, and drunken drivers who felt that the accounts of their inebriation had been exaggerated'.[48] Seventy-one per cent thought their sentences were unjust.[49]

Policy Differences

It can be argued logically that if a community does not want its motoring laws enforced it should either repeal them completely or modify them in such a way that motoring misbehaviour clearly falls outside the domain of the police.[50] Implementation of one or the other of these policies is, of course, what motorists have wanted all along, and there have been movements towards implementing both of them. With reference to the first policy, for example, England's Law Society has proposed that trivial infractions be called 'traffic breaches', not 'traffic offences', and that they be dealt with by a civil rather than a criminal procedure.[51] Elliott and Street have argued, however, that this proposal really would not decriminalize even 'traffic breaches'. They conclude:

> A procedure less markedly criminal than at present would have many solid advantages, and could probably be made acceptable to the public in respect of traffic breaches. However, the opposition will certainly make use of the argument that something new in English criminal jurisprudence is being proposed. It is

[48] See Willett, *Drivers After Sentence*, op. cit., p. 79.

[49] Ibid., p. 91.

[50] Daniel Patrick Moynihan, 'Public Health and Traffic Safety', *Journal of Criminal Law, Criminology and Police Science*, May–June 1960, **51**, 93–7; Daniel Patrick Moynihan, 'The War Against the Automobile', *The Public Interest*, Spring 1966, 10–26. For the contrary view, see Quinn Tamm, 'The Police: Pivot for Highway Safety Efforts', *Traffic Quarterly*, April 1964, **18**, 251; and Wilbur S. Smith, 'Widening the Traffic Enforcement Front', *Annals of the American Academy of Political and Social Science*, January 1954, **291**, 73–77.

[51] *Motoring Offences*, Memorandum by the Council of the Law Society, June 1965, para. 20. Cited by Elliott and Street, op. cit., p. 144.

important not to deny this, nor to attempt by juggling with labels to disguise a reality which will remain obstinately visible.[52]

The second policy has been tried in New Zealand, where control of traffic is no longer regarded as a job for the police. In most areas of the country, the local authorities have handed over their traffic functions to the Department of Transport, which employs its own traffic officers. One consequence is greater respect for the police. A 1967–8 study indicated that 23 per cent of a sample of New Zealand motorists had, at best, only 'mixed feelings' about the 'way the police do their job', as compared to 19 per cent of the non-motorists. In neighbouring Australia, where traffic is controlled by the police, the comparable figures were 33 per cent and 22 per cent.[53] Further, in Australia the percentage of persons with mixed feelings about the police increased regularly with the number of miles driven per year, but in New Zealand this figure remained at a constant 22–24 per cent. A congruent survey indicated that 23 per cent of the Australian police and 20 per cent of the New Zealand police thought that the public's opinion of the police had changed for the worse in the last ten years. The significant finding, however, was that of the Australian policemen who thought public opinion had changed for the worse, 22 per cent gave 'public resentment over enforcing petty traffic regulations' as the reason; but not one New Zealand policeman advanced that reason.[54] The researchers concluded:

> The survey data show clearly that one of the main factors contributing to lack of public respect for the police is motorists' resentment toward police handling of minor traffic regulations. The motorists' resentment appears to overflow to the police force generally. If a separate traffic organization was established, as in New Zealand, public respect for the police might improve significantly.[55]

A third policy, briefly alluded to above, asks for compromise. Here, the police continue to be assigned the responsibility for dealing with traffic offences as these are defined by criminal law, but they are asked to deal with them as if they were not crimes. This policy has been developed and implemented in communities all over the world. Conceivably, the policy represents a fuzzy, frail, and unwitting attempt to transfer traffic matters from the law-enforcement sector of police activity to the peace-keeping or

[52] Ibid., p. 157.

[53] D. Chappell and P. R. Wilson, *The Police and the Public in Australia and New Zealand,* St. Lucia, Queensland, University of Queensland Press, 1969, p. 121.

[54] Ibid., p. 62. The 1960 British Home Office survey, made for the Royal Commission on the Police, indicated that 69 per cent of the British police thought the public's opinion of the police had changed for the worse; of these men, 33 per cent attributed the change to resentment about enforcement of traffic regulations.

[55] Ibid., p. 127.

service sector. Wilson's discussion of the service style of police work, with its stress on discretion and warnings in traffic cases, certainly suggests that this is the case.[56]

The presence of unannounced service policies of this kind helps make sense of the fact that some police officials, prosecutors, and judges acknowledge that their authority to deal with traffic violations stems from the criminal law but nevertheless insist that these offences are not 'real crimes'. This seeming contradiction has become official in New York, where the Vehicle and Traffic Act provides: 'A traffic infraction is not a crime, and the penalty and punishment therefore shall not be deemed for any purpose a penal or criminal penalty or punishment'. Yet the New York police are still expected to deal with these non-crimes—to issue tickets and make arrests so that the non-penalties and non-punishments can be imposed by courts. The apparent contradiction diminishes but does not disappear if it is understood that the New York police have in a vague way only been asked somehow to handle traffic infractions in their capacities as servants of the public or as peace agents, rather than in their capacities as law-enforcement officers.

But the policies which have asked the police to handle traffic matters in some way that does not involve, or stress, their law-enforcement rôle have not been a resounding success. In the first place, many police chiefs and other high officials seem obligated to emphasize the law-enforcement functions of their departments and to characterize service and peace-keeping activities as 'not real police work'. Police manuals, police training programmes, and policemen themselves are likely to emphasize the officers' expertise in law enforcement, even if policemen in private conversation confess that little of their work involves the dramatic detecting and chasing of criminals one sees in films and on television. Further, the efficiency or effectiveness of a police department tends to be judged in terms of law-enforcement expectations rather than public-service expectations.

In the second place, and of more specific relevance to traffic matters, the law-enforcement rôle is thrust upon the police as they are asked to behave proactively in dealing with traffic offenders. No matter how many warnings are issued, no matter how loudly it is said that punishment is not punishment, no matter how enthusiastically the police direct traffic, no matter how many assistance vehicles the police put on the highways, and no matter how effectively the police in some cities plan traffic flow, designate one-way streets, locate traffic signals and stop signs and find additional parking spaces, motorists and policemen alike continue to view the policeman's rôle in traffic affairs as that of the law-enforcement officer. Wilson found that high-

[56] Wilson, *Varieties of Police Behavior*, op. cit., p. 221.

status traffic offenders accuse even the members of service-style police departments of harassment.[57]

Both Wilson and Gardiner have presented statistical evidence suggesting that when police departments establish specialized traffic divisions or units, the law-enforcement function of the police in traffic affairs is exaggerated rather than diminished.[58] Theoretically, such specialized divisions might be concerned principally with peace-keeping and with services to motorists, but it does not work out that way. Gardiner found that the policemen working in specialized traffic units behave, in interaction with motorists, much more like 'law-enforcement officers and nothing else' than do general-duty policemen.[59] Probably the greater 'toughness' of the specialized men arose because they were expected to produce tickets, which is to say that they were *directed* to behave like law-enforcement officers, and not like servants of the motoring public.[60]

What Wilson calls the 'legalistic style of police work',[61] was not popular in some of the cities studied by Gardiner, especially those where a police department and a stable population had come to an understanding about the desirability of exercising police discretion in traffic cases. A statistical study indicated that, among 508 American cities larger than 25,000, there were moderately high negative correlations between traffic ticketing rates and several indicators of the stability of the cities' populations—the greater the stability, the lower the ticketing rate. Gardiner hypothesized that residents of rapidly changing cities *expect* their police departments to be stricter than do residents of more stable cities and that, stated conversely, 'stabilization produces demands for "political" enforcement of criminal law'.[62] The suggestion here is that powerful residents of stable cities, more than others, have asked their police to consider social status when determining what the criminal law in action should be.

Some General Effects

In combination, the three conditions I have discussed—the middle- and upper-class status of early motorists, proactive law enforcement, and

[57] Ibid., p. 222.
[58] Ibid., pp. 95–9; Gardiner, op. cit., p. 83.
[59] Ibid., pp. 152–3.
[60] Franklin Kreml, 'The Specialized Traffic Division', *Annals of the American Academy of Political and Social Science*, 291 (January 1954), 63–72. See also Herman Goldstein, 'Police Discretion: The Ideal versus the Real', *Public Administration Review*, 23 (September 1963), 140–8.
[61] Wilson, *Varieties of Police Behavior*, op. cit., pp. 172–99.
[62] Gardiner, op. cit., p. 145.

insistence that police enforce the law while at the same time overlooking offences—have had important consequences for police work generally. Most importantly, they have introduced a misconception of the nature of 'the crime problem' and its causes and, by personalizing law enforcement, have laid the foundations for accusations of inefficiency, bigotry, and corruption in police departments.

First, the crime statistics have been drastically affected. Offences which must come to the personal attention of a policeman before official action is initiated probably are greatly under-reported, as compared with offences that are complained about by the public generally. Barbara Wootton, who does not take the 'soft view' of motoring offenders, has declared that 'the typical criminal of today is the motorist'.[63] If the number of unreported crimes in the motoring area could be compared with the number of other unreported crimes, even those involving minor offences, it probably would exceed it by a large factor.

Second, the notion that motoring offences are not crimes, 'really', has itself contributed to the incidence of such offences. Moreover, this proposition stresses the creed that one need only obey those laws one believes in, and popularization of this creed could only lead to higher crime rates generally. If there is any validity to Sutherland's principle of differential association (which holds that crime rates are a function of the presentation of attitudes favourable to the violation of law, in comparison with the presentation of attitudes unfavourable to such violation) then we should expect the motoring laws to be violated with the great frequency any driver can observe daily.[64] The violation rate is high because motorists persistently teach each other that law obedience is both unnecessary and undesirable. Like white-collar criminals, motorists believe they are not criminals and, also like white-collar criminals, they insist on specialized criminal justice procedures which will help insure that the criminal label is not attached to them.[65] Such behaviour and attitudes, which make law violation into a harmless little game, certainly must contribute to a so-called 'decline in law and order'.

Third, official policies asking police to enforce traffic laws but also to

[63] Wootton, op. cit., p. 25.

[64] Edwin H. Sutherland and Donald R. Cressey, *Criminology*, 8th ed., Philadelphia, Lippincott, 1970, p. 75.

[65] In sociological circles it is now popular to use so-called 'labelling-theory' to stress the undesirability—to both the offender and his community—of attaching opprobrious labels to questionable behaviour. While there is merit in this proposition, the high rate of traffic offences suggests that failure to label might have unanticipated, and bad, consequences too. See Howard S. Becker, *Outsiders: Studies in the Sociology of Deviance* (New York, Free Press, 1963); and Stanton Wheeler and Leonard S. Cottrell, Jr., *Juvenile Delinquency: Its Prevention and Control*, New York, Russell Sage Foundation, 1966, pp. 22–7.

ignore traffic offences have contributed to a widespread belief that any arrest, even an arrest for burglary or robbery, is more or less just an expression of some official's personal prejudices. No longer is a wide range of citizens convinced that the police are an impersonal arm of justice. The traffic offender knows that officers can observe only an insignificant proportion of all traffic violations, that they take action in only a small proportion of those observed, and that they do not have to take action of any particular offence coming to their attention. When a motorist is ticketed, he, like Bruce Smith, the police expert, is likely to suspect the worst:

> In traffic cases the police officer can favor local offenders over those who are non-residents, and vice versa. He can indulge in racial, religious, political, fraternal, national, regional, and social prejudices almost at will. He can put a cash price on his nonenforcement with little danger of detection. When he does act, it is often because he personally feels impelled to do so; that is, because his own sense of justice or propriety have been offended. From this personal element in law enforcement inevitably spring the harsh and overbearing attitudes and abusive language so often attributed to traffic offenders.[66]

From this 'personal element in law enforcement' also springs the belief that almost any arrest is merely an expression of bias against poor people, or blacks, or some other segment of the society. For that matter, this personal element also helps foster the notion, now popular among radicals, that traditional crimes such as larceny and assault are 'political crimes' against the controllers of the prejudiced and power-seeking police, who are said to exercise discretion in a blatant attempt to subordinate the poor and the powerless.

It appears, then, that the discretion demanded of the police by motorists and openly granted the police in traffic affairs, has put the policeman in a game he cannot win. If he enforces the law in a routine and efficient way, as one part of the public and one set of penal law theory say he should do, he is damned for being inhumanly overzealous. But, if he exercises discretion, thus overlooking instances of law violation, as another part of the public and a different set of penal law theory ask him to do, he is damned for operationalizing discriminatory attitudes. The automobile driver, faced with the alternative of being labelled a villain or of making villains out of the police, has clearly made his choice.

---

[66] Smith, op. cit., p. 58.

PERSPECTIVES ON THE RIGHT TO SILENCE

Kent Greenawalt

Introduction

Sir Leon Radzinowicz's systematic consideration of the administration of criminal justice, in his monumental *History of English Criminal Law* and his other writings, has had a great deal to do with the increased attention modern criminologists have paid to the criminal process; and his own eloquent defence of the 'right to silence',[1] at a time when the scope of that right is the subject of acute controversy in both the United States and England, makes its treatment particularly appropriate for this volume in his honour.

Although some advocates of a curtailed or expanded right to silence may treat a particular argument or their position as conclusive, a considered judgement about any proposed change involves assessment of some very different kinds of arguments. Since the wide range of these arguments is not always apparent, I distinguish them and evaluate them separately before proceeding to a brief conclusion.

The 'right to silence' embraces the right of suspects not to respond to police questioning and the right of defendants to be free from testifying at their own trials. In the United States both these rights are aspects of the 'privilege against self-incrimination', a phrase used as a shorthand for the constitutional bar against the government's compelling a man in a 'criminal case to be a witness against himself'.[2] Whether this provision of the Fifth Amendment reaches police interrogation of suspects was in some doubt

---

[1] Leon Radzinowicz, 'Them and Us', *Camb. L.J.*, 1972, **30**, 260, 275–6.

[2] This language is from the Federal Constitution. State constitutions have similar protections. In *Malloy* v. *Hogan*, 378 U.S. 1 (1964), the Supreme Court held that the federal protection was made applicable to state proceedings by the Fourteenth Amendment, adopted after the Civil War.

The constitutional language has long been interpreted to reach testimony by ordinary witnesses in civil and criminal cases and compelled production of incriminating documents, matters not covered in this essay.

until 1966, when Chief Justice Warren's majority opinion in *Miranda* v. *Arizona*,[3] took pains to confirm its applicability and used it as the basis for establishing new rights for suspects. In England, where linguistic usage is not so interwoven with constitutional interpretation, the term 'privilege against self-incrimination' may be used more narrowly to refer to the privilege of a witness not to respond to an incriminating question, which he nevertheless may quite properly be asked.[4]

The phrase 'right to silence', commonly used in England, evades the confusing differences in American and English usage, and I shall use it in this essay. The 'right to silence' does, however, have an either-or ring about it that unfortunately contributes to overblown rhetoric. In fact, a suspect may or may not remain silent at various stages in the criminal process, and at each stage a variety of possible consequences may impose greater or lesser penalties on silence and create greater or lesser pressures to speak. Few now would urge that a defendant's silence be treated as contempt of court or a legally conclusive confession of guilt, or that physical torture be used to loosen the tongues of recalcitrant suspects. The debate is over more moderate pressures, such as intensive police questioning of uncautioned suspects and natural inferences from silence drawn by those determining guilt or innocence. Those who would contract the existing right to silence would eliminate or alter the rules designed to prevent these moderate pressures; those who would expand the right seek more effective protections against them.

A suspect or defendant would have a 'perfect' right to silence if no one could draw any adverse inference from his decision to remain silent, if he were free from any other pressures to speak except those produced by his own conscience and by the possibility that speaking would help establish his innocence, and if he could make an informed decision whether speaking would be likely to help or hurt him. Such a person would speak only if he freely wished to confess his guilt and expose himself to punishment or if he intelligently concluded that speaking would be likely to help him. A 'perfect' right to silence is unrealizable in practice. First, most persons feel strong social pressures to be polite and co-operative, to speak when spoken to, and no one likes to appear guilty.[5] Second, the police will focus special investigative attention on a suspect who declines to answer relevant questions, and it is hard to see how any rule could prevent this, even were it

---

[3] 384 U.S. 436 (1966).
[4] See, e.g., G. Williams, *The Proof of Guilt*, 3rd ed., London, Stevens & Sons, 1963, pp. 37–38.
[5] See E. D. Driver, 'Confessions and the Social Psychology of Coercion', *Harv. L. Rev.*, 1968, **82**, 42, 57–8.

thought desirable. Thus, the suspect's natural feeling that his chances of appearing innocent may depend on his explaining himself are reinforced by the predictable police response to silence. Third, jurors sometimes will draw adverse inferences from a defendant's failure to testify, even if they are told not to, since they will suspect that the defendant's decision not to speak was based on a wish to hide his guilt. A return to the pre-1898 English law making a defendant incompetent to testify might meet this difficulty, but no one would consider that change an acceptable price for strengthening the right to silence. Damaging inferences may also be drawn, despite contrary judicial comment, when jurors are made aware that a defendant has refused to answer police questions.

Because the law is powerless to guarantee a perfect right of silence, considerable pressure to speak must remain on the best advised suspects and defendants whatever the applicable rules.[6] But in neither England nor the United States does the law go as far as it might to create an effective right to silence. Instead it compromises between protecting silence and satisfying competing interests, namely the usefulness for determinations of guilt of having suspects and defendants make statements and of allowing silence to be given its natural evidential significance. In both England and the United States the major impetus for change is now towards diminution of the existing right to silence, an impetus that is largely the result of acute fear of rising crime.

In the United States many of the rules that protect silence are based on constitutional interpretation. Not only do the 'rules' themselves vary considerably from their counterparts in England, the structure of the debate over them is different. Although proposed constitutional changes and legislative initiatives within existing constitutional principles are discussed, most arguments are about the proper interpretation of the Fifth Amendment as it stands. In England, on the other hand, the major debate now is over proposed legislative alterations of the right to silence, and particularly the influential proposals of the Criminal Law Revision Committee. I shall pay special attention to these because, whether or not they are adopted in whole or part, their comprehensive approach to narrowing the right to silence makes them an excellent vehicle for considering basic disagreements about the right.

The Committee would permit broader adverse inferences than are now

---

[6] Perhaps a perfect right could be realized if police never questioned suspects at all, if no admissions or confessions could be presented in evidence, and if defendants could not testify, but such drastic changes in the criminal process are beyond the realm of suggested alterations. Cf. L. Levy, *Origins of the Fifth Amendment* (New York, Oxford U.P., 1968), pp. 433–41, describing the Talmudic rule that even voluntary confessions are inadmissible.

allowed when suspects and defendants remain silent; it would eliminate the present caution of a right to silence, and it would relax the standards for inadmissibility of confessions obtained by threat or inducement. The Committee argues that these changes would enhance the accuracy of the process of guilt determination, without having an undesirable effect on police practices or directly violating any fundamental individual rights. The improved pursuit of the guilty is a common theme of those who wish to curtail individual rights; those who defend existing rights or propose their expansion are most likely to emphasize fundamental individual rights, protection of the innocent, and the need to prevent unacceptable police practices. Supports of change in either direction are also likely to contend that the law will be made more rational in some respect by what they propose. The broad questions, then, that need to be asked about the Committee's proposals are those raised by almost any proposals to alter rights in the criminal process: (1) Would they make the law more or less rational? (2) Would they make determinations of guilt and innocence more or less accurate? (3) Would they be consistent with or violate fundamental individual rights? (4) Would their effect on police practices and other institutions be desirable or undesirable? Much of what I say about the Committee's suggestions will have obvious application to other suggested changes in the right to silence, and less direct relevance for proposals regarding other controversial rights in the criminal process.

A recurrent question in such discussions is the utility of existing empirical data and the likely utility of further empirical research. The Criminal Law Revision Committee has been attacked for failing to ascertain vital facts before making its proposals, and *The Times* concluded in a leading article that 'there is not yet sufficient information for a rational judgment on some of the report's more controversial proposals'.[7] Not everyone agrees; some defenders of the report believe the suggestions can stand independent of relevant empirical data,[8] while others doubt that any new data can add significantly to the combined wisdom of the Committee members, most of whom are knowledgeable participants in the criminal process. In a volume devoted to a pre-eminent criminologist, it is certainly appropriate to enquire how far empirical research about the criminal process can aid decisions about the proper scope of individual rights; and, though not myself experienced in such research, I do briefly consider in which areas it appears most likely to be helpful. As we shall see, many of the relevant questions are not empirical and others, though 'empirical' in theory, require estimates about

---

[7] 'How Many Guilty Men Go Free', *The Times*, Feb. 16, 1973, p. 19, col. 1.

[8] R. Cross, 'A Very Wicked Animal Defends the 11th Report of the Criminal Law Revision Committee', *Crim. L.R.*, [1973], 329–33.

so many interrelated social variables that useful research 'projects' are hard to conceive. Still, many questions remain as to which empirical studies can prove most helpful.

Rationalization of the Law

Of the many circumstances in which legal rules suffer defects that might be thought to call for 'rationalization', I shall touch on four: when legal rules draw irrational distinctions; when they conflict with common sense; when they conflict with ordinary practice; and when they draw distinctions that are difficult to apply or lend themselves to evasion of their underlying purposes. Aspects of the right to silence suffer from each of these defects, but perception of the need for rationalization does not establish the best form for it to take or, in at least one instance, even whether rationalization is possible.

A. *Irrational Distinctions*

Sir Rupert Cross, a Committee member as well as a distinguished authority on the law of evidence, has written, 'Even if it were the case that the present rules of evidence produced no wrongful acquittals, I would still be in favour of most if not all of the Committee's recommendations for the simple reason that their adoption would spare the judge from talking gibberish to the jury, the conscientious magistrate from directing himself in imbecile terms and the writer on the law of evidence from drawing distinctions absurd enough to bring a blush to the most hardened academic face'.[9] It is quite possible that prohibited instructions might have a different impact on the average juror than permitted ones, even if careful analysis reveals no reasoned distinction between the inferences these instructions allow. How instructions strike most laymen is a proper subject of empirical research, though one made more difficult by the secrecy of jury deliberations.[10] In any event, however juries actually respond to different instructions, legally required 'gibberish' is hardly desirable, and if the present law on silence requires it that is a powerful argument for change, though not necessarily in the direction the Committee proposes.

Insofar as Professor Cross maintains that there is no rational basis for distinguishing the instructions a judge may sometimes give from those he may not give concerning a defendant's failure to testify or his earlier silence

[9] Ibid., at 333.
[10] See H. Kalven, Jr., and H. Zeisel, *The American Jury*, Chicago, Univ. of Chicago Press, 1966, pp. 127–30, 177–80.

in response to police questions, I think he is right. It is consistent with this contention, however, that the Committee's proposals would lead in many cases to instructions that are substantially different and rationally distinguishable from those given now, and it would thus be mistaken to treat the Committee's suggestions on permitted inferences as minor repair work. The crucial point is that the judge now enjoys wide discretion; he may instruct in a way that comes pretty close to the Committee proposals, but he may instruct in a way that is widely divergent from them.

Let us look first at a defendant's failure to testify. Under present law the judge, but not the prosecution, may comment. In no circumstances may he suggest that jurors can assume that a defendant is guilty because he has not testified.[11] He may, however, comment strongly on the failure to testify, at least when the evidence is quite damaging to the defendant. In *Nodder* (1937), a case involving the abduction and murder of a small girl, Swift J. commented, 'There is one man in the world who knows the whole story, and when you are trying to elicit that which is true he sits there and never tells you a word'.[12] The judgement of Lord Justice Lawton, a member of the Criminal Law Revision Committee, in *Sparrow* [1973] 2 All E.R. 129, acknowledges that informed opinion at the Bar would now question the propriety of that instruction, but implies that such strong comment is warranted when the evidence implicating a defendant in a crime is persuasive.

Whatever the precise boundaries are of permitted comment, clearly it may go well beyond reminding jurors that they should not necessarily assume a defendant could have rebutted unrebutted evidence or resolved all factual uncertainties in his own favour if he had decided to testify. Such comment would be consistent in theory even with a 'perfect' right to silence since a mere caution not to treat silence like favourable testimony does not invite the jury to draw any adverse inference from silence.[13] But judges may plainly go further and invite the jury to give added weight to the evidence against a defendant because he has failed to answer it. It is the invitation to give this weight, appropriate only when there is already strong evidence against a defendant, that is so hard to distinguish from permitting an inference of guilt.

Comment on silence is often much less damaging to defendants, however.

---

[11] *Mutch* (1973) 57 Cr. App. R. 196, [1973] 1 All E.R. 178; Bathurst (1968) 52 Cr. App. R. 251.

[12] G. Williams, op. cit., n. 4, at 60.

[13] Such a reminder would, for example, be appropriate in a case in which the activities of a dead man were crucial and counsel propounded a theory about them favourable to his clients. The judge might comment that counsel's theory was not the equivalent of sworn testimony, without inviting an obviously inappropriate adverse inference from the dead man's silence.

Another recent judgement by Lord Justice Lawton reviewed the following instruction: 'the jury are entitled to draw inferences unfavourable to the prisoner where he is not called to establish an innocent explanation of facts proved by the prosecution which, without such explanation, tell for his guilt'.[14] The Court of Appeal held this comment inappropriate when the accused's defence was mistaken identification; it indicated that the comment should be limited to cases in which the accused is undisputedly involved in apparently incriminating circumstances but contends that his involvement is innocent. For other cases the court recommended the form of comment suggested in *Bathurst* (1968) 52 Cr. App. R. 251, at p. 257: 'while the jury have been deprived of the opportunity of hearing his story tested in cross-examination, the one thing they must not do is to assume that he is guilty because he has not gone into the witness-box'. The *'Bathurst'* instruction is somewhat ambiguous. It does seem to go beyond merely reminding the jury that it should not treat a suggested version of defendant's activities as if it were supported by sworn testimony by the defendant maintained in the face of cross-examination. But if it also invites the jury to give some weight to the defendant's silence in considering the evidence against him, it does so in the most mild and oblique form and with the counterbalancing statement that guilt should not be assumed.

In many cases judges have modelled their comments on those of Mr. Justice Devlin (now Lord Devlin) in R. v. *Adams* (1957), whose flavour is fairly reflected in the following excerpt: '. . . it would be utterly wrong if you were to regard Dr. Adams' silence as contributing in any way towards proof of guilt. . . .' In *Sparrow* the court regarded these instructions as proper when the case against a defendant is very weak, but it speaks of a 'duty' to comment 'in strong terms' when the evidence is very damaging.[15] Despite this latter dictum it is far from clear that a trial judge, given his extensive discretion, would fail in his duty if he gave a Devlin-like instruction, not because the case against a defendant was weak but because he took a generous view of the scope of the right not to testify.

What is the import of the Committee's proposals? They would have the court or jury 'draw such inferences from the refusal [to testify] as appear proper',[16] proper inferences being 'such as common sense dictates'.[17] In the Committee's view, 'it should be regarded as incumbent on [the defendant] to give evidence in all ordinary cases'. Even defendants who did not wish

[14] *Mutch* (1973) 57 Cr. App. R., at 199.
[15] [1973] 2 All E.R., at 135. For analysis of the weight to be attached to failure to testify in various circumstances, see R. S. O'Regan, 'Adverse Inferences from Failure of an Accused Person to Testify', *Crim. L.R.,* 1965, 711.
[16] Draft Criminal Evidence Bill, § 5 (3).
[17] Criminal Law Revision Committee, *Eleventh Report, Evidence (General)* (1972), § 110.

to testify would actually be called to do so,[18] and would have to refuse to take the stand openly before the jury. Counsel for the prosecution as well as the judge could comment on a refusal to testify.[19] (The Committee also would allow silence to count as corroboration but that suggestion is not crucial to its other suggestions on silence, and I shall put it aside.[20])

If common sense determines the propriety of an adverse inference of guilt, it will ordinarily be warranted, because most innocent people wish to speak in their defence. While the Committee indicates that 'failure to give evidence may be of little or no significance if there is no case against [a defendant] or only a weak one', the unenforceable 'obligation',[21] to testify apparently applies to any case strong enough to go to the jury; and it will be a rare case in which the evidence is so weak that a person exercising only common sense would not draw some inference of guilt from the accused's failure to testify. This does not mean, of course, he will conclude that the defendant is guilty beyond a reasonable doubt, only that he will think the likelihood of guilt greater than if he put the failure to testify out of his mind. If the Committee's standards were conscientiously applied, in many cases the instructions on silence would be markedly more unfavourable for defendants than they are now. The judge would no longer be free to moderate the dictates of 'common sense' by a protective attitude towards silence, which he may now do by stressing that guilt should not be assumed and by declining to invite the jury to give evidential weight to silence or by inviting it in very weak language. And the prosecution's new power to comment on the failure to testify would mean that possible adverse inferences could be suggested to the jury even were the judge not inclined to do so.

In short, the Committee's proposals would significantly alter the actual comments on silence and their likely impact on jurors in many cases, and justification for the proposals must rest on something more than their elimination of the anomalous distinction between what is now permitted in the worst instructions from the defendant's point of view and the now forbidden inference of guilt. Rationalization is, of course, a two-way street. The same anomalous distinction could equally well be removed by forbidding judges ever to instruct that jurors can give additional weight to the

---

[18] Draft Criminal Evidence Bill, § 5(2).

[19] *Eleventh Report,* § 110.

[20] Draft Criminal Evidence Bill, § 5(3). Whether it would be irrational to permit adverse inferences from silence but not to permit silence to count as corroboration is itself an interesting and complex inquiry, but one that would take us too far from the central concerns of this essay. Compare *Eleventh Report,* §§ 40–2, 111, with General Council of the Bar of England and Wales, *Evidence in Criminal Cases,* Memorandum on the Eleventh Report of the Criminal Law Revision Committee, Evidence (General) (1973), §§ 27–9.

[21] *Eleventh Report,* §§ 110, 112.

prosecution's evidence because of the defendant's silence. This is the law in the United States, as a matter of federal constitutional interpretation. Some states including California previously allowed judicial and prosecutorial comment on a defendant's silence, but in a case involving comment similar to that in *Nodder*, the Supreme Court, with two dissenters, held that any invitation to the jury to draw adverse inferences from the defendant's silence was an unconstitutional penalty on the exercise of his right not to testify.[22]

Comparison of the Committee's proposals with the law governing instructions on a suspect's silence in response to police questions yields similar conclusions. The prosecution as well as the judge may now comment on defendant's pre-trial silence, but neither may suggest that the jury may infer guilt from that silence. In *Ryan* (1966) 50 Cr. App. R. 144, 148, the Court of Criminal Appeal considered proper the following kind of comment: 'This accused, as he was entitled to do, has not advanced at any earlier stage the explanation that has been offered to you today; you, the jury may take that into account when you are assessing the weight that you think it right to attribute to the explanation.' This specific language leaves open the reason why the jury may take the earlier failure to speak into account, and a juror thus instructed might well suppose that it is because that failure indicates the story now told is a subsequent fabrication.[23] If the defendant's earlier silence covered the major facts of his defence, as it did in *Ryan*, and not just some peripheral fact, then the inference apparently allowed by *Ryan* that those asserted facts are untrue is indeed not very different from the forbidden inference of guilt, and the stirring defence of that distinction by the Council of the Bar is puzzling.[24] A jury will not often disbelieve the major aspects of a person's defence and still think him innocent.

The leading case before 1966 upholding comment as permissible, *Littleboy* (1934) 24 Cr. App. R. 192, is much narrower than *Ryan*. The defendant had withheld his alibi defence until trial and the trial judge noted that when an alibi is told to the police it gives them 'an opportunity of making their own enquiries to test the truth of the statement', but that by reserving his defence an accused 'deprives the prosecution of any opportunity of testing that statement'. This comment is not free from ambiguity. The word 'deprives' might be taken to imply that a suspect wished not to have his statement tested, from which it might be inferred that the statement is untrue. No doubt by careful choice of words and inflection a judge can intimate that a

---

[22] *Griffin* v. *California*, 380 U.S. 609 (1965).

[23] The language actually reviewed in *Ryan* was much stronger than the court's model language; it rather clearly invited the jury to disbelieve the accused's testimony because he had not before offered an explanation of his apparently incriminating behaviour.

[24] Council of the Bar Memorandum, op. cit., no. 20, § 59.

C.C.P.P.—9*

defendant is lying while following the outline of the *Littleboy* comments. But the main thrust of these comments is quite different and theoretically is consistent with a perfect right to silence. The probability of any story being true becomes greater when it has been thoroughly checked by the police and no gaping holes have been discovered. A judge might remind the jurors that an account presented for the first time has not been subject to the extensive check that would have bolstered its credibility, without implying that defendant's earlier silence may be taken as an indication that the account is untrue.[25] I have seen no direct indication how often a suspect's pre-trial silence is the subject of comment, and whether when it is the comments usually follow *Littleboy* or *Ryan*, but the Criminal Law Revision Committee evidences some question about the general appropriateness of the *Ryan* comments when it indicates they are 'apparently' all right.[26] Since distinguished judges were members of the Committee, perhaps this qualifying doubt is at least a reflection that comments like those in *Ryan* are rather uncommon. English law, like that of most American states, now requires advance notice of alibi defences, so the person raising that defence no longer has Littleboy's option of depriving the police of the opportunity to check his story, but similar comments would be appropriate for other defences not revealed until trial.

Under the Committee proposals the court and jury could draw such inferences 'as appear proper' from the suspect's failure to mention facts later relied on in his defence when he was questioned by the police or charged.[27] From its discussion, one concludes that the Committee would think it appropriate in some settings for a judge to comment to the jury that 'it might well think that if a man is innocent he would be anxious to answer questions', language used in *Sullivan* [1966] 51 Cr. App. R. 102, 104–5, that the Court of Criminal Appeal considered sensible but beyond bounds allowable at present.[28] I agree with Professor Cross that the distinction between *Sullivan* and *Ryan* is hard to defend, but, as with the Committee's suggestions with respect to failure to testify, the 'common sense' standard of proper adverse inferences would mean that many defendants who had been silent at the stages of questioning and charge would be subject to comments substantially more unfavourable than those they would receive now. Again, rationalization is not a sufficient argument for the Committee's proposals; again, rationalization could be equally well accomplished by change in

---

[25] As the judge might try to do, for example, in the case of a witness who had certifiably suffered from amnesia from the time of the relevant events to the day of trial.

[26] *Eleventh Report*, § 29.

[27] Draft Criminal Evidence Bill, § 1.

[28] See more recently R. v. *Lewis*, Court of Appeal, *Crim. L.R.* [1973] 576.

favour of defendants, namely by forbidding any negative comment or by limiting comment to mention of the inability of the police to check facts first asserted at the trial; and again, the law in the United States, where no adverse inference is to be drawn from the suspect's decision to remain silent,[29] reflects rationalization in this direction.

B. *Conflicts With Common Sense*

The Committee's proposals would rationalize the law of evidence in a way the American decisions do not; they would bring the permissible inferences from silence more nearly in line with ordinary understandings of its significance. In personal and private business relationships we expect responses from persons accused of wrongdoing. This is particularly true if the accusation is based on something substantial, but persons often bother to confirm their innocence even when an accusation is farfetched. Silence in the fact of accusation by no means establishes guilt, but it does point in that direction. And given the inevitable pressures to speak on those accused of crime, jurors understandably may believe that the suspect or defendant who remains silent is more likely to be guilty. In *Sullivan* the defendant charged with smuggling watches had refused to answer the questions of Customs officers when the watches were discovered in his bag. The Court of Criminal Appeal rightly supposed that the jurors must have been thinking how odd, if the defendant was innocent, that he did not try to explain what the watches might have been doing in his bag.[30]

It is desirable, other things being equal, that inferences permitted by the law of evidence conform with the rational dictates of common sense, not only because evidence is then more generally accorded its real weight, but also because jurors and magistrates are not required to perform mental gymnastics. Empirical research could shed further light on what assumptions about silence people ordinarily have and on their responsiveness as jurors to instructions that contradict common sense, but few informed persons doubt that negative inferences are drawn in ordinary life and that they are drawn with some frequency by jurors in criminal cases regardless of instructions.

Only a substantial justification can support a rule asking jurors to disregard their own common sense. One possible justification for limiting permissible inferences from silence is the gravity of the danger that inferences drawn by common sense are wrong in particular cases; another is that independent policy reasons underlie a right to silence that requires protection by means of a rule limiting inferences. Whether either of these justifications is adequate is the subject of subsequent parts of this essay.

[29] *Miranda* v. *Arizona*, 384 U.S. 436, 468, n. 37.
[30] 51 Cr. App. R. at p. 105.

A rule that withholds relevant trustworthy evidence from the jury, and makes harder its accurate determination of facts, may also be thought to conflict with common sense, although this kind of rule at least does not require the jurors themselves to refrain from drawing ordinary inferences. The present law in England is that confessions of suspects are not admissible in evidence against them if they are obtained by threat or inducement, or result from oppression. Confessions made after the police have failed to caution suspects or have engaged in improper questioning under the Judges' Rules may also be excluded from evidence, even in the absence of inducement or oppression; the decisions whether to admit these confessions are within the discretion of the trial judges. Somewhat different but similar rules of exclusion govern in the United States; a confession is inadmissible as a matter of constitutional law if it is not 'voluntary' or is given after the police have disregarded the *Miranda* requirements that a suspect in 'custody'[31] not be questioned in the absence of counsel, unless he has been warned of and has voluntarily waived his rights to remain silent and to have the assistance of counsel, which must be provided by the state if he is indigent. (The Supreme Court has actually backtracked somewhat from the original *Miranda* opinion by allowing introduction of statements made after violations of the *Miranda* rules for the limited purpose of attacking the credibility of defendants who give inconsistent accounts at their trials.)[32]

The Committee proposes effective elimination of the warnings in the Judges' Rules, which it rightly concludes are inconsistent with the inferences from silence it would permit; and it would allow much freer scope for police questioning than under existing law. Thus, it would indirectly eliminate failures to conform with the Judges' Rules as grounds of inadmissibility. The Committee also suggests admitting confessions made in response to a threat or inducement unless the threat or inducement was 'of

[31] In *Orozco* v. *Texas*, 394 U.S. 324 (1969), the Supreme Court held the *Miranda* requirements applicable to questioning of a murder suspect regarded as under arrest at 4:00 a.m. in his boarding-house bedroom. Professor Cross suggests that that ruling makes the law look 'an ass' (R. Cross, op. cit., note 8, at 330). Whatever the wisdom of this extension of *Miranda* to the field, it hardly follows that the original absolute rules for station-house questioning are necessarily unsound.

[32] *Harris* v. *New York*, 401 U.S. 222 (1971). This decision, in Professor Cross's view, makes the law look 'a hypocrite'. Cross, op. cit., note 8, at 330. The *Miranda* decision was by a narrow 5–4 majority. The Supreme Court's membership had shifted by the time of *Harris* so that a majority were no longer sympathetic to the original decision. Each remaining member of the original majority dissented from the new majority's limitation on *Miranda*'s application. Perhaps the law is always a hypocrite when the majority of a court are unsympathetic to the doctrine of an old case and instead of overruling it outright cut it back by drawing a distinction that is not fully persuasive. But, again, this hardly establishes that the original doctrine was unsound.

a sort likely, in the circumstances existing at the time, to render unreliable any confession which might be made . . .'.[33] As far as rules of evidence themselves are concerned, admitting 'reliable' confessions obviously conforms with common sense. The Committee itself, in declining to take the further step of admitting reliable confessions obtained after oppression or of admitting all confessions and leaving the determination of reliability to the jury,[34] acknowledged the need to curb improper police practices. The crucial questions about the present strict rule on threats and inducements are whether it is needed for the same purpose or to protect the right to silence.

C. *Conflicts Between Legal Rules and the Common Practice of Those To Whom They are Directed*

In both England and the United States most observers believe that there are substantial failures by the police to comply with rules protecting silence. Sometimes their import is evaded. In England suspects may be invited in rather strong terms 'to help the police with their enquiries'; in the United States warnings are often given in a way that minimizes likely comprehension. Sometimes outright violations occur. The police may invent damaging admissions, called 'verbals' in England, or obtain actual confessions by using impermissible methods that are later denied in court. Since the police may wish to conceal violations, researchers cannot establish the precise degree of noncompliance, but close study of interactions between the police and suspects can certainly contribute to a more accurate picture of what takes place. Observations of police practices and interviews with policemen and suspects after the *Miranda* decision were surprisingly productive in showing police responses to the rules it established.[35] In England, Michael Zander had shown convincingly through interviews with convicted defendants that access to solicitors by suspects in custody is denied by the police much more frequently than the limited reasons for denial specified in the preamble to the Judges' Rules would appear to warrant.[36]

[33] Draft Criminal Evidence Bill, § 2(2).

[34] A minority of the Committee members proposed this course, believing that jurors can weigh the value of a confession fairly and that inadmissibility has little deterrent effect on police improprieties. *Eleventh Report*. §§ 62–3.

[35] See 'Interrogations in New Haven: The Impact of *Miranda*', *Yale L.J.*, 1967, **76**, 1519; R. J. Medalie, L. Zeitz and P. Alexander, 'Custodial Police Interrogation in Our Nation's Capital: The Attempt to Implement Miranda', *Mich. L. Rev.*, 1968, **66**, 1347.

[36] M. Zander, 'Access to a Solicitor in the Police Station', *Crim. L. Rev.*, [1972], 342. Seventy-four per cent of the convicted defendants who reported requesting a solicitor also reported that the police denied their request. Since Mr. Zander relied exclusively on their statements, and, as he acknowledges, some of them may have been untrue, the actual percentage of requests denied may be somewhat lower, but even if the reported figure is a good bit inaccurate, access to a solicitor is being denied with disturbing frequency.

Since a wide discrepancy between the law and common practice is generally thought to breed cynicism and disrespect for legal rules, one way to rationalize the law is to bring rule and practice into congruence. One approach to remedying an apparently unacceptable gap between rule and practice is to free the police to do what they think is reasonable. Under the Committee's proposals, the discrepancy between the legal model of investigation and present police views of what should happen would be much less great. No warning would be required before a suspect is charged, and the warning given then would encourage revelation of facts to be relied on in one's defence. Another way to remedy this kind of gap is to encourage better compliance with existing rules by education, more severe sanctions, and closer surveillance of the process, for example by recording conversations between suspects and policemen. This approach is not necessarily inconsistent with relaxation of the rules themselves, and a minority of the Committee would make implementation of the Committee's suggestions to alter the rights of suspects contingent on a pervasive system of accurate recordings of suspects' conversations with policemen at the station-house.[37]

One risk of the 'relaxation' remedy is that police attitudes and practices will shift with the rules themselves. It is possible that engaged as they are in the pursuit of criminals, the police will almost always think the rules set by society at large too inhibiting, and that they will strain and even break whatever rules are imposed.[38] Under this hypothesis, a gap between rule and practice is inevitable, and the rules should be set with that gap in mind. A researcher can judge how police respond to either kind of remedy only if he has a reasonable picture of previous as well as subsequent practice. Empirical data, including studies of police attitudes, may also contribute to predictions about the effects of proposed changes, but these are necessarily more uncertain.

D. *Distinctions That Are Unsound in Practice*
Some distinctions drawn by the law make sense, but are too elusive to apply in practice or too easily subject to having their purpose evaded. The Judges' Rules require an initial caution that the suspect need not speak when the 'officer has evidence which would afford reasonable grounds for suspecting that a person has committed an offence'.[39] This point is very hard to

[37] *Eleventh Report*, § 52.

[38] If police attitudes and practices are influenced by administrative rules and applicable court decisions but remain 'tougher' than those rules and decisions, a decision forbidding any custodial interrogation without counsel may, for example, at least persuade the police that physical coercion is wrong.

[39] Rule II. See R. v. *Osborne*, Court of Appeal, *The Times*, Dec. 12, 1972, p. 12. col. 1, on what constitutes 'evidence' on which reasonable suspicion is based.

determine, and the fact that it may be reached at a time when a caution would seriously interrupt the flow of questioning may encourage officers to postpone the caution in some instances. The second caution, and in most cases, termination of questioning are supposed to occur when a 'person is charged . . . or informed that he may be charged'.[40] This is much more objective, but lends itself to police manipulation by delays of charge until useful questioning is finished.[41] The exceptions the rules create to the termination of questioning[42] are themselves so general that they provide only a limited restraint on police discretion.

Empirical research like Mr. Zander's can amplify understanding of the application of the rules in practice, but much is already known about the difficulties with some of the lines drawn in the Judges' Rules, which would be eliminated by the Committee's proposals. Again, however, as with many of the other matters thus far discussed, identifying defects in the present law does not establish the direction of desirable change, and most of the dubious standards could be scrapped equally easily by expanding the rights of suspects.

Silence and the Determination of Guilt and Innocence

The major argument in the *Eleventh Report* for its proposed changes in the right to silence is that they will contribute to the conviction of the guilty, and particularly to the conviction of sophisticated professional criminals.[43] Opponents of the changes emphasize the danger that they will lead to the conviction of the innocent, a danger the Committee does not believe is real.

A moderate understanding of the criminal process can carry us some of the way in establishing the effect of the right to silence on accurate determinations of guilt. Some crimes, where physical evidence is inconclusive and neither a victim nor another witness can make a convincing identification, can be solved only if a suspect confesses or makes damaging admissions. When for example, a murder is committed by a family member or close acquaintance the evidence against a person strongly suspected may be inconclusive without his admissions. Some suspects admit their guilt spontaneously but apart from situations in which someone is caught 'red-

---

[40] Rule III.

[41] In *Collier* (1965) 49 Cr. App. R. 344; [1965] 3 All E. R. 136, the court declined to hold that the police must stop questioning when they have a basis for charging a suspect. There is a description of how charges were delayed in the Moors Murder case in R. N. Gooderson, 'The Interrogation of Suspects', *Canadian Bar Review*, **48**, 270, 281–8 (1970).

[42] Rule III (b).

[43] *Eleventh Report*, §§ 21 (vi), 30.

handed', admissions in response to police questioning are much more frequent, at least in the United States. The questioning may expose palpable contradictions in the suspect's story or at least persuade him of his inability to maintain a plausible account of his innocence; or it may 'resolve' his psychological conflicts between concealing his guilt and making a clean breast of it.[44] Under existing practices, the level of confessions is fairly high. The ordinary willingness to respond initially to police questions is largely a consequence of 'natural' pressures to appear innocent and co-operative. But often it is also a consequence of ignorance; ignorance, despite a warning, of the full significance of the right to silence, or ignorance of the significance of some kinds of admissions. The latter may occur when a suspect wrongly supposes that oral statements can not be used against him or fails to understand that one who drives the getaway car for armed robbers is as culpable as those who commit the robbery.

Some suspects remain silent. Increased pressures to speak to the police would result in fewer instances of silence and, therefore, in more damaging admissions and confessions; and since those who admit their guilt typically plead guilty in the hope of a lighter sentence, the percentage of cases resolved without a trial, already over 70 per cent, would probably rise. If juries were invited to draw broader adverse inferences the conviction rate of those who did not speak and went to trial would increase somewhat. The vast majority of those who admit their guilt and are convicted are in fact guilty, and the vast majority of those who would admit their guilt because of the Committee's proposed changes would also be guilty. Conceivably a few guilty but silent suspects who are now convicted might 'talk their way out' if forced to speak to the police, but these instances must be very rare. Thus a contraction of the right to silence at the stages of investigation and charge would result in more convictions of the guilty.

Greater pressures to speak at the trial would probably have a similar effect. However, since many lawyers in England already advise most defendants to take the stand in order to avoid a negative judgement by jurors, and the effect of testimony by those who now remain silent is problematic, the impact on conviction of the guilty of the Committee's proposed changes in the right not to testify is less certain and almost surely slighter.

All this is non-controversial. The real debate is over the percentage of cases in which admissions of the guilty are needed for conviction, and

---

[44] On the strong psychological pressures to confess, sometimes felt even by persons who are completely innocent, see T. Reik, *The Compulsion to Confess: On the Psychoanalysis of Crime and Punishment*, New York, Farrar, Straus & Cudahy, 1959; Driver, op. cit., note 5, at 57–8.

obtainable. Though this is an empirical question, it is rarely possible to answer with certainty whether any particular conviction would have been lost without a confession or whether any silent suspect not prosecuted or not convicted was in fact guilty and would have been induced to confess by now impermissible tactics. And general statistics on convictions and acquittals are by themselves not very revealing, either about how many guilty people escape conviction[45] or about how often their silence contributes to that escape. A study in Pittsburgh, Pennsylvania, after the *Miranda* decision, employed the more useful approach of correlating guilty pleas and convictions to confessions and comparing the rates of confessions and convictions before and after the changes in the right to silence dictated by the Supreme Court's decision.[46] In a New Haven, Connecticut, study, law students observed police interrogations in many cases and interviewed detectives, prosecutors, defendants and defence attorneys about the cases.[47] They estimated that confessions would be necessary for conviction in twelve out of the ninety cases they observed (and in some other cases the evidence was so clear the police did not bother with interrogation); confessions were actually obtained in forty-nine cases, but these included only four of the cases in which confessions were deemed 'necessary'.[48] The New Haven study was done shortly after *Miranda* and the police were inconsistent about giving the required warnings; the observers judged that the warnings did not in any way reduce the success of interrogation in more than 10 per cent of the cases in which they were given. In Pittsburgh, the rate of confessions in cases handled by the detective branch dropped from nearly half to just over a quarter; the authors estimated that confessions were 'necessary' for conviction roughly one-fifth of the time. One interesting conclusion of the New Haven study was that confessions were more often crucial for getting the names of accomplices or tracking down stolen goods than for conviction of those confessing.[49]

Impressionistic as the conclusions of these studies are, they do indicate persuasively that in the great majority of cases in which the police have focussed their attention on a particular suspect, they have sufficient evidence

---

[45] See Council of the Bar Memorandum, § 67; A Muir, 'The Rules of the Game', *Crim. L.R.,* [1973], 341–2.

[46] R. H. Seeburger and R. S. Wettick, Jr., '*Miranda* in Pittsburgh—A Statistical Study', *Univ. Pitt. Rev.,* 1967, **29,** 1.

[47] 'Interrogations in New Haven: The Impact of *Miranda*', *Yale L.J.,* 1967, **76,** 1519.

[48] Ibid., at 1584–9. The twelve cases in which interrogation was deemed important included two in which the suspects were 'probably innocent', two in which the 'necessity' of a confession derived from the unwillingness of the police to use an informer at the trial, and three in which detectives already had sufficient evidence to obtain a conviction for a lesser offence.

[49] Ibid., at 1580, 1594–6.

to obtain a conviction without getting a confession. Warnings about the right to silence affect the ability of the police to get confessions in a minority of cases. Even if these studies produced more authoritative and precise estimates than they do, they could not be transposed confidently to the English situation for a host of reasons,[50] but the exercise is worth undertaking simply to give the grossest kind of idea of the magnitude of change in convictions of the guilty which the adoption of the Committee's proposals might cause. Suppose, to take the Pittsburgh estimates, 20 per cent more of those arrested as suspects would confess[51] if the warnings of the Judges' Rules were replaced as the Committee suggests; and suppose that in 20 per cent of these cases confessions were necessary for conviction;[52] out of one hundred suspects arrested, four more would be convicted than are now. If, to use the New Haven estimates, the elimination of the present warnings affected only 10 per cent of those questioned and confessions are 'necessary' in less than 13 per cent of the cases of those arrested, the increase in convictions would be little more than one per cent of those arrested. Even if the proposed comments to the jury regarding silent suspects and defendants caused a further slight increase in convictions, there would be no vast increase in the percentage of guilty persons convicted. Whether, as the Committee supposes, sophisticated criminals take more frequent advantage of the right to silence than others, the Council of the Bar may well be right that the main reason they escape conviction is because the cases against them are often weak;[53] and one might guess that these professional criminals will

[50] The percentage of 'necessary' confessions is affected by the kinds of crimes committed, the methods of investigation other than interrogation, the willingness of witnesses to testify and the willingness of the police to use certain witnesses, such as informers. A correspondence on these matters cannot be assumed for different areas within one country, let alone different countries. The *Miranda* warning is more thorough than the warnings of the Judges' Rules; and the right of a suspect to counsel is absolute in the United States but not in England. On the other hand the American police probably have more latitude in interrogating suspects who have waived their right to silence than the English police have. For these reasons, it cannot be assumed that the American warnings have the same effect on American interrogations as English warnings on English interrogations. Moreover, the Committee proposals cannot properly be treated simply as eliminating existing warnings, since the suspect would be informed that silence might count against him.

[51] I have not seen a general estimate of the rate of confessions in England. Over a three-year period, an astonishing ninety-four per cent of those convicted for homosexual offences confessed in writing, see P. Devlin, *The Criminal Prosecution in England*, London, Oxford U.P., 1960, p. 49, but the rate for most other offences must be much lower.

[52] Presumably the resistance to confessing is usually greater when the police have less evidence against a suspect, that is when a confession would be 'necessary'. Whether any given contraction in the right to silence would have more or less impact on interrogations in which confessions are necessary than on those in which they are not is difficult or impossible to guess, so I am assuming in the text the same impact.

[53] Council of the Bar Memorandum, § 63.

also lie more successfully than the average culprit if faced with increased pressures to speak.

What is the likely effect of an increased conviction rate of this general magnitude upon the rate of crime itself? According to Sir Leon Radzinowicz probably only about 15 per cent of the crimes committed are reported;[54] Howard Jones believes the figure is about 25 per cent.[55] In only about a quarter of the crimes reported are arrests made.[56] The percentages are higher than this for more serious crimes and lower for less serious ones, but even for the most serious offences, arrests follow crimes only in a minority of cases.[57] Insofar as increases in confessions lead to increases in identification of accomplices, a limitation of the right to silence would have some impact on the rate of arrests but probably not a major one. Whatever the precise effects on arrests and convictions of a cut-back in the right to silence, the odds that a person will be convicted of a particular crime will rise only infinitesimally, certainly not enough to affect his decision whether to commit it. Of course, if more guilty persons are convicted, more will be isolated and temporarily unable to commit other crimes. And it is also possible that a publicized change towards 'toughness' in the criminal process might have some diffuse deterrent effect on the attitudes of potential criminals. Even a slight increase in convictions of the guilty is to be welcomed, especially since public confidence in the administration of justice is shaken seriously when persons assumed to be guilty cannot be convicted, but it would be fatuous to believe that moderate changes in the right to silence will significantly influence the rate of crime.

How much protection the innocent get from the right to silence is even harder to estimate than its probable effect on the guilty. Most jurisdictions in the United States routinely allow evidence of prior crimes to impeach defendants who testify, and this practice frightens many previously convicted but innocent defendants from taking the stand.[58] England does not labour

[54] L. Radzinowicz, 'The Criminal in Society', *J. Royal Soc. Arts,* 1964, **112**, 916–29.
[55] H. Jones, *Crime in a Changing Society* Harmondsworth, Penguin Books, 1965, p. 18. See generally R. Hood and R. Sparks, *Key Issues in Criminology*, London, World Univ. Lib., 1970, pp. 11–45.
[56] Cf. ibid., at 16, for a table comparing crimes estimated to have been committed with convictions in England; testimony of James Vorenberg, Hearings on H. Res. 17 before the Select Committee on Crime of the House of Representatives, 91st Cong., 1st Sess. 267, 271–8 (1969), summarizing conclusions about American crime of the Report of the Commission on Law Enforcement and Administration of Justice.
[57] Cf. Hood and Sparks, op. cit., n. 5, at 16.
[58] See W. Schaefer, *The Suspect and Society* Evanston, Northwestern U.P., 1967, pp. 67–68. The fact that many innocent defendants may be afraid to take the stand in the United States strengthens the arguments there for protecting silent defendants from adverse inferences.

under this unjust rule, but some few innocent defendants still must refrain from testifying for fear they will make a bad showing. Assuming that they are now receiving sound advice from counsel, the effect of more substantial adverse inferences from silence and the resulting increase in pressure to testify is more likely to be hurtful than helpful. It is impossible to know how many innocent defendants who are now silent and acquitted would make such a bad showing on the stand they would be convicted, but the number must be small. In the United States a study indicated that 82 per cent of the defendants, and 91 per cent of those not liable to impeachment by prior conviction, testified.[59] One might expect the figure to be even higher in England, where adverse comment is still a possibility. If so, it must be very few innocent defendants who do not testify, and fewer still whose acquittals would have turned into convictions had they testified.

Silence in response to police questioning or at the time of charge may prevent an innocent person from being cleared as fast as he might and it may result in unnecessary detention, but it will rarely increase the chances of his conviction.[60] He still has the opportunity after consulting counsel to tell his story well enough before trial so it can be checked, and thus can avoid the jury's giving his defence less weight because the police have had no opportunity to investigate it. When counsel advises silence until trial, we must assume that the benefits of earlier disclosure probably do not outweigh the benefits of surprise.

If initial silence rarely leads to convictions of the innocent it need not follow that innocent persons really require silence; perhaps earlier statements would do them no substantial harm. Bentham and others have assumed that innocent persons will want to establish their innocence as soon as possible. No doubt this is usually true. But in a fair number of cases the line between guilt and innocence is not clear.[61] A suspect who kills in response to an

---

[59] See Kalven & Zeisel, op. cit., n. 10, at 137, 146.

[60] With respect to cases where the crime itself or the suspect's possible involvement is minor enough to make non-prosecution a serious option, the police may be more inclined to drop a case against someone who has made a plausible assertion of innocence than against someone who remains silent; in that context an initial decision to remain silent might conceivably lead to a conviction.

[61] In *The Jury At Work*, Occasional Paper Number Four of the Oxford University Penal Research Unit (1972), Sarah McCabe and Roger Purves concluded, after observation of jury trials at selected courts of Quarter Session and Assize, that 80 of the 115 defendants who were acquitted admitted 'being involved in something which could have been interpreted as criminal activity' but claimed that 'this involvement did not amount to a crime' (p. 41). Some of these factual settings were ones in which the line between innocence and guilt was murky and an innocent defendant might have hurt himself by talking to the police, but more typical were cases in which the issue was quite clear and an initial explanation to the police by an innocent person would not have been likely to have been harmful. For example, in a shop-lifting case one would not suppose

attack by an angered acquaintance or one who is peripherally involved in some fraudulent scheme may not know whether he has committed a crime. Though in fact innocent of a crime, he may reasonably fear that responding fully to police questions will make prosecution and conviction more likely. The danger that this may happen is increased by the possibilities that under intensive questioning he will make some slightly inaccurate but very damaging admission whose significance he does not understand, or that he may even come to believe his degree of guilt was greater than it actually was. Further risks are that the police will understand him to have admitted something he has not, or that believing him guilty, they will fabricate an admission of guilt. Since silence may be quite important for uncounseled suspects who have come close to the borderline of criminal activity, a contraction of the pre-trial right to silence might do them considerable harm. By allowing broader adverse inferences to be drawn from silence, the Committee would make silence evidentially much more significant than it is now. This change would amplify the existing opportunities for inaccurate evidence resulting from police misunderstanding of what a suspect has or has not said. It is doubtful if the police would often engage in outright lies that suspects remained silent when in face they spoke, since fabricated admissions would still be more damaging to defendants than fabricated silence and almost as easy to invent. But a genuine failure of communication might lead an officer to think a suspect unresponsive when in fact he failed to understand a question. Or, a suspect might make cryptic mention of a fact that is passed over by the officer because it seems unimportant. Later in the investigation when the significance of the fact emerges, the officer might forget the suspect's earlier mention of it and mistakenly recall that nothing had been said about it.

A minority of the Committee were concerned enough about inaccurate versions of what transpires during police questioning to suggest that the Committee's proposals should not be put into effect until a general system of station-house recording exists.[62] This change, despite the reservations of the Committee majority about its feasibility,[63] would be a substantial protection for the innocent that might well be worthwhile whether or not the law governing silence is altered.[64]

---

that a shopper who had actually forgotten that she had unpaid goods under her arm would be led into making slips or damaging admissions if she told that to the police when accused by the store-owner.

[62] *Eleventh Report*, § 52.

[63] Ibid., at §§ 50–1.

[64] See C. J. Miller, 'Silence and Confessions—What Are They Worth?' *Crim. L.R.,* [1973], 343, 350.

There is a special kind of circumstance in which the right to silence may hurt the innocent. That is when an innocent person is convicted because a guilty person remains silent in response to police questioning and refuses to incriminate himself at the trial instead of establishing the defendant's innocence. One of the most distinguished jurists in the United States, Judge Friendly of the United States Court of Appeals for the Second Circuit, has urged that because of such situations the innocent are more often harmed than aided by the right to silence,[65] but one wonders how he reaches this conclusion. If the guilty suspects who now remain silent are forced to talk, they may do their best to cast the blame on others, including possibly innocent defendants and other innocent people previously unsuspected. Of course, falsehoods in their statements may be exposed, but on other occasions their attempt to throw the dirt on someone else will be successful. Greater pressures on guilty persons to talk will almost certainly aid conviction of other guilty people; indeed this is the rationale for granting immunity (indemnity) to some suspects involved in complex crimes. But whether these pressures would lead to more or fewer convictions of others who are not guilty is uncertain. My own guess would be that if innocent suspects did benefit on balance from the pressures on other suspects to speak, that benefit would not offset the damage done to them more directly by a retraction in their own right to silence.

We can tentatively conclude that limits on the right to silence will increase the numbers of guilty persons convicted but will also increase to a much smaller extent convictions of the innocent. That leads to the crucial and non-empirical question what the acceptable 'trade-off' is between the two kinds of convictions. The Committee's comment that 'It is as much in the public interest that a guilty person should be convicted as it is that an innocent person should be acquitted'[66] fails to give due regard to the deep belief that acquittal of the guilty is more tolerable than conviction of the innocent. The Council of the Bar, on the other hand, in suggesting that society should assure 'certain acquittal of the factually innocent',[67] proposes a standard that is unattainable and obviously out of line with convictions now rendered on less than certain evidence, such as momentary eye-witness identifications. Nevertheless, given the rather limited effect at best these proposals are likely to have on the commission of crimes, the possibility that they might prejudice some innocent suspects counts heavily against them, at least in the absence of some substantial offsetting protections for the innocent such as

[65] H. Friendly, 'The Fifth Amendment Tomorrow: The Case for Constitutional Change', *U. Cinn. L. Rev.,* 1968, **37,** 671, 680–1.

[66] *Eleventh Report,* § 27.

[67] Council of the Bar Memorandum, § 4.

those proposed by the Committee minority for recording station-house questioning.

The Right to Silence and Basic Individual Rights

The right to silence has often been defended as an inherent right of free people,[68] worth preserving regardless of its effects on accurate determinations of guilt. Few would disagree that some methods of obtaining statements, such as physical torture, extreme deprivation of sleep, and interminable questioning, are so abhorrent to liberal notions of individual autonomy they would be morally unacceptable in ordinary criminal investigations even if the admissions they produced were consistently reliable. What is at issue is whether it would be morally objectionable to discourage silence by legal sanctions such as confinement for contempt or adverse inferences about the credibility of an account of innocence not testified to at trial or withheld at earlier stages in the criminal process. Insofar as the argument is that protections against these sanctions are needed as safeguards against deteriorations of police techniques, it is dealt with in the next section; what is of concern here is whether the Committee is right to reject the simple contention that requiring someone to accuse himself is intrinsically unfair.

In ordinary social relationships between family members, friends and business associates, a person who has a substantial basis for thinking that another has caused unjustifiable injury often asks the 'suspect' whether or not he has done so, and the questioner expects a response. Suspicion does not confer a right to coerce an acquaintance by physical force or extreme browbeating, but if he declines to talk without giving a persuasive reason why he remains silent, it is ordinarily inferred that he is 'guilty'. The person who remains adamantly silent in the face of an accusation that he has shown contempt for a friend behind his back is likely to lose the friend; the teller who makes no effort to defend against the charge that he has taken money from the till is likely to lose his job. And few would think anything morally objectionable in the friend and the employer acting on the inference of probable guilt.

The situation is different when persons are questioned about possible guilt on the basis of flimsy rumour or as a part of a systematic effort to uncover previously unsuspected crimes. Many persons will wish to establish their

---

[68] In the United States, the Fifth Amendment establishes the privilege against self-incrimination as a fundamental legal right, and lawyers and judges interpreting the law must start from this premise. But it does not necessarily follow that the protections the Amendment affords are based on fundamental moral or social rights.

innocence clearly even in response to malicious rumours, and employees of some companies in the United States periodically take lie detector tests to ascertain if they have been up to anything wrong. But an outraged subject may well assert that he will not respond to unfounded rumours or 'fishing expeditions' and his claim that no one can justifiably treat him as guilty because he remains silent would be widely accepted. The moral basis for a right to silence in these situations is in part the general interest in privacy; persons should not have to expose matters they wish to keep private unless a substantial interest in exposure has been demonstrated. There is also the further special notion that since the commission of anti-social actions is a failing of most of humanity[69] people may be made nervous and insecure if they have to come forward to produce the initial evidence against themselves or demonstrate their innocence when no one has good reason to think they are guilty. Those subjected to periodic innocence-establishing examinations may also forfeit the sense of dignity that comes from being trusted.[70] Thus, the periodic lie detector test is objectionable even if employees are asked only about possible actions that, if they had occurred, would be the legitimate concern of the company.

If in ordinary relationships there is no 'right to silence' in response to substantial charges, do the state-individual relationship and the penalties of the criminal law change the moral assessment? By the time one has been committed for trial, a substantial basis for the charges against him has been demonstrated; compelling trial testimony is not inherently wrong unless it is made so by some special aspect of the administration of criminal justice. In a leading Fifth Amendment case, Justice Goldberg wrote for the majority of 'our unwillingness to subject those suspected of crime to the cruel trilemma of self-accusation, perjury or contempt'.[71] It may be thought immoral to force a defendant to tell the truth and be convicted, remain silent and be subject to contempt penalties, or perjure himself. The argument used to be made that it was wrong to give an individual so strong a temptation to lie under oath, thereby damning himself; but even for those modern witnesses for whom the oath itself has little intrinsic significance, the chance of being exposed as a liar, or possibly prosecuted for perjury,[72] is still enough to

[69] See Hood & Sparks, op. cit., n. 55, at 46–63, summarizing studies that indicate that a very small percentage of the population indeed denies ever committing criminal acts.

[70] Cf. C. Fried, *An Anatomy of Values*, Cambridge, Mass., Harvard U.P., 1970, pp. 137–52.

[71] *Murphy* v. *Waterfront Commission*, 378 U.S. 52, 55 (1964).

[72] Presumably defendants are not often later prosecuted for perjury. If they are clearly lying they are likely to be convicted in the first place. If they are believed by the jury, it will usually be difficult to establish that they have lied, and to prosecute for perjury may seem too close to trying a man twice for the same offence. Insofar as the 'trilemma' is

make the trilemma a cruel one. It is considerably modified but by no means eliminated if the consequence of silence is not a contempt penalty but a substantial adverse inference. However, compulsory testimony often forces cruel choices on individuals. A defendant in a civil case, if he is to avoid perjury or contempt, may have to admit actions that mean a crippling civil liability for him, a witness in a criminal case may have to admit highly embarrassing activities and see his words 'convict' an intimate friend or even family member. The choice may usually be even more painful for the criminal defendant faced with jail, but so long as a society judges rightly that its interests justify the 'cruelty' of jail sentences for criminals, the 'cruelty' of putting pressure on defendants to testify does not render the practice inherently immoral.

A somewhat different contention is that defendants should not be penalized for silence because the proper balance between the state and the individual requires that the state 'shoulder the entire load' of proving guilt.[73] This contention is not very persuasive, unless it rests on assumptions about harmful indirect effects of putting greater pressure on defendants to speak. If the state has the burden of making out a substantial case against an accused, and if conviction requires belief in guilt 'beyond a reasonable doubt', it is hard to understand why proper relationships between the individual and the government are breached by asking a defendant to give his own account of the relevant facts or have natural inferences drawn from his refusal to do so.

The simple fact that state prosecution for crime is involved is not a sufficient basis for establishing a right to silence in the face of substantial charges which does not exist in ordinary social relationships. There is, however, very good reason for giving legal recognition to the moral right to remain silent in the absence of substantial charges. Even during the worst days of the Holy Inquisition, Aquinas and other canon law authorities wrote that persons should not be required to confess to hidden crimes whose existence was unknown, and the theory was maintained that persons brought before the Inquisition had been 'accused' in some manner, even if only by vehement suspicion or common report.[74] In England those who early refused to take the oath ex officio and answer questions put by the prerogative courts claimed a right not to respond in the absence of due

---

troublesome because of the possibility of a perjury prosecution, it might make sense, as Professor Cross has suggested in correspondence, to immunize an accused from that danger.

[73] *Tehan* v. *Shott*, 382 U.S. 406, 415 (1966); 8 Wigmore, *Evidence* (McNaughton rev. 1961) 317.

[74] See L. Levy, *Origins of the Fifth Amendment*, New York, Oxford U.P., 1968, pp. 95–6.

accusation;[75] only later was a right not to incriminate themselves asserted by those who had been indicted. Despite the interrogation of suspects by magistrates well after the privilege against self-incrimination was established, there are, therefore, some analogues in legal history to the moral right to remain silent in the absence of substantial charges.

Pressure on suspects to respond to police questioning may violate this moral right to silence. The matter is complicated somewhat if one accepts, as I believe any thoughtful person must, the notions that people have a social duty to aid the police in solving crimes and that they should ordinarily respond helpfully to police inquiries, even if they are effectively free of legal obligation in this respect. In many cases initial police questioning of relevant persons is part of a general investigation of what happened. By the time the police treat someone primarily as a suspect rather than a possible witness, that is are questioning him primarily to establish his own guilt or innocence, they usually have a substantial basis for thinking him guilty. If someone is discovered in compromising circumstances he will of course be a suspect from the beginning of an investigation, but then also there is a substantial basis for thinking him guilty. Unfortunately, however, if adverse inferences could be drawn from silence as the Committee proposes, there would still be circumstances in which a person might be under pressure to incriminate himself or to respond to charges before there is a substantial basis for thinking him guilty. When a person is being questioned as part of a general investigation and realizes that a true answer to a particular question will incriminate him, he now has the right not to answer it, although he has received no warning of his right to silence. The Committee would allow juries to draw adverse inferences from a refusal to answer questions in this context. Also, the police sometimes treat people as suspects well before there is substantial evidence against them. The jury could draw adverse inferences from a suspect's failure at this early point to answer questions designed to elicit his guilt or innocence.

It might be suggested that the Committee has largely met this objection by limiting the occasions on which silence can lead to adverse inferences. These can be drawn only from a suspect's failure 'to mention any fact relied on in his defence' which he 'could reasonably have been expected to mention'.[76] How significant are these limitations? It is an unusual case in which the prosecution has presented enough evidence to go to the jury and defence counsel is still so confident of the weakness of the evidence against the defendant that no evidence for the defence is presented. If the defence does produce evidence and this goes beyond merely casting doubt on the

[75] Ibid., at 62.
[76] Draft Criminal Evidence Bill, § 1(1).

prosecution's evidence, the crucial facts relied on will typically be within the knowledge of the defendant, whether he or someone else testifies to them at trial, and would cover matters he might well have revealed earlier to the authorities.

When would a defendant not 'reasonably have been expected to mention' exculpating facts later relied on at his trial? He might contend that it would be unreasonable to expect him to give an account of his activities before the evidence against him was substantial, but in most circumstances most people would do just that, wishing to clear themselves as quickly as possible from any hint of suspicion. Thus if the standard of reasonableness is what people ordinarily do, an innocent person questioned by the police could reasonably be expected to exculpate himself at an early stage of the investigation.[77] Now, a judge might conceivably conclude that whatever people usually do, a person should not have to give an account of his activities at that point and that therefore it would not be reasonable to have expected him to do so. But the Committee gives no indication that its 'reasonable expectation' standard incorporates respect for a moral right to silence or indeed, is meant to be anything other than a shorthand for common sense understandings of how people usually act.

Even if silence at preliminary stages can sometimes count against a defendant, a particular defendant may, of course, try to persuade a court or jury that no inference is proper in his case because he felt strongly he should not respond to insubstantial charges. But a judge or jury might view with scepticism the suggestion that a defendant against whom substantial evidence exists at the time of trial first remained silent because of the absence of such evidence. Moreover, persons questioned often do not know what information the police have, so even if silence in the face of insubstantial accusations were never harmful, suspects would sometimes overestimate the case against them and feel under pressure for that reason.

In summary, the Committee's proposals about silence in response to police questions contain nothing approximating the 'probable cause' safeguard of search and seizure law. Persons may be later penalized by a jury for refusing to answer questions before probable cause of guilt exists. In practice the addition of this pressure to speak may be slight in comparison with the natural and inevitable pressures to do so, but this legally approved pressure would conflict with the moral right to remain silent in the absence of substantial charges.

[77] An exception may be some cases in which at the trial the defendant acknowledges some degree of participation in an apparently criminal activity, but claims his involvement was innocent. If he had been questioned before any involvement on his part was established, he understandably might not have made the damaging admissions that are an integral part of his exculpatory account.

This moral argument is not a conclusive one against the Committee's proposals. Violation of the moral right in a few cases might be thought an acceptable price for pressure in the greater number of cases in which a substantial case against a suspect does exist, it being unfeasible to try to draw a line between the two. Or, the need to solve crimes might be thought to outweigh the interest in silence even when the moral claim is applicable. But if the moral argument is not conclusive, it does reveal a serious objection to allowing silence before the police to be treated as incriminating.

One other matter requires discussion in this section. Is reliance on ignorance and weakness to obtain statements morally objectionable? Insofar as the legal system is a contrivance to resolve actual disputes, the forfeiture of rights through ignorance is not a problem, and the right to silence could be viewed as the system's grudging concession to the recalcitrant. Insofar as legal rights define a desirable norm in social relations, it is unfortunate if individuals are unaware of their rights or too weak to act rationally with respect to them, even though informing them may take some effort and even create psychological conflicts that have not previously existed. Forfeiture through ignorance and weakness inevitably also reflects inequality of rights in practice, since the intelligent and strong will enjoy rights that others will not. Even when warned, many suspects remain ignorant of the real significance of the right to silence and the right to counsel and of the import of admissions they may make. Many are psychologically vulnerable to persistent questioning and other ploys that are within legal bounds. The spirit of the warnings required by the Judges' Rules and the *Miranda* decision is that suspects should not forfeit rights through ignorance and should be placed on a roughly equal footing,[78] but the warnings alone do not have those effects. It is indeed hard to think of anything short of representation by competent counsel that would have such effects, though allowing questioning of suspects only in front of magistrates would moderate present inequalities.

Judgements can reasonably differ about the respective importance of obtaining useful statements and having informed decisions and approximate equality in respect to the right to silence. I would give considerable weight to the latter.[79] From this perspective, the Committee's proposed inferences from silence are not objectionable since they treat all suspects and defendants equally and allow a rational judgement to determine whether speech or silence is preferable; its suggestions that the first warning be delayed until

[78] Warnings also reduce the plausibility of many later claims that statements were not made voluntarily. See P. Devlin, op. cit., note 51, at 32.

[79] In defending the caution of the Judges' Rules, Sir Brian McKenna says, 'If the law gives a man a right, it is good that he know it'. 'Criminal Law Revision Committee's Eleventh Report: Some Comments', *Crim. L.R.,* [1972] 605, 607.

the charge, and its failure to guarantee access to counsels do, however, mean that the ignorant, poor, and emotionally weak will remain at a distinct disadvantage when questioned by the police.

Impact on Existing Institutions

Changes in legal rules have broader ramifications than those necessarily implied by the changes themselves, and differing predictions about the effects of proposed changes in the right to silence are often the basis for opposing judgements about their desirability. Without attempting full enumeration or exhaustive analysis I shall indicate some of the major questions about the likely indirect effects of diminution of the right to silence.

Some of these questions involve the necessity for prophylactic rules that preclude some practices in themselves acceptable in order to curb abuses that would arise if restrictions were relaxed. The Committee's proposals on silence and police questioning may be opposed on the ground that investigating officers would be given too much additional leverage to overbear suspects by improper but undetectable techniques of interrogation and too much additional opportunity to make unintentional but damaging mistakes about the words of the accused. How far one trusts the police has a good deal to do with how seriously one views these risks.[80] If they are taken seriously, they could be largely avoided by the presence of counsel, a neutral magistrate, or protected recording devices during interrogation, any of which could also curb abuses under the present rules.[81]

The need for broad protective rules is also raised by the Committee's proposal to make admissible confessions given in response to a threat or inducement unless the threat or inducement is 'of a sort likely, in the circumstances, existing at the time, to render unreliable any confession which might be made . . .'.[82] The Committee itself recognizes that part of the purpose for excluding confessions is to deter improper behaviour, and it accordingly would keep inadmissible any confession obtained by oppressive treatment, regardless of reliability.[83] But it does not believe the present strict rule regarding threats and inducements is necessary to foreclose police im-

---

[80] Even if the general level of confidence in the integrity of the English police has declined somewhat in recent years, it is still very much higher than the level of confidence in most American police forces.

[81] See A. R. N. Cross, 'The Right to Silence and the Presumption of Innocence— Sacred Cows or Safeguards of Liberty', *Journal of the Society of Public Law Teachers*, 1970–71, 11, 68, 71–2.

[82] Draft Criminal Evidence Bill, § 2(2).

[83] *Eleventh Report,* § 60.

proprieties.[84] The Council of the Bar, on the other hand, asserts that if any threats or inducements are 'encouraged' by allowing resulting confessions in evidence, the police will slide into acts of oppression.[85] This danger is made more serious by the elusiveness of determining whether the circumstances make an unreliable confession likely.[86]

A different objection to the Committee's formulation is that it might admit statements resulting from inducements that are not oppressive or likely to lead to false confessions but that do seriously undercut the suspect's choice whether or not to remain silent. This objection is far less serious if one accepts the Committee's general thesis that freedom from moderate pressures to speak is inappropriate than if one accepts the premises of the existing right to silence. Detached from the other Committee proposals, the suggested change on confessions cuts too far into the right to silence. But even if one accepts that right, the present law may be too strict. There is no good reason for refusing to admit statements following trivial inadvertent inducements that do not seriously affect a suspect's choice,[87] and the Council of the Bar's fear that even a rule formulated in such terms would lead to oppression appears exaggerated.[88]

Another fear about police practices if the right to silence is cut back is that increasing reliance on confessions would replace more reliable, less intrusive techniques of criminal investigation. An argument in these terms requires some qualifications. One is that in some cases alternative techniques simply cannot suffice. A second is that some typical kinds of proof, such as eye-witness identification, may often be less reliable than admissions. A third is that some 'alternative' techniques, such as informers and electronic surveillance, may be even more intrusive on individual liberty than pressures to answer questions. Still the argument remains that in systems relying

[84] Even in respect to threats and inducements, the Committee's decision not to admit all confessions and leave reliability to the jury, and its decision to have 'reliability' rest on the circumstances before the confession, rather than the terms of the confession and evidence confirming its accuracy, reflect a wish to deter improper practices. See ibid., §§ 64–5.

[85] Council of the Bar Memorandum, §§ 71–4.

[86] The Council's prediction of great unevenness in judicial application of the Committee's standard, ibid. at § 71, is a ground for doubting its desirability even apart from the effect on police practice.

[87] I am less sure than the Committee (see *Report*, § 57) that the inducement in *Northam* (1967) 52 Cr. App. R. 97, was 'trivial'. It is true that in response to Northam's inquiry concerning the offence on which he was being questioned, the officer said only that the police would have no objection to its being taken into consideration at Northam's trial for another offence. But to Northam this response might well have meant that he would not be charged separately for the offence in question if he confessed and perhaps that he would be free to go home to his pregnant wife rather than be held for trial.

[88] Council of the Bar Memorandum, § 74.

heavily on confessions, there is a tendency to overbear suspects rather than establish guilt by independent means.[89]

The more fruitful questioning is likely to be, the greater the incentive to examine those against whom there is only slight suspicion. This added power to engage in fishing expeditions against 'undesirable characters' may seem acceptable if used against 'known' professional criminals, but threatening if turned against political or personal enemies. Again one's trust or distrust of the police has much to do with whether one views this prospect with alarm. Close study of investigative methods in countries without such a significant right to silence might be of limited use in predicting the likely consequences of a change, but so many social variables affect police methods, it would be impossible to single out the precise influence of the way silence is treated in the legal system.

A shift in a right with historical and ideological roots as deep as the right to silence is bound to have broader symbolic overtones. While publicized contraction might symbolize a 'toughening' of the law to potential criminals more significant than its actual impact on them, it might also symbolize for many citizens an indifference to individual liberty far out of proportion to its actual effect on liberty. Such a change might also ease the path for other adjustments in the criminal process; these might be viewed as further rational alterations in obsolete rules or the dismantling of a 'venerable fortress' 'to protect the innocent'.[90] Predicting symbolic fallout and effect on future proposals is so difficult, the main focus for judgement must be on the more direct arguments for and against a particular reform, but only a substantial justification should support diminishing rights that have a heavy ideological weight. This principle is of special importance when diminishment would take the form of amendment of entrenched rights in a written constitution, as in the United States.

Conclusion

I have considered a variety of arguments about the right to silence primarily in relation to changes proposed by the Criminal Law Revision Committee,

[89] Drastic changes in modes of investigation may alter the kinds of crimes which can usefully be investigated. The silence of suspects makes it particularly difficult to establish crimes committed in secret, without victims, and involving little physical evidence, such diverse crimes as bribery, deviant sexual acts and, historically, heresy. If it is thought that a proposed alteration in the right of silence would have a substantial effect on investigative methods, it is relevant in weighing the alteration how important enforcement is against the crimes most affected.

[90] Letter to *The Times*, 5 Oct. 1972, p. 17, col. 4, of Dr. Manfred Simon, a distinguished French judge who was consulted by the Committee.

but most of these same arguments are, with little transposition, relevant to other proposals to contract or expand existing rights. On many of the relevant issues empirical research could make some contribution, but any particular study is unlikely to resolve clearly even one of those issues, much less the broader question of the overall desirability of a proposed change in the existing law. That answer depends on a whole host of empirical assessments or guesses and a number of non-empirical and sharply contested judgements of value. Realistically, it is doubtful if any empirical studies in the near future will change very many minds about the proper scope of the right to silence. My own conclusions on the basis of existing data follow.

The argument that it is inherently wrong to put pressure on a defendant to testify is not persuasive; such pressure would harm very few if any innocent defendants as long as prior convictions are not routinely introduced to impeach their testimony; and there appears little possibility of abuse if such pressure is introduced upon a counseled defendant in the public setting of a trial. Therefore, I see no major objection to the Committee's basic proposal to allow broader adverse inferences to be drawn from a defendant's silence at trial.[91] My reservation about that proposal, standing alone, concerns the slightness of its likely effect on present practices, since most defendants now testify and juries probably draw adverse inferences from silence even despite contrary instruction. Perhaps the actual change would be too insignificant to justify the symbolic fallout.

Because of the danger to the 'borderline' innocent of damaging distortions in memory and slips in answers to police questions, because the police may misconstrue what a suspect has or has not said, because of the moral right not to respond to insubstantial charges, and because juries may wrongly draw adverse inferences from justified silence at pre-trial stages, the Committee's proposals regarding silence before trial raise much more serious problems. Some of these could be cured by an accurate recording system safeguarded against manipulation[92] but not all.

Present rules governing silence and pre-trial interrogation are defective in both England and the United States because there is more danger than there

[91] Its subsidiary proposals on the failure to testify are more subject to attack. Calling the defendant to take the stand even when he wishes to remain silent would be a demeaning ritual not fully consistent with the Committee's comment that in some circumstances adverse inferences from silence may not be warranted. *Eleventh Report*, §§ 110, 112; Council of the Bar Memorandum, § 82. Allowing silence to count as corroboration, *Eleventh Report*, § 111, even when corroboration is required by law for a conviction, is of doubtful consistency with the premise that the state should have to make out a substantial case against an accused before he should have to answer it.

[92] See Council of the Bar Memorandum, § 26, recommending control by an independent person.

need be that an inaccurate version of what transpires between a suspect and the police will be accepted, and because the rules shield the intelligent and emotionally strong much better than the ignorant and weak. While recordings could remedy the accuracy problem in large part, only the advice and continuing support of a non-hostile participant can help the ignorant and weak if persistent police questioning of suspects is to be permitted. The participant might be a specially trained layman rather than a fully fledged solicitor. If interrogation of suspects could be carried on only in the presence of counsel, the right to silence that now exists would be genuinely protected, but perhaps the price of fewer admissions and confessions would be considered too high. If so, some combination of effective counsel and legally authorized pressures to speak, such as adverse inferences from silence, would be fairer than the grossly uneven effect of the pressures under existing practice, since these legally authorized pressures would call for the exercise of rational choice and fall with rough equality on all suspects. Perhaps the fairest procedure of all would be to have police questioning of suspects in front of magistrates,[93] with those questioned represented by counsel who would be provided for by the government if necessary. The magistrate might have the responsibility of protecting the moral right to silence by assuring that no one would be 'penalized' for refusing to answer questions unless there were already some substantial reason for thinking him guilty.

Entirely apart from government payments to provided counsel, a system such as this would involve a considerably greater drain on manpower and monetary resources than does the present form of police questioning. But fairness to criminal suspects and accurate determinations of guilt are important enough social goals to warrant great efforts to improve the criminal process. That the suggestions advanced here are far from novel is some reflection both that thoughtful people have long been troubled by the defects of police interrogation and that the presence of counsel or magistrates or both have appeared to be possible correctives.[94]

[93] A simple requirement that questioning be before magistrates, without any assurance of counsel, would provide a good deal more protection than a suspect has now. If rights are to be specially protected when persons become 'suspects' or are arrested, there still would be possibilities of abuse and the forfeiture of rights through ignorance during preliminary field investigations. Drawing the line now required for the first warning of the Judges' Rules would remain extremely difficult and would be even more important. These difficulties might simply be accepted as an unfortunate drawback of a desirable plan, or they could be moderated by making inadmissible against a defendant any admissions made outside the 'protected' procedure.

[94] See, e.g., Indian Evidence Act of 1872; Justice, *The Interrogation of Suspects*, London, Stevens and Sons, 1967; R. M. Jackson, *Enforcing the Law*, London, Macmillan, 1967, pp. 72–3; W. Schaefer, *The Suspect and Society*, op. cit., note 58, pp. 76–81; H. Friendly, 'The Fifth Amendment Tomorrow', *U. Cinn. L. Rev.*, 1968, **37**, 671, 713–15.

Change in the United States is complicated by the Fifth Amendment. It must take the form either of rule-making within existing constitutional principles, amendment, an exceedingly difficult process, or new interpretations of the existing Constitution. The Bill of Rights has never been altered by amendment, and I strongly doubt if interpretations of the privilege against self-incrimination are likely to be damaging enough to society in the foreseeable future to warrant amendment. Although the Supreme Court has not overruled *Miranda* v. *Arizona* the present Court includes, among its membership of nine, two of the dissenters, and four new Justices who are generally less sympathetic than the Supreme Court to claims of criminal suspects. Its ungenerous attitude towards *Miranda* is reflected by its decision that statements obtained in violation of the decision can be used to cross-examine defendants who testify.[95] Expansion of *Miranda* to make the right to counsel effective by sharply restricting waivers is not likely to come soon from the Court. Legislative guarantees of this kind would be desirable, but are also unlikely in the present climate, especially since American legislatures are used to relying on the courts for such protections.

The principle that adverse inferences from silence are impermissible is based on constitutional interpretation,[96] and so is safeguarded against legislative change, as are the *Miranda* warnings on the right to silence and the right to counsel. Supreme Court overruling of one or more of the existing precedents on the content of privilege against self-incrimination or the applicability of the federal constitutional privilege to the states[97] is a long-run possibility, but, barring such action, significant legislative diminution of the right to silence is foreclosed.[98]

As valuable as entrenched constitutional limitations are in curbing the excesses of legislatures and administrators, the Fifth Amendment does preclude a systematic attempt to redefine the ground rules for questioning of suspects in a way that will be fairer to them without curbing the information the police are likely to obtain. The proposals of the Criminal Law Revision Committee and the present debate over the right to silence may give Parliament that opportunity.

---

[95] *Harris* v. *New York*, 401 U.S. 222 (1971).

[96] See *Griffin* v. *California*, 380 U.S. 609 (1965); *Miranda* v. *Arizona*, 384 U.S. 436, 468, n. 37 (1966).

[97] See footnote 2, above.

[98] Congress has attempted to make a violation of the *Miranda* requirements only one relevant factor for the inadmissibility of a confession, Omnibus Crime Control and Safe Streets Act of 1968, 18 U.S.C. § 3501, but the effort is unconstitutional if the central doctrines of *Miranda* are authoritative.

THE RELATIONSHIP BETWEEN CRIMINOLOGY AND 'POLITIQUE CRIMINELLE'[1]

Marc Ancel

It is undoubtedly difficult to make a choice from an output so rich and diverse as that of Sir Leon Radzinowicz; but the continuity of his thought may be perceived with ease. Over and beyond the normative study of law—with which he is fully conversant—the scientist, the researcher and the teacher to whom we are paying tribute in this volume has always sought to involve himself in the concrete problems of criminality considered from the perspective of society's organized reaction against crime. From such pre-occupations derive not only his monumental *History of English Criminal Law since 1750*, which remains unrivalled in the literature of crime studies, but also his diverse work as a criminologist—in international organizations and as Head of the Cambridge Institute of Criminology. A common thread running through many of his writings is the concern to re-orientate society's reaction to crime by bringing to bear the resources and methods of criminology and a better understanding of the evolution of institutions and ideas concerning the prevention and repression of crime. This is precisely the field of *politique criminelle*—whose origins and terminology, Sir Leon asserts, are French.[2] It is from this perspective that I intend to concentrate on the relationship between the science of criminology and that particular discipline —both science and art—that is *la politique criminelle*.

In order to do this usefully it is important first of all to emphasize fully the necessary link which exists, in my opinion, between criminology and *politique criminelle*, as much from an historical point of view as from a methodological one. It is also appropriate to recall and measure the contribution of criminology to the practical policies involved in dealing with

[1] This term, as Sir Leon Radzinowicz himself notes, though encompassing the English term of 'penal reform', is in fact much wider in its application and 'cannot be rendered into English' see L. Radzinowicz, *In Search of Criminology* London, Heinemann Educational Books, 1961, pp. 65–6. For this reason it has been left in French rather than translated to 'criminal policy'.

[2] Ibid., p. 66.

crime. Finally, we must guard against misjudging the obstacles which hinder *de jure contendo* the influence or diffusion of criminological notions in the field of the traditional study of penal law. It is important to discuss in more detail these three major aspects of the problem.

Forging the Link

It is necessary to make a clear distinction between *la politique criminelle* and the actual criminal law that is in force at any given moment. Any organized society possesses a penal system consisting of infractions and penalties, a procedural machinery to pronounce sanctions, and an executive body. *La politique criminelle* on the other hand makes its appearance and comes into existence only when, side by side with the existing laws, three deliberate and correlated positions are taken up: (1) a meticulous critical examination of the system of penal law in force; (2) an articulated and complementary body of reforms intended to improve this system; (3) a coherent guiding principle in the movement for reform which guarantees it both a methodological cohesion and a social relevance.

It is clear—and Sir Leon Radzinowicz has demonstrated this admirably—that these three conditions were fulfilled, for the first time, at the end of the eighteenth century. The reform movement which developed on the continent with Beccaria, Montesquieu and Voltaire, and in England with William Eden, Sir Samuel Romilly and Bentham, worked separately, in one place and another, upon systems of criminal law that were essentially different. The continental countries were to expend a great deal of energy in the attempt to establish some of the guarantees that (as Blackstone noted with due pride) the historical development of the common law system already gave to the citizen of Great Britain. England had thus spared itself a sharp break with the old penal law. This is perhaps one of the reasons why the notion of *politique criminelle*, in so far as it virtually implies a revolutionary change of approach, has remained foreign to England for a long time; whereas it has been possible in Europe to see that Montesquieu was the instigator of this conception and that Feuerbach was one of those who contributed towards shaping it. But, from all sides too, the 'reform movement' implied criticism of an inhuman system of punishment, the replacement of capital punishment by sanctions restricting freedom, the search for a new direction in the basis of punishment: the appearance of such words as 'correctionel' in France and 'reformatory' in England is significant in this respect. The effect was to combine the movement for legislative reform with prison reform.

It would doubtless be excessive to claim that this new movement could be ascribed to an as yet unconstituted science of criminology. But it is nonetheless certain that this penal reform, was only possible and even 'thinkable' from the moment when criminal law was no longer regarded as an organization for legal expiation. A prime example was the confrontation between Charles Lucas and Ducpetiaux which followed the developments on the continent after 1830 which were marked by the appearance of the Franco-Belgian reformatory school. A severe indictment was drawn up against the old system, with its manifold punishments; the intention was to put in its place a system of retribution for offences better adapted to the Enlightenment's conception of free and sovereign man. This meant the deliberate adoption of an aim that combined both punishment and respect for human dignity, and which was reformatory both because of its deterrent value and the regime of contrite meditation that imprisonment entailed.

However, this movement for reform, comprising as it did an attempt to broaden basic ideas and evolve what today would be called a multi-disciplinary approach, was arrested in its progress by the advent of classical penal law. This system, in all its differing legislative forms and legal techniques, was essentially founded upon the precept of legality which defined infractions and punishment in terms of a dual aim of individual retribution and collective intimidation. Social reaction against crime from then on was enclosed solely within the framework of penal law; the campaign against crime fell to the lot of legal specialists. In this way, during the nineteenth century and particularly in its second half, a powerful penal dogmatism was established which made the criminal offence into a 'judicial entity', to use the formula of Carrara who, contemplating the magnificent construction of the jurists, considered that penal law no longer had any need for improvement. The sovereignty of the jurist rendered unnecessary all recourse to a *politique criminelle*.

However, in spite of the legislative triumph of the jurists' dogma in the promulgation of the Italian penal code of 1889, it had already been challenged more than a decade earlier, by the advent of the Anthropological and Sociological School. It is curious to note that the inspiration for this school came from a doctor of medicine, a professor of penal law and a magistrate: an interdisciplinary encounter in which the practical and the theoretical were in close association. Lombroso, Ferri and Garofalo took as their point of departure the individual offender, and not crime in the abstract. Anthropology and the sociology of crime became the two branches or main directions of the new-born criminology. On these scientific foundations the elaboration of a new *politique criminelle* began, put forward by the International Union for Penal Law, also founded in 1889. Its instigator, von Liszt, reformulated and developed criminal policy in the light of the lessons of the Positivist school. From then on, the necessary conjunction between *politique criminelle* and the science of criminology was established and remained unchallenged.

This link was no longer to be lost from sight. When after the interesting, but limited, experience of penal legislation between the wars (emerging from a turmoil in which the very notion of law appeared to have been lost) a fresh movement for penal reform came into sight, M. Hurwitz could go as far as to write that *politique criminelle* was, ultimately, no more than applied criminology. Perhaps this is a rather absolute and overstated formula, but it is one that illuminates perfectly the close relationship which was established quite naturally between the discipline that saw as its aim the rationalization of social reaction against crime and the science whose object is to study crime and the offender—both personally and in the context of his social environment.

Criminology and Practical Policy

The task remains of assessing, in a more precise way, the direct influence of criminology on *la politique criminelle*; that is, the impact of the science of criminology upon the positive content and conceptions of penal law. If indeed criminal law is essentially a normative discipline founded upon *lex lata*, the normal area of *politique criminelle* is that of *lex ferenda*.

As we are unable in the present context to undertake the vast study of comparative law which might allow us to answer fully this question we shall have to limit ourselves to sketching in some remarks, firstly about those areas where the influence of extrajudicial scientific concepts can be felt, and secondly about the consequences of this movement from the methodological point of view.

We may recall that after the 'positivist revolt', that preceded and accompanied the promulgation of the Zanardelli Code in Italy, the scientific study of crime, of the offender and his milieu made it necessary to revise the solutions of 'classical penal law'. This movement for legislative reform found its particular expression in the codifications of penal laws on the continent ranging from the Norwegian legal code of 1902, the instigator of which, Bernhard Getz, was a fervent follower of the International Union for Penal Law, to the Swiss legal code of 1937, the immediate impulse for which came from the famous project of Carl Stooss which von Lizst had enthusiastically greeted in 1894. Schematically, this reform movement was concentrated in three areas:

(1) that of childhood—and later also adolescent—delinquency; for it was progress and research in psychology, psychiatry and sociology that had brought to light the inadequacy and erroneous character of a repressive system based upon the search for the degree of culpability of the young offender;

(2) in the case of adults, progress in psychiatry showed that many offenders, especially amongst those with multiple convictions for petty offences, were in reality mentally ill, or at least mentally deficient. It was unscientific to judge and punish them in relation to a notion of responsibility which was considered to be either total or, in the event of madness, entirely in abeyance. The system of the Napoleonic legal code of 1810 (article 64) coincided in this respect with the famous English *McNaghten Rules* of 1843. Penal legislation following upon the positivist movement established gradations by introducing the idea of diminished responsibility, and proposed for such offenders specialized establishments and non-punitive treatment;

(3) criminal anthropology, confirmed both by the sociological research of Ferri and Garofalo's *Criminology*, distinguished the categories of criminals by nature and professional and habitual offenders, and emphasized the notion of dangerousness (*pericolosità*). In the case of the latter criminals, the threat of punishment was ineffective and the application of sanctions of no avail. It was necessary, without any preoccupation with moral retribution, simply to protect society against these criminal elements. The French measure of transportation of 1885, the English preventive detention of 1908, the precautionary internment provided for by the penal codes of 1930 (and, in part also, the Belgian law of social protection of the same year) were nothing other than the translation into legislative terms of criminological notions.

In addition to these particular categories of criminals (without forgetting the influence, notably between the wars, of research into 'criminal typology') criminological preoccupations can be discerned equally in two wide areas. The first of these lies in the way punishments were carried out: the whole of prison reform, from the Gladstone Committee of the late nineteenth century to the Section for Social Defence of the United Nations (which has as its object 'the prevention of crime and treatment of offenders') was given its first stimulus, its subsequent direction and has been continually transformed by the lessons of the human sciences—penology itself is an integral part of criminology in the widest sense of the term. The second area is that of penal procedure, the technicality of which had seemed, in spite of these developments, impenetrable by criminology. The concern for individualization of punishment is asserted by the legal codes of the twentieth century. The Italian legal code of 1930 went as far as to grant the penal judge discretionary powers in the individualized choice of punishment. Later, others (such as the French code of penal procedure of 1958) instituted an examination of the personality of the offender far beyond the old psychiatric appraisal.

If we pass from the penal legislation of the inter-war years to that following 1945, we can see a strengthening and widening of the influence of criminology upon the policies of penal legislation. The Swedish penal code of 1962 was the subject of lengthy and meticulous preparation, which took account of the lessons of all criminal sciences and, at the instigation of Karl Schlyter, it was at one time even envisaged entitling the document 'Code of protection'. The revision of the German penal code, which gave rise notably to the two great reform laws of 1969, was carried out in the light of an extensive judicial and sociological enquiry. Although the text of the official commission remained within the framework of classical penal law, an 'alternative project' elaborated by a group of dissident jurists and criminologists—many propositions of which were finally accepted by the legislature —was based upon the needs of a *politique criminelle* which was largely inspired by the human sciences. The typical Latin American penal code, put forward by a commission set up in 1963 on the initiative of Professor Novoa Monreal of Santiago (the general section of which was published in 1971) while striving to maintain a strict judicial relevance, was equally concerned with criminological ideas and findings. Sir Leon Radzinowicz has shown how in the United States the movement created at the beginning of the century by the setting up of the *American Institute of Criminal Law and Criminology* (which published its *Journal* from 1910 onwards) had so developed between the wars that it came to the conclusion after World War II that the connections between criminology and penal law were 'fundamental and inescapable'.[3] The outcome of this was the *Model Penal Code*, drawn up by the American Law Institute. The Federal penal code project, decided upon by Congress in 1966 and presented to the same Congress in January 1971, bears witness to the same preoccupations—especially with the theory of responsibility (the four degrees of the moral element in crime as can be seen in section 302), the creation (wilful or by negligence) of a public danger (sections 1613 and 1704) and the possession, use of and trafficking in drugs. This scientifically inspired legislative movement is no less familiar to the countries of Eastern Europe (the so-called socialist law legislations), as can be seen from the 1958 basic Principles for penal legislation of the U.S.S.R.

[3] L. Radzinowicz, *The Need for Criminology*, London, Heinemann Educational Books, 1965, pp. 18 et seq, and pp. 33 et seq.

and the 1960 penal code of the RSFSR as well as from the establishment, under the aegis of the Prokuratura, in Moscow, of a Research Institute for the causes of criminality. The recent penal codes of the people's democracies demonstrate this in the same way, notably the Polish legal code of 1969, replacing that of 1932, and the revision, adopted by the Yugoslav Federal Assembly on 30 June 1959, of the penal code of 1951.

These are only a few examples; many more could be found. Let us try now to elaborate the consequences of this evolution which has, as I have emphasized been due largely (to use once again Sir Leon Radzinowicz's phrase) to the 'intense and stimulating' collaboration of criminology and penal law.

The first of these consequences has been to bring about in the theoretical field of penal law a wide-reaching reconsideration of values. In this way, on the continent, a powerful doctrine—affirmed notably by the French Court of Appeal—draws the distinction between the criminal intention, which consists in the awareness on the part of the offender of the illicit nature of his act, and the concrete motives that impel him to act. This distinction, which rests, once more, upon the fiction of a human being completely free to choose between good and evil, is today very widely questioned; for, criminologically speaking, only the motives explain the act—they are the driving force. Similarly, it was the same legislative conception that led the continental system to decide that the judicial proof of the material fact of the felony should entail the immediate pronouncement of the punishment provided for by the law, without the judge being able to postpone his decision for a subsequent evaluation of the personality of the offender. The movement in favour of what is called (incidentally rather inexactly) the 'break in the penal process' which tends ultimately to introduce into legal systems derived from Roman law the distinction, traditional within the common law system, between conviction and sentence arises from criminological considerations and from a wish to personalize penal law.

A further consequence of the activities of criminology has consisted in questioning the permanence and stability of legal rules and institutions. The science of penal law takes the judicial norm as a definitive and logically immutable first principle. The science of criminology, however, is the science of mobility, of the relative and the contingent. This can lead to an occasionally spectacular surrendering of previously held scientific positions. Since the end of the last war, criminological analysis has been seen to lead in this way to the relinquishment of certain former opinions held by criminologists: protective security measures, such as transportation in France and preventive detention in England (which had been one of the great ideas of the beginning of the century) were finally rejected, and the

C.C.P.P.—10*

indiscriminate internment of psychopathic sexual offenders, an American innovation during the years before or immediately after the beginning of the Second World War, has been increasingly criticized. The notion of dangerousness (the novelty and dynamism of which we have already mentioned), borstal training and its continental equivalent, the prison-school, the very notion of 'treatment' of offenders, or at any rate the search for institutional 'methods of reformatory treatment', from once having been major demands on the part of criminologists become from this moment on subject to debate and are occasionally rejected by certain modern schools of thought. After considering criminality as a product of the poor and dis-inherited classes, or of individuals undermined by biological defects, after seeking lengthily in the criminal the atavistic signs of an inferior type of human being, criminologists, especially following the work of Kinberg and De Greeff, have shown that the offender is a person like any other and that the true problem is less that of the criminal himself than that of the individual circumstances and situations in which crime is committed.

This has led to fresh currents of thought, the most symptomatic of which is without doubt the distinguishing of the phenomenon of 'deviance' in addition to that of criminality. The criminal is without doubt the deviant *par excellence*, but there also exist many deviants who are not, in the strict and traditional sense of the term, offenders. Sutherland, introducing the notion of white collar crime, has widened the boundaries of criminal law and emphasized the inadequacy of its techniques. Notions of criminal contagion, group criminality, sub-culture and differential association encourage us to revise many of the accepted analyses as to the causes and manifestations of crime. At the other end of the spectrum much attention is paid nowadays to the criminality of the affluent society. The Welfare State itself can no longer have the rigour, unity and, one might say, the simplicity it had when in the past the legislator, on the basis of established values, determined, with the threat of penal sanctions, the indivual rules of social behaviour.

At the present time, recent legislation is tending towards a wide ranging 'decriminalization'. For a considerable time now heresy, sacrilege or blasphemy have no longer been pursued penally. The penal punishment of adultery, which still may be applied in numerous countries, seems like an anachronism. A strong current of thought tends to decriminalize immoral behaviour when it takes the form of pornography, homosexuality between consenting adults, various forms of voluntary intoxication and even, in quite a widespread way, abortion. This decriminalization of behaviour is accompanied by a 'depenalization' which challenges the old system of penal law, especially its indiscriminate recourse to punishments restricting freedom. Prison, like the whole system of repression itself, is put into the dock. It is indeed the development of the sciences of man and of criminological thought which has lead to the often energetic revision of old notions about the appropriate action to be taken against crime; and it is modern penology that has shown the extent to which imprisonment acts as the germ of further crime. Thus, progressively, and at times without open acknowledgement of it, *la politique criminelle* draws upon the lessons of criminology.

Obstacles to Collaboration

Is this to say that we have reached a state of true co-operation? To believe this would be without doubt an illusion. Already Mr. Sheldon Glueck, wishing to examine the relationship between psychiatry and penal law, had pinpointed the real question: cold war or entente cordiale? We have at most reached the stage of peaceful co-existence; and, as in international politics, this co-existence is not without its crises and mutual misunderstanding. Let me attempt in conclusion to state more precisely the obstacles against complete collaboration between criminologists and jurists.

There is, in the make-up of the traditional jurist, an old defensive reflex against the intrusion of criminology. The jurist is brought up in the cult of the law and, in penal terms, the actual crime interests him only in its legal character. The personal conditions of the individual and the social factors surrounding the offence are traditionally taken into consideration only in order to determine the proportion of the punishment, i.e. when all questions concerning the material fact of the infraction and the penal responsibility of the offender are resolved—or deemed resolved. Thus there is a necessarily and, in principle, legitimately different approach to the phenomenon of crime.

In the countries of the continent of Europe and Latin America the jurist is moulded in the spirit of Roman Law. Judicial logic is his normal mode of argument. He is the inheritor of an historical tradition which he intends to maintain in the face of distortions from outside. The penal judge is finally conscious of expressing social reproof towards the act adjudged as crime and of having as his essential responsibility the assertion and protection of values acknowledged as fundamental by the consciousness of the collective body. The legal norm, moreover, indicates just as much the degree to which the state has the right to intervene in personal affairs as it does the leeway of the citizen's lawful activity. If the modification of this norm can be influenced by social or scientific considerations, its elucidation and application are the lot of judicial technique alone. This technique will thus be regarded as an expression of the state of law; and the 'rule of law' constitutes without question an essential guarantee of civil liberties. A fresh reason will be found here to reject all intrusion by criminology, which might be liable to weaken the rule of law.

The field of activity of the jurist has thus a natural tendency to remain self-contained and to assert its supremacy. We have already said that penal dogmatism in the last century strove towards the setting up of a system owing nothing to the human sciences. The *tecnico-juridisme* originating in Italy, which has developed widely in Latin America, had made similar claims to limit the jurist to the dogmatic meaning of legal regulations, ignoring any social context.

Resistance on the part of judges towards scientific innovations, especially as far as blood tests and blood-alcohol analyses are concerned, is an almost universal experience. Their mistrust of psychology and psychoanalysis is equally traditional. In any case, this resistance, fostered moreover, at least indirectly, by the legislature, has often resulted in reducing to nothing at least a substantial number of the reforms motivated by criminological considerations. Indeed, these reforms are bound to be simply inserted into a system of repression, the foundations of which are meant to be maintained at the same time. They often constitute isolated experiments, which are sporadic and limited. In this way, the examination of personality, imperatively set out by article 81 of the French procedural code of 1958, was for some time put into abeyance, because a particular jurisprudence favoured recourse to traditional rules of procedure.

The hostility of jurists towards criminology has at times taken more subtle and apparently more scientific forms. For example, the existence of a 'dark figure' is invoked to support the argument that since there exists an unknown degree of criminality, greater than that studied by criminologists, the analyses presented by the latter are incomplete or inexact. It is asserted that the criminals studied are, in fact, convicted detainees; and it is further argued on the one hand that their very condition as detainees falsifies all examinations of their personality, and on the other hand that these sample cases are the least significant, since the true danger comes from offenders who 'don't get caught'. Why, if this is the case, should we ask criminology to guide the steps of a *politique criminelle*?

Up to now, we have appeared to disagree with the jurist in his challenging of the criminologist. Let us not forget, however, that there are cases in which criminology can be at fault. We have already had occasion to recall that neutralizing measures such as transportation or preventive detention, brought in due to criminological considerations, had later to be abandoned. So also were institutions such as the 'work-house' or the 'short, sharp shock' of internment for young offenders. Reformatory experiments of 'treatment' in detention have gone for thirty years from failure to failure. Certain specialists in child delinquency have at present reached the point of recommending a return to constraint, i.e. to punishment as a substitute for therapeutic re-education.

Criminologists, on the other hand, do nothing to help matters when they in turn reject the jurists and pursue the mirage of a 'criminological definition of crime' owing nothing to legal definitions. They further nourish the atavistic mistrust of the jurist when they declare that after so many efforts— and injunctions requiring the legal specialist to bow to the imperatives of science—we must now start once more from the beginning, dedicate ourselves for an unlimited time to basic research and consider as null and void all that has been so brilliantly extolled for over a quarter of a century. Criminological imperialism (which has been denounced only recently by certain jurists) runs the risk of leading to a lofty isolation of the criminologist which would deprive him first of any authority, then of any influence.

Co-operation between criminologists and jurists has developed for a long time in an atmosphere of illusions. They have sought successively to define the ideal prison system suitable in all cases and for all offenders, to classify the different criminals in groups and to organize appropriate modes of social action against each type, and claimed to discover the causes of criminality and provide the means of preventing them or rendering them inoperative. Their efforts remain more or less haunted, despite official protestations to the contrary, by the old Lombrosian image of the criminal, whose distinguishing traits, whose stigmata even, could be scientifically recognized. The appeal of criminology has at times taken on the semblance of recourse to the soothsayer of ancient times, or the medieval invocation of the sorcerer.

Collaboration between criminologists and jurists, between criminologists and judges, remains nonetheless indispensable, and must be strong and coherent enough to surmount nostalgia for lost illusions or to avoid the wish-fulfilment of future illusions. In any case, *la politique criminelle* depends neither on jurists alone nor on criminologists alone. Ideological factors, such as the scale of values in social ethics, religious influences, economic and political conditions and, finally, the general conception of crime, of punishment and the collective reaction to criminal offences play a considerable rôle. Sir Leon Radzinowicz has helpfully recalled this point in his excellent recent lecture in which he calls upon both jurists and criminologists to undertake a critical examination of their respective positions.[4] This is the very heart of *la politique criminelle*, and it is reassuring to see that interdisciplinary conferences are being held periodically (as recently, in Bellagio in May 1973), and are

[4] Sir Leon Radzinowicz, 'Them and Us', *Cambridge Law Journal*, 1972, **30**, pp. 260–79.

bringing together qualified representatives from the four major scientific associations involved in studying the prevention of crime and methods of dealing with offenders. The one amongst these most directly concerned with *la politique criminelle*, the International Society for Social Defence, sees itself as a meeting-place for specialists both in judicial science and in criminological science. This organized co-operation has the striking merit of making better known the combined and sometimes contradictory interplay of all the elements at stake, and thus making possible the working out of a policy for the struggle against crime founded simultaneously on the lessons of science and the inevitable exigencies of the rule of law.

(Translated by Leslie Hill and Alison Finch.)

UTILITY AND SOCIAL VALUES IN COURT DECISIONS ON PUNISHMENT

Nils Christie

Introduction

An air of coolness pervades both the concept and practice of punishment. This can be sensed both by those who receive it and by those who dispense it. It is a type of activity that does not fit in with the spirit of the times. Yet a great deal is done to cloak the coolness and the dissent. Words can cloak so many things. In my first draft of this article I started off by using the word 'sanctions' instead of punishment. It is often referred to in this way, so as to draw a decent and suitable veil over the whole subject.

But this is, of course, quite wrong. It separates us from the core of the problem. This article therefore will be mainly concerned with punishment, with penalties that are meant to be painful. We want punishment. I want it. I find it to be the right thing sometimes. But often it is concurrently both wrong and harmful. And so I, like so many others, try to get out of this dilemma by using words like sanctions instead of punishment, inmate instead of prisoner, attendant instead of prison warder, single room instead of cell, and of course, first and foremost training or treatment instead of punishment.

Some will object that such terms can have a persuasive effect. By styling a prisoner a patient, it is possible that he will come to be treated as a patient, by calling an institution a school, one may become forced to provide proper training. But the history of criminal policy is full of examples to the contrary. The use of particular terms does not regularly lead to treatment that gives these terms a proper meaning; on the contrary, their effect often only persuades us to accept conditions that we would not have accepted if the terms employed had been less misleading. In my opinion, on the whole, the best protection is afforded to the weakest party in a system employing compulsory measures if these measures are given their harshest names.

But it is not just a case of stumbling over words. Not only is punishment a deliberate infliction of suffering, but it is also a form of suffering that includes seemingly irrational features. It is difficult to satisfy contemporary demands for a rational justification of *why* and *how* we react to criminal offences and criminal offenders. It is, moreover, not in line with our future-orientated culture that we should direct our aim *backwards* against misdeeds committed in the past. Nor is it in line with our pain-relieving culture that we should *inflict suffering* for suffering's sake. And it is difficult for us with our equalitarian ideology to accept that so much of the punishment is concentrated on *sections of the population that are known to be severely handicapped at the outset.*

We have in Norway as in most other industrialized countries attempted to correct this. We have tried to modernize the system by substituting *treatment* for punishment. We have also tried to protect ourselves by a system of *preventive detention.* And, we have tried to increase the level of rationality by gearing the infliction of punishment to what is necessary in order to *deter others* from committing criminal offences—through *general prevention.*

These are three rational goal-orientated justifications in sweet harmony with the spirit of the times. I will, however, attempt to show that these justifications are not really so well founded as they are often made out to be, and that they obscure other important tasks relating to the administration of justice. The arguments now prevalent in favour of the rehabilitation of criminal offenders and the elimination of dangerous criminals can, in my opinion, generally be refuted as a foundation for a rational criminal policy. As regards general prevention or deterrence, however, it is necessary to draw a distinction between arguments that are applicable at the legislative and general control levels and those applicable at the judicial level. At this latter stage—individual decisions made by the courts—I am of the opinion that the deterrent line of argument does not provide any useful basis for the decisions.

What then remains? On what are the courts to base reactions against criminal offences if the three rational justifications put forward above are shown to be untenable? My suggestion will be that the judge will almost certainly be bound to grope his way back to certain venerable notions about justice and morality, and that he has perhaps gone astray by giving too free a rein to his desire to respond to contemporary demands for rational, future-orientated objectives in making decisions in individual cases. He is not in a position to do so. Moreover, the attempt to do so causes him to *forget* to take into account *other important social needs.*

Little claim to originality is made as regards what follows. Much of it is part of the common stock of Norwegian sociology of law, criminology, and criminal law research,[1] even though we quarrel about the conclusions which

---

[1] Some of the major works are: Johs. Andenæs, 'General Prevention—Illusion or Reality', *Journal of Crim. Law, Criminology and Police Science*, 1952, **44**, 176–98; and 'The General Preventive Effects of Punishment', *Univ. Penn. Law Rev.*, 1966, **114**, 949–83. Vilhelm Aubert, 'Legal Justice and Mental Health', *Psychiatry*, 1958, **21**, 101–13; and

can be drawn from it all. But information and ideas within this field are seldom looked at as a whole. By co-ordinating all the arguments we might more easily recognize the need to find another basis for inflicting the suffering that we may eventually decide to apply.

Treatment for Crime

The treatment of offenders has been a main theme in the ideology of modern criminal policy. In Norway, forced labour for alcoholics was originally introduced on the assumption that it was providing recuperative treatment, and subsequently this idea has cropped up in many different connections. A great deal of idealism, good intentions and thought lay behind this development, even if we—wise after the event as we have now become—can rather sceptically observe that these ideals fitted in with the ideology of the day and, in particular, made it a great deal easier to apply force to large sections of our fellow citizens than it would have been had one not asserted that they were receiving treatment. Today we can see quite clearly that ideas about the treatment of criminal offenders can not be used as a foundation for the construction of a rational system of reaction against criminal offences. Why?

Firstly, because a great deal of legal transgression is committed by rational people. It is common to commit criminal offences, and they are committed by ordinary people. It will probably become more and more common the weaker the primary social ties which control behaviour in society become. Any attempt to construct one's system of reaction on a basis of sickness must founder in its own unreasonableness. Secondly, on the occasions when the attempt has been made, the results have been poor. Treatment is linked with knowledge gained from experience—and this opens the door to research. In this type of research there are two main paths to follow. The first is to analyse the measures which are applied to criminal offenders, and then to ask oneself whether they resemble what is usually provided in the name of treatment or training. The research is focused on the *phenomenon* itself, what is done to the criminal offender as part of the process of treatment, and then a comparison is made—point for point—with what happens in, for example, a hospital or a nursing home. There are important similarities

---

'Avskrekking med omsorg', *Kontrast*, 1968, **2**, 11–39. Nils Christie, *Tvangsarbeid og Alkoholbruk* (Oslo, 1960); and 'Noen kriminalpolitiske særforholdsreglers sosiologi', *Tidsskrift for samfunnsforskning*, 1962, **3**, 28–48. Thomas Mathiesen and Vilhelm Aubert, *Crime and Illness. Transactions of the Fifth World Congress of Sociology*, International Sociological Assn., 1964, IV, pp. 393–403. Thomas Mathiesen, *The Defences of the Weak*, London, Tavistock, 1965. Tove Stang Dahl, *The Emergence of the Norwegian Child Welfare Law*, Institutt for kriminologi og strafferett, Universitetet i Oslo, Stensilserie 1971.

between these phenomena. The prison and the hospital both bear the marks of what we call *total* institutions; in such institutions the inmate almost completely abandons his former identity; he is there at all hours of the day and night, and the staff share with each other information relating to the prisoners or the patients; in such institutions there is a rigid dividing line between the employees and the others; the institution forms a world of its own, and what happens internally is of paramount importance. Nevertheless it is the differences that predominate. The hall-mark of a criminal offence is the *disgrace* attached to it. Some wrong has been committed, otherwise society would not have intervened. But this wrong is not, of course, a *permanent condition*. The criminal offence is a concrete act in the past, but to be a criminal is to have a certain rôle. Only a minority of those who have committed a criminal offence regard themselves as criminals. The usual thing is to regard one's own offence as distinguished by quite special circumstances. An additional punishment for very many of those who are sent to prison is that they thereupon come into *contact* with 'real criminals' whom they contrast with the image they have of themselves as persons who have committed something that is hardly a crime at all. A vital aspect of the treatment of an offender must presumably be to prevent him from assuming a criminal identity, i.e. to prevent a person from regarding himself as having assumed a criminal rôle. It is somewhat unrealistic to set about trying to achieve such prevention by bringing together in one building a number of persons suffering from the same disgrace and with the same need for protection against degradation. Added to this is the fact that the starting point for the whole thing—the criminal offence—has almost certainly been part of *a total social situation*. It is not just a question of attributes connected to a *person*.

The second main path one can follow in studying the 'treatment of criminal offenders' is to conduct research into the effects of the sanctions. This is, in principle, a simple procedure. One takes a criminal offender, does something to him, and sees how it works. In practice it proves to be both heavy going and costly. Prisoners who have been subjected to different forms of reaction have different rates of recidivism. But this is not necessarily due to differences in the type of punishment or treatment. It can be due to differences between the prisoners or those treated, for it is not just chance which controls which method is chosen for dealing with them. These differences between prisoners undergoing the punishments or treatments which are being compared must be neutralized. To some it appears to be perfectly obvious that if one succeeds in establishing this type of control, one will discover that some forms of punishment or treatment must be more effective than others. Detention in a treatment centre or in a hospital must presumably offer great possibilities for preventing recidivism than detention in a prison or in a forced labour camp, small institutions must undoubtedly be better than large ones, treatment at liberty must be more effective than treatment behind bars, active supervision must be better than passive supervision. There is no lack of reasonable suppositions, and scientific research has faithfully committed itself to the thankless task of proving the obvious, of proving what everyone was so well aware of before, namely that the findings that researchers produce are simply a confirmation of their own naïve ability to squander a million kroner on proving what all reasonable people have known to be the case all along.

But the research worker's consolation in this situation is that he has generally *not* been able to confirm any of these hypotheses which have been so obviously taken for granted. Nearly all investigations[2] relating to individual effects have been deeply disillusioning. Generally speaking, one has *not* been able to confirm all the usual assumptions: that treatment is better than punishment, that small prisons are better than the large ones, or that active supervision of criminal offenders is better than the superficial variety. Indeed, treatment experiments conducted at liberty do not even appear to yield demonstrably better results than old-fashioned prisons. Nor do they yield worse results.

To be sure, Bengt Börjeson's enquiry[3] suggests that non-prison leads to less recidivism than prison. Karen Berntsen's and Karl O. Christiansen's investigation[4] indicates that intensive social work in prison leads to somewhat reduced recidivism. A third investigation by Karl O. Christiansen, Mogens Moe and Leif Senholt[5] can be interpreted in the same way. It is an excellent study of the effectiveness of detention and special prisons compared with the more traditional prison. The main conclusion is, 'In spite of considerable efforts, we have not succeeded in demonstrating any significant difference in the results from the four types of treatment' (state prison, special prison, detention in Horsens, and detention in Herstedvester). In reply to a supplementary question from the Criminal Law Committee, how-

---

[2] R. Hood and R. Sparks have adopted a slightly more optimistic tone. It is at least questionable whether they would maintain it today. Cf. their *Key Issues in Criminology*, London, World Univ. Library, 1970.

[3] Bengt Börjeson, *Om påföljders verkningar. En undersökning av prognosen för unga lagöverträdare efter olika slag av behandling* (Stockholm, 1968).

[4] Karen Berntsen and Karl O. Christiansen, 'A Resocialization Experiment with Short-Term Offenders', *Scandinavian Studies in Criminology*, London, 1965, 1, 35–54.

[5] Karl O. Christiansen, Mogens Moe and Leif Senholt, in collaboration with Ken Schubell and Karin Zedeler, *Effektiviteten af forvaring of særfængsel m.v. En kriminologisk efterundersøgelse af lovovertrædere henført under straffelovens § 17, stk. 1, og indsat i forvaring, særfængsel eller statsfængsel, samt et forsøg på en vurdering af disse reaktioners effektivitet. Foretaget på foranledning af straffelovrådet.* Statens trykningskontor, Danmark. Betænkning nr. 644, Kopenhavn, 1972.

ever, some of the authors modify this conclusion to the effect that they think they can demonstrate, as a result of a fresh analysis, that the detainees— who have received an indeterminate sentence—show significantly better long-term results than the inmates of prisons. But the differences are *very small* in practice. The result—based on statistical corrections—conflicts with what Kassenbaum, Ward and Wilner[6] found in a large-scale experimental investigation recently published in the U.S.A.

The main trend in the great flood of investigations which have been published in the years following the Second World War is towards results which emphasize the lack of differences between the effects of different sanctions on similar offenders. If the object is to ensure that the criminal offender should not relapse into fresh crime, it is of little consequence what form of reaction is chosen. The small and questionable differences that may be found cannot under any circumstances be sufficient to provide a justification for fashioning a system of reaction against criminal offences in accordance with a 'treatment model'.

Prevention of Dangerousness

But if they cannot be rehabilitated, they can at any rate be incarcerated, so as to get them out of the way for the time being. This is also a solution, although an unpractical and expensive one. We send 10,000 people to prison every year in Norway. There would rapidly be a great number locked up if we did not release an equal number. And it is expensive to keep them there. The daily upkeep of a prisoner amounts to 100 kroner. If we are to extend these facilities, it will rapidly become even more expensive.

But cannot we at least keep the dangerous ones out of the way?

Yes, we can succeed in doing so in the case of a few of them, but only a few. This is due to the fact that most dangerous actions are committed by persons who have not previously shown any sign that they would commit such actions. Consequently, we have not much to go on in advance. More- over, we soon find ourselves in trouble even in the case of those who have previously shown signs of being dangerous. Using statistical methods we are able to predict recidivism to crime. We know that a man who has previously been punished eight times is more than 80 per cent certain to commit a ninth offence; so in this instance we are in a good position to forecast a high probability of recidivism. But obviously even in such cases we would make a mistake in 20 per cent of decisions if we acted as if all such

[6] Gene Kasselbaum, David A. Ward and Daniel M. Wilner, *Prison Treatment and Parole Survival: An Empirical Assessment*, New York, John Wiley, 1971.

men were to be reconvicted. The problem is that when forecasting dangerous actions we do not just occasionally make a mistake, but very often. *Our chance of accuracy is*, as shown by Rosen,[7] *less the rarer the action we are attempting to foresee.* For every correctly predicted violent criminal, one must as an absolute minimum reckon with three 'false positives', that is to say persons who are equivalent as regards every measurable characteristic but who nevertheless will not commit any form of violent crime. And this relates to forecasts made by means of statistical methods, and not by the far less dependable 'clinical judgements' that is usually applied. Attempts to predict the really hard core of very dangerous criminals would of necessity— because of the low frequency of their crimes—result in a considerable increase in the number of the 'false positives'.

This brings us face to face with both practical and ethical dilemmas: practical, because we get an accumulation of essentially undangerous persons in prison, and ethical because in this instance we engage in a radical breach of our normal rules of conduct. We are usually willing to let ten guilty persons go free in order to avoid condemning one innocent person. But if we resort to incarcerating possibly dangerous criminals, we must lock up several who are not dangerous in order that a few should not get an opportunity to commit a fresh offence.[8]

Instilling Fear into Others

A final possibility of supplying a rational basis for punishment is to let one person suffer in order to instil fear into others. The one who is made to suffer is not improved by it. But others may be improved—or at any rate be made to refrain from criminal offences they otherwise would have committed. This is what is often called the general deterrent effect.

It is here necessary to draw a distinction between arguments that are applicable at the legislative and general control levels and those applicable at the judicial level.

As regards the *legislature*, the power of compulsion is the vital factor behind many of its injunctions. A traffic sign saying 'Stop' means stop; offenders are threatened with punishment, and those who are caught are punished. But also in this connection there are limits to rationality. One does not threaten to impose the death penalty for misdemeanours, or a fine

[7] Albert Rosen 'Detection of suicidal patients. An example of some limitations in the prediction of infrequent events', *J. Consulting Psychology*, 1954, **18**, 397–403.

[8] Alan Dershowitz, 'The Law of dangerousness: Some fictions about predictions', *J. Legal Ed.*, 1970, **23**, 24–51. Andrew von Hirsch, 'Prediction of criminal conduct and preventive confinement of convicted persons', *Buffalo Law Review*, 1972, **21**, 717–58.

for maiming. A general weighing of values serves to prescribe upper and lower limits to the pains that can be inflicted.

The deterrent argument is also a valid one as regards the operation of the *police force*. Here we have some experiences which at any rate tell us something about the extreme case, when the police force is withdrawn altogether. The result is quite disastrous. Periods without police in Copenhagen and Montreal indicated a very sharp rise in criminal activity in such situations until the citizens themselves eventually took the matter in hand and organized a substitute police force. Formal control seems to be absolutely necessary, at any rate in towns in an industrialized society. But *how much* police control is needed? And particularly *how much more* is needed *in addition* to direct control we know practically nothing about?

With regard to the latter question, we are first of all without any information regarding the 'necessary' *volume* of punishment in society. Does it make any difference as regards general law abidance if *nothing* happens apart from arrest and police interrogation for several hours, or if one per cent of those apprehended are later punished, if 10 per cent are later punished —or 50 per cent, or all?

The total amount of punishment meted out by society is probably to a great extent determined by traditional limits. It will depend upon the capacity of the penal system, upon the number of staff available, the number of prison places, and old-established custom. There will rarely be any co-ordinated plan, any clear conscious design behind the total amount. So one should not expect any striking results if this amount increases or decreases. Two interesting examples of this have quite recently come to light. In California, the increase in the number of prisoners, especially in institutions for young persons, has for a long time caused great disquiet. This disquiet has not perhaps primarily been inspired by humanitarian reasons, rather by the increasing expense. Consequently, from 1966, a major campaign has been waged to encourage local probation services *not* to send juvenile offenders to institutions, but instead to gamble on keeping as many as possible at liberty. The services receive an additional financial grant in respect of every juvenile offender they would normally have sent but now do not send to a young persons' institution. The financial grant is but a fraction of what it would have cost to have the young person concerned incarcerated. It is claimed that as a result there has been a dramatic fall in the number of juvenile prisoners in California. Well-known institutions are standing empty; other projected ones have not been built.[9]

[9] Robert L. Smith, *A Quiet Revolution: Probation subsidy* Washington D.C., U.S. Dep. of Health, Education and Welfare, 1972. Karl O. Christiansen, 'Om at affolke fængsler', *Politikens kronik*, 1972, **6,** Juni.

In the State of Massachusetts even more radical steps have been taken, and in the course of the last couple of years all the closed institutions for juvenile criminals have been shut down. Out of a total of several thousand, a couple of hundred at the most (as far as I have been able to make out, possibly fewer) have been transferred to mental hospitals and other institutions. From this State no co-ordinated report is as yet available,[10] but neither of these experiments appears to have had any dramatic impact on the level of crime—in any direction. There are presumably very wide limits to the necessity for any reaction.

Nevertheless, in a society where people do not live so closely together that sufficient control is provided by the opinion of the neighbourhood, it is reasonable to assume that stronger remedies are required—that formally apportioned penalties must sometimes be a consequence of unlawful behaviour so that others do not follow the bad example. But in this connection the core of the problem is the wide and unknown boundaries of the behaviour types which need to be legally proscribed. For they mean that in reaching decisions in actual cases we receive remarkably little guidance from our stock of knowledge about general deterrents.

The second major problem here has to do with *type* of sanction. Again we are without relevant information. How great an effect does the severity of the punishment have? Does it make any difference whether those apprehended suffer retribution in silence or are exhibited in the market place, or whether they make atonement for days, or months, or years, or decades —or whether they answer with life and limb? I am of the opinion that it *does* make a difference—but again within extraordinarily wide and at present unknown limits. The English experience relating to drunken driving is not very helpful, at least not abroad. The sentences have been milder than those imposed in Norway, and no research has been directed to the effects of these sentences in a context independent of police control. In particular we know nothing for certain as to what effect a suspended prison sentence combined with a heavy fine and the possibility of a suspended driving licence would have. Recent research seems to indicate that a heavy fine would be regarded as a more severe penalty than a short prison sentence by a large section of the drunken driving clientele.[11]

Both regarding the amount and type of punishment the judge, in particular, is worse off with regard to relevant information than he often seems to think. Nearly all the examples relating to the effects of general prevention apply

[10] Loyd Ohlin and his staff at Harvard are currently preparing an evaluation.
[11] Anders Bratholm and Ragnar Hauge, 'Reaksjonene mot promille-kjørere', *Lov og Rett*, forthcoming, 1974.

to a *situation quite different from that confronting the judge when he has to choose a particular reaction in the individual case*. The judge is bound by a tradition of imposing punishment which normally requires him to choose between sanctions that rather closely resemble one another—three or six months' imprisonment, or suspended rather than an unsuspended sentence—while the examples of general prevention are concerned with such huge differences in stimuli as the presence or total absence of a police force. The examples of general prevention show that external social control is especially effective in relation to forms of criminal activity that are not inspired by deep and spontaneous inner impulses. But when the question is one of the general deterrent effects of the individual court decision, then we have no data to fall back on. Faced by the vital question, namely what effect is produced on person A by the infliction of a certain penalty on person B, we are driven back to common sense and intuition. They are not the worst bases for action. But it is important not to assume that the intuition is also based on solid scientific grounds.

It has, at least within theoretically oriented segments of the criminal justice system, been relatively easy to gain acceptance of the fact that no data indicate that one type of treatment produces less recidivism than any other type of treatment. But this insight could easily lead to the conclusion that general prevention has the scientific foundation which treatment lacks. Thus it is important to make clear how limited knowledge on general prevention actually is. It cannot provide the judge with a rational 'scientifically founded' base for decisions made about an individual case. Research on general prevention does not help him except in blocking out one rather extreme alternative: he ought not to cancel all activities.

Of course the totality of sentences imposed has consequences. Were no punishment imposed, the bottom would fall out of the system of reaction. We should find ourselves in a situation similar to that which arises when the police go on strike, and we should experience an increase in certain types of crime. And, conversely, if all drunken drivers received a sentence of 15 years' imprisonment, this also would presumably have consequences —this time in the direction of fewer cases of drunken driving (and a speedy amendment of the law). But, of course, these examples are not particularly practical. The judge has to choose between shades of retaliation a long way removed from artificial examples. In making this choice he certainly finds great consolation in referring to general prevention. But it is precisely in the area where he must function that the references to general prevention are on an especially shaky basis.

Something ought to follow certain actions—but we do not know what, how much, or in what way. Research on treatment effects leaves the judge without rational guidance, but so also does research on general prevention. This might be changed, relevant knowledge might sooner or later appear. But we do not have that sort of knowledge today.[12]

Functions for the Courts

But a negative result also has its positive sides.

Once we are freed from the belief that the judge can substantiate his arguments in favour of the individual and general deterrent effects and preventive incarceration, we are emboldened to ask whether the predominant faith in these objectives can have had detrimental effects *additional to* the lack of justification for them. One such effect has already been touched upon: it is the injustice to individuals which can occur in the name of treatment and preventive detention. But another detrimental effect is perhaps more important from the point of view of the interests of society as a whole. It is the neglect of *that function of punishment that has to do with the weighing of moral values,* or to put it another way, *the court's side-tracking of the politics in criminal policy.* How can we appreciate the evilness of the evil acts when the punishment is motivated by a wish to change future behaviour? How can we come to know the justness of the penalties when the punishment is disguised as welfare treatment? How can we evaluate mitigating circumstances when future behaviour-modification is the stated goal? Not only is the recent goal-orientated judicial tradition based on sand, but its whole short-range goal orientation also deprives the courts of the very type of service that only they can provide. There are no other institutions available that are so clearly designed for evaluating conflict. There are no alternative arrangements for the subtle weighing of evils in society. We are therefore at a loss when the relevant institution is used for other purposes.

We are left without evaluative guidance. And we are also left without facilities for controlling the new decision-makers, who can oscillate in their aims and moral reasoning, and in addition claim that basically the sanction is not a punishment at all. Thus, we have reduced the system's possibilities for giving moral guidance, but at the same time increased the power of the decision-makers within the system. But let me add: This is all a question of degrees. Parallel to the rational giving of reasons, the old tradition has all the time been vividly alive. A report from one of the valleys in my country indicates that up there the word of God and reasoning from Natural Law is seen as a perfectly sufficient base for all legal decisions. And this is not

[12] For a more detailed discussion see Andenæs, op. cit., 1950 and 1966, and Christie, op. cit., 1971.

only so in the valleys. Orientation towards future goals and use of rational means for reaching them is certainly much more dominant a feature in debates on criminal policy and legal theory than in the *practice* of the courts, and the lower courts in particular. Many a judge will, probably rightly so, be of the opinion that what really lies behind the conclusions with regard to punishments are values and moral views. To keep up with the demands of modern times, however, some fashionable reflections are mixed into it all— usually some remarks indicating that the decision is influenced by what is best for the individual's treatment or necessary for general prevention. But this cover-up reduces the possibilities of clarifying the real reasons, and the possibilities for constructive criticism are likewise reduced. We need courts as clearly defined arenas for decisions on values—uncontaminated by other aims. Nothing is thereby implied about severity. The morality applied can be severe or mild; it can lead to the infliction of great pains, or minor ones. The point is that we should be made quite conscious of what is going on, so that we can thereby embark upon a rational discussion of what type of morality should form the foundation of the penalties imposed by the courts.

I am not implying that society possesses a set of shared values which would without a doubt command general approval as a result of public discussion and that the rôle of the judge is primarily to help to start the discussion. On the contrary, it will be a normal feature of a society such as ours that disagreement and conflict are rife with regard to both what are and what ought to be society's basic values, and even more so with regard to how these values are to be applied in the individual case. The point is precisely that the courts through their adoption of clear-cut moral positions would be able to bring these conflicts into focus. The courts thereby could regain their value-crystallizing function. What the courts condemn and why and how they do it must be *clearly visible* so that any subsequent conflict relating to these values can be subjected to a constructive debate within the society concerned. In the short term, judicial pronouncements about these values will be authoritarian; it will be the voice of one individual judge. But in the long term, a clear pronouncement makes it possible to bring about changes in these values if powerful groups so wish. But this possibility is lost when the courts operate under an illusion that they are concerned with rehabilitation or are directly influencing general obedience to law. Paying regard to such illusory effects makes things far too easy for the judge.

Three Types of Evaluation

There are in particular three types of values that we can clarify by this means. Firstly, there is the evaluation of the *criminal offence*. How serious are cases of petty theft in an affluent society? How serious are embezzlement of tax funds, high treason, dishonest acquisition of social security benefits, or defamation of another person's character? In some circles there is a gnawing doubt whether some of these transgressions merit any special attention at all on society's part. This doubt ought to be made public and become the subject of political debate.

Secondly, and this is equally important, we shall thus be able to pursue a more open discussion about the *choice of the type of suffering* that can be inflicted in the course of punishment. It will then be a question not of what penalties are *effective*, but of what *in the name of decency can properly be inflicted*. Which types of intended suffering accord with the basic values? Death has a different meaning in different societies and at different periods, and so does physical suffering. Death is a more severe punishment in a society in which people live long and endure less physical suffering in their lifetime than in one in which they die young and normally suffer a great deal. Imprisonment is more grievous in a society in which life at large is easy and enjoyable than in one in which it is difficult and dangerous. Loss of one's reputation depends on whether it occurs in a society in which reputation counts; the imposition of a fine is a heavier punishment in a society in which money counts most than in one in which other benefits—for example cleanliness or contact with the next world—happen to be of paramount importance. And if one means of punishment is to be substituted for another, what yardstick is to be applied if one wishes to give 'equally severe punishment', that is to say inflict equally great suffering? How great a loss of freedom corresponds to how much money or how much physical suffering or how much public disgrace? What measure is the equivalent of what other; what *ought* to be the equivalent of what else? Again, these are questions that must be exposed so that they may become the subject of public debate and political decisions.

Thirdly, release from empirical considerations will make it possible to set in progress a moral debate about what characteristics *of the criminal and his situation* ought to count as extenuating or aggravating circumstances. It has not been possible to conduct such a discussion in recent years. It has been set aside by treatment enthusiasts, with appropriate ideologies, in favour of a discussion about what reactions most effectively prevent recidivism in the individual criminal offender. Many of the most important characteristics of the individual concerned have been dismissed as irrelevant. Nothing can be done with poverty except to get rid of it. Bad living conditions, a bad environment, lost opportunities, a boring job, an angry wife or no wife, bitterness occasioned by injustice and ignominious defeats, such factors do not perhaps provide especially suitable starting points for treatment, but some of them might be perceived to have a vital bearing on the question of the degree of individual guilt. Advocates of treatment have not had the resources to relieve poverty, improve living conditions, or appease angry wives. At the most they have been able to strive to adjust the individual to his fate, and have had to be on the lookout for characteristics which could be altered. A mass of difficulties and handicaps caused by an orphaned upbringing may have created reading disabilities. For those who have such disabilities, treatment is provided in institution X, and so, for example, a car thief may be sent there. And in this way the core of the problem created by the mass of difficulties and the lack of parents is passed over. But the knowledge of all this ought to be accorded a quite independent significance as regards the evaluation of the individual's *blameworthiness*. People who have grown up in difficult surroundings and without parental care ought perhaps to be more leniently dealt with in respect of their transgression than other people. An evaluation of the justice of the case might perhaps require the sentence to be a warning accompanied by a recommendation for a pension— not on the basis of any hope that it would help, but on the basis of a reasoned assessment that it would be a decent and just solution for one who has had such a difficult start in life.

Against the background of all the dislocations brought about by concentrating on individual characteristics, and especially in view of all the misuse of power that has taken place, one can well understand why the American Friends Service Committee in their report, *Struggle for Justice*[13] propose that individual characteristics should be entirely ignored and instead punishment fitted exclusively to the gravity of the crime. This is quite understandable in the context of the special conditions prevailing in the U.S.A., with the tremendous use of indeterminate sentences and the consequent problems relating to legal safeguards. But this point of view is also of relevance for us, though from quite a different angle. Even if we should completely succeed in freeing ourselves from the temptation to make use of individual characteristics as a basis for a treatment-orientated judgement when a crime has been committed, it is nevertheless clear that paying attention to individual characteristics can easily obscure the other two evaluations that also must be made: the evaluation of the gravity of the crime, and the evaluation of how serious the punitive measures to be inflicted really

[13] American Friends Service Committee, *Struggle for Justice*, New York, Hill and Wang, 1971.

are. It will be expecting a great deal from a judge if he is to clarify, in one and the same judgement, the relative importance he has attached to these three factors.

But there is really no other avenue open. The judge has had an easy time of it for so long. He must now shoulder a heavier burden. The same applies to the theoreticians in the field of criminal law who have failed to present us with a developed theoretical structure and a coherent system relating to these themes. We cannot, at any rate in a society such as ours, avoid taking up the questions of individual extenuating or aggravating circumstances. Most of us are not in favour of a system based on the extraction of an eye for an eye, and a tooth for a tooth. We need an elaborate categorization of the factors which a reasonable society thinks it should be concerned with when considering the mildness or severity of its penalties. We need a systematic exposition of what characteristics of criminal offenders a society such as ours ought to take into consideration. What weight is to be attached to the fact that an offender is young; not to heal him, but because one cannot expect ordinary good sense or thoughtfulness or responsibility from those who are excluded from many of the most important resources in society? Likewise, is some allowance to be made for great age, sickness, illegitimate birth, an unfaithful husband, or a drunken father? How great an allowance? And what about those who have previously enjoyed privileges? Is it reasonable that a person who has received a good education shall be punished as leniently as a person who has been badly educated, or that as little retribution shall be exacted from rich persons as from poor persons, or that the strong shall get off as lightly as the weak? Or as regards the weak—should some upper limit be set to their extenuating suffering? Among recidivist prisoners the expression 'served in advance' is sometimes used. They sometimes have the feeling that it is society that owes them something and not the other way around, and that for every day they spend in prison they acquire a constantly increasing claim upon society.

Where are the radical or even socialist ideas on punishment? They are not even evident in welfare states where social democrats have been in the majority for most of the latter part of the century. Maybe the line of thought I have been pursuing is particularly vulnerable in rational industrial societies. Why develop a socialist-oriented penal theory with regard to acts, types of sufferings, and extenuating as well as aggravating circumstances if the basic problems are perceived as treatment or prediction of dangerousness? With the utmost goodwill one might be able to say that the debate between the proponents of general prevention and those advocating treatment reflects a debate between conservatives and radicals. Personally I think this debate has been a dead end, distracting attention from the major political questions.

Encouraged by theory, the courts have shirked the task of clearly enunciating the fundamental considerations they apply in each individual case. Only when they undertake such an exposition, will it be possible for others to take up a firm position. Only in this way can the courts preserve their important *conflict-creating* function. The courts have for a long time been drifting in a stagnant lagoon protected by the belief that they are, through expertise, striving to reach attainable utilitarian goals. It is time that they were forced out of this and into the flowing waters of a clearly expressed and exposed morality.

JURISPRUDENCE
EMPIRICALLY TESTED

Adam Podgorecki

'The relation between criminal law and morality . . . has been considered an essential preliminary to all legal textbooks. Whatever its length its contents have been pretty much the same: they include such truisms as "The relationship between law and morality can be metaphorically expressed as that between two intersecting circles"; or "A legal system which would prohibit, or even punish, a basically immoral act *per se*, would defeat itself and prove unenforceable in practice"; or, "the penal law is, and should be, less wide than social morality . . . because the penal law should forbid and punish only actions which are harmful and dangerous to the social order . . . and should, whenever it is not rigorously necessary, abstain from intervention out of respect for individual liberty. . . . On the other hand, certain actions, though morally indifferent, are forbidden by penal law . . . because, though they do not harm others directly, they involve a potential danger or are harmful to certain institutions and measures provided for by the constructive legislation of a country."

Perhaps these things have to be said, but they do not lead very far when it comes to the consideration of particular measures.'[1]

Introductory Remarks

Traditionally, the theory of law (jurisprudence) dealt with the following problems: social norms, legal norms, elements of norms, sanctions, law versus morality, natural law, legal systems, legal reasoning, legality, equality, justice, rights, duty, obligation, etc. Over a long period each author has stubbornly taken the same path: criticizing the notions of previous writers and presenting his own set of new and 'original' concepts. But the growing amount of semantic misunderstanding and the increasing range of mutually

[1] Leon Radzinowicz, *Ideology and Crime*, London, Heinemann Educational Books, 1966, pp. 101–2.

untestable arguments produced an atmosphere of theoretical sterility. Dissatisfaction with this state of affairs among research workers has now shifted the focus of enquiry, directing it to new areas. Problems such as respect for the law, legal awareness, effectiveness of the law, and deviance have become the main targets of empirical studies. This changing spirit and methodological orientation has gradually altered the traditional approach to the field of jurisprudence. The scope of this new jurisprudence is still not clear. It has begun to emerge through empirical research but has not yet fully reformulated basic problems or become aware of its own achievements.

Before I attempt to translate several abstract traditional notions into operationally testable concepts, it is necessary to consider some general methodological issues.

Analytic or descriptive definitions are particularly important in the social sciences, for they try to grasp encountered social reality. Synthetic (projective) definitions, arbitrarily stipulating the meaning of a term, are more significant in the deductive disciplines (like mathematics and logic), the basic pursuit of which depends upon propositions and statements entailing each other, and systems being coherent. Although analytic definitions which attempt to describe the basic concepts referring to social reality are so important in the social sciences in general, and in legal disciplines in particular, it remains rather difficult to construct them—the reason being the multiplicity of meanings that a term may possess—and this applies particularly to basic terms. M. Ossowska, who is an authority on matters of semantics and sociological disquisitions on morals, said: 'We do not regret the effort once spent to outline the concept of morality, for we have learned a lot from these attempts; today we still insist that any efforts to build up an analytical definition of morals, i.e. a definition respecting the apparent common sense intuitions related to this term, are doomed to failure in advance. Any analytical definition ought indeed to be formulated only after the public opinion has been polled. But in this particular instance we have very good reasons to suppose that the method of opinion polling, even if it was limited to a single social group, would not produce compatible results.'[2] It is apparent that we might gain from giving up attempts to construct analytic definitions and turn towards the building of synthetic ones, taking care to make them methodologically useful. Doubtless, this might obviate the difficulties in a situation both methodologically and theoretically bewildering. However, such an approach would not be without problems for it would impose limitations on the scope of communication, caused not by ambiguity of terms, but by the abundance of different meanings attributed to them. Doubtless, if every writer in any discipline of the social sciences

[2] M. Ossowska, *Sociologia Moralności*, Warszawa, P.W.N. 1969, p. 252.

insisted on the meanings which he had stipulated by his own arbitrary decisions (as would happen, if any and all synthetic definitions were respected), then the meaning of the term used in each isolated publication might well be clear in its context, but the consequent multitude of untranslatable meanings would soon constitute another barrier against intersubjective understanding. In what follows I shall suggest a tentative solution which avoids this vicious circle.

Hitherto, the intuitions underlying analytic definitions were drawn from accidental experiences and observations, selected unsystematically and by way of illustration, according to idiosyncratic semantic tastes. These experiences and those tastes, in spite of their tendency to similarity which results from some communication, and the stock of data available, in academic environments, may still differ in important ways. Consequently, the systems of concepts and the models based on them may differ widely from each other. The alternative is *not* to base the analytic definitions upon private terminology, but instead upon suggestions drawn from an analysis of operational definitions (i.e. those adopted for research purposes) and from the results of empirical investigations of public opinion. Even though such investigations are still in their initial stage, some synthesis can be attempted even now. We can also make use of the existing investigations which allow us to generalize from existing historical, psychological and sociological data, drawing from both the output of particular writers and from the general body of established knowledge.

It might be objected that such an approach will arbitrarily select its starting points, analyse only a few selected definitions relating to the law, consider only a few sociological investigations concerning public opinion on law and morality, dismiss the extensive literature concerning various concepts widespread in the legal sciences, etc. The charges could be multiplied, but they neglect some essential points, namely that the number of legal definitions which *could* be analysed is enormous and that some selection or other is absolutely necessary; that on the contrary there are only a few relevant sociological investigations; that spurious problems have piled up relating to discussions such as those on the so-called levels or surfaces of the legal sciences, and that a Gordian knot of misunderstandings can be cut only by leaving these spurious issues aside. All these objections would miss what is the ultimate objective of the proposed approach: its aim is *not* to make a full survey of all the possible definitions taking into account their methodological shortcomings and merits, but simply to focus attention upon those data which promise to be particularly useful for our purpose.

Problems

Recent studies dealing with attitudes towards the law, relations between legal and moral norms, different types of legal sub-cultures, links between actual behaviour and legal values which pertain to this behaviour, types of conformity and deviation along with reflections on basic questions arising from jurisprudence, now present new possibilities of formulating some hypothetical statements in a more operational way. These are:

1. that the acceptance of the law differs in different social systems;
2. that the acceptance of the law differs in different areas of social behaviour;
3. that the acceptance of the law differs depending upon the different levels of generality with which it is expressed;
4. that the legal condemnation of certain anti-social behaviour induces also moral condemnation of this type of behaviour;
5. that the acceptance of the law varies with different social backgrounds, different personality traits and different interpersonal patterns of human relations;
6. that 'anti-legal' (illegal) behaviour does not lead to the erosion of legal and moral values but nevertheless generates negative attitudes towards law enforcement officers;
7. that the knowledge of the law differs as far as the primary and secondary rules of law are concerned;
8. that there are different stages in the socialization of legal values;
9. that the acceptance of the legal system of a given social system does not warrant the acceptance of the political version of this system;
10. that the acceptance of the law lies somewhere between two extremes: the '*autotelic*' orientation towards the law and the '*heterotelic*' one.[3]

Relevant Findings

A synthetic overview will be presented below in order to test the empirical foundations of the propositions listed above.

Proposition 1: That the acceptance of the law differs in different social systems
   There are several ways to measure the acceptance of the law. The traditional way consists in conducting enquiries on the crime rate characteristic of a given period of time or country, the type of anti-social behaviour, etc.

---

[3] These terms are explained below, see p. 316.

There also exist other areas which might be investigated in order to establish the nature of legal prestige: the scope and intensity of appeals made against legal decisions, the activities of various pressure groups aiming to change the existing law or trying to enact a new one, and the extent to which the charisma surrounding a particular law is due to the traditional label attached to that law.

The most recent approach has been to study attitudes related in some way to the law. The first thing these studies reveal is that the law is rooted in entirely different ways in different types of societies. Some societies based on values shaped by differentiated, stable social structures do not perceive law as the basic element of their generally accepted value code. Other societies have a tendency to treat the law as the linchpin of their standards for individual and group behaviour. This is illustrated in two studies.

In Korea 57 per cent of the population under investigation said that the man capable of living without the law was a good and gentle man and 17 per cent of this population said that he was a foolish man.[4] An American enquiry produced the opposite results; 86 per cent of the population studied felt that a man was not able to live without law.[5] The simple findings of these studies (which should be continued as they point to new avenues for research) reflect the divergence of the roots and social settings of different legal orders. In one culture, the law is a secondary additional device which enters the social picture when other traditional well-established instruments for control fail to work effectively. In the other culture, the lack of a legal dimension to the fabric of social behaviour would be deemed unthinkable. Thus, the first distinction to be made in considering the role of the law is in the traditional, cultural and philosophical set of values prevailing in a given society. According to the results of the studies mentioned above (however simplified they might be), it is possible to suggest that the law plays a different rôle in societies with a traditional Chinese culture: they rely more on the concept of a decent man (who knows how to conduct himself according to the traditionally accepted norms of courtesy, duty, etiquette) than on the recognition of rules which stem from the legal order as an abstract body of regulations reflecting possible alternative behaviours.

Societies belonging to the so-called western culture are from the point of view of philosophical framework homogeneous enough to be compared,

[4] Pyong-Choon Hahn, 'The Decision Process in Korea' in G. Schubert and D. J. Danelski (eds.), *Comparative Judicial Behaviour*, Oxford University Press, 1969.

[5] Research conducted in Philadelphia in 1972 by A. Podgorecki with co-operation of students participating in a seminar on the sociology of law at the University of Pennsylvania: J. Eigen, B. Epstein, P. Pietrovito, B. Simon, V. Vournas. The sample taken randomly from different strata of Philadelphia population (quota system) consists of 100 subjects.

and several studies are available for comparison. They usually assume that the law is supported by custom, morals and ethical concepts. However, the law often appears to rely not on this reservoir of supportive feelings but on the sense of legal imperative which produces an obedience to the law whatever the conditions might be in the situation covered by the law.

A Polish study in 1964 of a nationwide representative sample of the Polish population (2,820 subjects) has sought to examine this problem empirically and to measure the degree of average compliance with the law prevailing in the society.[6]

It focused its attention on public attitudes including the degree of eagerness with which orders from superiors are accepted (a factor which seems to be crucial when administrative decisions are made) and the intensity of feelings about the rejection or acceptance of a possible bribe. The essential question, which was later taken up also in Dutch, Belgian,[7] German[8] and American[9] studies, was formulated as shown in Table 1.

These findings clearly show that the general prestige of the law varies in different societies. Strangely enough, the degree of acceptance of the law is the same in Holland (a country which did not go through the complicated process of political and social revolution in which one political and social system was rejected and another one was imposed) as it is in Poland (which was moulded by such a process). In the U.S.A. the emphasis on the law is stronger than in Holland or Poland, a phenomenon which may reflect the strong American reliance on the law as an egalitarian device for regulating interaction and competition. It could also express the social need for obedience to law (because of the rising crime problem). The heavy reliance of Germans on the law is not a new discovery. German society is traditionally known as a law-abiding state and nation. These simple findings might also indicate that 'the divorce' (e.g., in Germany) between the acceptance of the law and its moral evaluation can lead to anomie in the social system as a whole (which is different from the anomie existing inside of a given social system). In such a situation the whole social system could be induced to

[6] A. Podgorecki, *Prestiz Prawa*, Warsaw, Książka i Wiedza, 1966.

[7] The fullest description of the Dutch and Belgian studies may be found in J. Van Houtte and P. Vinke, 'Attitudes Governing the Acceptance of Legislation Among Various Social Groups' in, A. Podgorecki *et al., Knowledge and Opinion about Law*, London, Martin Robertson, 1973.

[8] W. Kaupen and R. Merle, *Knowledge and Opinion of Law and Legal Institutions in the Federal Republic of Germany (Preliminary results)*, 7th World Congress of Sociology, Evian, 1965 (unpublished) and W. Kaupen, H. Volks and R. Merele, *Compendium of Results of a Representative Study Among the German Population on Knowledge and Opinion of Law and Legal Institutions*, Atbeitskreis für Rechtssozologie ander Universität za Köln, 1971, *mimeo*.

[9] Op. cit.

accept any skilfully advertised ideology, because the internalized moral standards would not offer sufficient guidance for the evaluation of the principal values which underlie the legal order.

TABLE I

Compliance with the Law

	Poland	Holland	U.S.A.	Germany	Japan*
The law should always be obeyed even if in your opinion it is wrong. Agree	45%				
Do you think a law should be obeyed even when you feel this law is unjust? Yes		47%			
The law should always be obeyed even if in your opinion it is wrong			51%		
You should obey the law even if you do not think they are just. Agree				66%	
We should obey the law under any circumstances, because it is laid down to assure a peaceful society. It is expedient to avoid violating it so far as possible although it is not always just					73%

* Japanese data should be interpreted with some caution. The above-mentioned figure is based on Government research conducted in 1969 (as reported by M. Chiba, *Results and Problems of K.O.L. Research in Japan, A Preliminary Report,* Nordwijk, 1972, unpublished material, p. 9). The following questions were used: (a) we should obey the law under any circumstances, because it is laid down to ensure a peaceful society— 39.3 per cent, (b) it is expedient to avoid violating it so far as possible although it is not always just—34.1 per cent; (c) I have never thought of this specifically, because the problem scarcely affects me—14.2 per cent; (d) we are not required to respect the law, because it is laid down for the advantage of older people and the establishment; (e) no answer and Don't Know—8.6 per cent. These findings contradict the notion that the law in Japan (as it is in other Oriental societies) is regarded as a secondary element of social control. The adherence to traditional values seems to be the basic regulatory force in the society. At the present time apparently we witness in Japan two parallel, somewhat contradictory currents: a modern one (as expressed by results which have been quoted) and an older traditionally oriented one. This observation explains the seeming contradiction with M. Chiba's conclusion: ' . . . peoples' consciousness of individual rights and the law was likely to be weak, uncertain or even non-existent, in view of their attachment to traditional feelings toward unity of the family, community, and nation and so on' (page 20).

Proposition 2: The acceptance of the law differs in different areas of social behaviour

The study of the legal and moral attitudes of the Polish population[10] produced some evidence that different types of 'anti-moral' and illegal behaviour are condemned (as punishable) in different ways. According to this research, behaviour endangering human life was at the top of the list of legally condemned actions; abuses of the norms of legal procedure—strangely enough—were ranked second (even higher than behaviour which violates traditionally established moral norms), and behaviour which violates norms relating to ownership was at the bottom of the list.

The Dutch and Belgian study[11] investigated these problems in a more penetrating way. Quite clear differences were found in the degree of legal condemnation.

TABLE 2

Legal Condemnation of Behaviour

Offences which deserve punishment	*Holland and Belgium** The condemning percentage of the population
1. Offences involving danger to human life and direct abuse of the legal system	100–70
2. Serious fiscal offences	70–50
3. Offences against morality	50–30
4. Lighter fiscal offences	less than 50

* The American study supports these findings.

TABLE 3

Condemnation of Behaviour by Others

Offences which deserve punishment	*Holland and Belgium* The belief that this type of offence is condemned by others	
	condemned by all %	*condemned by most* %
1. Immoral behaviour	5	60
2. Serious fiscal offence	5	46
3. Traffic violation	5	39
4. Lighter fiscal violation	2	28

[10] A. Podgorecki, J. Kurczewski, J. Kwaśniewski and M. Łoś, *Poglądy Społeczeństwa Polskiego na Moralność i Prawo*, Warszawa, Książka i Wiedza, 1971.

[11] Van Houtte and Winke, op. cit.

These findings indicate, further, that social systems tend to require different levels of 'internal force' to cope with various deviant behaviours.

It is possible to assume that the trial and error procedure embodied in a given social system (the mechanism which L. Petrazycki called *unconsciously ingenious adjustment*) selects, in the long run, some violations of the norms of conformity as more dangerous to the society and consequently attacks them more with severe condemnation and punishment, and that conversely some violations are selected as relatively less important and accordingly assigned more flexible and appropriate means of social control. It could be interesting to study the shift in the focus of social attention paid to different types of deviance as reflected in changes in the level of condemnation which different types of socially deviant behaviour receive. It would be also interesting to find links between the vested interests being defended and parallel social changes.

Proposition 3: The acceptance of the law differs depending upon the different levels of generality with which it is expressed

As a Danish study has clearly shown, acceptance of the law and the consequent strength of condemnation of violations differs according to whether it is being considered on the more general and abstract level or on a more concrete level.[12]

A study conducted by G. Zellman and D. O. Sears found a similar pattern: 'The combination of widespread support for the abstract principle of free speech, alongside opposition to its extension to concrete situations is a crucial characteristic of both children's and adults' opinions.'[13]

The American study examined this problem in more detail. It posed two sets of questions: one set dealing with the general aspect of law and the other with questions of a more specific nature.[14]

In all these answers, the tendency to apply informal sanctions was stronger than a tendency to react with formal sanctions. But only in one case (car speeding) was the tendency to use the informal sanctions as high as the percentage expressing a general respect for the law shown in Table 4. Even so it should be recognized that active support for the generally expressed attachment to legal values might manifest itself not only in the use of formal means of social control but also in the different ways of informal social control. If this were taken into account, the gap between respect for the law

[12] B. Kutschinsky, 'Regarding Legal Phenomena in Denmark', in Nils Christie (ed.), *Scandinavian Studies in Criminology*, **2**, Oslo, Universitetsvorlaget, 1968.

[13] G. Zellman and D. O. Sears, 'Childhood Origins of Tolerance for Dissent', *The Journal of Social Issues*, 1971, **27**, 2 (Special issue on Socialisation, the Law and Society).

[14] Cf. footnote 5, above.

expressed on the abstract and concrete levels might not be so wide as it otherwise appears.

TABLE 4*

Acceptance of the Law

	Percentage Agreeing
There are different opinions as far as observance of the law is concerned. Choose the particular opinion which is closest to your own.	
(a) the law should always be obeyed even if in my opinion it is wrong	51
(b) when the law is wrong people should only pretend to obey it and in practice should try to get around it	3
(c) wrong laws should not be obeyed at all	17
(d) difficult to say	28
Most people have moral principles which they try to live up to. What do you think a person should do if obeying a law contradicts a personal moral principle?	
(a) he should obey the law because it is the law	39
(b) he should obey the law because he is afraid of what might happen if he breaks it	8
(c) he should disobey the law and follow his principles despite the consequences	23
(d) difficult to say	23
Sometimes it is difficult to obey the law in exceptional situations. For example, when a soldier is told to shoot those whom he believes to be innocent but who are suspected to be the enemy, he should:	
(a) shoot because it is an order	30
(b) not shoot because he thinks the order is not right	30
(c) difficult to say	39
Should laws always be obeyed?	
(a) yes	60
(b) no	37
Please explain your answer.	

All answers to these questions display, in a consistent pattern, a relatively high respect for the law as it is expressed by the general principles. The comparison of these answers with answers to questions having a more concrete character, as given below, leads to interesting conclusions.

---

* If the 'no answers' were included percentages would equal 100.

TABLE 5*

Preferred Action on Perceiving Law-breaking

	Percentage Agreeing
If the driver of the car in which you are riding is speeding, how would you react?	
(a) would not do anything about it	9
(b) try to convince him to slow down	72
(c) report it to the police	2
(d) don't know	8
If an official of a private company whom you know is unlawfully charging personal items to the company account, how would you react?	
(a) not do anything about it	28
(b) try to convince him to stop it	47
(c) bring it to the attention of the authorities	15
(d) don't know	10
If you find that an adult you know commits a homosexual act with a consenting adult, how would you react?	
(a) will not do anything about it	81
(b) try to convince him to stop this behaviour	11
(c) bring it to the attention of the authorities	4
(d) don't know	4
If a government official whom you know is unlawfully charging personal items to official expenses, how would you react?	
(a) don't know	18
(b) not do anything about it	21
(c) bring it to the attention of the authorities	27
(d) try to convince him to stop it	33

* If the 'no answers' were included percentages would equal 100.

Proposition 4: The legal condemnation of certain anti-social behaviour induces also moral condemnation of this type of behaviour

Contrary to the usually expressed expectations of jurisprudence, the legal condemnation of certain illegal behaviours (usually a contravention of a procedural rôle) also induces moral condemnation of these types of behaviours. This is shown clearly both by the data on legal and moral attitudes of the Polish population and the findings of the American study. A pilot study undertaken in England also supports these data.[15]

[15] Replications of Polish study based on a questionnaire prepared by A. Podgorecki, J. Kurczewski, J. Kwaśniewski, M. Łoś (cf. footnote 10). Study conducted by A. Żebrowska. The sample used consists of 100 randomly selected subjects of the British population (1972).

TABLE 6

Attitudes Towards Condemnation and Punishment*

Suppose that somebody:	Would I condemn?						Should the law provide punishment?					
	% Yes, to some extent			% Strongly			% No			% Yes		
	Poland	U.S.A.	England	Poland	U.S.A.	England	Poland	U.S.A.	England	Poland	U.S.A.	England
(1) violated pedestrian rules	45·7	20	39	38·6	67	26	23·0	18	30	56·9	67	43
(2) did not register his TV or radio although he used it	40·5		30	40·5		52	23·2		13	57·0		73
(3) did not turn up as a court witness without a good reason	36·7	61	52	40·8	30	39	21·4	27	16	54·7	70	56
(4) didn't register his gun†		35			55			12			80	

* Don't Know's not included.   † Only U.S.A.

The Dutch findings support the Polish, American and English data:

TABLE 7

Attitudes Towards Condemnation and Punishment in Holland

Suppose that somebody:	Would I condemn? % Yes	Should the law provide punishment? %
(1) did not register his TV or radio	82·3	64·3
(2) did not turn up as a court witness without a good reason	85·4	53·6
(3) did not follow residence regulations	58·3	30·0

As mentioned above, the bulk of these findings contradicts certain well-established ideas in jurisprudence. According to traditional thought, law and morals affect three areas of behaviour: (1) behaviour governed exclusively by morals; (2) behaviour governed exclusively by law; and the main area of human behaviour; (3) behaviour governed simultaneously by law and morals. Data collected in Polish, American, English and Dutch studies rule out the second possibility, namely behaviour governed exclusively by law.

M. Łoś proposed the following explanation to elucidate the inconsistency between theoretical expectations (which are to some extent supported by common-sense intuitions) and empirical evidence. The moral condemnation arising where legal condemnation takes place is, according to this explanation, a secondary one. It does not pertain so much to the condemned behaviour itself, as to the fact that the legal order, its logic and structure, has been impaired. This type of condemnation tries to defend the legal order against violations which, although they often attack neutral elements of this order, nevertheless might, and usually do, attack non-neutral elements of it. And yet the West German data (W. Kaupen and A. Merle)[16] unexpectedly contradict these, surprisingly consistent, findings.

Although these data are not sufficiently substantial, they lead to some interesting speculations. If they find further confirmation, then the following explanation might be offered: if the legal system has strong legalistic support

[16] Kaupen and Merle, op. cit.

(as this system has: 66 per cent of the German population, said that it would obey the laws even if they were not just), then this particular social system does not need to strengthen the motivational forces which it has at its disposal by using additional moral motivations. This strategy (applied by 'unconsciously ingenious adjustment mechanisms') seems to permit the rational allocation of social energy. Nevertheless, it involves some potential dangers which, as noted earlier, consist in the lack of corrective mechanisms for morally evaluating laws and thus for preventing the use of law to achieve undesirable goals.

TABLE 8

Knowledge and Opinion of Two Laws in West Germany

	*Are the following behaviours prohibited or not?**		*Is the behaviour?*		
	Prohibited %	Not prohibited %	Very bad %	Fairly bad %	Not bad %
Someone changes his domicile without registering his new address	84	11	4	16	78
A workman has a weekend job and does not declare this income (200 DM a month) for tax purposes	69	22	4	19	74

* Don't Know's not included.

Proposition 5: Acceptance of the law varies with different social backgrounds, different personality traits and different interpersonal patterns of human relations

This three-step hypothesis was formulated in an earlier article;[17] its essential features might be summarized in the following way. The hypothesis of the three-factor functioning of the law means that an 'abstract binding law' influences social behaviour by means of three basic variables or 'meta-standards'. The first independent variable is the content and significance assigned to the given legal enactment by the type of socio-economic relationship within which it operates as a binding element of the legal system. The second independent variable (which may differentially modify the functioning of an abstract law—within the framework of a given socio-economic system— as a link between the legislator's directives and the social behaviour of those bound by the law) is the type of legal sub-culture. The third independent variable (which may variously modify the functioning of an abstract law—

[17] A. Podgorecki, 'Three Modifiers of the Operation of the Law', *Polish Sociological Bulletin*, No. 1, 1966.

within the framework of a given socio-economic system and a legal sub-culture) is the type of personality of the subjects ultimately affected by the law. Abstract laws begin to function and to be expressed in terms of social behaviour in conjunction with their human subjects, and it is into this context of human relations that the law itself and the 'meta-standards', or variables, which influence social behaviour enter. This general hypothesis is supported by a lot of empirical data,[18] but in the light of further enquiries, it needs some extension and modification. The essential modifying factor would be the introduction of a new concept of 'invisible factors'.[19]

Proposition 6: Illegal behaviour does not lead to the erosion of legal and moral values but nevertheless generates negative attitudes towards law enforcement offices

B. Kutchinsky formulated these generalizations in the following way: 'The empirical evidence . . . leads to the conclusion that, generally speaking, criminals and non-criminals, delinquents and non-delinquents, persons who have committed crimes and persons who have not, share more or less the same attitudes, as expressed in questionnaire studies.' And, again, in a more specific way: 'first of all, we found an overall tendency among criminals or persons who had committed criminal offences, to be slightly more tolerant towards crime and criminals, to believe somewhat more often that punishments are too severe, that the police and courts do not treat all citizens alike, that criminality is more widespread than most people think, and so on.'[20] The Polish study also supports these general statements.[21]

The findings which suggested these generalizations are quite puzzling. An expectation that behaviour had a tendency to be consistent with the values pertaining to it (or that 'positive' social values lead to 'positive' social behaviour, and 'negative' social values generate 'negative' social behaviour) seems to be reasonably supported by common knowledge and also by Festinger's theory of cognitive dissonance. In fact these findings directly contradict the theory that through a process of assimilation there is a general tendency to reduce contradictions between opinions and behaviour. Another Polish study on divorce was quite consistent with these general findings.[22] The overwhelming majority of a sample of the Polish

[18] A. Podgorecki, 'Law and Morals in Theory and Operation', *Polish Sociological Bulletin*, No. 7, 1969.

[19] The concept of 'invisible factors' will be developed later on in this paper.

[20] B. Kutchinsky, 'Knowledge and Attitudes regarding Law and Law-Breaking', in A. Podgorecki *et al., Knowledge and Opinion About Law*, London, Martin Robertson, 1973, pp. 118 and 120.

[21] Podgorecki, Kurczewski *et al.*, op. cit.

[22] A. Podgorecki, *Zjawiska Prawne w Opinii Publicznej*, Warszawa, Wydawni-ctwo Prawnicze, 1964, Chapter 2. (Nationwide study conducted in 1962 based on interviews with 2355 subjects).

population declared itself to be religious.[23] Even so, the same sample of the population on the whole accepted divorce (a new institution, established in 1945 which, of course, directly contradicts the general religious beliefs). While 30 per cent of the population rejected divorce when a question was formulated in a general way only 7 per cent rejected it when the questions were more specifically formulated (e.g., would you accept the idea of divorce in a case when the husband committed a crime, is cruel, etc.). These findings point to the existing dissonance between diverging values, namely, religious beliefs on the one hand and values which govern family life on the other. Nevertheless, this contradiction could be explained in terms of cognitive dissonance theory. The dissonance between these values may exist as a price paid for the reduction of another dissonance which otherwise would exist between social practice and values which guide this practice—for lots of people are divorced, this is a socially recognized fact, the rate of divorce is increasing and divorced people are socially accepted. What this study shows is that pressure of socially accepted behaviour is such that it induces values which are ambivalent and contradict more widespread values rooted in tradition—values consistent with much behaviour. If this is so, why is the situation in relation to illegal behaviour different?

The following is a possible explanation: the social ('positive') values still held (by people actively engaged in anti-social and illegal behaviour) are transformed through the intervention of 'invisible factors' ('germs') and in this way become 'immune' and unresponsive to social activity. If so, what are these invisible factors? They are not personality traits because these factors usually constitute a set of traits or a configuration which incorporates several personality traits in a structural unit. They are not 'neutralization techniques' or 'rationalizations' because they actually generate these neutralization factors and rationalized excuses. They might be defined as general orientations which combine many attitudes into a unified pattern of response. These patterns of response are not influenced by biological factors (as apparently is the case with introverted or extroverted orientations) but instead are influenced by the principal social changes which create such psychic and social responses. In the study of the moral and legal attitudes of the Polish population,[24] three of these patterns of response were recognized, defined, operationalized and investigated: (1) principled and instrumental attitudes, (2) individualistic and social orientations in ethics, (3) affiliated or not affiliated approach to life. The 'principled attitude' can be

[23] Catholic religion: around 60 per cent of the population say that they 'believe'; around 20 per cent do not consider themselves as attached to the religious tradition; around 8 per cent define themselves as not religious persons.

[24] Podgorecki, Kurczewski *et al., op. cit.*

defined as a direct, spontaneous acceptance or negation of some rule, relative to imaginary or actual behaviour. The 'instrumental attitude' is, according to the proposed definition, one where the acceptance or negation of an imaginary or actual behaviour depends upon the calculation of different possible alternatives of behaviour and the evaluation of their different aspects. Individually oriented ethics refer to those systems where the predominating norms regulate the social behaviour of people towards other members of small, more or less, informal groups. On the other hand, norms of socially oriented ethics give priority to the social rôles and positions which are, or can be, occupied by an individual. The extent of involvement in the society and affiliation with its basic values can reveal the degree of social adherence and social affiliation. Lack of this adherence produces anomie; its existence provides the instruments of social control.

How are these concepts related to the basic question? Why does illegal behaviour not lead to the erosion of legal and moral norms? Instrumental attitudes, individualistic orientation in ethics, an approach to life without social affiliation, when combined and inter-related, are able to transform and immunize inherited values, neutralize them, invest them with rationalizations, and, in this cumulative way, produce anti-social behaviour.

Proposition 7: The knowledge of the law differs as far as the primary and secondary rules of law are concerned

The overview given by B. Kutchinsky of studies in the knowledge of the law leads to an enigmatic conclusion: 'Knowledge about the law is neither a necessary nor a sufficient condition for conformity to the law.'[25] Another Polish study of knowledge of the law provides, perhaps, more informative data.[26] The research findings show the following categories of the population as having relatively better knowledge of the law: males of the 35–49 age group, persons of a higher educational level (those with an elementary education show a better acquaintance with the law than those without any formal education; those who have completed secondary schooling know more than those with only an elementary education); persons involved in social service work; those with legal experience (criminal or civil) associated with appearance in court; persons who have declared a past or present need for legal advice; persons interested in following press reports, radio or television broadcasts dealing with legal matters. Thus the average knowledge of the law has an instrumental purpose. It is characteristic of those better

[25] B. Kutchinsky, 'Knowledge and Attitudes Regarding Law and Law-Breaking', op. cit., p. 104.

[26] A nationwide study conducted in Poland in 1970 by A. Kojder and A. Podgorecki. The random sample (quota sample) of the Polish population consisted of 2197 interviewed subjects.

situated socially (better acquainted with social life). Greater knowledge of the law, it may be assumed, facilitates their adaptation to complex and changing social reality which requires of them more elaborate patterns of personal behaviour if they are to function. Knowledge of the law is a means to effective action where there are intricate social relations.

The average population, according to this study, knows the law (basic norms which describe the duties and obligations of the people) quite well. In contrast to the relatively widespread knowledge of the primary rules (elementary rules of social order which describe the structure of legitimized claims and duties), the data collected in this research indicates that the man in the street has limited knowledge of the secondary rules—which describe the norms of legal procedure. Law officials are trained to know these rules and how to use them.

Proposition 8: There are different stages in the socialization of legal values

Traditional, abstract, and speculative jurisprudence assume that the law is assimilated by subjects to whom it is addressed—directly, absolutely, on its own merit and through its charisma. For the traditional philosophy of law, this assumption seems so obvious that investigation of the ways, conditions, obstacles, etc. which could influence the internalization of legal values would seem pointless. However, recent psychological and sociological studies show clearly that this point of view is obsolete and superficial.

A growing amount of evidence suggests that the process of socialization of legal values is quite complicated. Some authors[27] distinguish three stages in the general process of socialization. These are (1) the pre-conventional level when labels of 'good' or 'bad' are interpreted in terms of physical consequences; (2) the conventional level when there is active support for the fixed rules of authority in a society, and (3) the post-conventional level when an effort is made to achieve autonomous moral principles which are supposed to have validity despite possible divergent opinions of dissenting groups and individuals. According to the empirical studies based on these assumptions the state school and the legal system are the two most important institutions in stimulating legal development. Another study, with a different theoretical background, supports these overall conclusions. It states in a general way: '. . . children's ideas about the functions performed by laws are similar to their ideas about school rules and may be transferred from that realm.' The same study provides some more detailed findings: 'The origin of many attitudes towards the legal system may be found, therefore, in attitudes towards personal authorities. In summary, what is observed

[27] J. L. Tapp and L. Kohlberg, 'Developing Senses of Law and Legal Justice', *The Journal of Social Issues*, 1971, **27**, No. 2 (Special Issue on Socialisation, the Law and Society).

here is a statistically significant tendency for the lower middle-class children to glorify authority as represented by the policeman . . . on all five dimensions, girls rated the policeman more positively than did boys.'[28]

More studies need to be conducted in this area. Nevertheless, it is quite easy to foresee that such reference groups as the family, peers, teachers, schoolmates, companions at work, etc. could initiate, stimulate, hinder, change and influence different types of attitudes towards the law. So far some questions have simply been posed, for example: What are the consecutive stages of development of legal attitudes in a life span? What is the importance of particular reference groups? What is the impact of the legal system itself? What is the rôle of the image which social and legal institutions project to individuals and social groups? There is a growing need to try to find answers for them. No longer can traditional jurisprudence pretend that they do not exist.

Proposition 9: The acceptance of the legal system of a given social system does not warrant the acceptance of the political version of this system

Several Marxian and Weberian analyses, which have shown a strong interrelation between social systems (especially their economic components) and legal systems have also shown that social systems strongly influence the content of the legal systems attached to them. But it would be an oversimplification to think that the social and economic system shapes the image of the whole legal system. The legal system, although partially determined by its social, political and economic counterparts, also has its own values created by tradition, has links with customs and morals, and ethnic, regional and national institutions. Despite such ramifications, the legal system still has its own imponderables which cannot be reduced to the values existing outside the world of legal order. Essential elements in this are the scope and intensity of the prestige which the legal system enjoys in a given society. Different parts of the legal system apparently command different types of respect. Different social, political and economic factors might weaken or strengthen this respect. But despite these interrelations, an essential element still remains outside the influence of these factors. This element has strategic bearing on the social behaviour of the average citizen who will more often comply with basic social values when he is motivated by respect for the law *as law*. A theoretical approach to legal problems which overlooks the social, political, and economic roots of the law is too simplistic, but so is also the approach which simply reduces the law to the interplay of social, political, and economic factors.

[28] J. V. Torney, 'Socialization of Attitudes Towards the Legal System', *The Journal of Social Issues*, 1971, **27**, No. 2 (Special Issue on Socialisation, the Law and Society), esp. pp. 145–8.

Proposition 10: The acceptance of the law lies somewhere between two extremes: the autotelic orientation towards the law and the heterotelic one

The autotelic orientation treats action, behaviour and goals as ends in themselves. This type of orientation does not seriously take into consideration any other aspects, benefits or points of view, other than those expressed by this orientation. According to the autotelic orientation, the law should be obeyed just because the law is law. This orientation stresses the legitimacy of the law, its charisma, and its unconditional binding force. The law expresses the categoric imperative which requires an action to be performed exactly as it is prescribed by the binding rule. This type of orientation creates a sense of duty, obligation, responsibility and especially, respect for the law. It is not difficult to understand why this orientation might be regarded as socially 'sound and healthy' when it prevents anomie and disorder, and motivates people to comply with basic social values. Nevertheless, this type of orientation could also lead to extreme injustice when, for example, extraordinary circumstances are ignored by law enacted without possible knowledge of these types of circumstances. Higher values than the law itself should decide when a legalistic, autotelic orientation is 'good' and when it is 'bad'. Because law is usually a necessity of social life, different means of social control try to internalize legal rules as autotelic entities. This procedure, if successful, could produce harmful by-products which might also support—using law as a powerful absolutist, autotelic device— evil and/or criminal ideologies.

The heterotelic orientation towards law is instrumental. It reflects the social fact that the law is regarded as an instrument designed to smooth relations between people: solve conflicts, inform about accessible, licit alternatives, and restrict those who seek gains detrimental to society. The greater one's knowledge of the law, the more opportunities to use it in a profitable way. Generally, the law is likely to be used as an instrument of social adjustment, but it could also be used as an instrument of the *a priori* intended (political and economic) oppression or of an oppression which was not intended *a priori* but was identified as such later.

The purpose of this argument is to emphasize the point that respect for the law does not necessarily have value in itself (although the autotelic orientation in law can give it an additional and sometimes very useful social force), but depends upon the higher values which should be realized and preserved by law. The combination of careful empirical diagnosis and clear recognition of accepted values can also provide guidance to the development of a reasonable social policy—that is, it can play a part in social engineering.

Conclusions

Certainly this recent checking and testing of the basic ideas of jurisprudence was not planned or anticipated in any systematic way. It occurred on the one hand as a result of the growing dissatisfaction with the apparent futility of the theory of law in its present form, and on the other as a spontaneous expansion of the use of sociological methods. Despite the rapid increase of empirical studies it is still too soon to attempt a definitive comprehensive translation of the old jurisprudential problems. It would be methodologically more sound to wait for additional data before undertaking a final synthesis rather than rush now into dubious generalizations.

Some idea of the directions in which future enquiry and reasoning will move has already emerged from the collected material. The crucial problems and approaches which have been identified and which appear especially promising theoretically seem to be the following: (a) enquiries into the relations between actual legal behaviour and legal values and attitudes (studies of legal knowledge and opinions might be of a special interest here); (b) existing studies, conducted in the area of criminology and deviance (and inadequately used in jurisprudence) have the virtue of empirical evidence gathered on a large scale, relatively advanced methodology and some new and valid knowledge; (c) an interdisciplinary approach could give a more humanistic insight into the relationships between the law and other elements of social life—for instance, social psychology and anthropology have shown the limitations of a purely sociological point of view; (d) comparative studies of legal and social systems might disprove the spurious belief that a particular legal system can be used as a final framework for all types of comparisons (this approach could especially aid the study of the limits and conditions of effectiveness of legal norms); (e) a greater emphasis should be put on legal policy as an independent legal discipline. Legal policy as a branch of social engineering could give reliable guidelines for legislation, since legal policy's main concern is the task of finding the proper legal norms to achieve, in a tested way, socially desired goals.

Jurisprudence expirically tested might be weak at the beginning; data being scarce and vulnerable to criticism on methodological grounds. Furthermore interpretations are often contradictory or unacceptably generalized. But despite these shortcomings an empirical approach has the potential of accumulating a continuous stream of findings rather than accumulating misunderstandings and quarrels which are merely abstract and semantic.

ON THE DECRIMINALIZATION
OF ENGLISH JUVENILE COURTS*

A. E. Bottoms

In 1969 the United Kingdom Parliament passed the Children and Young Persons Act, relating to juvenile justice in England and Wales. If it is ever fully implemented, this Act will have, *inter alia*, the following effects:

(i) It will be impossible to prosecute any child under fourteen for a criminal offence (excluding homicide); and it will also be impossible for compulsory civil care measures to be applied to an offender of this age unless the court is satisfied not only that he has committed an offence but also that 'he is in need of care or control which he is unlikely to receive unless the court makes an order' (section 1 (2)).

(ii) As a corollary of (i), wherever possible children should not have to go to court when they have committed an offence, but treatment should be voluntarily agreed between parents and social workers (unless it is to be residential treatment, which should only be permitted with a formal court order).

(iii) Young persons (aged 14 and under 17) may be prosecuted in certain specified cases, but the non-criminal 'care proceedings' (see (i)) will be available as an alternative, and should be preferred in most cases, with voluntary agreements (see (ii)) an even more desirable possibility.

(iv) Two main 'disposals' will be available for persons successfully prosecuted or found in need of compulsory care, i.e. the 'care order' and the 'supervision order'. In both, supervising social workers will have a significant element of discretionary power which is not subject to court review or scrutiny.

* An earlier version of this paper was first presented at the First British–Scandinavian Research Seminar in Criminology, held at Bolkesjø, near Oslo, in September 1971, at which Sir Leon Radzinowicz was the leader of the British delegation. I am grateful to a number of participants at the Seminar, particularly W. G. Carson, Martin Davies, and Paul Wiles, for their helpful comments. I also wish to thank John May for some useful discussions and Allison Morris for advice on the developments in Scotland.

Although the Act leaves the formal composition and constitution of the English juvenile courts virtually unchanged,[1] it is clear that the jurisdiction of these courts is intended to be radically altered by the provisions. There is a substantial move towards either voluntary agreements or civil proceedings rather than criminal proceedings; hence it is correct to speak of the Act as a decriminalizing Act, though in the rather special sense of 'substitutory decriminalization', i.e. 'substituting one kind of formal control for another kind of formal social control'.[2] The Act is also quite clearly a move towards a more explicitly 'welfare' oriented jurisdiction, and is in large part based on classical social work concepts. In particular, it enshrines two major assumptions:

(i) That delinquency is to be understood, as in psychoanalytic thought, as a presenting symptom of some deeper maladjustment;[3] hence the problems of delinquents are similar to the problems of other children in need, and the two should be dealt with together and not separated by the accident of whether the symptom calling attention to the need happened to be an offence or (say) truancy or persistent bedwetting.

(ii) That court appearances, especially on a criminal prosecution, cause stigma and should be avoided wherever possible in favour of more informal treatment decisions by professional social workers.

This is not the place for a full discussion of the Act and its detailed provisions,[4] nor of the limited extent to which it is likely to be implemented in the forseeable future. The purpose of this essay is rather to see how the Act came to reach the Statute Book.[5]

[1] The courts are composed of part-time unpaid magistrates, sitting in an informal atmosphere, in private, and with restrictions on press reporting: see generally W. E. Cavenagh, *Juvenile Courts: The Child and the Law*, Harmondsworth, Pelican Books, 1967. The 1969 Act alters this only by giving the Lord Chancellor greater power over appointments to the juvenile bench.

[2] See I. Anttila, 'Conservative and Radical Criminal Policy in the Nordic Countries', *Scandinavian Studies in Criminology*, 1971, 3, 9–21.

[3] 'The new legal framework should enable greater weight to be given, in deciding what treatment a child needs, to the background and causal factors underlying his behaviour, although it must still be recognised that presenting symptoms in the form of difficult or anti-social behaviour should also receive attention in the treatment situation', Home Office, *Care and Treatment in a Planned Environment: A Report on the Community Homes Project*, London, HMSO, 1970, para 1.

[4] For general legal accounts of the Act, see Home Office, *Part I of the Children and Young Persons Act 1969: A Guide for Courts and Practitioners*, London, HMSO, 1970; A. E. Bottoms, J. D. McClean and K. W. Patchett, 'Children, Young Persons and the Courts —A Survey of the New Law', *Criminal Law Review* [1970], 368–95; and J. A. F. Watson, *The Juvenile Court—1970 Onwards*, London, Shaw, 1970.

[5] The Conservative Party gained power at the General Election of June 1970, before most of the Act was implemented. Subsequently, the new Government announced that

Recent sociologists of deviance have rightly turned their attention to the sociology of law, since the process by which law is created and enforced is obviously central to a full understanding of deviance.[6] We are here particularly concerned with studies of law creation (rather than enforcement) and, as it happens, two of the seminal works in this area, by Platt and Lemert, have been concerned with laws relating to juvenile courts in the U.S.A.,[7] while other important work is proceeding in relation to the establishment of Norwegian child welfare legislation.[8] An English contribution in the same field may therefore be apposite although—as I cannot stress too often—this essay is more speculative in nature than that of any of the other authors' work, as I have neither carried out fully exhaustive research on the topic, nor had access to any of the confidential files and correspondence which would be necessary for a full explanation of the Act in question. Nevertheless, even a less than full study of the English experience may be of special interest in one respect, since only some three years before the Act, an earlier proposal for legislation in the same field had failed. Lemert rightly says that why one movement succeeds where an earlier one failed is 'among the more challenging questions that a sociology of law must answer',[9] though his own comments on this in the Californian case are fragmentary in the extreme.

The English experience is also illuminated by contrasts with two other countries' experience in the 1960s. In Scotland, a revolutionary change in juvenile court law was established in the substitution of 'children's hearings' for juvenile courts by the Social Work (Scotland) Act 1968. This change was in the same general direction as the English Act, but was accomplished with very much less opposition than in England, and this raises important problems for explanation.[10] Conversely, the U.S.A. in the 1960s saw changes

---

it will never increase above twelve the age below which no criminal prosecutions may be brought; that it will not impose any administrative restrictions on the bringing of prosecutions for persons aged 12–16, for whom a free choice of care or criminal proceedings is therefore available to the police; and that it will not implement certain treatment provisions for the time being: *Government Statement on Children in Trouble*, Home Office Press Release, October 1970. This and later Conservative reaction to the Act could also be examined in sociological terms, but for convenience I have imposed a cut-off point for exploration at the time of the passing of the Act.

[6] For a classic early statement see H. Becker, *Outsiders*, Glencoe, Ill., Free Press, 1963.

[7] A. M. Platt, *The Child Savers*, Chicago, University of Chicago Press, 1969; E. M. Lemert, *Social Action and Legal Change: Revolution within the Juvenile Court*, Chicago, Aldine, 1970.

[8] T. Stang Dahl, 'The Emergence of the Norwegian Child Welfare Law', paper presented at First British–Scandinavian Research Seminar in Criminology, Bolkesjø 1971 (revised and extended version forthcoming from Martin Robertson & Co.).

[9] Lemert, op. cit., p. 217.

[10] Both English and Scottish Acts were of course passed by the same body, the United Kingdom Parliament. But there was relatively little cross-reference during the Parlia-

in the opposite direction from those in England and Scotland, towards a more legalistic juvenile court, and it is important to consider why these opposite movements should have occurred.

Changing the Juvenile Courts: A Decade of Debate

The essential core of the explanation of the English Act lies, it is submitted, in a conjunction of interests and ideology between the British Labour Party and those in key positions in British social work. However, although this is a necessary kernel of the explanation, it is not a sufficient explanation, since this conjunction existed (though perhaps in a different context) both at the time of the failure of 1965–6 and in the later success of 1968–9. The additional elements of the explanation can only be understood in the light of the social history of the various debates preceding the legislation, to which we now turn.

The history begins with the setting up in 1956, quietly and almost as a matter of post-war routine enquiry, of a Departmental Committee under Viscount Ingleby, with strangely bifurcated terms of reference: to enquire into the working of the law on juvenile courts in all its aspects, *and* 'whether local authorities should be given new powers to prevent or forestall the suffering of children through neglect in their own homes'. The committee was of fairly unadventurous composition: apart from the distinguished child psychiatrist Peter Scott, it was composed entirely of lawyers, administrators, and magistrates—in particular, it should be noticed, there were no social workers. It reported in 1960, and declared that the juvenile courts should be retained and that, with very minor exceptions, the then existing range of treatment orders and treatment facilities was adequate.[11] The committee was clear that the answer to the second question referred to it was in the affirmative, but thought that any question of the reorganization of the social services to meet this need lay 'well outside our terms of reference', although important for 'further study'. In these respects it was by no means unfair for Donnison to describe the general tenor of the report as 'respectable and cautious'.[12]

Nevertheless, the committee did unearth one major 'weakness' in the juvenile court system, and what it considered to be the logic of this situation

---

mentary debates, especially because of the Parliamentary custom of leaving the discussion of Scottish Bills to Scottish Members of Parliament.

[11] *Report of the Committee on Children and Young Persons*, Cmd. 1191, London, HMSO, 1960.

[12] D. Donnison, 'Social Services for the Family' in *The Ingleby Report: Three Critical Essays* (see footnote 19 below).

led it to its most radical proposal. The 'weakness' was the discrepancy between the expectation of 'just deserts' raised by the forms of a *criminal* trial, which were adhered to in the juvenile court up to the time guilt was proved or admitted; and the subsequent specific direction that in considering treatment, it was the duty of the court to 'have regard for the welfare of the child or young person'.[13] In a now famous passage, the committee pointed out that (para. 66):

> It results, for example in a child being charged with a petty theft or other wrongful act for which most people would say that no great penalty should be imposed, and the case apparently ending in a disproportionate sentence. For when the court causes enquiries to be made . . . the court may determine that the welfare of the child requires some very substantial interference which may amount to taking the child away from his home for a prolonged period. It is common to come across bitter complaints that a child has been sent away from home because he has committed some particular offence which in itself was not at all serious.

To get around this logical difficulty, however, there was no suggestion that the 'welfare' ethic at the sentencing stage should be abandoned, as many would now certainly demand. Rather, it was thought that in 'offence' cases, one should move away from a criminal-type jurisdiction for younger children, so that the inappropriate expectations aroused by a criminal trial should be lessened. Hence the solution propounded was that the age of criminal responsibility should be raised from eight to twelve immediately, and perhaps to fourteen eventually; below that age, only civil 'welfare' proceedings could be brought, but a child would be proved to be in need of protection or discipline under these if he had acted 'in a manner which would render a person over that age liable to be found guilty of an offence'.

Whether this is a solution to the problem posed by the committee is doubtful on intellectual grounds.[14] Of more interest to this essay, however, is the way the committee related its proposed procedures to its assumptions about delinquency. These, set out fully in its paras. 107–8, are that responsibility for crime in juveniles is shared between the child and 'those responsible for his upbringing'. By and large, children come to court because those responsible for their upbringing (i.e. parents, school and general community) have 'been unable in different degrees and for various reasons to bring the child up in the way he should go. They have been unable . . . to teach him to behave in an acceptable manner'. For the younger

---

[13] Children and Young Persons Act 1933, section 44; described by Watson, op. cit., as a key section 'enshrining the spirit' of 'that great Act'.
[14] See Cavenagh, op. cit., pp. 261–2; Barbara Wootton, 'The Juvenile Courts', *Criminal Law Review* [1961], 669–77 at 673–5.

child, most of the responsibility lies 'squarely' with the upbringers; but later on 'the child must learn to stand on his own feet and accept greater responsibility for his actions'. In other words, the model was, in crude terms, one of social pathology for the younger child, but more classical assumptions about choice of evil for the older child; and these models were to be reflected in the differing procedures—civil proceedings for the younger child and criminal for the older.

Duster has pointed out a central problem in the way Western societies typically deal with the offender: he is treated as a 'rational being' in the early stages of police processing and the determination of guilt by the court, but in later stages, notably in prison and probation treatments, the emphasis is on pathology or psychic disturbance.[15] Taking this idea further, one can see that in the adult court, where sentencing to prison, fine or whatever is in the majority of cases carried out on retributive and deterrent principles, the potential clash between the ideology of the first stage of court proceedings (the trial) and the second stage (the sentence) is a manageable one. But in the juvenile court, with its much greater typical emphasis on 'treatment' or 'the welfare of the child' at the dispositional stage, the conflict of two incompatible ideological models within one courtroom case may appear acute. This, one suspects, lies at the heart of the 'problem of the juvenile court', and is the reason why the rôle of the juvenile court or its equivalent raises so much controversy in so many countries. The Ingleby committee perceived the problem: their solution was, in effect, to inject the pathological model into the *whole* of the court proceedings for younger children, and for older children to reduce the force of the conflict by stressing moral responsibility for crime and thus minimize the pathological model at the sentencing stage.

This point has been spelt out in some detail because it is related to the varying reaction to the Ingleby report. The Conservative Party, then in power, and at the time busy dealing with the aftermath of serious disturbances at an approved school,[16] as well as warding off the strong pressure of its grass-roots supporters for the re-introduction of corporal punishment for juvenile delinquents,[17] was in no mood to minimize the moral seriousness of juvenile crime. Hence its reaction to the Ingleby proposal to raise the age of criminal responsibility was a distinctly cool one; in November 1961 the Home Secretary (R. A. Butler) made it clear that he did not intend to raise

[15] Troy Duster, *The Legislation of Morality*, Glencoe, Ill., Free Press, 1970.

[16] *Disturbances at the Carlton Approved School: Report of Inquiry by Mr. Victor Durand, Q.C.*, Cmd. 937, London, HMSO, 1960.

[17] Advisory Council on the Treatment of Offenders, *Corporal Punishment*, London, HMSO, 1960. The then Home Secretary, R. A. Butler, subsequently commented after his retirement that this was one of the most difficult campaigns with which he had to deal in his political career.

the age, and, although the Government was subsequently forced to compromise and raise the age to ten, it did so with noticeable reluctance.[18] This type of reaction, stressing the seriousness of much juvenile crime and the moral responsibility of offenders, was a typical one in subsequent Conservative attitudes throughout the ensuing years of debate.

The Labour Party's reaction to Ingleby was very different. It thought the report far too timid, as evidenced in speeches in Parliament and in a special critical Fabian Society pamphlet on the report.[19] The proposal to raise the age of criminal responsibility was generally welcomed, but this was not thought sufficient, and two main additional points were stressed.

The first of these was that, though Ingleby had located the family as an important source of delinquency, too little had been suggested to help the family: 'there is no doubt that the Ingleby committee's recommendations were a great disappointment, [and] those who hoped to find the outline of a statutory service of help to the family in need looked in vain'.[20] The background to this was that during the 1950s, significant elements in Labour thinking began to regret some of the philosophy of the Labour administration of 1945–51 which had largely created the apparatus of the Welfare State in Britain. At that earlier time 'it was clear that social workers would be needed to do various jobs in the big [new] specialist statutory services, but many people assumed that old-fashioned general social work, or family casework, would gradually wither away'.[21] Now an opposing movement had gained force, partly due to the typical plight of the problem family with multiple needs, knocking on the doors of one specialist agency after another; and partly influenced by emerging notions among social workers of so-called 'generic social work', which had emerged from the common psychoanalytic base of social work practice in the 1950s, and was increasingly affecting social work training. But, though pressed to do so by evidence from Labour organizations, the Ingleby committee had given no lead to the creation of a unified 'family service'.

The second Labour criticism of Ingleby rested on a version of stigma theory. It was argued that the committee, despite its endorsement of special

---

[18] In the House of Lords debates on the Children and Young Persons Bill 1963, the Government's decision not to raise the age was strongly attacked, particularly by Lady Wootton, and an Opposition amendment to raise the age to twelve was surprisingly carried by one vote. The Government, no doubt feeling that it would be politically very difficult to make no concession in these circumstances, subsequently succeeded in forcing a compromise by proposing the age of ten. This became law in the 1963 Act.

[19] D. Donnison, P. Jay and M. Stewart, *The Ingleby Report: Three Critical Essays*, London, Fabian Research Pamphlet No. 231, 1962.

[20] Peggy Jay, 'A Plan for Family Bureaux', in Donnison *et al.*, op. cit.

[21] Donnison, op. cit.

statutory powers of prevention, was not sufficiently concerned about keeping children out of courts altogether. As Miss Alice Bacon, leading for the Opposition in a 1963 debate put it:[22]

> I want to ensure not only that young children are not charged with having committed a crime—which is important—but that as far as possible we shall keep young children out of the courts altogether. This is the important thing. It is not just the nature of the charge made in court; it is the appearance in court which can do so much damage to a young child.

These two strands of Labour thinking, the 'family service' concept and stigma theory, were both to be of central importance in the next stage of proposals. It is important to note, however, that although Ingleby was attacked for its timidity, the Labour stress was not for a more pathological view of the deviant than Ingleby's, but rather if anything a modification of Ingleby's social-pathological concept towards a broader view of the delinquent in relation to the wider society—or, in Duster's terms, the delinquent as a 'victim of external forces' rather than as 'psychically inadequate'. For example, Labour accounts of the family indicated the difficulties of the family unit in coping with problems of accommodation in the private rented sector and of stress caused by conflicting policies of different social agencies.[23] Nevertheless, the Labour view did not stress the view of the offender as morally evil, and, particularly in view of the emphasis on the family, its ideology allowed much greater possibilities of conjunction to Ingleby's notion of social pathology—and subsequently, to more social work-based notions of individual and family maladjustment—than did the Conservative ideology. This was to remain the position for the rest of the decade.

In retrospect, then, we can see the Ingleby Report as important in identifying an apparent anomaly in the juvenile court system, and as having to some extent polarized the position of the two political parties vis-à-vis the juvenile justice issue. Although the most controversial Ingleby proposal did not become law, to ignore the symbolic importance of the Ingleby debates in relation to subsequent events would be a serious mistake.[24]

By 1964, the Labour Party was confidently girding itself for power after

[22] H. C. Deb. vol. 672 col. 1288.

[23] Jay, op. cit.

[24] Nevertheless, some of the Ingleby recommendations did become law in the Children and Young Persons Act 1963, notably the proposal to empower local authorities to carry out preventive work with juveniles. As a consequence of this, the following year the Conservative Government issued a circular to police forces (Home Office circular 20/1964) asking them to consult with local authority children's departments before prosecuting children under twelve. These arrangements were supported by the Labour party, and there was thus in these respects a consensus on certain steps to keep some younger children out of courts altogether.

the forthcoming election. In readiness for it, a private party committee on criminal policy was set up under the chairmanship of Lord Longford (subsequently a Cabinet minister), with a very strong membership including the future Lord Chancellor and seven other future Ministers as well as two criminologists, Terence Morris and T. C. N. Gibbens. As with Ingleby, however, the committee contained no professional social worker.

The committee's report[25] was very wide-ranging, but certainly one of its major proposals was for the total abolition of juvenile courts, based on the philosophy that 'no child in early adolescence should have to face criminal proceedings: these children should receive the kind of treatment they need, without any stigma'. Instead, non-judicial and entirely informal consultations between the child, his parents, and a new Family Service were envisaged: proposals as to treatment would be put by the social worker, and only if no agreement could be reached (or in certain other serious cases aged over thirteen referred by the Family Service) would the matter go to court. If it did go to court, this would be to a new 'Family Court', the establishment of which for many kinds of family problems was held by the committee to be of the 'highest importance'.

In considering these proposals, the two characteristic strands of Labour thinking in the response to Ingleby are again very evident. The second of them, stigma theory, was reinforced in this committee by Lady Wootton, who according to Lord Longford was a witness who powerfully and decisively influenced the committee[26] and who previously and subsequently made very strong statements about the stigma of court appearances.[27]

The receptivity of Labour politicians to these ideas perhaps needs a little elaboration, though it is readily understandable. Especially on the strong trade union wing of the party, there has always been a deep suspicion of courts and lawyers,[28] based on a justifiable feeling that in English industrial history, lawyers had always been on the side of the property owners and industrialists. At the same time, the egalitarian orientation of the party made it very aware that, as the Longford Report put it, 'the machinery of the law is

[25] *Crime: A Challenge to Us All:* Report of the Labour Party's Study Group, London, 1964.

[26] Speech at Symposium held at the Institute of Criminology, Cambridge, July 1968.

[27] Wootton, op. cit., 1961; also B. Wootton, 'The White Paper on Children in Trouble', *Criminal Law Review* [1968], 465–73, e.g., 'every child in respect of whom a court order has been made is inevitably stigmatised thereby, and initiated into a delinquent fraternity'.

[28] E.g. the remarks of Mr. James Callaghan, Home Secretary, during debates on the 1969 Bill: 'there is a natural tendency for these distinguished lawyers . . . with their legal minds trained in the majesty of the law, accepting its exactness and integrity, [that] they should believe that the view put forward about the law is one which must triumph above other considerations. We are dealing here with growing and developing children, not questioning the supremacy of the law': H.C. Deb. vol. 779 col. 1189.

reserved mainly for working class children who more often than not are also handicapped by being taught in too big classes in unsatisfactory school buildings', while middle-class parents often managed to cloak their sons' delinquency and have it dealt with elsewhere.[29] As for the Family Service concept, as well as the matters already referred to (above, p. 325) this appealed not only to the paternalism of upper-class Socialists like Lord Longford, but also to the strong lower-middle-class/nonconformist traditions of family solidarity, which are often very influential in Labour politics.

It is important to see, however, that the Longford Report does not bear any strong imprint of 'pure' social work ideas—there is for example no hint of the later view of delinquency being merely a symptom of deeper maladjustment—but rather is the expression of a general social democratic ideology. Nevertheless, social workers were not slow to appreciate how the tenor of the report chimed in with their own ideology. This, based on psychoanalytic concepts, stressed particularly the 'presenting symptom' theory, and the consequent adoption of a medical-treatment analogy in considering delinquency prevention. It was also critical of courts and lawyers, partly on the basis of a stigma theory very similar to Labour's, and partly on the grounds that lawyers operated with over-rationalistic concepts of human behaviour. These ideas had, at that time, come closest to official recognition in the Kilbrandon Report for Scotland.[30] A typical social work reaction to Longford stressed the extent to which it had come close to these notions: 'the ideas expressed by the (Longford) group, although not exactly identical with the Kilbrandon Committee's . . . had at least this much in common with them: avoidance of criminal proceedings for young offenders, and, instead, merging the treatment of young offenders with that of other school age children who require specialized provisions.'[31] Social workers, with the exception of probation officers (discussed further below) were therefore glad to be able to use the Longford proposals to press their own case, and certainly found Longford much more congenial than Ingleby.

Labour gained power, albeit with a precarious Parliamentary majority, four months after the publication of the Longford report. Ten months later came the famous but abortive White Paper, *The Child, The Family and the*

[29] This strand of thought was particularly evident in Lady Wootton's desire to abolish juvenile courts completely and have all treatment dealt with informally: this view she justified on the grounds that a child does not have comparable civil liberties to an adult: Wootton, op. cit., 1961, p. 673.

[30] *Children and Young Persons: Scotland*, Cmd. 2306, Edinburgh, HMSO, 1964; see further below.

[31] Peter Boss, *Social Policy and the Young Delinquent*, London, Routledge and Kegan Paul, 1967, p. 86. Even here, note that Boss has evaluated to a major place the concept of treating delinquents and non-delinquents together, while in Longford (p. 30) the idea is implied but not stressed.

Young Offender,[32] in which the Government published 'provisional proposals' subject to 'discussion'.

The White Paper substantially reproduced the Longford proposals on the abolition of the juvenile courts, except that the purely informal consultations with the Family Service proposed in the earlier document were to be replaced by a formal 'Family Council' in each area, consisting of 'social workers of the children's service and other persons selected for their understanding and experience of children'. This change, however, hardly affected the major issue of abolishing juvenile courts, and few people found the difference important enough to affect their overall attitude to the two reports.[33] Nevertheless, the change is possibly symptomatic of a slightly greater direct social work influence in the concepts of this report as against Longford, another sign of which is a stronger stress on the family and the absence of comment as to the class-biased clientele of the juvenile courts.

The Longford Report had attracted some criticism in professional and academic circles, but its reception was quietness itself compared with the flood of criticism which now descended upon the new White Paper. In retrospect, it is difficult to recall the heat of the battles in those days, though a rereading of, for example, the special issue of the *British Journal of Criminology* (April 1966) shows the bitterness of the struggle seeping out behind the intellectual debating points. This greater degree of controversy reflects not so much the detailed differences between the two reports, as the fact that the second contained Government proposals which seemed likely to lead to imminent legislation, especially after the Queen's Speech in October 1965 when it was announced that the Government would 'promote the provision of improved services for the family [and] the development of new means of dealing with young persons who come before the courts'.

The main opposition came from lawyers, magistrates, and probation officers. The last group is of particular interest, as they shared much of the psychoanalytic ideology of other social workers; but they also had a long tradition of independence of local authorities, and of service to courts, and it was from this standpoint that their critique was made.[34] On the other side of the debate, the main supporters of the proposals were other social workers,

[32] Cmd. 2742, 1965.

[33] An exception was Lady Wootton, who presumably approved of the entirely informal consultations of the Longford Report, but who criticized the 1965 proposals for their complexity, wasteful duplication, and probably total incomprehensibility: Wootton, op. cit., 1968, p. 466.

[34] See, e.g. the statement by the National Association of Probation Officers, 'The Child, The Family and the Young Offender: Observations by N.A.P.O.', *Probation*, 1965, **11,** 83–91 at p. 84: 'no action should be taken to interfere with the liberty of an individual on grounds of his conduct, or with the rights of parents on allegations of their failings, except as the result of a judicial assessment'.

particularly members of the child care service, and many of these talked openly of their gaining through the proposals much more professional prestige and recognition for their service which was still less than twenty years old.[35]

Eventually the opponents of the paper triumphed, and the proposals were withdrawn. Since, as has been seen above, they appealed to significant strands in Labour ideology, it is important to ask why the campaign of resistance was successful, especially as the abandonment was by no means immediate.[36] Although no certain answer can be given, the probability seems to be that there were two main reasons: the strength of the opposition, and a change of Home Secretary.

In gauging the effect of opposition, one has to bear in mind the general political difficulties of the Government. Until the General Election of spring 1966, it had only a hair's breadth majority of three in the House of Commons, and was no doubt not anxious to risk defeat on matters not central to its political programme—as this was not. After the election, it very quickly ran into very great economic difficulties which for some time were a major preoccupation. More generally, the Government must have been aware that the strong opposition of the legal lobby and the probation officers would cause some of its own supporters to waver, and it may have been especially important that on this issue the specialists engaged in the detailed controversy were able to appeal to a wider constituency which in general was prepared to uphold the value of courts as defenders of individual rights.

Speculatively, one might also suggest that the civil servants within the Home Office were less than wholeheartedly sympathetic to the proposals. In the nature of the case, there is no firm evidence to support this; but the inference may perhaps be drawn from the facts that (i) the original proposals in Longford were drawn up without civil service advice, and (ii) that the proposals which emerged three years later, which were demonstrably much influenced by civil servants, were of a rather different nature. If this speculation is correct, it could have been of considerable importance in view of the known importance of the civil service in modifying Government policy on certain occasions.

[35] The local authority children's departments were set up in 1948 to deal with deprived children, leaving probation officers to deal with delinquents. Inevitably there was always some overlap, and inter-service rivalry as to their relative professional competence in handling child delinquents. For a children's officer's view of the 1965 White Paper see B. J. Kahan, 'The Child, The Family and the Young Offender: Revolutionary or Evolutionary?', *British Journal of Criminology*, 1966, **6**, 159–69.

[36] Miss Alice Bacon, Minister of State at the Home Office, declared as late as September 1966 that allegations of the withdrawal of the White Paper were 'absolutely untrue': Boss, op. cit., p. 1.

An additional factor of some importance was almost certainly the change of Home Secretary in December 1965. For Mr. Roy Jenkins, who took over the post from the ailing Sir Frank Soskice,[37] is not the kind of Socialist to whom any of the arguments against courts or for a Family Service make a strong emotional appeal. Rather, as has been said in an assessment of other aspects of his Home Secretaryship, he is a 'technocrat Socialist, seeking cures for economic malaise by efficient achievement' and believing in a 'civilized bourgeois socialism', with a 'concern for the individual and his place vis-à-vis the bureaucracy'.[38] In the field of penal policy, these concerns were manifested in his strong drive for greater police efficiency through amalgamations of forces, better equipment, etc. and in his liberal reforms in the Criminal Justice Act 1967, such as the parole system and (in intention though not in practice) the suspended sentence. The juvenile court reforms do not loom large in such a perspective, and no doubt the intellectual in Jenkins was also deterred by the frankly rather poor and simplistic general level of the argument in the 1965 White Paper, and in the Longford Report before it.[39]

The 1965–6 reform movement, then, was unsuccessful. But two to three years later, in April 1968, the Government produced a second White Paper *Children in Trouble*[40] which, with minor modifications, became law as the 1969 Children and Young Persons Act (for the main provisions, see the introduction to this paper). The problems raised by *Children in Trouble* are (i) why did it emerge, after the abandonment of the earlier proposals; (ii) why was it not successfully opposed, as the previous paper had been?

A clue to the first problem lies, perhaps, in a careful reading of the paper itself in comparison with the 1965 predecessor. Undoubtedly the level of the argument presented is higher, whatever one may think of its substantive merits. But more importantly, the argument has much more of the influence of professional social work thinking than of the Fabian politico-social thinking, which tended to characterize the earlier Labour papers, especially Longford. This seems to reflect the growth to power in the three-year

[37] Soskice seems not to have been much involved with the White Paper proposals, but was apparently content to leave them in the hands of his Minister of State, Alice Bacon, who subsequently defended them doggedly against the mounting attack.

[38] E. J. B. Rose *et al.*, *Colour and Citizenship: A Report on British Race Relations*, London, Oxford University Press, 1969, pp. 513–14.

[39] See, for example, Lord Kilbrandon's ironic comment: 'I see in para 4 of the English White Paper the following sentence: "A high proportion of adult criminals have been juvenile delinquents, so that every advance in dealing with the young offender also helps in the attack on adult crime." This is where my inadequate training begins to show, because I thought of another premise to which I was unable to fit an appropriate conclusion, that is: "An extremely high proportion of juvenile delinquents do not turn into adult criminals".' 'Children in Trouble', *British Journal of Criminology*, 1966, **6**, 112–22, at p. 113.

[40] Cmd. 3601, 1968.

interim of a very strong team of civil servants at the top of the Children's Department of the Home Office. This group, led by the late D. H. Morrell and Miss Joan Cooper, was committed to a 'child care' view of delinquency in a strong form. The published works of Morrell and Cooper make this very clear:[41] for them, delinquency is a presenting sympton of a deeper maladjustment; children will grow up deviant if they are denied the advantage of early social work intervention at crisis periods; and residential institutions they maintained, should take the form of therapeutic communities. A comparison of the *treatment* proposals of the 1965 and 1968 White Papers is especially instructive in seeing how a more consistently professional social work approach has in the intervening years been applied to various aspects of the proposed reorganizations. For example, though both papers intended to replace the approved school order with the care order (giving parental rights to the local authority), only in 1968 had a systematic plan for 'community homes' and their philosophy been evolved;[42] or again, the 1965 White Paper intended to retain both attendance centres and detention centres, whereas by 1968 the intention was to phase these out because of their punitive connotations, and to bring replacements within the concept of 'intermediate treatment'—which, however, would be solely in the discretion of the social worker.

Of course, some aspects of the 1968 proposals were allied closely to the earlier Labour philosophy, in particular the proposal to avoid court proceedings and prefer voluntary agreements wherever possible, aimed at eliminating the effects of stigma.[43] But the section of the Act by which courts were empowered to explore the possibility of a voluntary agreement (section 1(2)) could be and was attacked on the grounds that it was class-biased against the working-class boy.[44] By a deep irony, it was the *Conserva-*

[41] D. H. Morrell, 'The Educational Role of the Approved Schools', in *The Residential Treatment of Disturbed and Delinquent Boys*, ed. R. F. Sparks and R. G. Hood, Cambridge Institute of Criminology, 1968; J. Cooper, 'Social Disadvantage and Social Help', *Approved Schools Gazette*, 1969, 643–5; J. Cooper, 'Social Care and Social Control', *Probation*, 1970, 15, 22–5.

[42] Morrell, op. cit., Home Office, *Care and Treatment in a Planned Environment*, op. cit.

[43] In one major respect the 1968 paper went less far towards the social work position than did its 1965 predecessor; this was in the retention of the juvenile court, on which see below, p. 335.

[44] The wording of the section is, in part, 'and also that he is in need of care or control which he is unlikely to receive unless the court makes an order'. It was argued that it would be easier to prove this to mainly middle-class magistrates against a working-class than against a middle-class boy; since for under-14's no intervention could be made unless this matter were proved, the result could be no action against one child and a major intervention against another, arising out of the same offence incident. See D. R. May, 'Delinquency Control and the Treatment Model: Some Implications of Recent Legislation', *British Journal of Criminology*, 1971, 11, 359–70, at pp. 364–5.

tives in parliament who raised this objection: not surprisingly, Labour spokesmen never seemed very comfortable in dealing with it.[45] The irony can be explained as the result of the greater social work influence of 1968: from a classical social-work position, the section can be defended much more easily than from a typical Labour position,[46] though why the Labour Government allowed itself to adopt the clause must remain a matter of difficulty.

The apparently strong influence of the Home Office Children's Department in the formation of the Act requires some further comment. For it is unlikely that this group would have had either the influence or the confidence which it had, were it not for some parallel developments in English social work.

Throughout the 1960s, many social workers in England and Wales were pressing for two goals which they saw as closely related: (i) the unification of various statutory local authority social services into a single Social Services Department for each authority; (ii) the creation of a unified professional body for social workers, instead of the then existing multiplicity of organizations (Association of Child Care Officers, Association of Psychiatric Social Workers, National Association of Probation Officers, etc.). At the time of Longford and the 1965 White Paper, both these aims seemed relatively remote, for although the professional organizations had taken a crucial step in 1963 by coming together into a consultative group (Standing Conference of Organizations of Social Work), this still essentially reflected an ideological, pre-organizational, stage of development. By 1968–9, however, all was different. In 1968, a major Inter-Departmental Committee report was published, urging the creation of unified local authority departments[47] and this became law in the Local Authority Social Services Act of 1970, though the probation service has remained separate from the new departments. Also in 1970, the professional social work organization was finally achieved in the form of the British Association of Social Work, and it had been clear for some little time previously that this would be the result. These twin developments, it can be argued, probably crucially assisted the institutionalization of professional social work concepts within the Home Office at the relevant time. They also, and perhaps just as importantly, debilitated the National

[45] E.g. the Bill 'aims to ensure as nearly as we can real equality for all children of all classes and backgrounds. When I say "equality" I mean "equality" and not "uniformity".' Mr. James Callaghan, H.C. Deb. vol. 779 cols. 1176–7; see also cols. 1190–93.

[46] Because from a social-work premise the act, as a presenting symptom, is irrelevant, while anything that is done by way of intervention concentrates on 'treatment needs, and therefore what is done is done in the interests of his welfare' (Boss, op. cit., p. 91) regardless of class—even if the result is more interventions against working-class children.

[47] *Report of the Committee on Local Authority and Allied Personal Social Services,* Cmd. 3703, London, HMSO, 1968. (Seebohm Report)

Association of Probation Officers, which throughout the period 1966–70 was fighting a severe internal battle as to whether or not it should merge itself into the proposed B.A.S.W. Those probation officers in favour of unification tended to be very critical of those who opposed the 1965 and 1968 White Papers too vigorously, in case other social workers thought probation officers too reactionary and too much on the side of lawyers. This was more important in 1968 than 1965, since the influence of this group was then stronger; and N.A.P.O. was no doubt thankful that the retention of courts in the 1968 proposals allowed it, consistently with its earlier position, to give a much greater welcome to *Children in Trouble* than to its predecessor.[48] Nevertheless it still was unhappy about some aspects of the proposals, but arguably had less influence precisely because its own internal squabbles had partly deprived it of external credibility.

One other irony deserves comment. The social work concepts employed in the 1969 Act were what I have described as the 'classical' ones, derived from the strong dependence of British social work on psychoanalytic theory in the 1950s and early 1960s. This common conceptual base was also one of the major origins of the suggestion to merge professional organizations. But from the vantage point of the early 1970s, we can see that in the late 1960s those ideas were beginning to change rapidly at a grass roots level, towards a more sociological stance; though in 1968 the challenges which this involved were all at a non-institutionalized and hence powerless level in the professional organization of social work. The interaction between social work conceptions of knowledge, professional reorganization, and legislative activity for juvenile offenders in the 1960s is certainly a highly complex one which is deserving of further study.

But we have not yet shown why the 1968 White Paper succeeded where the 1965 one failed. Certainly, the strong commitment of civil servants of the Home Office Children's Department, not present at least to the same extent in 1965, must be considered a factor; and in this case a further change of Home Secretary a few months before publication of the White Paper does not seem to have been a decisive event.[49] An additional factor was no

[48] E.g. the editorial comment in the N.A.P.O. journal, *Probation*, in July 1968: 'the new White Paper is a great advance on its predecessor . . . the Government must be congratulated on having been prepared to consider and meet so many criticisms'. N.A.P.O., of course, was in any case not as opposed to the introduction of social work concepts as were some other bodies: nevertheless, it had some reservations about the Bill and expressed these in a detailed memorandum—see 'N.A.P.O. and the Children and Young Persons Bill', *Justice of the Peace*, 1969, **133**, 296–7.

[49] Mr. James Callaghan replaced Mr. Roy Jenkins in November 1967. But the 1968 paper (published in April) must have been in reasonably advanced preparation before Callaghan took office. The greater professionalism of the 1968 paper is consistent with the thesis that Jenkins was partly responsible for the demise of the 1965 paper, though

doubt the Government's insistence that some legislation on the subject must be carried: it is embarrassing to a Government to withdraw proposed egislation on a subject twice in one term of office.

The decisive difference appears to have been the lesser degree of opposition to the new proposals. It is true that the Magistrates' Association again took a very critical stance, but their opposition, together with that of some lawyers and probation officers, had much of the sting taken from it by the retention of the juvenile court, the proposed abolition of which had caused so much opposition in 1965. It is much easier to appeal to a wider constituency with opposition to the abolition of a court than with opposition to some of the more technical matters the 1969 opposers were fighting. Indeed, the retention of the court, while radically altering the jurisdiction and conceptual basis of the court's operation, seems in retrospect a masterly manoeuvre by the Home Office. At the grass roots level if not at the level of the Magistrates' Association, juvenile justices seem to have thought they had won a victory in 1969 with the retention of the court. But after the Act had been implemented in part in 1971 a serious magisterial revolt took place. Major conflicts with the local authority social workers[50] led to the almost unprecedented step of a full-scale conference of interested groups with the responsible Government Minister in January 1973.[51] The main ingredient in this dispute was, by common consent, the different operating philosophies of magistrates and social workers: yet this conflict had not led to really sustained pressure by magistrates against the 1968 White Paper. Almost certainly, the reason for this is that the symbolic retention of the court in the 1968 proposals meant that magistrates had failed to realize how far the traditional functions and operating philosophy of the juvenile court were being eroded by the details of the new framework.

To sum up then: it is submitted that the main framework of an explanation of the English Act is approximately as follows. The Ingleby committee brought to the fore a central anomaly in juvenile justice, and helped to

---

of course it is impossible to say whether the paper would have been different, or introduced at a different time, had he remained in the Home Office.

[50] See Brian Harris, 'Children's Act in Trouble: An Appreciation of the Children and Young Persons Act 1969 in Operation', *Criminal Law Review* [1972], 670–84; G. Smith, 'The Children Act: What is Going Wrong?' *New Society*, 1972, **22**, 681–3.

[51] At this conference, representatives of the Magistrates' Association pressed for a full-scale reconsideration of the whole Act, but this was decisively rejected by the Minister. (Incidentally, directly as a result of the 1969 Act, the responsible Minister was no longer the Home Secretary, but the Minister for Health and Social Security, Sir Keith Joseph.) The degree of conflict leading to the conference is particularly remarkable in view of the fact that the Act was intended to be only very partially implemented by the Conservative Government (see footnote 5) and that at the time of the conference compulsory care proceedings even for 10–12 year old offenders were not in force.

polarize the political positions of the two major parties on the issue. From different but conjoining standpoints, both the Labour party and social workers wanted a more welfare-oriented juvenile justice system. The first attempt was put forward by Labour, relatively unassisted by professional social workers but strongly backed by them. This attempt failed, due to the strength of the opposition, the wider issues it was able to raise, the political difficulties of the Government, and a change of Home Secretary. The second attempt was—aside from the retention of the court—much more by professional social work ideas, but was still backed by Labour because of the conjunction of concepts. The emergence of this attempt can be mainly traced to a very influential group of social-work oriented civil servants, but they in turn would not have been so influential but for parallel developments towards professional and organizational unity in British social work. The success of the attempt as against the failure of the earlier attempt is attributable to a number of technical matters, but particularly to the retention of the juvenile courts in the second White Paper, which deprived the opposition of its most evocative symbol. This outline is tentative, and certainly in need of further research, but I believe its main thrust is likely to be correct.

Theoretical Issues

Previous work on the sociology of lawmaking does not appear strikingly helpful in dealing with the case of the Children and Young Persons Act. One main strand of theory has been concerned with 'moral entrepreneurs'[52] or 'symbolic crusaders',[53] the difference being that the former have a vested interest in the passage of the law, while the latter have not. Most such analyses, as Lemert points out, have been on 'issues like alcohol and drug use, gambling and sex', where the notion of a moral entrepreneur or crusader is readily applicable.[54] This is not wholly so, however: for example, Platt specifically invokes Becker's theory in dealing with the 'child savers' who were responsible for the campaign to create the first juvenile court law in Illinois.[55]

Platt's analysis, however, serves also as a warning of the deficiencies of this type of theory. For, apart from a reference to the support gained from the Chicago Bar Association, he never examines critically the way in which the various organizations comprising the child-saving movement—itself

[52] Becker, op. cit., 1963.
[53] J. Gusfield, *Moral Crusade,* Urbana, University of Illinois Press, 1963.
[54] E. M. Lemert, *Human Deviance, Social Problems and Social Control,* 2nd ed., Prentice-Hall, 1972, Englewood Cliffs, New Jersey.
[55] Platt, op. cit., 1969.

somewhat vaguely defined—had any impact on the actual passage of the 1899 Bill. By ignoring legislative and bureaucratic process, he tends to give the impression of the inevitability of the success of the movement; yet as Lemert says—

> Acquaintance with the workings of legislatures reveals the multi-faceted inter-action they have with (crusading) groups, as well as the intricacies of their own internal interaction through committees, majorities and minorities . . . To understand the interplay of so many groups in the development of new categories of legal and moral control requires a model of group interaction rather than inter-personal interaction.[56]

Lemert thus aptly characterizes moral enterprise as a *reductio ad personam* theory. In a not dissimilar vein, Dickson has pointed out that Becker's illustrative case, the Marijuana Tax Act, is capable of being understood as much in bureaucratic terms as in terms of a moral crusade.[57]

Suitably complicated by reference to these and other matters, the concept of the moral entrepreneur or symbolic crusader may be helpful in some contexts.[58] In our present context, however, it is not. The most likely candidates for the rôle are the child-care officers and other social workers, including those in the Home Office Children's Department. But, while the final legislation did indeed represent the victory of a relatively 'pure' classical social work position, this legislation can only be viewed in the context of earlier reports which were not in the same conceptual framework. The process summarized at the end of the previous section is assuredly not that of classical moral enterprise.

On the other hand, Lemert's work seems a good deal more appropriate, particularly in his explicit adoption of a pluralistic framework of group interaction.[59] In discussing the process of achieving revolutionary procedural (not substantive) law, Lemert applies Kuhn's theory of the genesis of revolutions in natural science,[60] complicating it only by reference again to

[56] Lemert, op. cit., 1971, p. 20.

[57] D. T. Dickson, 'Bureaucracy and Morality: an organisational perspective on a moral crusade', *Social Problems*, **16**, 143–56.

[58] Cf. Stang Dahl's (op. cit.) analysis of the Norwegian child welfare legislation, where she refers carefully and fully to the organisational and legislative context, including the reasons why both political parties supported the law; but where nevertheless Bernhard Getz played a crucial pioneering rôle which could apparently be brought within the concept of the moral entrepreneur, though Stang Dahl does not specifically use this notion.

[59] Lemert, *Social Action and Legal Change*, especially pp. 10–11. Many recent sociologists of law have of course repudiated a pluralistic model in favour of a conflict model, but in the context of legislation of the type discussed in this paper, a pluralistic framework seems most appropriate, and the various interest groups themselves impliedly operate within such a framework.

[60] T. S. Kuhn, *The Structure of Scientific Revolutions*, Chicago, University of Chicago Press, 1962; Lemert, *Social Action and Legal Change, passim*.

group interaction, e.g. in the organized support and direction of science by major institutions. Hence, following Kuhn, Lemert sees procedural law revolution as characterized by the appearance of a new paradigm, and this is explicable through the growth of 'anomalies' in the old law, though for anomalies to result in change of law, there must first be the creation of the anomaly into a social *issue*, and 'strong involvement, effective leadership, and ingenuity in creating qualitatively different ways of looking at facts'. Procedural law will also typically go through long periods of evolution as 'normal law' before revolutionary change can be achieved, 'although no particular cyclical form or periodicity can be claimed for the process'.

If we are prepared to grant that the Children and Young Persons Act is revolutionary law,[61] the Lemert thesis appears to fit it well. The Ingleby Committee exposed an anomaly; the Labour party and the social workers in different ways turned it into an issue; and successful legislation eventually resulted, following a long period of evolution since the establishment of the juvenile courts in 1908.

Despite the apparent fitness of his thesis, however, doubts arise as to Lemert's theorization. Some have expressed such doubts on the ground of lack of applicability of the concepts of scientific revolution to legal revolution. In fact, however, in one major respect the theory is *more* applicable to legal than to scientific revolution. For the epistemological basis of Kuhn's paradigm theory is relativism: he himself is only partially willing to admit this,[62] but close analysis renders the conclusion inescapable.[63] In relation to science, such a basis is a fatal flaw, but this is not so for legal revolutions since no one pretends that legal paradigms are anything but relativistic.

But another contrast between law and science renders Lemert's thesis highly problematic. For within the framework of a single scientific paradigm, the concept 'anomaly' has a restricted meaning. This is not so in law, and to apply Kuhn's theory Lemert is forced to widen the concept considerably, to include 'discrepancies between practice and legal precept'. Logically, it seems, there is also no case against a further extension to cover perceived injustice from a different value stance from that enshrined in the legal paradigm.[64] But if the concept is as wide as this, it becomes relatively useless,

[61] The post-Act conflicts between magistrates and social workers would suggest that it is; but a case can be made for saying that it is evolutionary: see Kahan, op. cit. There is obviously no clear definition of the term 'revolutionary'; this is important in relation to Lemert's view that revolutionary procedural law involves paradigm change, since on some definitions this could collapse into tautology.

[62] T. S. Kuhn, 'Reflections on my Critics', in *Criticism and the Growth of Knowledge*, ed. I. Lakatos and A. Musgrave, London, Cambridge University Press, 1970.

[63] R. Trigg, *Reason and Commitment*, London, Cambridge University Press, 1973, pp. 99–118.

[64] Lemert describes anomalies as 'objective phenomena, which can be brought to light

for there will always be some discrepancy between legal precept and practice, this being an integral feature of law as a symbolic system; and there will always also be the possibility of value-challenge. Hence there will always be anomalies, and in view of the breadth and vagueness of the concept, it will be difficult to speak—as one meaningfully can with scientific paradigms—of 'the *growth* of anomalies'. Nor, to take Lemert's analysis further, is it very helpful to say that anomalies must be converted into issues, for this is simply the truism that someone must promote legislative change. If predictive power is the hallmark of good sociological theory, it is significant that little of Lemert's theory is genuinely predictive; the sole exception relates to the suggestion that difficulty will be found in achieving further revolutionary change shortly after revolutionary legislation—itself an apparently sound proposition which is supported in the English case by the Conservative Government's rejection of proposals to review the Act in 1973 (see footnote 51), despite the strong Conservative opposition to the original Bill in 1969.

At this stage in the sociology of law, it may in any case be premature to seek for theories of law creation of a high degree of generality, rather than specific explanations of particular legal changes. If it is objected that this is history or political science, and not sociology, the danger may be conceded —but if the sociological dimension is kept firmly in view, it should be minimized. In any case, as one scarcely needs to emphasize in a *Festschrift* to Sir Leon Radzinowicz, there is much to be said for that historical tradition which insists on seeing historical events in the full richness of their contemporary context. Certainly in the case of the Children and Young Persons Act, only an analysis which keeps close to the richness of the data seems likely to offer an adequate explanation.

In this connection I should like to emphasize again that this paper is not based upon extensive research. A full explanation, as well as making a fuller exploration of primary sources, would need to consider a number of wider background issues of relevance to the eventual passage of the legislation. For example, the developing ideology of the Labour Party would need to be analysed, to consider why, at a particular moment in time, it was placing so much stress on the rôle of the family as against other social institutions, and thus rendered itself particularly susceptible to an alliance with psycho-analytically oriented social workers. It would also need to consider different ideological strands within the Labour Party more fully, just as it would also need to consider the relation between ideology, types of explanation, and professionalism in British social work (see above, p. 328), as well as the

---

by critical research or comprehensive appreciation of all possible consequences of patterns of action' (p. 88). But again, they are not quite 'objective' in the same sense in the contrasting cases of science and law.

formal and informal network of communication between social workers and influential members of the Labour Party. Pending elaboration or falsification for more detailed work of this kind, it is nevertheless hoped that the analysis in this paper casts some light on the legislation in question.

The Scottish Contrast

The Social Work (Scotland) Act established a new system of non-judicial 'children's hearings' for juvenile justice in Scotland.[65] According to most commentators, this Act is more revolutionary than the English Act of 1969;[66] yet it was passed with much less controversy and bitterness than the English Act. Why?

Prior to the 1968 Act, Scotland was in the anomalous position of having no less than four different types of juvenile courts in different areas. A third of all cases were handled by sheriffs, i.e. legally qualified judges sitting alone; just under a half of all cases were handled by burgh courts presided over by elected lay town councillors sitting alone; while the remainder (one-fifth) were handled by two different types of lay justice of the peace (or magistrates') court. These differences could only be explained historically, and when a committee was established to consider the situation it was more or less inevitable that some rationalization should be propounded, especially as criticisms were not infrequently heard that, unlike English juvenile courts, the Scottish ones were not very different from adult criminal courts.

But no one could have predicted the radical outcome of this committee's deliberations when it was set up in 1961, especially as its composition was almost as unadventurous as Ingleby's: 'two judges of the sheriff court . . . three magistrates . . . an expert in probation work, a professor of law, an approved school manager, a clerk to a juvenile court, a very distinguished child psychiatrist, a well known headmaster, and a chief constable',[67] pre-

---

[65] For descriptions of the new Scottish system see J. P. Grant, 'Juvenile Justice—Part III of the Social Work (Scotland) Act 1968', *Juridical Review* [1971], 149–175; R. W. Renton and H. H. Brown, *Criminal Procedure according to the Law of Scotland*, 4th ed., Edinburgh, W. Green & Son., 1972, ch. 19.

[66] E.g. D. R. May and G. Smith, 'Policy interpretation and the children's panels: a case study in social administration', *Applied Social Studies*, 1970, **2**, 91–98, speak of the Scottish Act moving more 'outside the context of criminal law and into the ambit of professional social work'. But global judgements are difficult: e.g. the English care order gives total power to the local authority social workers, whereas the Scottish 'residential supervision requirement' is controlled by the lay panel. Hence the post-Act conflicts in England about social workers sending juveniles placed on care orders straight home to their parents, could not arise in Scotland.

[67] Lord Kilbrandon, op. cit., p. 114.

sided over by a High Court judge. Yet the Committee's report (see footnote 30) was not only radical, it was also by far the longest and incontestably the best argued British policy document in this field in the 1960s, and it completely dominated the subsequent scene in Scotland.

The Kilbrandon committee identified precisely the same problem as Ingleby, i.e. the difficulty of the criminal trial followed by the duty to consider the welfare of the child. Kilbrandon, too, like Ingleby, was sure that the solution to this was to move in a more 'welfare' direction. But Kilbrandon, unlike Ingleby, reacted to these conclusions by proposing a complete new structure, spelt out in detail. Mack's suggestion that this difference between the two reports was due to a Scottish tradition of Civilian rather than Common Law jurisprudence[68] is a possibility, but it is more likely that the greater heterogeneity in the unreformed Scottish situation prompted a resort to first principles.

The Kilbrandon approach is on the whole, a meticulously consistent application to the juvenile justice issue of a medical treatment approach to delinquency.[69] Only in one major respect were the Committee's proposals altered in the ensuing legislation, and this concerned the issue of the type of 'matching fieldwork organization', or social service, required to back up the new children's panels. Kilbrandon, drawing on a long Scottish tradition of the importance of education, proposed that this fieldwork service should be in new Social Education Departments under the Director of Education for each local authority. But when the Labour Government announced its acceptance of the main Kilbrandon recommendations in 1965, it also announced that it did not accept the proposal for housing the support social workers in the Education Department, but was considering other alternatives. This decision appears to have been the result of strong grass roots pressure among social workers, resisting entry into local authority education departments perceived by the social workers as over-dominated by academic and didactic learning traditions.[70] After a period of uncertainty as to the eventual outcome, proposals were ultimately made to set up unified local authority social work departments,[71] and these became law in Part I of the same Act which established the children's hearings. Of very great interest in contrasting the English and Scottish situations, is that this reorganization

[68] J. A. Mack, Lecture on the Kilbrandon Report at Glasgow University, 1968; cited in article by Carmichael (below, footnote 70).

[69] See Allison Morris, 'A Criminal Law in Practice: Children's Hearings in Scotland', paper presented to Fifth National Conference on Research and Teaching in Criminology, 1973 (mimeo).

[70] Catherine M. Carmichael, 'Development in Scottish Social Work: Changes in the Law and Implications for the Future', *Applied Social Studies*, 1969, **1**, 35–42.

[71] *Social Work and the Community*, Cmd. 3065, Edinburgh, HMSO, 1966.

came about directly *because* of the acceptance of the Kilbrandon approach, which necessitated some broader field organization than had previously existed in the impoverished state of Scottish social work.[72] Without the stimulus of Kilbrandon, it is extremely doubtful if anything like the Scottish social work departments would exist today; whereas in England there was a strong *independent* move towards social work unification, which in turn created pressure towards a more 'welfare' orientation in the juvenile courts.[73]

But, though there was plenty of controversy in Scotland about what form the fieldwork organization should take, objections to the central Kilbrandon proposals for children's panels were 'most extraordinarily . . . muted in public discussion in Scotland itself'.[74] It is difficult to account for this. One possible reason is the obvious anomaly of the old heterogeneous system for Scottish juveniles: May comments that things might have been different had more than a few local authorities taken advantage of a permissive power in a 1932 statute to create specially constituted juvenile courts akin to those in England.[75] Again, it is possible that the very thoroughness of the Kilbrandon Report was itself a silencer, as people were unable to think of more convincing replacements for the previous heterogeneity.

Perhaps a more likely reason for the lack of controversy is that those groups who in England were most critical of the proposals—lawyers, magistrates and probation officers—were for different reasons, less likely to offer opposition within Scotland. Except in a few areas, J.P.s were not involved in the old juvenile courts and had little reason to oppose the new system, especially as the lay element would be substantially greater when the panels came into existence. Scottish lawyers, accustomed to a legal system which interposes an independent official (the procurator-fiscal) between the police and the courts, were perhaps not as disposed as their English colleagues to oppose the non-judicial body being proposed, especially as an appeal to the sheriff court was retained in the new system.

---

[72] See, on this, Carmichael, op. cit., who attributes the lack of development of Scottish social work (in contrast to England) to a number of factors such as the lack of early involvement of philanthropists, a strong Calvinist tradition, and a tradition of environmental reforms rather than humanistic perspectives among the powerful Scottish socialists. The Scottish probation service was considered and found wanting in an official report in 1962: *Report of the Departmental Committee on the Probation Service*, Cmd. 1650, Edinburgh, HMSO, ch. 9.

[73] It is true that the setting up of the English Seebohm Committee (see footnote 47) was first announced in the 1965 White Paper on juvenile courts (para. 7), but, as indicated earlier in this essay, there had prior to this been considerable independent pressure for unification.

[74] J. A. Mack, 'The Scottish Reforms: II—The Social Work (Scotland) Bill 1968', *British Journal of Criminology*, 1968, **8**, 242–6.

[75] May, op. cit., 1971, p. 359.

As for the probation officers, they were organizationally very weak in Scotland and in any case too busy fighting their forthcoming incorporation into social work departments[76] to concentrate overmuch on the children's panels themselves, although some token opposition was offered.

Even in the strictly political arena, there was less controversy. It is true that there was Conservative criticism during the Parliamentary debates on the 1968 Bill,[77] and it is at least possible that, had the Conservatives been in power, the Kilbrandon Report would not have been so easily translated into legislation. Nevertheless, Conservative opposition was not nearly as strongly pressed to the 1968 Scottish Bill as it was to the English 1969 Bill—for example, there was no attempt to divide the House to a vote on the Second Reading—and the acceptance of Kilbrandon seems to have been much less decisively influenced by party political considerations than was the case in England.

The suggestions in this section are highly tentative, but seem the most probable explanations of a social contrast between the two countries which is itself of the greatest interest, and well worthy of further study. Such a study would of course need to consider the background and development of the Scottish system in its own right, on which see the essay by Allison Morris elsewhere in this volume.

The American Contrast

The English–Scottish comparison is of particular interest because of the close integration of these two countries in so many ways. The British–American contrast is obviously of a rather different order, and is of interest mainly because the trends on the two sides of the Atlantic were in such different directions during the 1960s.

As is well known, the American move towards a more legalistic and 'due process' model of the juvenile court has been manifested in a number of ways. In California, a State law to this effect was passed as early as 1961, and it is this legislation whose genesis is extensively described by Lemert. The Task Force on Juvenile Delinquency of the President's Commission

[76] The Social Work (Scotland) Act 1968 abolished the Scottish probation service and merged it into the local authority social work departments; the corresponding English Act of 1970 retained a separate probation service.

[77] E.g. Mr Ian MacArthur, winding up for the Opposition on the Second Reading debate: 'We have considerable reservations about this Part of the Bill, all centred on the legal rights of the child and the protection of the child, whose rights must not be ignored in the local authority's understandable anxiety to act *in loco parentis*', H.C. Deb. vol. 764, col. 139.

recommended moves in the same direction: 'in theory the court's operations could justifiably be informal . . . because it would act only in the best interest of the child; in fact it frequently does nothing more nor less than deprive a child of liberty without due process of law.'[78] And the Supreme Court of the U.S.A., in a series of cases of which the most celebrated is *In Re Gault* (1967) 387 U.S.1, promulgated a similar view. In the later stages of this movement, but not in the Californian campaign, powerful support for the trend was forthcoming from deviance sociologists impressed with the evidence of labelling theory about the power of social institutions to criminalize rather than rehabilitate.

It is important not to exaggerate. A more recent Supreme Court decision, ruling that jury trial was not essential in juvenile courts, noted that the Court was 'disinclined to give impetus' to a total formalizing of American juvenile courts.[79] As the Court correctly stated, the Task Force Report had also declined to go so far; and it is noteworthy that even after the American 'formalizing' reforms and the English and Scottish 'welfare' reforms, the former may in some situations offer less chance for formal challenge than the latter.[80]

Nevertheless there have undoubtedly been different movements of opinion in America and Britain. Why? Again answers are not easy to give, and must be largely speculative. On the face of it, the American movement seems the more easily explicable, in view of the increasing maturity and independence of youth in contemporary Western societies. This is undoubtedly reinforced in the American case by the growing awareness of the civil rights problem and its meaning for individual liberty; and also by the kind of sociological critiques already mentioned.

At least some of these movements are also now apparent in Britain, though still at present often in a nascent stage. In the case of the 1968–9 legislation, however, they had no influence. They are as yet relatively powerless: the social work ideology is far more entrenched in positions of power than the radical sociological philosophy.

Additionally, we need to consider the previous history of the institutions

[78] President's Commission on Law Enforcement and the Administration of Justice, *Task Force Report: Juvenile Delinquency*, 1967, Washington D.C., U.S. Gov. Printing Office, p. 9.

[79] *McKeiver* v. *Pennsylvania* (1971) 403 U.S. 528.

[80] For example, the California Youth Authority has enormous power of discretionary decision, and even in the reformed system 'attorneys and court officers' regard this as 'beyond the scope of legal protections', Lemert, op. cit., 1970. By contrast, in the new Scottish system, the panel must review and renew each supervision requirement annually at least, and the child has right of appeal to the Sheriff, with legal representation, on each such renewal.

which have been reformed. This is not just a lawyer's or an historian's point, if (as seems likely) Lamert's revolutionary/evolutionary thesis is correct, because successful change can only occur after a relatively long evolutionary period. In the American case, the *parens patriae* juvenile court of the 1900s was a sufficiently paternalistic interventionist institution to allow the subsequent growth of professional social work to be easily incorporated into it. This meant, for example, that no reform in that direction was necessary at the time of the strong influence of psychoanalytic ideas in the United States in the 1950s. On the other hand, such courts were ripe for reform when viewed from the individual liberties perspective. Conversely, the British juvenile courts were, at their inception and on beyond the 1933 reforms, essentially private, informal criminal courts. Hence they were more prone to reform by the social work ethic when it became sufficiently powerful.

But the subject of juvenile justice is full of ironies, and one of the ironies of the British–American contrast is that in one major respect the new philosophies on each side of the Atlantic are heading in a similar direction: namely, the tendency to make the court or panel more of a 'last resort' than formerly. In the American case, this comes from sociological critiques based on labelling theory; in the British case, it comes from stigma theory based on the social work view of delinquency. So we find an American audience being offered, in a recent article, section 1(2) of the Children and Young Persons Act as being 'shrewdly drafted' for the purpose of keeping children out of courts,[81] while in England it is attacked as opening the door to class bias (see footnote 44). And, by a double irony, both may be right: for if the words are applied by persons operating on social work concepts, they could well be class-discriminatory, while if they are applied by persons operating on sociological labelling theory, they will not.[82]

In the Foreword to the first volume of Leon Radzinowicz's *History of English Criminal Law*, Lord Macmillan said:

Behind [legislation] lies a vast area of discussion and controversy in which the formation of public opinion discloses itself . . . Without knowledge of this background, the significance of legislation cannot be fully appreciated.

This essay is offered in the spirit of Lord Macmillan's comment, and in the hope that directly or indirectly it may stimulate further consideration of the significance of the recent English legislation for juvenile offenders.

[81] J. A. Seymour, 'Youth Services Bureaux', *Law and Society Review*, 1972, 7, 247–72.
[82] One further irony may be mentioned: the American movement was virtually unknown in Britain—even to some criminologists—at the time of the 1965–69 debates and discussion, and it was never used by any of the opponents of the English 1969 legislation.

SCOTTISH JUVENILE JUSTICE: A CRITIQUE

Allison Morris

Introduction

The method of dealing with children in need of compulsory measures of care in Scotland involves a movement away from legal processes towards a social welfare approach and, for that reason, is an innovation worthy of attention. To understand an institution requires knowledge of the motives and aspirations of those who created it and of those who operate it. One must consider not only what an institution consciously attempts to do, but also what it in fact does. This paper hopes to provide some understanding of the philosophy and implementation of Part III of the Social Work (Scotland) Act 1968, which introduced the system of children's hearings.

The Act is based on the recommendations of the Kilbrandon Committee[1] and the White Paper *Social Work and the Community*.[2] To put it briefly,[3] it replaces appearance before a juvenile court with appearance before a hearing consisting of three persons drawn from a panel of laymen. Children are referred to a hearing by a local authority official known as the reporter. Before the hearing can deal with the child the reporter must establish the ground of referral. Section 32 of the Act sets out the available grounds which include, for example, lack of parental care, and the commission of an offence. The grounds are normally established by the child's admission; if they are disputed the reporter (provided the hearing wishes to proceed with the referral) must apply to the sheriff court for a finding as to whether they are established. The disposals open to the hearing, once the grounds are established, are discharge or a supervision order which may or may not require the child to reside in a named residential establishment. Both the

---

[1] *Children and Young Persons, Scotland*, The Kilbrandon Committee Report, Cmd 2306, HMSO, 1964.
[2] *Social Work and the Community*, Cmd. 3065, HMSO, 1966.
[3] For a more detailed description see R. W. Renton and H. H. Brown, *Criminal Procedure according to the law of Scotland*, Ch. 19, 4th ed., Edinburgh, W. Green and Son, 1972.

child and his parents have a right of appeal to the sheriff against the hearing's disposal. The hearing may review its decision as to the appropriate disposal at any time, and must do so annually, at which times it may change or terminate the order. The jurisdiction of the hearing continues until the child reaches the age of eighteen unless the referral is discharged before then.

Thus, although both Scotland and England considered the appropriate method of dealing with child offenders and other 'problem' children in the 1960s, what emerged in the two countries differs. The difference is not in the philosophy underlying the changes—both stress that a child should not be brought before a court or tribunal unless his problems cannot be dealt with on a voluntary basis, and that offences by children should be seen as symptomatic of their needs—but rather in the implementation of that philosophy. England chose to retain the juvenile court; Scotland chose to replace it with a lay tribunal. This difference may not matter. Cavenagh, for example, writes:

> The most important question is perhaps not whether to deal with young offenders in criminal or civil courts or welfare boards, but how, under whatever system is in use, to ensure that the public is protected from crime, that liberty is preserved, and the young offender gets the treatment he needs.[4]

But in terms of understanding the motives of the Scottish reform the distinction between lay tribunal and court does matter. The Kilbrandon Committee explicitly saw the move from court to tribunal as a solution to the conflict which arose from the juvenile court's attempt to perform a treatment function, the conflict between the existing concepts of criminal courts and the directive to have regard to the welfare of the child.[5]

This conflict has been a critical element in the field of juvenile justice.[6] Those referred to juvenile courts or welfare tribunals are children as well as offenders. Thus, although treating child offenders differently from adult offenders is normally seen as having its roots in humanitarian attitudes,

[4] W. E. Cavenagh, *Juvenile Courts: The Child and the Law*, Harmondsworth, Pelican Books, 1967.

[5] Kilbrandon Committee Report, paras. 71, 72 and 73.

[6] See also para. 60 of the *Report of Committee on Children and Young Persons*, Cmd. 1191, HMSO, 1960. 'The court remains a criminal court in the sense that it is a magistrates' court, that it is principally concerned with trying offences, that its procedure is a modified form of ordinary criminal procedure and that, with a few special provisions, it is governed by the law of evidence in criminal cases. Yet the requirement to have regard to the welfare of the child, and the various ways in which the court may deal with an offender, suggests a jurisdiction that is not criminal. It is not easy to see how the two principles can be reconciled: criminal responsibility is focussed on an allegation about some particular act isolated from the character and needs of the defendant, whereas welfare depends on a complex of personal, family and social considerations.'

humanitarianism in this context covers a wide variety of attitudes and standpoints. In its 'pure' form it means simply that child offenders, just because they are children, should be treated differently from adult offenders. This can be expressed in two ways: it is inhumane to subject children to such harsh penalties as are provided for adults, and it is unreasonable to expect the same standards of conduct from immature and uneducated children as are expected from adults. The punishment therefore, can be mitigated. Humanitarian motives have also led the state to intervene when a child was not being looked after properly by his parents. As it was assumed that the delinquent was, by definition, not well looked after and that there were deficiencies in his upbringing, the state could place itself *in loco parentis* to that child. Linked with this attitude, but separate from it, is humanitarianism based on the interests of society. The state intervenes because of the child's behaviour rather than his needs; because it is morally 'better' for the child to be a conforming citizen than a delinquent; and because it is the duty of the state to save him from recidivism. Thus, control of the child's behaviour also appears under the guise of humanitarianism.

These motivations exist whether the agency for dealing with child offenders is a court or a welfare tribunal. The Kilbrandon Committee clearly reflect these ambivalent attitudes when they state that:

> this small minority of children who are offenders are, and must remain, a continuing source of public anxiety because children's misdemeanours must naturally cause concern, because of the forms which such delinquency sometimes takes, and the worry, distress and loss which in particular cases they may cause for the persons whose property is the subject of these attentions and because they form a recruiting ground for the adult criminal.[7]

This paper discusses to what extent the system of children's hearings in Scotland is in fact a solution to this conflict.

The Emergence and Acceptance of the Kilbrandon Committee Report

A confused and confusing picture of juvenile courts in Scotland no doubt created a desire in the 1960s for a reconsideration of the appropriate method of dealing with child offenders. In Scotland, after the Children Act 1908, there were three courts with concurrent jurisdiction; the sheriff, the justices of the peace in the counties, and the magistrates in the burghs. These courts acted in the main in their ordinary capacity as criminal courts dealing with adults, and only acted as juvenile courts on certain days. The court procedure

[7] Kilbrandon Committee Report, para. 8.

was modified and simplified on these days in an attempt to enable the child to understand what was happening, but there was no fundamental alteration in the principles of criminal procedure. These first juvenile courts were criticized in 1928 by the Morton Committee.[8] That Committee felt that magistrates (who were town councillors chosen by the electorate to administer the town government) and sheriffs (who were legally trained) were not the appropriate persons to deal with child offenders. 'In these circumstances it is not surprising that there should be a lack of constructive or settled policy in the treatment of juvenile offenders.'[9] The Committee recommended that jurisdiction in the case of children should be transferred to a justice of the peace court specially constituted for the purpose and staffed by people 'carefully chosen on account of their specialized qualifications'. These were defined as 'concern for the problems of childhood and of adolescence, and an insight into young life and that knowledge of local conditions which will enable them to estimate the influence of parents, the effect of the environment, and the moral atmosphere of the district in which the offender lives'.[10] This recommendation was accepted, and the new legislation also imposed a duty on magistrates to have regard to the welfare of the child in making their decision as to the appropriate disposal for him.[11]

The parliamentary debates on the 1932 Bill show in fact the continuing process of incorporating changing ideas and attitudes. Referring firstly to the Children Act 1908, the Earl of Feversham stated that 'twenty-four years ago there were certain provisions in that Bill which were regarded by some as revolutionary, but 24 years of progress and increased understanding of the problems of child life have shown those who have been closely connected with working with the children in the juvenile courts that what was then considered revolutionary is now looked upon as almost obsolete'.[12] He went on to say of the new Act—'We no longer concentrate on the offence. We look now to the offender.'[13]

In practice, however, although the clear intention of the legislature was that there should be one juvenile court, the old system continued except in four areas of Scotland where special juvenile courts were established.[14] The provisions of section 1 of the 1932 Act were never extended beyond these areas. The reasons for this are no doubt numerous and complex, but the

[8] *Report of Committee on Protection and Training*, HMSO, 1928.
[9] Ibid., p. 42.
[10] Ibid., p. 43.
[11] Children and Young Persons (Scotland) Act 1932, s. 16.
[12] Parliamentary Debate on the Children and Young Persons Bill 1932, *H.L. Debates*, vol. 84, col. 478–9.
[13] Ibid., col. 482.
[14] The four areas were the Counties of Fife, Renfrew and Ayr, and the city of Aberdeen.

war years of 1939–45 must have prevented further developments. Subsequently local authorities, on whom the financial burden of providing the
new juvenile courts lay,[15] may have been reluctant to commit themselves to
the further development of the special courts unless it could be established
that those already in existence were effective in reducing juvenile delinquency.
Thus the juvenile courts remained essentially criminal courts, and, as such,
their first function was to deal with a specific offence. As a result, when the
judge came to the disposal stage, he was influenced by the facts of the case
and his decision was related to these. In addition to this, the major part of
the judge's duties was dealing with adult offenders where considerations such
as the gravity of the offence and protection of the public could not be ignored.
Despite the obligation to have regard to the welfare of the child, these other
aspects still loomed large.

Also operative in setting the scene for radical changes in the method of
dealing with children was the revolution in social policy which had occurred
in Britain after the Second World War.[16] Concern for the lot of children
was very much part of the plans for a new Britain. Committees were set up
to consider provisions for the care of children deprived of normal home
life.[17] And, although services for the delinquent child had, in the main, been
separate from services for children without adequate family care, there was
a greater recognition that their various forms of misbehaviour or handicap
might be rooted in broadly similar circumstances. Thus the field of enquiry
of the Ingleby Committee covered not only the constitution, jurisdiction
and procedure of juvenile courts, but also whether or not new powers
should be given to local authorities 'to prevent or forestall the suffering of
children through neglect in their own homes'.[18] The establishment of this
Committee provided the Civil Service in Scotland with an opportunity to
evaluate the situation there. It is, moreover, worth noting that the Civil
Service was criticized by such organizations as the Scottish branches of the
British Medical Association and of the Howard League for setting up two
separate Committees to discuss these questions and, thereby, for not recognizing the underlying similarities.[19]

[15] *Boase* v. *Fife County Council*, 1937, *S.C.* (*H.L.*) 28.
[16] The starting point was the report prepared by Sir William Beveridge on *Social
Insurance and Allied Services* in 1942, HMSO, Cmd. 6404.
[17] *Interdepartmental Committee on the Care of Children* (the Curtis Committee), HMSO,
Cmd. 6922, 1946, and its equivalent in Scotland, the Clyde Committee, Cmd. 6911,
HMSO, 1946.
[18] *Report of the Committee on Children and Young Persons*, Cmd. 1191, HMSO, 1960.
[19] Children and Young Persons Committee (the Kilbrandon Committee), op. cit., and
the Committee on the Prevention of Neglect of Children (McBoyle Committee), Cmd.
1466, HMSO, 1963.

From the 1950s too, the 'teenager' emerged as a separate rôle in society. Teenagers were recognized as a new market, and distinctive clothes, magazines, etc. were provided for them. This helped to crystallize and give substance to their identity and led to the increasing recognition of their special needs and problems. But this interest in children was coupled with distrust and misunderstanding. 'Many adults seem to use the term "teenager" and "juvenile delinquent" as if they were synonymous; to them, the youth problem is one of law enforcement or treatment for the emotionally disturbed.'[20] The press carried reports of the rising rate of juvenile delinquency and of changes in the type of delinquency, particularly the spread of violence among teenage gangs. In their presentation of this, the media to some extent created and to a large extent encouraged the belief that 'something had to be done'[21] to protect society.

How then, in the light of this climate of opinion, did the Kilbrandon Committee's major recommendation—the abolition of the juvenile court and its replacement by a 'welfare' tribunal—gain acceptance from the legislature and the public? The rôle of the media in shaping public attitudes is now well documented[22] and it appears that the media in Scotland prepared the way for popular acceptance of the Kilbrandon Committee's recommendations. Before the publication of the Report there was considerable criticism of the juvenile court. Lord Kilbrandon, for example, was widely reported as saying in a speech to the Association of Child Care Officers that the delinquent child's first contact with the law should not be in the juvenile court where he is dealt with by 'nice people', but in an atmosphere of rigid formality at police headquarters, where he is faced with 'an ugly police superintendent in full uniform, who will tell the little perisher exactly what he thinks of him'. In describing the juvenile court Lord Kilbrandon continued:

> He is shown into a room and faced by a benevolent old gentleman and a kindly old lady who do their best to put him at his ease. He then listens to his mother telling the court what a good boy he is and how he has been led astray by bad companions and would not have thought up anything of this kind for himself. This surprises the boy nearly as much as when he hears his school-master giving

---

[20] E. Friedenberg, 'Adolescence as a Social Problem', in H. Becker, *Social Problems, A Modern Approach*, New York, John Wiley, 1966.

[21] For a discussion of the emergence of a social problem, see R. C. Fuller and R. R. Myers, 'The Natural History of a Social Problem', *Amer. Soc. Rev.*, 1941, **6**, 320 and H. Becker (ed.), op. cit., Introduction.

[22] F. J. Davis, 'Crime News in Colorado Newspapers', *Am. J. of Soc.*, 1952, **57**, 325–30; R. J. Roshier, 'Crime and the Press', *New Society*, 1971, **18**, 502; R. Hauge, 'Crime and the Press', in N. Christie (ed.), *Scandinavian Studies in Criminology*, Vol. 1, London, Tavistock, 1965.

him a glowing reference. After this encomium, the boy begins to feel quite genuinely that he is not a bad chap after all, and he is confirmed in this by the kindly admonition which is handed out to him by the elderly gentleman, and so he leaves the court.[23]

The juvenile court was blamed by implication for the failure to stem the increase in juvenile crime. The juvenile court having been discredited, the way was open for alternative solutions, and it is significant that stress was laid, after the Report's publication, on those aspects of it which were designed to strengthen the means available for the protection of the public and, in particular, on the wider powers which the hearings would have, e.g. continuous jurisdiction over the child until he reached the age of eighteen. This may have been done to make the proposed removal of most child offenders from the courts acceptable to a public opinion concerned with the growth of juvenile crime. However, the wider powers possessed by the hearings were an important feature of the Kilbrandon proposals. In addition the media hailed the Report as radical and controversial, and presented it in such a way that its acceptance became an issue in national identity. It was stated that the Report 'would bring Scotland into the mainstream of world penal reform',[24] and that it was 'more refined than anything already in practice anywhere in the world'.[25] References to cultural identity have always weighed heavily with the Scots,[26] and in these circumstances sustained criticism was difficult.[27]

The only consistently critical group were sections of the Scottish Branch of the National Association of Probation Officers who presented arguments similar to those which carried the day in England—for example they argued that children's hearings 'would not meet the requirements of a judicial system', and that the appointment of a reporter would not 'satisfactorily safeguard the liberty of the individual',[28]—but they had no great influence in Scotland. Furthermore, with the publication of the Social Work (Scotland)

[23] Quoted in *The Scotsman*, 13 April 1964.

[24] Ibid., 23 April 1964.

[25] *Glasgow Herald*, 23 April 1964.

[26] See the traditional toast: 'Here's tae us, wha's like us!' From the mid-fifties onwards there also occurred a growth of interest in Scottish nationalism—see N. MacCormick (ed.), *The Scottish Debate*, Oxford Univ. Press, 1970.

[27] One issue on which there was some disagreement in the editorials was the recommendation in the Kilbrandon Committee Report that parents should not be fined for the misdeeds of their children. The *Scottish Daily Express*, for example, stated that 'most Scots will agree that youngsters should, in most cases, be kept out of the criminal courts'. The editorial headline, however, was 'Make the Parents Pay!' (*Scottish Daily Express*, 23 April 1964).

[28] Quoted in *The Scotsman*, 1 February 1965, from a memorandum prepared by the Scottish branch of N.A.P.O. on the Kilbrandon Committee Report.

Bill, the important issue for the probation service became the proposed absorption of the probation service in a general social work organization which had been suggested not by the Kilbrandon Committee[29] but in the White Paper *Social Work and the Community*. Social workers in general were in favour of the Kilbrandon Report, and in fact had much to gain in status from its implementation, as it was published at a crucial time in the development of the professionalization of social work. The movement from the concept of 'social education' on which the Kilbrandon Committee relied to that of 'social work' which emerged in the White Paper can be described as a moral victory for social workers, but it was not a battle fought by social workers themselves.[30] Judith Hart, then Under-Secretary of State for Scotland, made a number of statements that the Government were planning to use the Kilbrandon Committee Report as a basis for the re-organization of social work. The fact, however, that the three advisers appointed to advise on the proposals for the re-organization of social work were either social workers or social administrators undoubtedly influenced the end result. The major opposition to the re-organization, apart from the National Association of Probation Officers, came from the medical profession, particularly the Scottish section of the British Medical Association and Medical Officers of Health on the ground that 'the social needs of the community cannot be separated from the mental and physical health of the community'.[31] Teachers were not particularly interested in the concept of 'social education'; they remained more interested in traditional academic pursuits.

It is relevant to discuss this movement from 'social education' to 'social work' in terms of 'moral' victory and 'status gains' for, when one considers what the Kilbrandon Committee meant by 'social education', it appears largely indistinguishable from what one generally means by 'social work'.

> It is intended . . . not to supersede the natural beneficial influences of the home and the family, but whenever possible to strengthen, support and supplement them in situations in which for whatever reason they have been weakened or have failed in their effect . . . Such a process of education in a social context . . . essentially involves the application of social and family case-work.[32]

---

[29] The Kilbrandon Committee's recommendations did raise difficult questions as to the future of the probation service as the Committee saw probation as a 'court-centred service concerned almost exclusively with adult offenders' (para. 249). Probation Officers were, therefore, already concerned about this and, after the publication of the White Paper, concentrated on the re-organization rather than the other Kilbrandon Committee proposals.

[30] Probably the most active group was the Association of Child Care Officers whose members felt that a multiplicity of authorities militated against good casework but that it would be a retrograde step to make family care part of the educational services. See the memorandum quoted in *The Scotsman*, 26 October 1964.

[31] *Glasgow Herald*, 6 March 1967.

[32] Kilbrandon Committee Report, op. cit., para. 35.

There was some criticism from the sheriffs of the proposed abolition of the juvenile courts but this was balanced by praise of other features;[33] and they, too, after the publication of the White Paper, concentrated on the separate issue of the retention of the probation service to deal with adult offenders. In any event sheriffs still retained their traditional rôle as guardians of individual liberty.[34] The magistrates of the four areas of Scotland which did have juvenile courts took a minor part in the debate[35] and, in fact, formed too small a group for any criticism they made to be effective. The status and expertise of the members of the Committee, particularly its Chairman, who was a respected member of the Scottish Bench, may also have prevented criticism. The report could not merely be dismissed as the ideas of radicals with no real knowledge of the problem. There was, also, an awareness of the anomalies in the Scottish juvenile court system and of a need for rationalization.[36]

Juvenile justice has been a fruitful area in the past for studies on the emergence of legislation[37] and the emergence of the Social Work Scotland Act would clearly repay further study. What can be said at this stage is that the acceptability of the proposals was due to a wide mixture of factors, rather than to the influence of particular interest groups.

The Influences on the Kilbrandon Committee

The Kilbrandon Committee was much concerned with the conflict in the juvenile court between what it called the 'punishment' concept and the 'preventive' concept:

[33] E.g. Sheriff Aikman Smith in a speech to the City and Counties Society quoted in *The Scotsman* stated that the abolition rather than the improvement of the juvenile courts might be 'throwing out the baby with the bath water', but also said that 'other proposals in the report were imaginative and challenging' (*The Scotsman*, 27 April 1974).

[34] When the child does not admit the ground of referral, the reporter, if the hearing wishes to proceed, must refer the case to the sheriff for establishment of the ground; the child and parents also have the right to appeal to the Sheriff Court on the disposal of the hearing and to the Court of Session on a point of law.

[35] There were, for example, some letters to newspapers and the County of Ayr Quarter Sessions set up a Special Committee to discuss the Kilbrandon Committee's proposals. Nothing came of this.

[36] Nor did the report become a political issue to the same extent as its English counterparts. See A. E. Bottoms, 'On the decriminalisation of English Juvenile courts', in this volume; pages 319–45.

[37] See A. E. Bottoms, ibid.; E. Lemert, *Social Action and Legal Change*, Chicago, Aldine Publishing Co., 1970; A. Platt, *The Child Savers*, University of Chicago Press, 1969; T. Stang Dahl, 'The Emergence of the Norwegian Child Welfare Law'—paper delivered at the First British–Scandinavian Research Conference in Criminology, 1971, University of Oslo, Institute of Criminology, *mimeo*.

... The emphasis which statute law places on the 'welfare' of juvenile offenders, serves to indicate society's concern that effective preventive measures should be applied at the earliest possible stage. Since, however, judicial action in relation to juvenile offenders in all cases takes place within a framework governed by criminal procedure, the proceedings as a whole and, in particular, the consideration of measures to be applied once the offence is established, cannot avoid being coloured by the underlying general concepts of responsibility and punishment.[38]

The Committee went on to say that

the shortcomings which cause dissatisfaction within the present juvenile court system seem to us to arise essentially from the fact that they seek to combine the characteristics of a court of criminal law with those of a specialised agency for the treatment of juvenile offenders, proceeding on a preventive and educational principle. In our view, criminal procedure does undoubtedly affect the whole atmosphere and manner of procedure in the juvenile courts ... it also colours the entirely separate stage of proceedings at which ... the question of practical action in the form of training measures appropriate to the needs of the individual falls to be resolved.[39]

The Committee felt that such a conflict of aims could never be wholly eradicated, but that their recommendations were capable of *reducing* it considerably.[40] Accordingly they recommended a procedure whereby juvenile offenders would be brought before a specialized agency whose sole concern would be the measures to be applied on what amounted to an agreed referral. 'The agency would exercise jurisdiction only on the basis of facts established by admission of the child in the parent's presence and with their agreement ... It would have no concern whatsoever with the determination of legal issues, its sole function being the consideration and application of training measures appropriate to the child's needs.'[41] A major factor leading the Committee in this direction appears to have been the evidence that in almost 95 per cent of the cases appearing before the juvenile courts there was no dispute as to the facts alleged.

A number of influences appear to have shaped the Committee's thinking and consequently, its recommendations. Firstly, it is clear that there were civil servants who were very conscious of the conflicts in the existing arrangements and who felt that the possibility of a welfare approach deserved examination by a Committee. Work had already been done on the contrasts between a 'crime-responsibility-punishment' concept and a 'prevention' concept—contrasts which, as modified by the Kilbrandon Committee,

[38] Kilbrandon Committee Report, para. 67.
[39] Ibid., para. 71.
[40] Ibid., para. 57.
[41] Ibid., para. 73.

appeared as paragraph 54 which is basic to much of the Committee's approach. It states:

(1) *Early preventive measures:* the 'crime-responsibility-punishment' concept militates against preventive action against potential delinquents. Because of the high degree of personal responsibility which it attaches to the criminal, a stigma is attached in the public eye to conviction of a crime, which bears no necessary relationship to the harm done by the action itself or the actual responsibility of the person who did it. Because it is concerned with the deserts of a criminal, the standard of proof is high. In the absence of such proof—even though it is clear that the surrounding circumstances are such as to call urgently for preventive action—no such action can be taken since it would involve treating as criminals persons who have not been convicted by a criminal court.

(2) *Environmental factors:* punishment cannot be extended to any substantial degree beyond the individual offender . . . But treatment can be applied beyond the individual who committed the act, to others, an alteration in whose behaviour might result in a substantial improvement in that individual.

(3) *The needs of the individual:* the 'crime-responsibility-punishment' concept, because the punishment must fit the crime, may inhibit the court in ordering the treatment the offender needs. . . . No such difficulties would arise on the 'preventive' principle since there the prime consideration would be the need for treatment measures.

(4) *Alteration of treatment:* punishment by its nature is 'once for all'. This concept, however, is unhelpful from the point of view of treating or training an individual.

Briefly, the paragraph implies that, by moving from a court to a tribunal and by replacing punishment with treatment, it becomes possible to treat not only the child referred to the hearing but also the family of the child and the potential delinquent.[42] The paragraph also sets the scene for one of the most radical of the Committee's recommendations: that the hearing's jurisdiction may continue until the child reaches the age of eighteen and that the hearing must review, and may change, its decision throughout that period.

Two other influences can be identified in the report: medical-psychological and criminological. To some extent these influences are interrelated, for criminological writing and research was, until recently, dominated by psychiatrists and psychologists—but for the purpose of this discussion it is easier to treat each in turn.

The use of the medical analogy in the understanding of delinquency does, of course, have a fairly lengthy history. Platt, in his discussion of the

[42] It is worth noting that the powers of the children's hearings do not enable them to go as far as this. The potential delinquent, for example, could be dealt with by a hearing only if he satisfied the requirements of one of the grounds of referral, e.g. lack of parental care.

American juvenile court, describes the rôle model of the judge as a 'doctor-counsellor' who sees his court room as a clinic:

> 'Judicial therapists' were expected to establish a one-to-one relationship with the delinquent in the same way that a country doctor might give his time and attention to a favourite patient. The court room was arranged like a clinic and the vocabulary of the participants was largely composed of medical metaphors.[43]

Similarly, in the Kilbrandon Committee Report, such words as 'symptom', 'diagnosis', 'assessment' and 'treatment' are frequently used,[44] and an analogy between the treatment of the delinquent and of the physically ill is the basis of the recommendation that the hearing should have continuing jurisdiction and not be restricted like a court to a once-for-all disposal:

> A doctor treating even a comparatively well-understood disease could not operate in this way. The doctor prescribes a course of treatment and observes the patient's response to it over a period. On the basis of his observations he continues the treatment or prescribes a different course, more drastic or less, as the situation appears to him to require. But he does not continue a course of treatment where, as a result of his observations, he is satisfied that it is doing no good, or that it has served its purpose and its continuation is either unnecessary or positively harmful.[45]

The Committee's recommendations follow closely the medical model of treatment: full investigation and assessment of the needs of the child; diagnosis of the causes; appropriate treatment and continuing contact with the child; and change of treatment if the original treatment 'fails'.

The medical model can be associated with the predominance of medical-psychological groups among those who gave written or oral evidence to the Committee, whereas the criminological influence was not a direct one in the sense that any criminological or sociological body presented written evidence to the Committee. Nevertheless, the Report reflects, and accepts, aspects of criminological thinking at that time. Cohen, in a review of the development of criminology in Britain, characterized it as reformist, pragmatic and positivistic.[46] These aspects are present in the report, which states, for example, the traditional criminological aim of[47] 'the reduction and ideally

---

[43] A. Platt, *The Child Savers*, University of Chicago Press, 1969, p. 142.

[44] See, for example, para 13, 'It might be that the child's quite minor delinquency was simply a symptom of personal or environmental difficulties.' Also paras. 54 and 146.

[45] Ibid., para. 54.

[46] S. Cohen, 'Criminology and the Sociology of deviance in Great Britain: A recent history and a current report'. Paper to British Sociological Association, April 1971.

[47] It is also the aim of the 'new criminology'. 'The abolition of crime is possible under certain social arrangements.' The somewhat naive and romantic aim is 'to create a society in which the facts of human diversity, whether personal, organic or social, are not subject to the power to criminalize'. I. Taylor, P. Walton and J. Young, *The New Criminology*, London, Routledge and Kegan Paul, 1973.

the elimination of delinquency'.[48] The notion of delinquency as a probable symptom of personal or environmental difficulties is the basis of the Report. It is described as affecting 'a very small minority within the child population as a whole',[49] and the delinquent is assumed to be different from the law-abiding child though not from truants and other 'problem' children. '. . . For the purposes of treatment measures, these various classifications could not in practice be usefully considered as presenting a series of distinct and separately definable problems. The basic similarity of underlying situations far outweighs the differences . . .'.[50] Delinquency is seen as symptomatic, as an indicator of the need for intervention.

> There were cases in which . . . no very drastic steps appeared to be justified on the basis of the offence itself. But . . . looking to the whole background, it might be that the child's quite minor delinquency was simply a symptom of personal or environmental difficulties, so that for the prevention of more serious offences and for the future protection of society as much as in the child's own interests, more sustained measures of supervison were equally called for.[51]

The root of the problem, the characteristic which differentiates the delinquent from the normal, is the 'shortcomings in the normal "bringing-up" process—in the home, in the family environment and in the schools'.[52]

The Kilbrandon Committee explicitly dismissed, as explanations of delinquency, the environmental factors which the Morton Committee, in a similar discussion in 1928, concentrated on: overcrowding, poor housing, lack of playing facilities for youth and juvenile unemployment.[53] Comparing these reports one can see a shift in emphasis from crime as a symptom of the 'unhealthy society' to crime as a symptom of the 'abnormal individual'. In the words of Lord Kilbrandon, '. . . the problem is primarily one of arrested or deformed development. There has been a growth failure'.[54]

---

[48] Kilbrandon Committee Report, para. 12.

[49] Ibid., para. 8.

[50] Ibid., para. 15.

[51] Ibid., para. 13.

[52] Ibid., para. 87.

[53] 'In our own century it was in earlier years fashionable to attribute delinquency in large measure to social and environmental factors. It has been long observed that many of those convicted of delinquency came mainly from poorer elements largely to be found in certain districts of urban communities—districts whose names in time became, some-times undeservably, local or even natural bywords. The environmental argument, it is now recognized, could, however, never offer a universal answer; in a great many delin-quents a degree of maladjustment, of malfunction personal to the individual, has always been observable . . .' Ibid., para. 77.

[54] 'The Kilbrandon Report—The Impact on the Public', *B. J. Criminol.*, 1968, **8,** 236.

Criticisms of the Kilbrandon Committee's Report

Broadly speaking, the model used by the Kilbrandon Committee assumed that deviant behaviour is the product of antecedent causes, that these causes can be discovered and that this discovery makes possible the control of that behaviour. The Report assumes that criminals are different from other people and have a special set of problems which explain their deviance. This approach fails to recognize that while some delinquents do have such problems, and that these problems set them apart from others and help to explain their deviance, deviance is more complex than this if only because what counts as criminal behaviour varies from time to time and place to place. The definitional element in crime and deviance, i.e. questions such as who defines certain activities as deviant and why, are ignored; the importance of society's response is also ignored. Concepts of societal reaction and secondary deviation point to the inadequacy of concentrating solely on the personal history of the delinquent in explaining deviance. Hidden delinquency studies[55] show that criminal behaviour is more widespread in society than was at one time appreciated, and studies of decision-making among agents of social control[56] show the importance of the interaction between the controlled and the controller in determining which rule-breakers will become defined as deviant.

Furthermore the Committee adopted a particular explanation of delinquency: 'growth failure'. There was no reference to or discussion of the writings of sociological criminologists. Admittedly the most important work in this area was done after 1965,[57] but the significant contribution of ecological criminology[58] was largely overlooked. These writers, at the very least, raise the question of the cultural normality of certain kinds of delinquency in certain areas and of the behaviour of many delinquents as reflecting the distinctive processes of socialization found in these subcultures.

In practical terms too, the treatment model, however appropriate in the

[55] See, e.g., M. Gold, 'Undetected Delinquent Behaviour', *J. of R. in Crime and Delinquency,* 1966, **3,** 27.

[56] See, e.g., I. Piliavin and S. Briar, 'Police encounters with Juveniles', *Amer. J. of Soc.,* 1964, **19,** 206.

[57] Particularly D. Downes, *The Delinquent Solution,* London, Routledge and Kegan Paul, 1966; D. Hargreaves, *Social Relations in the Secondary School,* London, Routledge and Kegan Paul, 1967; P. Willmott, *Adolescent Boys of East London,* London, Routledge and Kegan Paul, 1966.

[58] See, e.g., T. Morris, *The Criminal Area,* London, Routledge and Kegan Paul, 1957; J. Mays, *Growing up in the City,* Liverpool Univ. Press, 1954; M. Kerr, *The People of Ship Steeet,* London, Routledge and Kegan Paul, 1958; P. Jephcott and M. Carter, *Social Background of Delinquency,* Nottingham University, *mimeo,* 1955.

field of medicine, cannot be applied so readily to the field of delinquency.[59] Firstly, the process of becoming delinquent differs from that of becoming ill; the patient with a broken leg is universally recognized as such, whereas rulebreaking may at one time be dismissed as of no significance and at another seen as problematic, though the actions are identical. Secondly, it is stated in the Report that measures applied to the child should be determined on 'an informed assessment of the individual child's actual needs',[60] and by a 'procedure which from the outset seeks to establish the individual child's needs in light of the fullest possible information as to his circumstances, personal and environmental'.[61] But, unlike the position in treating physical illness, there is an absence of objective criteria by which the nature and extent of the needs of the delinquent child can be determined.

The Committee also appear to assume too readily that those charged with the operation of the children's hearings will be able to disregard the difference between the delinquent and the non-delinquent 'problem' child. Regardless of changes in society's attitude to children who offend, the offence of the child still evokes certain types of responses in society, and where the limits of tolerance are reached action is demanded. The form of action may be determined by external factors such as the age of the child, but the demand is based on the commission of an offence rather than on the existence of a 'deprived' or neglected child. In practice decision-makers in the children's hearing system are interested in the nature of the offence, the previous record of the child, etc. Reference to such factors is clearly relevant in making the types of decision these people are called upon to make. Society demands that 'something should be done' about offenders, irrespective of their status as children or adults. The point is that the Committee is wrong to talk of decision-making *only* in terms of the child's needs, and is somewhat naïve in its attempt to disregard the relevance of the offence. What Allen says about juvenile courts is equally applicable to children's hearings.

> The court is not simply a laboratory or a clinic and the tendency to conceive of it in these terms, largely to the exclusion of the other functions it is called upon to perform, contributes neither to a sound understanding of the institution nor to its proper use in serving the public interest. Self-knowledge is as vital to the proper growth of an institution as it is to the moral and intellectual development of the individual.[62]

[59] For further discussion of this point see D. May, 'Delinquency control and the Treatment Model: some implications of recent legislation', *B. J. Criminol.*, 1971, 11, 359; A. Morris, 'Criminal law in practice: Children's Hearings in Scotland', paper presented to the Fifth National Conference on Research and Teaching in Criminology, Cambridge, 1973.
[60] Kilbrandon Committee Report, para. 12.
[61] Ibid., para. 78.
[62] F. Allen, *The Borderland of Criminal Justice*, University of Chicago Press, 1964.

Moreover, the Committee appear to accept the appropriateness of control in certain situations. 'It is generally recognized that a fair proportion of juvenile offences, particularly among younger children, amount to acts of petty mischief *which must be dealt with* [my italics], but which are unlikely to call for elaborate and lengthy measures of training and supervision.'[63]

The continuing interest in the offence is seen in the 1968 legislation itself. An offence is a self-sufficient ground for referral. There is a statutory duty on the reporter to refer the child to the hearing only where it appears to him that the child is in need of compulsory measures of care, but the reporter need only establish this to his own satisfaction. The 'double-barrelled' test of the Children and Young Persons Act 1969 may be implied in the Scottish system, but it need not be applied.[64] Furthermore, the power to prosecute child offenders in the courts is retained. If the offence is symptomatic of underlying disorder there should be no reason for referring children who commit certain types of offence to a court. Or are only minor offences symptomatic of underlying personality or family disorder? One answer to this puzzle is that notions of general deterrence and protection of the public are relevant considerations in dealing with child offenders who commit serious offences, and may take precedence over the interests of the child.[65] The Committee, in preserving the power to prosecute, state that 'its exercise would arise only exceptionally and on the gravest crimes, in which major issues of public interest must necessarily arise and in which, equally as a safeguard for the interests of the accused, trial under criminal procedure is essential'.[66] In practice it is not only 'the gravest crimes' which are prosecuted, and it is difficult to see a consistent principle in those cases reserved for prosecution.[67] Another answer to the puzzle is the notion that the

[63] Kilbrandon Committee Report, para. 85.

[64] The Social Work (Scotland) Act 1968, s.39 (3) states 'where it appears to the reporter that the child is in need of compulsory measures of care, he shall arrange a children's hearing . . .' The Children and Young Persons Act 1969, Part I, para. 2, states that a child should be 'guilty of an offence . . . and also . . . in need of care or control which he is unlikely to receive unless the court makes an order under this section in respect of him . . .'.

[65] It is worth noting that the Court of Criminal Appeal, in substituting a three-year probation order with a condition of psychiatric out-patient care, for an order of detention for up to 18 months in the case of a nine-year old Glasgow girl who stabbed her eleven-year old playmate, said '. . . The interests of *justice* can be served by domiciliary treatment of this young girl'. It made no reference to the needs of the child not being met by the detention order. *The Scotsman*, 6 October 1973. This case was discussed in the press from 18 September onwards.

[66] Kilbrandon Committee Report, para. 125.

[67] The cases referred to the procurator-fiscal include offences committed by children whilst acting along with an adult, offences which may lead to a court ordering forfeiture of an article or disqualification and, more generally, serious offences. In practice although

seriousness of the offence is an indicator of the seriousness of the disturbance, and consequently the more serious the disorder is the more 'serious' the intervention must be. The prior assumption, however, holds no empirical basis and, as the hearings have in fact greater powers of intervention than the sheriff (for example the power to review the case until the child reaches the age of eighteen), this cannot be the reason for the referral of some cases to a court.

The Committee assumed that offenders were no different from other children who need help: 'in terms of the child's actual needs, the legal distinction between juvenile offenders and children in need of care and protection was—looking to the underlying realities—very often of little practical significance'.[68] Government Committees have been criticized in recent years for making recommendations on the basis of unfounded assumptions or without regard to empirical research. The Kilbrandon Committee cannot be entirely faulted on this ground, but there is at least some doubt that persistent delinquency is simply a 'presenting symptom', and not a problem which should be treated in its own right. The criticism made by Hood and Sparks of the White Paper *Children in Trouble* is also relevant in this context.

Whatever one may think the predisposing causes of delinquency are, few will deny that delinquency often involves the young person taking a certain attitude towards property and personal relationships, and that these attitudes with their supporting rationalisations may be learned and re-inforced through association with other delinquents. Thus, a child may be 'acting out' aggression because of family disturbance, but whether or not this aggression is channelled into housebreaking and whether or not he develops attitudes expressing aggression to school, work and property, may depend partly upon whom he has been associating with. To ignore this *seems to deny completely one of the fundamental planks of the sociological view of delinquency* . . . Persistent delinquents should be recognised as a special group for the purposes of treatment centering around attitude change as, at least, a basis for dealing with their underlying problems.[69]

Although research does show that similar factors are associated with both child offenders and children in need of care and protection, research also shows that there are differences. Philip and McCulloch have suggested that juvenile delinquency is primarily associated with social disorganization,

---

the majority of such cases are referred by the police to the fiscal, the fiscal subsequently refers many to the reporter. See Parliamentary Questions 27 Nov. 1973 and 3 Dec. 1973 referred to in 1973 *Scottish Law Times*, 14 Dec.

[68] Kilbrandon Committee Report, para. 13.

[69] R. Hood and R. Sparks (eds.), *Community Homes and the approved school system*; papers presented to the Cropwood Round-Table Conference, Cambridge, Institute of Criminology, 1969.

while child care rates are associated with family disorganization.[70] In a replication study, McAllister and Mason also found differences between the two groups of children.[71] Although such distinctions may have little meaning in practice given present resources, it is at least arguable that social policy and action should be framed to take account of these divergencies rather than to conceal them.

There is also a fundamental difference in principle between the two types of case. Care and protection cases are genuinely welfare cases where children are being looked after for their own good. The child offender is not being dealt with primarily for his own good, but because he is behaving in a way which is a nuisance to other people. 'A child who persists in being honest despite parental neglect is not a danger to society, but he has a right to be properly looked after; a child who persists in being dishonest despite parental care is not in need, but society may be in need of dealing with his dishonesty.'[72] One must be aware of these differences and their implications, otherwise a realistic analysis of the operation of the children's hearings cannot be made.

Another criticism which can be made of the Report and the Act is that they are an example of 'legislation by euphemism'. Euphemisms are frequently used to disguise the true state of affairs, to pretend that things are other than they are. Courts become tribunals, probation becomes supervision and approved schools are renamed residential establishments. But few are deceived by these verbal devices. 'An altered semantic of child care, liberally slanted euphemisms, cannot alone transport the maladjusted child to the imaginary correctional utopia where he will find understanding and moral reconstruction.'[73] The most important factor which remains unchanged is compulsion. The child, and his parents, are compelled to attend the hearing, and the order of the hearing is binding. In defence of this the Committee pointed out that children had fewer rights than adults, and that one of the obligations laid on them was to undergo compulsory education. But there is a difference between all children undergoing compulsory education, and some children being singled out for special forms of compulsory education, e.g. compulsory residential education. The stigmatizing aspects of this compulsory selection remain. The Committee's argument may have had

[70] A. E. Philip and J. W. McCulloch, 'Uses of social indicators in psychiatric epidemiology', *B. J. of Prev. Soc. Med.*, 1966, **20**, 122. Juvenile delinquency was associated with overcrowding, fewer owner-occupied houses and a high infant mortality rate. The child care rate was associated with separation and trauma in parent–child relationships.

[71] J. McAllister and A. Mason, 'A comparison of juvenile delinquency and children in care: an analysis of socio-economic factors', *Br. J. Criminol.*, 1972, **12**, 280.

[72] G. H. Gordon, unpublished address to Dundee University Law Society, 1969.

[73] P. Tappan, *Juvenile Delinquency*, New York, McGraw-Hill, 1969, p. 219.

superficial plausibility when it was talking about compulsory education, but even this disappears with the shift to social welfare, particularly when one compares Part II and Part III of the Act. Part II deals with the 'promotion of social welfare by local authorities', and although the powers of the local authorities to take children into care are wide (covering children whose parents are ill, have abandoned them, or are unable to cope) the assistance given to parents and children is mainly on a voluntary basis.[74] Part III, on the other hand, deals by and large with cases with a criminal element, the offenders and 'the potential' offenders (truants, children in moral danger, etc.) and cases for whom compulsory measures of care are thought to be necessary, and so stigma is embodied in the legislation itself. The fact that under the Act the reporter is prevented from transferring to the hearing those cases which he initially decided to deal with under Part II, but for whom voluntary measures are not working, unless there is a subsequent ground of referral, reinforces the separation and implies that certain types of children are better dealt with under Part II.[75]

The rehabilitative ideal has in the past led to a number of instances of increased use of compulsory therapeutic measures and a corresponding movement away from criminal procedure. The Kilbrandon Committee accepted that extensive intervention in the lives of children and their families would follow from their recommendations: '. . . If these arrangements are to be effective, we consider that they may be expected to result in a wider use of continuing supervision of the delinquent child within the community, and in some cases in a greater readiness to apply residential training measures involving removal from home at much earlier stages than apply at present.'[76] Similarly, though legal procedures are by no means excluded in the Report, they have become secondary to what is seen as the main task: the assessment of the child's needs and the disposal appropriate for them. No doubt those who hold the rehabilitative ideal are sincere in their beliefs, but 'there is a tendency for such persons to claim immunity from the usual forms of restraint and to insist that professionalism and a devotion to science provide sufficient protection against unwarranted invasion of individual rights'.[77] One must question the value of therapy purchased at the expense of other

---

[74] 5,868 children were placed in care during 1971 under the provisions of Part II of the Social Work Scotland Act 1968, s 15. Parental rights were assumed by the local authorities in about 200 cases (*Scottish Social Work Statistics 1971*, HMSO, Table 2.2, and verbal communication with Statistics Branch, Social Work Services Group in Edinburgh).

[75] The reporters referred to the social work departments for voluntary care 7 per cent of their cases in 1971 and 5 per cent in 1972 (*Social Work in Scotland in 1972*, Edinburgh, HMSO, 1973, p. 11. A footnote to this table states that the figures may be incomplete).

[76] Kilbrandon Committee Report, para. 76.

[77] F. Allen, op. cit.

values of the community, such as individual liberty, due process, justice and fairness. Matza graphically drew attention to the sense of injustice perceived by the delinquent boy:

> Why should persons so important and influential as the judge and his helpers lie to him regarding the true bases of disposition? Why should they insist, as they frequently do, that it is not what he did—which strikes delinquents and others as a sensible reason for legal intervention—but his underlying problems and difficulties that guide court action? Why do they say they are helping him when patently they are limiting his freedom of action and movement by putting him on probation or in prison? What on earth could they possibly be hiding that would lead them to such heights of deception?[78]

It may be argued that there are differences in this respect between the court and a welfare tribunal. But this is at least open to doubt where they both have compulsory powers.

Moreover the Kilbrandon Committee intended the hearings to have a wide discretion. '. . . The agency would have the widest discretion to vary or terminate the measures initially applied.' But any extension of the powers of official bodies must be viewed with caution in light of the inadequacy of our understanding of crime and its treatment or control.

If it is agreed that the recommendations of the Committee are based on certain premises now felt to be inadequate, it follows that the social policy and action which have their origin in the Report are similarly inadequate. An interesting question then arises of whether the operation of the children's hearings can avoid the inadequacies of the model and adapt to meet criminological developments.

The Operation of the System of Children's Hearings

A number of criticisms of the philosophy underlying the Act were made in the preceding sections. These were, in summary, the lack of objective criteria for assessing the needs of the child; the conflict between the needs of the child and the needs of society; the continued existence of stigma; and the possibility of greater intervention in the lives of children and their families. The discussion which follows deals with the extent to which the operation of the system of children's hearings meets or exemplifies these criticisms.

Little research except that on the membership of the children's hearings[79] has been completed, and any views must, because of this, be of a tentative nature. The comments made and figures presented are derived from a

[78] D. Matza, *Delinquency and Drift*, New York, John Wiley, 1964, pp. 133–4.

[79] A. J. B. Rowe, *Initial Selection for Children's Panels in Scotland*, London, Bookstall Publication, 1972. E. Mapstone, 'The Selection of the Children's Panels for the County of Fife', *B. J. of S. W.*, 1972, **2**, 4.

number of Government publications, and from research currently being carried out in the Department of Criminology, University of Edinburgh. That research is the continuation and extension of a survey, begun in 1967,[80] on the juvenile courts in two areas of Scotland, and so some comparative information is available on the base of which one can attempt to measure the changes which have occurred.

A caveat must first be given: one cannot talk of *the* system of juvenile justice in Scotland. There are quite a number of systems operating within the same statutory framework but with different results in practice. Each area is influenced by the differing organizational structure of the police and the social work department within it, and by the ideology of such key figures as senior police officers and reporters. 'In essence decision making and judicial outcomes in the juvenile courts are phenomena of social organiza- tion rather than law *per se*.'[81] Procurators-fiscal were a fairly homogeneous group, with similar background and training, as well as being all subject to central control by Crown Office. Yet their attitudes to child offenders differed, and this affected the way in which such offenders were treated in different areas. Reporters come from many different backgrounds, and are not subject to any comparable central control, so that the differences between areas are likely to be greater than before.[82] Nevertheless, some general points can be made.

It was suggested in the preceding section that there are in fact no objective criteria for the assessment of 'need'. The children referred to the children's hearings present the familiar picture of deprivation: parents with high unemployment rates, financial and domestic problems within the home, poor family or interpersonal relationships, etc. But there is little point in recount- ing the wealth of social characteristics available, for what conclusions can be drawn from them? The picture may well reflect some association between these factors and delinquent behaviour, but, more importantly, it reflects the way in which a child is *defined* as in need of care. Factors which are *assumed* to be linked with delinquency are often the factors which *determine* whether action will be taken or not, or, indeed, the form of the action. Often these factors are no more than assumptions and are without empirical basis, or

---

[80] J. Duncan and A. Arnott, unpublished research on the juvenile courts in Scotland, University of Edinburgh.

[81] E. Lemert, *Instead of Court*, National Institute of Mental Health, Chery Chase, Maryland, 1971, p. 2.

[82] Similar comments can be made about sheriffs and the members of the children's hearings. Thus although the average rate of referral to the children's hearing by the reporter is 56 per cent this varies between 23 and 73 per cent; and although the average use of residential supervision as a percentage of all disposals is 16 per cent, this varies between 2 and 30 per cent (*Scottish Social Work Statistics 1971*, op. cit.).

are dependent on research since discredited. The significance once attributed in criminological writings (and consequently in social background reports prepared for courts) to such factors as 'the broken home', and 'the working mother', is an example of this point.[83]

The decision-maker in this context, i.e. the reporter or the individual member of the hearing, has to assess the significance and meaning of a set of actions. The factors he uses, discredited or not, such as attendance and behaviour at school, attitude to the offence, involvement in organized youth activities, the nature of the offence, previous findings of guilt, and family circumstances (employment of the parents, income, expenditure, leisure activities, etc.), are incapable of objective measurement, and are therefore liable to be interpreted by the standards of the life-style of the interpreter and his particular model or stereotype of delinquency.[84] The result is an impressionistic assessment, and tends to be related to *social conformity* rather than to *individual need*. The decision-makers are seeking reinforcement or disproof of the original diagnosis of 'delinquent' or 'problem' child, yet the factors referred to can relate only to their own conception of what a 'good', 'difficult' or 'troublesome' child is. Considerable attention, for example, is paid to the child's family situation, but studies on the effects of family disorganization have been far from adequate. Those who are assessing the situation must do so again by reference to their own beliefs about what does or does not constitute a 'good' family. Members of the children's hearings are predominantly middle-class,[85] and the previous occupations held by reporters reveal a similar class background. Thus the danger, to which David May directed our attention, of creating a system of juvenile justice in which class bias becomes institutionalized, is a real one.[86]

This part of the discussion has centred on reporters and children's hearing members, but clearly anyone who presents a report to either of these groups is a decision-maker, and is perhaps more influential than the reporters or members of the hearing, as he presents information to them and can shape his report in such a way as to influence their decision. At present approximately 85 per cent of the recommendations made by social workers are accepted by members of the hearing.[87] This raises the important question

[83] See, e.g., D. J. West, *The Young Offender*, Harmondsworth, Pelican Books, 1967, and M. Rutter, *Maternal deprivation reassessed*, Harmondsworth, Penguin Books, 1972.

[84] Studies of police discretion, for example, have shown the importance of the values and beliefs of individual officers in the official processing of delinquents. See Piliavin and Briar, op. cit.

[85] A. J. B. Rowe, op. cit.

[86] D. May, op. cit.

[87] A. Morris, M. McIsaac and J. Gallagher, *Interim Report on the Children's Hearing System in Scotland*, University of Edinburgh, unpublished.

of the function of a *lay* panel and leads to the suggestion that their major rôle may well be that of controlling the expert.

The Kilbrandon Committee was also criticized for its exclusion of the relevance of the nature of the offence. It stated that the sole function of the children's hearing was 'the determination and application of training measures appropriate to the child's needs'.[88] It has already been suggested that it is not possible to do this, and in practice the nature and seriousness of the offence, and the existence of previous findings of guilt are criteria used both by the reporter and the children's hearing members. There is, for example, some relationship between persistency and seriousness of offending and the decision made by the reporter whether or not to refer a child to a hearing.[89] A similar pattern is observed when the child's previous record is considered.[90] Clearly these factors are not, in the main, operating in isolation, but they *are* operating and are influential. It can, of course, be argued that the relationship between these factors and the decisions made can be explained on the basis that they suggest that the offending is not casual but is part of an established pattern. But, even so, this does not necessarily mean that the child needs 'compulsory care'; it may indicate that the child is in need of compulsory control. It can also be argued that the seriousness of the offence is an indicator of the seriousness of the disturbance. This is often assumed but, as I have already pointed out, there is little empirical evidence for it.[91]

Community pressures, as well as community resources, are a constraint on decision-makers and those pressures may curtail any attempt to operate solely on the basis of the child's needs. It is expected that 'something should be done' about children who continue to offend. At this level, then, the

[88] Kilbrandon Committee Report, para. 73.

[89] In the unpublished Edinburgh University survey, while 17 out of the 18 children with 5 or more offences were referred to a children's hearing only, only 16 out of the 83 children with one offence went to a hearing, and while 19 out of the 31 children involved in property offences exceeding £25 were referred to a hearing only 11 out of the 37 children involved in property offences of value less than £5 were referred to a hearing. The offences of children warned by the police or given a 'no action' disposal by the reporter tend also to be minor.

[90] In the same survey, of the 82 children with no previous record only 21 were referred to a hearing, while of the 67 with some previous record 39 were referred to a children's hearing. The majority of the children given police warnings or 'no action' disposals also have little or no record.

[91] That this is assumed can be seen from recent newspaper discussions of the case of Mary Cairns (see, for example, *The Scotsman,* 18 Sept. 1973). After the Sheriff Court trial the Director of Social Work in Glasgow was reported as saying that there was nothing in Mary's background to suggest an abnormal personality, etc. The Court of Criminal Appeal, however, replaced the detention order with a supervision order and *a condition of psychiatric out-patient care.*

adequacy of the notion of 'treatment' as a description of society's response to those children may at least be questioned, as may claims to have reconciled the conflicting interests of the child and the community. The conflict is inherent in *any* system which deals with offenders.

The Kilbrandon Committee also envisaged the probability of increased intervention in the lives of children and their families, and of the greater use of residential facilities. Certainly more children are referred to the reporter than were referred to the fiscal in the court system,[92] but whether there has been increased intervention is open to doubt. Ninety per cent of the referrals to the reporter in 1971 came from the police and were for offence behaviour. The general picture, as previously, is predominantly one of petty delinquency, of social nuisances rather than social problems.[93] But many of the children referred to the reporter for offence behaviour are *not* subsequently referred by him to the children's hearing. In 1971, only 56 per cent of the total number of children referred to the reporters on this ground were referred to the children's hearing.[94] The Kilbrandon Committee stated that '. . . referral should be made to juvenile panels for one reason only, namely, that *prima facie* the child is in need of special measures of education and training'.[95] The Committee was aware that this involved a substantial change in the nature of the discretion involved, for the procurator-fiscal's task in the juvenile court was primarily to assess whether prosecution was in the public interest and whether there was sufficient evidence to establish the commission of the offence. This change is clearly reflected in the rate of referral to the juvenile court by the procurators-fiscal and to the children's hearing by the reporters: 95 per cent[96] and 56 per cent respectively. Thus it can be argued that because of the change in criteria relevant in decision-making fewer children reach the 'formal' social control agencies in the children's hearing system than in the court system.

It is difficult to compare the disposals of the juvenile court with those of the children's hearing. Because of the differences in the referral rates of the reporters and the fiscals and in the different types of decision made by them,

[92] The number of children within the court system in 1966 was 23,452 compared with 27,917 within the children's hearing system in 1971. (See *Criminal Statistics 1971*, HMSO). The figure for 1972 is 29,790.

[93] More than half the offences concern property, the value being under £5 in the majority of cases. In very few cases is the value over £25. Other offences were minor incidents of breach of the peace and assaults, mainly children fighting at football matches or after school.

[94] *Scottish Social Work Statistics 1971*, HMSO, Table 2.45.

[95] Kilbrandon Committee Report, para. 138.

[96] J. Duncan and A. Arnott, op. cit., an interesting point from this study is that where a special juvenile court existed the referral rate of the fiscal was lower than in ordinary juvenile courts and closer to that of the reporter to the children's hearing.

one would expect the number of discharges by the children's hearings to be less than those by the juvenile courts. The reporters should be sifting out, earlier than the court system did, those children who do not need compulsory care. Previously this was the function of the sheriff or magistrate rather than of the fiscal. But the discharge rate from the children's hearings is surprisingly high. Though there are regional variations, the average is 28 per cent;[97] the rate of discharge in the court system was between 30 and 40 per cent. The former figure suggests that the children's hearings *continue* to sift out, on the basis of further information, those who do not need compulsory measures of care. The information available to the children's hearing is, of course, fuller than that available to the reporter.

It initially appeared that the children's hearings were making less use of residential establishments than had the juvenile courts. Placement in a residential establishment accounted for only 16 per cent of all disposals made by the hearings;[98] in March 1972 there were 183 fewer children in List D establishments than in March 1971.[99] But the picture has changed. List D schools are now full, as are regional assessment centres where children await transfer to the List D school.[100] Without additional information it is impossible to explain this but, in discussing the level of intervention in children's lives, it may be worth drawing a distinction between more intervention in some cases and some intervention in more cases. Many cases which previously would have been prosecuted now do not reach the children's hearings—intervention in fewer cases—but the interference is greater in those cases which are referred, e.g. removal from home because of the family circumstances though the offence itself is minor. Another possible explanation would, of course, be that the members of the children's hearings are committing an increasing number to List D establishments because of the lack of alternative facilities, and because they feel that they must 'do something'.

Little is yet known about the operation of the review procedure, and it may be too early to assess the full impact of the continuing jurisdiction of the children's hearings, but the 1971 figures show that the hearings terminated supervision requirements in 28 per cent of their cases, continued them in 35 per cent and varied them in 36 per cent.[101] These figures, and the fact that very few of the requests for review came from the child or parent (64 out of 1906), suggest that the children's hearing members do

[97] *Scottish Social Work Statistics 1971*, op. cit.
[98] *Scottish Social Work Statistics 1971*, ibid.
[99] *Social Work in Scotland 1972*, op. cit., p. 13.
[100] Verbal communication from the Statistics Branch, Social Work Services Group.
[101] *Scottish Social Work Statistics 1971*, op. cit.

scrutinize their decisions and are prepared to terminate their jurisdiction.

Another aim of the Kilbrandon Committee was to eliminate or reduce stigma. Doubts have been cast on the possibility of this as, despite euphemisms, the system of children's hearings is still part of the system of formal social control and still deals predominantly with offenders. This criticism cannot yet be answered. The many children whose cases are dealt with by 'no action' by the reporter may well escape the stigmatizing effect associated with formal social control mechanisms. Whether the high 'no action' rate can continue will depend to a large extent on whether decision-makers can resist the criticisms currently being made by the police. It appears that the police and the reporter do not share the same working philosophies, and that the police are still using the criteria which they used in the court system. The major functions of the police are, of course, the prevention and detection of crime, and, at least with respect to adults, they expect socially harmful and undesirable behaviour to be punished. Whether they feel that traditional values (for example, respect for law) are threatened in the new system is difficult to determine, but some change from their traditional rôle is essential for the handling of child offenders. The Kilbrandon Committee foresaw this need for change by describing the police as 'one of the primary sources of the identification of children in need of special educative measures as well as being part of the sifting or assessment agency'.[102] This has not yet been achieved.[103]

Differences between idealized models and reality are frequently found, and the children's hearing system is no exception. But in this particular case it appears that in some major aspects of its operation the system has avoided or corrected deficiencies in the ideal. It would be wrong to create the impression that the Committee felt that all delinquency resulted from underlying family or personality disorder.[104] The Committee states: 'It would moreover in the great majority of such [i.e. acts of petty mischief] cases be quite absurd to postulate either serious emotional disturbance in the child

[102] On the publication of the Report, Dan Wilson, Scottish Police Federation secretary, said, 'The police haven't the time to go dishing out warnings. Police are being paid to be police officers—not social workers. Fear is still one of the great deterrents. Give these juvenile offenders back some of what they gave out.' *Scottish Daily Express*, 23 April 1964. Since then there has been continued criticism of the rate of 'no action' by the reporters. It was referred to, for example, in the speech made at the conference of I.S.T.D. in Scotland in November 1971 by David Gray, H.M. Chief Inspector of Constabulary in Scotland.

[103] Kilbrandon Committee Report, para. 143.

[104] Cf. Kilbrandon Committee Report, para. 15 which states 'The basic similarity of underlying situation far outweighs the differences, and from the point of view of treatment measures the true distinguishing factor, common to *all* the children concerned, is their need for special measures of education'.

or parental neglect.'[105] But it also states: 'The child's quite minor delinquency was simply a symptom of personal or environmental difficulty. . . .'[106] Taken together these paragraphs imply that every child who commits an act of delinquency, however minor, should be the object of investigation and assessment. This is clearly impossible on a practical level and undesirable on a theoretical one. Moreover, it is unnecessary. The police in many areas continue to give police warnings to children, and reporters often make decisions to take no action. Both of these courses are taken on the basis of a minimal amount of social information (and one could, therefore, argue that both police and reporters may be failing to identify certain disturbed children) but both agencies appear to be relatively successful at selecting those children who do not require assessment or special measures. In the Edinburgh University's survey approximately two-thirds of those warned by the police or given a 'no action' decision by the reporter did not reappear in the system within a twelve-month period after the initial decision.

The Committee admitted the possibility of no action being taken by the children's hearings, but saw it as arising 'occasionally' and where there had been 'some relatively minor legal infringement'.[107] This reveals both the Committee's confusion about the appropriateness of 'control' in the new system, and its acceptance that the commission of a serious offence *per se* indicates an underlying personality disorder. Yet, in fact the hearings do discharge referrals fairly frequently, even where the child has committed more than a 'minor legal infringement'. Edwin Lemert set out the ideal model of a juvenile court in the following way:

> The juvenile court is properly an agency of last resort for children, holding to a doctrine analogous to that of appeal courts which require that all other remedies be exhausted before a case will be considered. This means that problems accorded for action by the juvenile court will be demonstrably serious by testable evidence ordinarily distinguished by a history of repeated failures at a solution by parents, school and community agencies.[108]

Whatever the deficiencies in the Kilbrandon approach one can nevertheless suggest that the children's hearing system is moving towards this ideal.

Scotland has put into novel form the caring philosophy that underlies most systems of dealing with child offenders. In the introduction to this

---

[105] Kilbrandon Committee Report, para. 85.

[106] Ibid., para. 13.

[107] Ibid., para. 161.

[108] E. Lemert, *The Juvenile Court—questions and realities*, Presidential Commission on Law Enforcement and Administration of Justice, Washington D.C., U.S. Gov. Printing Office, 1967.

paper it was suggested that the system in England and Scotland had a number of common characteristics. The criticisms I have made should not, therefore, be construed as applying solely to the Scottish experiment, or as indicating that any other system (English or whatever) is 'better'. The criticisms may well apply, perhaps with even greater force, elsewhere.

CRIMINOLOGY AND PENAL CHANGE:
A Case Study of the Nature and Impact of some recent Advice to Governments

Roger Hood

The influence of criminological research upon the development of the penal system has probably been rather small. Most existing methods of dealing with offenders have 'evolved . . . under the influence of growing social consciousness, of religious movements and philanthropic stimulus, from some temporary measure, or just from straight-forward common sense supported by experience'. As a result, they reflect conflicting assumptions about the nature of criminality . . .[1]

Introduction

There seems little doubt that the prevailing mood of penal administrators and legislators in the years leading up to the Second World War was one of optimism. Alexander Paterson's daring (for the time) experiments with the borstal system were being extended into the prisons. There was a feeling in the air that institutional 'training for freedom' could be so devised as to cut off the roots of recidivism. Some elements of this optimistic spirit could still be seen in the Criminal Justice Act of 1948: the eligibility for borstal training was based solely upon the need for training, a new longer sentence of corrective training was introduced for young adults on the verge of habitual recidivism, compulsory after-care was extended to these and certain other prisoners as well as a single form of imprisonment substituted for the old divisions which included penal servitude and hard labour. It is significant that

[1] Memorandum submitted by the British Psychological Society to the Royal Commission on the Penal System, England and Wales.

Written Evidence of Government Departments, Miscellaneous Bodies and Individual Witnesses, Vol. II, Miscellaneous Bodies, para. 4, p. 178. Quoting from Leon Radzinowicz, *In Search of Criminology*, Heinemann Educational Books, 1961, pp. 178–9.

The B.P.S. went on: 'most of the penal theories which are presently being applied are based (sometimes rather tenuously) upon assumptions about the nature of criminality which have no foundation in modern criminological theory: they have grown up piecemeal and generally reflect the philosophies of human behaviour that were current at the time of their inception'. (para. 20, p. 182)

the Act introduced no entirely new forms of punitive non-custodial measures for adults[2] and, except for young offenders, no curbs upon the use of imprisonment. The underlying philosophy, it is true, was opposed to the use of short sentences and greatly in favour of reserving prisons for those who would benefit from the training it was assumed would be provided there. Men who did not need to be sent to prison could be dealt with either by an absolute or conditional discharge, a fine or by probation. The pre-war view prevailed that offenders who were in need of, or deserved, more than a nominal penalty should be dealt with either by social workers in the community or by longer 'training' in institutions. In either case the belief in the value of the therapeutic approach prevailed.[3] For young offenders, however the mood had already hardened, the Howard Houses—hostels within the community—included as the short-term alternative to Borstal in the 1938 Bill had been changed by 1948 to the detention centre with the strict and 'shocking' regime.[4] The mood and expectations were to change also in relation to penal measures for adults.

A quarter of a century of rising rates of recorded crime, of minimal progress in the provision of penal facilities which might give even the semblance of 'treatment institutions' and the lack of evidence that longer incarceration increases the likelihood of reform have caused a retreat from this period of penal optimism. Emphasis is no longer on providing measures which increase the opportunities for prisoners to be detained longer in order to achieve their reform: corrective training has been abolished. The growth of serious crime has itself ensured an increasing prison population and an increased tariff of penalties.[5] The problem has been to find means of

[2] It did, however, introduce the possibility of probation with a condition of mental treatment (S.6), made formal provisions for absolute and conditional discharge and introduced the general power to fine an offender for any conviction on indictment of felony (S.13).

[3] Leon Radzinowicz records the 'atmosphere of justifiable optimism' that prevailed in 1938 and 1948. The Act of 1948, he says, 'was no hasty measure, nor was it the utopian project of some lofty and unrealistic penal reformer. It was firmly grounded in the many gradual developments, experiences and achievements which had taken place since the Gladstone Committee had laid down its programme of reconstruction . . . in many ways (the Act) was a faithful reflection of the new social attitude of which the Welfare State itself is both a manifestation and a case'. L. Radzinowicz (1964), *Criminology and the Climate of Social Responsibility*, an address to the Howard League for Penal Reform, 7 May 1964, W. Heffer, Cambridge.

See also, Rupert Cross (1971), *Punishment, Prison and the Public*, London, Stevens, esp. pp. 99–100 in which he contrasts the 'penological optimism' of 1939 with the current 'era of penological pessimism'.

[4] See V. Choppen, 'The origins of the philosophy of detention centres', *Brit. J. Criminol.*, 1970, 10, 158–68, and Roger Hood, *Borstal Re-assessed*, London, Heinemann Educational Books, 1965, pp. 69–73.

[5] In 1951 only 4,777 men received into prison under sentence had been sentenced to

restricting the use of imprisonment and of releasing those within through the parole system before they 'deteriorate'.[6] Post-war penal policy has therefore been set upon a task of contriving alternatives to custody in a political climate where the increasing alarm about crime and the growing scepticism about the relevance of welfare measures to the 'criminal of the affluent society' (the major puzzling paradox, it seems, to politicians),[7] has dispelled some of the earlier enthusiasms for dealing with the more serious offender within the community as a problem solely for social casework and supervision. In analysing recent changes in policy it is less difficult to understand why imprisonment is being seen as a punishment of 'last resort' than it is to understand why *particular* alternatives have been devised for it.[8]

But, of course, political attitudes towards the punishment and treatment of offenders are extremely complex. While in general (as I shall show) there has been a concern to ensure that the alternatives to imprisonment should reflect the new social situation, by relying upon a combination of straightforward deterrence and some form of restitution to the 'wronged' community, there have been extensions of welfare measures to offenders formerly dealt with by imprisonment. The redefinition of the habitual drunken offender as someone suffering from the disease of alcoholism[9] and the re-categorization

---

terms of over 1 year, and only 790 for terms of over 3 years. The corresponding figures in 1971 were 12,096 and 2,017. In 1951 those receiving over 3 years comprised 2·6 per cent of those sentenced, in 1971, 6·3 per cent.

[6] This was the officially stated *raison d'être* of the parole system introduced in the Criminal Justice Act 1967.

Mr. Jenkins in introducing the Bill referred to 1965 White Paper *The Adult Offender* (Cmd. 2852) which stated that a number of prisoners reached 'a recognisable peak in their training at which they may respond to generous treatment, but after which, if kept in prison, they may go downhill' *H.C. Debates*, Vol. 738, col. 70, 12 Dec. 1966.

I shall not discuss parole in this paper, but for an analysis of its origins and present dilemmas see Roger Hood, 'Some Fundamental dilemmas of the English Parole System and a Suggestion for an Alternative Structure', in *Report of Cropwood Conference on Parole* Institute of Criminology, Cambridge, 1974.

[7] See Leon Radzinowicz, (1964) op. cit., p. 12. He refers 'to a strong feeling of frustration, not to say irritation, that these unpleasant changes in the number and quality of transgressions should appear so difficult to check—and in spite of the improvement in economic and social conditions which might have been expected to neutralize so many of the traditional causes of crime'.

[8] For a discussion of the economic motives for devising alternatives to prison see Keith Hawkins, 'Alternatives to imprisonment', in S. McConville (ed.), *Imprisonment in England*, London, Routledge, 1974.

[9] S. 91 of the Criminal Justice Act, 1967, removed the penalty of imprisonment for the offence of being 'drunk and disorderly', to be implemented when the Home Secretary was satisfied that satisfactory and sufficient available alternatives were available for 'the care and treatment of persons convicted of that offence'.

See Home Office, *Habitual Drunken Offenders*, Report of the Working Party (Chairman T. G. Weiler, London, HMSO, 1971.

of the former persistent petty thief and old lag as an 'inadequate'[10] has ensured that they can receive benefits by virtue of their 'sickness'. The habitual drunks will be removed from the prison system as treatment centres become available (and the progress here is far too slow, reflecting I believe public lack of sympathy for these offenders), and the provision of day training centres and increased number of hostels (used often in conjunction with a liberal parole policy) is at last providing some alternative for the persistent petty prisoner.[11] This policy is, I believe, not just a result of long experience of the futility of imprisoning these men, but their redefinition as categories 'entitled' to special consideration. It mirrors the selective application of social benefits developed in other branches of social policy since the fifties.

The problem of devising alternatives to imprisonment for those who have no claims for special treatment has been extremely difficult. It might seem at first sight that the logical step would have been to expand the probation service so as to provide within the community a degree of supervision, control and social aid which apparently had formerly been the aim of their treatment within prison. But there seem to have been a number of reasons why this was not acceptable. First, whatever happened within prison (and it was rarely anything that could be called treatment anyway) the purpose of the sentence—whether short or long—had usually been to deter. Secondly, in the context of what was regarded as widespread public anxiety about crime,[12] alternatives without a 'bite' may not have been politically acceptable. Third, the constant repetition of the stereotype of the new affluent criminal created an image to which social casework hardly seemed appropriate. Fourth, and perhaps most important, in these circumstances it would have been hard for governments to justify a vastly increased expenditure on the

[10] The term first seems to have come into use in the penological literature in the late 1950s, and was taken from Henderson's classification of psychopathy.

[11] S. 20 of the Criminal Justice Act 1972 provided an order of probation with the requirement to attend a day training centre. They were described by Mr. Carlisle as: 'being more likely to be used for the person who has already developed a bad work record, a record of irresponsibility and a record which shows that he is socially inadequate and needs training of this kind'. *H.C. Debates*, Standing Committee G. 13th Sitting, 10 February 1972, col. 539. It is worth noting that this measure was *not* recommended by the Advisory Council on the Penal System's report *Non-Custodial and Semi-Custodial Penalties* (Home Office, Chairman Lady Wootton, 1970). It seems to have been recommended by a Home Office Working Party which discussed the Wootton proposals.

[12] In general the popular press made more of this 'concern' than did well-informed Members of Parliament. Even so, the report of the Labour Party's Study Group *Crime— A Challenge to Us All* (1964), while recognizing that crime 'is one of the gravest social problems of our time', (p. 7), was cautious in interpreting statistics. The Conservative Party Study Group's *Crime knows no boundaries* (1966) spoke of a 'background of rising crime and mounting public concern', p. 7.

'treatment' of offenders, on measures which were undoubtedly generally regarded as soft. Expenditure upon control was of course a different matter, public anxiety about that ensured there was no difficulty in expending very large sums on tightening security after the Mountbatten report on the 'scandal' of escapes.[13] It is very unlikely that any government would have been able to spend this amount on the provision of professional or social services for improvements within prisons or outside. Generally speaking, expenditure on controlling crime is not in competition with expenditure on social services where those who have offended, a clientele with no political power, consistently have the lowest priority. In political terms it is not so surprising that the repeated claim that intensive social work is far less expensive than imprisonment still falls largely upon deaf ears. This is why alternatives which relieve over-worked social workers, and if possible actually reimburse the community, have gained in popularity.

The post-war years have seen, therefore, some major shifts in ideology and in the penal measures themselves. It is not possible to discuss all of them in one paper. My purpose here is to analyse the arguments which led to the adoption of the most significant non-custodial measures—the suspended sentence, financial reparation and community service by the offender. In particular, I shall attempt to uncover the underlying criminological and penological assumptions of those who have been appointed to advise governments on penal policy[14] and of those who have supported the measures in Parliament during the passage of the Criminal Justice Acts 1967 and 1972.[15]

[13] Lord Mountbatten's report lists the major escapes between 1964 and October 1966 when the escape of the spy George Blake led to the setting up of the enquiry (para. 5). There was at the time an exceptional press coverage of all escapes from open as well as closed prisons. *Report of the Inquiry into Prison Escapes and Security* (Mountbatten report) Cmd. 3175, HMSO, 1966.

The amount spent was some £2 million. See J. E. Hall Williams, *The English Penal System in Transition*, London, Butterworths, 1970, p. 96.

[14] According to Sir Frank Newsam, *The Home Office*, 2nd ed., London, Geo. Allen and Unwin, 1955, p. 124, the Advisory Council on the Treatment of Offenders was established in 1944. Michael Wolff, *Prison*, London, Eyre & Spottiswoode, 1967, records that the Prison Commissioners submitted a report to the Council on open prisons in 1945, see p. 54. The first report publicly discussed was on mentally abnormal offenders. See *The Lancet*, 17 June 1950, p. 1120. The first report, published by HMSO, appeared in 1957. As noted below A.C.T.O. was dissolved in 1966 and replaced by the Advisory Council on the Penal System (A.C.P.S.). For a general discussion of the functioning of the A.C.P.S., see Dr. Bolt's interview of Sir Kenneth Younger, its Chairman, in *Justice of the Peace*, 1972, 136, pp. 621–2.

[15] For a discussion of the sociological questions raised by the study of government reports for the sociology of knowledge—in particular those where there is 'deviance from social science rationality'—see G. Smith and N. Stockman, 'Some suggestions for a sociological approach to the study of Government Reports', *Sociological Review*, 1972, 20,

These measures provide an interesting contrast in at least one important respect. The suspended sentence was introduced despite the Advisory Council on the Treatment of Offenders (A.C.T.O.) having twice recommended against its adoption as being 'wrong in principle'.[16] On the other hand, community service was almost solely based on the enunciation of the idea by the Advisory Council on the Penal System (A.C.P.S.). The Council's report on the suspended sentence became ideologically out of date but the reparation and community service ideas were the apotheosis of the post-war attitude towards offenders. My argument is that the adoption of both these methods of punishment was due to the appeal of their ideologies and that, particularly in the case of community service, there was no attempt to justify the new penalty in terms of a coherent analysis of crime, criminal behaviour or the effects of penalties. In other words, the part played by criminological analysis, theory and research was minimal. Some would claim that this was inevitable because of the piecemeal way in which policy was formulated and argue instead for an overall analysis of the penal system in the light of knowledge about those who commit crime, in order that a consistent master-strategy could be implemented. Others would argue that there is no criminological knowledge which is of use in formulating legislation and that change can only be on a trial and error basis fully supported by evaluative research. This general issue is, of course, of major consequence to the way in which committees of enquiry work, and as Sir Leon Radzinowicz was at the heart of the controversy on this matter it is appropriate to begin with it.

59–77. For a detailed analysis of the assumptions of recommendations relating to social policy see G. Smith, 'Some research implications of the Seebohm Report', *Brit. J. Sociol.*, 1971, **22**, 295–310.

[16] Home office, *Alternatives to short terms of imprisonment*, Report of the Advisory Council on the Treatment of Offenders (A.C.T.O.), HMSO, 1957, para. 27, p. 9 and Appendix D. This was not the only example where the Advisory Council's advice was ignored.

The Parole system (although endorsed by the Labour Party's paper *Crime—A Challenge to Us All*, 1964) was never referred to A.C.T.O.: it was simply announced in a White Paper. But A.C.T.O., in putting forward the view that the selection of some prisoners for early release from preventive detention was a major factor adversely affecting the morale of these prisoners, had indicated that they were opposed to an indeterminate element involving selection by penal officials. In addition, when considering the extension of compulsory after-care, both A.C.T.O. and the Scottish A.C.T.O. had specifically stated that any system of selection by prison staff or any board acting on their advice would tend simply to pick those who were able to conform to the prison regime and through its invidiousness be a major cause of prison discontent. See: *Preventive Detention*, Report by A.C.T.O., HMSO, 1963, paras. 34–7, pp. 13–15, also; Home Office: The *After-care and Supervision of Discharged Prisoners*, Report of A.C.T.O., HMSO, 1968, paras. 31–3 and Scottish Home Department, *The Extension of Compulsory After-care to Additional Categories of Inmates and Prisoners*, Report of the Scottish A.C.T.O., Edinburgh, HMSO, 1961, para. 25, pp. 12–13.

Ad-Hoc Advice or Master-Plan?

Of course it must be recognized that many committees and advisory bodies have terms of reference which limit their considerations to problems of penal administration. For example, the A.C.T.O. report on *The Organisation of After-Care*[17] was entrusted with making recommendations about how a new policy for extending after-care should be administered.[18] Also, the important Working Party on the *Habitual Drunken Offender*, with its excellent exhaustive review of the problems of treatment of public drunkenness, was reporting within the framework of the legislative intentions to provide alternative facilities so that imprisonment as a penalty could be abolished.[19] Some of the most important and influential committees have also been virtually tribunals of enquiry, set up to investigate the case for or against a particular proposal. An outstanding example is A.C.T.O.'s report on *Corporal Punishment*[20] which effectively demolished the case (strongly supported in the ranks of the Conservative Party) for its reintroduction not only by re-iterating the moral objections[21] but more persuasively by bringing to the fore the weighty empirical evidence collected by the Home Office. The evidence, on which a government decision could have been taken, already existed, but it was known of course that Mr. Butler was opposed to corporal punishment. A.C.T.O. provided that element of prestigious independent assessment which put the matter beyond political debate. In a similar way (although it was not a politically contentious issue) A.C.T.O.'s report on

[17] Home Office, *The Organisation of After-care*, Report of the Advisory Council on the Treatment of Offenders, HMSO, 1963.

[18] Even so it could be claimed that the note of dissent, signed by Leon Radzinowicz and his colleagues, objecting to an integrated probation and after-care service and favouring a more central and 'dynamic' control of after-care, was based on a wider appreciation of the tasks and organization of the probation service in general and of the different reactions of offenders to the concepts of probation and post-prison supervision. See, Memorandum of dissent by Professor Leon Radzinowicz, the Hon. Lady Inskip and the Rev. E. Shirvell Price, ibid., 83–6. For example, one of the main grounds of dissent was that the locally organized probation service was an inappropriate body to administer a service that needed 'centralized initiative and effort'. The signatories of the memorandum accused the Council of a 'distorted vision which is so preoccupied with casework problems that it ignores the broader questions of community provision'.

[19] Op. cit.

[20] Home Office, *Corporal Punishment*, Report of the Advisory Council on the Treatment of Offenders (A.C.T.O.), Cmd. 1213, HMSO, 1960.

[21] The Committee strongly expressed the opinion that it would be a retrogressive step— 'putting the clock back not twelve years but a hundred years [and damaging] our reputation as the country which has been a pioneer in the use of enlightened methods of penal treatment'. Ibid., paras. 85–6.

Preventive Detention[22] was an enquiry into a system which already had few, if any, strong supporters. It made effective use of the available criminological research that had been carried out within the Home Office at Cambridge and elsewhere and again acted as an independent body of assessment whose recommendations could form a firm and uncontested basis for legislation. There have been other examples of Committees of Enquiry which have had a substantial impact on penal policy. Foremost was the report of the Mount-batten Committee whose recommendations for new security categories and for an ultra-high security prison had a traumatic effect on prison regimes. Here again the Advisory Council on the Penal System, through a committee under Leon Radzinowicz's chairmanship, was asked to assess within a short period, the problems of providing a humane regime for very long-term prisoners kept in conditions of maximum security. Drawing upon evidence from overseas, interviews with prison staff as well as with prisoners, upon the available research and upon a study of the characteristics of the men con-cerned, the Committee reported in favour of dispersing the highest security risks to a number of prisons and against Mountbatten's Isle of Wight 'Alcatraz'.[23] Bold and politically necessary as this enquiry was at a time when the Home Office was under strong pressure to begin work on the new fortress, there has not been a dispassionate review of the basic premises of Lord Mountbatten's wider conclusion—namely that prison security needed tightening drastically not just for the handful of category A men but also for a substantial percentage of the remainder of the prison population placed in Category B.[24] It is clear that the present practices in relation to security

[22] Home Office, *Preventive Detention*, op. cit. The research relied upon was published by W. Hammond and E. Chayen as *Persistent Criminals*, HMSO, 1963; by D. J. West, *The Habitual Prisoner*, London, Macmillan, 1963, and R. S. Taylor, 'The habitual criminal', *Brit. J. Criminol.*, 1960, 1, 21.
Of course, this report did make some tentative recommendations for future policy, but it is interesting that it is in that area that its views have been least remembered.

[23] Home Office, *The Regime for Long-Term Prisoners in Conditions of Maximum Security*, Report of the Advisory Council on the Penal System (A.C.P.S.) (Chairman Leon Radzin-owicz), HMSO, 1968. Mr. Castell of the Prison Officers' Association claimed that the Radzinowicz Committee had gone beyond its terms of reference, which were, in his opinion 'simply to recommend a suitable regime for a prison built for this purpose'. See Hall-Williams, op. cit., p. 103, quoting F. Castell, 'Prisons—has the Home Office Blundered?' *Police*, Oct. 1968.

[24] Defined as those 'in respect of whom the very high expenditure on the most modern escape barriers may not be justified, but who ought to be kept in very secure conditions', Mountbatten report, para. 217, p. 58. The report called for the allocation of prisoners to those categories 'to be kept under continuous review and subjected to careful research' (para. 218) but did not say how many prisoners might be in category B. The White Paper *People in Prison* stated that experience suggested that about 30 per cent of convicted prisoners would be in Category B. One wonders if the Prison Department were defining this category in the same way as Mountbatten. It appears to include a number almost

classification, home leave, parole, open prisons, hostels and prison welfare, because of the piecemeal way in which they have been developed, contain many inconsistencies and anomalies that could only be made coherent by a review of the system as a whole.

But it is especially when a government seeks advice on *alternative* penal measures that it unequivocally poses for its committees a consideration of wider issues of penal policy. The first occasion on which this occurred after the war was in 1957 when A.C.T.O. was asked to consider alternatives to short terms of imprisonment after the Howard League for Penal Reform had proposed the setting up of a Departmental Committee.

The Home Secretary replied that a departmental committee was not the appropriate body and that his Advisory Council (A.C.T.O.) would first make a general survey.[25] He agreed that if any of the suggestions were acceptable they might repay closer examination by a Departmental Committee. In fact only very limited proposals were made.[26] The Committee felt that they were dealing with a 'comparatively narrow sector of penology [which] is not self contained and in considering it we have found that wider issues, falling outside our terms of reference, emerged'. As examples they gave the questions of requiring offenders to pay compensation or make restitution and the problems of remanding offenders for social enquiry reports in the higher courts as they were organized at the time. Considering that such matters went far beyond their terms of reference, the Committee concluded: 'We have been struck by the fact that there has been no authoritative enquiry for a long time into such fundamental problems as the objects of punishment, the suitability of the existing methods of dealing with offenders, the desirability of introducing new ones, and the procedure for determining what is the appropriate method in a particular case—problems which lie at the root not only of our work as defined by this enquiry but that of the Council itself.'[27] Among the signatories was Leon Radzinowicz.

Mr. Butler's view, upon becoming Home Secretary in 1957, was that his desire to map out a plan for penal reform was thwarted by 'the very limited amount of information and knowledge which I have found at my disposal'. As he has said in his contribution to this volume (see page 1 above) this was why he gave research top priority. But the hope of being able to formulate the basis for a *policy* remained. In his White Paper *Penal Practice in a*

---

equivalent to the number of prisoners in the daily average population, serving three years or more. Cmd. 4214, 1969, p. 69, and Table 5, p. 118.

[25] *H.C. Debates*, Vol. 542, col. 1497, 23 June 1955, and 554, cols. 535–6, 21 July 1955, reply by Major Lloyd-George.

[26] Home Office, *Alternatives to Short Terms of Imprisonment*, Report of the Advisory Council on the Treatment of Offenders, HMSO, 1957, pp. 18–19.

[27] Ibid., para. 62, p. 19.

Changing Society the case was made for a fundamental re-examination of penal methods which 'could be a landmark in penal history and illuminate the course ahead for a generation'. It would be:

> based on studies of the causes of crime, or rather of the factors which foster or inhibit crime, and supported by a reliable assessment of the results achieved by existing methods. . . . Such a re-examination, though based on practical studies, need not—and indeed should not—be purely pragmatic. If it were not merely to assess past progress, but also to point the way forward, it must concern itself with the philosophy as well as the practice of punishment. It must consider the fundamental concepts underlying our treatment of offenders, and examine not only the obligations of society and the offender to one another, but also the obligations of both to the victim.

But the paper went on

> Until we are ready for the more fundamental examination. . . . Existing forms of penal treatment, continuously adjusted in the light of deeper insight and greater information must be developed to the limit of the good we believe to be in them. Only when their potential power to turn men from crime has been fully tested can we judge how far other methods may be required to reinforce and, if need be, to replace them.[28]

So much is important in these paragraphs: the clear statement that penal changes can only be based on knowledge of the behaviour they are presumed to be affecting, the need for a thorough development and assessment of existing penal measures before proceeding with change, the review of penal philosophy with particular emphasis on relocating the basis of punishment in some form of compensation: a subject referred to warmly by Mr. Butler in his first speech as Home Secretary in 1957. Clearly what was implied was a lengthy period for experiment and research, for only on the basis of the information it supplied could any review of penal measures be satisfactorily conducted. Finally as Leon Radzinowicz pointed out, 'with great conviction it made the point that penal policy in a modern, large-scale state, like so many other kinds of policies, economic, fiscal, social or educational, requires much more than makeshift isolated advances here and there. Long-range planning, the choice of priorities, and firm commitments to meet these in pre-arranged stages, were at last fully recognized as the responsibility of government'.[29] But politicians could not be so patient. Only five years later, in 1964, the Home Secretary, Mr. Henry Brooke, announced the establishment of a Royal Commission on the Penal System. The White Paper, *The War Against Crime in England and Wales 1959–1964* outlined a number of

[28] Cmd. 645, HMSO, 1959, paras. 24–5, p. 7.
[29] Op. cit. (1964), p. 14.

reasons why it was now felt that the time was right to undertake the 'funda-mental re-appraisal'. These reasons included the increase in crime, police changes following the Royal Commission on the police, the report of the Streatfeild Committee, especially in relation to providing the courts with more information on which to base their sentences and various changes in criminal law and within the administrations of the prison and probation services.[30] None of these appear at all relevant to the case made in the 1959 White Paper, with the possible exception of the Streatfeild Report.[31] But that Inter-departmental Committee had been set up in response to the Advisory Council's plea in 1957[32] for a consideration of how the higher courts could have more information provided before sentencing and, in endorsing a 'reductivist' penal philosophy (to stop offenders from offending again),[33] its proposals were generally in line with the current thinking on the need to 'individualize' sentences where possible. In particular the report reflected the view that research would eventually provide sufficient informa-tion on the comparative effectiveness of the various sentences open to a 'sentencer' to enable him to make the correct 'disposal'. It was concerned with sentencing as a technical problem of allocation and did not question the appropriateness of the available penalties to which an offender might be allocated. In this sense there was certainly nothing revolutionary about its proposals, but the prestige of the Committee undoubtedly ensured that its views would come to have a substantial impact upon the practice of the courts. While the White Paper mentioned research as an area where there had been a remarkable growth in government financial aid, it was admitted that 'rapid progress cannot be expected. Research projects in this field are inevitably complex and take time to complete'.[34] Actually within this period very little had been published that could justify the view that there had been a marked change in the state of criminological knowledge. Indeed almost none of the research had anything to do with the 'factors which foster or inhibit crime'. The Commission was much more the creature of political pressure. In the face of concern about rising crime, and particularly that committed by adolescents (who were singled out for priority treatment) and in the light of the paucity of solutions, the Government fell back on the 'wise men' approach to seeking alternatives. It is indicative of Mr. Brooke's attitude towards sources of information that he had appointed a 'strong and

[30] Cmd. 2296, HMSO, 1964.

[31] Home Office, *Report of the Interdepartmental Committee on the Business of the Criminal Courts,* Cmd. 1289, 1961, HMSO, para. B.

[32] Op. cit., para. 62, p. 19.

[33] See Nigel Walker, *Sentencing in a rational society,* London, Allen Lane, The Penguin Press, 1969.

[34] Op. cit., para. 27, pp. 8–9.

widely based Advisory Committee on Juvenile Delinquency to consider and advise on the problems of juvenile delinquency and on measures for its reduction'. He took the unprecedented step of taking the chair at this large gathering of forty, comprising magistrates, voluntary workers, youth leaders, a pop star with an involvement in youth clubs and a young man recently out of a detention centre, a psychiatrist and two academics.[35] Whatever the qualifications of the members might have been, the vast majority had no special expertise, and not surprisingly within a very short time the Committee was disbanded.

The proposed Royal Commission had very wide terms of reference, repeating the emphasis in the 1959 White Paper on the need to re-examine both penal theory and practice 'in the light of modern knowledge of crime and its causes' and the need to assess how far the available methods of punishment achieve their objectives and to review the way in which the services actually operate and are administered. In addition it was charged with reporting whether any changes in penal methods were desirable, including 'the arrangements and responsibility for selecting the sentences to be imposed on particular offenders'.[36]

Soon afterwards, in an address to the Howard League, Leon Radzinowicz raised a number of trenchant criticisms of the traditional notion and method of work of Royal Commissions. First he suggested that the terms of reference were too wide. The Gladstone Committee of 1895, to which the new Commission was being compared was much more restricted in scope: 'The new Royal Commission has been given a general framework of investigation rather than specific terms of reference, and it seems to me that solid progress can be hoped for only if it selects, within this framework, a series of specific and related themes and tackles them in their appropriate order.'[37] He believed that 'the subjects for enquiry are not novel and the range of solutions is not unfamiliar'. That being so, questions such as the use of the indeterminate sentence, parole and hostels could be tackled as discrete issues. But it was the method of enquiry which most concerned him: 'To elicit the experience and views of the usual list of organizations and of various meritorious individuals and weigh them up in an hour or two's discussion from time to time is not enough.'[38] The more technical know-

[35] Ibid., paras. 16–17, pp. 5–6. See *The Times*, 13 February 1964.

[36] Ibid., paras. 34–5, pp. 13–14.

[37] Op. cit., p. 22.

[38] See, for an excellent critique of oral evidence, Sidney and Beatrice Webb, *Methods of Social Study*, London, Longmans, Green and Co., 1932. 'Of all recognised sources of information the oral "evidence" given in the course of these enquiries has proved to be the least profitable. Considering the time spent in listening to it, or even in rapidly reading and analysing these interminable questions and answers—still more, the money spent

ledge is required to define and examine a problem, the less likely is the traditional procedure of the Royal Commission to result in useful conclusions.[39] The Commission should, therefore not rely 'on an able young secretary, just about to learn his penological trade', but needed to have a real secretariat made up of young energetic people with experience and knowledge; it should mobilise the resources of research groups and set up working parties staffed by criminologists conducting commissioned research. 'By such means the Commission may obtain vital information, factual and critical, which is at present still largely unavailable.' In other words the Commission should be used as a means to ensure that appropriate research was conducted, rather than await its completion before beginning work. Leon Radzinowicz was appointed one of the Commissioners, but that did not silence him. Rather, it served to reinforce his view that the collection of memoranda and cross-examination in oral evidence was getting the Commission nowhere. Indeed a study of the published evidence submitted to the Committee shows that with the exception of a few papers which were especially commissioned, the evidence consisted of official pronouncements from government departments and various suggestions from penal reform pressure groups and from legal bodies and associations: none of them based on any firm evidence. The oral evidence, in particular, is pitifully weak as a whole and sometimes inaccurate.[40]

There was no sign anywhere of the consideration of the issues in the light

---

over them—the yield of solid fact is absurdly small' (p. 142) . . . 'what seems to be the aim of the keenest members of the committees of enquiry is to get some practical opinion "on the notes" so that they can use it to back up their side in the eventual report' (p. 155) . . . 'the great mass of oral "evidence" given before committees of enquiry relates to opinions on general questions, and not to actual occurrences, whilst even the modicum of fact given in evidence is not checked or verified by other enquiries' (p. 155) . . . 'It must be remembered that these bodies are seldom designed for scientific research: they are primarily political organs, with political objects' (p. 156).

[39] Ibid., p. 25. In rather similar vein others have suggested that 'small investigatory groups . . . charged with the duty of having evidence from all the conflicting interests would be better than a Commission composed of representatives of these different interests' whose reports if they are to produce agreement 'must be vague, general, ambiguous, or perhaps even express conflicting views in different corners', Jenifer Hart, 'Some Reflections on the Report on the Royal Commission on the Police', in Richard Rose (ed.), *Policy making in Britain*, London, Macmillan, 1969, pp. 238–55.

[40] As an example see the interchange about the results of various American experiments in the treatment of offenders in the oral evidence of the Howard League for Penal Reform, Royal Commission on the Penal System (R.C.P.S.) England and Wales, *Minutes of Evidence Taken Before the Commission, Witnesses*, HMSO, 1967, The Howard League for Penal Reform, p. 171 (on the Grant and Grant Study) and p. 178 (on the Highfields Study). It is no criticism of the persons involved that they could not remember details in oral discussion.

of any knowledge about offenders: no surveys, no reviews of criminological theory to glean any relevant information, no special studies of the effects of measures nor even a thorough-going enquiry into prison conditions and the current status of prisoners. Four volumes of evidence (much of it papers by government bodies) by and large repeat the same platitudes and general observations. Even specific suggestions, such as those in favour of suspended sentences, indeterminate sentences and forms of compensations were not based on any reliable evidence. The cross examination of oral evidence invariably failed to elicit the basis of criminological or penological knowledge, or even assumptions, upon which the suggested new proposal rested. In fact, the Commission seems to have spent a very large amount of its energy debating the niceties of penal philosophy: an approach to which Leon Radzinowicz was unsympathetic. In cross-examining Mr. Klare of the Howard League he asked:

> Is it really necessary to agree specifically what the purposes of punishment have to be in order to introduce important changes in our penal system. Can we not really introduce a great number of changes without putting down on paper in a form which must always necessarily be irritating and which must produce conflicts?

Mr. Klare replied that the Howard League agreed with this pragmatic approach. When Lady Wootton asked,

> Does this really mean you think you could make desirable reforms without being able to put into words what the object of the reform is, without being able to say what you are aiming at?

Radzinowicz replied:

> Once we have this common objective (to control crimes as far as we can and give some kind of protection satisfactory to society) is it not true to say that we can reshape our policy in a very drastic way without bringing to the forefront rigid principles which may antagonise public opinion and in some ways weaken penal reform?[41]

It is clear he considered it more politically expedient, within broad objectives, to proceed upon an empirical basis of attempting to find out which measures were likely to produce the best results rather than label the system

---

[41] Ibid., p. 160. Similarly in *Criminology and the Climate of Social Responsibility* (1964), he asked 'I sometimes wonder how far . . . we should pursue arguments about the principles of punishment. . . . It is not, at least nowadays, arguments about first principles that influence the strength or direction of public opinion or awaken public response to the need to cope with crime and criminals. What does appeal to the imagination, and move public feeling, is the successful salvage operation. . . . It is this empirical approach, rather than jurisprudential disquisition on the calculus of utility of punishment that has produced progress' (p. 21).

as a whole with a particular penal philosophy—say reformation—which itself could become the basis for political divisiveness.

It is hardly surprising that Professor Radzinowicz was a leader of the dissident group of Commissioners who decided that such endless debates were achieving nothing and whose resignations led to the dissolution of the Commission. In view of Radzinowicz's conception of a research-based enquiry, the British Commission had suffered even more by comparison with President Johnson's Commission which began work in 1966 with enormous academic resources. In place of the Commission, the Advisory Council on the Treatment of Offenders was reconstituted with an almost entirely new membership as a smaller Advisory Council on the Penal System (A.C.P.S.). This body, with a much greater proportion of experts with a knowledge of criminology among its members, was intended to consider some major problems of penal policy of more limited scope and in more depth. To what extent did it do so?

Only two of the members of A.C.T.O. were appointed to A.C.P.S., Professor Radzinowicz and Dr. Mortimer, the Bishop of Exeter. Whereas A.C.T.O. had among its members two experts in childrens' problems and juvenile delinquency, Professor Moncrieff and Dr. Pearce, the new Council had, including Leon Radzinowicz, 6 out of 17 with academic qualifications in criminology—all of them having lectured and published extensively in the field. One would imagine therefore, that the reports of A.C.P.S. with its greater preponderance of 'experts' (from an academic point of view) would, in contrast to those of A.C.T.O., pay more attention to empirical evidence and be more likely to formulate its arguments in relation to academically derived knowledge—both theory and empirical data—about crime and the effects of penal sanctions. In my opinion, the change in membership did not bring about a new approach to the task more in keeping with academic enquiry. This undoubtedly was partly, and perhaps mainly, due to lack of facilities in the form of expert working parties of consultants which Leon Radzinowicz had said were so necessary in his criticisms of the traditional form of Royal Commission. In fact the Advisory Council continued to use the same means of enquiry: written and oral evidence supplemented by visits of observation and enlightening foreign trips to pick up some comparative material and opinions. And while I can find nothing in favour with the composition or method of approach of the 1965 Royal Commission, the swing back to the other extreme of dealing with each question on a pragmatic basis obviously has the major drawback of limiting the opportunity for the development of a coherent and logical penal strategy.[42]

[42] Manuel Lopéz-Rey comments: 'The series of official reports produced by committees and councils in charge of finding solutions have never gone beyond the stage of suggesting

The image of committees as vehicles for research is still far off: and the reports of A.C.P.S. have given little indication that it might be getting near at hand. The Widgery Committee on *Reparation by the Offender* and the Wootton Committee on *Non-Custodial and Semi-Custodial Penalties* both relied far more upon opinion than on any theory or research.[43] It is true that the Wootton Committee's task, to consider what new non-custodial penalties might be introduced, was extremely difficult. But even if it were unable to conduct any enquiries itself the formula of the 1959 and 1964 White Papers still appeared most appropriate, namely to base recommendations upon knowledge of the factors fostering or inhibiting crime and upon an assessment of why the present methods were proving unsatisfactory. It is the thesis of the last part of this paper that the committee conspicuously failed to do this. Instead it based its proposals for community service by offenders on the implicit ideological appeal of the scheme. Its social science orientation lay not on a theoretical basis but on a commitment to the evaluation of the scheme through 'experimentation' and follow-up. Here, par excellence, was the pragmatic approach of British penology.[44] This does not mean that I am not strongly in favour of careful evaluation of new penal measures—if possible through controlled experimental conditions. But I do believe that in the long run it can be counter-productive to produce a series of ineffectual remedies, and that from the point of view of both society and the offender each innovation should be backed by a reasonable case based on available knowledge of why it is considered it *might* be a useful and just addition to the penal measures already available.

---

arrangements within existing situations or systems. The result is that although some progress has been made it is mostly peripheral'. 'Administrative penology (England and Wales)', *Brit. J. Criminol.*, 1965, 5, 4–21. *The Times* in a leading article on 17 April 1964, had commented on the Royal Commission: 'The terms of reference appear to expect the Commission to get their theory right first and then to examine its practical implications. This is sensible. It is possible to contend that this is a false antithesis, in the sense that theories may be modified by practical experience. But to accept this is only to acknowledge the inevitability of *ad hoc* innovation: it is better to make the attempt to fashion a new, cogent and informed philosophy . . . it would be unworldly to underestimate the difficulties'.

[43] Despite the fact that Mr. Jenkins announced that a Standing Sub-committee on Criminological Research had been set up 'which will keep my department informed of research which the Council would like to see instituted in connection with its operations', reported in *The Times*, 22 February 1967.

[44] For a discussion of the development of this pragmatism see Leon Radzinowicz, *Ideology and Crime*, London, Heinemann Educational Books, 1968, Ch. 4.

Changing Attitudes and Changing Policy:
the example of the Suspended Sentence

It is intriguing that when in 1957 A.C.T.O. reported on the possibility of providing alternatives to short terms of imprisonment they failed to conceive of any new measures for adults other than improving the machinery for collecting fines and reminding the courts that they should limit imprisonment to those cases where it was essential. It is true, as I have already pointed out, that the Committee felt that compensation and restitution were matters outside their terms of reference, but no one, it seems, seriously proposed these alternatives in a practical form. Also, the Committee reiterated its view, first put forward in 1952, that the suspended sentence was wrong in principle and impracticable. Yet ten years later the suspended sentence was introduced and fifteen years later two measures of restitution and community service. Why had these changes taken place?

A great deal has been written recently about the use made by the courts of the suspended sentence of imprisonment which was introduced in the Criminal Justice Act 1967. But little attempt has been made to understand why A.C.T.O.'s opinion held sway in the fifties but was disregarded in the sixties. Rupert Cross has suggested that the main reason why the Council had considered the suspended sentence impracticable 'was thought to be due to the difficulty of ensuring that it was not automatically made operative by a conviction for a venial offence during the period of suspension' and that this objection had been adequately met by the provision in the 1967 Act by allowing the court convicting for a second offence not to invoke the suspended sentence if it considered it to be unjust to do so.[45] But it was not just seen as impracticable. It was wrong in principle. Which principles were being applied?

The prime mover in support of the suspended sentence in 1951 was Sir Leo Page, the distinguished Metropolitan magistrate, supported by the Magistrates' Association. The main argument was that the hand of the probation service needed strengthening. A definite threat, pronounced at the time of the probation order, would, Sir Leo claimed, avoid the practice of making ordinary probation orders for a second or third time; 'a practice which tended to bring the probation system into contempt'.[46] It would also allow the courts to indicate the gravity of the offence but avoid sending the offender to prison. In other words, he believed it was necessary to add a deterrent and retributive element to the current non-custodial provisions.

[45] Rupert Cross, op. cit., p. 113. See generally, pp. 112–16.
[46] *Alternatives to Short-term Imprisonments*, Appendix D, paras. 1 and 2.

The Advisory Council reported in 1952. They were not convinced that there was any evidence to justify change and insisted that *'to justify any new form of penal treatment there must be strong reasons to show that the suggested innovation would be likely to be a positive improvement on existing methods'* [my italics].[47] They dismissed the supposed deterrent advantages of a known future penalty over an unknown penalty, claiming that people would react in different ways, but that 'the dictum *"omne ignotum pro magnifico"*[48] seems to stand the test of time'. They also claimed that at the time of sentence the court could hardly know whether in a particular case a known suspended sentence would be more of a deterrent than probation or conditional discharge 'with its liability to punishment of a degree of severity not then known'.

Of course the argument for the suspended sentence rested upon assumed facts, namely that probation was being used over and over again to its discredit because breaches were leniently dealt with. If this were so, the Council's deterrent argument could not be sustained except by exhorting judges and magistrates to behave differently in future: there being nothing wrong in principle with the law, only with its application. In fact there was no evidence other than some favourable oral reports from the probation service, stressing that probationers were aware that if they breached the order they would be dealt with for the original offence. But, of course, the argument about how breaches should be dealt with depends very much upon the purpose of probation. If it is viewed as a form of 'let-off', then failure to enforce breaches severely is a major fault. But if it is considered a form of 'treatment', then abandonment of the service upon a 'breakdown' (as it was often called) would not necessarily, or even often, be interpreted as a cue for imposing punishment. The commitment of the Council to such a treatment philosophy was more important in their rejection of the suspended sentence than any supposed empirical evidence or the practical difficulties of the problem of enforcement. It is reflected in a number of their views. The belief that 'swords of Damocles' were not likely to have a special effectiveness indicates a view of the offender as living in a complex set of circumstances where his choice of action is unlikely to be affected only by the consequences of potential punishment: the offender in need of help, guidance and support is not necessarily going to behave rationally in relation to the sole goal of avoiding reconviction. For this reason the Council were completely opposed to the mandatory invocation of the suspended sentence upon a breach: and if it were not mandatory they said, what advantages

[47] Ibid., para. 9.
[48] Translated by Dr. Nigel Walker as 'Anything sounds wonderful in an unknown language'. See 'The Case for more use of Suspension', *The Times*, 13 April 1965.

would it have over probation and conditional discharge? They wanted complete flexibility, and especially for those who had co-operated with their probation officer but 'at a later stage in the period succumbed to sudden and strong temptation'. As far as the original offence was concerned a retributive standpoint was rejected: to ignore the new circumstances because of the original offence 'savours of the doctrine that the offence rather than the offender should be punished . . . the question of the court dealing with the subsequent offence is not so much what the offender deserved for the earlier offence as what form of treatment would, in the circumstances relevant at the time when it is imposed, be most likely to serve the three purposes of protecting the public, reforming the offender and deterring others'. This non-retributive standpoint perhaps explains why the council gave short shrift to the argument for using the suspended sentence as an alternative to imprisonment rather than probation in more serious cases. The idea of 'marking the severity of the crime' and then letting the offender free within the community without supervision did not commend itself. Indeed this 'meretricious attractiveness' of the suspended sentence was regarded as a great disadvantage, because its appeal to retributive feelings might distract attention 'from the more solid advantages of probation'. If a non-supervisory sentence were needed the Council thought that more hope lay in the reform of certain aspects of conditional discharge, such as increasing the period from one to three years and perhaps changing the name which had an 'unfortunate connotation'. Furthermore it seemed rather an anachronism that while many foreign countries were moving towards probation from the suspended sentence of imprisonment, England and Wales should seek to move in the opposite direction.

Without doubt the Council looked with disfavour upon a retributive or deterrent sentence which would be a form of mitigated imprisonment. If the offender need not be in prison for training then he should be supervised and aided (trained) in the community. The dominant ideology undoubtedly still saw the offender as disturbed, maladjusted or socially incompetent and so in need of rehabilitation. Sentencers should therefore concentrate, in the words of the Streatfeild Report, on 'the needs of the offender as a person'.[49]

The belief in the value of a reformative approach was also at the root of the objection to the proposal to combine the suspended sentence with probation. It was felt that the 'essential character' of probation would be 'altered for the worse'. Threat of punishment was regarded as likely to put the offender in a 'negative spirit, seeking to avoid [its operation] rather than build up a positive will to reform' through 'the help and guidance of the probation officer'. Of course, the probation service had no empirical basis

[49] Op. cit., para. 259, p. 76.

for such an assertion but it was plainly based upon the dominant themes of casework and psychiatric diagnosis which were in their full ascendancy in the fifties.

In 1957 A.C.T.O. reported again. In considering alternatives to short terms of imprisonment evidence had been given from the Association of Chief Police Officers in favour of the suspended sentence to replace, in the more serious cases, the power to discharge conditionally: it was claimed that this would both be more acceptable to the courts and have more impact on the offender. No mention was made of it as an alternative to immediate imprisonment and no mention was made of its advantages over or use with probation. In a terse paragraph the council reiterated its view that it was 'wrong in principle and to a large extent impracticable'. Despite the publication of Home Office White Papers in 1959, 1964 and 1965, the last of which, *The Adult Offender*, was specifically concerned with airing the intention to establish a parole system and abolish corrective training and preventive detention, the suspended sentence was not again publicly discussed until it appeared in the Criminal Justice Bill 1967. But there had been rumbling in the wings for some time. The Labour Party's *Crime—a challenge to us all* report had recommended use of the suspended sentence, but without dealing with any of the objections raised by the Council.[50] Similarly the Conservative Party's *Crime knows no boundaries* suggested the idea needed fresh examination particularly as being 'more effective than the present form of probation' in certain cases.[51] In April 1965 Nigel Walker published an article in *The Times* entitled 'The case for more use of suspension' in which he claimed that it had not only advantages over imprisonment but 'even over probation', mainly because 'it is less costly . . . in terms of money and specialized manpower. . . . For offenders who have not yet experienced imprisonment, and whose offences do not involve physical harm to others, the suspended sentence seems especially suitable'. He suggested that the Advisory Council had dealt with the subject at the 'level of armchair psychology', and expressed the hope that it would be re-examined by the Royal Commission on the Penal System. In evidence to the Commission several bodies and Mr. Bryan Leighton J.P., in particular, commended it on the grounds of its greater deterrent effect than probation or conditional discharge.[52] The Council of

[50] Op. cit., p. 46. The suspended sentence is simply mentioned *en passant* as the section was mainly devoted to recommending support for the probation service.

[51] Op. cit., p. 34.

[52] Evidence for the Magistrates' Association: 'Many members are of the opinion that the deterrent effect of the suspended sentence is far greater than that of probation or conditional discharge,' R.C.P.S. (E & W), *Vol. II, Miscellaneous Bodies*, p. 5. The Association added that they felt it was 'particularly effective in cases . . . with whom the shock of detection and exposure have already made a repetition of the offence unlikely' (p. 18)—

the Law Society, for example, felt that the weakness of the current probation order was that 'the offender continues to hope and often to assume, that should he commit a further offence he may still be visited with only lenient punishment. In many cases this hope is, in practice fulfilled and, in any event, the nature and extent of the punishment which is notionally held *in terrorem* is neither predetermined nor expressed. The sanction is much stronger if the offender knows from the outset the punishment which he invited by committing a further offence'. It was the deterrent value, creating 'in the mind of the offender (an) active state of "fluid anxiety"' which the Law Society considered should predominate. They admitted that they could produce no 'results of any medical or scientific data or research' but based their view upon 'intelligent guesswork and intuition drawn from experience'.[53] The National Association of Probation Officers remained opposed in principle mainly on the grounds that a suspended sentence not rigidly applied was little different from the element of suspension implied in the probation order. They were unconvinced that closely controlled discretion to allow mitigation of the penalty, if circumstances had changed drastically or the new offence was trivial or of a completely different nature, would meet the objection. No doubt they thought this would only cover the greatest exceptions to the rule.

Nevertheless the support given for the proposal to the Royal Commission (which of course was dissolved before it could give an opinion) was invoked by Mr. Jenkins when he introduced the clause. He said he believed that 'it

---

thus indicating its retributive or denunciatory value. Mr. Bryan Leighton, J.P., suggested that the suspended sentence was called for not only because of conditions of overcrowding in the prisons but because probation 'excellent though it is when the offender responds to help, [has] inherent weaknesses which could with advantage be strengthened' and was 'valuable for certain types of crime to mark society's disapproval . . . acting as a strong deterrent'. 'Probation alone has its limitations', some offenders not recalling the threat inherent in the sentence and being 'of such character that the alternatives of fine, probation and conditional discharge are inappropriate and where used draw contempt on the decisions of the court'. Thus the suspended sentence would, he claimed, be a deterrent and lighten the load not only of the prisons but the probation service as well. Vol. III, pp. 36–8.

[53] R.C.P.S. (E & W) Written Evidence, Vol. II, *Miscellaneous Bodies*, HMSO. Evidence from The Council of the Law Society, para. 12, p. 59. It is interesting to note that even the Howard League for Penal Reform asked for suspended sentences to be re-examined 'in the light of whatsoever knowledge may become available regarding the effects of deterrence on certain types'—although they must have known that no such evidence would be made available to the Commission. The League supported the suspended sentence because of the shortage of probation officers and in cross-examination it became clear that they really favoured a variation on conditional discharge and deferred sentence. Their evidence on this point is a good example of a confused rationale for a new penalty. See *Witnesses*, pp. 153 and 186.

should have a substantial deterrent effect on those who may be hesitating on the verge of a life of crime'.[54] But by now the proposal had changed quite radically from that considered by the Advisory Council: instead of a sentence to add teeth to a probation order it had become a mandatory alternative to immediate short terms of imprisonment up to six months, as well as a discretionary alternative for the higher courts when imposing sentences of up to two years. The logic of the Government's proposal was that a sentence should only be suspended where imprisonment would otherwise have been chosen. In response to an opposition proposal to combine the suspended sentence with probation it was argued, first, that it was inconsistent with the principle of probation and, secondly, that 'to allow it to be used in conjunction with probation would suggest that it was intended mainly as a reinforcement of the probation system and might detract from its [of the suspended sentence] status as a serious deterrent and sanction in the eyes of the public'.[55] The reason for the new penalty as far as the Government was concerned was to provide an alternative to imprisonment at a time when the prisons were particularly overcrowded and appeared both ineffectual and costly as a means of dealing with many petty offenders. Its policy recognized implicitly that in a climate of rising crime and changing attitudes to the offender the belief of the Advisory Council—that probation, conditional discharge (even renamed) and fines were sufficient alternatives to imprisonment—was no longer politically acceptable. Not only had probation itself come to be used proportionately less often for adults, especially in the magistrates' courts,[56] but the realities of the amount of aid which a vastly overworked and underpaid service could offer had become apparent. Suspended sentences *were* cheaper, they were at least symbolically more severe, whatever the actual deterrent effects might be, and only seemingly severe measures would be acceptable as alternatives to prison at a time when there were clamours for more 'law and order' combined with some disillusion with the claims of social work and an increasing reluctance to accept the criminal as a victim of social disadvantages.

I am inclined to interpret the Labour Government's position as a pragmatic response to these pressures. They had not lost faith in probation, but they were more concerned to find ways of emptying the prisons, which were seen as non-reformatory, having little deterrent effect once experienced and

[54] *H.C. Debates,* Vol. 737, col. 66, 12 December 1966.
[55] *H.C. Debates,* Standing Committee A, 11th Sitting, 22 February 1967, cols. 579–80.
[56] The *Criminal Statistics* show that for males aged 21 and over convicted of indictable offences in magistrates' courts the proportion placed on probation fell from 15·5 per cent in 1938 to 9·3 per cent in 1965. For 17–21 year olds the fall had been even more spectacular, from 45·3 per cent to 17·4 per cent.

actually likely to increase the chances of re-offending.[57] The argument was that the threat of imprisonment was a greater deterrent than the experience itself—the contaminating experience and stigma of which worked in the opposite direction. Lord Stonham went so far as to say:

> When a man goes to prison for the first time he is not only well on the way to recidivism, but he is labelled for the rest of his life . . . the mandatory suspension would ensure them a second chance and keep most of them crime-free for the rest of their lives. We can say that from experience.[58]

Furthermore, it was hoped that by freeing the prison staff from the burdens of many short-term prisoners 'the prison regime will come closer to the ideal of fitting the prisoner to lead an unoffending and productive life when he is released'.[59]

A rather different attitude can be discerned on the Conservative side. They were strongly opposed to the mandatory suspension of short sentences on four grounds: they were in principle against fettering the discretion of the court,[60] they believed that the suspended sentence should strengthen the deterrent effect of the existing non-custodial penalties, they thought that short-term imprisonment was sometimes appropriate and lastly that mandatory suspension would weaken the deterrent element provided in the last resort by imprisonment itself. Thus, although they agreed it was a more effective penalty than other non-custodial measures they did not wish to see it entirely replacing imprisonment, even though the Government's proposals did make some substantial exceptions to the rule. Mr. Carlisle (he was to be the Minister of State in the following Conservative Government) felt that the measure

> would make a considerable psychological difference to the person who today is conditionally discharged

---

[57] Mr. Jenkins, *H.C. Debates*, Vol. 751, col. 802, 26 July 1967. See Keith Hawkins, 'Alternatives to imprisonment', op. cit.

[58] *H.L. Debates*, Vol. 285, col. 1133, 27 July 1967.

[59] *The Times*, Leading Article, 30 Nov. 1966.

[60] Mr. Hogg, *H.C. Debates*, Vol. 751, col. 812, 26 July 1967: 'I think that not a bad rule of thumb would be found in the general proposition that a mandatory sentence or mandatory fetter on sentencing . . . is almost always productive of injustice.' Lord Stonham, on the other hand, had argued that magistrates had not even used their discretion properly in regard to the First Offenders' Act 1958, and that he did not regard the Lord Chief Justice's Practical Directions as having much impact on the courts (op. cit.).

The Conservatives thought that the mandatory element would simply mean that many more cases would be sent to the Higher Courts for sentence. See: Lord Brooke, *H.L. Debates*, Vol. 285, col. 1127, and Sir John Hobson and Mr. Carlisle, *H.C. Debates*, Vol. 751, cols. 803 and 806.

thereby implying its use in cases other than where imprisonment would be imposed,[61] and that imprisonment was in any case not necessarily to be avoided except for first offenders; rather he felt that the first short sentence in appropriate cases was effective and that the suspended sentence was better reserved for the petty recidivist:

> while we should all try to prevent the proliferation of short sentences, it may also be advisable to remember that for a person who has never been to prison before it has often been said that the first three months are the worst and that the short sentence on many people as a first sentence may have an equally reformative effect on them and have the effect of preventing them committing crime, just as a longer period of imprisonment would. The Home Secretary knows that of people going to prison for the first time, something like 80 per cent never return. What we have to avoid is the continuation of the short sentence for a man who has gone back, but that does not mean that there is not a place for a short sentence, on the man who has committed a crime before but not been to prison.[62]

That was, indeed, a major difference of opinion from Mr. Jenkins's.

There was also the deterrent argument. Lord Brooke said that the measure was a

> blow at the maintenance of law and order . . . a man can be tempted by other wrongdoers by the argument that it will be alright for him to join in with them because he will not get more than six months, and it would not mean going to prison anyway . . . This is exactly the sort of situation which a responsible Government ought not to allow to arise in days like these, when by common consent crime is too rife, and far too many weak characters are being tempted by more experienced criminals into criminal ways.[63]

Although the government persisted in its intentions to use the suspended sentence as a form of mitigated imprisonment rather than a new form of alternative non-custodial measure, it is quite clear that the substantial support from magisterial, judicial and other legal circles for the penalty was based on their belief that it was an additional deterrent to imprisonment not a replacement for it. The reason why it had become so popular was precisely the same as the case originally made after the war—a strengthener to the current non-custodial measures, but falling short of actual confinement. As the courts became more and more reluctant to pass very short sentences they had been forced to use alternatives which they clearly regarded as too lenient, especially at a time when there seemed to be an inexorable rise in

[61] *H.C. Debates*, Vol. 737, col. 105, 12 December 1966.

[62] *H.C. Debates*, Vol. 751, col. 807, 26 July 1967; also, Vol. 745, col. 1957, 27 April 1967.

[63] *H.L. Debates*, Vol. 285, cols. 1137 et seq., 27 July 1967. Mr. Carlisle maintained that 'local courts will never be able to take into account particular crime waves', Vol. 751, col. 806.

crime. The suspended sentence was the deterrent *via media* they desired.[64] And that of course is why it was not used as the Government intended: a story which everyone is familiar with.[65] The Government had certainly not taken heed of the Advisory Council's warning that new forms of penal treatment could only be justified if there were strong reasons for thinking they would be an improvement on existing methods. Nor was there any substance in Mr. Jenkins's claim that this bill

> would give us a penal system more able to do its proper job in accordance with civilised standards and *modern criminological knowledge* [my italics].
>
> It is based as all our crime and punishment policies should be, on a mixture of hope and realism, without subordinating either to the other . . .[66]

But as Leon Radzinowicz said, the suspended sentence was based much more 'upon a pious hope than upon examination of hard evidence'.[67]

There was indeed no basis in criminological knowledge for this change. But there was a political reason why it was chosen instead of, for example, attempting to make the probation service more effective. It is interesting to note that those who were generally disappointed in, or opposed to the bill were the proponents of the master-plan approach to penal change. In reply to Mr. Jenkins's speech about hope and realism, Mr. Hogg (later Lord Hailsham) pointed out that corrective training and preventive detention which were being abolished in the bill had been introduced in a similar spirit of hope and realism in 1938 and 1948, and

> that a potpourri of intelligent suggestions from high-minded and experienced men is not what is wanted at present. Indeed it is not better in principle than what has already failed over the period of 28 years which I have been examining the subject, in a mixture of hope and realism. What I believe is wanted is a new appraisal of the fundamental assumptions of our penal system, a new rational and coherent approach to English criminal law.[68]

Mr. Deeds added that much of the Bill was 'based on very little reflection and very little has been based on very long-term thinking', a view echoed by

[64] Mr. Edmund Dell in 1972 quoted from the Magistrates' Association Memorandum 'what is more natural than that courts which were previously torn between fines and imprisonment for offenders who drive while disqualified should regard the new sentence as an appropriate *via media*?' Standing Committee G. Seventh Sitting, 18 January 1972.

[65] See Leon Radzinowicz, 'A foreseeable failure', *Sunday Times*, 24 Jan. 1971. The proportion of offenders placed on probation fell even further (see footnote 56, above)—for those aged 21 + to 5·8 per cent (from 9·3 per cent in 1965) in magistrates' courts and to 7·2 per cent (from 14·3 per cent in 1965) in the higher courts.

[66] *H.C. Debates*, Vol. 737, col. 75, 12 December 1966.

[67] Foreword to Marc Ancel, *Suspended sentence*, London, Heinemann Educational Books, 1971.

[68] *H.C. Debates*, Vol. 737, col. 77, 12 December 1966.

others who regretted the abandonment of the Royal Commission and a reversion to piecemeal legislation lacking a 'comprehensive philosophical base'. Mr. St. John Stevas even went so far as to attribute the inadequacies of the Bill 'to our rudimentary knowledge of criminological science in this country'.[69] Without doubt it was hard to see that the matters of principle which had concerned the Advisory Council in 1952 and 1957 had been adequately discussed or the likely effects predicted from any empirical evidence of the attitudes of the courts. One can only assume the 'principles' had changed.

When the Advisory Council reported again in 1972 on Non-Custodial and Semi-Custodial Penalties it strangely made no reference to the arguments for a mandatory suspension of short prison sentences: what is more, no comment at all was made about the case for or against the suspended sentence. It was simply considered, or so it would appear from the report, as a fact of life and the sole question raised was whether it should be combined with a probation order. As I have already said, this was rejected vigorously by Mr. Jenkins in 1967 on the grounds that the suspended sentence had to be seen as a tough alternative to imprisonment. It had also been rejected by the probation lobby. But while there was still no case for adding suspension to probation, the matter was rather different looked at the other way round. Some of those given suspended sentences might be in need of supervision. In recommending this the Wootton Committee endorsed a penal philosophy which would have been unacceptable to its predecessor a decade earlier. It implicitly accepted that offenders who courts decided need not, for reasons of public protection, be sent to prison and who would benefit from advice and support from the probation service could nevertheless also receive a 'declaratory' sentence to mark the seriousness of the offence: and a sentence which was extremely likely to be imposed if there were a subsequent offence, whatever the impact of supervision might have been. In the words of 1952 this certainly 'savours of the doctrine that the offence rather than the offender should be punished'. That the Committee gave in so easily on what had formerly been regarded as a matter of principle is perhaps explainable in terms of their assessment of the reality of the courts' sentencing practices.[70]

[69] Vol. 737, Mr. Deedes, at col. 93, Mr. Silkin, at cols. 177–8, Mr. St. John-Stevas, at col. 178, and Sir John Hobson, cols. 189–90, 12 December 1966.

[70] As Mr. Edmund Dell commented, 'When one comes to what the Wootton Committee actually says in support of this proposal, I think the principal impression one has is how thin the argument is compared with the categoric nature of recommendations'. *H.C. Debates*, Standing Committee G. Ninth Sitting, 25 January 1972, col. 383 and again, 'In paragraph 189, it is said: "the matter will have to be further examined in the light of the operation of the suspended sentence. . . ." But no further examination took place between paragraph 189 and the firm recommendations in paragraph 33 of the Conclusions.

The higher courts have tended to regard probation as too lenient a penalty for some offenders and insisted on the gravity being marked by a particular term of imprisonment.[71] That they are willing to suspend it in some cases is probably regarded by many (including I believe probation officers) as the best that can be hoped for. To add supervision is then seen as better than no supervision whatever the merits of probation without a suspended term might be. The Committee may have seen their task as simply trying to improve the suspended sentence system rather than endorsing its principles. But this did not stop Mr. Edmund Dell from pointing to the defects:

> [this] tougher form of suspended sentence is undesirable, and contains great disadvantages, in that it will dilute the work of the probation service, increase the use of suspended sentences, reduce further the use of probation and increase the number of people going to prison.[72]

It was all very well for Mr. Carlisle to reply that 'the courts should never get as far as a suspended sentence if they think the right order is a probation order',[73] for experience of the *via media* between probation and prison had surely been otherwise.

Given that all the Conservative spokesmen in 1967 were absolutely opposed to the mandatory provision, it is hardly surprising that they should have taken the opportunity to repeal it in 1972. The reasons were, however, rather curious in view of the Conservative opinion that the courts could be relied upon to exercise their discretion sensitively within an overall policy of using short-term imprisonment only in exceptional circumstances. Mr. Jenkins believed that the control of discretion was necessary to limit dis-

---

I believe if that examination had taken place . . . it might have hesitated much longer before recommending the suspended sentence supervision order.' *H.C. Debates*, Vol. 838, cols., 1957–8, 15 June 1972.

The Wootton Committee's recommendation on the combination of probation supervision with a suspended sentence was accepted, but only in those cases where sentences of over six months' imprisonment were awarded: thus the power was denied to magistrates' courts. An amendment to abolish the restriction on awarding a suspended sentence and a probation order in respect of one conviction (involving multiple offences) was rejected by the government on the grounds that although the suspended sentence supervision order 'had made a hole in it' the general principle of not combining penalties with probation was still right. See Mr. Carlisle, Standing Committee G. Twenty-Third Sitting, 23 March 1972, col. 1080.

[71] See D. A. Thomas, *Principles of Sentencing*, London, Heinemann Educational Books, 1970, Ch. 3.

[72] Op. cit., col. 385.

[73] Ibid., col. 395. According to Mr. Carlisle it was supported in principle by the Advisory Council on Probation and After-care and by the National Association of Probation Officers; the only bodies opposed were the Conference of Principal Probation Officers and the British Association of Social Workers.

parity in sentencing practice. Mr. Hogg and his colleagues believed it would lead to injustice. But Mr. Maudling claimed that it was the mandatory provisions themselves which had led to the increase in the use of short sentences, when clearly it was the way the sentence was being used by magistrates in place of existing non-custodial penalties. In a blistering attack on the logic of the Government's argument, Mr. Edmund Dell pointed out that if the aim really was to reduce the use of short imprisonment terms it was paradoxical to increase the range of sentences at the discretion of magistrates when experience clearly showed that they had not used their discretion in the way intended by Parliament. He even used statistical material from the Home Office study to suggest a compromise whereby a particular category of 'poor risks' should be excluded from the mandatory provisions. 'After all', he asked, 'what is the point of Home Office research unless one learns from it and takes action in accordance with what it shows?'[74] Mr. Carlisle admitted that there was 'clear evidence that the suspended sentence had been used more widely than was intended and also that the sentences given have been longer'.[75] But as the 1967 debate had already shown the Government was unshakenly against any legislative controls on sentencing discretion and neither shared the Labour Party's almost complete aversion to the short sentence nor their view that suspension was only to be used as a mitigation of actual imprisonment. Although the Government accepted a clause which drew attention to the decision of the Court of Appeal that suspension should be reserved for cases which would otherwise have *merited* imprisonment, such a clause is of course capable of wide interpretation by the courts.[76]

Crime, the Criminal and Community Integration

Even before the Bill introducing the suspended sentence had been introduced to Parliament the Home Secretary had asked the new Advisory Council (A.C.P.S.) to 'consider what changes and additions might be made in the existing range of non-custodial penalties, disabilities, and other requirements

[74] *H.C. Debates*, Vol. 838, cols. 139–1941, 15 June 1972. Mr. Dell suggested that the exception would be: 'that the offender had at any time before the commission of the offence been sentenced to any custodial sentence or has three or more previous convictions'. This was based on a Home Office study of 1,000 men given a suspended sentence in 1968 which showed that offenders subject to the mandatory suspension had a relatively low rate of breach—1 in 3—but that the two groups included in the amendment had a high breach rate.

[75] Ibid., col. 1081.

[76] R. v. *O'Keefe*, (1969) 1 All E.R. 426.

which may be imposed on offenders'.[77] A fact which emphasizes even more that the suspended sentence was regarded as an 'obvious' solution that need not await examination by the Home Secretary's 'impartial' expert advisers. But the remit to the Council does indicate that the Government were searching for new approaches. In addition they asked the Council 'to consider how the principle of personal reparation by the offender might be given a more prominent place in the penal system, and in this connection to consider specially the position of the professional criminal'.[78] The fact that the Wootton Committee's most novel non-custodial proposal was to introduce the penalty of community service by the offender meant that, on two fronts, a new element in the penal system was in the process of being forged.

Of course, the general idea itself was not new, it had been raised by Mr. Butler in 1957 and again, as I have already indicated, in the White Paper, *Penal Practice in a Changing Society* in 1959. Mr. Butler asked whether the 'simple conception of punishment' had 'occupied too dominating a position in our penal philosophy . . . was there not . . . some ethical value in the older conceptions . . . of restitution and compensation'.[79] The White Paper re-emphasized:

> the redemptive value of punishment to the individual offender . . . if it were made to include a realisation of the injury he had done to his victim as well as to the order of society, and the need to make personal reparation for that injury.[80]

But it was not only the moral or redemptive aspect that was seen as attractive. It was suggested that as the more reformative aspects of punishment were emphasized (presumably both within the prisons and especially in the extension of non-custodial measures):

> the assumption that the claims of the victim are sufficiently satisfied if the offender is punished by society becomes less persuasive . . . Indeed in the public mind the interests of the offender may not infrequently seem to be placed before those of his victim.[81]

Intertwined here are two intriguing elements, each of which was to find expression in different ways in the Wootton and Widgery Reports. On the one hand, the redemptive feature of restitution reflects a concern voiced frequently in the post-war years of a fragmenting social fabric; of a lack of

---

[77] Wootton Report, p. V.
[78] Widgery Report, p. V.
[79] *H.C. Debates*, Vol. 566, col. 1154, 13 March 1957.
[80] Op. cit., Cmd. 645, para. 25, p. 7.
[81] Ibid., para. 24, p. 7.

sense of community obligation and respect for authority. 'The growth in the crime rate', said the Conservative Party study group, 'may be largely attributed to the breakdown of social disciplines exercised in the past—by the family, the community, religion, and by personal loyalties. . . . In the impersonal society, concepts such as "the public good" and "social well-being" tend to lose their significance. Motives frequently become selfish and community loyalties and values diminish in their influence.'[82] The penal system was seen as one means of reintegrating offenders within the community, not through the older ideas of casework and support but by 'bringing home to them' their obligations. The second element rests upon this view of the criminal as having obligations, rather than being simply a social misfit. In part it probably had its roots in the belief that criminal behaviour could no longer be regarded as explainable merely in terms of social or personal disadvantage. To many the image of the contemporary delinquent was the undisciplined hooligan (so leading to a large growth in the use of detention centres) and of the criminal as a parasite, an abuser of the privileges of an affluent welfare society, who consequently should not simply be a burden to the state, but made to repay, in some form, the damage he has caused. Although one consequence of this view was the adoption of Miss Margery Fry's proposed scheme for compensating victims of violence, its operation as a state scheme did not involve a contribution from the offender himself.[83] The arguments and assumptions which led the Advisory Council to its conclusions have been so little debated that they are worth considering in detail.

The ideas in the White Paper were not, as far as I am aware, taken up seriously[84] until the Royal Commission began to gather evidence. Then, a number of organizations put forward proposals ranging from the offender making personal reparation to the victim,[85] through making repairs to community property,[86] taking part in schemes of public work either at

[82] Op. cit., p. 41 and p. 15.

[83] For a concise review of this legislation, see Hall-Williams, op. cit., pp. 296–7.

[84] For example, a critical examination of *Penal Practice in a Changing Society* was published by the I.S.T.D. (Institute for the Study and Treatment of Delinquency) in August 1960 in which only a passing reference was made to the proposals for restitution. See p. 6.

[85] Evidence of the Magistrates' Association, R.C.P.S., Vol. II, *Miscellaneous Bodies*, para. 68, p. 18, and Free Church Federal Council, para. 37, p. 215, and Society of Labour Lawyers, para. 2, p. 83.

[86] Such as litter droppers sweeping streets and damagers of communal property helping in its repair. Evidence of Justices' Clerks' Society, ibid., para. 15, p. 29. See also the Memorandum of the Law Society in 1970 which suggested offenders might perform menial public duties such as sweeping hospital floors, *The Times*, 21 February 1970.

In a speech to the Conservative Party in 1970 Mr. Heath proposed that 'it might be salutory if a compensation principle in sentencing could be erected for offences such as

subsistence 'adequate' or full rates of pay[87] to a scheme to use the bankruptcy proceedings in order to reveal all the offender's wealth and assess financial restitution.[88] It is significant, though, that the idea of personal restitution was not mentioned in either of the academic papers on the purposes of punishment submitted by Dr. Walker and Professor Sprott; significant because it indicates that the pressure came from a grass-roots public reaction rather than from academic discourse.

None of the measures for community service were canvassed during the debates on the 1967 Bill, but an attempt was made to introduce a new clause for compensating the victim. It received the fullest discussion at the Report stage, when many Conservative and some Liberal members expressed their disquiet that no immediate action was being taken.[89] The object of the clause was to allow the court 'in addition to or in lieu of any other penalty' to give a judgement for restoration of the property or payment for damage or injury by the accused to the victim.[90] The most novel feature of this was the possibility it gave for the avoidance of imprisonment. As Mr. Hogg said: 'if he [the criminal] would make it clear that there was something serious he meant to do to put things right, he might get probation or a conditional discharge—criminal courts could avoid sending people to prison who otherwise would attract prison sentences. This, after all, is one of the main objects of the Bill. . . .' In particular he stressed the ethical value of reparation which he considered should be 'one of the principal motives underlying our treatment of serious offences'.[91] The Government opposed the clause then,

---

squatting and trespassing in demonstrations' . . . 'there is one common element, a distinct and obvious lack of a sense of social obligation on the part of the offender'. *The Times*, 17 March 1970.

[87] R.C.P.S., Vol. II, Evidence of Society of Clerks to the Peace, para. 12, p. 51, in Evidence of the Inns of Court Conservative and Unionist Society, s. 6, p. 89 and the Penal Affairs Committee of the Society of Friends, p. 245.

[88] Ibid., evidence of the Council of the Law Society, 1st Memorandum, para. 16, p. 61, and expanded in the Second Memorandum.

[89] It had originally been brought forward by the Liberal M.P. Mr. Winstanley in the Standing Committee on 22 March 1967 and was raised at Report by Mr. Hogg (Lord Hailsham), with the support of Mr. Iremonger (a member of the dissolved Royal Commission) who had published an article in *The Times* entitled 'Britain's penal system lacks clarity of purpose', 26 April 1967, calling for restitution as a more appropriate response to the professional criminal than parole: 'the treatment idea and reformation of character and early release under brief supervision is pious humbug in certain cases'.

Sir John Foster complained that the idea was being referred to A.C.P.S.: 'all Governments when civil servants or Ministers do not like an idea or cannot be bothered with it, refer the question to Committee'. *H.C. Debates*, Vol. 745, col. 1695, 26 April 1967.

[90] New Clause No. 12 (Compensation for victim), s(1). *H.C. Debates*, Vol. 745, col. 1684, 26 April 1967.

[91] Ibid., cols. 1686-7.

and again when it was introduced as a private members' bill in 1970[92] on the grounds that the Advisory Council would soon report. In the event, the conclusions of the Widgery and Wootton sub-committees of A.C.P.S. were markedly different, not only because they dealt with rather different categories of offender but because their basic philosophies diverged on the purpose of restitution. The Widgery report, dealing mainly with professional or large-scale criminals considered that reparation should reduce 'the specific consequences of the offences' for the victim,[93] while the Wootton Committee considered that their scheme should not 'compel the offender to undergo some form of penance directly related to his offence, which would have only a limited application, but to require him to perform service of value to the community or to those in need'.[94] It owed nothing to the ideas of community work, either for pay on public projects or as a form of direct punishment, which had been canvassed by various bodies before the Royal Commission.

First, I shall briefly consider the Widgery proposals in the light of what the supporters of personal reparation hoped might be achieved. The Committee felt that the deterrent element in the criminal law would be increased by a system of redress. In particular it noted 'the affront to public opinion' of an offender 'still able to enjoy the proceeds of crime after he has paid the penalty imposed by the courts'. Indeed, the Committee considered that such a situation was a 'positive inducement to crime'. There is no doubt that this attitude had greatly affected sentencing practice in increasing sentence lengths where large sums were involved. Thus the Committee saw the possibility of reparation adding to the general deterrent effects of punishment and, by denuding the offender of his 'ill-gotten gains' and so reducing public reaction to the crime, making it possible to reduce the length of custodial sentences 'or even to rely in some cases on non-custodial penalties alone'.[95] Thus, it could also be part of the strategy of relieving the overcrowded prisons. The Committee also ventured to suggest that there might be some redemptive value in making the offender repay: 'a realization of the injury he has done to his victim as well as to the order of society',[96] but the argument was not developed, nor, more significantly, was it referred to when the

[92] Mr. Iremonger introduced the Restitution Bill on 21 April 1970. *H.C. Debates*, Vol. 800, cols. 255–7. He mentioned the popularity of the notion, its basis in 'a principle of morality' and that the fulfilment of an order for 'restoration of stolen property or compensation for injury, loss or damage . . . would be a condition of the criminal's getting a suspended sentence, probation or conditional discharge'.

[93] *Reparation by the offender*, para. 4, pp. 1–2.

[94] *Non-Custodial and Semi-Custodial penalties*, para. 41, pp. 14–15.

[95] Op. cit., pp. 3–5.

[96] Ibid., para. 9, p. 3.

proposal was debated in Parliament. The major proposal discussed was the Law Society's scheme for introducing bankruptcy proceedings. The Committee immediately recognized that there was little hope of getting any repayment from

> the feckless and improvident offender who derives little profit from his offences and who might be driven further in crime if compelled to pay compensation, or from the hardened professional who is contemptuous of authority and skilled in concealing the proceeds of theft . . . it is doubtful whether the additional deterrent effect, in the sense of a harassment or a curb on criminal activities, either on the offenders or on the criminal fraternity at large, would be significant.

Indeed the only type of criminal who might be a promising candidate were those 'offenders who are in the main honest and law abiding but succumb on a single occasion when temptation is placed in their way'; the Committee particularly had in mind 'white collar' criminals 'who have committed isolated but nevertheless serious offences'.[97] And it was these cases, 'especially fraud' which were picked out by Mr. Maudling when introducing the measure in the 1972 Criminal Justice Bill.[98] Although for these offenders compensation might well reduce the need for a long prison sentence, the Committee did not enquire in how many such cases there was evidence that the offender had any assets remaining[99] or whether those who had would not pay back with alacrity rather than suffer a prison term, without the need for bankruptcy. A very small proportion of prisoners serving long prison terms are white collar criminals and they are hardly the class of criminal which the Committee suggested cause so much public concern. The proposals (with their experimental lower limit of crimes amounting to £15,000 for bankruptcy proceedings) would also according to the Committee's own figures account for well under a hundred cases a year. It is obvious that the impact of the proposals could only be extremely limited and, as Mr. Maudling said, 'not easy to enforce'.[100] It is therefore important to note that the Committee rejected another suggestion, namely that the maximum term of imprisonment in default of payment of compensation should be raised above the present maximum of one year. This meant that it was impossible, in effect, to offer offenders a choice of reparation or long terms of imprisonment, as suggested in the attempts to introduce legislation

[97] Ibid., para. 13, pp. 4–5.

[98] *H.C. Debates*, Vol. 826, col. 970, 22 November 1961.

[99] What limited research there is on embezzlers for example, would indicate that the money is taken often to deal with an 'unshareable problem', is disposed of gradually and taken often with the intention of repayment—which as the amount grows becomes increasingly difficult for the offender to achieve. See D. R. Cressey, *Other People's Money*, Glencoe, Illinois, Free Press, 1953.

[100] Op. cit.

in 1967 and 1970; or, even more radical, a system of 'prison discount' so that what the court might regard as a substantial repayment could be offset against a part of the prison term.[101] This is, after all, not such an extraordinary idea: parole boards regularly take such factors into account in deciding whether to release an offender on licence. If, in fact, the aim of reparation is to return property where possible, and minimize the use of imprisonment as a penalty, with all its destructive aspects, then a system of this type (even allowing for the enormous problems of assessing the amount to be repaid) might have received closer examination. But there was no investigation of the attitudes of criminals and presumably the assumption was made that such 'bargaining' would be either useless or inappropriate. Yet it is equally hard to believe that for professional criminals it would not have some success; after all they will regularly leave everything if they are in danger of being caught, so why should they not return property if the major incentive is to avoid long incarceration? The Committee without such research was only able to make *assumptions* about the reaction of offenders to a method of punishment which could have an impact on the most intractable of penal problems: the substantial reduction of the prison population by substituting alternatives to medium- and long-term penalties. In its present form, reparation by the offender through criminal bankruptcy is likely to be a penal measure of purely symbolic significance.

The Wootton Committee proposals are much more complex in their intentions. They were put forward as likely to appeal to those holding any theory of punishment:

> To some, it would be simply a more constructive and cheaper alternative to short sentences of imprisonment: by others it would be seen as introducing into the penal system a new dimension with an emphasis on reparation to the community; others again would regard it as a means of giving effect to the old adage that the punishment should fit the crime; while still others would stress the value of bringing offenders into close touch with those members of the community who are most in need of help and support. These different approaches are by no means incompatible.[102]

But the Committee itself was most attracted by 'the opportunity which it could give for constructive activity in the form of personal service to the community, and the possibility of a changed outlook on the part of the offender. We would hope that offenders . . . would come to see it in this light, and not as wholly negative and punitive'.[103] Fundamentally, the Committee believed that offenders' attitudes could be changed if they could

[101] See Rupert Cross, op. cit., 1971, pp. 178–9.
[102] Wootton Report, op. cit., para. 33, pp. 12–13.
[103] Ibid., para. 34.

either become part of, or be subject to 'the wholesome influence' of the voluntary service movement which 'has deep roots in the social life of this country'.[104] Although undoubtedly it gained its public appeal from the notion of repairing specific damage[105] the concept of voluntary community *service,* rather than compulsory community *work,* was a response to the idealistic spirit of the Community Service Volunteers movement: a movement of mainly middle-class educated youth for the alleviation of hardship among the old and under-privileged. Attachment to the work of these young volunteers was presumed not only to be of help to the community but mainly to introduce offenders to constructive rather than destructive attitudes towards others in the community. The proposition that such service would be effective must, of course, have been based upon some assumptions about why crimes are committed or, indeed, why they are not committed. But none of them are made explicit.[106] One can only guess that the Committee believed, either that offenders failed to realize the personal or social consequences of their actions or that their offences derived from a general lack of consideration for others—rather than from a set of circumstances more specific to the offence, and/or that offenders were not well integrated into the social life of the community within which they lived and that joining with volunteers might effectively change the pattern of their previous associations and leisure activity.

Later on, in the passage of the Bill through Parliament, Lady Wootton mentioned the possibility of friendships with volunteers giving the offender 'a rather different outlook on society' and spoke in particular of the evidence

---

[104] Ibid., para. 35.

[105] For example, Lord Gardiner in discussing the provisions in the Bill gave as his example of the use of community service as a means of winning 'the voluntary co-operation of such people in the rules of society . . .'. 'Young hooligans come down from London . . . to a seaside town and make an infernal nuisance of themselves. What could be more sensible, or more just than, if they agree, that they should be told, "Instead of being sent to prison or fined, we are going to ask you to help us with community work for this town. We have had an oil slick outside and this oil slick is making a confounded mess of the beach. Come along! Will you agree to help the citizens of this town (in which, you must admit, you made a bit of a nuisance of yourselves) by clearing away the effects of the oil slick on the beach?".' In reply Lord Colville pointed out that this was not the idea: 'Indeed . . . I felt the whole concept of this was not to rub the offender's nose on the beach where he had offended' and that in any case the court would not be able to order any particular form of service; it 'simply sentences the person to the system run by the Probation Service'. *H.L. Debates,* Vol. 333, cols. 635–6 and 642, 17 July 1972.

[106] On the problems of analysing sociologically the arguments used by Committees of Enquiry see G. Smith and N. Stockman, op. cit. (1972). For a discussion of the relationship between theories of crime and delinquency and proposals for prevention see W. B. Miller, 'Ideology and Criminal Justice Policy: some current issues', *J. Crim. Law. Criminol. & Poli. Sci.,* 1973, **64**, 141.

from borstal boys who helped bath the totally disabled at Cheshire Homes: 'It is found that the opportunity of helping such people, has a very beneficial effect on their *attitudes*'[107] [my italics]. But, as the Committee recognized, the involvement of offenders in such service was not a new phenomenon: it had particularly been a long-standing element (even if in a more limited form) of the open borstal system since the 1930s.[108] Although, of course, giving aid of this kind will almost certainly be seen as a more purposeful and socially valuable activity than that available in the ordinary regimes of penal institutions, there has in fact been no clear evidence that it has led to significant attitude changes of a kind which result in lessening the likelihood of reconviction. But the belief in the possibility of changing attitudes was taken up as one of the strong arguments for the scheme. Lord Colville suggested that such service would 'also impress upon the offender that there are other needs in society than his own selfish requirements, and perhaps by the example of the volunteers and others with whom he works he will learn the satisfaction of giving to others rather than exploiting them'. That, he admitted, 'may sound a little high-flown' but it was, he contended, based on the experience of those engaged in voluntary effort.[109]

These views both reflect assumptions about the nature of social learning[110] —particularly that responses learned as appropriate in one situation are readily transferred to others[111]—as well as about the nature of the 'average run of minor offender . . . not steeped in criminal behaviour' with which the report claimed to deal. And here the report completely failed to reveal its assumptions. Did they believe, for example, that such offenders are any different from the majority of the population in the value they place upon mutual support and in the sympathy they feel for the sick, disabled and incapacitated aged? After all, relatively few of the law-abiding majority are

[107] *H.L. Debates*, Vol. 332, col. 610, 26 June 1972.

[108] See R. G. Hood, *Borstal Re-assessed*, op. cit., pp. 116–19.

[109] *H.L. Debates*, Vol. 332, col. 583, 26 June 1972.

[110] See J. Stuart Whiteley, 'Coming to terms with deviance: opportunities in the Criminal Justice Act', *Howard J. of Penology*, 1973, **13,** 270. Whiteley is particularly concerned with arguing for a therapeutic content to community service—an argument which Lady Wootton was later interested in, in the hope that community service might be associated with residential weekend centres, such as have been established in New Zealand. See *H.L. Debates*, Vol. 333, col. 644, 17 July 1972.

[111] The Evidence of the British Psychological Society to the Royal Commission specifically took as an example, 'the principle that habits of honesty, self-control, industry and so on that have been practised in one social environment, will necessarily be transferred to another was widely regarded as self-evident during the nineteenth century; few modern psychologists would subscribe to this belief, as attempts to demonstrate its worth have usually yielded negative results'. *Vol. II*, para. 20, p. 182. It has, of course, been hoped by many supporters of the community service approach that some offenders would after the experience themselves become voluntary workers.

active in organized voluntary movements. Was the offender viewed as basically lacking empathy, and that this could be remedied by revealing the true state of the sick? Or was he seen as labouring under a feeling of inferiority, with a 'chip on his shoulder' which would be dispelled by revelation of the truly underprivileged? Or was he simply hedonistic and selfish; a fact to be brought home to him by the selflessness of volunteers? Where was the consideration of the problem in the light of criminological ideas and knowledge? Most sociological research and theory, emphasizing as it does the importance of the delinquent subculture, the complexity of the interactions which shape the delinquent's sense of identity, the broader problems of attaining status in school and work and the 'dissociation' from conventional leisure activities,[112] indicate a picture of the delinquent, let alone the adult criminal, who may have moved far beyond the point of being influenced simply by the 'wholesome influence of those who choose voluntarily to help in the community'. But then, in trying to understand the report, one is also faced by the fact that it does not try to define the types of offender concerned. Presumably, if community service were to be a genuine alternative to imprisonment, they were already well on their career, having experienced the majority of other nominal alternative penalties, or were first offenders who had committed an offence of the type the courts wished especially to deter. In either case it is not self-evident why the remedy of community service is appropriate. To the extent that many repetitive minor offenders are among the most deprived members of the community—those lacking parental support, affection, educational or work skills, stability and friendships— they are hardly in need of 'bringing . . . into close touch with those members of the community who are most in need of help and support'.[113] Of those who are involved in particular situations which result in relatively serious offences, such as violence or property damage, there is as far as I am aware no evidence that the majority are especially lacking in social awareness at other times or in other spheres of their lives. If there is such evidence the committee could have referred to it or even set out to try to collect it. In its absence one is reminded of Howard Becker's observation that

> possession of one deviant trait may have a generalised symbolic value, so that people automatically assume that its bearer possesses other undesirable traits allegedly associated with it . . . apprehension for one deviant act exposes a

---

[112] Among the vast literature on this subject, see D. Downes, *The Delinquent Solution*, London, Routledge & Kegan Paul, 1966, esp. pp. 255–69.

[113] Op. cit., para. 33, p. 13, unless, of course, one subscribes to the 'conservative' (and in my opinion, unpalatable) view that social control should be achieved by showing the badly-off that there are others even less fortunate than themselves. But this is not to deny that some offenders, like other people, will get genuine satisfaction from social service.

person to the likelihood that he will be regarded as deviant or undesirable in other respects.[114]

There are many other similar questions: such as why the Committee felt that a general service to repay *the community* might have meaning to the person who had stolen from work or private property or from stores or the relatively wealthy.

But I am not here trying to argue the case for one view of the offender over another or even to claim *a priori* that the concept of Community Service is wrong or likely to prove particularly ineffective as a suitable alternative to imprisonment for at least some offenders. The important point is that the committee failed to provide any analysis of the case for its proposals in terms of criminological and penological knowledge: basic pre-requisites for the consideration of change as far as the 1959 White Paper had been concerned. It was what Rupert Cross once called, 'a mass of unexplained and unfounded assumptions'—at least as far as a reader of the Report can judge.[115]

In another sphere, also, the committee conspicuously failed to follow the earlier formulae: namely, to provide a convincing analysis of why the methods already available had failed or needed 're-inforcing'.[116] It could, of course, be said that the Committee's only problem was to suggest alternatives that would be acceptable to courts and to parliament in order to decrease the overcrowding within the prisons. But the issue should have been conceived in broader terms than this. Firstly, it was essential to know why the existing alternatives (especially probation) were not being used more frequently or could not be extended in use, why were they regarded as unsatisfactory or unsuccessful or both? Secondly, as the Committee was charged particularly with devising alternatives to prison, it was necessary to establish some basis for believing that any new proposals would be at least as acceptable to the courts, and *at least not less successful* for whatever purpose imprisonment was being used.[117] In other words, one would have expected to see an analysis of the extent to which imprisonment is used, for what purposes and for what types of offence and offender, a discussion of why the alternative penalties were not used and a justification of the proposed alternatives both from the standpoint of satisfying the courts that their sentencing aim when formerly using imprisonment could still be achieved and that the 'measures' being advocated appeared likely to be at least not less effective than imprisonment and to have a different effect upon offenders than the range of non-custodial penalties already available. Lastly, the Committee should have

[114] Howard S. Becker, *Outsiders* New York, The Free Press, 1963, p. 33.
[115] *Criminal Law Review*, [1966], 184.
[116] *Penal Practice in a Changing Society*, para. 27, p. 7.
[117] See below, p. 414.

satisfied itself these available penalties were themselves working satisfactorily and at their maximum effectiveness—for if they were not, the solution might lie in first improving them before embarking on anything new. The Committee may have taken these steps, but the report does not indicate that they did. The method of enquiry appears to be very similar to a 'mini' Royal Commission of the type so strongly criticized by Leon Radzinowicz. There was no specific research conducted, and virtually no discussion of the problem along the lines outlined above: there was no analysis of the prison population, of sentencing practice, of those who were regarded as unsuitable for available alternative penalties even though the A.C.T.O. in 1957 had specifically stated that it would need 'the most extensive research to form even a tentative estimate of the numbers' of prisoners who could be dealt with by means other than imprisonment.[118]

In presenting its recommendations to the Minister, the Advisory Council as a whole stressed that 'probation as such must clearly play an increasing part in the non-custodial treatment of offenders being a more economical and often more valuable sanction than deprivation of liberty'. But, in fact, there was no discussion of probation and of the ways in which that service might be improved: on the grounds that it had already been 'fully reviewed' by the Morison Committee which reported in 1962. A reading of that report will, in fact, show that it was much more concerned with administration, recruitment, training and outlining a philosophy for the service than with radical change to make it more acceptable to the courts as a measure to be used in the more serious cases. In fact the provisions in the Criminal Justice Act 1972 which most increased the work of the probation service and its control over offenders—the new day training centres and the expansion of probation hostels—resulted from the recommendations of a Home Office Working Party set up to consider the Wootton Committee's proposals and not from the Committee itself. But in any case the Committee was not content 'merely to suggest modifications to existing forms of non-custodial treatment' which would have been 'a very meagre achievement, quite out of proportion to the recognized facts of the situation. Formidable though the practical difficulties might be, we could not but be impressed by the need for some new and radical development'.[119] The reason was that 'sentencers' complained of lack of appropriate alternatives to imprisonment, in particular to those cases

[118] Op. cit., para. 8, p. 4. In fact little research of this kind into prisons has been conducted by the Home Office or other bodies—despite Mr. Butler's insistence in 1957 that prison research should have priority—and the House of Commons Estimates Committee was particularly critical of this in its Seventh Report of 1966-7.

[119] Wootton Report, para. 30, p. 12.

where the offence required the imposition of an effective deterrent both to the offender and to others; where a fine was in effect no penalty, because the offender was either well to do or dependent on his parents; and where a custodial sentence was in all the circumstances, and with all it involved, too harsh or inappropriate in the sense that it would be likely to embitter or contaminate an offender who was not already steeped in criminal behaviour.[120]

Presumably they were cases in which a suspended prison sentence was not thought to be a sufficient deterrent or was otherwise inappropriate; but, whether significantly or not, this alternative was never mentioned. The sentencers themselves apparently admitted to being 'generally baffled by the difficulties of devising any satisfactory alternative'. One of the major difficulties must have been that there was no definite indication which offenders the Committee considered might be subjected to community service by the courts, and in putting forward the case specifically for community service they completely ducked the issue of whether they thought it would solve the sentencers' dilemma in the extraordinary statement:

> We have not attempted to categorise precisely the types of offender for whom community service might be appropriate, nor do we think it possible to predict what use might be made by the courts of this new form of sentence.[121]

They mentioned as examples 'some cases of theft, for unauthorized taking of vehicles, for some of the more serious traffic offences, some cases of malicious damage and minor assaults'. Thus while it was hoped it 'would be felt by the courts to constitute an adequate alternative to a short custody sentence', it would also be available for offenders not previously sent to prison[122] as well as 'a welcome alternative in cases where the court imposes a fine for want of any better sanction, or again in some cases where it is desired to stiffen probation . . .'.[123] Thus, the new penalty might in many

---

[120] Ibid., para. 37, p. 14.

[121] Ibid., para. 37. This was an argument supported in Parliament by Mr. Dell, but with the interesting proviso—reminiscent of the prison-discount idea already discussed in this paper—that an offender sentenced to imprisonment might *apply* to 'discharge his penalty through a community service order'. *H.C. Debates*, Standing Committee G. Twelfth Sitting, 8 February 1972, col. 468.

An indication of the uncertainty of the situation is Lord Colville's remark: 'I am in a certain amount of difficulty in explaining how this community service will work out.' *H.L. Debates*, Vol. 333, col. 644, 17 July 1972.

[122] The subsequent Act did, however, limit the application of a C.S.O. to persons convicted of offences punishable by imprisonment and excluded certain traffic offenders which the Committee would have included.

[123] Op. cit., para. 37. It is interesting to note that the Wootton Committee considered carefully the arguments for and against making community service a condition of a probation order. While they accepted that this might be the right course in some cases, they thought that a new form of order 'would be a guarantee that the courts would see

cases be yet another *via media* to join the suspended sentence: a point emphasized by the Minister, Mr. Carlisle (formerly a member of the Wootton Committee), in 1972 when he stressed that 'one of the advantages of community service is that it is punitive in that it deprives a man of his free time' and 'I am not suggesting for a moment that in future everyone will receive a sentence of community service where previously he would not receive a custodial sentence. I believe it will be used where people are now dealt with in other non-custodial ways'.[124] The Government did, however, insist on inserting a minimum period of 40 hours and a maximum of 240 instead of 120 hours to stop the new proposal being seen by the public as 'the soft option of all time', and to make its deprivation of leisure a more realistic alternative to terms of imprisonment of up to six months.[125] It is important to recognize that the Committee was suggesting that a penalty was needed of sufficient severity to replace imprisonment as a punitive measure—that is, a penalty of what might be called 'equal dimension on the tariff' (even though the maximum number of hours this should involve was in dispute). But by emphasizing the rehabilitative aims of the proposed order the Committee did not confront fully two thorny issues. First, what criteria were to be used in fixing the length of the order? Was it to be on a tariff (related to the offence) or treatment basis? Secondly, the question of the aim of the penalty is of crucial importance in assessing the effectiveness of the scheme. If it is to be regarded as an equally severe but less degrading and contaminating penalty than imprisonment (i.e. simply as 'sufficient punishment') then it will be acceptable if the rate of reconviction during and following the orders is not greater than the rate following imprisonment. If it is to be regarded as more rehabilitative than imprisonment (even if a lesser penalty) then it would be expected to show commensurate results. In leaving the

---

it in that light and use it accordingly and that they would not regard it merely as an "extra" in a probation order' (para. 55). The Home Office Working Group which considered the proposals were, however, firmly of the opinion that to link community service with a probation order would 'blur the traditional concept of a probation order and emphasize the probation officer's controlling function rather than his rôle of advising and assisting'.

[124] *H.C. Debates*, Standing Committee G, Twelfth Sitting, 8 February 1972, cols. 471–3. It is also important to note that the government felt that 'to incorporate community service in a probation order would be likely to blur the additional concept of a probation order; it would emphasize the probation officer's controlling function rather than his rôle of advising and assisting'—an argument that was not used with the suspended sentence supervision order (col. 480).

The Times leading article of 4 January 1972 called the community service orders 'the counterpart of intermediate treatment' for children.

[125] Lord Colville, *H.L. Debates*, Vol. 333, col. 642, 17 July 1972. See also Lord Donaldson's concern at Mr. Carlisle's emphasis on the punitive side of community service, cols. 644–5.

question open the Committee gave no guidelines as to how its proposed experiment was to be evaluated.[126]

It is, I hope, obvious from the foregoing discussion that although the Wootton Committee and the Government regarded the new proposals as 'experimental',[127] the enthusiasm with which it was embraced in both Houses of Parliament simply reflected its *ideological* appeal. It was seen as likely to be 'particularly valuable to the young offender'[128] because of its roots in young people's voluntary service and was especially appealing in a climate of opinion much concerned about adolescent crime and the need to make sanctions more appropriate to their changed social situation. Any measure which could appeal to a demand to make delinquent adolescents realize their responsibility to the community while at the same time being more punitive than probation was likely to prove popular, especially as much adolescent crime has been blamed upon the loss of respect for authority and lack of concern for 'the community'. The volunteer movement could be seen as providing shining examples of adolescent responsibility and concern, and it was hardly surprising that they should have been seen as a source of salvation for the 'irresponsible'. But as far as adults were concerned, the only group the Committee could put its finger on were those who were 'thought to be suffering from domestic isolation'.[129] It is difficult to imagine that the Committee thought that either the tasks themselves or the association with volunteers, young or old, could help overcome the multiple problems the older petty recidivist faced in terms of family and community relations, employment and income, housing and often chronic drinking.

[126] It has since, for example, been suggested that because offenders subject to community service will be at risk in the community, the scheme will have to prove *more* successful than prison: 'This is a risk which it is hoped the community will tolerate if its limits can be seen and the ultimate benefits of the system, *in terms of criminals made less delinquent*, demonstrated' [my italics]. See Report by the Inner London Probation and After-Care Service, *Community Service by Offenders*, January 1974.

However, after the Act had been passed, Lady Wootton suggested that the scheme could be expanded massively if 'it ever did turn out that the C.S.O. *was at least as successful* a treatment as imprisonment, judged by the rate of subsequent recidivism, for a substantial number of offenders' [my italics], in *Criminal Law Review*, 1973, 19–20.

[127] The Committee were very careful to emphasize the need for systematic study and the dangers of drawing premature conclusions. It is not clear what they had in mind, but in practice the scheme has been run on an 'experimental basis' only to the extent that it has been attempted to see whether it is 'workable' in practice. There has, to my knowledge, been no experimental evaluation (difficult as that is to accomplish) and plans are now afoot in 1974 to expand the scheme to a number of other areas.

[128] Op. cit., para. 38. For data on the importance attached to securing reparation from young offenders by various 'social control agents' in the community, see Stanley Cohen, *Folk Devils and Moral Panics*, London, MacGibbon & Kee, 1972, pp. 89–91.

[129] Loc. cit.

And such men, of course, form the bulk of the petty repeaters in the prison population. It seems to me that the Widgery report was right in saying: 'There seems little doubt that treatment of offenders along these lines could at best have only a limited application.'[130] The future will show whether it can have in the long run—after the initial impetus provided by the enthusiasm generated by the new scheme—more than a symbolic appeal.

From all these points of view, theoretical and empirical, it is hard to resist the conclusion that the deliberations of the Wootton Committee, which provided the justification for the introduction of an entirely new penal measure in the Criminal Justice Act, 1972, failed to provide a coherent and convincing criminological argument for its proposals. And this is not simply an indictment of its distinguished chairman and members, among them a number of notable criminologists, but rather of the method of approach and resources traditionally associated with government advisory bodies which at best can only lead to suggestions for unstructured 'experiments'. Without facilities for research and academic enquiry their conclusions and recommendations will probably remain a 'potpourri of intelligent suggestions': their acceptance or rejection will depend more upon their political appeal than their likelihood of making a major impact upon what is in danger of becoming an intractable problem: the provision of alternatives for that 'three quarters of the prison population' for whom a distinguished judge, not renowned for sentimentality, said 'loss of liberty is an inappropriate, useless and expensive sanction'.[131] Indeed, Lady Wootton herself, pointing to the ideological basis of the Victorian belief in hard work and the Edwardians' hope for the influence of the public school ideal, said, 'Now I am not sure whether we are at all clear what we are trying to do with people who are in custody'.[132] Her own recommendations are, I believe, as ideologically based as those of Ruggles-Brise and Alexander Paterson.[133] Indeed, the belief that expert advice based on criminological and penological research is the foundation for penal change, is only a screen behind which ideological and political factors, perhaps inevitably, shape those attitudes which imbue legislation.

---

[130] Widgery Report, para. 5, p. 2.

[131] Lord Justice Lawton, quoted by Lord Gardiner, *H.L. Debates*, Vol. 332, col. 594, 26 June 1972.

[132] *H.L. Debates*, Vol. 332, cols. 615–16, 26 June 1972.

[133] It is intriguing to note how much of a similarity there is between Paterson's idealism about 'service' and the Wootton ideas. See R. G. Hood, *Borstal Re-assessed*, op. cit., pp. 103–112.

Note

United States penal law is currently undergoing extensive and rapid revision. Florida, for example, has enacted a new penal code (FLA. LAWS 1974, CH. 74–383; effective 7/1/1975). Statements given in the following chapter respecting the various jurisdictions were accurate at the time of writing – January 1974.

THE MODEL PENAL CODE AND THE CODIFICATION OF AMERICAN CRIMINAL LAW

Herbert Wechsler

Introduction

Criminal law in the United States began on independence with reception of the English common law, which in the eighteenth century was both a crude and bloody system, fraught with technicality and using for its major sanctions only death and transportation—as Sir Leon Radzinowicz's *History* so brilliantly makes clear.[1] One might have thought the Age of Reason would have yielded an incentive to refurbish this inheritance but efforts of this kind were all abortive. Legislation did no more than fix the penalties for major crimes, happily reducing the number of the capital offences, but trusting to the common law for definitions and defences, not to speak of principles and doctrines measuring the scope of liability.

Attack upon this state of things was vigorous, as Perry Miller's posthumous volume so richly shows.[2] But neither Edward Livingston's draft code of 1824 nor that prepared in Massachusetts some two decades later was enacted. The lawyers glorified the common law and they prevailed. Almost half a century elapsed before a fresh assault was mounted in New York by David Dudly Field. His crusade for written law was not by any means a full success but one of his achievements was a penal code proposed in 1865 and passed in 1882. The draft was copied or adapted in a number of the western states, most notably in California. It was, however, less of an achievement than one might have hoped, for Field was poorly versed in penal law and little given to confront its basic problems. In this area he purported only to compile and rearrange existing statutes, with minor

---

[1] L. Radzinowicz, *A History of the English Criminal Law*, Vols. 1–4, London, Stevens, 1946–68. It does not depreciate Sir Leon's other contributions to say that this work of scholarship alone would merit the tribute of this volume.

[2] P. Miller, *The Life of the Mind in America*, New York, Harcourt, Brace & World, 1962, pp. 99 et seq.

additions that he thought restated common law. Even the systematic treatment he developed was abandoned in New York in later years in favour of an alphabetical arrangement, with bankers preceding barratry, bedding, bigamy and bribery as titles, as trespass followed treason and receiving followed rape. The code became a dictionary of the statutes, totally obscuring any sense of function, order or proportion in the norms that they declared.

This bare sketch must suffice to indicate why our burgeoning society entered this century without a coherent, rational articulation of the law on which men placed their ultimate reliance for protection against all the deepest injuries that human conduct can inflict on individuals and institutions, the law that also governs condemnation and disgrace and punishment, with all the suffering that they entail and their irreparable scars. Viewing the country as a whole, such penal statutes as we had were fragmentary, old, disorganized and often accidental in their coverage and content. They drew upon and were supplemented by common law concepts of uncertain meaning and were steadily augmented on an *ad hoc* basis by a multitude of most particular enactments, often inconsistent or redundant, responding to the pressures and excitements that arose from time to time.

There was ameliorative progress, to be sure, such as the introduction of probation and parole, but even such developments, important as they were, were most unevenly employed. They were, moreover, superimposed upon the corpus of the law and thus reflected in their scope and impact many o the arbitrary features of the underlying system.

Dissatisfaction with this situation was, of course, long-standing and intense. It played a major part in the deliberations leading in 1923 to the establishment of the American Law Institute as a permanent organization of judges, lawyers and academics devoted to the clarification and improvement of the law. That was a time much like our own when there was a widespread sense that the cement that holds society together was dissolving, as attested by the magnitude of disrespect for law. The merit of the Institute's proponents was that they were not content to denounce lawlessness to comfortable, applauding audiences[3] but were ready to assume the burden of so nurturing the law that it should become worthy of respect, even by those least attuned to its necessities and its commands.

It was natural that penal law should have a high place on the Institute's agenda when its work began. Initial efforts led, however, to the obvious conclusion that the method of restatement that the Institute was using in attempting to bring clarity and order to fields largely governed by the common law—contracts, torts, agency, trusts, property and the like—could

[3] See, e.g., F. B. Smith (ed.), *Law Versus Lawlessness*, New York, Fleming H. Revell Co., 1924, *passim*.

not be used effectively in dealing with the law of crime. Its statutory content was too large and too uneven for such treatment and the need, in any case, was less for a description and reaffirmation of existing law than for a guide to long-delayed reform. A second proposal calling for the formulation of a model code was, accordingly, advanced in 1931. The prospectus for the project called, however, for empirical investigations too elaborate and expensive to be financed in depression years. Hence, notwithstanding strong support from President Roosevelt, the undertaking was abortive. A second effort, which began in 1950, did obtain the generous assistance of the Rockefeller Foundation. A large Advisory Committee was established, drawn from all the many disciplines concerned with understanding and dealing with problems of crime and penal law administration, and work on the planning and the drafting of the Code began in 1952.[4]

In the succeeding ten years there were numerous meetings of Advisers, usually lasting for three days, at which basic issues of policy were debated and resolved, studies and drafts prepared by the Reporters or Consultants were considered and revised, criticisms of the tentative drafts examined and reviewed, and the entire work subjected to a final critical revision. The product of the Reporters and Advisers was in turn considered by the Council in some thirty-one Council Drafts examined and debated in the years from 1953 to 1962. After consideration and revision or approval by the Council, the material with supporting commentary was put before successive meetings of the Institute in Tentative Drafts numbered 1 to 13, followed by a Proposed Final Draft dealing with sentence and correction submitted in 1961, and the Proposed Official Draft of 1962, which both supplemented the previous submissions and reflected all the changes made in the revision of the drafts of prior years.

This critical evaluation carried on within the Institute was supplemented by extensive consideration of the published tentative drafts by interested groups and individuals, whose views were given weight in the revision. Such criticism was particularly valuable with respect to the correctional provisions, which were discussed with representatives of organizations interested in these problems[5] and at numerous meetings of the Congress of Correction,[6] leading to important changes in the drafts.[7]

---

[4] On the background of the project and the initial concept of its scope and possibilities, see H. Wechsler, 'The Challenge of a Model Penal Code', *Harv. L. Rev.*, 1952, **65**, 1097.

[5] The most significant of these discussions was a meeting with representatives of the Advisory Council of Judges and the Advisory Council on Parole of the National Probation and Parole Association (now National Council on Crime and Delinquency) and of the American Correctional Association on December 21 and 22, 1956. A transcript of the session is on file at the Philadelphia office of the American Law Institute.

[6] See, e.g., *American Prison Association, Proceedings*, 1952, **125**; *American Correctional*

Not everyone involved in this extensive process was, of course, content with the positions taken upon all the major points, not to speak of matters of detail. There were propositions on which the Reporters were unable to convince the Advisers or the Council or the Institute and issues on which these distinguished bodies were divided or in conflict with one another. Viewing the product as a whole, it is, however, fair to say that a remarkable approach to a consensus was achieved. The Code the Institute approved in 1962 by the concurrent votes of the Council and of the members in attendance at the Annual Meeting is thus the work of many heads and many hands, the stronger for the fact that it reflects collective judgement of this kind.

Writing in 1955, I undertook to state the object and approach of the Institute as follows:

> We are attempting to think through the problems of the law that governs the determination of what conduct constitutes a crime—at least within the major areas of criminality—and also governs what is done or may be done with the offender. In thinking through these problems we are seeking all the help that we can get. We look for legal wisdom—a quality that we believe to be both real and relevant—for we are dealing after all with law. We also look, however, for the knowledge, insight and experience offered by the other disciplines and occupations concerned with crime and its prevention. Armed with collaboration of this order, we mean to act as if we were a legislative commission, charged with construction of an ideal penal code—properly regardful of realities but free, as legislative commissions rarely are, to take account of long-range values as distinguished from immediate political demands.[8]

Viewing these words in retrospect, I am content with their description of the effort. Whether or how far it is reflected in the product, I shall not attempt to judge.

It should be noted, however, that it was not the purpose of the Institute to achieve uniformity in penal law throughout the nation, since it was deemed inevitable that substantial differences of social situation or of point of view among the states should be reflected in substantial variation in their penal laws. The hope was rather that the model would stimulate and facilitate the systematic re-examination of the subject needed to assure that the prevailing law does truly represent the mature sentiment of our respective jurisdictions, sentiment formed after a fresh appraisal of the problems and their possible solutions. Of course, the Institute was not without ambition that in such an enterprise the model might seem worthy of adoption or, at

---

Association, Proceedings, 1956, 114, 257, 348; 1958, 11, 314; 1960, 57.

[7] See, e.g., S. Bates, 'Treatment and Correction of Criminals as Proposed by the Model Penal Code', *Notre Dame Law,* 1964, **39,** 288.

[8] H. Wechsler, 'A Thoughtful Code of Substantive Law', *J. Crim. L. Criminol. & Pol. Sci.,* 1955, **45,** 524, 525.

least, of adaptation. It coupled that ambition with the recognition that legislators working with the model might well find it unacceptable on given points and helpful upon others. It also recognized that much useful legislative work is addressed to particular problems of the penal law rather than to general revision, and wished the Code to be of aid, so far as possible, in undertakings of this kind.

These goals have been achieved to a significant extent. Revision work was started in a number of the states even as the Institute began its work, producing new codes in Wisconsin in 1956, Illinois in 1961, Minnesota and New Mexico in 1963. A major undertaking in New York was authorized in 1961, resulting in the present Penal Law enacted in 1965 and effective in 1967. New codes were passed in Georgia in 1968, Connecticut and Kansas in 1969, Colorado, Idaho,[9] New Hampshire and Oregon in 1971, and in Delaware, Hawaii, Kentucky, Montana, North Dakota, Ohio, Pennsylvania, Texas and Utah within the past year. Completed codes are pending in the legislatures of thirteen other states and in Puerto Rico, with work in progress at one stage or another in ten additional states, work contemplated in three more, and only three with no plans for revision at this time.[10] Finally, and certainly not least important, Congress in 1966 established a National Commission to re-examine the federal criminal law and propose a full reformulation in an integrated code. That work is now completed and the Report of

[9] The Idaho Penal and Correctional Code was effective 1 January 1972. Opposition that was silent in the process of enactment succeeded, however, in obtaining its repeal as of 1 April. See D. G. Stone and T. L. Hall, 'The Model Penal Code in Idaho?', *Idaho L. Rev.,* 1972, **8,** 219.

[10] The codes and drafts referred to in the text are listed in the Appendix, *infra* pp. 466-8. The largest collection of this material in Europe is in the Radzinowicz Library of the Cambridge Institute of Criminology.

For discussion of particular enactments or proposals, see, e.g., 'Symposium on the Proposed California Criminal Code', *U.C.L.A. L. Rev.,* 1972, 525; 'Symposium, The Proposed Ohio Criminal Code', *Ohio St. L. J.,* 1972, 351; 'Oregon Criminal Code', *Ore L. Rev.,* 1972, **51,** 427; 'Symposium, The Revised Washington Criminal Code', *Wash. L. Rev.,* 1972, **48,** 1; Bowman, 'The Illinois Criminal Code of 1961 and Code of Criminal Procedure of 1963', *J.L. Reform,* 1971, **4,** 461; Baldwin, 'Criminal Law Revision in Delaware and Hawaii', ibid., 1971, 476; Lawson, 'Criminal Law Revision in Kentucky', *Ky. L.J.,* 1969-70, **58,** 242 and 695; 'Symposium on Revised New York Penal Law', *Buffalo L. Rev.,* 1968-9, **18,** 213; 'Symposium on the New Kentucky Penal Code', *Ky. L.J.,* 1972-3, **61,** 620-7292; 'Symposium—Proposed Missouri Criminal Code', *Mo. L. Rev.,* 1973, 361-430, 549-611; S. J. Fox, 'The Proposed Criminal Code for New Hampshire', *N.H.B.J.,* 1969, **11,** 262; 'Symposium on the Proposed Michigan Revised Criminal Code', *Wayne L. Rev.,* 1968, **14,** 772; W. P. Keeton and W. G. Reid, 'Proposed Revision of the Texas Penal Code', *Texas L. Rev.,* 1967, **45,** 399; F. Cohen, 'Reflections on the Revision of the Texas Penal Code', ibid., 1967, 413; Note, 'The Proposed Penal Law of New York', *Colum. L. Rev.,* 1964, **64,** 1469. See also P. E. Wilson, 'State Criminal Law Revision', *Am. Crim. L.Q.,* 1965, **3,** 198.

the Commission is before the Judiciary Committees of the Congress.[11] Hearings have been held which thus far consume some seven published volumes; bills have been introduced in both Houses based in some measure on the Commission's draft;[12] and the President has also submitted a draft code prepared in the Department of Justice.[13]

This is the magnitude of the recent and current legislative interest in criminal law codification in the United States. It is a movement that has gathered strength without a pre-commitment to particular reforms. Its impetus has been essentially a moral sentiment, the need for reassurance that when so much is at stake for the community and for the individual, care has been taken to make law as rational and just as law can be. The enactments and drafts, with their supporting commentaries,[14] are indeed creating a new literature of the substantive criminal law—viewed from the aspect of its legislative policy—that is comparable and in some respects superior to that developed in connection with the continental codes.

It is true, of course, that the new codes adopted and proposed are far from univocal in their scope and content; they by no means always follow the submissions of the Model Code. There are respects in which improvements on the model have been made, as there are instances in which its insights were rejected or ignored.[15] Georgia, Kansas, Minnesota and New Mexico were content with much less ambitious efforts than, for example, Delaware, Hawaii, New York, Pennsylvania and Utah or the drafts in Massachusetts, Michigan and New Jersey. What is important is, however, that the legislative process has at long last made explicit effort to determine the content of the penal law, the prohibitions it lays down, the excuses it admits, the sanctions it employs, and the range of the authority that it confers, by a contemporary

---

[11] *Final Report of the National Commission on Reform of Federal Criminal Laws* (1971). See E. G. Brown and L. B. Schwartz, 'New Federal Criminal Code', *A.B.A.J.,* 1970, **56**, 844, 935, 1181; J. L. McClellan, 'Codification, Reform and Revision: The Challenge of a Modern Federal Criminal Code', *Duke L.J.,* 1971, 663, summarized in 'The Challenge of a Modern Federal Criminal Code', *A.B.A.J.,* 1971, **57**, 585.

[12] The only bill that embodies the Commission draft as such is H.R. 10047, 93d Cong., 1st Sess. The Senate Committee's hearings have been focused primarily on S. 1, 93d Cong., 1st Sess., which embodies a revision of the Commission draft prepared by the Committee's staff.

[13] S. 1400, H.R. 6046, 93d Cong., 1st Sess. For a careful analysis of the important differences among the Commission draft, S. 1 and S. 1400, see L. B. Schwartz, 'The Proposed Federal Criminal Code', *Crim. L. Rep.,* 4 July 1973, **13**, 3265.

[14] The jurisdictions in which the code proposals were accompanied by substantial commentary are indicated in the Appendix, *infra* pp. 466–8.

[15] On the practical difficulties of the process of revision, especially on controversial issues, see, e.g., A. H. Sherry, 'Criminal Law Revision in California', *J.L. Reform.,* 1971, **4**, 429; 'The Politics of Criminal Law Reform: The United States', *Am. J. Comp. L.,* 1973, **21**, 201; S. J. Fox, 'Reflection on the Law Reforming Process', *J.L. Reform.,* 1971, **4**, 443.

reasoned judgement. It is as if there had been a concerted judgement in this field to heed Lord Radcliffe's counsel that 'every system of jurisprudence needs . . . a constant preoccupation with the task of relating its rules and principles to the fundamental moral assumptions of the society to which it belongs'.[16]

It should be added that the Institute was right in thinking that the model might be useful in relation to specific problems, quite apart from its utility to codifiers working on a general revision. Individual provisions of the Code, such as those relating to jurisdiction, double jeopardy, responsibility, attempts, abortion and obscenity have been enacted separately and there has been a gratifying use of the material by courts in areas where they have felt some freedom to restate or reshape important concepts, rules and doctrines.

The uniformities and variations in this massive legislative and judicial product would require a large volume to expound. The process of re-assessment has, however, often—if not usually—been attended by consideration of the formulations of the Model Penal Code. It will, accordingly, serve as an introduction to the whole development to turn to the model and its treatment of important legislative issues, noting insofar as feasible the influence that it has had. That is the course that will be followed here.[17]

Plan and Scope of the Model Penal Code

Pursuant to a decision taken early in the work, the Code was organized into four main parts: (I) General Provisions; (II) Definition of Specific Crimes; (III) Treatment and Correction; and (IV) Organization of Correction.

Part I is devoted to provisions that are general in the sense that they apply whatever the specific crime that is involved. The effort here was to exhaust the possibilities of useful generalization about the use of penal sanctions, going far beyond the fragmentary formulations found in penal codes drafted in the Anglo-American tradition and even beyond the more extensive statements of the newer European codes.

Thus, in addition to dealing with such problems as jurisdiction, limitations and double jeopardy, the Code attempts a full articulation of the basic principles that govern the existence and the scope of liability. These include the mental elements of culpability; causality; strict liability; complicity; the

[16] C. J. Radcliffe, *The Law and Its Compass,* Evanstone, Illinois, Northwestern University Press, 1960, pp. 63–4.

[17] The discussion of the model in the succeeding portion of this paper draws heavily on my report to the Third National Conference on Research and Teaching in Criminology held by the Institute of Criminology, 3–7 July 1968, published as 'Codification of Criminal Law in the United States: The Model Penal Code', *Column. L. Rev.,* 1968, **68,** 1425.

criminal liability of corporations and associations; the defences that negate *mens rea* or otherwise remove the moral basis of conviction; the justifications recognized for conduct that would otherwise be criminal; and the effect on responsibility of mental disease or defect and of youth. It also deals in comprehensive terms with the general inchoate crimes, that is, attempts, solicitation and conspiracy to commit substantive offences, as well as the possession of the instruments of crime and prohibited offensive weapons. Finally, it undertakes to specify the types of disposition authorized upon conviction, to define the court's authority in sentencing and to prescribe criteria to be considered in imposing sentences of different kinds, especially a sentence of imprisonment.

It may be useful to note here that the length of the prison sentences that may be passed depends on (1) the classification of the offence of conviction among the three degrees (or categories) of major crimes, for which the name of felony has been retained, and two degrees of misdemeanour; and (2) a distinction between ordinary and extended terms, the latter being reserved for recidivists, professional criminals, certain psychiatric categories and offenders who commit a multiplicity of crimes for which the sentences would otherwise be cumulated. This classificatory scheme has vital bearing on the definitions of specific crimes, since they not only mark the bounds of criminality but also differentiate among offences or degrees thereof, in terms of a legislative judgement of their gravity. How many such distinctions should be drawn, based on the nature, circumstances or results of criminal conduct, is a question to be faced in any system before the definitions of specific crimes are drawn. Those definitions will be narrower or broader, as the case may be, depending on the number of discriminations to be made. In the Code scheme it was regarded as sufficient to distinguish between major crime and minor criminality and to draw only three distinctions among major crimes. Part II was drafted in the light of this conclusion.

Part II does not purport to be exhaustive in its definition of specific crimes. Some special topics such as narcotics, motor vehicles, alcoholic beverage control, gambling offences and offences against trade and tax laws were omitted, either due to lack of time or in the view that they are better treated in a regulatory statute placed outside the penal code. There is, however, a full treatment of (1) offences involving injury or danger to the person, such as homicide, assault, bodily injury, reckless endangering, threats, kidnapping, false imprisonment and criminal coercion; (2) the sexual offences; (3) the major offences against property, including arson, criminal mischief, burglary, robbery, theft, forgery and fraudulent practices; (4) offences against the family, such as bigamy, incest, abortion, endangering child welfare and persistent non-support; (5) offences against public administration, including bribery, corrupt influence, perjury and other falsifications, obstructions of governmental operations and abuse of office; and (6) offences against public order and decency, including riot, disorderly conduct, public drunkenness, crimes of desecration, violation of privacy, lewdness, prostitution and obscenity. In totality, this is, of course, most of the proper conduct content of a penal code, as distinguished from the vast corpus of the regulatory legislation that, insofar as it employs a criminal sanction, should normally be governed by the general provisions of the Code but will be better classified or codified in other contexts.

In Part III each of the methods of treatment and correction authorized in dealing with offenders is treated in detail, with a view to their legal regulation, to the extent that it was deemed appropriate to prescribe legislative norms. The topics thus included are: suspension of sentence and probation, including revocation and resentence; fines and their collection; short-term imprisonment, including work release; long-term imprisonment (meaning terms in excess of one year); release on parole (which in the case of long-term sentence would be mandatory on a first release of any prisoner), including the term of a conditional release and consequences of its revocation; and, lastly, the loss of rights incident to conviction or imprisonment and their subsequent restoration.

Part IV is addressed to the organization of the public services involved in the administration of the system of correction. It contemplates the establishment of an integrated Department of Correction responsible for the administration of the state correctional institutions as well as for parole and certain aspects of probation. Institutional commitments would be to the custody of the Department, not to a specific institution as is the case at present in many states. The classification, distribution and transfer of inmates among state facilities would thus be in administrative hands. The obligation to define and provide a suitable corrective programme is articulated, the rights of prisoners are to some extent defined, responsibility for training personnel and for maintaining operational research is allocated and powers of visitation over local institutions are conferred. The adjudicative aspects of parole, i.e., the timing of release and the decision to discharge or to revoke, are made the function of an independent Board in the Department, with a separate Young Adult Division designated by the Board. All first releases from state institutions would, moreover, be upon parole, with power in the Board to terminate supervision or grant absolute discharge at any time. Where prior law commits release decisions to the absolute discretion of parole authorities once legal eligibility arrives, the Code prescribes criteria to guide the judgement of the Board, though its decisions are still insulated from judicial review.

Developing a model framework for administration of correction was in many ways the hardest task attempted by the Code, given the variety of our administrative structures, the distribution of authority between the state and local governments and the immense unevenness in institutional and other correctional services throughout the country. But recognizing that the model necessarily requires adaptation before it is put to use in any given jurisdiction, the Code goes far towards setting forth the standards that the best of our correctional administrators have articulated during recent years.[18] Those standards can and ought to be reflected in prevailing legislation far more generally than they are.

As the foregoing summary makes clear, it is an integral and vitally important object of the Code to view the substantive problems of criminal law, i.e. the wise delineation of the conduct that is declared to be criminal, and the problems of sanctions and penology, i.e., the wise determination of the treatment of offenders on conviction, as analytically separable for some purposes but ultimately closely intertwined. It accepts 'as basic' Sir Leon's proposition that the 'connection between criminology and criminal law is fundamental and inescapable'.[19] Sound judgement in determining the elements and scope of liability or the definition and gradation of offences presupposes a concern about the consequences of those judgements when applied. By the same token, useful thought about the problems of correction presupposes a concern that the indicia by which it is determined that an individual presents a problem of this order reflect valid social policy. The aim of the whole process, after all, is to define and within reasonable limits to enforce what Professor Henry M. Hart aptly called 'those minimum obligations of conduct which the conditions of community life impose upon every participating member if community life is to be maintained and to prosper'.[20]

The tension in existing systems, when inconsistent premises have been embraced in different aspects of the process, shows the need for their revaluation in these unifying terms.

It is not possible in a paper of reasonable length to render a full statement of the content of the four parts of the model, which comprise a volume that, with its short background notes, runs to 346 pages. I must content myself, therefore, with presentation of the Code's position on a number of the basic issues that arise in any legislative effort to give fresh articulation to a system

[18] See *American Correctional Association, A Manual of Correctional Standards* (1966), 3rd ed.; S. Bates, op. cit., *supra*, note 7.

[19] L. Radzinowicz, *The Need for Criminology*, London, Heinemann Educational Books, 1965, p. 33.

[20] H. M. Hart, 'The Aims of the Criminal Law', *Law & Contemp. Prob.*, 1958, **23**, 401, 413.

of criminal law. Those positions will afford an indication of the animating concepts of the effort and the progress I believe to have been made.

The Purposes of Criminal Law and the Requirements of Justice

A. *The Purposes of Criminal Law*

It should be said *in limine* that while the Model Code declares a dominant preventive purpose in its statement of objectives,[21] it offers no extraordinary remedies to meet the mounting incidence of many common crimes reported generally in the country. The Code sponsors would, indeed, deny that penal law presents the possibility of any major breakthrough of this kind, within the framework of the values we affirm. There are provisions in the model, like the use of the extended term, that have a certain relevancy to the crime preventive effect of the system as a whole; but the results of this or any other dispositions will depend in the long run on the resources our nation is prepared to use in the elaboration and development of genuine corrective programmes. In the past few years, priority in allocation of resources has been given to police, including the enlargement of the forces and improvement in their training and equipment, and to the broad social programme in the cities. Attention is now turning to the courts. Correction has been badly slighted in the past and, notwithstanding current protest, it is likely to be slighted in the future.[22]

To say this is not, however, to depreciate the practical and theoretical importance of the dominant preventive purpose of the Code. That purpose has important implications in determining the scope of criminality as well as in the sentencing and treatment of offenders.

The implication for defining criminality is that the Code confines its

---

[21] § 1.02. Here and hereafter section citations of the Model Penal Code are to Proposed Official Draft (1962).

[22] For recent influential protest by Chief Justice Warren E. Burger, see, 'No Man Is an Island', *A.B.A.J.*, 1970, **56**, 325; 'Our Options Are Limited', *Vill. L. Rev.*, 1972, **18**, 165. See also, e.g., *President's Commission on Law Enforcement and Administration of Justice, The Challenge of Crime in a Free Society*, 1967, p. 183; *National Advisory Commission on Criminal Justice Standards and Goals, A National Strategy to Reduce Crime* (1973), p. 173.

Federal financial aid for state criminal justice programmes, authorized by Congress in 1968, has been increasing steadily. It totalled $529 million in fiscal 1971 with $177·6 million reported to be allocated to correction. In fiscal 1973, the total authorized was $750 million with correction receiving some 35 per cent. See L. E. Ohlin (ed.), *Prisoners in America* (American Assembly, 1973), p. 7; *Federal Law Enforcement & Criminal Justice Assistance Activities, Attorney General's First Annual Report* (1972), p. 113. This finding could, of course, begin to make a difference in the situation.

prohibitions to conduct that can usefully be made a target of preventive effort, given the potentialities and limitations of the sanctions that the penal law provides; and that the penal law should not be used merely to express the pious sentiment of the community. Unless conduct 'unjustifiably and inexcusably inflicts or threatens substantial harm to individual or public interests',[23] it is not deemed to be a proper subject of a penal prohibition— a declaration designed to be given weight in the interpretation of the Code. The principle is given legislative application in significant delimitations of the scope of penal law, achieved in some part by the general provisions and more directly by the definitions of offences, especially in such familiar areas as conspiracy, compounding, sexual misconduct, abortion, obscenity and disorderly conduct.[24]

With respect to sentencing and treatment, the Code's preventive purpose necessarily excludes dispositions motivated by merely vindictive or retributive considerations or determined by routine tariffs of the sort some courts employ. It is, however, recognized that the threat and imposition of a penal sanction may advance preventive ends in different ways—by fortifying normal instincts to refrain from substantially injurious behaviour, by deterrence both general and special, by incapacitating persons who are dangerously disposed to engage in criminal conduct and by correcting those who have such disposition. The Code does not attempt to state a general priority among these goals of dispositions, all of which are means to crime prevention. It proceeds rather in the view that when these values are in conflict, as they often are, what is demanded is a viable accommodation.

To state the point in more detail, the Code assumes that when the legislature makes conduct criminal, its purpose is that those who are convicted of defiance of the prohibition should be dealt with by a disposition that does not depreciate the gravity of the offence and thus imply a licence to commit it. This minimal objective presupposes that the impact of a sentence upon others, and not only its effect on the defendant, will be given proper weight in passing sentence following conviction. In many cases, to be

---

[23] § 1.02(1) (a).

[24] See, e.g., L. B. Schwartz, 'Morals, Offenses and the Model Penal Code', *Colum. L. Rev.,* 1963, **63,** 699; 'The Model Penal Code: An Invitation to Law Reform', *A.B.A.J.,* 1963, **49,** 447.

The model does not present submissions in the important areas of narcotics and gambling, to which the quoted principle would arguably have important application. See, e.g., H. L. Packer, *The Limits of the Criminal Sanction,* Stanford, Cal., Stanford Univ. Press, 1969, pp. 296, 332; S. H. Kadish, 'The Crisis of Overcriminalization', *Annals Amer. Acad. Pol. & Soc. Sci.,* 1967, **374,** 157. Professor Packer's criticism of the omission ('Criminal Code Revision', *U. Toronto L.J.,* [1973], **23,** 1, 12) takes no account of the specialized attention being given to these topics by other professional and official bodies at the time.

sure, the formal condemnation that is normally implicit in conviction will achieve this purpose, with the consequence that the tribunal can concern itself primarily with the offender in determining the disposition to be made. In other cases there may be small danger that the individual will be disposed or able to repeat the crime but a substantial deprivation may be thought essential if the legislative prohibition is to carry reasonable force. Still others may present a situation where the offence is of such minor moment that the use of any major sanction would be patently oppressive, however adverse the offender's record, and would distort the scale of values that the law endeavours to maintain.

This is, of course, to view the problem at the time of the initial disposition. If that results in institutional commitment, or even in an order of probation, the correctional authorities must be expected and encouraged to emphasize the rehabilitative goal while working within the framework of the sentence, including, most importantly, the nature and duration of the restraint that it involves. This argues for a prudent limitation on how much may be conclusively determined at the time when the offender is committed to the organs of correction. If decisions of importance are reserved for later times, there may be room for some reordering of values; there will, at least, be different data and experience to guide the choices to be made.

These general considerations are reflected in the Code provisions with respect to sentencing and treatment, especially the broad discretion to forego a sentence of imprisonment and the criteria for such determinations;[25] the nature and extent of indeterminacy of the duration of an institutional commitment, whether for an ordinary or extended term;[26] the requirement that all long-term prisoners have first releases on parole;[27] and the criteria for the decision to release.[28]

I shall return to these provisions later.[29] It suffices to say here that the Code's approach to dealing with offenders differs from that sketched in Baroness Wootton's Hamlyn Lecture[30] mainly in demanding that the sentencer devote more attention than she seems to contemplate to the impact of a sentence upon others in addition to the factor she most emphasizes, its influence upon the future conduct of the individual defendant. The Code does not, however, put this as a scientific question, recognizing the uncertainties involved. It goes no further than to justify

[25] §§ 6.02, 7.01.
[26] §§ 6.05, 6.06, 6.07, 6.09.
[27] § 6.10.
[28] § 305.9.
[29] See pp. 458–66, *infra*.
[30] 'Sentencing Policy in a Preventive System' in B. Wootton, *Crime and the Criminal Law*, London, Stevens, 1963, pp. 91 et seq.

a judgement that imprisonment of an offender may be necessary for protection of the public because 'a lesser sentence will depreciate the seriousness' of his crime; and to acknowledge that the release of a prisoner who otherwise is eligible for parole may legitimately be postponed upon such grounds.[31] No system that precluded some such judgement—granting how far it is matter of opinion—could maintain for long the norms that it prescribes. That legislators take this view in the United States is very clear and universally reflected in the current codes and drafts.

B. *The Requirements of Justice*

Preventive purpose notwithstanding, it is the distinctive feature of the penal law that it condemns offenders as wrongdoers, marshalling the formal censure of conviction and coercive sanctions on this ground. This is not a feature of the system that is open to manipulation or can really be re-structured in our time. Even if restructuring were possible, its wisdom would assuredly be doubtful, given the extent of deprivation that the sanctions may entail. When censure or deprivations of this kind are not required, cases can be dealt with, as so commonly they are, by other social agencies.[32] The penal law is, in a sense, a last resort precisely for the reason that it operates by condemnation and correction. There is a qualitative difference between criminal conviction and compulsion to attend a school or even an involuntary hospital commitment. To maintain that difference is important both for penal law and for the social programme. This point of view is strongly embraced by the Model Penal Code.

Preventive purpose does not, therefore, insulate the penal law from the demands of justice with respect to allocating blame and punishment, as those demands have been conceived and rationalized for so long in our culture. If fault is to be found with human conduct because it is offensive in its nature, potentialities or consequences, it surely is essential that the actor knew or should have known the facts that give it this offensive character. Unless that much can be affirmed, how can it possibly be judged that he should not have acted as he did? History, as has been said, shows little tolerance of reasonable judgements that have turned out to be wrong, but those whom it condemns have passed away. The law deals with the living and must exercise a greater circumspection.

[31] §§ 7.01, 305.9.

[32] For comment on such diversion from the criminal process, see, e.g., *President's Commission on Law Enforcement and the Administration of Justice, The Challenge of Crime in a Free Society* (1967), p. 133; *Task Force Report: The Courts* (1967), p. 4; E. and J. Vorenberg, 'Early Diversion from the Criminal Justice System, Practice in Search of a Theory', in L. E. Ohlin (ed.), *Prisoners in America*, op. cit., p. 151; *National Advisory Commission on Criminal Justice Standards and Goals, Task Force Report on Courts* (1973), p. 27.

Criminal law cannot, accordingly, escape the task of recognizing and defining the essential mental elements of culpability, including the defences that negate them; nor can it ignore mental factors in determining the gravity of different crimes. It has, of course, been urged that there should be totally objective definition of offences, presumably in terms of the evil actually caused or threatened by behaviour, giving weight to the subjective situation only in connection with the disposition to be made of the defendant. The Institute Advisers spent much time on this submission before recommending its rejection, on the ground that it ignores the distinctive nature of the penal law both as it is and as it ought to be.

What is involved is not only that this conception would deny all moral force to the proscriptions of criminal law and generate in individuals a sense of gross injustice. The law promotes the general security by building confidence that those whose conduct does not warrant condemnation will not be convicted of a crime. This is a value of enormous moment in a free society. It is in jeopardy when that assurance is withdrawn. The tendency of present thought in the United States is to consider this so fundamental that criminal liability without regard to culpability would raise the gravest constitutional question, at least if major sanctions are involved.[33]

The Mental Element in Crime :
Criteria of Culpability and Responsibility

The underlying concepts summarized above are reflected in the general provisions of the Code, especially those dealing with the significance to be accorded to the actor's state of mind in determining criminal liability. The Model's treatment of *mens rea* and responsibility has exerted a pervasive influence upon the current formulations. Its restatement is, accordingly, in order here.

1. *Mens Rea and the Modes of Culpability.* In America, as in England, the statutes and decisions have employed a plethora of *mens rea* terms both in defining crimes and in the grading of offences. Words and phrases like 'general' and 'specific' intent, 'malice', 'scienter', 'wilful', 'reckless', 'negligence', 'wanton recklessness or negligence', 'wilful, wanton negligence', 'criminal negligence', 'corruptly', 'feloniously', and the like, illustrate what Mr. Justice Jackson in a famous Supreme Court opinion called 'the variety, disparity and confusion' of 'definitions of the requisite but elusive mental

---

[33] Cf. *Robinson* v. *California*, 370 U.S. 660 (1962); *Powell* v. *Texas*, 392 U.S. 514 (1968); see H. L. Packer, 'Mens Rea and the Supreme Court', *Supreme Court Review* (1962), 107.

element'.[34] Systematic study of the federal criminal law disclosed, for example, some 78 different words and combinations of words used to denote how far subjective factors are encompassed in the conduct sought to be proscribed.[35]

There is no conceivable justification for this profusion of terms to describe or differentiate among the mental states that are potentially significant in penal law and it has been a standing grievance that the verbiage has confounded juries and perplexed the courts. Even the most innocent appearing 'wilful' has had such contrariety of interpretation that Judge Learned Hand was led to say: 'If I were to have the index purged, "wilful" would lead the rest in spite of its being at the end of the alphabet.'[36] Clarification plainly was essential and was undertaken systematically in the Code, in terms that are reflected very widely in the legislation since enacted[37] or in draft.

The Model begins[38] by classifying the material objective elements of crimes as involving either the nature of the actor's conduct (shooting a gun, driving a car, writing a cheque, etc.) or the attendant circumstances (e.g., a crowded street, an empty bank account) or a result of conduct (e.g., causing death, injury or deception). The problem of the mental element arises obviously with respect to each of the objective elements that give the actor's conduct its offensive quality (or negative a defence that would otherwise obtain) and are included for that reason in the definition of the crime.

Starting with the explicit declaration that 'a person is not guilty of an offense unless his liability is based on conduct which includes a voluntary act or the omission to perform an act of which he is physically capable', the Code proceeds to exclude from the category of voluntary acts a reflex or convulsion, movements during unconsciousness or sleep, conduct during hypnosis or resulting from hypnotic suggestion and, finally, any 'movement that otherwise is not a product of the effort or determination of the actor, either conscious or habitual'. Possession is declared to be an act only if 'the possessor knowingly procured or received the thing possessed or was aware of his control thereof for a sufficient period to have been able to terminate his possession'.[39]

[34] *Morissette* v. *United States*, 342 U.S. 246, 252 (1952).

[35] *National Commission on Reform of Federal Criminal Laws, Working Papers*, Vol. 1 (1970), pp. 119–20.

[36] *A.L.I., 32d Annual Meeting, Proceedings* (1955) (unpublished), quoted in H. F. Goodrich, 'Two Great Men', *A.L.I., 39th Annual Meeting, Proceedings* (1962), p. 523.

[37] The new codes in which the model formulations were adopted or adapted very closely are those in Colorado, Connecticut, Delaware, Hawaii, Illinois, Kentucky, Montana, New Hampshire, New York, North Dakota, Ohio, Oregon, Pennsylvania, Texas and Utah. See Appendix, *infra* p. 467.

[38] § 1.13(9), (10).

[39] § 2.01.

It is important to observe that the formulation demands only that liability be based on conduct that *includes* the voluntary act or the omission but it need not be based on the act or omission alone. If the driver of a car loses consciousness with the result that the car kills a pedestrian, none of the movements or omissions that occur during unconsciousness may themselves give rise to liability. If liability is imposed, it must be attributed to prior voluntary action or a prior omission included in the course of conduct culminating in the homicide, such as the act of driving or the failure to stop when the driver felt that illness was approaching. The further elements of culpability, discussed below, must have been present at that time. If they were, the liability may be established notwithstanding the fact that the fatal loss of control was due to the later loss of consciousness.

The definition of the further elements of culpability was one of the hardest drafting problems in the framing of the Code. The solution advanced proceeds on the premise that for purposes of liability (as distinguished from sentence) only four concepts are needed to prescribe the minimal requirements and lay the basis for distinctions that can usefully be drawn. These concepts are purpose, knowledge, recklessness and negligence. The minimal statement is that one may not be convicted of a crime 'unless he acted purposely, knowingly, recklessly or negligently, as the law may require, with respect to each material element of the offense'.[40] This way of putting the matter acknowledges that the required mode of culpability may not only vary from crime to crime but also from one to another element of the same offence—meaning, it will be recalled, by material element an attribute of conduct that gives it its offensive quality—including attendant circumstances that negative a defence. In murder, for example, the law may require proof that the defendant killed purposely or knowingly, demanding that degree of culpability with respect to the result element of the offence: the homicide. But if self-defence is claimed in exculpation, it has frequently been held sufficient for conviction that the actor's belief in his peril did not rest on reasonable grounds. When that is so, negligence is all the law requires with respect to the existence of the attendant circumstances negativing that defence—which it is useful in this context to treat as an element of the crime.

One of the virtues of this method of articulation is, of course, that it invites attention to the wisdom of such stark distinctions as to culpability respecting different elements of an offence. The Code makes some attempt to promote uniformity upon the issue by providing that when 'the law defining an offense prescribes the kind of culpability that is sufficient', without 'distinguishing among the material elements thereof, such provision

[40] § 2.02(1).

shall apply to all the material elements of the offence, unless a contrary purpose plainly appears'.[41] It also states what is believed to be the common law position that when 'the culpability sufficient to establish a material element of an offense is not prescribed by law, such element is established if a person acts purposely, knowingly or recklessly with respect thereto'.[42] The legislature when it defines specific crimes may thus draw such distinctions among crimes or elements thereof as it deems wise; but if it fails to make explicit judgements of this kind, the Code prescribes the norms that shall prevail.

The basic culpability conceptions are, of course, defined.[43] The discrimination between acting purposely and knowingly is very narrow.[44] Knowledge that the requisite external, attendant circumstances exist is a common element in both conceptions. But action is not deemed purposive with respect to the nature or results of an actor's conduct unless, as the Code puts it, 'it was his conscious object to engage in conduct of that nature or to cause such a result'.[45] Though acting knowingly suffices to establish liability for most offences, there are situations where our law has deemed it proper to require purpose; for example, treason and crimes of subversive speech, solicitation, complicity, attempts, conspiracy, and probably obtaining property by false pretences. The Code formulations on these subjects so provide. Moreover, in determining the gravity of crimes for purposes of sentence, it is often useful to lay stress on purpose. This is frequently the case under the older law as well as in the Code.

Recklessness, as the Code employs the term,[46] involves conscious risk creation. It resembles acting knowingly in that a state of awareness is involved, but the awareness is of risk, short of practical certainty with respect to a result[47] or of high probability with respect to existence of a fact.[48] The

[41] § 2.02(4).

[42] § 2.02(3).

[43] § 2.02(2).

[44] But cf. § 2.02(7): 'When knowledge of the existence of a particular fact is an element of an offense, such knowledge is established if a person is aware of a high probability of its existence, unless he actually believes that it does not exist.'

[45] § 2.02(2) (a). See also § 2.02(6): 'When a particular purpose is an element of an offense, the element is established although such purpose is conditional, unless the condition negatives the harm or evil sought to be prevented by the law defining the offense.'

Many of the codes and drafts employ some form of the term 'intent' in preference to 'purpose', defining it, however, to mean 'conscious object'. The danger of perpetrating the obscurities and ambiguities of old judicial exploitations of intention, often resulting in a concept indistinguishable from recklessness or negligence, is thus eliminated by the definition.

[46] § 2.02(2) (c).

[47] § 2.02(2) (b) (ii).

[48] See note 43 *supra*.

matter is, in short, contingent from the actor's point of view.[49] Since risk is indeterminate, however, it would usually be oppressive to hold an actor criminally liable whenever he knew that there was some risk that his conduct might prove to be of the kind forbidden or that the requisite circumstance might exist or that the untoward consequence might follow. Hence, the Code requires that the risk consciously disregarded be 'substantial' and, moreover, that it be 'unjustifiable', since even substantial risks often may be taken properly, depending on their nature and the character and purpose of the conduct. A surgeon may perform an operation though he knows it very likely to be fatal, if he thinks that it affords the patient's only chance. The ultimate question put, when all is weighed, is whether the actor's disregard of the known risk 'involves a gross deviation from the standard of conduct that a law-abiding person would observe in the actor's situation'. Analysis can do no more than point, as the Code does, to the factors to be weighed in answering that question when it arises in a concrete case.

Negligence[50] is distinguished from acting purposely, knowingly, or recklessly in that it does not involve a state of awareness. It is the case where the actor inadvertently creates a substantial and unjustifiable risk of which he ought to be aware, given its nature and degree, the character and purpose of his conduct, and the circumstances known to him. Here the ultimate issue is conceived to be whether the actor's failure to perceive the risk 'involves a gross deviation from the standard of care that a reasonable person would observe in the actor's situation'. Much more than the 'ordinary negligence' of tort law is thus deemed to be involved.

Of the four kinds of culpability thus recognized and defined by the Model Code, there is, no doubt, least to be said for treating negligence as a sufficient basis for imposing criminal liability; and vigorous attack upon acceptance of this standard has been made, especially by Professors Glanville Williams and Jerome Hall.[51] The Code position is defended in the commentary in these terms:

---

[49] The precision of this formulation is not always followed in the codes and drafts. In Colorado, for example, the code provides that a person acts 'knowingly' when 'he is aware *or reasonably should be aware* that his conduct is of that nature or that the circumstance exists'. One of the federal bills, S. 1, *supra* note 12, would attribute knowledge of circumstances to one who is aware that they 'probably exist' (regardless of his contrary belief) and hold one for knowingly causing a result who 'is aware that his conduct will probably cause the result'. Cf. *Law Commission, Published Working Paper No. 31, The Mental Element in Crime*, pp. 40 et seq. ('second alternative').

[50] § 2.02(2) (d).

[51] See G. L. Williams, *Criminal Law: The General Part*, London, Stevens, 2nd ed. 1961, p. 123; J. Hall, 'Negligent Behavior Should Be Excluded from Penal Liability', *Colum. L. Rev.*, 1963, **63**, 632.

Knowledge that conviction and sentence, not to speak of punishment, may follow conduct that inadvertently creates improper risk supplies men with an additional motive to take care before acting, to use their faculties and draw on their experience in gauging the potentialities of contemplated conduct. To some extent, at least, this motive may promote awareness and thus be effective as a measure of control. Certainly legislators act on this assumption in a host of situations and it seems to us dogmatic to assert that they are wholly wrong. Accordingly we think that negligence, as here defined, cannot be wholly rejected as a ground of culpability . . . though we agree that it should not be generally deemed sufficient. . . .[52]

In formulating the specific crimes, negligence, as the Code defines it, is occasionally accepted as sufficient to establish liability, as in the case of homicide,[53] causing bodily injury with a deadly weapon[54] and damaging property by fire or other enumerated highly dangerous means.[55] It is accepted far more rarely, however, than it was in prior law and only in two types of situations: (1) where maximum preventive effort is essential; or (2) where it alleviates strict liability or enlarges the defences hitherto established by the law.[56]

2. *Strict Liability*. Whatever may be thought about accepting negligence as a sufficient mode of culpability, the problem is of less significance than that presented by the widespread use of strict liability in penal law—not only in the constantly proliferating corpus of the regulatory statutes but even with respect to some of the elements of the more serious offences, such as bigamy and statutory rape. Even in homicide or in assault, some jurisdictions have held that one who uses force in what he reasonably thinks to be the necessary defence of another person acts at his peril if he proves to be assisting the aggressor. The felony–murder rule presents an analogous problem, at least when the homicide is truly accidental.

For the reasons previously stated, the Model Code mounts a frontal

---

[52] § 2.02, Comment, 126–7 (Tent. Draft No. 4, 1955).

[53] § 210.4.

[54] § 211.1.

[55] § 220.3.

[56] See, e.g., § 230.1 (defence to bigamy that actor 'reasonably believes that he is legally eligible to remarry'); § 213.6 (defence to corruption of minor or sexual assault that actor reasonably believes that consenting female older than 10 is above critical age).

It may be said in general that insofar as the newly enacted codes have departed from the model, the tendency of the departures is ambivalent, limiting liability for negligence in some situations and extending it in others. For a careful and informative analysis of the provisions found in eighteen of the codes and seven of the drafts, see S. Z. Fisher, *Criminal Liability for Negligent Conduct in the United States*, a paper prepared for the forthcoming International Congress of Comparative Law (American Section), which will be published in J. N. Hazard and W. J. Wagner (eds.), *Law in the United States of America in Social and Technological Revolution*, Brussels, Establissements Emile Bruylant, 1974.

attack on such rejection of a culpability prerequisite to criminal conviction. The Code attempts, however, to meet the argument that strict liability is needed for effective regulation in many of the areas involved, if only because neither time nor personnel will be available for proving culpability. The practical solution offered is the creation of a grade of offence called a violation, for which no sentence other than a fine or fine and forfeiture or other civil penalty may be imposed upon conviction. The Code declares that a violation 'does not constitute a crime' and that conviction 'shall not give rise to any disability or legal disadvantage' based upon a criminal conviction.[57] Crime has, in short, been equated with the possibility of sentence of probation or imprisonment. If sanctions of that order are demanded, the principles of penal law apply.

The Code would impose this resolution on the full body of the regulatory law, amending *pro tanto* all the statutes found outside the Penal Code. Whatever sanctions such laws now employ, and most permit a sentence of imprisonment, the Code provides that only when it has been charged and proved that they were culpably infringed may a sentence of probation or imprisonment be passed. However, as previously noted, negligence is accepted as sufficient in the situations where strict liability is now in force.[58] This goes as far as was thought feasible to reverse the prevailing trend and may go further than most jurisdictions are yet willing to advance.

The Code's thrust has served, however, to produce a reconsideration of the problem. The Revised Penal Law of New York provided, for example, that a 'statute defining a crime, unless clearly indicating a legislative intent to impose strict liability, should be construed as defining a crime of mental culpability'.[59] The concept of a 'violation' was embraced, but with the difference that a sentence of imprisonment for up to fifteen days was authorized upon conviction.[60] Other states have followed New York's example on this point more often than they have adopted the position of the Model Code.[61] To the extent, and the extent is large, that corporations are charged with offences of strict liability, this difference is, of course, deprived of practical significance.

3. *Intoxication*. There is one point on which the Code has been charged with infidelity to its principles respecting proof of culpability, namely, in its

---

[57] § 1.04(5).
[58] § 2.05(2).
[59] *N.Y. Rev. Pen. Law* § 15.15.2 (McKinney 1967).
[60] Ibid., §§ 55.10.3, 70.15.4.
[61] The model has thus far been enacted fully only in Hawaii, Montana and New Hampshire. For a middle position, see, e.g., Pennsylvania, adopting the model with the qualification that strict liability offences may constitute a 'summary offense', punishable by imprisonment for not more than 90 days. §§ 106(c), 305(b), 1105.

treatment of intoxication when adduced in exculpation. The potential significance of drunkenness for this purpose is the same as that of ignorance or mistake of fact—namely, that it may negate a mental state that otherwise would be established circumstantially by proof of the defendant's conduct. Ignorance or mistake is ordinarily accorded its full probative significance, whatever that may be, and the Code provides that it is a defence if it 'negatives the purpose, knowledge, belief, recklessness or negligence required to establish a material element of the offense . . .'.[62] Intoxication is, however, given less significance.

The Code grants, as did the prior law (with its unhappy distinction between crimes involving 'general' and 'specific' intent), that intoxication is admissible to disprove purpose or knowledge insofar as it may logically do so. But when recklessness suffices to establish culpability, the Code provides that 'if the actor, due to self-induced intoxication, is unaware of a risk of which he would have been aware had he been sober, such unawareness is immaterial'.[63] The problem normally does not arise when only negligence is charged, since it is judged by an objective standard.

This provision of the Code has been attacked as arbitrary and unprincipled, discriminating against the inebriate by sanctioning conviction not for his inebriation but for other crimes, of which, on the hypothesis, an element has not been proved.[64] Judge Learned Hand, the most distinguished of the Code Advisers, was strongly of this view. Why then was the position taken in the draft? The major reason was a sense of the enormous weight of the existing law, which in the United States has tended towards a special rule for drunkenness in cases of so-called general intent. Seeking to rationalize that rule, many thought that awareness of the potential consequences of excessive drinking on the capacity of human beings to gauge the risks incident to their conduct is so widespread that it is not unfair to postulate a general equivalence between the risks created by the conduct of the drunken actor and the risks created by his conduct in becoming drunk. Some also were impressed by the substantial difficulty posed in litigating the foresight of any particular actor at the time when he imbibed as well as by the rarity of cases where intoxication really does engender unawareness, as distinguished from decrease of inhibition.

I fully realize that there is weakness in these answers, but I have no doubt

[62] § 2.04(1) (a). A further exculpative import is accorded to mistake when induced by official statements or rulings. § 2.04(3): These formulations are included generally in the codes and drafts.

[63] § 2.08(2).

[64] See, e.g., G. L. Williams, *Criminal Law: The General Part,* op. cit., p. 571, n. 12; H. L. Packer, 'The Model Penal Code and Beyond', *Colum. L. Rev.,* 1963, **63,** 594, 599.

of the political necessity of dealing specially with drunkenness.[65] Nor do I think that this necessity could have been met merely by providing a rebuttable presumption of awareness, a suggestion that Professor Packer advanced.[66] That would moreover be quite ineffective without placing the burden of persuasion on the issue upon the defendant, a course to which the Institute was much opposed in principle.

Of course, the Code provision applies only in the case of self-induced intoxication, which is defined to exclude action upon medical advice or under such exculpating circumstances as duress.[67] When drunkenness is 'pathological', meaning intoxication grossly excessive in degree, given the amount of the intoxicant, to which the actor does not know he is susceptible, a broader exculpation also is supplied,[68] analogous to that in cases of insanity.

4. *Responsibility.* The hardest issue in the area of culpability is that of the significance of mental disease or defect as a ground of exculpation.

All would agree that illness like any other evidence may negative existence of the mental element required for commission of particular offences and the Code so provides.[69] One who appropriates another's property believing it to be his own is not a thief, whether his erroneous belief involves a simple error (two umbrellas look alike) or a symptom of delusional psychosis. To limit exculpation to such cases, as is sometimes urged,[70] would, however, yield results that are too arbitrary for acceptance. The psychotic would be acquitted of stealing in the case supposed but would be convicted of criminal homicide if he killed in the deluded thought that he was imminently threatened and must act in self-defence, since such a belief does not exculpate in general unless it rests on reasonable grounds. The same problem would arise in any other situation where negligence suffices to establish culpability and might arise as well in the more common case where recklessness is deemed to be sufficient, since the justifiability of risk creation is determined generally by objective standards.[71] It is clear, therefore, that the culpability

---

[65] The general acceptance of the model on this point may be thought relevant in this connection.

[66] Op. cit., *supra* note 64, at 600.

[67] § 2.08(5) (b).

[68] § 2.08(5) (c).

[69] § 4.02(1).

[70] See, e.g., J. Goldstein and J. Katz, 'Abolish the Insanity Defense—Why Not?', *Yale L.J.,* 1963, **72**, 873; N. Morris, 'Psychiatry and the Dangerous Criminal', *S. Cal. L. Rev.,* 1968, **41**, 514; N. Morris and G. Hawkins, *The Honest Politician's Guide to Crime Control,* University of Chicago Press, 1970, p. 176; R. C. Allen, 'The Brawner Rule—New Lyrics for an Old Tune', *Wash. U.L.Q.,* 1973, 67.

[71] The critics characteristically ignore the point involved. Cf. J. Goldstein, 'The Brawner Rule—Why?', *Wash. U.L.Q.,* 1973, 126, 130, n. 15: 'For purposes of this discussion, the lesser degrees of culpability, recklessness and negligence, have generally been

requirements, formulated with reference to competent individuals, call for adaptation with reference to the disordered or defective psyche. In our system, as in others, this adaptation is effected by an independent criterion of criminal responsibility as affected by mental disease or defect.

When work upon the Model Code began, a majority of American jurisdictions found that criterion in strict adherence to the *M'Naghten* rule, putting the question whether the actor by reason of mental disease or defect did not know the nature or quality (i.e., potentialities) of his act or know that it was 'wrong'—meaning by 'wrong' in some states only contrary to law, in others both immoral and illegal. A minority of jurisdictions recognized a further exculpation if the actor's conduct was the product of an 'irresistible impulse' or, as it was sometimes said, occurred when madness had destroyed his will.[72]

Malaise with these solutions had grown apace for many years and reached a peak in 1954 when Judge Bazelon's opinion in the *Durham* case[73] adopted for the District of Columbia a standard long ago propounded in New Hampshire—whether the defendant's conduct was 'the product of mental disease or defect'. Many who did not approve that formulation were persuaded that there was some need for change.

The Institute worked through the problem and the various views as to its right solution with the aid of three psychiatrists, all of whom urged adoption of the *Durham* rule.[74] It was an exceedingly productive collaboration, not because it ended in complete agreement—it did not—but rather because it enabled an eclectic group, starting without any pre-commitments, to reach judgements that were totally responsive to the psychiatric points, while advancing a fresh solution.

The judgements can be stated very simply: the problem is the drawing of a line between the use of public agencies and force (1) to condemn the offender by conviction, with resulting sanctions in which that ingredient is present no matter how constructive one may seek to make the sentence and the process of correction, and (2) modes of disposition in which that condemnatory element is absent, even though restraint may be involved. When the sentence

---

left out.' The omission does not contribute to the wisdom of the author's judgement o the issue. Cf. A. Goldstein, *The Insanity Defense*, Newhaven, Yale University Press, 1967, 18; H. Wechsler, 'Insanity as a Defense', *F.R.D.*, 1965, **37**, 380, 381.

[72] See Comment, § 4.01, Appendix A, 161 (Tent. Draft No. 4, 1955).

[73] *Durham* v. *United States,* 214 F.2d 862.

[74] See Freedman, Guttmacher and Overholser, 'Mental Disease or Defect Excluding Responsibility—A Psychiatric View of the American Law Institute Model Penal Code Proposal', *Am. J. Psychiatry*, 1961, **118**, 32. My own effort to achieve a meeting of minds with Dr. Guttmacher is indicated by our correspondence on the subject published in Appendices B & C to § 4.01, Comment, 170–92 (Tent. Draft No. 4, 1955).

may be capital there is, of course, a starker contrast between the punitive reaction and a reaction of the second kind. Stating the matter differently, the problem is to etch a decent working line between the areas assigned to the authorities responsible for public health and those responsible for the correction of offenders. As previously stated, it is important to maintain this separation, not least in order to control the stigma involved in a hospital commitment.

Viewing the problem in these terms, no one can doubt that the *M'Naghten* rule is right as far as its principle extends; that those who are mad according to the *M'Naghten* rule are plainly beyond the reach of the restraining influence of law; and that their condemnation would be futile and unjust. The question is whether the rule goes far enough to draw a fair and workable discrimination. Almost all informed opinion holds that it does not, insofar as it confines attention to the actor's cognitive capacity; for even though cognition may obtain in some degree, mental disorder or defect may destroy capacity for self-control. Stephen[75] and others[76] sought, indeed, to save the test from this reproach by urging that the knowledge test requires more than merely surface intellection, demanding a capacity to function in the light of knowledge or, as the point is sometimes put, integration of perception, that is understanding as distinct from mere verbalization. This conception was, however, given no substantial recognition by our courts and a psychiatrist who wished to testify in these terms in defence would normally encounter grave resistance.[77] It was, therefore, concluded that a practical reform should treat capacity for self-control as a separate question and not merely as to some extent implicit in the question of cognition.

Beyond this, and more importantly, the judgement was that no test is workable that calls for the complete impairment of ability to know or to control; and that the extremity of these conceptions, as applied in court, posed the largest difficulty in the situation. Disorientation, we were told, might be extreme and still might not be total; what clinical experience revealed was closer to a graded scale with marks along the way. Hence, an examiner confronting a person who had performed a seemingly purposive act might helpfully address himself to the extent of awareness, understanding and control. If, on the other hand, he must speak to utter incapacity *vel non*, he could testify meaningfully only as to delusional psychosis, when the act would not be criminal if the facts were as they deludedly were thought to be,

---

[75] Stephen, *History of the Criminal Law of England*, London, MacMillan, Vol. ii, at 171 (1883).

[76] See, e.g., J. Hall, *Principles of Criminal Law*, 2nd ed. Indianapolis, Bobbs-Merrill, 1960, p. 520; F. Wertham, *The Show of Violence*, London, Gollancz, 1949, p. 86.

[77] See, e.g., J. Van Voorhis, dissenting in *People* v. *Horton*, 308 N.Y. 1, 20-1 (1954).

although he knew that there were other situations in which the disorder was no less extreme. To meet this aspect of the difficulty, it was thought that the criterion should ask if there was, as a result of disease or defect, a deprivation of 'substantial capacity' to 'appreciate the criminality' or 'wrongfulness of his conduct' or to 'conform his conduct to the requirements of law'[78]— meaning by 'substantial' a capacity of some appreciable magnitude when measured by the standard of humanity in general, as opposed to the reduction of capacity to the vagrant and trivial dimensions characteristic of the most severe afflictions of the mind. It was recognized, of course, that 'substantial' is an open-ended concept but its quantitative connotation was believed to be sufficiently precise for purposes of practical administration. The law is full of instances where it explicitly confronts or authorizes courts and juries to confront an issue of degree. Such an approach was deemed to be no less essential and appropriate in dealing with this issue than in the case of recklessness and negligence.

It should be added that the Code does not attempt to define 'mental disease or defect' but does include a cautionary limitation, namely, that the terms, as used in the Code, 'do not include an abnormality manifested only by repeated criminal or otherwise antisocial conduct'.[79] The limitation was, of course, designed to disallow the circularity of reasoning involved in grounding a diagnosis of disease for purposes of determining responsibility upon no other basis than repeated conduct of the kind which, by hypothesis, must be attributed to such disease for irresponsibility to be established. Some critics have regarded this as a presumptuous legal intervention in the realm of psychiatric theory[80] but there are conceptions of psychopathy and sociopathy as forms of mental illness that were thought to warrant caution of this kind.[81] Apart from this qualification, the Code pursues the only course that was deemed feasible. It treats the question of disease as one of fact, to be determined by the court or jury on the evidence presented in the cases that arise. As medical understanding may develop in such areas, for example, as brain chemistry, it can thus have its proper impact on the application of the law.

[78] § 4.01(1).   [79] § 4.01(2).

[80] See, e.g., J. Biggs, *The Guilty Mind* (New York, Harcourt Brace & Co., 1955), p. 160; H. L. Kozol, 'The Psychopath Before the Law', *Mass. L.Q.*, 1959, 44, 106, 116; H. Wei-hofen, 'The Definition of Mental Illness', *Ohio St. L.J.*, 1960, 21, 1, 6; F. Guttmacher, 'Current Trends in Regard to Criminal Responsibility', *Am. J. Psychiatry*, 1961, 117, 690.

[81] For further discussion of this problem, see H. Wechsler, 'On Culpability and Crime: The Treatment of Mens Rea in the Model Penal Code', *Annals*, 1962, 339, 24, 39–40. See also the thoughtful analysis by the Court of Appeals for the District of Columbia in *United States* v. *Brawner*, 471 F.2d 969, 992 (1972), concluding that the *caveat* should be considered by the court in ruling on the admissibility of prior antisocial conduct as evidence of 'mental disease', but should not be made a basis for instructions to the jury.

Cast in the terms described, the model formulation has exerted a large influence upon the course of legal change. It has been enacted *verbatim* or in substance in eight of the new codes (Connecticut, Delaware, Hawaii, Illinois, Kentucky, North Dakota, Oregon and Utah) and adapted in three others (Montana, New York[82] and Texas). It has been adopted or adapted separately by statute in three states (Maryland, Missouri and Vermont)[83] and by judicial decision in six others (Idaho, Indiana, Massachusetts, Ohio, West Virginia and Wisconsin).[84] Ten of the eleven federal courts of appeals have approved the formulation for their circuits,[85] including even the Court of Appeals for the District of Columbia, which overruled the *Durham* case a year ago.[86] Most of the draft codes now pending or under development also

[82] The New York formulation limits the criterion to lack of 'substantial capacity to know or to appreciate', eliminating any separate reference to capacity to conform. The redundancy was introduced with the explicit purpose of insisting on a cognitive capacity for genuine perception, a requirement accorded further emphasis by the inclusion of 'substantial'. Cf. notes 75 and 76 *supra*. A distinguished panel of New York psychiatrists, consulted in the framing of the statute, was opposed for the most part to this departure from the model but failed to adduce specific kinds of cases in which testimony would be hampered or the result probably affected. The variation was, however, crucial in allaying prosecutive opposition to abandoning the strict *M'Naghten* test that was in force. See *People* v. *Adams*, 26 N.Y. 2d 129, 257, N.E. 2d 610 (1970).

In Montana and Texas, on the other hand, the criterion enacted extends the inquiry to capacity to conform but makes the more important change of eliminating the allusion to 'substantial' (e.g., 'unable either to appreciate . . . or to conform . . .').

[83] *Md. Ann. Code* art. 59, § 9 (1968); *Mo. Amm. Stat.* § 552.030 (Supp. 1967); *Vt. Stat. Ann.* tit. 13, § 4801 (1958).

[84] *State* v. *White*, 93 Idaho 153, 456 P.2d 797 (1969); *Hill* v. *State,* 252 Ind. 601, 251 N.E. 2d 429 (1969); *Commonwealth* v. *McHoul*, 352 Mass. 544, 226 N.E. 2d 556 (1967); *State* v. *Staten*, 18 Ohio St. 2d 13, 247 N.E. 2d 293 (1969), 25 Ohio St. 2d 107, 267 N.E. 2d 122 (1971); *State* v. *Grimm,* 195 S.E. 2d 637 (W. Va. 1973); *State* v. *Shoffner*, 31 Wis. 2d 412, 143 N.W. 2d' 458 (1967). It had also been adopted in Kentucky prior to its enactment in the new criminal code. *Terry* v. *Commonwealth*, 371 S.W. 2d 862 (Ky. 1963); *Graham* v. *Commonwealth*, 420 S.W. 2d 575 (Ky. 1967).

[85] *United States* v. *Freeman*, 357 F.2d 606 (2d Cir. 1966); *United States* v. *Currens*, 290 F.2d 751 (3d Cir. 1961) (limited to 'substantial capacity to conform his conduct to the requirements of the law he is alleged to have violated'); *United States* v. *Chandlr*, 393. F.2d 920 (4th Cir. 1968); *Blake* v. *United States*, 407 F.2d 908 (5th Cir. 1969); *Unitede State* v. *Smith*, 404 F.2d 720 (6th Cir. 1968); *United States* v. *Shapiro*, 383 F.2d 680 (7th Cirs 1967); *Pope* v. *United States*, 372 F.2d 710 (8th Cir. 1967), *rev'd on other grounds*, 392 U.S. 651 (1968); *Wade* v. *United States*, 426 F.2d 64 (9th Cir. 1970); *Wion* v. *United States*, 325 F.2d 420 (10th Cir. 1963). The courts are divided as to the appropriateness of the *caveat* in § 4.01(2).

[86] *United States* v. *Brawner*, 471 F.2d 969 (1972) (en banc). The Court (ibid. 983) retains the definition of 'mental disease or defect' articulated in its earlier opinion in *McDonald* v. *United States*, 312 F.2d 847, 851 (1962): 'any abnormal condition of the mind which substantially affects mental or emotional processes and substantially impairs behavior controls'. Needless to say, this explication is consistent with the underlying theory of the model, subject to the *caveat* in § 4.01(2).

propose the standard for enactment. There is, therefore, reason to believe that it may ultimately become the prevailing rule in the United States.

In addition to redefining the criterion of responsibility, the Model Code deals fully with the procedural problems involved in litigating the issue of responsibility, requiring that the defence be raised by the defendant on notice to the prosecution,[87] making provision for psychiatric examination by court-appointed experts,[88] facilitating psychiatric testimony,[89] prescribing mandatory commitment of persons acquitted on this ground and regulating their release.[90] Though these provisions have drawn less attention than the

[87] § 4.03.

[88] § 4.05.

[89] § 4.07(4). On the extent to which refusal to submit to psychiatric examination may be made a basis for precluding the defence without infringing the constitutional privilege against self-incrimination, see, e.g., *Matter of Lee* v. *County Court of Erie County,* 27 N.Y. 2d 432, 267 N.E. 2d 452 (1971); *United States* v. *Wade,* 13 Crim. L. Rep. 2315, 489 F.2d 258 (9th Cir. 1973); S. J. Brakel and R. S. Rock (eds.), *The Mentally Disabled and the Law,* rev. 1971 (Chicago), p. 401; S. L. Lefelt, 'Pretrial Mental Examinations: Compelled Cooperation and the Fifth Amendment', *Am. Crim. L. Rev.,* 1972, **10,** 431.

[90] § 4.08. The commitment for 'custody, care and treatment' must be to the public agency concerned with public health, not to the correctional authorities. The release decision, which may be conditional, is to be made by the committing court on application of the health officials recommending discharge or of the committed person but the latter may not make the application until six months from the date of the commitment or more frequently than once a year thereafter. Whoever makes the application, the Court is called upon to designate two qualified psychiatrists to make an independent examination. It may accept their recommendation of discharge but otherwise must hold a hearing. The criterion to be applied is whether 'the committed person may be discharged or released on condition without danger to himself or others'. A discharge may be conditional for up to five years.

Though this approach has been adopted or continued in some of the recently legislating jurisdictions (Colorado, Delaware, District of Columbia [hearing within 50 days], Maryland, Minnesota, Missouri, Montana, New York, Ohio, Wisconsin), others have adhered to the much more prevalent position in the United States, conditioning commitment on a hearing and a finding of continuing disorder or defect presenting a present danger on release (Connecticut [after examination limited to 90 days], Hawaii, Illinois, Kentucky, New Hampshire, North Dakota, Oregon). See *The Mentally Disabled and the Law, supra,* note 89, at p. 404.

When the model was prepared, the substantial number of decisions sustaining the validity of mandatory commitment and of a bar to applications for release within a prescribed period deemed long enough for thorough observation, led to the conclusion that the problem fell within the realm of legislative policy. See § 4.08, Comment, 199 (Tent. Draft No. 4, 1955); Note, 145 A.L.R. 892 (1943). See also *Lynch* v. *Overholser,* 369 U.S. 705, 715, 724–8 (1962); *State* v. *Taylor,* 158 Mont. 323, 491 P.2d 877 (1971). It was thought both fair and politic that a defendant who had sought and won exculpation on the ground of his derangement be required to submit to institutional examination for the suggested six-month period before litigating the contention that a change in his condition had occurred, eliminating present danger.

Recent Supreme Court decisions suggest, however, that a stark differentiation of the

substantive proposal, they too have had substantial influence upon the course of legislation.

These developments do not imply a judgement that many more cases should result in a commitment to the agencies of mental health, as distinguished from a sentence on conviction. Such cases will inevitably be infrequent, given the rigour of the criterion of exculpation, the prudential reasons for foregoing the defence to any but the gravest charges, the preponderance of dispositions upon guilty pleas and other practical considerations.[91] The judgement implied is rather that it is important to the justice of the system that the defence be available; that it be defined in terms susceptible of viable administration; and that in the rare contested cases where a psychiatric judgement is in issue, the forensic situation be acceptable to those who are requested to collaborate in the administration of the law. Needless to say, the merit of that judgement does not turn upon the number of acquittals and convictions.

5. *Justification.* What has been said should serve to illustrate the Code's approach to the articulation of those principles of liability and exculpation that measure the right scope and limits of the use of penal sanctions and thus qualify or supplement the definitions of specific crimes. The point involved is that it is essential to subordinate or to accommodate preventive goals to other purposes, including, as the Code declares in its enumeration of objectives, 'to safeguard conduct that is without fault from condemnation

---

standards and procedures for commitment of acquitted persons from those generally employed for civil commitment may be condemned as an unreasonable discrimination or a denial of due process. *Jackson* v. *Indiana*, 406 U.S. 715 (1972) (automatic commitment of defendant incompetent to stand trial must be limited to time reasonably required to restore competency, or civil commitment standards and procedures must be followed); *Baxstrom* v. *Herold*, 383 U.S. 107 (1966) (deranged prisoner at expiration of sentence); *McNeil* v. *Director, Patuxent Institution*, 407 U.S. 245 (1972) (extended commitment as 'defective delinquent' beyond expiration of term of prison sentence). See also *People* v. *Lally*, 19 N.Y. 2d 27, 224 N.E. 2d 87 (1966) (defendant acquitted as irresponsible and mandatorily committed accorded same procedural rights on application for discharge as on civil commitment, including right to jury trial); cf. *In re Davis*, 106 Cal. Reptr. 178, 505 P.2d 1018 (1973); Leavy, 'The Mentally Ill Criminal Defendant', *Crim. L. Bull*, 1973, 9, 197. The most important aspect of the problem may well be whether there is a shift in the burden of persuasion from the proponent of commitment, as in the ordinary civil situation, to the proponent of discharge. See *United States* v. *Brawner*, 471 F.2d 969, 996–8 (1972). The justification for such shift may well turn upon the character of the defendant's conduct and the length of time involved.

[91] The criterion reducing murder to manslaughter when homicide is committed 'under the influence of extreme mental or emotional disturbance' is noted hereafter. See also § 4.02(2) providing that evidence of impaired capacity is admissible against capital sentence, if such sentence is discretionary, a possibility that since has been precluded on constitutional grounds.

as criminal' and 'to differentiate on reasonable grounds between serious and minor offenses'.[92]

The pursuit of that accommodation is involved in other general provisions, as well as in the definition of specific crimes. Of the former, I shall merely note in passing the formulations on causality,[93] complicity,[94] the liability of corporations and associations,[95] and the defences based upon duress,[96] military orders,[97] *de minimis* violations[98] and entrapment,[99] reflected in some measure in the codes.[100] The major effort to state general principles of justification,[101] greatly aided by Professor Glanville Williams as consultant, has, however, been so influential that it calls for brief description here.

With respect to conduct 'involving the appropriation, seizure of, damage to, intrusion on or interference with property', the model accords the defence in any 'circumstances which would establish a defence of privilege in a civil action', save as the law defining a particular offence may otherwise provide.[102] This is, of course, the sole alternative to undertaking a complete restatement in the penal code of the law of torts and property. There is, perforce, a similar incorporation by reference of the law governing the functions and duties of public officers, the execution of legal process, court orders and judgements, the armed services and the laws of war. With respect, however, to 'the use of force upon or toward the person of another' in self-defence or in defence of others, for the protection of property, in law enforcement (including crime prevention) and in discharge of special responsibilities for the care, discipline or safety of others, there is no such deference to norms developed elsewhere. The governing standards are embodied in the Code.[103]

The Code standards are, moreover, more detailed than a mere rule of reason,[104] especially in limitations on the justifiability of deadly force in self-protection,[105] protection of property[106] and law enforcement.[107] The limitations are, however, so defined that the actor's belief in the existence

---

[92] § 1.02(1).   [93] § 2.03.   [94] § 2.06.

[95] § 2.07.   [96] § 2.09.   [97] § 2.10.

[98] § 2.12.   [99] § 2.13.

[100] Most of the codes and drafts employ or adapt the provisions on complicity and corporate liability. The causality formulation will be found in Delaware, Hawaii, Kentucky, Montana, Pennsylvania and Texas, as well as in a number of the drafts (e.g., Michigan, New Jersey, Washington). The defence for duress is often formulated more strictly than the model. The other problems are unevenly addressed.

[101] Article 3.

[102] § 3.10.   [103] § 3.03.

[104] E.g., Criminal Law Act 1967, Pt. I, 3.

[105] § 3.04. See also § 3.05 (protection of other persons).

[106] § 3.06.   [107] § 3.07.

of the justifying circumstances will suffice for exculpation if the charge is an intentional offence. Recklessness or negligence in having such belief (the traditional absence of reasonable grounds) bars the defence only if the prosecution is for an offence for which recklessness or negligence, as the case may be, suffices generally to establish culpability.[108] The *mens rea* schema earlier described is thus preserved in this important area, where even homicide is frequently involved.[109]

Beyond this, the Code provides in an important innovation a broad defence based on a necessary choice of evils, applicable if neither the Code nor the law defining the offence deals with the specific situation involved. The justification is established by the actor's belief that his conduct is 'necessary to avoid a harm or evil to himself or to another', provided that it is objectively established that the 'harm or evil sought to be avoided by such conduct is greater than that sought to be prevented by the law defining the offense charged'. Here too the actor's recklessnes or negligence—either in creating or appraising the necessity—bars the defence if the crime charged may be committed recklessly or negligently.

Though many of the codes omit this general provision, deeming it perhaps too open-ended, it has been enacted or adapted in nine of the legislating jurisdictions (Delaware, Kentucky, Hawaii, Illinois, New Hampshire, New York,[110] Pennsylvania, Oregon and Texas) and included in a number of the pending drafts.

---

[108] § 3.09(2).

[109] This approach has thus far been enacted only in Delaware, Hawaii, Kentucky and North Dakota. Connecticut, Illinois, Michigan, Montana, New York, New Hampshire, Oregon and Texas preserve the traditional requirement that a belief in justifying circumstances and necessity be reasonable, with the result that an unreasonable belief may lead to a conviction of an intentional crime. In the case of homicide, the crime may thus be murder, save as the reduction to manslaughter on grounds of emotional disturbance may apply. Illinois and Pennsylvania make the reduction explicitly to voluntary manslaughter but do not otherwise afford relief in cases of unreasonable belief.

The model has been much more influential in the limitations it proposes on justification for the use of deadly force to prevent the commission of a felony or to effect an arrest. §§ 3.04(2) (b), 3.06(3) (d), 3.07(2) (b) (iii), 3.07(5) (a) (ii).

[110] The New York adaptation, followed or reflected in a number of the formulations, is as follows (§ 35.05.2): 'Such conduct is necessary as an emergency measure to avoid an imminent public or private injury which is about to occur by reason of a situation occasioned or developed through no fault of the actor, and which is of such gravity that according to ordinary standards of intelligence and morality, the desirability and urgency of avoiding such injury clearly outweigh the desirability of avoiding the injury sought to be prevented by the statute defining the offense in issue. The necessity and justifiability of such conduct may not rest upon considerations pertaining only to the morality and advisability of the statute, either in its general application or with respect to its application to a particular class of cases arising thereunder.'

The Definition of Specific Crimes:
Problems of Coverage and Grading

The problems of coverage and grading confronted and resolved in the model's definition of specific crimes are far too numerous for presentation in this paper. Since selective treatment is essential, I shall deal with homicide in some detail, in view of its importance in all systems. In other areas, I must content myself with a bare statement of the dominant objective, hoping to invite attention to the formulations by those interested in the subjects.

1. *Homicide.* The general provisions with respect to culpability, causality and justification greatly simplify the problem of defining criminal homicide. The definition merely encompasses causing the death of another human being either purposely, knowingly, recklessly or negligently, with a special provision for causing or aiding suicide embodying some limitations.[111] The decision to treat negligence as a sufficient mode of culpability when death is caused has previously been discussed.[112]

The issue of importance was reduced, therefore, to that of working out a proper grading of the crime for purposes of sentence. While American law had followed the English in distinguishing for this purpose between murder and manslaughter, all but ten states had followed the early lead of Pennsylvania and Virginia in further differentiating murder into two degrees, with the death penalty (where it was used) reserved for first degree and becoming in the course of time discretionary even then in all our jurisdictions. That was the position when the problem was considered in the drafting of the Model Penal Code.[113]

The usual determinants of first degree murder were that the killing was 'wilful, deliberate and premeditated' or that it occurred in the commission of or the attempt to commit enumerated felonies, usually arson, rape, robbery, burglary and kidnapping.[114] The test of deliberation and premeditation was interpreted in general to require no more than that the homicide be intentional and it was criticized throughout the years. The basic difficulty was, of course, that no single aspect of mentation could provide a viable criterion for this purpose without reference to other circumstances too complex to be encompassed in the rule.[115]

---

[111] §§ 210.1, 210.5.

[112] See p. 441, *supra*.

[113] The details are presented fully in Tent. Draft No. 9, 1959, at 65–80 (Comment), 115–26 (Appendix C). The mandatory death penalty referred to in the District of Columbia, New York and Vermont (ibid. 66, 125) was later abolished in those jurisdictions.

[114] Ibid., 33–9.

[115] Ibid., 68–70.

These reflections led to the decision to propose abandoning degrees of murder, structuring the offence in the three categories of murder, manslaughter and negligent homicide, constituting, respectively, felonies of the first, second and third degree for purposes of sentence. When homicide is committed purposely or knowingly, it was placed in the murder category, permitting, however, a reduction to manslaughter on the basis of a standard much broader than the concept of provocation as developed at the common law. This standard refers to a homicide which would otherwise be murder 'committed under the influence of extreme mental or emotional disturbance for which there is reasonable explanation or excuse', with reasonableness determined 'from the viewpoint of a person in the actor's situation under the circumstances as he believes them to be'.[116] The purpose was explicitly to give full scope to what amounts to a plea in mitigation based upon a mental or emotional trauma of significant dimensions, with the jury asked to show whatever empathy it can.[117]

When homicide is committed recklessly, it normally is viewed as manslaughter rather than murder,[118] but a murder category was reserved in the model for very heinous cases of this kind. Such a case was identified by saying that 'it is committed recklessly under circumstances manifesting extreme indifference to the value of human life',[119] a formula that Glanville Williams has found wanting,[120] though I confess he has not led me to repent.

We should have liked, within this scheme, to follow the British example[121] by dispensing with constructive murder wholly, but such a course was thought to be impolitic, given the weight of prospective opposition. The case made for felony-murder always is, however, that the actor who engages in a felony of violence is recklessly endangering the lives of others, even though he does not mean to kill. The point suggested to us what we thought to be a viable solution, namely, the creation of a rebuttable presumption of recklessness manifesting extreme indifference to the value of human life, if the actor was engaged in the commission, attempted commission or flight after commission of forcible intercourse, arson, burglary, kidnapping or felonious escape.[122] The presumption rests on an empirical foundation and accords all that can be said for the prevailing law. Since it is rebuttable, the

[116] § 210.3(1) (b).
[117] Comment (Tent. Draft No. 9, 1959) 46–8.
[118] § 210.3(1) (a).
[119] § 210.2(1) (b).
[120] G. L. Williams, *The Mental Element in Crime*, Jerusalem, Magnes Press, Hebrew University, 1965, pp. 91–6. In New York the adjective 'depraved' was substituted for 'extreme'. *N.Y. Rev. Pen. Law* § 125.25.2 (1965).
[121] Homicide Act § 1 (1957).
[122] § 210.2(1) (b).

defendant has the opportunity to establish, if he can, that this was the unusual case in which the death was really a fortuity. The absence of that opportunity is certainly the major vice of the old rule.

Even this degree of relaxation was too great to be acceptable in New York, though some alleviation was attained. The crimes that give rise to the constructive liability were reduced from all felonies to those enumerated in the model; the death must have been caused 'in furtherance' of the crime or of 'immediate flight therefrom'; and, finally, an accomplice who did not himself commit, incite or aid the homicidal act, was unarmed and had 'no reasonable ground to believe that any other participant was armed' or 'intended to engage in conduct likely to result in death or serious physical injury' was given an affirmative defence.[123]

Trivial as the New York alleviation is, it has been followed in Colorado, Connecticut, North Dakota and Oregon as well as in a number of the drafts. New Hampshire, on the other hand, followed the model, as did Delaware (requiring recklessness but dispensing with the presumption). Utah required at least proof of negligence and Texas that the causative conduct be 'clearly dangerous to human life'. Hawaii and Kentucky took the further step of abolishing felony-murder, while Georgia, Illinois ('forcible felony'), Kansas, Louisiana, Minnesota, Montana, Ohio, Pennsylvania and New Mexico preserved it in substantially its antecedent form. The Model Code has thus had some effect within this controversial area, though less than was its due upon the merits.

The model did not propose the abolition of the punishment of death in jurisdictions where it could be imposed for murder; the Institute took no position on the question. Thorsten Sellin's study for the Code[124] was, however, a potent force for the repeals that were achieved in recent years in Iowa, New York, Oregon, West Virginia and Vermont, increasing to thirteen the jurisdictions that outlawed the death penalty for homicide entirely or with very few exceptions. The Institute did give much thought to when the penalty should be available in a system that continues to employ it and to the procedure for determining its imposition in such case.

The solution offered in the Model Code is to enumerate a set of aggravating and of mitigating circumstances. A capital sentence is excluded if the court is satisfied that none of the aggravating circumstances was established by the evidence at the trial or would be established on a further proceeding to determine sentence; that substantial mitigating circumstances calling for leniency were established at the trial; that the defendant was under eighteen

---

[123] N.Y. Rev. Pen. Law § 125.25.3 (1965).

[124] T. Sellin, The Death Penalty (1959), first published as an attachment to Tent. Draft No. 9, American Law Institute (1959).

years of age at the time of the crime; that his mental or physical condition calls for leniency; or that the evidence does not foreclose all doubt respecting the defendant's guilt. If no such finding is made, a further proceeding is initiated before the court or court and jury. Much scope is given to the evidence admissible in that proceeding. The court or jury is directed to take into account the enumerated aggravating and mitigating circumstances and any other facts considered relevant. Capital sentence is again excluded unless the tribunal finds that one of the aggravating circumstances and no mitigating circumstance sufficiently substantial to call for leniency are established. Apart from this, the sentence is discretionary but if the jurisdiction puts the issue to the jury, it must be unanimous for penalty of death and the court must concur in its opinion for the sentence to be passed.[125]

This approach reflects agreement with the Royal Commission on Capital Punishment that 'the factors which determine whether the sentence of death is the appropriate penalty in particular cases are too complex to be compressed within the limits of a simple formula'.[126] This insight leads to the rejection of a mandatory sentence. It does not, however, preclude the delineation of cases where the sentence is entirely inappropriate; nor does it argue against the attempt to guide the exercise of sound discretion by pointing to the main circumstances of aggravation and of mitigation that should be weighed and weighed against each other when presented in a concrete case. The required finding goes a step beyond this to assure that such a balancing takes place.

The model was far less influential in this area than in promoting the elimination of degrees of murder and liberalizing the criterion for mitigation to manslaughter in cases of emotional distress.[127] Some jurisdictions, to be sure, adopted the bifurcated trial[128] but the general legislative disposition was to maintain full discretion with respect to death or imprisonment for murder, or, if degrees were employed, for murder in the first degree. Starting in 1967, however, a concerted attack on the constitutionality of capital punishment produced a moratorium on executions.[129] The United States

---

[125] § 210.6.

[126] *Report* 174 (1953).

[127] The mitigation formulation was enacted or adapted in Connecticut, Delaware, Hawaii, Kentucky, Montana, New Hampshire, New York, North Dakota, Oregon and Utah and is embodied in most of the pending drafts.

[128] A two-stage proceeding of this kind had long been utilized in court martial in the United States. It was proposed by the Royal Commission on Capital Punishment in 1953 (*Report* 194–8) and had been adopted in simplified form in California (*Pen. Code* § 190.1), Connecticut (*Gen. Stat.* § 53–10), New York (*Rev. Pen. Law* § 125.35) and Pennsylvania (*Stat. Ann.*, tit. 18, § 4701, apparently repealed by the Crimes Code of 1972).

[129] The plan and progress of this litigation are described in detail in M. Meltsner, *Cruel and Unusual: The Supreme Court and Capital Punishment*, New York, Random House, 1973.

Supreme Court considered and rejected the contentions that the bifurcated trial and statutory standards were compelled by constitutional considerations.[130] Surprisingly, however, in June 1972, the Court held 5–4 that the discretionary system as administered, with its random selection of cases for capital sentence, constituted cruel and unusual punishment forbidden by the Eighth and Fourteenth Amendments.[131]

The result was a permanent reprieve for the six hundred prisoners throughout the country then held under sentences of death. The further result was a resurgence of legislation to restore capital sentence on a basis that could arguably overcome the constitutional objection.[132] Some states reverted for this purpose to a mandatory sentence in such cases as the murder of a law-enforcement officer, murder by a prisoner serving a life sentence, murder for hire, a second murder or even felony-murder.[133] Others turned to the Model Code proposals, prescribing a similar catalogue of aggravating and mitigating circumstances and either authorizing[134] or requiring[135] a death sentence if one of the aggravating circumstances is established and no sufficient mitigating circumstance.[136] As capital sentences are imposed under these new provisions, the constitutional attack will, of course, be renewed.

Many believe the Court will hold the constitutional safeguard infringed whatever system for imposing sentence is involved. It would be anomalous, indeed, if a simplistic statutory mandate should ultimately be upheld and a regime of guided discretion, designed to eliminate the arbitrariness of such a mandate, held unconstitutional. Until and unless that anomaly has been decreed, legislators unhappily determined that capital punishment remain on the books may wisely resort to the Code provisions.[137]

2. *Inchoate Crimes: Attempt, Solicitation and Conspiracy.* The Model Penal

---

[130] *Crampton* v. *Ohio, McGantha* v. *California,* 402 U.S. 183 (1971).

[131] *Furman* v. *Georgia,* 408 U.S. 238 (1972).

[132] As of 31 January 1973, such legislation had been passed in twenty-one states.

[133] Such mandates were prescribed in Idaho, Indiana, Louisiana, Nevada, New Mexico, Oklahoma, Rhode Island and Wyoming, qualified in some instances by authority to convict of a lesser included offence. In Montana, the mandate applies unless the sentencer finds 'mitigating circumstances', which are undefined.

[134] Arizona, Arkansas, Connecticut, Florida, Georgia, Nebraska, Tennessee, Texas and Utah preserve such qualified discretion. On the Florida development, see C. W. Ehrhardt, P. A. Hubbart, L. H. Levinson, W. M. Smiley, Jr., and T. A. Wills, 'The Future of Capital Punishment in Florida: Analysis and Recommendations', *J. Crim. L. & Criminology,* 1973, **64,** 2; C. W. Ehrhardt and P. A. Levinson, 'Florida's Legislative Response to Furman: An Exercise in Futility', ibid., 10.

[135] California and Ohio.

[136] The new statutes provide for a bifurcated trial in Arkansas, Arizona, California, Connecticut, Florida, Georgia, Nebraska, Ohio, Tennessee, Texas and Utah.

[137] A similar view is expressed in L. A. Wollan, Jr., 'The Death Penalty After Furman', *Loyola U.L.J.,* 1973, **4,** 339.

Code deals systematically with the general inchoate crimes (sometimes described as 'anticipatory' or 'relational' offences) of attempt, solicitation and conspiracy, presenting a complete reformulation of the standards that determine criminality and the sentences authorized upon conviction.

The provisions are too complex for restatement here[138] but their main thrust may be summarized as follows:

(a) to extend the criminality of attempts by sweeping aside the defence of impossibility, including the distinction between so-called factual and legal impossibility, and by drawing the line between attempt and noncriminal preparation further away from the final act, in terms of 'a substantial step' towards consummation; the crime becomes essentially one of criminal purpose implemented by an overt act strongly corroborative of such purpose;

(b) to establish criminal solicitation as a general offence;

(c) to limit the unity and scope of criminal conspiracy by emphasizing the primordial element of individual agreement to commit or to assist in the commission of a crime, while preserving so far as possible the procedural advantage of joint prosecution of related segments of an organized criminal enterprise;

(d) to eliminate as objectives that may make conspiracy a crime such vague determinants as 'oppressive', 'corrupt', 'dangerous to public health or morals', and the like, limiting the general offence to cases where the purpose is to engage in conduct that would constitute a crime;

(e) to establish in attempt, solicitation and conspiracy a limited defence in cases where there was a true renunciation of the criminal objective; and

(f) to establish these inchoate crimes as offences of comparable magnitude to the completed crimes that are their object, while precluding conviction for both conspiracy and the substantive offence that was its object.

These formulations are exerting a substantial influence upon the course of legislation and decision.[139]

3. *Reckless Endangering.* It was typical in American criminal law to deal with homicide and the infliction of bodily injury but to give scant attention to conduct that creates grave risk of such results if the results do not ensue. In some jurisdictions, the law of attempts (with its requirement of a 'specific intent') and provisions addressed to firearms and motor vehicles provided the only sanctions that obtained. The model proposed to fill this gap by defining two general crimes of reckless risk creation, committed when a

[138] They are discussed at length in H. Wechsler, W. K. Jones and H. L. Korn, 'The Treatment of Inchoate Crimes in the Model Penal Code of the American Law Institute: Attempt, Solicitation and Conspiracy', *Colum. L. Rev.,* 1961, **61,** 571 and 957.

[139] See especially the treatment of these subjects in the new codes enacted in Colorado, Delaware, Hawaii, Kentucky, Montana, New Hampshire, North Dakota, Oregon, Pennsylvania, Texas and Utah.

person 'recklessly engages in conduct which places or may place another person in danger of death or serious bodily injury' or, in the case of the graver offence, 'recklessly creates a risk of catastrophe' by dangerous means.[140] The appropriateness and utility of such enlargement of the scope of criminality have been widely recognized in the new codes and drafts.

4. *Property Destruction.* The Code provides a unified, simple and consistent treatment of crimes of property destruction,[141] an area that formerly was dealt with by uneven definitions of the scope of arson and an incredible proliferation of offences of malicious mischief treated on an *ad hoc* basis through the years. Starting a fire, even on one's own property, would be made a serious offence—an extension of the law in many states—if it recklessly endangers other persons or a building of another.

5. *Burglary and Kidnapping.* These two offences were permitted to run wild in many of our statutes, arbitrarily converting into major crimes much conduct that upon analysis involves no more than the inception of some petty criminality. The Code would cut these awesome categories down to proper size.[142]

6. *Theft.* The undisciplined proliferation of offences, with concomitant complexity of content and frequent inequality in grading, is nowhere better illustrated than in theft. The Code would unify these crimes of acquisition, not only with respect to larceny and criminal conversion, but also in the situation where the acquisitive method is fraud, improper threats or subsequent receiving.[143] Unification calls, of course, for safeguarding the right of a defendant to due notice of the particulars of the charge, but that is not a major problem. What is most important is to draw a clear and rationa line between forbidden and permitted acquisition and to end acquittals that are based on minor technicalities.

The Code would also make extensions of importance of the scope of criminality, notably by reaching promissory fraud and intentional deception as to relevant matters of law, value or opinion, if the statements are likely to deceive ordinary persons in the group addressed. The theft of services is also comprehended.[144]

The unified law of theft is supplemented by provisions[145] addressed to forgery and fraudulent practices, including provisions that apply whether or not property has been obtained or theft or attempted theft could otherwise be proved. Such matters as simulating antiques or works of art, tampering with records, issuing bad cheques, misuse of credit cards, deceptive business practices, commercial bribery, rigging public exhibitions, and frauds in insolvency are dealt with *inter alia* in this context.

---

[140] §§ 211.2, 220.2.   [141] Article 220.   [142] Articles 212, 221.
[143] Article 223.   [144] § 223.7.   [145] Article 224.

All of the foregoing formulations have been widely copied in the codes and drafts.

7. *Sexual Offences and Abortion*. Private sexual relations, whether heterosexual or homosexual, are excluded from the scope of criminality, unless children are victimized or there is coercion or other imposition.[146] Penal sanctions also are withdrawn from fornication and adultery, contrary to the law of many states. Prostitution would continue to be penalized, primarily because of its relationship to organized crime in the United States, but major sanctions would be reserved for those who exploit prostitutes for their own gain.[147] Forcible rape would be extended to include coerced deviate intercourse but relations between spouses would be excluded entirely, which was not generally true.[148] Sanctions are maintained against intercourse with minor females notwithstanding their willing participation, but the crime is not denominated 'rape' unless the child is under ten years of age. When the girl is older but below the recommended age of consent (16 years), the offence is treated as corruption of a minor. It is not committed, moreover, unless the male is four years older than the female, and a defence is provided if it is shown that she had previously engaged in promiscuous relations with others.[149] The crime of incest was preserved but the enormous sentences then permitted in some states would be much reduced.[150]

Finally, the model proposed that abortion performed by a physician in a hospital be justifiable when it was considered necessary not only to safeguard the life of the woman but also to protect her physical or mental health, or when there was a substantial risk that the child would be born with a grave physical or mental defect, or when the pregnancy resulted from rape or incest.[151] This was a modest change but very few considered its acceptance to be possible. To our surprise, it was enacted promptly in many of the states[152] only to be followed by the much more permissive statutes in Hawaii and New York, drafted on the British model,[153] and then by the Supreme Court decision holding any prohibition of abortion in the first trimester of pregnancy, to be a deprivation of the woman's right of privacy repugnant to the Constitution.[154] There is no better illustration of the magnitude and pace of fundamental change in penal law than these developments in this most controversial field.

8. *Support for Police Intervention*. There are, of course, some serious offences

---

[146] Article 213. [147] Article 251. [148] Article 213.
[149] §§ 213.3, 213.6. [150] § 230.2. [151] § 230.3.
[152] California, Colorado, Georgia, Maryland and North Carolina, followed by Alabama, Arkansas, Delaware, Florida, Kansas, Mississippi, New Mexico, Oregon, South Carolina and Virginia.
[153] Abortion Act, c. 87 (1967).
[154] *Roe* v. *Wade*, 410 U.S. 113 (1973); *Doe* v. *Bolton*, 410 U.S. 179 (1973).

against public order, such as riot, to which major sanctions are applied.[155] More commonly, however, the prime function of the penal law in its proscription of disorderly behaviour is to lay a basis for preventive police action. The significance of the arrest is largely spent once police custody has been established.

It has been characteristic to authorize such intervention by defining minor offences in catch-all terms that neither yield a norm of conduct nor a guide to the police. Much time was spent in working on this problem, which has overtones of great importance for the disadvantaged and presents an issue with respect to civil liberty that may rise to constitutional dimension. New formulations were proposed for the offences of disorderly conduct,[156] harassment[157] and loitering or prowling,[158] which achieve much greater specificity than older law and make a studied effort to accommodate conflicting values. The cases in which there may be an arrest for disobedience to a police command to move also were defined.[159] The statute would make clear that one whose sole offence is that he is regarded with dislike by others who observe him in a public place, is not a proper target for preventive intervention.[160] It ought not to be necessary to articulate that point, but I believe that it unfortunately is.

The Sentencing and Treatment of Offenders

The concept of the purposes of penal sanctions that the Model Code embraces has been set forth above and the approach to sentencing and treatment that derives therefrom has been described in general.[161] It remains to indicate in more detail some of the main positions taken in developing the system that the Code undertook to prescribe.[162]

1. *Foregoing Sentence of Imprisonment; Probation.* One of the most important dispositions in the Code is assuredly its disapproval of all legislative efforts to require sentence of imprisonment upon conviction of particular offences, with the possible exception of murder—where a mandatory sentence may be thought to be the only possible alternative to capital punishment. This

---

[155] § 250.1.   [156] § 250.2.   [157] § 250.4.

[158] § 250.6.   [159] § 250.7.

[160] The constitutional dimension of these issues is indicated by the following recent Supreme Court decisions: *Bachellar* v. *Maryland*, 397 U.S. 564 (1970); *Coates* v. *Cincinnati*, 402 U.S. 611 (1971); *Palmer* v. *City of Euclid*, 402 U.S. 544 (1971); *Papachristou* v. *City of Jacksonville*, 405 U.S. 156 (1972); *Gooding* v. *Wilson*, 405 U.S. 518 (1972); *Colten* v. *Kentucky*, 407 U.S. 104 (1972).

[161] See above.

[162] The antecedent situation is described in detail in Note, 'Statutory Structures for Sentencing Felons to Prison', *Colum. L. Rev.*, 1960, **60**, 1134.

is, of course, to disapprove the very widespread statutes that precluded the suspension of sentence or probation when defendants were convicted of crimes that the legislature wished to denounce with special emphasis of when they had a record of some designated kind. The point involved is, or course, that no legislative definition or classification of offences can take account of all contingencies. However right it may be to take the gravest view of an offence in general, there will be cases comprehended in the definition where the circumstances are so unusual, or the mitigations so extreme, that a suspended sentence or probation would be proper. Indeed, unless this power is overtly vested in the courts, experience makes clear that it will be assumed covertly by plea bargaining or charge reduction that involve a greater evil for the reason that the process is concealed.

The Code went further than merely to abandon arbitrary limitations on avoiding institutional commitments. It prescribed criteria that should be followed by the court in withholding sentence of imprisonment, directing[163] that the court 'shall deal with a convicted person' without passing such a sentence unless it is of the opinion that imprisonment is necessary for the protection of the public on one or more of the following grounds:

(a) there is undue risk that during the period of a suspended sentence or probation the defendant will commit another crime; or

(b) the defendant is in need of correctional treatment that can be provided most effectively by his commitment to an instutition; or

(c) a lesser sentence will depreciate the seriousness of the defendant's crime.

The position expressed in these criteria is that dispositions that do not involve imprisonment should be accorded a priority unless the sentencer believes that a good reason for imprisonment obtains. This would reverse the attitude of many courts, which ask themselves if there is special reason for dispensing with a prison sentence and thus put the emphasis in the wrong place. Probationary dispositions are, however, now so numerous and widespread in America that it is believed the Code criteria articulate and ratify what the best practice has achieved.

In many jurisdictions the suspension of a sentence necessarily involved an order of probation. That practice too was disapproved. There obviously is no necessary correlation between the conditional release of an offender and the need for his supervision by a probation officer. Both the conditions that ought to be applicable and the need for or degree of supervision should rather be determined in the light of the needs of the case. Hence, probation was envisaged in the Code as an independent mode of disposition.[164] If the

---

[163] § 7.01.   [164] § 6.02.

court does not perceive a need for supervision, a suspension, on such conditions as the court may specify within the statutory limits,[165] is the indicated disposition.[166]

In many jurisdictions a suspension and probation start a regime that may last as long as the maximum sentence of imprisonment that could have been imposed. The Code regarded this as both unnecessary and excessive, fixing a limit of five years for the conditional discharge on any felony conviction and for the lesser crimes a limit of two years.[167] If nothing untoward happens in that time, the defendant would be finally discharged; and there would be a power in the court to discharge earlier, if so advised.

These formulations have, upon the whole, been well received, though there are variations in how far criteria have been articulated, as well as in the standards that have been declared.[168] The New York Revised Penal Law moved somewhat in this direction, even following the British example in permitting a sentence of unconditional discharge.[169] Its approach has been highly influential but has not deterred others from a closer reproduction of the model.[170]

2. *The Nature and Duration of Prison Sentences.* There is nothing short of anarchy in the American statutes governing the prison sentences that the law authorizes on conviction of specific crimes. In California, for example, thirteen different maxima are employed in the statutes defining felonies. There are twelve in Pennsylvania and there were twelve in New York before the recent revision.[171] Nor do these computations take account of all the variables. A study in Oregon revealed that of the 1,413 different offences that could be identified, there were before the enactment of a new code 466 different and unique sentences (not all imprisonment) authorized by law.[172]

---

[165] § 301.1(2).   [166] § 6.02(3).   [167] § 301.2.

[168] Cf. Illinois Unified Code of Corrections § 1005–6–1 (a): 'The court *shall* impose a sentence of imprisonment if, having regard to the nature and circumstance of the offense and to the history, character and condition of the offender, the court is of opinion that: (1) his imprisonment is necessary for the protection of the public; or (2) the offender is in need of correctional treatment that can most effectively be provided by a sentence to imprisonment; or (3) probation or conditional discharge would deprecate (*sic*) seriousness of the offender's conduct and would be inconsistent with the ends of justice.' See also note 184 *infra*.

[169] N.Y. Rev. Pen. Law. § 65.20 (1967).

[170] E.g., Connecticut, Delaware, Hawaii, Kentucky, New York, North Dakota, Oregon, Texas, Utah. See also *A.B.A. Standards, Sentencing Alternatives and Procedures* § 2.5(c) (Approved Draft, 1968).

[171] For the details, see H. Wechsler, 'Sentencing, Correction and the Model Penal Code', *U. Pa. L. Rev.,* **109**, 465, 472–5; *A.B.A. Standards, supra* note 170, § 2.1, comment **a**, 50. See also the valuable memoranda by Professor Peter Low for the National Commission on Reform of Federal Criminal Laws, *Working Papers,* vol. II, 1245–337 (1970).

[172] See W. A. Beckett, 'Criminal Penalties in Oregon', *Ore. L. Rev.,* 1960, **40**, 1, 71.

There can be no rational defence of such a plethora of legislative judgements, the existence of which merely shows the failure of the legislature to perceive the limits—psychological and logical—of reasonable determinations of this kind. Too many distinctions of this order either must reduce the force of all and thus be nullified in practice or must produce results that are unjust and an impediment to the administration of correction.

The Code offered a remedy upon this point that has proved workable in drafting, permitting us upon the whole to take account of the discriminations that seem worthy of attention at the legislative level. The remedy, as stated above,[173] was to establish for the purposes of sentence only three degrees of felony, carrying as maxima, respectively, imprisonment for life, for ten and for five years. All major crimes and different forms thereof are distributed among these categories. Lesser crimes are, in turn, divided into misdemeanours and petty misdemeanours, with limits of one year and thirty days.[174]

Using this classification, the fifty felonies defined in the Model Code were distributed as follows: first degree: four (murder; kidnapping, rape and robbery in their most aggravated forms); second degree: twelve (manslaughter; aiding or soliciting suicide in its most aggravated form; aggravated assault; the lesser forms of kidnapping and rape; deviate sexual intercourse by force; arson; the lesser forms of robbery; burglary; forgery; causing catastrophe and abortion in their most aggravated forms). The other thirty-four felonies were classified as third degree.

There is, of course, an inescapable element of arbitrary judgement involved in the selection of precisely three decisive categories in relation to the serious offences and many variations are embodied in the codes and drafts. In New York, where the theory of the plan was adopted, five classes were employed; and many think that five are an improvement on the three. I should not take a brief on either side. The important point is that a small number of distinct sentencing categories ought to represent the entire range of the permitted prison sentences for crime; and that the legislature, once it has adopted such a plan, should adhere to it in future legislation. Such a step is vital to accord minimal deference to reason and equality in the administration of penal justice and to start to make an inroad on the problem of disparity of sentence, which everywhere is felt to be extreme. All of the current revisions of penal codes proceed, as far as I know, on this premise. It is, indeed, the one submission of the Code that no one has challenged.

Given a system of this order, there are two controversial questions as to the extent of influence the court should be empowered to exert on the duration of imprisonment, assuming that a prison sentence is imposed.

[173] See above.   [174] §§ 6.06, 6.08.

The first issue is whether the judicial power should extend to fixing a minimum. The Code answers this affirmatively, in the view that there is often need for the reassurance of the community that only imposition of a minimum is able to provide. It was, however, thought that whether any minimum should be prescribed ought to be discretionary with the court,[175] except that any sentence to a state institution should import at least a year's duration as an institutional necessity for diagnostic work and shaping of a programme. Beyond this, under the model the minima the court would be empowered to impose are relatively short: up to two years for the third degree of felony where the maximum is five; up to three years for the second degree where the maximum is ten; and up to ten years for the first degree where the maximum is life imprisonment. Eligibility for release on parole would, of course, arise upon the expiration of the minimum, less the reductions for good time that the Code provides.[176]

The second issue is whether the court should have authority to fix a maximum term shorter than that fixed by statute for the degree of felony involved. There was substantial disagreement in the Institute upon the answer to this question, resulting in alternative provisions.[177] If such control is given to the court, there was, however, full agreement that a minimum imposed should not be longer than one-half the maximum, whatever that might be.

3. *Special and Extended Terms.* The authorized prison sentences I have described are what the Code denominates the ordinary terms. A departure from these norms would be permitted in two different situations.

The first is the case of what the Code calls the Young Adult Offender, meaning a person between the ages of sixteen and twenty-two at the time of sentencing. Such an offender, the Code provides,[178] may in lieu of any other sentence of imprisonment upon conviction of a felony be sentenced to a special term without a minimum and with a maximum of four years, if the court is of opinion that such special term is adequate for his correction and

---

[175] The general acceptance of this view in the New York Revised Penal Law of 1967 was highly influential in promoting its acceptance in the later codes and drafts. Amendments enacted in 1973 have, however, mandated sentence of imprisonment upon conviction of certain (usually drug-related felonies), as well as on most second-felony convictions, prescribing a range of minimum and maximum terms but requiring the minimum to be one-half the maximum. *N.Y. Rev. Pen. Law* §§ 60.05.3, 70.06. It is too early to predict the influence that this regrettable regression may exert in other jurisdictions.

[176] §§ 305.1, 305.6.

[177] § 6.06 and Alternate § 6.06. The competing arguments upon this issue and the issue with respect to judicial authority to fix a minimum are canvassed in Wechsler, *supra* note 171, at 475–80. See also, *A.B.A. Standards, supra* note 170, §§ 3.2, 6.2 and accompanying comments.

[178] § 6.05.

rehabilitation. The object here is to protect the young from longer sentences in meritorious cases and to give an impetus to greater emphasis on the development of special programmes for their needs. This much deference to the miracle of youth has had general support in the United States, however ominous the crime reports may be.

The second departure inheres in the authority to impose imprisonment for an extended term in dealing with four categories of offenders: (1) persistent offenders; (2) professional criminals; (3) dangerous, mentally abnormal persons; and (4) multiple offenders, i.e. persons convicted of numerous offences without the spread in time that justifies a finding of persistence.[179] When an extended term may be imposed, the court would be empowered to lengthen the maximum otherwise available up to twice its length for felonies of second and third degree and within limits to extend the minimum as well. Sentence for an extended term would, however, always be discretionary with the court, avoiding the mistake of our earlier habitual offender laws, which have been largely nullified in practice. The concept is, moreover, of substantial criminological significance, since the criteria for the extended term employ three criminological categories of offenders, whose danger to the public the court is thus invited to explore.[180]

4. *First Release on Parole and the Parole Term.* The Code provides, as previously stated, that all long-term prisoners must have their first release upon parole; and to implement this provision it declared that every sentence of imprisonment for felony includes, in addition to the terms I have described and as a separate portion of the sentence, a parole period up to five years, terminable sooner by the Board of Parole in its discretion.

The statement of this proposition gives a first impression that all of the maximum terms that I have noted should be increased by five years; and many critics of the Code appraised it in this way.[181] The important fact that they ignored is that the only case in which this is a fair description is that in which the Board retains the prisoner until the expiration of the maximum, a course that would be followed only when there is the gravest apprehension of repeated crime. In the normal situation, the separate parole term gives the prisoner a large advantage. The reason is that what the Code puts forward is the novel proposition that the maximum of the original sentence should

---

[179] §§ 6.07, 7.03.

[180] For a comparison of these proposals and the somewhat different submissions of the Model Sentencing Act, prepared under the auspices of the Advisory Council of Judges of the National Council on Crime and Delinquency, see *A.B.A. Standards, supra* note 171, at 82–116; G. F. Flood, 'A Higher Level of Penal Law', *Crime & Delinq.*, 1963, **4,** 370, 374–5.

[181] See, e.g., S. Rubin, 'Sentencing and Correctional Treatment Under the Law Institute's Model Penal Code', *A.B.A.J.*, 1960, **46,** 994. But cf. Bates, op. cit., *supra* note 7.

cease to operate after a first release has taken place. Its function, in other words, is confined to stating how long the prisoner may lawfully be held in custody before that first release occurs. Once there has been a first release, that portion of the sentence would be over. The parole term then would be the only operative basis of restraint, measuring both the period of supervision and the duration of a recommitment if a recommitment should be ordered for a violation of parole. In the result, a person sentenced to a maximum of ten years, for example, and released after two, would be subject to restraint for only five years more, instead of the eight that present systems would allow.

This drastic change in concept had the very simple purpose of removing an anomaly that otherwise obtains. Prisoners who are conceived to present the worst risks upon release and thus are held the longest time must be released with a short period of supervision or with none at all. The best risks, given earliest release, are, on the other hand, subjected to the longest period of supervision, a regime that often carries on for many years. We saw no better way to reverse that absurd result than the proposal I have described.[182]

5. *Criteria for First Release*. Finally, I would direct attention to the Code's attempt to formulate criteria for the parole release decision, a judgement heretofore committed to the free discretion of the Board.

The Code provides[183] that when the Board considers first release of a prisoner whose minimum term, if any, has expired, it shall be the policy of the Board to order his release unless it is of the opinion that release should be deferred because:

(a) there is a substantial risk that he will not conform to the conditions of parole; or

(b) his release at that time would depreciate the seriousness of his crime or promote disrespect for law; or

(c) his release would have a substantially adverse effect on institutional discipline; or

(d) his continued correctional treatment, medical care or vocational or other training in the institution will substantially enhance his capacity to lead a law-abiding life when released at a later date.

These criteria express the policy that there should be a first release when prisoners are eligible under the judicial sentence, unless a substantial reason for postponing the release appears. We knew of no substantial reason for

---

[182] On the alternative mechanism recommended by the National Commission on Reform of Federal Criminal Laws, namely, a prescribed 'parole component' in all prison sentences for felony, see Low, *supra* note 171, at 1292–7, 1330–3.

[183] § 305.9(1).

postponement of release other than those specified; and critics of the formulation, who are numerous, have not thus far advanced a reason of this kind. Some parole boards, on the other hand, are using the criteria, and there are indications that they find them sound.

I am not optimistic that the Code's parole provisions will achieve enactment in the calculable future, since the Boards are naturally zealous to protect the full autonomy they have enjoyed.[184] They are, moreover, fearful that if all first releases take place on parole, the record of parole success will fall because the worst risks then will be included in the calculation. But as Commissioner Frederick A. Moran, once Chairman of the New York Board, said more than thirty years ago: 'As long as parole is limited in its use to carefully selected prison inmates, its value to prison administrators, to the prisoner, and to the community must necessarily be limited.'[185] The American Law Institute agreed with Moran and saw quite clearly that the only answer was to view parole as the proper method for all first releases. The problem for the Board should not be thought to be *whom* to release but rather *when* a first release ought to be made.

In resisting the adoption of this concept, many parole administrators have performed like neurotics clinging to their symptoms What makes them vulnerable now is that they do assume to underwrite the future of each parolee, with the resulting implication that a failure on his part involves a failure of the Board. When they and the public recognize that failure and success are both inherent in the system, as it is recognized respecting sentence of the court, parole will finally have come of age.

When the Model Penal Code had been completed, a generous commentator characterized its 'dominant tone' as 'one of principled pragmatism'[186]—an

---

[184] The opposition has, however, grown increasingly articulate and influential in the recent past. See, e.g., K. C. Davis, *Discretionary Justice* (Baton Rouge, Louisiana State Univ. Press, 1969), p. 126; M. E. Frankel, *Criminal Sentences: Law Without Order* (New York, Hill and Wang, 1973), p. 95; F. Cohen, 'Sentencing, Probation and the Rehabilitative Ideal: The View from Mempa v. Rhay', *Texas L. Rev.*, 1968, **47**, 1; S. H. Kadish, 'Legal Norms and Discretion in the Police and Sentencing Processes', *Harv. L. Rev.*, 1962, **75**, 904; S. H. Kadish, 'The Advocate and the Expert—Counsel in the Peno-Correctional Process', *Minn. L. Rev.*, 1961, **45**, 803; V. O'Leary and J. Nuffield, 'Parole Decision-Making Characteristics—Report of a National Survey', *Crim. L. Bull*, 1972, **8**, 651.

Attention should be called to the sad irony of the provision in the Illinois Unified Code of Corrections (§ 1003-3-5(c)) enacting the model criteria in reverse: 'The Board shall not parole a person eligible for parole if it determines that: (1) there is a substantial risk ...' etc. Since the Board is given no instruction if it does not make the negative determination, it would perhaps be justified in reading the formulation as an affirmative pregnant!

[185] *N.Y. Division of Parole, Trends in Parole* 6–7 (1940).

[186] H. L. Packer, 'The Model Penal Code and Beyond', *Colum. L. Rev.*, 1963, **63**, 594.

appraisal I was no less ready to accept than Browning to adopt a reader's version of the meaning of his poem. If the description is correct, it articulates how far the model and its legislative progeny reflect the spirit of Sir Leon's contributions to the field of criminal and penal policy—avowedly pragmatic but insistently humane, ardent to increase our knowledge but attentive to its grievous limitations, rejecting ideology[187] in favour of accommodation when conflicting values call for reconciliation. We celebrate that spirit in this volume.

APPENDIX

STATUS OF SUBSTANTIVE PENAL LAW REVISION
(Asterisk indicates publication of substantial commentary)

I. REVISED CODES; EFFECTIVE DATES:

*COLO. REV. STAT. ANN., CH. 40 (1971 Perm. Cum. Supp.); 7/1/1972.

CONN. GEN. STAT. ANN., TIT. 53A; 10/1/1971.

*DEL. CODE ANN., TIT. 11; 7/1/1973.

*GA. CODE ANN., TIT. 26; 7/1/1969.

*HAWAII LAWS OF 1972, ACTS 9 & 102; 1/1/1973.

*ILL. ANN. STAT., CH. 38; 1/1/1962.

ILL. UNIFIED CODE OF CORRECTIONS; 1/1/1973.

*KAN. STAT. ANN., § 21–3101 (1972 Supp.); 7/1/1970.

*KY. REV. STAT., CH. 433A (1972 Supp.); 7/1/1974.

LA. REV. STAT., TIT. 14; 1942.

MINN. STAT. ANN., CH. 609; 9/1/1963.

*MONT. REV. CODE ANN., TIT. 94 (1973 Sess. Laws, Ch. 513); 1/1/1974.

*N.H. REV. STAT. ANN., TIT. 62 (1972 Supp.); 11/1/1973.

N.M. STAT. ANN., CH. 40a; 7/1/1963.

*N.Y. REV. PEN. LAW; 9/1/1967.

N.D. CENT. CODE, TIT. 12.1 (1973 Supp.); LAWS OF N.D. 1973, CH. 116; 7/1/1975.

*THE NEW OHIO CRIMINAL CODE; 1/1/1974.

ORE. LAWS 1971, CH. 743; 1/1/1972.

*PA. STAT., TIT. 18; 6/6/1973.

*TEXAS PEN. CODE (S.B. 34, passed by 63rd Reg. Sess. of Leg., signed by Governor 6/14/1973); 1/1/1974.

UTAH CODE ANN., TIT. 76 (1973 Supp.); 7/1/1973.

*WIS. STAT. ANN., TIT. 45; 7/1/1956.

---

[187] See, e.g., L. Radzinowicz, *Ideology and Crime*, London, Heinemann Educational Books, 1966, pp. 60–128.

II. CURRENT SUBSTANTIVE PENAL CODE REVISION PROJECTS:

A. *Revision completed; not yet enacted:* (17 in all)

Alaska (Proposed Code not reported out of Judiciary in 1972 Legislative session; not re-introduced in 1973 Legislature).

*California (Proposed Criminal Code, Sen. Bill 39, introduced in Senate; Sen. Judiciary Comm. to hold hearings).

Florida (Proposed revision of Tit. 44 introduced in Legislature April 1973).

Idaho (IDAHO PENAL & CORRECTIONAL CODE, TIT. 18, enacted effective 1/1/1972 but repealed effective 4/1/1972).

Iowa (Iowa Criminal Code [Final Draft 1973] to be considered by 1974 Legislature).

*Maryland (Proposed new Code & Commentary: Part I published; Part II to be published autumn 1973; may be introduced in 1974 Legislature).

*Massachusetts (Code & Commentary re-introduced in 1973 Legislature).

*Michigan (Revised Criminal Code re-introduced in 1973 Legislature: House Bill 4086; Sen. Bill 82; pending in Senate & House Judiciary Committees).

*Missouri (Plan to introduce Code in 1974 Legislature).

Nebraska (Proposed Criminal Code [Final Draft, Oct. 1972] introduced in Jan. 1973 Legislature).

*New Jersey (Proposed new Penal Code & Commentary submitted to Governor & Legislature 12/1/1971).

Oklahoma (Revised Code re-introduced in 1973 Legislature [Sen. Bill 22]; pending in Sen. Judiciary Comm.).

*Puerto Rico (Proposed Code: Sen. Project 19 & House Project 27 rejected by 1972 Legislature; a new revised Bill will be considered soon).

*South Carolina (Proposed Code with Commentary introduced in Legislature 4/5/1973; recommitted to Sen. Judiciary Comm.).

*Tennessee (Plan to introduce Code in 1974 General Assembly).

*United States (Criminal Code Reform Act of 1973: S. 1400 & H.R. 6046 introduced March 1973. Criminal Justice Codification, Revision & Reform Act of 1973: S. 1 introduced Jan. 1973. H.R. 6046 in House Judiciary Committee. Sen. Judiciary Subcommittee on Criminal Laws & Procedures began holding hearings April 16 on S. 1 & S. 1400).

*Washington (Proposed Criminal Code to be re-introduced in autumn 1973 Legislature).

B. *Revision well under way:* (4 in all)

Alabama (plan to introduce Code in 1975 Legislature).

Arkansas.

Indiana (plan to introduce Code in 1974 Legislature).

Maine.

C. *Revision at varying preliminary stages:* (3 in all)

Arizona, Virginia, West Virginia.

D. *Revision authorized—work not yet begun:* (1)

North Carolina.

E.   *Contemplating revision:* (3 in all)
Rhode Island, South Dakota, Vermont.

III. **NO OVER-ALL REVISION PLANNED:** (4 in all)
D.C., Mississippi, Nevada (recodification with minor changes enacted 1967), Wyoming.

THOUGHTS ON SEX LAW REFORM

D. J. West

General Principles

Crime occurs when the needs or desires of some individuals clash with the well-being of others. Criminologists are students of social conflict and their observations necessarily impinge upon social policy. A political dialogue between legislators and criminologists seems both desirable and inevitable. This is acknowledged when government departments invite criminologists to serve as expert advisors on official committees. The discussions cannot be expected always to run smoothly. Sometimes the administrators' expectations, assumptions and rules of patronage conflict with academic notions of intellectual freedom, so much so that certain of our younger colleagues prefer to criticize from a safe distance.

Controversy is unavoidable because discussion of social policy must involve value judgements. Criminological observations are not simple physical measurements of a psychologically neutral character, they depend in part upon the eye of the beholder. Moreover, deciding what to do about the 'facts' reported by social investigators involves setting up priorities and balancing conflicting needs. In making recommendations the criminologist may be better informed than the man-in-the-street, but he still has to use some personal scale of values. I believe that the criminologist should not try to hide behind a smoke-screen of pseudo-scientific objectivity, but should state his values plainly. This is particularly necessary in relation to the legal control of sexual behaviour, since this is a topic about which ideas are changing and different sections of the community adhere to very different value systems.

In his famous essay *On Liberty* John Stuart Mill asserted: 'The only purpose for which power can rightfully be exercised over any member of a civilized community, against his will, is to prevent harm to others'. In the abstract, this liberal maxim seems to offer a sound guide to the proper function of the criminal law, which is to prohibit only those acts which cause harm to others. Historically, sex law has attempted to be much more restrictive, and to condemn forms of behaviour, such as unconventional coital positions, which, though not demonstrably harmful, are considered unusual or distasteful. In his Beckley Lecture for 1972, the Rt. Rev. John Robinson, Dean of Trinity College, Cambridge, argues that the same libertarian values considered appropriate in other branches of the criminal law should also be applied to the statutes relating to sex, and that the law should intervene only when needed to safeguard persons, their privacies and freedoms. Otherwise, citizens should be free to express their own opinions, tastes and preferences, and to behave according to their own ideas of morality. I personally subscribe to these principles with one addition. I think the burden of proof of the alleged harmfulness of an activity should rest with those who seek to prohibit it. In other words, behaviour should not be made criminal that has not been shown to be harmful to others.

These principles may not seem particularly revolutionary. Some years ago, the distinguished American sociologist Stanton Wheeler[1] pointed out that the modern trend in criminal law, as exemplified by the American Law Institute's Model Penal Code, is to punish only those acts which are socially dangerous, independent of their moral character. 'Throughout the discussion of code provisions,' says Wheeler, 'emphasis is clearly placed on control of behaviour that appears to show some immediate social harm, either through the use of violence, through the exploitation of children, or through the nuisance of public indecency.' This modern aim of the criminal law replaces the previous emphasis on law as an expression of moral condemnation.

When virtually the whole community accepted Christian teaching about the evils of sexual activity outside of marriage, and about the particular abomination of conduct described as 'unnatural', it was perhaps reasonable for the criminal law to follow a similar line. Today, as Wheeler points out, 'Increasing social differentiation makes it difficult to find sexual acts that are universally condemned'. A criminal law that does not have common assent becomes difficult to enforce in a democratic country. This, I believe, was a powerful factor in bringing about changes in the English law concerning attempted suicide and homosexuality. It was not merely that the law was frequently flouted. After all, laws against theft are frequently broken, but that is no reason for abandoning them. It was rather that the spectacle of unfortunate individuals being condemned for actions that harmed no one else, which others were known to have committed with impunity, began to arouse a feeling of injustice among an influential section of the community.

A glance at contemporary English sex laws shows that they are still a long way from being guided solely by the utilitarian aim of preventing demonstrable harm to victims. They consist of a strange medley of enactments,

[1] S. Wheeler, 'Sex offences: A sociological critique', *Law and Contemporary Problems*, 1960, **25**, 258–78.

often couched in quaint language, originating at different periods, and providing a tariff of maximum penalties that have hardly any connection with the supposed harmfulness or prevalence of the offences in question. For instance, intercourse *per anum* by a man with his wife, the crime of buggery, is subject to life imprisonment (Sexual Offences Act, 1956, S.12), whereas the same act between two males in private is not a crime in England. However, any form of sexual behaviour, even without actual physical contact, which involves two males, is gross indecency and punishable by imprisonment in Scotland or Northern Ireland. Sexual fondling of a girl under sixteen, even if she initiates the activity, is a crime of indecent assault punishable by imprisonment for two years (S. 14). Similar behaviour with a man under twenty-one is punishable as gross indecency with a penalty of imprisonment for five years (Sexual Offences Act, 1967, S.3).

These anomalies are less important than breaches of the general principle that the criminal law should direct itself exclusively to preventing harm to others. It seems to me justified to view critically all laws directed against so-called 'crimes without victims', such as drunkenness, gambling, drug abuse and attempted suicide, in which dispute arises as to whether the offending behaviour harms anyone else. There have been a particularly large number of 'crimes without victims' linked with sexual behaviour. Abortion, prostitution, fornication, miscegenation, obscenity, living on immoral earnings, homosexuality and sex under the age of consent spring to mind, although of course not all of these are currently crimes. In the days when birth control was primitive and syphilis a devastating and incurable scourge, it may have been realistic for legislators to regard any manifestation of sex outside marriage as socially dangerous, but circumstances have changed.

The root problem is to decide what behaviour is sufficiently harmful to merit definition as a sexual crime. The most diverse interpretations have their ardent supporters. The protagonists of homosexual law reform used to point to the non-criminal status of heterosexual adultery, and argue that homosexual conduct posed a lesser threat to the family. This argument could equally well be used in support of legislation against adultery, with penalties even heavier than those against homosexuality. This is, in fact, the present position in some Islamic countries. In Afghanistan, adultery is still, theoretically, a capital crime, but sexual relations between unmarried persons, and homosexual conduct, are considered much less grave transgressions.

Sexual legislation aimed at the protection of the institution of marriage and the nuclear family has been attacked by radical sociologists as positively harmful. Marcuse[2] has pointed to 'surplus repression', that is the limitation of erotic interest to marital procreation, as one of the undesirable features of

[2] H. Marcuse, *Eros and Civilisation*, Boston, Beacon, 1965.

the capitalist system. Restrictions of personal freedoms, and the imposition of a static, predictable life style, is necessary for the full economic exploitation of industrial workers. Imaginative art, with its strong erotic overtones, and unconventional or 'perverse' sexual conduct, reveals sexuality as a hedonistic rather than a utilitarian function, and is therefore anathema to capitalistic puritanism. The sexual subservience of women, who are not supposed to have needs of their own, but are given bed and board in return for catering to their husbands' wants, is another aspect of traditional economics operating in the sexual field.

This kind of radical challenge has been taken up by several militant reformist movements, especially in the United States. Dennis Altman,[3] in a lucid account of some of these developments, shows the close connections which exist between womens', homosexuals' and blacks' liberation movements, all of which demand an end to forms of oppression so long taken for granted by society that even the victims have tended to accept unquestioningly their own inferior status. The gay liberation front demands for homosexuals much more than the removal of legal sanctions. They insist that tolerance, in the sense of an absence of positive discrimination, is not enough. They want full recognition of homosexual life styles as legitimate and respected alternatives to heterosexual living. Altman sees the campaign as part of a sexual revolution that will be of immense benefit to all, regardless of their sexual orientation. He writes (p. 223): 'Gay liberation is part of a much wider movement that is challenging the basic cultural norms of our advanced industrial, capitalist society and bringing changes in individual consciousness and new identities and life styles. . . . Unlike liberalism, the movement in America today recognizes no barriers between politics and culture, art and life, public and private. Gay liberation is both an affirmation of the right to live as we choose and an intent to extend that right to others.'

The sexual behaviour of some lower animals is highly stereotyped and genetically programmed by means of the endocrinological control of sexual responses. Dramatic reversals of normal patterns can be induced by manipulating hormone levels experimentally. In man, however, sexual behaviour is very largely a matter of learning and experience. The socialization processes begin virtually from birth, and are mediated through parental training of infants and young children. Many of the cues are non-verbal and unwitting. Disgust reactions and shuddering avoidance are as powerful suppressors of an infant's manifest sexual interests as deliberate punishments. Differential training of male and female also begins very early. Many cases are recorded in which inappropriate handling at critical stages of development has

[3] D. Altman, *Homosexual: Oppression and Liberation*, Sydney, Australia, Angus and Robertson, 1972.

produced physically normal males or females with the psychological identities and sexual preferences of the opposite sex. Humans are susceptible to sexual conditioning in many different ways. In some cultures the stimuli of kissing, or oral-genital contact, are highly prized for their erotic value, whereas other cultures find such practices revoltingly unclean and unnatural.

If one considers the matter with sufficient detachment, it becomes difficult to say by what right certain erotic preferences are condemned and others accepted. Lars Ullerstam[4] a Swedish physician, takes this line of thought to its logical conclusion in a highly revolutionary but singularly unpolitical book about erotic minorities. He argues that homosexuals are unfairly privileged among sexual minorities in being recognized as a group and having meeting places where they can make contact with others able to reciprocate their unconventional desires. Other kinds of deviants, exhibitionists, fetishists, voyeurs, etc. suffer severer legal and social sanctions, and have less opportunity to satisfy their needs. Ullerstam argues that the intolerance of sexual minorities is irrational and inhumane, and in many ways comparable to the worst atrocities of racial persecution. He thinks the coupling of inferior personality and moral turpitude with unconventional sexual interest is an unjustified slur, perpetuated by the ignorance and prejudice of psychiatrists. He advocates a wholesale relaxation of current sex laws. In particular, he proposes that the law should permit specialized brothels, where the physically or mentally handicapped, the sexually deviant, and the sexually impotent might find charitably minded persons to minister to their needs.

These arguments are all concerned with redefining many forms of sexual behaviour as non-criminal on the grounds that they are not really harmful to others. However, even where the criminal law is seeking to control actions that are demonstrably harmful, it is not always the most appropriate means for the purpose. Where alternatives to prosecution are available, they may be preferable. In cases of cruelty to children, for instance, an educational and welfare approach to the family is often less damaging in the long run than sending a parent to prison. Similarly, in cases of sexual interference with children by a member of the family it may be preferable, in the interests of the child, to have the matter dealt with by medical or social workers than to break up the home with a criminal prosecution.

Leaving matters to the discretion of prosecuting authorities has the disadvantage that the law may seem to be applied arbitrarily or unevenly. The minority of offenders who are prosecuted may be thought to be unfairly selected scapegoats. Sometimes it proves possible, with surprisingly little disruption, to remove offences altogether from the penal code and allow the

[4] L. Ullerstam, *The Erotic Minorities* (transl. A. Hollo), New York, Grove Press, 1966.

situation to be dealt with by other methods of social control. For instance, with the raising of the age of criminal responsibility, the management of unruly children becomes more and more the business of the medical, educational and social services rather than of the courts. The abolition of some minor offences may prevent more serious abuses. For instance, permitting drug addicts a legitimate medical supply may discourage the black market in drugs, thereby reducing many associated crimes. Similarly it might be argued that by permitting certain sexual outlets, such as licensed brothels, or clubs for homosexuals, nuisances such as street soliciting or indecencies in lavatories would be correspondingly reduced.

In the discussion which follows, some specific aspects of English sex law are reviewed critically in the light of the general principles and considerations that have been mentioned.

The Age of Consent for Girls

The governing statute is the Sexual Offences Act, 1956, as amended by the Indecency with Children Act, 1960. However willing they may be, girls under the age of sixteen cannot legally consent to participate in any form of sexual activity. An attempt to have sexual intercourse with a willing girl under sixteen renders the male participant liable to two years' imprisonment, or to seven years' imprisonment, should she be under thirteen years. A completed act of sexual intercourse with a girl under thirteen carries a possible 'life' sentence. Furthermore, any kind of sexual approach to a girl under sixteen constitutes an indecent assault rendering the offender (whether male or female) liable to two years' imprisonment, or to five years' imprisonment if the girl is under thirteen. If the girl is under fourteen, it is not necessary to touch or threaten to touch her in order to commit a crime; indecent behaviour in her presence, or encouragement of the girl to act indecently of her own volition, suffices. 'Any person who commits an act of gross indecency with or towards a child under the age of fourteen, or who incites a child under that age to such an act with him or another' is liable to two years' imprisonment (Indecency with Children Act, S.1, i). It will be noted that such behaviour is an offence regardless of the sex of either the child or the offender. However, so long as he is over fourteen, a woman can let a young boy have intercourse with her without committing an offence (R. v. *Mason*, 1968, Cri. App. R., *53*, 12–19).

The majority of convictions for indecent assaults upon females involve girls under sixteen. There are two elements to the offence, the assault, that is some physical act, or the threat of it, plus 'circumstances of indecency'.

Any behaviour that would have been an indecent assault in the case of an adult woman who refused consent is automatically an assault if the girl is under sixteen, regardless of her willingness. Hence, the merest touch may be held to be an assault. There must, however, be circumstances of indecency. The use of force for chastisement or restraint is not an indecent assault. According to the Cambridge report on *Sex Offences*[5] police practice as to the type of conduct which should be charged as indecent assault has varied. 'In some areas, for instance, there has been a reluctance to charge indecent assault unless there has been a touching of the bare flesh of the victim; in others a more strict attitude has been adopted.' If the offender avoids touching the victim, but instead invites her to manipulate him, this has been held not to be an assault (R. v. *Burrows* (1952) 1 All E.R. 58, n.). However, as has been explained, such conduct can now be charged as gross indecency, if the girl is under fourteen, but not otherwise. The fixing of the age at fourteen for this purpose followed a report of the Criminal Law Revision Committee (1959, Cmd. 835). The Committee felt that children of fourteen and fifteen were already sufficiently protected by the provisions against indecent assault and attempted intercourse. They commented: 'Moreover, those provisions already present problems for both courts and prosecuting authorities in relation to girls approaching sixteen, and the creation of a further offence would tend to increase these difficulties.'

There is a statutory defence to a charge of sexual intercourse with a minor if the man is under twenty-four, has not previously been charged with a like offence, and had reasonable cause to believe that the girl was over the age of consent (Sexual Offences Act, 1956, S.6, iii). Curiously, this defence is not available to an offender charged with indecent assault, even though his conduct may have fallen a long way short of attempted intercourse. For this reason, a charge of indecent assault is occasionally used to get round this defence even if sexual intercourse has taken place (1971, Crim. L.R. 299).

The age of consent to sexual intercourse used to be only twelve (Offences against the Person Act, 1861). It was first raised to thirteen in 1875 and then to sixteen by the Criminal Law Amendment Act, 1885. In contrast, the age at which a lawful marriage could be contracted remained at twelve years until the Age of Marriage Act, 1929, raised it to sixteen also. In the intervening period, it was lawful for a man to have sexual intercourse with a girl under age provided she was his wife.

Historically, the fixing of the age of consent at sixteen arose out of the appalling social conditions of the working class in Victorian England.[6] For

[5] L. Radzinowicz (ed.), *Sexual Offences*, a report of the Cambridge Department of Criminal Science, London, Macmillan, 1957, p. 408.

[6] Ann Stafford, *The Age of Consent*, London, Hodder and Stoughton, 1964.

young girls, prostitution was often a happy relief from intolerable poverty, and their overburdened parents had little incentive to restrain them. Owing to the celebrated double standard of sexual morality, respectable gentlemen who treated young girls of their own class with the utmost delicacy, thought nothing of satisfying their lust with children of the brothels. Procurers had little difficulty finding fresh virgins to supply to the brothel-keepers at home or abroad, and the police did not seem to want to intervene. The situation was commented upon by the Royal Commission on Contagious Diseases, 1871. Their main task was to consider the laws concerning control of venereal disease by compulsory examination of women prostitutes, but they drew attention to the notorious traffic in children for infamous purposes in London and other large towns. It was not until 1885, following some unsavoury and sensational revelations in the *Pall Mall Gazette* by the famous editor W. T. Stead, that Parliament was moved to pass, with considerable haste, the Criminal Law Amendment Act. The age of consent suddenly jumped to sixteen, heavy penalties were introduced for taking girls under eighteen out of the possession of their parents or guardians for immoral purposes, and girls escaping from premises used for immoral purposes in clothes not their own were no longer to be prosecuted for theft.

The dangers of sexual exploitation of the poor are much reduced in modern conditions, and the retention of the age of consent at sixteen is generally justified on other grounds. Young girls are thought to need protection from their own impulsiveness. Those who are too immature to take the decision for themselves, or too young to appreciate the full implications of sexual permissiveness, are prevented by law from giving consent to sexual approaches. It is hoped that this discourages sex among adolescents, which is socially undesirable because of the risk of producing babies. It is also emphasized that the law is still needed to discourage older seducers and procurers from recruiting among the very young.

There are a number of practical reasons for doubting the wisdom of the present law. First of all, it bans, at least in theory, even the mildest forms of sexual experimentation between young adolescents. Since such behaviour is widely regarded as a normal part of growing up it is surely inappropriate to stigmatize it as 'criminal'. Admittedly the law is not normally enforced in this way, but that could be a good reason for changing it. Even the law against intercourse under age is enforced only exceptionally. Less than a thousand males are prosecuted annually for sexual intercourse with girls under the age of consent, but some three thousand girls under sixteen either give birth to illegitimate babies or have legal abortions. The spread of venereal diseases among the young, and the production of unwanted pregnancies, are the immediate evils of undisciplined sexuality. Instead of seeking to control these complications by criminalization of sex, it might be better to deal with them by providing more frank and practical sex education in schools, and by giving easy access to contraceptives. Well-informed and relatively sophisticated adolescents are likely to be more responsible in sex, as in other matters.

One aspect of the law appears peculiarly unjust. However willing or even importunate the female, her contribution is not recognized in law, only the male is an offender. In R. v. *Tyrell* (1894) 1 Q.B. 710, Lord Coleridge, C.J., referring to the Criminal Law Amendment Act, 1885, which raised the age of consent from thirteen to sixteen, pronounced: '. . . it is impossible to say that the Act, which is absolutely silent about aiding and abetting or soliciting or inciting can have intended that the girls for whose protection it was passed should be punished under it for offences committed upon themselves.' Since naming her lover can result in criminal prosecution, a young girl may be placed in a very difficult position when authorities demand to know his identity.

It seems to me that the concept of an age of consent could be abolished with advantage and still leave girls adequately protected from exploitation. Any unwanted sexual approach would still be an assault, and it could be made a rebuttable presumption that a girl under fourteen would not want such behaviour. Procuring of minors for immoral purposes, including prostitution, would remain an offence. Young girls who willingly indulge with older men might still present a problem beyond the power of parents to cope with, but in such cases the Childrens' Acts provide for the imposition of care orders on grounds of exposure to moral danger. At present, any person under seventeen who absconds from the parental home and leads a disorderly life can be brought back by the police and is liable to be dealt with as in need of care, or control.

It needs to be emphasized that this proposed change in the law leaves non-consenting behaviour a crime, so that any show of aggression towards a child would still be a criminal offence. In practice, however, child molesters are rarely aggressive. In Kinsey's survey, among his 4,441 female subjects he found only one clear-cut case of serious injury done by a child molester. The strongest objection that might be raised against relaxing the law in the way suggested is that it would abolish all legal restraint upon an adult who takes unfair advantage of the willingness of small girls, who may not realize the full implications of their behaviour, to participate in sexual games.

The results of research surveys have some bearing upon the importance to be attached to this objection.[7] They suggest that many of the victims are

[7] J. W. Mohr, 'A child has been molested', *Medical Aspects of Human Sexuality*, 1968, **15**, 43–50.

girls who seek a relationship with other adults because they have not found emotional security with their own parents. The cases coming to official notice usually involve girls of 6 to 11, the adult concerned is often a relative or family friend, and the mutual fondling and exhibitionism which occur reflect the sexual curiosity and play common among pre-pubertal children. The after-effects of such incidents are likely to be minimal unless, upon discovery, the parents react with horror, and bitter family recriminations or police questioning ensue. As an investigation by Professor Gibbens confirmed, molested children made to appear in court are more likely to show emotional disturbance subsequently than similar children dealt with informally by social workers.[8] This is a powerful reason for trying to de-criminalize such incidents. An amendment of criminal procedures to allow written statements to be admitted in these cases might go some way towards helping child victims, but would not eliminate stress from family recriminations.

Most of the offenders are timid, socially inadequate men who find contact with children easier than a relationship with another adult. Some are intellectual dullards with childish mentality, some are lonely old men, and some are immature adolescents. Only a small proportion of detected offenders become recidivists. Even without the intervention of the criminal law, it is likely that the severe social disapproval which this behaviour incurs would suffice to discourage these offenders once their behaviour comes to light. Moreover, any complaint on the part of the child, to the effect that the man had behaved improperly against her wishes, would render him liable to criminal prosecution.

It might be further objected that, without an official prosecution, which serves to draw the attention of employers and prospective employers, positions of trust in schools and children's homes might become more readily open to men with paedophiliac tendencies. In practice, such abuses are best prevented by a careful staff recruitment policy, the dismissal of anyone found misbehaving, and the reporting of incidents to the bodies which regulate or discipline professional workers. The occasional criminal prosecution is not a particularly effective means of general control, and has the great disadvantage of exposing the individual children concerned to an unnecessarily harrowing experience.

---

[8] T. C. N. Gibbens and Joyce Prince, *Child Victims of Sex Offenders*, London, I.S.T.D., 1963.

Incest

In English law, a man commits incest if he has or attempts to have sexual intercourse with a female whom he knows to be his daughter, sister, half-sister, granddaughter or mother. A woman of sixteen or over who permits a man who stands in such a relationship to her to have sexual intercourse with her also commits a crime (Sexual Offences Act 1956, S.11). (In Scotland, incest between uncle and niece is also incestuous.) Incest by a man with a girl under thirteen is punishable with life imprisonment. Incest with an older person is punishable by up to seven years' imprisonment.

Where, as is often the case, the behaviour occurs by mutual consent, incest is an example of a crime without a victim. However, the female partner is usually the man's adolescent daughter, and it is certainly arguable that these girls might not be so ready to participate if they fully appreciated the damaging social consequences that can ensue. Many of the cases which come before the courts involve varying degrees of callousness, intimidation or brutality towards the girl involved. In the absence of a law specifically directed against incest, these cases could still be prosecuted as sexual assaults. Indeed, before the Incest Act of 1908 first made this a statutory crime, it was frequently prosecuted as rape or as sexual intercourse with a girl under age.

The reasons for the incest taboos have been discussed *ad nauseam* by psychologists and sociologists (for example Freud and Parsons).[9] Anthropological research reveals that although such taboos are widespread they are very variable. In some communities incest may be permitted on special occasions or within particular groups, and there are societies which have no taboo on incest at all.[10] Moreover, cultures which preserve an official ban on incest do not necessarily discourage the practice of masturbatory handling of children by their parents. In our own culture, however, it is evident that the incest ban serves some useful purposes, encouraging the young, as they grow towards independence from their parental homes, to look outside for mates and ultimately set up new families of their own. The worst effects of incest are not so much in the sexual activity itself as in the disturbance to social development which arises from criminal prosecution, unwanted pregnancy, or the possessiveness of a sexually jealous father.

The cases of incest which come to the attention of doctors or the courts characteristically arise from situations of obvious family conflict. A wife may

[9] T. Parsons, *Essays in Sociological Theory*, Glencoe, Ill., The Free Press, 1954; S. Freud, *Totem und Tabu*, London, Routledge, 1950.
[10] H. Maisch, *Incest*, London, André Deutsch, 1973, pp. 35 ff.

be ill, absent, neglectful or turning sexually frigid. A husband is thrown into close contact with a sexually maturing daughter, or stepdaughter, of stimulating attractiveness. Girls brought up in an atmosphere of marital tension feel a particular need for love, protection and attention. This may lead to deliberately seductive behaviour, and the ready acceptance of a special relationship with the father. Some incestuous men are habitually tyrannical and demanding with their families, so that the sexual exploitation of a daughter fits in with their general style. In contrast to the behaviour of the true paedophile, the typical incestuous father does not begin offending until the girl is mature enough to be sexually responsive. The relationship often continues until the girl is in her later teens and starts forming sexual attachments outside. The abnormal possessiveness and jealousy displayed by the father when this occurs is not infrequently the cause of the offences coming to notice or being revealed by the girl herself. Another common circumstance leading to denunciation is a continuation of the marital conflict that predisposed to the incest in the first place.

Only a minority of incest crimes known to the police and 'cleared up' actually lead to a conviction. The laws of evidence require the girl's statements to be corroborated. Apart from acquittals, and discretion exercised by the police in instituting proceedings, there must be an enormous dark figure of unreported cases. Some of these are known or suspected by doctors and social workers, and dealt with informally.

There is a conflict of view about the likely consequences to the girl of permitting an incestuous relationship. Brother–sister incest is probably less serious psychologically, since it is often a brief and 'experimental' interlude in sexual development. Weinberg suggests that most victims of father–daughter incest settle later to a normal heterosexual life.[11] Everyone agrees that the effects of a prosecution for incest can be disastrous to the girl involved. If the father is imprisoned, she suffers the guilt of being in part responsible, she loses his protection and economic support, her parental home is broken up, and she herself may be taken into a children's home. Moreover, since the social service departments have a statutory duty to remove from the home of a convicted sex offender any minor thought to be in moral danger, the family's troubles do not end when the prisoner is due for release. The wife may be forced to choose between having no husband or having no children. Because the social service departments are not always willing to commit themselves in advance to what they will do when an incestuous prisoner comes home, the man's chances of release on parole are likely to be adversely affected.

Sentences for incest are extremely variable and sometimes very severe.

[11] S. K. Weinberg, *Incest Behavior*, New York, Citadel Press, 1963.

In commenting upon the sentences considered appropriate by the Court of Appeal, Thomas noted that in all cases involving parents and children, sentences in the region of six years of imprisonment were commonly confirmed, even when there was no question of threat or force.[12] In reducing one sentence from six years to four, because the man was 'mentally very backward and not able to stand up to the buffets of an unhappy marriage', the Court emphasized the need for 'an adequate measure to show that this is a crime which society looks upon with horror. . . .' In this case the victims were two daughters aged eighteen and twelve (*Smith* (1967), 51 Cr. App. R. 376). More recent cases suggest that the Court may now be taking more account of mitigating circumstances. Perhaps the Court of Appeal is more horrified by incest than the trial courts, for the sentences which they approve are much longer than those received by the majority of incest offenders. Because incest is one of those crimes about which people hold opposing views, individual offenders are likely to be dealt with very differently.

For the sake of the victims and their families, and because the concept of incest arouses unhelpful emotions, I should be glad to see the crime deleted from the statutes and offenders prosecuted only when a charge of sexual assault is appropriate. Lesser degrees of sexual immorality involving children could be dealt with, when necessary, by the legal power to remove from their parents children exposed to moral danger.

The Anti-Homosexuality Laws

As was mentioned earlier, the focus of discussion on this topic has undergone a radical change. Spokesmen for the homosexual minority have emerged who challenge the right of the majority to define them as deviant, undesirable, problem people, inferior or sick. Homosexual people demand, as of right, equal status before the law and the abolition of discriminatory practices in employment, housing and social services. Their demands echo those of the campaigns for equal rights for women, for coloured people, and for religious or political minorities.

One may doubt whether the militant homosexuals are right that their lifestyle is as healthy, satisfying, and worthwhile as heterosexual living; but the existence of the homosexual subculture proves that it is at least a viable alternative. Scientific knowledge of the ways in which sexual learning is acquired, and sexual attitudes and feelings develop, is as yet at a primitive level, due to the social inhibitions which hamper research in this field.

[12] D. A. Thomas, *Principles of Sentencing*, London, Heinemann Educational Books, 1970, pp. 111 ff.

Consequently, the influences which bring about homosexuality or hetero-sexuality are little understood. A substantial majority of the population might agree that universal heterosexuality is a desirable social aim, but there is no evidence that criminal sanctions against the adult deviant make any positive contribution to this end. It appears that, in some cases patterns of sexual behaviour are surprisingly firmly established early in life, and are resistant to change thereafter. My own hunch is that the exposure of children to practical training in sexual response would have a more powerful effect in encouraging the development of heterosexuality than any amount of moral exhortation or criminal legislation. However that may be, child train-ing in sex is obviously not a practical proposition in the present climate of opinion, notwithstanding the advent of the so-called permissive society.

In view of our ignorance in this field, it is my view that the criminal law should interfere as little as possible, and then only for the purpose of pre-venting demonstrable harm in situations in which other methods of control are ineffective. The present state of English law on the matter is curiously inconsistent. Homosexual behaviour between females is broadly controlled in the same way as heterosexual behaviour. No sanction exists if both parties are consenting and over sixteen, but sexual 'assaults' upon under-age girls, and indecency with children, committed by female offenders, are regarded as crimes.

The key statutes for the control of homosexual behaviour between males are the Sexual Offences Acts of 1956 and 1967. Homosexual behaviour is referred to as gross indecency or, if anal penetration occurs, as buggery. Buggery with an unwilling male over the age of sixteen carries a maximum penalty of ten years' imprisonment, while buggery with a consenting partner carries only a two-year penalty, provided that the participants are either both over twenty-one or both under twenty-one. Should one be older and the other younger than twenty-one, the older man becomes liable to five years' imprisonment (1967 Act, S.3, i). Buggery with a boy under sixteen (or with a woman or an animal) carries a penalty of life imprisonment (S.4a). An act of gross indecency between two consenting males is punishable by two years' imprisonment, or by five years' imprisonment if the man is over twenty-one and his partner under twenty-one. The same penalty applies if he merely procures or attempts to procure a male under twenty-one to commit an act of gross indecency with a third party (1967 Act, S.3, ii). Indecency with a boy under sixteen is an assault punishable by ten years' imprisonment.

The 1967 Act introduced one important exception to the above-listed sanctions. In England and Wales (but not in Scotland or Northern Ireland) buggery and gross indecency by male couples are no longer punishable as crimes provided both participants are consenting civilians over twenty-one years of age, and provided their conduct occurs in private with no third party present. Members of the Forces, however, are still subject to court martial for homosexual conduct, and similarly the exemptions do not apply to homosexual behaviour on U.K. merchant ships by members of the crew (1967 Act, S.2, i).

Males are also subject to penalties for persistently soliciting or importuning for immoral purposes (1956 Act, S.32), misconduct which carries a maximum penalty of two years' imprisonment. This offence stems from the Vagrancy Acts, and it is likely that the legislators originally had in mind annoyances caused by the male touts of female prostitutes. In practice, however, the law is not much used to suppress solicitation for prostitution, whether male or female, but is usually directed against homosexual males trying to make the acquaintance of others similarly inclined. Men who loiter in the vicinity of public conveniences, or around notorious picking-up places in parks etc., are liable to prosecution on these grounds. The statute has been interpreted extremely strictly by the courts. Evidence of annoyance caused to members of the public is unnecessary. Charges are normally brought on the evidence of police officers, frequently in plain clothes, who are on the lookout for suspicious behaviour. It has been held that suggestive smiles directed towards strangers are sufficient to constitute an offence, and that the person solicited need not necessarily be aware of the offender's signals (*Horton* v. *Mead* (1913) 1 KB. 154). It has often been alleged in the past, by men charged with importuning, that they were led on by young policemen in attractive civilian attire who behaved in a provocative and inviting manner in order to secure an arrest. On the other hand, it is also said that the police are compelled to fall back on their own resources in these cases because members of the public are embarrassed and reluctant to come forward to give evidence against homosexuals who have propositioned them. If the police took no action, the public would be annoyed and scandalized by the misuse of public facilities for immoral purposes.

Laws designed to preserve public order and decency are sometimes applied in a discriminatory way against homosexuals to make them conform to stricter standards of decorum than are required of heterosexuals. For instance, public bars or clubs which develop a homosexual clientele may fail to get their licence renewed, even though there is no question of improper behaviour occurring on the premises. In Sept. 1968, a club owner pleaded guilty before the Manchester magistrates to allowing behaviour likely to cause a breach of the peace, namely males dancing together. Men who use the personal columns of magazines or newspapers for advertising for male travel companions or flat mates risk police enquiries, and the advertisements themselves may be held as evidence of conspiracy to corrupt public morals—as in the *International Times* prosecution of 1970.

Among the more obviously unsatisfactory aspects of contemporary legislation in this area are the extreme severity of the maximum penalties (which makes for wide variation in sentencing), and the glaring discrimination between homosexuals and heterosexuals in such matters as soliciting and the definition of acts in private. Males can, it seems, solicit women with impunity, but not other men. Women can solicit men, but not if they do so in the streets for purposes of prostitution. The Director of Public Prosecutions must be consulted before proceedings are taken for any homosexual offence involving a person under twenty-one, but this provision has not prevented prosecutions from taking place when all concerned were under that age. In fact the criminalization of all homosexual acts by or with men under twenty-one is perhaps the worst feature of the law. One effect is that very mature young adults who choose to participate in forbidden sex with older men, whether for pleasure or for gain, are placed in a position in which they can threaten, abuse or blackmail the older person, knowing the victim will not complain for fear of a heavy prison sentence. Another effect is that social workers and professional counsellors are inhibited in providing appropriate advice and guidance to young homosexuals for fear of getting to know about, or being accused of encouraging, conduct defined as serious crime.

It is tempting to suggest, by way of radical reform, a simple abolition of any distinction between homosexual and heterosexual misconduct. Sexual behaviour could be regulated by a single set of laws which would apply equally whatever the sex of the participants. This, broadly, is what the campaigners for homosexual equality would wish. It would require some modification of existing statutes. For instance, on present legal definitions, males cannot be the victims of rape, and females cannot perpetrate rape, (except as accomplices), although they can be respectively the victims or perpetrators of sexual assault with violence. Some offences, such as 'obscenely exposing his person with intent to insult a female' (Vagrancy Act, 1824), were obviously formulated with male offenders only in mind for the reason that the acts in question (in this case unwanted exhibition of the genitals to strangers of the opposite sex) are in practice rarely committed by women.

The crucial difficulty about an integration of homosexual and heterosexual laws is the matter of the age of consent. If the laws as they now stand were integrated, boys of sixteen would become legitimate targets for homosexual relationships. If, as was suggested in a previous section, the notion of an age of consent were to be abandoned altogether, then boys of any age could, if they wished, form homosexual relationships with other boys or with older men without breaking the law.

These consequences would be deplored by a great many people. Rightly or wrongly, there is a stronger reaction against the man who encourages young boys to behave homosexually than against one who encourages young girls to behave heterosexually. Likewise, adults are even more shocked at the idea of letting children behave homosexually than letting them behave heterosexually. These revulsions stem from the idea that homosexual indulgence when young may lead to permanent homosexual fixation in later life, an outcome which, in a heterosexually oriented community, is surely best avoided if possible.

Clinical studies suggest that casual sexual experience does not usually result in the permanent conditioning of erotic responsiveness to deviant situations. Extensive homosexual experience in adolescence is quite compatible with a contented heterosexual adjustment subsequently. There is far more to sexual development than merely learning the easiest mechanical technique for achieving orgasm. If that were all there was involved there would be no urge to progress beyond solitary masturbation. In reality, sexual activity is a complex social activity that involves the imagination and fulfils a variety of symbolic functions. By the time a child reaches puberty he has a well-learned gender rôle to play, a rôle which has become essential to himself and to his acceptance by others. Homosexual activity may produce orgasms, but it does not satisfy the social needs that make heterosexuality additionally rewarding. Hence normal youngsters, unless they are in some way discouraged or frightened, will go on to seek opposite-sex partners, because this is what they have long since learned is part of their gender rôle. Once heterosexual responsiveness is well established, it is rare for it to be lost again however many homosexual incidents occur subsequently. This is exemplified by the male prostitute, who happily finances his own heterosexual requirements on the proceeds of repeated homosexual indulgence.

Early homosexual experience is probably not an important factor in the development of homosexual fixations in adulthood, except where there are pre-existing disturbances of gender rôle or concomitant hindrances to heterosexual contacts. The abolition of an age of consent for boys as well as for girls is a less dangerous step than might be supposed. The law would still provide for juveniles of either sex, found to be in need of care, protection or control, to be compulsorily removed from undesirable sexual associations with adults. Unwanted sexual approaches would remain criminal assaults. Finally, responsibility for the guidance and control of children's developing sexual behaviour would be placed firmly where it ought to rest, namely with parents, educationists and child guidance agencies. The criminal process need be invoked against children only if they commit violence.

General Conclusions

This paper has considered several spheres of sexual control, namely adolescent sexuality, children involved in sex with older persons, incest, and homosexuality. In all these spheres it appears to the present writer that the criminal law as it stands is unnecessarily rigid and harsh, and not the best means for preventing social evils. Other topics might have been discussed, with similar conclusions. For instance, the control of prostitution, an activity which is theoretically legal, is hedged about with restrictions on advertising, profit-making by a third party, or the use of premises for the purpose. Furthermore, these restrictions on a supposedly legitimate business activity are enforced by harsh criminal sanctions. It is argued that these penalties are necessary because prostitution encourages criminal activities, such as exploitation by pimps, robbery, blackmail, drug peddling etc. How far these evils are intrinsic to prostitution, and how far they are the consequence of legislation which reinforces the near-criminal status of the prostitute and her associates is for me an open question.

Another example is pornography. At present, a vigorous campaign for stricter control and harsher legislation is in full swing. It seems to be tacitly assumed that the dissemination of pornography lowers standards of sexual morality and promotes sexual misconduct. The evidence, such as it is, suggests that in reality the ready availability of pornography reduces rather than increases sexual nuisance, by giving frustrated and inadequate individuals a harmless outlet. Imprisoned sex criminals are not, in general, particularly avid users of pornography. Perhaps it would have been better for them if they were!

All these examples point to a conflict of values between those who support sexual permissiveness or tolerance, and those who wish to set out a straight and narrow path of restricted conduct supported by restrictive legislation. The supporters of restrictions argue that selfish hedonism causes unhappiness, breaks up marriages, and threatens the stability on which the upbringing of children depends.

In essence, the argument turns on a matter of values. Freedom of choice is an important value. Applied to sex it means tolerating minorities with deviant styles of sexual conduct. Stability of the home is also an important value, especially where children are concerned. If the two were irreconcilable, it would be difficult to decide between them. In this writer's opinion the dilemma does not arise. The sexual habits and attitudes of the community as a whole change only very slowly. Public protests of sexual liberation co-exist with conservative practice in private. Toleration of minority practices, such as prostitution and homosexuality, does not cause the majority to change their ways. Indeed, paradoxically, by making the requirements of law and custom more flexible and less insistent, more people rather than fewer might attain to ideal sexual standards, and fewer would become social casualities on account of sexual inadequacy. These are the beliefs underlying the values advocated in this paper.

UNITED NATIONS SOCIAL DEFENCE POLICY AND THE PROBLEM OF CRIME[1]

Manuel López-Rey

The Foundations

The programme, activities and machinery of the United Nations in the field of Social Defence are based on the terms of reference of the Social Commission as described in United Nations document E/41, 1946 and resolution 155 of the Economic and Social Council 1948. Both clearly state the importance of the study of the prevention of crime and the treatment of offenders at the international level, and that the United Nations should assume leadership in promoting this activity. This leadership was reaffirmed by General Assembly resolution 415,V,1950, governing the transfer of the functions of the International Penal and Penitentiary Commission (I.P.P.C.) to the United Nations. The references are of importance for two reasons. First, General Assembly resolution 415, V, 1950 cannot be regarded as the *ratio essendi* of United Nations Social Defence policy, and it certainly cannot be taken to signify a 'contract' between the United Nations and the old I.P.P.C. designed to continue the functions performed by the latter.[2] Secondly, leadership by the United Nations demanded from the very beginning a policy far broader than that which had been pursued by the I.P.P.C.

Whether or not the transfer was justified cannot be discussed here. It is

[1] Nothing of what is said here is based on restricted information acquired by the author as a former international civil servant of the United Nations but on unrestricted documents and publications of the United Nations. Accordingly the analysis of facts and social defence policies is that made by a professor of Criminal Law and Criminology of a policy which, like any other, is open to professional consideration.

[2] See *Official Records* of the corresponding joint meetings of the Second and Third Committees and General Assembly, 1950, at which the representative of the Secretary General stated that 'if adopted, the plan [of transfer], would of course imply the intention to apply it, but the plan did not constitute a rigid contract and alterations could later be made by the United Nations if in the light of the experience any changes should be made necessary'.

sufficient to say that, to a great extent, it was forced upon the I.P.P.C. and the Social Commission by the United States who invoked the then widely accepted policy against 'overlapping activities', which had resulted in several international organizations being absorbed by the United Nations. Another and no less important factor was the growing American dissatisfaction with the 'French working' of the I.P.P.C. which was bluntly brought into the open by the American representative at the decisive session held in Bern shortly before the transfer.[3] Moreover, although markedly European, the I.P.P.C. was financially too dependent on United States contributions.

It was obvious that, at the international level, the activities of the League of Nations relating to the prevention of crime and the treatment of offenders (with the co-operation of several international organizations, among them the I.P.P.C.), were unsatisfactory. This was partly because the problem of crime was regarded as marginal and partly because the organizations, mostly of a European character, which dealt with crime problems, were powerful enough to assert themselves in the limited international community of the period between the two world wars. The organization of the United Nations reflected a new and rapidly expanding international community, the penal and criminological needs of which, even if still approached from a traditional angle, could not be satisfied by the I.P.P.C. Its European character and approach to the crime problem as well as its limited means constituted serious obstacles to leadership in the prevention of crime and the treatment of offenders. With all its importance and splendour, The Hague Congress of 1950 clearly showed that the I.P.P.C. was a spent force. In that year, after the expulsion of Franco's Spain the number of member states was 24, of which the non-European were Argentina, Egypt, Japan, New Zealand, the Union of South Africa and the United States, i.e. 25 per cent of the total membership. This apparently led the U.S.S.R. to consider the I.P.P.C. as 'a minor international organization' and to oppose the transfer of its functions to the U.N. The remark was unfair, inasmuch as the limited international community to which the I.P.P.C. belonged did not demand the huge organizations of our time. Moreover, the rôle played by the I.P.P.C. was not minor and deserves praise.[4]

From the beginning, the foundations of the social defence policy were regarded as forming part of a broad socioeconomic policy which did not exclude, under the term social, the psychopsychiatric consideration of some crime problems. In the last ten years these foundations have been expanded

[3] See Proceedings of the I.P.P.C., 1949.

[4] It is significant that the International Penal and Penitentiary Foundation which, in some respects, may be regarded as a survival of the old I.P.P.C., has not greatly succeeded in altering its marked European character by enlarging its membership internationally.

and social defence activities are now supposed to become an integral part of socioeconomic development or national planning. Therefore, with some fluctuations, there is continuity between the socioeconomic foundations of the social defence policy, set up in 1948[5] and resolution 1086B XXXIX, 1965, of the Economic and Social Council. Indeed the documents *International Action in the Field of Social Defence, 1966–1970* (1966) and *Progress Report on Programmes in the Field of Social Defence* (1967) maintained that 'the prevention and control of juvenile delinquency and adult criminality should be undertaken as part of a comprehensive economic and social development' and 'social defence problems lay deep in the process of economic and social development and had to be solved within them'. The 1966 Committee of Experts—of a marked governmental character—'recognized the wisdom of this approach'. This socioeconomic foundation has occasionally been attenuated in some of the more recent documents prepared by the Secretariat,[6] but was stressed as recently as the Kyoto Congress in 1970—which, in one of its conclusions, stated that 'social defence planning should be an integral part of national planning'. In his exposition as General Rapporteur of the Congress, Sir Leon Radzinowicz rightly, in my view, criticized this conclusion. Even assuming that national planning embraces more than socioeconomic planning, the foundations instead of being reinforced become even more shaky.

The foregoing remarks do not mean that the socioeconomic foundations of social defence policy lack historical justification. However, even in 1946 and 1948, when the provisional and definitive programmes of social defence were formulated, that justification had steadily been losing ground—in spite of the support received from socialist ideologies and from statements inside and outside the United Nations. In fact, the socioeconomic thesis of crime may be regarded, in many respects, as more the expression of traditional approaches or ideological thinking than as the result of the analytical appraisal of the problem of crime. I shall explain later that both attitudes are largely the result of regarding as one two different (though related) things: namely (1) *the problem of crime* and (2) *crime problems*. The fact is, that while some *crime problems* are determined by socioeconomic conditions, the *problem of crime* as a global sociopolitical phenomenon (of which *crime problems* are aspects) cannot be dealt with purely through socioeconomic policies or through planning or by assuming that it is only an element of national development. The conclusion is that the present foundations are only partially valid and should be revised.

---

[5] Documents E/CN 5/13, E/260 and E/578.
[6] See *Criminality and Social Change,* 1971.

Operational Concepts and Activities

The formulation of social defence policy requires the use of some basic operational concepts which, owing to their instrumental character, should not be regarded either as foundations of this policy or as establishing the boundaries within which the policy should be confined.

Thus, the term 'social defence', which had originally been linked to the Social Defence school of thought, was promptly abandoned and in accordance with the 'neutral' character of international policies it was stated that 'the purpose of the programme of social defence was to deal practically with the necessities in the field of the prevention of crime and the treatment of offenders since, in the opinion of the members (of the Social Commission) this was the major practical issue'.[7] Since then this pragmatic approach has been maintained, and it therefore cannot be said that the United Nations social defence policy implies recognition of the Social Defence school of thought. As an administrative classification of services the term 'social defence' means that the prevention of crime and the treatment of offenders is concerned with 'immediate necessities' as well as those of the near future. Nowadays in some documents prepared by the Secretariat the term 'control' is also used. Although having a different meaning, control should for all practical purposes be regarded as part of prevention and treatment.

The term 'social change' is also used as a major operational concept to explain the problem of crime, and as one of the foundations of social defence policy.[8] The ambivalent character of social change as a general explanation of crime was demonstrated when the item *Prevention of types of criminality resulting from social changes and accompanying economic development in less developed countries* was discussed at the 1960 United Nations Congress. Unfortunately the clear findings of the Congress have been obliterated by the discussions and findings on social change and social forces at the 1965 Congress. One has only to read the report to see that such vague terms inevitably lead to confusion and generalities of no scientific or policy-making value.

The analysis of the phenomenon of crime shows that the still much favoured term 'social change' is a misleading metaphorical concept which tries to explain everything (not only crime) but actually explains very little, if anything. Social change has been going on for millenia and, as an unlimited and complex process, cannot be used as an operational or explanatory concept. Experience shows that social change does not occur in every direction and place in the same way; its effects are often prevented in many

[7] Document E/799, 1948.
[8] A/8372, C/CN, 5/461, 1971 and related documents.

ways; people are affected differently according to a series of variable circumstances and many persons remain unaffected. All this applies to individual
as well as collective attitudes and values. In sum, social change may eradicate
certain forms of crime, increase or reduce others and create new ones. The
study of these variations shows that in many cases the changes are in the
forms (modalities) of an unchanged type of crime. Some of the new manifestations can be related to social change but many others reflect political
aims or technological progress. The distinction between modalities and types
of crime is important in criminal policy matters, and this importance was
already pointed out at the 1960 United Nations Congress in connection with
the item *New forms of Juvenile Delinquency*. Indirectly the point is also made in
the very informative study *Towards a Strategy for Crime Prevention*,[9] prepared
by the Secretariat, but its obvious implications for the use of the term
'social change' are not fully developed. If, as a general explanation, 'social
change' is used, the following questions among many others may be raised:
what modalities and types should primarily be taken into account? Are
all those selected for prevention purposes due to social change or to political,
technological and other factors which have very little to do with social
and economic conditions? Which are the aspects of social change that
prevent crime?

The study of the structure and functioning of any society shows that
changed and unchanged patterns of thinking, acting and living, whether
individual or collective, coexist in various degrees everywhere. As in all
societies change has always taken place in an uneven rather than in a uniform
way, the current expression 'crime in a changing society' makes very little
sense. In addition to social and economic factors, the physical environment,
ethnological characteristics, different structures and rôles of the population,
varied cultural aspects, the rôle of ideologies and political parties, religion,
technological progress, opposition, protest and revindication and many
other factors play a definite rôle in the fluctuations of crime. Only a grossly
distorted meaning of social change can embrace all of them. Yet the term
is still used. Before continuing with this 'wishful thinking' about the
causation of crime it would be better to pause and ascertain whether a more
limited use of the term, besides being criminologically justified, would
facilitate the prevention of crime and the treatment of the offender.

The question is not rhetorical inasmuch as operational terms in many
respects determine policy making as well as research. Actually it has already
been suggested that the 'causal' conception of social change should be
replaced by the 'agential' or 'institutional' conception of it. Guy Rocher,[10]

[9] Document E/AC. 57/3, 1972.
[10] Guy Rocher, *Le changement social*, Vol. 1, 1968, Paris.

pointed this out by indicating the significant rôle played by élites (a term which embraces groups of many sorts). If we look at the phenomenon of crime as a global problem and not only at some problems of crime, it can be concluded that groups and institutions often play a greater criminal rôle than individuals in the problem of crime. No doubt ultimately every crime is committed by individuals but this does not exclude—in fact it often stresses—the rôle of élites and institutions. A great amount of crime cannot be explained by contemporary criminology even if the term 'macro-criminology' is coined to cover this neglected area.

Terms such as 'deviation' and 'social change' are ineffectual from a policy-making point of view. For example, when, where and how should social defence policies intervene in order to prevent 'criminogenic' deviation or social change? Not all social change is 'criminogenic'. In fact in many cases it has an 'anti-criminogenic' character. If pinpointed, can the areas or factors leading (or possibly leading) to crime be regarded as unalterable or as allowing intervention? These and other questions show that in actual fact the use of social change, and for that matter of deviation, maladjustment and other terms, barely hide the failure of contemporary criminology.

As a result of the growing subordination of social defence policies to socioeconomic matters, the terms 'national development', 'socioeconomic planning', 'trends' and the like, are widely used in social defence pro-grammes. This preference has been reinforced by certain assertions of the Kyoto Congress, by resolution 1584 L 1971 of the E.C.O.S.O.C., by the Com-mission of Social Development, by some recent resolutions of the General Assembly and by the Committee of Experts on Prevention and Control of Crime.

Certainly, prevention of crime and the treatment of offenders are related to socioeconomic planning and also to national development although the amplitude of both terms, particularly the latter, raises many difficulties which are apparently usually overlooked. Thus the correlation implicit in the title of the U.N. Report, *Crime and Development: The socioeconomic context*, and the assertion that 'there was, in general, agreement that the main aspects of development considered potentially criminogenic were urbanization, industrialization, population growth, internal migration, social mobility and technological change; they were so considered because of their indirect effect upon the behaviour of some people', deserve a series of comments which lack of space does not allow. Suffice it to say that besides being a repetition of what has been said many times, the 'indictment' is worded in such a way that it deflates itself. Thus the terms 'potentially', 'indirect' and 'some' amount to very little because no less potentially and indirectly urbanization, industrialization, etc. may prevent 'some people' from becoming offenders. If so, what is the purpose of such imprecise generalities? If what is meant is that a better planning of all that is enumerated would prevent crime, the question again is what kind of crime did the drafters have in mind? Is it conventional crime, some crime problems or the whole crime problem? With others this mistaken premise led to a series of conclusions, among which the first reads as follows: 'Social defence planning should be an integral part of national planning. No country can afford to exclude the social defence element in its over-all social and economic planning and its allocation of adequate resources to that end. The prevention of crime and the treatment of offenders cannot be effectively undertaken unless it is closely and intimately related to social and economic trends. Social and economic planning would be unrealistic if it did not seek to neutralize criminogenic potential by the appropriate investment in development programmes.'[11]

The intention to improve conditions, which in many countries go from unsatisfactory to criminal and in others are simply bad in spite of the claims made by governments, is of course, praiseworthy. On the other hand, the excessive subordination of social defence matters to socioeconomic policy or development is unjustified. The operative terms are 'integral', 'cannot be effectively undertaken', 'socioeconomic' and 'closely related'. Has all this been reasonably demonstrated? Socioeconomic planning certainly plays a definite rôle in social defence planning and vice versa, but only with respect to some problems of crime and not to the whole problem of crime. Even the socialist countries are already aware of this. And the word 'integral', without further specification, is rather perplexing. What does it mean? These and other questions show again that present operational concepts and approaches are obsolete, and that in order to be more constructive the United Nations Congresses must be organized in a different way.

In a moderate way the informative study, *Towards a Strategy for Crime Prevention*,[12] itself contradicts the oversimplified approach I have been criticizing. It enumerates a wide variety of criminal offences such as hijacking, kidnapping, subversive activities, murder, robbery, violence and others which quite often have nothing to do with socioeconomic planning. The fact is, that although still ignored by many people, sometimes purposely, crime is first a sociopolitical entity and only second a causal event. Unfortunately governmental and professional considerations are still very much against this approach.

The fact is that socioeconomic policies and planning and (even more so) national development, are too vast, complex and fluctuating to offer a reliable basis for the integration of social defence planning. Moreover, social

[11] *Report*, United Nations Publication E. 1971, IV 8.
[12] See above, p. 493.

defence possesses its own planning of which many aspects have little or nothing to do with socioeconomic matters. In a pioneering way the Secretariat has rightly promoted the publication of a series of articles in the *International Review of Criminal Policy* and more recently in the volume *A Policy Approach to Planning in Social Defence*, published in 1972. On the other hand, the United Nations Asian and Far East Institute (U.N.A.F.E.I.) has published some of the lectures given at its first training course on social defence planning.[13] Apparently the recently created United Nations Cairo Institute has also initiated this training.

The material published shows that sometimes the meaning of social defence planning is misunderstood. The following cases deserve special mention: cost-benefit is indiscriminately used without taking into account that its transplantation into the social defence field requires a readaptation. If cost-analysis means that one does 'A' if the benefits exceed those of the best alternative course of action and not otherwise,[14] the first thing to do is to examine this concept in the light of the different types of treatment, the character and extent of the personnel to be used, the criminal clientele and the aims of criminal justice (which, at the present time, cannot be confined to the rehabilitation of the offender). The same applies to any other sector of social defence planning. Accordingly the already widespread use of concepts such as cost-effectiveness, input, output, sectoral (with all its variations), interconnectness, saving of time, uncertainty, risk and many others should be screened before being used by sometimes over-eager planners. Other concepts often distorted beyond recognition are 'system' and 'criminal justice system'. Thus, in *A Policy Approach to Planning in Social Defence*, Leslie T. Wilkins says, 'The idea of a system connotes something that is what it is by reason of its interconnectedness. Anything consisting of parts connected and working together may be called a "system". . . . Thus a pair of scissors may be called a system, but the expanded system in which someone cuts with the scissors is also itself a genuine system. . . . The difficulty in accepting the phrase "criminal justice system" arises from the difficulty of describing its exact purpose. . . .' It is to be lamented that such a distinguished professor should make such unfounded assertions. Neither a pair of scissors nor a motorcar—also cited by him—should be regarded as a 'system' (whether or not between quotation marks). As for the difficulties in describing the exact purpose of the criminal justice system, it is obvious that the difficulties in describing any given purpose are something apart from the system serving it. In his curious reasoning Wilkins reminds me of Norbert Wiener's irritation in his book *The Human Use of Human Beings: Cybernetics*

[13] UNAFEI, *Resource Material Series*, 4, 1972.
[14] See R. Layard (ed.), *Cost Benefit Analysis*, Harmondsworth, Penguin Books, 1972.

and Society,[15] where he complained about the diversity of purposes assigned to criminal justice and demanded that the first duty of law should be to determine what it wants for communication and cybernetic purposes. The fact is that criminal justice implies a plurality of purposes, all of them centred around that of justice. The concepts of interconnectedness and purpose are not enough to characterize a system. Organization, sociopolitical needs, social values and political and administrative power are also essential elements. Therefore the vulgar meaning of 'system' as something merely instrumental or operational, and 'system' conceived as part of a complex sociopolitical structure in a given society are two entirely different things. Only the *latter* should be used by experts when dealing with criminal justice and in our case social defence planning.

Neither sociology nor economics are the exact disciplines that they pretend to be and even less so is socioeconomic planning. As I have already stated in *Crime, An Analytical Appraisal*,[16] the term 'social' lacks precision; social and economic development may be associated but they may also oppose each other. The notion of balanced socioeconomic development is often more wishful thinking than reality and is, in any case, in a precarious state. As a cadre of reference for social defence planning and integration the thirty social desiderata of E.C.O.S.O.C. resolution 1139 XLI, 1966, demand a serious analytical selection before being used as such.

As for economics and economic planning, experience shows that both are much too often ineffectual—partly because of the shaky foundations of economics as a science and partly because economic planning is never purely economic but is to a considerable extent, psychological and political. If social change is merely a metaphor the same must apply to economic change. No doubt metaphors are useful in some respects, but they cannot be transformed into general explanations or regarded as foundations of any policy.

If economics is what some claim, i.e. an eclectic collection of bits of ideas, experiences and purposes, it is difficult to visualize how, with its companion sociology not much better equipped, socioeconomic planning can be regarded as the base on which social defence planning should be built. As stated in my contribution to the volume on policy planning, there are four different kinds of planning, 'first, national development; secondly, socioeconomic national development, which can be only partially identified with the previous one; thirdly, social defence planning, which although closely related to the second, is in many respects outside of it; and fourthly, the

---

[15] N. Wiener, *The Human Use of Human Beings: Cybernetics and Society*, London, Eyre & Spottiswoode, 1954.

[16] M. López-Rey, *Crime, An Analytical Appraisal*, London, Routledge and Kegan Paul, 1970, Chapter 4.

planning of the criminal justice system related to all three, but also autonomous in some relevant aspects'.

Perhaps the most crucial conceptual question is to determine what is meant by 'national development' and what is the operative meaning of it in general as well as in specific cases. Up to now, the general impression has been that development is understood mostly in socioeconomic terms—in economic terms particularly—partly as the result of capitalistic penetration in newly developing countries professing a socialism *sui generis* and partly because of the lack of imagination and inventiveness in setting up the basis for better socioeconomic, cultural and political structures in these countries. In this respect, it is significant that many of these 'socialist' or 'nationalist' countries still preserve colonial penal systems that cannot be adapted to national and social defence planning. This lack of imagination is still marked, after more than 150 years of independence, in Latin American countries, the vast majority of which have penal systems which are a mixture of neo-colonialism, neopositivism and fashionable transplantation. The Latin American Model Penal Code (General Part) of 1971 can hardly be regarded as appropriate to national or social defence development and planning.

Obviously a socioeconomic notion of development is not enough. Although in theory development means co-ordination and, in many respects, even harmony, in practice it means contradiction and frustration: i.e. the beginning of new forms of crime and the continuation of others. Still another question is whether some forms of development are not more 'criminogenic' than certain forms of under-development. These and other problems again illustrate that, as a frame of reference for social defence planning, national development must be carefully examined before being accepted as a basis for policy. When examined carefully its value would be far more limited than its supporters claim.

The foregoing fully justifies the initiative of the Secretariat in preparing a basic outline for the courses on social defence planning. The justification would be even stronger if the theme 'Analytical consideration of Concepts and Aims in Social Defence Planning' were added.

The subordination of social defence to socioeconomic policies has also led to a rapid decline of social defence manpower in the Secretariat and also of technical assistance. The main reasons are (1) the erroneous belief that the improvement of material socioeconomic conditions will eventually 'take care' of the crime problem and (2) that the kind of political regimes prevailing in the vast majority of the 132 member states are not conducive to the reinforcement of a more effective United Nations leadership in social defence. This explains the already numerous resolutions passed by the policy-making bodies, particularly those of the General Assembly in the last few years.

However, experience shows that the greater the number of resolutions on a given matter the less practical action is taken. The recent case of terrorism is significant. No less significant are the following data: during the 1950s the Section of Social Defence had 11 professionals, in 1973 the equivalent body (the Social Defence Programmes Section) has only five; in 1952 with 50 member states, 45 fellowships in social defence were granted, in 1963 with 123 member states only three and in 1972 with 132 member states only six fellowships and two experts. According to the 1969 *United Nations Yearbook* the amount spent on social defence assistance in that year was 0·2 per cent of the total. Actually, if it is remembered that this includes US$20,397 for the Funds-in-Trust (in itself a minute amount) for the controversial United Nations Social Defence Research Institute (U.N.S.D.R.I.) of Rome, the percentage becomes infinitesimal. What then is the practical value of G.A. resolution 3021, XXVII, 1972, which stressed the gravity of crime as well as the importance of social defence policies, if at the same time the United Nations policy-making bodies do not provide greater funds for social defence? Admittedly the question is very complex. On the other hand, the fact remains that the greater the number of member states—the majority of which are developing countries—the smaller has been the number of requests for social defence technical assistance. Probably it can be partly explained by the existence of direct bilateral aid from member nations. As for the answer that the relative frequency of regional meetings reduces the need for such assistance, it is enough to look into the contents and purpose of these meetings to see that their technical assistance value is very limited. No doubt the regional institutes may partly fill the gap, but apart from the fact that there are only two at present, their functions require the reinforcement of technical assistance. The organization of training courses and the commission of some research is not enough.

Unfortunately from the beginning social defence was too closely tied up with either a narrow social welfare policy or with a not much broader socio-economic policy. As a reaction against this approach the 1953 *Programme of Concerted Practical Action in the Social Field of the United Nations and Specialized Agencies*,[17] stated: 'In implementing social defence programmes it should be kept in mind that by their very nature these programmes are directed toward the whole community and not to certain groups. Although reiterated on several occasions the thesis does not yet seem to have received due recognition, a fact which seems at variance with the importance attached to the problem of crime by several resolutions in the last ten years and the growing concern about crime outside the United Nations. Thus the 1967 *Report of the Commission for Social Development* continued to list the prevention

[17] Document E/CN 5/291, 1953.

of crime and the treatment of offenders under the heading of Social Welfare Programmes for families, communities and special groups, and in the 1970 *World Social Report* social defence matters are grouped with the rehabilitation of the disabled and community development.

It would take too long to examine the past and present activities and programmes of work. They have received world recognition. As a rule social defence publications command attention and are frequently referred to in research and criminal policy projects. The same applies to many of the findings and conclusions of United Nations Seminars and Congresses. As for regional institutes, U.N.A.F.E.I. has already gained a fully justified prestige. On the other hand, the scarcity of funds from which the United Nations chronically suffers explains why, in spite of the efforts made, not all projects are carried out, some being postponed or dropped and others not implemented as they should be.

Needless to say, other funds than those mentioned are spent on publications, organization and attendance at conferences and meetings, the organization of quinquennial congresses, co-operation with institutes, personnel, etc. Yet the question remains wide open: if the crime problem is what it is said to be (and there is little doubt about it) are present resources enough to enable the United Nations to take more effective leading part in the prevention of crime and the treatment of offenders? A cursory glance at the existing situation in the vast majority of countries, socialist or capitalist, shows—to put it mildly—that the situation is more than just unsatisfactory, particularly as far as the organization and functioning of criminal justice systems are concerned.

The main projects of the present programme of work are social policies in relation to development planning, organization of research for policy development in social defence, new and special problems in social defence such as violence, terrorism, hijacking, drug abuse, corruption, organized crime and criminal justice, the revision of the Standard Minimum Rules and the participation of the public in the prevention and control of crime.

A word must be said about the United Nations machinery for dealing with social defence. It consists of the Commission for Social Development, the Economic and Social Council, the General Assembly, the Advisory Committee on Crime Prevention and Control and in some respects certain specialized Agencies, other Commissions and Divisions of the United Nations and the Section of Social Defence Programmes which forms part of the Social Development Division.

Although this is not the moment to comment on such machinery, it is too heavy, complicated and, in some instances, of doubtful effectiveness. The main reason is that both the Commission and the E.C.O.S.O.C. have functions too broad to deal adequately with social defence matters. More-over, as stated, the crime problem goes far beyond socioeconomic policies. Another reason is that both policy-making bodies are too governmental in character. Certainly governments should play a predominant rôle but this should be shared with non-governmental organizations (the present rôle of which is minor) and with other organizations and groups which could effectively contribute to the renewal of the present policy of social defence. In order to compensate for the socioeconomic approach and the govern-mental character of the above-mentioned bodies, as well as to bring in more professional knowledge and experience, the *ad hoc* Committee on the Pre-vention of Crime and the Treatment of Offenders undertook advisory functions starting in 1949. It is enough to look into the proceedings and reports of its sessions to realize why its reputation was so high. One of the advantages was that its members were not permanent and were appointed by the Secretary General on purely individual professional qualifications with no interference from governments or the policy-making bodies. The list of experts who served on the Committees still defies comparison. The new Advisory Committee on Crime Prevention and Control has been geographically enlarged, its members are permanent and appointed by the E.C.O.S.O.C., a governmental body, with the result that the experts are government experts. The Secretary General nominates them but experience shows that such nominations are seldom made without previous government approval. Therefore, like mission delegates, the new experts, if unable to attend may designate their own substitutes after previous official approval. This performance by proxy is contrary to the idea of choosing an expert on the task to be undertaken. In the past the Secretary General appointed the experts for a given session according to the matters to be discussed. This practice assured greater independence and professional adaptability. At that time no one believed in all-embracing experts in crime problems acting on a permanent basis. The excessive governmental character of the Advisory Committee could be reduced by adding *ad hoc* experts to assist in the con-sideration of particular matters. This can easily be done inasmuch as no E.C.O.S.O.C. resolution can, by itself, supersede the functions granted to the Secretary General by G.A. resolution 415 V, 1950.

It is obvious that the Section of Social Defence Programmes, in spite of its reduced staff, is doing a remarkable job which deserves sincere praise. However, it is clear that the machinery is inadequate to the growing import-ance of the problem of crime at national, international and supranational levels—three different and closely connected areas in which the need for more effective policies justifies the transformation of the Section into an autonomous Division. Such a move would give the flexibility of action required by a leadership more in accordance with the social defence policies needed at this time. It would liberate these policies from the socioeconomic or welfare 'tutelage' which, although partly valid, can no longer offer the appropriate framework to social defence activities. An integral part of the Division should be the U.N.S.D.R.I. of Rome, reorganized to avoid unsatisfactory past experiences and reduce local influence. This would justify its existence particularly at a time when the number of the regional institutes is gradually increasing. No doubt the generosity and interest of the Italian Government would facilitiate such an amalgamation.

The Problem of Crime and Crime Problems

Although important, the main questions relating to planning are not its operational concepts and mechanics but the delimitation of its subject matter. Many of the difficulties of socioeconomic planning—so often disrupted by political and military aims—come from the vagueness of the terms 'social' and 'economic' even if reduced to specific aims. Thus the planning of education or industrialization is often more like an image than a clear delineation of these terms. In our case the key term is 'crime' since the way it is defined and its extent predetermines the corollaries of prevention, control, treatment, offender and criminal justice. Fortunately, the concept of crime is usually clear enough, being what is defined as such by law.[18] This means that as an object of planning the concept of deviation is useless. Yet if the concept of crime is clear enough for planning purposes its extent is not. The question is not one of dark figures but of the distinction between the problem of crime and crime problems.

When using the term the problem of crime I include the total consideration of all manifestations of crime, wherever they appear; those responsible and the reasons they invoked to commit crime, as well as the policies aiming at crime prevention and control. The term crime problems denotes only the consideration of some of the aspects of the problem of crime as a whole. As we shall see, the distinction is vital to three important aspects, namely: the effectiveness of social defence policies, international leadership and the *ratio essendi* of criminology.

The extent of the problem of crime embraces crimes committed (1) under

[18] Contrary to some distinguished authors' opinions, there is no such thing as a 'criminological' concept of crime. Moreover the thesis that the legal definition of crime is conventional and its boundaries cannot be recognized by science has no foundation since crime is not a scientific event but a sociological concept. It may be studied scientifically but unless logic and methodology are twisted the subject matter of this study is still a legal concept. See M. López-Rey, *Crime, An Analytical Appraisal*, op. cit., pp. 3–4.

cover of official and semi-official positions; (2) against international law; (3) as a sequel to patriotic, ideological, revolutionary and similar actions; (4) organized crime and (5) conventional crime. The last group are crimes committed by the 'man in the street', i.e. crimes usually dealt with by police and the courts involving, in most cases, persons of lower social groups.

As aspects of the same problem of crime all these manifestations are, from the legal point of view, identical, i.e. the murder or maiming committed by a policeman, revolutionary, secret service agent, partisan or the military is as criminal as the murder or bodily injury committed by the 'man in the street'. Political aims, the performance of duty, etc. are often put forward to justify non-conventional crime. Admittedly, in a few cases the justification is valid but this is not so with the vast majority. Nowadays such justifications are discredited enough and the exposé that follows will confirm this.

None of the categories enumerated above implies that there is a clear division between them. Thus, organized crime may be part of conventional crime, as well as part of crimes committed while taking advantage of official position, for revolutionary purposes or in resistance to enemy occupation. In many countries, political persecution becomes another form of organized crime, usually perpetrated by official agents or by the military. The examples are legion and in some countries with nationalist and anti-imperialist leanings are becoming an admitted feature of the enforced political regimes (Uganda is one of the most recent cases). Police corruption, particularly in some important cities of the U.S.A., is another form of organized crime with rules and commitments which may differ from those of the Mafia but are as effective as far as impunity and benefits are concerned.

The fact that many non-conventional crimes are fatalistically accepted, regarded as revolutionary or ideological tactics or simply transformed into historical events and often forgotten, does not deprive them of their criminal character. This is because in the first place, historical actions may be as criminal as any others. Actually the problem of crime itself is historically determined. Moreover, if admitted, political reasons would apply to crimes committed by rightists as well as by leftists. No aim can justify criminal atrocities. Finally, even from a legal point of view the lapse of time does not erase the criminal nature of the act. For purposes of convenience, statutory limitations prevent *prosecution* after certain periods of time but the criminal character of the act remains. Therefore the killings committed to maintain an established order whether capitalist, socialist or simply personal, by military operations against non-resistant civil populations (Vietnam offers recent examples), by partisans or organizations aiming at independence or revindication, etc. are seldom less criminal than those committed by gangsters. What follows is an *ad exemplum* exposé in which the countries, selected indiscriminately, confirm the distinction made between the problem of crime and crime problems.

Nazi Germany committed a series of crimes on such a huge scale—from robbery to murder through every criminal variety—that it will literally take centuries before conventional German crime can be compared with the non-conventional crimes which were committed under cover of official and semi-official positions or military action against individuals, groups, minorities and countries. The crimes were not only committed by members of the Nazi Party and its organizations. It is important to note that most of those caught and sentenced as criminals were leading honest and respectable lives. If rehabilitation means the development of willing attitudes to live without breaking the law, to work, to have self-respect and a sense of responsibility, then most of these criminals achieved it by themselves. Many others as criminal as those sentenced are still at large and leading lives in accordance with the postulates of contemporary criminological rehabilitation. Are the foundations of treatment and rehabilitation of the offender as firm as they claim to be? The most significant conclusion is that as soon as criminal law was restored in a non-Nazi dominated society its deterrent effect upon a different individual and collective consciousness was most effective. The question arises whether rehabilitative treatment would inculcate in many of these criminals greater willingness, self-esteem, etc. than they already have. Briefly, are the aims of contemporary rehabilitation fully justified? Would it not be better to admit that the real aim of criminal justice is simply justice and nothing else?[19]

Between 1936 and 1950, under Stalin's rule one million persons were executed and about 12 million died in labour camps. Some of them were rehabilitated after Stalin's death.[20] According to Soviet authors crime as a whole is declining in the Soviet Union and with reservations—as long as reliable police statistics are not produced—the assertion can be accepted with respect to some forms of conventional crime.[21]

According to available data one may say that if the number of con-

[19] By justice is understood social justice and not that at present 'administered' in the vast majority of countries. The matter has been dealt with by the writer in several papers.

[20] See Robert Conquest, *The Great Terror*, London, MacMillan, 1968; E. Crankshaw, *Khrushchev Remembers*, London, André Deutsch, 1971, and Boris Levytsky, *The Uses of Terror, The Soviety Secret Service 1917–1970*, London, Sidgwick & Jackson, 1971. Conquest's data are conservative and as far as the writer knows not seriously contested.

[21] See I. I. Karpets' contribution to *A Policy Approach to Planning in Social Defence*, which in many respects constitutes a more tempered ideological approach to the problem of crime than those much too often produced by other socialist authors. Free of any particular ideological content, some of his remarks on the planning of crime measures in the U.S.S.R., the planning of legal measures and social processes have general validity and should be taken into consideration by social defence planners.

ventional murders committed in the U.S.S.R. is 3,000, the number of non-conventional murders committed by special police action in the same period would be equivalent to the number of conventional murders committed by the entire U.S.S.R. population in 333 years. If the real average is lower, the corresponding period will be longer and vice versa.

All the parties concerned in the Vietnam war have committed non-conventional crimes, the most outstanding of which are murder, maiming, mental and physical torture of prisoners, liquidation of civil population, robbery, corruption and blatant violation of human rights at every conceivable level. Although scattered, there are already enough data to show that these crimes far exceed the number of the same kind of conventional crimes.

Terrorism in many forms, sometimes subsidized by certain member states of the United Nations, is responsible for the growing toll of crimes committed for political or ideological reasons. It may be possible to explain part of this criminality. For instance, the right to independence is undeniable but by itself does not justify everything done to attain it. In Northern Ireland sectarian crime far exceeds conventional criminal offences in the whole of the United Kingdom. The number of crimes committed by the Pakistani Army in East Pakistan will be greater than that of conventional crimes in Pakistan and Bangladesh combined, over a period of many decades. In sum, the killings, maiming, torture, robbery, rape, arson, kidnapping and sheer destruction for reasons of politics, ideologies or resistance is increasing in the majority of countries. Like a vicious circle, official terrorism is followed by terrorism by groups and organizations of many sorts and some of their members are officially treated as heroes.

As for the administration of justice and the protection of human rights, a comparison of the subjects dealt with by *Human Rights and the Administration of Justice*,[22] and the excellent *Study of Equality in the Administration of Justice*, 1972, published by the United Nations, shows that either by criminal negligence, or deliberate police and official action, human rights are frequently violated and criminal justice used for purposes foreign to it. In most cases these violations and uses are described as criminal offences by the respective penal codes but more often than not benefit from impunity; South Africa, Rhodesia, Uganda, Libya, Indonesia, Greece and Brazil are conspicuous in this respect.

The discussion and conclusions on the Standard Minimum Rules for the Treatment of Prisoners at the Kyoto Congress and the report on them by the Working Group of Experts,[23] show that after having been in the hands of governments for implementation for more than 25 years, the majority

[22] Document E/AC. 57/5, 1972.
[23] Document E/AC. 57/8, 1973.

of them are still not applied. Inhuman and degrading treatment and abuses by prison officials and systematic deprivation of fundamental human rights are still features of many prison administrations. As a reaction prison riots occur in developed and developing countries. Among other cases the Attica riot shows that whatever political motivation lay behind it, the living conditions of the majority of prisoners were often below those assuring human dignity, and seldom in accordance with the United Nations Minimum Rules. The use of 'tiger cages' in South Vietnam is another recent instance of criminal treatment of prisoners. The pictures of the released prisoners show them as 'shapes' who will be unable to stand upright for years to come. Brainwashing of prisoners is a typical feature of treatment in many countries, some of them calling themselves 'peoples' democracies'. In Libya, according to an Act passed in 1972, thieves will have their hands amputated by medical doctors, transformed suddenly into executioners. In some African countries capital punishment has not only proliferated but has been transformed into a public spectacle against the Universal Declaration of Human Rights and related Conventions.

Which is more dangerous sociopolitically as well as criminologically, conventional or non-conventional crime? The existence of the latter will be denied by many, yet in many countries its extent and gravity exceed that of conventional criminality. Those responsible are also far more varied. Compared with those who commit conventional crime there are among them far more politicians, revolutionary leaders, public officials, military men, party members, policemen of every sort, intelligence agents, diplomats, businessmen, industrialists, professional people, judges, prosecutors, prison officials, members of terrorist and resistance groups or associations, etc. But conventional crime is all that criminal law, criminology and the prevention of crime and the treatment of the offender deals with.

Final Remarks

(a) Can the problem of crime be tackled by dealing successively or simultaneously with some of the crime problems or should an effort be made to deal with it as a whole? In the latter case what should be the approach? If crime problems are to be chosen which should have the highest priority? If it is a question of impact it should be the criminal justice problem.

(b) As long as conventional and non-conventional crime are so far apart, the first almost exclusively the concern of criminal justice systems and criminology, and the second practically neglected by both, will a policy for prevention and control of crime and the treatment of the offender bring the results expected? What should be done to reduce non-conventional crime which is rampant in some countries, serious in many and endemic in others?

(c) The problem of crime (as well as most crime problems) far exceeds in its scope the problems of socioeconomic conditions and planning. Moreover, social defence planning has its own content and purposes. So it seems that the correlation between socioeconomic and social defence planning has been exaggerated and should be reduced to its proper size.

(d) As general explanations, or as basic operational terms, social change, deviation, maladjustment, labelling and the like are of little value for social defence planning and strategies. The greater the generality of the terms used the greater the failure of the planning concerned. Terms should not be borrowed without the most careful scrutiny and analysis first being applied.[24]

(e) The predicament of criminology is obvious. Should it be partly replaced (as has already been suggested), and divided into macrocriminology and microcriminology, leaving to the latter the so far unsuccessful task of dealing with conventional crime? Or should we dispense with both and build up an effective criminal policy?[25]

(f) The aims of prevention, control and treatment should be considerably reduced. This does not mean that problem of crime is less serious but that by dealing separately with particular crime problems all three purposes are magnified or distorted. A reduction in these activities would at least mean the minimum use of criminal law and an effective respect for human rights when using the penal system. It would also mean that as long as the present socioeconomic and political structures are imposed in the vast majority of countries the right to refuse rehabilitation should be admitted. In fact justice and not rehabilitation should be the sole aim of the penal system.

Given time and space, elaboration and discussion of the above points would be useful. They do not mean that social defence planning should be

[24] Terminological jargon is the main feature of most sociological, psychological, etc. 'methodologists' of our time. To them, method means more the manipulation of imported terms than conceptual analysis and basic knowledge of history, political science, logic and even some fundamentals of philosophy.

[25] 'Macro' and 'micro' have been used for methodological reasons in sociology by Gurvitch, Lazarsfeld, Rocher and others. See *Tendances principales de la recherche dans les sciences sociales et humaines*, I, 1970, UNESCO, where Lazarsfeld admits the obscurity of the term *macrosociologie*. If transplanted to criminology it would mean abandoning a great part of contemporary empirical research.

rejected. But it should be *subjected* to a thorough scrutiny before going further. I would go as far as to say that in some respects socioeconomic planning should be subordinated to social defence planning, particularly in so far as criminal justice is concerned.

As for United Nations leadership in the prevention of crime and the treatment of offenders, its effectiveness depends more on the willingness of governments than on the passing of resolutions by policy-making bodies. The failure in the implementation of the Standard Minimum Rules is one of the most flagrant contradictions between leadership and its effective endorsement. Very little can be achieved by the resolutions themselves if, at the same time, adequate ways and means are not provided to remedy the present shortage of staff in the Social Defence Programmes Section.

It would be naïve to consider what has been said as criticism of the bodies mentioned. They are sometimes too sensitive to appreciate that their rôle is subject to study, and that not everything done by them is as good as they think. United Nations social defence activities have a brilliant past and present but in maintaining effective leadership it seems that the rôle of governments has not always been what could have been expected.

MODERN CRIMINAL POLICY IN THE FEDERAL REPUBLIC OF GERMANY AND THE GERMAN DEMOCRATIC REPUBLIC

Hans-Heinrich Jescheck

Since World War II criminal law reform has been taking place in all parts of the world, in Western and Socialist countries alike. The reasons for this vast reform movement lie in the changes in social structure which in part began as a consequence of the war, in the revaluation of the position of the individual in relation to the state, in the altered assessment of the rôle of law in society, in the complete restructuring of the individual and collective conscience, in the advancements made in criminology, and in the new discoveries in criminal policy for the treatment of offenders. Anyone with an interest in law will find at present no field more attractive than criminal law. Together with his colleagues from the Cambridge Institute of Criminology, Sir Leon Radzinowicz, through his life-long work in criminology, has made a basic contribution to the understanding of the need for a complete reform of the criminal law, and at the same time has worked to discover what knowledge and procedures are necessary to accomplish this reform.

A review of current criminal law reform in Germany is particularly instructive. From a continuing common linguistic and cultural base, and from a previously uniform legal system, *two states* have been formed which are proceeding with criminal law reform along contrary lines: the Federal Republic of Germany (F.R.), a liberal democratic state, according to the Western model, and the German Democratic Republic (G.D.R.), a Socialist state, established on the legal theory of Marxism–Leninism, according to the Eastern European model.

Although at present criminal law reform in West Germany is not complete, it has advanced significantly. An essential part of the reform of the General Part of the criminal code, particularly that which concerns criminal sanctions, was enacted as law three years ago. The rest of the reform of the General

Part should have come into force on 1 October 1973. However, since it was considered desirable that the entire second part of the reform be adopted as a whole, and since deliberation in the Federal Parliament (Bundestag) on the introductory and corrections statutes has not finished, this latter enactment had to be postponed until 1 January 1975. The gradual reform of the Special Part is also progressing. The arduous debate on sexual offences has ended and has resulted in a far-reaching liberalization. The even more controversial reform of abortion law with legalization of pregnancy interruption up to the third month is approaching. The decriminalization of the criminal law by changing the classification of insignificant infractions from punishable acts to minor offences penalized by administrative fines (Ordnungswidrigkeiten) has made great progress. The reform of criminal procedure and judicial organization is also well under way.

In the G.D.R. criminal law reform is essentially completed.[1] The enactment of a Socialist criminal code in which legal unity with the Federal Republic is formally abolished was planned for many years with careful preparation. The new criminal code was enacted on 1 July 1968. In addition to the substantive criminal law reform, an extensive re-modelling of all areas of law has taken place. In the area of criminal law, as well as generally in the legal structure, the Federal Republic and the G.D.R. are set apart as two completely separate states. This development has been politically recognized by the recently concluded treaty (Grundvertrag) which sealed the division of Germany for the time being.

In this article the differences and similarities in criminal policy as well as their ideological backgrounds will be discussed in light of the *systems of sanctions* which are in force in the Federal Republic and the G.D.R. The originally existing opposed ideological positions on the purposes of punishment have been bridged somewhat as a result of the gradually proceeding development of theory in both countries.[2] On the one side, the previously dominating theory of the exclusive origin of crime in the class structure of a capitalist economy and the consequent absolute disappearance of crime in a completely Socialist state has begun to weaken in the G.D.R. as well as in other Socialist countries.[3] On the other side, in the Federal Republic, the

[1] For the history of criminal law in the G.D.R. see H.-H. Jescheck, *Lehrbuch des Strafrechts*, Allgemeiner Teil, 2nd ed. Berlin: Duncker u. Humblot 1972, pp. 66 et seq.

[2] The degree of harmonization, nevertheless, is greatly overestimated by G. Grünwald, 'Die Strafrechtsreform in der BRD und in der DDR', *Zeitschrift für die gesamte Strafrechtswissenschaft*, 1970, **82**, p. 225, with his statement 'that the fundamental decisions relative to criminal legislation in the G.D.R. and the Federal Republic are to a large extent corresponding'.

[3] See a statement by B. Zlatarić, *Zeitschrift für die gesamte Strafrechtswissenschaft*, 1970, **82**, pp. 286 et. seq. As to the dogmatism of the past and its abuses see H.-H. Jescheck. 'Delito y

once prevailing idealistic view that criminal law is a tool for achieving absolute justice has yielded to the more moderate and pragmatic attitude that the right to punish lies in the simple necessity of controlling the disturbing effects of crime on social life. As a result of this change, many of the irreconcilable differences separating both countries which were not subject to rational discourse have disappeared and an analysis of the developments in criminal law may be made apart from purely ideological differences.

The Death Penalty

One of the most striking and, with respect to the mentality of both systems, characteristic *differences* concerns the death penalty. It was abolished in the *Federal Republic* by Article 102 of the Constitution (Grundgesetz) and today is labelled directly as 'inadmissible'.[4] A decisive factor in the constitutional abolition of the death penalty was not simply indignation about its unprecedented misuse in the years 1933 to 1945, but an overriding acknowledgement of the humanitarianism and concern for human dignity which forbids extermination of an individual by the state even for the gravest crimes. In addition, experience has shown that the death penalty not only is unnecessary, since it is not a stronger deterrent than life imprisonment, but also that it can even be a psychological stimulus of crimes of violence.

In sharp contrast thereto, the G.D.R. criminal code has retained the death penalty for a few isolated particularly serious crimes.[5] In this case the penalty still serves a repressive function in the context of the revolutionary, ideological struggle against enemies of the ruling class and of the communist state and, therefore, is not found anachronistic for this particular purpose. The death penalty has never been questioned in the G.D.R., not even in the years between 1947 and 1950, when it was abolished in the Soviet Union[6]

---

sanción en la teoría y en la realidad del Marxismo-Leninismo', in *Estudios jurídicos en homenaje al Profesor Luis Jiménez de Asúa*, 1964, pp. 73 et seq. See also Thea Lyon, *Der Verbrechensbegriff in der Strafrechtswissenschaft der DDR*. Bonn: Röhrscheid, 1960, pp. 52 et seq.

[4] E. Schmidhäuser, *Strafrecht*, Allgemeiner Teil. Tübingen: Mohr, 1970, p. 611.

[5] See G. Grünwald, op. cit., pp. 276 et seq.; R. Maurach, 'Verbrechen und Strafe nach dem neuen Strafgesetzbuch der DDR', in: *50 Jahre Sowjetrecht*, 1969, pp. 184 et seq.; Thea Lyon, 'Kriminalpolitische Tendenzen und die "Massnahmen strafrechtlicher Verantwortlichkeit" nach dem neuen StGB der DDR', *Jahrbuch für Ostrecht*, 1968, IX/2, p. 106; H. Roggemann, 'Das Strafgesetzbuch der DDR von 1968', *Recht in Ost und West*, 1969, p. 158.

[6] Contrary to what is reported by W. Rosenthal, 'Neues Strafrecht in Mitteldeutschland'. *Recht in Ost und West*, 1968, p. 65, the death penalty was included in the Project of the new G.D.R. criminal code too; it is true that it was not mentioned in § 26, but it was provided for as a normal penalty in § 64.

and, in contrast to § 23 of the criminal code of the Russian Socialist Federal Soviet Republic (R.S.F.S.R.), death is *not* viewed as an unusual criminal measure which should be abolished (§ 60 G.D.R. criminal code). According to the semi-official commentary, the penalty even has an 'humanistic . . . character'.[7] This characterization quite clearly stresses the ideological differences in criminal law which still exist between East and West. To see the antithesis one need only consider the death penalty opinion of Justice Marshall of the U.S. Supreme Court, 28 June 1972: 'In addition, even if capital punishment is not excessive, it nonetheless violates the Eighth Amendment because it is morally unacceptable to the people of the United States at this time in their history.'[8] In this particular matter, consequently, there is still no bridge between two basically opposed conceptions of criminal law.

Prison Penalty

The similarities are somewhat greater where imprisonment is concerned.

1. The Federal Republic abolished penal servitude as a form of punishment and adopted a system of *one type of prison penalty* with implementation differentiated and designed according to the personality of the prisoner.[9] The criminal code of the G.D.R. speaks also of 'the' prison penalty (§§ 38 et seq.), which would seem to imply the adoption of a similar system.[10] In fact, however, the corrections system, similar to the Soviet model,[11] is tripartite, and implementation may be in either a severe, general, or mild form.[12] Prisoners are divided schematically (although there is, in fact, a possibility of variance) according to type of crime, severity of penalty, and previous conviction record. Although the ideal of 'socially useful work' is emphasized in all three forms of corrections, the characteristic consequences

[7] See 'Strafrecht der Deutschen Demokratischen Republik', (published by a collective of authors), *Lehrkommentar zum StGB*, Vol. I, 1970, § 60, note 1.

[8] See *Criminal Law Reporter*, 1972, 11, p. 3263. For more details see J. Herrmann, 'Der Supreme Court der Vereinigten Staaten erklärt die Todesstrafe für verfassungswidrig', *Juristenzeitung*, 1972, p. 615.

[9] Cf. H.-H. Jescheck, op. cit., pp. 574, 586 et seq.

[10] H. Roggemann, op. cit., p. 155 seems to believe it. The real implementation of the prison penalty, however, results from what is reported by Jauch in *Grundfragen des neuen Strafgesetzbuchs der DDR*, 1964, pp. 235 et seq.

[11] Cf. R. Maurach, 'Der sowjetische Freiheitsstrafvollzug', *Recht in Ost und West*, 1960, p. 189.

[12] On the conditions of implementation see H.-H. Bruhn, 'Das Straf- und Wiedereingliederungsgesetz der DDR', *Recht in Ost und West*, 1971, pp. 18 et seq.

of individualization inherent in the unified prison penalty of the F.R. do not occur in the G.D.R.[13]

2. The Federal Republic has made considerable progress in the restriction of the *short-term prison penalty*: § 14 F.R. criminal code in fact did not eliminate the short-term penalty completely (which would be misguided in the light of traffic and military offences, white-collar criminality, and multi-recidivism among those without regular employment) but did limit it essentially.[14] The practical effect of this limitation was considerable. In 1969 there were 132,161 prison sentences of less than six months' duration, while in 1970 this figure fell to 55,844 or less than one half of the 1969 figure. In 1971, even though the total number of prison sentences rose from 88,248 to 94,135, there were only 55,092 short-term penalties.

In the G.D.R. the minimum penalty is basically six months (§ 40(1) G.D.R. criminal code).[15] However, a prison penalty of three to six months is permissible 'by exception' if the offence also carries a penalty other than imprisonment (§ 40(2) G.D.R. criminal code) which is the case in many provisions of the Special Part. Otherwise, there is a custody penalty for the 'immediate and emphatic discipline of the offender' of one to six weeks which may be used, for example, in cases of hooliganism, unlawful assembly and anti-social behaviour.[16] Thus, the short-term penalty is applied exceptionally as a part of criminal law policy and regularly as a means of repressive discipline. To what extent it is in fact used cannot be reported since the G.D.R. publishes no statistics on the penalties the courts impose.[17]

3. In the Federal Republic there is a legal distinction between probationary suspension of a *sentence on parole* (§§ 23 et seq. F.R. criminal code), in which the entire penalty remains unexecuted, and *release on parole*, in which the penalty is executed in part (§ 26 F.R. criminal code). Both institutions were improved as part of the reform.[18] The suspended sentence is at present considered as the most effective means for resocialization since the dis-

---

[13] The same opinion is stated by R. Maurach, *50 Jahre Sowjetrecht*, op. cit., Stüttgart usw: Kohlhammer 1969, pp. 177 et seq.; Thea Lyon, *Jahrbuch für Ostrecht*, op. cit., pp. 102 et seq.; H. Aries, *Die freiheitsentziehenden Sanktionen nach dem neuen Strafrecht der DDR*, Dissertation, Hamburg, 1970, p. 61.

[14] Cf. H.-H. Jescheck, op. cit., pp. 574 et seq., 658 et seq.

[15] For the rejection of short-term imprisonment see E. Buchholz, 'Verwirklichung der Grundsätze sozialistischer Gerechtigkeit bei der Strafzumessung', *Neue Justiz*, 1968, p. 452; K. Ljutow, 'Die Effektivität der kurzfristigen Freiheitsstrafe', *Staat und Recht*, 1968, p. 796.

[16] Cf. Thea Lyon, *Jahrbuch für Ostrecht*, op. cit., 1968, pp. 100 et seq.; H. Roggemann, op. cit., pp. 154 et seq.

[17] On the principles directing the application of short-term imprisonment in the G.D.R. see H. Aries, op. cit., pp. 9 et seq.

[18] Cf. H.-H. Jescheck, op. cit., pp. 576 et seq., pp. 624 et seq.

advantages which attend imprisonment are avoided, the stimulus to work for one's own reintegration in the society under appropriate guidance is present, and the effect of general prevention remains intact. With favourable prognosis, prison penalties of less than six months are *always* suspended. Prison penalties of six months to one year are suspended in all cases *unless* they need to be implemented for the protection of society, and *in exceptional cases* prison penalties of one to two years are suspended when particular circumstances arise. The new rule relating to release on parole allows conditional release after two-thirds of the penalty is served and, in exceptional cases, permits release after one half of the prison period. Both types of early release can be associated with parole rules and regulations. The most important means of assistance and guidance to the individual on probation or parole is the probation officer.[19] In 1970 53·2 per cent of all prison penalties remained suspended, in 1971 58·5 per cent.[20] In 1969 12·8 per cent of all individuals sentenced actually went to prison, in 1970 9·3 per cent and in 1971 only 9·0 per cent. The number of persons incarcerated has decreased from 46,745 in 1969 to 35,927 in 1970 and to only 33,015 in 1971. In addition, 12,000 of the 57,520 existing places in prisons are needed for individuals awaiting trial, thus leaving more than 12,500 places unused. The critical overcrowding situation in prisons, therefore, has been overcome in Germany. Incarceration today has become a 'seldom used' penalty. The famous plea of Karl Schlyter 'Depopulate the prisons' has become a reality in the Federal Republic.

Although legally the probationary suspension of a sentence on parole in the G.D.R. (§ 45 criminal code) is not dependent on a prisoner partially serving his sentence,[21] in practice it functions only as conditional release from prison after implementation of a considerable part of the penalty.[22] No maximum period is defined as to when a sentence may be suspended. Rather, in cases of imprisonment for more than six years, a minimum implementation period is set as at least one half of the prison term (§ 349 (2) G.D.R. code of criminal procedure). Certain special probation measures, characteristic of the Soviet model, can be associated with the suspended sentence on parole in the G.D.R., viz., the pledge of collectives or individual citizens, education by the collective, occupational restriction, residential

[19] As on 31 December, 1971, 717 probation officers had to take care of 44,537 probationers.

[20] The ratio of suspended sentences is even higher in Switzerland. According to H. Schultz, *Einführung in den Allgemeinen Teil des Strafrechts*, vol. II, Bern: Stämpfli 1973, p. 41, in 1970 67 per cent of all prison sentences were suspended.

[21] Cf. Thea Lyon, *Jahrbuch für Ostrecht,* op. cit., p. 103; R. Maurach, *50 Jahre Sowjetrecht,* op. cit., pp. 179 et seq.

[22] See 'Strafrecht der DDR', op. cit., § 45, note 1; H. Roggemann, op. cit., p. 156.

restriction, requirement of submission to special medical treatment. What actual significance the suspended sentence and special probation measures have in the G.D.R. is unknown since no statistics are available.

4. There has been an attempt made in the Federal Republic to solve the *problem of recidivism* by raising the minimum prison term for recidivists to six months (§ 17 F.R. criminal code) and by adopting special measures, most important of which are preventive detention (§ 42 (e) F.R. criminal code) and institutional social therapy which will be provided in the future in the sociotherapeutic establishments to be modelled on Herstedvesta in Denmark (§ 65 F.R. criminal code 1975).[23] In Socialist countries, on the other hand, the double-track method is rejected in correspondence with the Soviet model.[24] In the G.D.R., therefore, there exists only a considerable aggravation of penalties for recidivism (§ 44 G.D.R. criminal code).[25] Furthermore, treatment of mental diseases is carried on in closed institutions, and repression of anti-social tendencies is accomplished by re-education through work (§ 42 G.D.R. criminal code)—a method which is, in fact, similar to that which existed in the former (now abolished) workhouses of the Federal Republic.[26] Also, measures against recidivism permissible in the G.D.R. *after* complete release from the corrections system are much more far-reaching than those which would be considered possible in the Federal Republic under the probation system (§ 24 (a–c) F.R. criminal code) or under the new measure of supervision called 'Führungsaufsicht' (§§ 68 et seq. F.R. criminal code 1975) which will be a stricter form of probation run by a specifically equipped administrative agency. The court may order certain controls over the individual (§ 47 G.D.R. criminal code) of which occupational and residential restriction are the most severe. Furthermore, rigorous police surveillance also may be inflicted (§ 48 G.D.R. criminal code). Finally, a decree of 15 August 1968 dealing with the problem of recidivism grants local authorities the right to re-socialize and control criminally dangerous persons. On the whole, the possibility of extensive state interference exists to a much greater degree in the G.D.R. than in the Federal Republic with its double-track system.[27]

[23] For 'Massregeln der Sicherung und Besserung' (measures of security and correction) in the F.R. criminal code, see H.-H. Jescheck, op. cit., pp. 59 et seq., 606 et seq.

[24] Cf. Thea Lyon, *Jahrbuch für Ostrecht*, op. cit., pp. 91 et seq.; R. Maurach, *50 Jahre Sowjetrecht*, op. cit., p. 172; H. Aries, op. cit., pp. 52 et seq.; H. Weber, in *Grundfragen des neuen Strafgesetzbuchs*, p. 35; L. Frenzel, ibid., pp. 254 et seq.

[25] See the critical discussion of this point by G. Grünwald, op. cit., p. 273.

[26] For this reason H. Roggemann, op. cit., p. 147, rejects the view that the G.D.R. criminal law is at all representative of the single-track system.

[27] Cf. Blüthner-Adam-Bohmüller, 'Die Bekämpfung und Verhütung von Erscheinungen der kriminellen Gefährdung', *Neue Justiz*, 1970, pp. 478 et seq.

Penalties without Imprisonment

With respect to penalties without imprisonment, the Federal Republic recognizes now only fines and a new sanction which is called 'Verwarnung mit Strafvorbehalt' (admonition with reserved sentence). In contrast thereto, the importance of the new criminal code of the G.D.R. consists in the establishment of a broadly differentiated system of such penalties and in the supplementation of these penalties through effective probation rules. The decisive change in criminal law policy which began in the G.D.R. in the early sixties has proved profitable in this respect.[28] The extreme severity of the criminal law during the revolutionary period has been replaced by an abundance of new techniques which are aimed not at repressing enemies of socialism but rather at redirecting the convictions of weak or ideologically backward citizens towards the Marxist–Leninist social ideal.[29] Jointly with these measures the educational and controlling power of the collective has been developed to help influence sentenced individuals in this direction. An assessment of the effectiveness of the new criminal law policy of the G.D.R. is difficult since numerical data concerning the frequency of application of the new measures are not published. An exception exists only with respect to the new technique of collective pledges for good behaviour of sentenced individuals which increased in application from 3,794 cases in 1964 to 4,945 cases in 1970.[30]

1. The *monetary fine* plays a decisive rôle in the Federal Republic as a substitute for short-term and also in many cases for average-term prison penalties.[31] The new § 14(2) F.R. criminal code provides for a fine in place of all prison penalties of up to six months unless imprisonment is indispensable for the protection of society. In practice the fine has become a significant penalty in the last few years: in 1969 the fine alone was given in 371,918 cases, in 1970 in 464,118 cases, and in 1971 in 476,785 cases. Although use of the fine has increased, sentences of imprisonment for non-payment have risen only slightly in proportion. In this same period the number of individuals sentenced to prison was as follows: in 1969 158,298, in 1970 88,248, and in 1971 94,135. Since, in the future, German law will adopt the Scandinavian system of day-fines (§§ 40 et seq. F.R. criminal code 1975), thus facilitating a fairer adjustment to the economic situation of the

[28] Cf. Irene Sagel-Grande, *Die Entwicklung der Sanktionen ohne Freiheitsentzug im Strafrecht der DDR*, Berlin: Duncker u Humblot, 1972, pp. 36 et seq.

[29] Cf. H. Creuzburg, 'Rolle und Funktion der Strafe im Kampf gegen die Kriminalität in der DDR', *Der Schöffe*, 1964, p. 267; E. Buchholz, op. cit., p. 452.

[30] Cf. *Statistisches Jahrbuch der DDR*, 1972, p. 488.

[31] Cf. H.-H. Jescheck, op. cit., pp. 589 et seq.; H. Zipf, *Die Geldstrafe in ihrer Funktion zur Eindämmung der kurzen Freiheitsstrafe*, Berlin, Neuwied: Lüchterhand 1966.

individual, the fine will be used in even more cases as a substitute for imprisonment. The new criminal code of the G.D.R. has abandoned the originally existing strong ideological opposition to the fine and has expanded its range of application using as a basis in the Marxist theory the principle of 'personal financial interest' (§§ 36 & 49 G.D.R. criminal code).[32] The fine should re-educate the offender 'by means of tangibly affecting his personal financial interests, towards respecting socialist legality and the rights of other citizens'. Nevertheless, legal provisions for the fine are not as abundant as for other penalties without confinement. It seems apparent, then, that certain ideological prejudices oppose the fine as a 'privilege of the rich' and that it functions worse as a prison substitute in a Socialist economy because of the uniformity and meagreness of wages and the unavailability of additional jobs or supplemental incomes.

2. The *sentence on probation* is of great importance in the G.D.R. (§ 33 G.D.R. criminal code).[33] This penalty is similar to Anglo-American probation in that it consists of a conviction and the stipulation of a probation period, and is associated with measures to promote the self-education of the offender under collective guidance. In contrast to Anglo-American law, the prison penalty, which will be executed if probation fails, is already pronounced at the time of conviction (§ 35(3) G.D.R. criminal code).[34] The implementation of the imprisonment, however, is dependent on the conduct of the probationer during the probationary period. Educational schemes of particular importance accompany this penalty of which the obligation to probation at the place of work is the most incisive (§ 34 G.D.R. criminal code). This particular programme consists in the obligation of the offender not to change his previous or assigned place of work and in the influence which the collective at the working place exercises in an effort to re-educate the offender towards 'a responsible attitude to Socialist labour and his other duties'.[35] Further, the sentence on probation can be associated with addi-

[32] Cf. K. Görner, 'Bemerkungen zur Anwendungsmöglichkeit der Geldstrafe', *Neue Justiz*, 1962, pp. 217 et seq.; U. Dähn, 'Strafen ohne Freiheitsentzug', *Neue Justiz*, 1967, p. 121; Schlegel-Pompoes, 'Kriterien für die Anwendung der Geldstrafe', *Neue Justiz*, 1970, pp. 196 et seq.

[33] For interesting case material see Irene Sagel-Grande, op. cit., pp. 95 et seq.; also J. Schlegel, 'Zu den Aufgaben der Gerichte bei der Verurteilung auf Bewährung', *Neue Justiz*, 1970, pp. 43 et seq.; G. Grünwald, op. cit., pp. 259 et seq.; *Grundfragen des neuen Strafgesetzbuchs*, pp. 216 et seq.

[34] Although, of course, England has recently introduced the possibility of a suspension order along with a suspended sentence, a probation order proper is still seen as incompatible with a suspended sentence. *Criminal Justice Act*, 1972, section 12, and the article by Roger Hood, 'Criminology and Penal Change', in this volume at page 400.

[35] Cf. U. Dähn, *Sozialistische Arbeitskollektive und bedingte Verurteilung*, Berlin: Staatsverlag der DDR, 1966, pp. 13 et seq.

tional penalties (cf. IV below) and with collective pledges (cf. III.3 below) in order to increase its effectiveness. In the Federal Republic, only the new *admonition with reserved sentence* can be compared to these G.D.R. institutions (§§ 59 et seq. F.R. criminal code 1975). The admonition with reserved sentence, however, is limited to a fine of minor or average amount and cannot be joined with educational programmes—thus completely failing to emulate the rehabilitation-oriented practices of G.D.R. law.[36]

3. Although with the sentence on probation the G.D.R. has established a criminal law institution completely of its own, it has taken the collective pledge (§ 31 G.D.R. criminal code) and the public reprimand (§ 37 G.D.R. criminal code) once again from Soviet law (Art. 52, 33 R.S.F.S.R. criminal code). The *collective pledge*,[37] which usually is associated with the sentence on probation, but which also may be joined with a fine, is a guarantee made by a work collective or in exceptional cases by a particular individual to take care of the re-education of the offender. The pledge has to be confirmed by the court. It is based on the power to reform and control the individual inherent in a socialist collective. The pledge may be undertaken not only by working collectives but also by athletic or residential collectives or by other communities.[38] When the individual maliciously refuses to participate in the reform programme, the collective may exercise its control by applying to the court for implementation of the prison term originally imposed as the sanction for non-compliance with the probation order.[39] The *public reprimand* (§ 37 G.D.R. criminal code) is the mildest principal penalty without imprisonment. It consists only in a judicial declaration of disapproval in an effort to exhort the offender 'conscientiously to fulfil his duties towards Socialist society'. The Federal Republic on the other hand does not recognize comparable sanctions. The authority of a socialist collective which is necessary if pledges are to be taken seriously and be effective is foreign to communities of workers in a liberal society. The severe moral denouncement of a criminal offence, which is an essential element in effective public reprimands is also lacking.

4. Another group of penalties not entailing imprisonment exist for those cases in which the criminal law of the G.D.R. allows *dispensing with 'measures of criminal responsibility'* so that conviction alone 'is considered as a sanction'. The guilt and responsibility of the offender nevertheless must be established.[40]

[36] For critical remarks concerning the entire institution see E. Dreher, 'Die Verwarnung mit Strafvorbehalt', *Festschrift für R. Maurach*, 1972, pp. 287 et seq.

[37] Cf. Irene Sagel-Grande, op. cit., pp. 226 et seq.

[38] Cf. Thea Lyon, *Jahrbuch für Ostrecht*, op. cit., p. 99.

[39] For more details see U. Dähn, *Sozialistisches Arbeitskollektiv*, op. cit., pp. 62 et seq.; case materials are reported by Irene Sagel-Grande, op. cit., p. 232.

[40] Cf. 'Strafrecht der DDR', op. cit., §25, note 4.

According to the law of the G.D.R. an act is not punishable even though it corresponds to the wording of a penal provision, if the guilt of the offender and the effects of the act are negligible (§ 3(1) G.D.R. criminal code).[41] This rule has a procedural counterpart in the Federal Republic in § 153, code of criminal procedure which permits the prosecutor to drop a case because of insignificance. But the law of the G.D.R. goes essentially further in that it also permits the taking into consideration of the subsequent evolution of the circumstances and of the personal development of the offender. Thus, according to § 25(2) of the G.D.R. criminal code, measures of criminal responsibility may be dispensed with if the act, regardless of the degree of guilt of the offender, 'has, as a result of the development of Socialist social relations, caused no harmful effects'. The far-reaching consequences of this concept of crime are justified in that a penalty in the G.D.R. 'is not given for the realization of an abstract notion of justice, but rather for the concrete service of the socialist . . . transformation'.[42] Not only a change in social relations, but also a change in the personality of the offender may lead to a total dispensation with penalty. Namely, the penalty will be dispensed with if the offender, through compensation for the injury or through other positive acts, has proved 'that he has drawn fundamental lessons for a conduct as a conscientious member of the community and can therefore be expected to adhere to Socialist legality'.[43] Even if one disregards, however, the party ideology implicit in this type of educational aim of criminal law,[44] such a far-reaching dispensation with measures of criminal responsibility would be impossible in the Federal Republic if only for reasons of certainty of law.[45] As a general rule a penalty may be dispensed with in this country only if the consequences of the act have so strongly affected the culprit in the sense of a 'poena naturalis',[46] that any supplementary penalty increasing his sufferings would obviously fail to have any reasonable effect and would appear as a mere cruelty (§ 16 F.R. criminal code).

[41] The ideological basis of this prescription, derived from Soviet law (art. 7, sect. 2, R.S.F.S.R. criminal code), is the 'material conception of crime'. For more details see Thea Lyon, *Der Verbrechensbegriff*, Bonn: Röhrsched 1960, op. cit., pp. 42 et seq.

[42] E. Buchholz, 'Gedanken zur ausserordentlichen Strafmilderung', *Neue Justiz*, 1959, pp. 561 et seq.

[43] For interpretation of this rule see H. Pompoes, 'Massnahmen der strafrechtlichen Verantwortlichkeit', *Neue Justiz*, 1970, p. 353.

[44] Cf. H.-H. Jescheck, *Strafrecht und Strafrechtsanwendung in der SBZ*, Tübingen: Mohr 1962, pp. 14 et seq.

[45] A more positive assessment of this institution is put forward by A. Eser, 'Absehen von Strafe—Schuldspruch unter Strafverzicht', *Festschrift für R. Maurach*, 1972, pp. 268 et seq.; cf. also G. Grünwald, *Zeitschrift für die gesamte Strafrechtswissenschaft*, 1970, **82,** p. 268.

[46] Cf. G. Maiwald, 'Das Absehen von Strafe nach §16 StGB', *Zeitschrift für die gesamte Strafrechtswissenschaft*, 1971, **83,** p. 671.

Additional Penalties

The principal penalties in the G.D.R. can be supplemented by various additional penal sanctions which are designed for the *re-education of the offender* as well as for the *protection of society* (§ 23 G.D.R. criminal code) and which in part assume the rôle of the measures of security and correction provided for in West German law.

1. The *fine* may be imposed as a penalty to supplement a sentence on probation or a sentence of imprisonment (§ 49 G.D.R. criminal code). Further, a *public announcement of conviction* (§ 50 G.D.R. criminal code) is permissible for all offences and is required if it is 'necessary for the elucidation of the population and their mobilization for the prevention of certain phenomena of crime'. The fine is recognized in West German law also as an additional penalty but only in cases of greed (§ 27a F.R. criminal code). Likewise a public announcement of conviction is provided for but only in rare cases and only for reparation to the injured party, not for reasons of general prevention (e.g. §§ 165, 200 F.R. criminal code).[47]

2. The most incisive additional penalty in the law of the G.D.R. is *local restriction* (§§ 51 et seq. G.D.R. criminal code).[48] It is based on the Soviet model (Art. 25, 26 R.S.F.S.R. criminal code) and can be imposed in addition to a sentence of imprisonment and a sentence on probation if it 'is necessary for the protection of society or the security of citizens to keep the convicted person away from certain places or areas'. Although the court passes only a *prohibition* of residence, the administrative authorities, on the basis of this judgement, are entitled to order the convicted person to a *forced place of residence* (§ 51(3) G.D.R. criminal code), thus making local restriction a measure similar to banishment.[49] Also, according to a decree of 1961, local restriction may be awarded independently of the commission of a punishable offence through a judgement on application of the administrative authority and may be accompanied by an obligation to work. This type of infringement on personal freedom and free choice of place of employment would be inconceivable in the law of West Germany. Although in connection with a probationary suspension of a sentence on parole, orders may be passed 'which relate to residence, education, work or leisure time' (§ 24b (2) nr. 1 F.R. criminal code), the requirement of a specific employment (Art. 12 F.R. Constitution) as well as of a specific residence (Art. 11 F.R. Constitution) would be considered as clearly unconstitutional.

[47] Cf. H.-H. Jescheck, *Lehrbuch*, op. cit., pp. 604 et seq.

[48] Cf. Neuhof-Schmidt, 'Anwendung von Zusatzstrafen', *Neue Justiz*, 1969, pp. 172 et seq.

[49] See the critical remarks by Irene Sagel-Grande, op. cit., pp. 211 et seq.

3. *Occupational restriction* (§ 53 G.D.R. criminal code) is also an additional penalty in East Germany established according to the Soviet model (Art. 29 R.S.F.S.R. criminal code), but it is in substantial correspondence with the provisions of the prohibition of profession in the Federal Republic (§ 42(1) F.R. criminal code).[50] *Cancellation of driver's licence* (§ 54 G.D.R. criminal code) unites the penalty of driving prohibition (§ 37 F.R. criminal code) with its corresponding measure of cancellation of driver's licence (§ 42m F.R. criminal code) in the Federal Republic.[51] According to § 55 of the G.D.R. criminal code other rights (e.g. trade licences, professional, hunting and other permits) may be cancelled as additional penalty. Such actions are provided for in West Germany only on the basis of a penal judgement by a special administrative hearing in which all legal rights are guaranteed.[52]

4. Furthermore, the additional penalty of *confiscation of property in total,* which is permissible in cases of serious crimes carrying prison terms of at least three years (§ 57 G.D.R. criminal code), is taken from Soviet law (Art. 35 R.S.F.S.R. criminal code). This penalty is not known in West German law because of its fundamentally destructive consequences. An even more destructive interference is the *deprival of civil rights* (§ 58 G.D.R. criminal code) which may be awarded only for murder and the most serious political crimes and which in effect deprives the sentenced individual of any possible participation in political or social life. On the contrary, deprival of civil rights has been abolished from the criminal law of West Germany in order to avoid any intentional stigmatizing of a convicted person. The forfeiture of official position and the deprival of eligibility to run for office and of the right to vote still remain within very restricted limits (§ 31 F.R. criminal code).

Social Courts and their Functions in Criminal Law

1. Deliberation and decision of criminal cases by *social courts* has become an independent and, for socialist legal thought, typical method of imposing sanctions in the G.D.R. (§ 28 G.D.R. criminal code). Social courts are based on the conception that state and law will die out in a fully developed communist society and that all regulatory functions still necessary in the future will pass on to free social associations.[53] Social jurisdiction in the G.D.R.

[50] See the critical remarks by Irene Sagel-Grande, op. cit., pp. 216 et seq.

[51] For more details concerning application of this rule see Neuhof-Schmidt, op. cit., pp. 173 et seq.

[52] Cf. Irene Sagel-Grande, op. cit., pp. 221 et seq.

[53] For more details about the ideological background of the social courts see A. Eser, *Gesellschaftsgerichte in der Strafrechtspflege*, Tübingen: Mohr 1970, pp. 12 et seq.; also

has developed through Article 92 of the new constitution of 1968, through statutory provision of social courts of 11 June 1968 and through §§ 28, 29 of the G.D.R. criminal code, from tentative beginnings within the internal management of factories[54] to a large-scale official institution incorporated in the state jurisdiction.[55] On the one hand, there are 'Konfliktkommissionen' (conflict commissions) established in the industries, in institutions of health, culture and public education as well as in all national and social organizations ('Konfliktkommissionsordnung' of 10 April 1968); on the other hand, there are 'Schiedskommissionen' (arbitration commissions) in the residential areas of both cities and villages and in the agricultural and handicraft co-operatives ('Schiedskommissionsordnung' of 10 April 1968). They are competent for all minor offences if 'an effective educational influence is expected to be brought about by the social court' (§ 28(1) G.D.R. criminal code). In such cases a criminal matter *must* be transferred from state jurisdiction to the commission, provided the factual circumstances have been clarified and the offender has admitted his guilt. The correctional measures available to the conflict and arbitration commissions extend from ordering the offender to apologize or to repair the damage he caused to inflicting a fine of up to 150 Marks (for property offences). The practical significance of social courts is great: the transfer of proceedings from state jurisdiction to a conflict or arbitration commission occurred in 38·5 per cent of all cases in 1965 and in 36·8 per cent in 1970[56]—and in an even greater percentage of cases for particular offences such as property crimes and bodily injury.[57] To this must be added jurisdiction over the very important new category of 'Verfehlungen' (offences of a minor degree) which no longer are regarded as criminal acts but nevertheless include thefts of up to 50 marks ('Verordnung über die Verfolgung von Verfehlungen' of 1 February 1968), and all cases of 'Ordnungswidrigkeiten' (infractions of the order) ('Gesetz über Ordnungswidrigkeiten' of 24 May 1968). The main objection to social courts—apart from the absence of rules of evidence and lack of judicial

---

Renneberg-Stiller-Weber, in, *Grundfragen des neuen Strafgesetzbuchs*, pp. 77 et. seq.; H. Keil, 'Die Verwirklichung der Leninschen Ideen über die gesellschaftlichen Gerichte', *Neue Justiz*, 1970, pp. 236 et seq.

[54] Cf. H. Schrader, 'Die Gesellschaftsgerichtsbarkeit in Mitteldeutschland', *Zeitschrift für die gesamte Strafrechtswissenschaft*, 1965, 77, pp. 512 et seq.

[55] See the decision of the Presidency of the G.D.R. Supreme Court of 9 August 1972 from which it appears that a sentence issued by an arbitration commission can be reviewed at four state levels including the Presidency of the Supreme Court which is the highest judicial authority of the G.D.R.

[56] Cf. H. Harrland, 'Die Kriminaltät in der DDR im Jahre 1969', *Neue Justiz*, 1970, p. 414; *Statistisches Jahrbuch der DDR*, 1972, p. 487.

[57] Cf. *Statistisches Jahrbuch der DDR*, 1972, p. 488.

independence—is directed at the completely public nature of the hearing and deliberation of punishable offences by colleagues and neighbours of the accused. There is always the possibility of constant influence from outside the court because people attending the trial, who are not a part of the bench, may interfere in the proceedings and deliberations by making observations, declarations and suggestions.[58]

2. Social courts established and organized by law do not exist in West Germany. There is, however, the social phenomenon of *'Betriebsjustiz'* (*factory justice*) which has attracted the attention of lawyers since the middle of the sixties[59] and is presently being studied empirically by the Max-Planck Institute for Foreign and International Criminal Law in Freiburg.[60] Various forms of factory justice have developed the responsibility for which may rest with management, the personnel officer or special regulatory commissions. Minor offences and other trespasses committed by employees and workers are controlled through sanctions internal to the organization in order to avoid reporting the offender to the police in criminal cases. State courts and offices of state administration do not participate in factory justice. Admonition, transfer within the factory, demotion, suspension from social benefits, fines and termination of the employment contract are possible sanctions. Factory justice is faster, less expensive and less stigmatizing than state justice. Since agencies exercising factory justice are more closely tied to the individuals concerned and their particular situations they may adjust their means more to the case at hand than the public courts. Legal protection of the accused party is secured to a certain extent by the 'Betriebsrat' (workers' council) if in fact it is participating in the proceedings which unfortunately is not always the case. The settlement of minor cases by factory justice is an advantage in that it relieves a large burden from state courts. As in the case of the G.D.R. social courts one criticism concerns the lack of formal rules of evidence and the position of the judges who are to a certain extent dependent on the staff. The main objection, however, is aimed at the non-existence of a state court of appeal which seems all the more

---

[58] See A. Eser, *Gesellschaftsgerichte*, Tübingen: Mohr 1970, op. cit., pp. 34 et seq. considering social courts from a more optimistic point of view; H.-H. Jescheck, *Strafrecht und Strafrechtsanwendung*, op. cit., pp. 24 et seq.; R. Lange, 'Was bedeutet die Änderung des Gerichtsverfassungsgesetzes in der Sowjetzone?', *Festschrift für E. Schmidt*, 1961, pp. 560 et seq.

[59] Cf. A. Arndt, 'Private Betriebs—"Justiz"?', *Neue Juristische Wochenschrift*, 1965, p. 26; Lederer, 'Betriebsjustiz—etwas ausserhalb der Legalität?', *Gewerkschaftliche Monatshefte*, 1965, **16**, p. 215; F. Baur, 'Betriebsjustiz', *Juristenzeitung*, 1965, p. 163.

[60] The actual state and the forthcoming results of this research project are reported by J. Feest, 'Betriebsjustiz: Organisation, Anzeigebereitschaft und Sanktionsverhalten der formellen betrieblichen Sanktionsorgane', *Zeitschrift für die gesamte Strafrechtswissenschaft*, 1973, **85**, pp. 1125 et seq.

necessary since the management often acts as both plaintiff and judge. Comparing the structure of social courts in East Germany with that of factory justice in West Germany it appears paradoxically that the former corresponds more to Max Weber's theory of the progressive bureaucratization and legalization of all social institutions whereas the factory justice of West Germany is more in line with the Marxist prophecy of the assumption of all state duties by free associations of workers—at least in so far as the competent commissions are really handled by workers and not by management.

With this background of the criminal policy of both countries in mind it is now possible to compare the *development and structure of criminality* in the Federal and the German Democratic Republics.[61] In the Federal Republic, as in other western industrial countries, we notice a high level and constant increase in the crime rate. The number of criminal offences (not including traffic violations) is reported as: 2,217,966 in 1969, 2,413,586 in 1970 and 2,441,413 in 1971. The frequency per 100,000 of the population therefore climbed from 3,645 through 3,976 to 3,983.[62] In the G.D.R. (with approximately seventeen million inhabitants) the reported crime (which, by the way, is somewhat more favourably counted but which includes traffic violations) is, in comparison with West Germany (with approximately sixty million inhabitants) considerably lower but nevertheless indicates a tendency to increase: 100,126 in 1968, 105,869 in 1969 and 109,101 in 1970. The frequency per 100,000 population went from 614 through 629 to 655.[63] The structure of criminality in both countries—bearing in mind the much lower incidence in the G.D.R.—appears nevertheless to have some common features. There is the same high percentage of property crimes (which is even higher in East Germany, being 50 per cent of total crime), the same high percentage of juvenile crime and a constant recidivism rate, which has fluctuated without significant change in both countries since 1964: around 20 per cent in the G.D.R. and around 38 per cent in the Federal Republic.

The difference in the extent of criminality cannot be explained solely by reference to the differences in social conditions in the two systems since then the recent parallel development and similar structure of criminality could not be fully explained. The main reason is that a regime with a powerful authoritative national machinery, a single-party structure, a constant social

[61] The following statements are to a large extent drawn from J. Hellmer, 'Zur Kriminalität in beiden Teilen Deutschlands', *Festschrift für R. Maurach*, 1972, pp. 641 et seq.

[62] Cf. *Statistisches Bundesamt, Bevölkerung und Kultur, Reihe 9, 'Rechtspflege'*, 1971, p. 11.

[63] Cf. *Statistisches Jahrbuch der DDR*, 1972, p. 486. Disappointment at the rising figure of crimes after a sharp decline since 1960 and much slower decrease from 1964 to 1968 is clearly expressed by J. Streit, 'Zu einigen theoretischen und praktischen Fragen des Kampfes gegen die Kriminalität', *Neue Justiz*, 1973, p. 131, and H. Harrland, op. cit., p. 470.

control exercised by organizations and collectives, and the strongest educational involvement of all state and party officials must, by definition, be more successful on all levels of the fight against crime than a liberal state.[64] Another reason is the more intensive administration of criminal justice in the G.D.R.[65] which is supported by more effective means of operation. It is exactly on this point, however, that the Federal Republic is limited. Many of the interferences permissible in the G.D.R. in the name of effective criminal police would be impossible in the Federal Republic because of the conception of liberty grounded in its constitution. Thus, one may to a certain extent view the high crime rate in the West as a price paid for liberty.

(Translation by Sharon Byrd, Scholar at the Max Planck Institute for Foreign and International Criminal Law, in co-operation with the author.)

---

[64] In Germany too, the conviction rate dropped from 1125 in 1931 to 838 in 1935 to probably less than 800 in 1938.

[65] In the G.D.R. four out of five identified suspects are brought to trial and sentenced; in the Federal Republic only one in three.

THE PUNISHMENT SCENE IN SOUTH AFRICA—Developments over the past Decade and the Prospects for Reform

Mr. Justice J. H. Steyn

The concepts Criminal Justice and Reform as they are used in this essay need to be defined. Criminal Justice encompasses a wide range of activities, and various disciplines are involved in its operation. The police who receive the first information of a crime, investigate it and apprehend the offender; the courts who, *inter alia*, determine guilt or innocence and assess an appropriate penalty; the probation officer who investigates, reports on and makes recommendations in respect of an accused; the prisons that receive and—it is hoped—correct and resocialize the offender; the after-care agency that facilitates the reintegration of the offender into the community are some of the disciplines that play a part in the process.[1] I cannot, in an essay of

[1] The Hon. John Turner, Minister of Justice of Canada, in an address to the John Howard Society in Ottawa on 24 February 1971, makes the point that the system must be viewed as a whole and warns against a categorized approach when he says:

It is no longer sufficient for us to think of criminal justice and penal rehabilitation as a series of connected events. We must see it as a convicted person does, *as a total system. We must work to achieve clearly enunciated goals that work for the entire system.* And we must do it from the point of view of the man or woman involved. We cannot talk of better criminal laws, or better police enforcement or more efficient penal systems unless we look at it as the convict must. As Professor Julius Stone has written, we must study the broad area of the interaction between law and legal institutions, on the one hand, and the attitudes and activities of men and women governed by these rules on the other. We must analyse the effect of law on men and men on law.

We can no longer work only in our own sphere of activity, oblivious to the needs, achievements and reforms being made in adjacent areas of the legal process. For instance, the new Law Reform Commission of Canada, under Mr. Justice Patrick Hartt, will shortly be starting a review of the Criminal Code. *Reform of the criminal law must now reflect the total criminal judicial process,* including rehabilitation programs. What must be analysed is the system as a whole and not just a component part. Only by adopting a *systems approach* to the criminal process and utilizing feed-back analysis can we achieve what we hope

this nature, attempt to deal with all these various aspects of the system, and I have confined myself to *sentencing or disposition* and related aspects.

Reform can have many meanings. For present purposes I interpret the concept as meaning change that has as its objective the establishment of a system which, (a) provides equal justice for all; (b) whilst directed at the protection of society also aims at the rehabilitation of the offender, achieving the objective of protection with 'the minimum of suffering to the offender and those connected with him'[2] and which (c) provides effective safeguards for the due recognition and protection of the worth and the dignity of each citizen.[3]

Criminal justice seeks to maintain order and tranquillity in a community. If it is capricious or ineffective, order is forfeited and survival jeopardized. If it is unduly harsh or oppressive either in content or enforcement it stifles growth and development and can give rise to unrest and revolt.

Herbert Wechsler[4] puts it thus:

> Its [the penal law's] promise as an instrument of safety is matched only by its power to destroy. If penal law is weak or ineffective, basic human interests are in jeopardy. If it is harsh or arbitrary in its impact, it works a gross injustice on those caught within its toils. The law that carries such responsibilities should surely be as rational and just as law can be. Nowhere in the entire legal field is more at stake for the community or for the individual.

I respectfully endorse this view. Reform must then be seen to be directed towards the attainment of the above-mentioned goals. Areas in which justice is weak or ineffective have to be strengthened; where criminal justice is harsh its impact has to be cushioned so as to protect the citizen

---

from the completed process. In so doing, we will find that such an analysis forces us to think in terms of total impact upon the individual as a person, rather than in terms of a series of isolated problems that somehow involve individuals.

Similar sentiments were expressed by the Chief Justice of the United States of America, Chief Justice Warren E. Burger in an address to the Association of the Bar of the City of New York on 17 February 1970, when he said:

> I hope we can change our thinking to see criminal justice as including the entire process from the detection of the crime, apprehension of the culprit, determination of his guilt, through the process of sending him back into society after a period of enforced education.

[2] Rupert Cross, *Punishment, Prison and the Public*, London, Stevens, 1971, p. 45.

[3] Mr. Justice Brennan in the recent U.S. Supreme Court decision of *Furman* v. *Georgia* concerning the constitutional permissibility of the death penalty says: 'The State even as it punishes must treat its members with respect for their intrinsic worth as human beings. A *punishment is cruel and unusual, therefore if it does not comport with human dignity.*' (Slip Opinion, p. 14.)

[4] 'The Challenge of a Model Penal Code', *Harvard L.R.*, 1952, **65**, 1097 at 1098.

and where it is arbitrary its provisions have to be recast to ensure participation and respect instead of distrust and non-compliance.

Sentencing Policy

(a) The Legislature

The South African Legislature has for some decades placed great emphasis upon sanctions as the principal means of sustaining law and order. Much legislation was enacted creating offences and prescribing penalties. The ambit of the death penalty was extended,[5] a system of compulsory sentences was introduced[6] and mandatory sentences were prescribed for offences viewed with particular disapproval.[7]

The results were not those sought by those who drafted and enacted these provisions. An abnormally high prison population was the result.[8] Yet crime increased apace[9] and little or no determinable long-term benefits

[5] By virtue of Sec. 4 of the Criminal Procedure Amendment Act, No. 9 of 1958, now Sec. 330(1) of Act 56 of 1965 the legislature extended the discretionary power of the Courts to impose the death sentence. Previously the Courts had the discretion to impose the death penalty (in addition to the mandatory power in the event of a conviction of murder without extenuating circumstances) in respect of the crimes of treason or rape. The amending legislation added robbery (including an attempt to commit robbery) if aggravating circumstances are found to be present and housebreaking or attempted housebreaking with intent to commit an offence, if aggravating circumstances are found to have been present. As Ellison Kahn in an incisive and informative article entitled 'Crime and Punishment 1910–1960' in *Acta Juridica*, 1960, at p. 191 states, these are crimes which, 'however much they may have attracted that penalty (the death sentence) in bygone times, had been treated as non-capital at least from 1840'. In 1965 by virtue of the provisions of Sec. 10 of Act 96 of 1965, kidnapping and childstealing were added to the list of 'capital crimes'.

[6] For a discussion of the system see the article by Ellison Kahn cited above at pp. 216–20 and see Secs. 334 (*ter.*), 334 (*quat.*) and 335 of the Criminal Procedure and Evidence Act, No. 56 of 1955 as amended.

[7] Act 33 of 1952 made a sentence of whipping not exceeding ten strokes compulsory for rape, robbery, culpable homicide where intent to commit rape or robbery was involved, assault with intent to commit rape and robbery, breaking or entering any house or building with intent to commit an offence. Certain persons were excepted such as, e.g. persons over the age of 50 years, habitual criminals and persons suffering from ill health as well as females.

[8] See Table 1, page 542 below, which shows the total number of committals pursuant to convictions and the daily average number of prisoners in South African jails every day. During the decade 1960–70 the South African population increased by 23 per cent whilst its prison population increased by 71 per cent.

[9] In 1958 'non-serious crime convictions' were given as 1,388,898; serious crime convictions as 85,636. The Reports of the Commissioner of Police for the years 1968/69, 1969/70, 1970/71 and 1971/72 reflect the following figures under the heading 'Cases sent for trial' and sub-headings 'Offences' and 'Law Infringements':

were experienced—in the sense of any significant decline in anti-social conduct. It is, of course, well known that convictions for both non-serious and serious crime are proportionately much greater among the non-white population than among the whites. This link between race and crime has many facets—economic, cultural, political, educational, etc.—and the system of sanctions can only be one aspect of the attack upon the problems which lie at the roots of crime in particular societies.[10]

The failure of some of the old penal measures appears to have been appreciated. Either because of their harshness and their unacceptability or because of the fact that the legislation had no apparent effect in reducing the incidence of the crime they were designed to combat, some measures were abandoned and other legislative provisions were amended so as to eliminate some of the inequities. So, for example, compulsory whipping introduced in respect of certain offences (see footnote 7 above) was abolished and the judicial officer's power to impose corporal punishment limited.[11] Compulsory sentences—although remaining on the statute book—were rendered discretionary, provided the judicial officer found circumstances justifying the imposition of a lesser penalty.[12]

John Citizen must, however, have been somewhat bemused when, shortly

---

[9] continued

	Cases Sent For Trial			
	1968/69	1969/70	1970/71	1971/72
A. Offences	413,428	433,297	447,836	484,662
B. Law Infringements	1,583,138	1,583,003	1,676,747	1,795,236

See Appendix 3 which is self-explanatory in respect of the incidence of the crime of murder. It indicates a steady increase in the number of persons charged with murder and those convicted of murder with or without extenuating circumstances despite the penal measures detailed above. The note to Appendix 3 gives comparative figures for a twelve-year period, 1935–46 and a five-year period, 1963–67 which are also self-explanatory. All statistics were obtained from the Department of Statistics.

For a valuable survey, see J. J. Labuschagne, 'Crime in South Africa', *Crime, Punishment and Correction* (NICRO Criminological Journal), 1, No. 2, November 1972. He points to the relatively very high incidence of serious violence as a proportion of all convictions (22 per cent) and the much greater incidence of these offences among the non-white population. The ratio for assault with intent to do grievous bodily harm was 1:75, whereas the ratio of whites to non-whites in the South African population is about 1:8. He shows that there is relatively little crime across the colour bar but that 'the sanctions applied by the white man are only partially accepted by the Bantu', p. 14.

[10] See J. J. Labuschagne, ibid.

[11] By virtue of the provisions of Sec. 12 of Act 96 of 1965. See *S. v. Kumalo*, 1965(4) S.A. 565(N) where the history of the South African legislation in respect of corporal punishment is analysed by a full-bench of the Natal Court.

[12] Sec. 335A introduced by Sec. 20 of Act No. 9 of the 1968 into the Criminal Procedure and Evidence Act.

after these more enlightened steps were taken, legislation was introduced, which once again sought to rely significantly upon broadly cast penal provisions and prescribed minimum sentences as a means of controlling offences particularly prevalent. In 1968 the so-called Dangerous Weapons Act (Act 71 of 1968) was passed. Section 4 of this Statute obliges the judicial officer (in the areas where the Act is made applicable) to impose a minimum sentence of two years' imprisonment on an offender found guilty of assaulting any person with a dangerous weapon,[13] unless there are circumstances which justify the imposition of a lighter sentence. No sentence other than imprisonment may be imposed and no portion of the sentence may be suspended.

Again the results were not those anticipated. No perceptible decrease in the prevalence of assaults with 'dangerous weapons' was experienced[14] and judicial officers occasionally had to resort to stratagems such as sentencing offenders to the 'rising of the Court' where imprisonment was manifestly an inappropriate form of punishment. Again, amending legislation followed. The General Law Amendment Act 102 of 1972 provided in Section 23 for an amendment to Section 4 of the 1968 Act which gave back to the Courts *some* of their discretion in imposing a sentence. Where there are circumstances justifying a lighter sentence the judicial officer now has a complete discretion, he need not impose imprisonment at all and, if he does, he may suspend it in whole or in part. Where, however, there are no circumstances justifying the imposition of a lighter sentence the minimum sentence of two years' imprisonment is compulsory and the judicial officer—somewhat anomalously—is not able to suspend any portion of the sentence of two years or more.

In the late sixties South Africa became conscious of the threat to stability and to the moral fibre of its people occasioned by the abuse of dependence-producing substances. A Committee of Enquiry was appointed to investigate

[13] A dangerous weapon is defined as follows: '... any object, other than a firearm, which is likely to cause serious bodily injury if it were used to commit an assault'. See also the incisive and amusing comments on this legislation by *Amicus Curiae* under heading 'The Big Stick' in *South African L.J.*, 1969, **86,** 486.

[14] Prosecutions or cases sent for trial—the statistical nomenclatures used by the Commissioner of Police in his Report, reflect the following:

Assaults with intent to cause serious bodily harm:

1969	73,934
1970	80,059
1971	82,741
1972	85,926

Whilst dangerous weapons may not have been used in all these cases, in view of the broad terms in which the definition is couched, it is likely that in all but a miniscule percentage of cases a dangerous weapon would have played a part in the infliction of the serious bodily injury.

the abuse of drugs and it reported in 1970.[15] The Committee stated specifically that 'except for necessary incidental references *alcohol and dagga (marijuana) would not be included in the present enquiry*'.[16] In paragraph 8[17] the Committee went on to say:

> The Committee was also aware of the fact that the problem of drug dependence manifests itself in different ways in the various ethnic groups in the Republic of South Africa. Up to now dagga has been the drug for which the non-white population groups have a predilection, although it is also abused by large groups of whites. The large group of synthetic drugs is, however, mainly preferred by whites *and the Committee therefore thought it advisable to restrict the inquiry to whites* [my italics].

The Committee also stated that:

> . . . while the illicit distributor should be prosecuted and punished mercilessly *the dependant is in a condition requiring treatment* [my italics].[18]

Act 41 of 1971 was introduced to give effect to the recommendations of the Committee: its imposing short title was 'The Abuse of Dependence-Producing Substances and Rehabilitation Centres Act, 1971'. The Act contains provisions and lays down penalties which subsequently led to the Supreme Court[19] describing the Act as one of *'manifest and unique severity and one which authorises punishments which the courts of the Republic would not have imposed had the Act not been passed'* [my italics]. The Court went on to say:[20]

> The history of the enforcement of the Act to date shows that a severe strain is being—and will to a progressively greater degree continue to be—placed upon the prison services to accommodate an unprecedented influx of convicted persons who have been sentenced to very substantial sentences of imprisonment. It is also the experience of Judges of this Division in conducting gaol inspection that remission of sentences for dagga offences is seldom, if ever, granted.[21]

Before citing the provisions of the Act which the Court had in mind and giving a brief resumé of its penal provisions, two matters have to be emphasized. Firstly, the legislature included dagga as one of the substances called 'prohibited dependence-producing drugs' along with drugs such as heroin, lysergide and prepared opium. Secondly, it drew no distinction between population groups in respect of which an investigation had not been made

[15] See the Report of the Committee of Enquiry into the Abuse of Drugs, 1970 R.P. 97/70.
[16] Ibid., p. 4.
[17] Ibid., p. 4.
[18] Para. 550 of the Report, p. 90.
[19] *S.* v. *Shangase and Others*, 1972(2) S.A. 410(N) at p. 415.
[20] At p. 416.
[21] All Judges have the right to visit all prisons at any time.

and the group in respect of which the Committee had enquired and recommended.

The relevant sections of the Act creating offences and prescribing penalties are the following:

2. *Dealing in, use or possession of prohibited or dangerous dependence-producing drugs prohibited.*—Notwithstanding anything to the contrary in any law contained, any person—
    - (a) who deals in any prohibited dependence-producing drug or any plant from which such dependence-producing drug can be manufactured; or
    - (b) who has in his possession or uses any such dependence-producing drug or plant; or
    - (c) who deals in any dangerous dependence-producing drug or any plant from which such drug can be manufactured; or
    - (d) who has in his possession or uses any dependence-producing drug or plant referred to in paragraph (c),

    shall be guilty of an offence and liable on conviction—
    - (i) in the case of a first conviction for a contravention of any provision of paragraph (a) or (c), to imprisonment for a period of not less than five years, but not exceeding fifteen years;
    - (ii) in the case of a second or subsequent conviction for a contravention of an offence referred to in paragraph (i), to imprisonment for a period of not less than ten years, but not exceeding twenty-five years;
    - (iii) in the case of a first conviction for a contravention of any provision referred to in paragraph (b) or (d), to imprisonment for a period of not less than two years, but not exceeding ten years;
    - (iv) in the case of a second or subsequent conviction for an offence referred to in paragraph (iii), to imprisonment for a period of not less than five years, but not exceeding fifteen years.

3. *Dealing in, use or possession of potentially dangerous dependence-producing drugs prohibited.*—Notwithstanding anything to the contrary in any law contained, any person—
    - (a) who deals in any potentially dangerous dependence-producing drug; or
    - (b) who uses or has in his possession any drug referred to in paragraph (a),

    shall be guilty of an offence and liable on conviction—
    - (i) in the case of a conviction for a contravention of any provision of paragraph (a), to imprisonment for a period not exceeding ten years;
    - (ii) in the case of a conviction for a contravention of any provision of paragraph (b), to imprisonment for a period not exceeding five years.

7. *In case of mitigating circumstances another sentence may be imposed in lieu of certain prescribed compulsory sentences.*—Whenever a court is bound to impose upon a person convicted by it of an offence, a punishment prescribed by section 2 (iii) or (iv) and is satisfied that there are circumstances which justify the imposition of a lighter sentence than such prescribed punishment, it shall enter those circumstances on the record of the proceedings and shall—

(a) if it is bound to sentence such person to the punishment prescribed by section 2 (iii), impose upon him, in lieu thereof, a sentence of imprisonment for a period not exceeding two years; or

(b) if it is bound to sentence such person to the punishment prescribed by section 2 (iv), impose upon him, in lieu thereof, a sentence of imprisonment for a period not exceeding five years.

In addition there are presumptions which aid the State when it seeks to prove that 'possession' was for purposes of 'dealing in' such drug. So, e.g. Sec. 10(1) (a) provides:

If in any prosecution for an offence under section 2 it is proved that the accused was found in possession of—
　(i) dagga exceeding 115 grams in mass;
　(ii) any prohibited dependence-producing drugs,
it shall be presumed that the accused dealt in such dagga or drugs, unless the contrary is proved.

It can be seen that the comments made by the Supreme Court in *Shangase*'s case are fully justified. The actual impact of the legislation was far-reaching especially in respect of sections of the community that had for many years, albeit unlawfully, used dagga. It is to be stressed that the penalties prescribed both in respect of possession and use of dagga and dealing therein, are the same as those provided for in respect of heroin, cocaine and morphine. In an introductory note to an article by Dr. Bensusan in the *South African Law Journal*,[22] Prof. Ellison Kahn points out that the use of dagga goes back to the beginning of our historical records, and that the name dagga was taken over from the Hottentots. (The Committee in its report confirms this fact and says: 'The South African word dagga is derived from the word 'dachah', a name given by the Hottentots to the plant *Cannabis Sativa*, various varieties of which are found in different parts of the world.') In the period 1 July 1969 to 30 June 1970, 37,539 contraventions were reported and 37,420 prosecutions were initiated; 5,145,635 pounds of dagga were confiscated.[23]

Principally the Act has most pertinently affected those groups in respect of whom the Committee specifically made no investigation or recommendation and in respect of a substance which, save for necessary incidental references, was not included in the enquiry. The Committee had, after all, specifically stated dagga was the drug for which the 'non-white population groups have a predilection'. The legislature apparently chose to disregard the specific recommendation of the Committee that '*another committee of*

---

[22] *South African L.J.*, 1972, **89**, p. 105 at p. 113.

[23] R.P. 45/1971—pp. 6–7. For a full discussion of the topic see Prof. Kahn's article, op. cit., and the article by Dr. Bensusan which follows. See also T. W. Bennet, 'Alcohol, Drugs and the Criminal Law', *South African L.J.*, 1973, **90**, p. 69.

enquiry be appointed to enquire into the dagga problem as it exists in the Republic today, because the abuse of dagga is so closely connected with the abuse of other drugs'[24] [my italics].

The penal measures caused a great deal of uncertainty and confusion, the nature and extent of which are not relevant for present purposes. What is significant, however, is that the Courts were, in respect of those who 'possess' or 'use' prohibited or dangerous dependence-producing drugs (the latter include amphetamine, pethedene, cocaine and morphine), also deprived of the discretion to impose, in the case of adults, sentences other than imprisonment—even though they were, in the circumstances stated in Section 7, entitled to suspend such sentences either in whole or in part. Probation, postponement of sentence, fines and other non-institutional forms of punishment were not appropriate forms of correction in terms of the provisions of the Act.[25]

In respect of those who 'deal' in prohibited or dangerous dependence-producing drugs the legislature obliged the Court to impose a minimum sentence, but did not deprive it of the power to suspend all but a part of the sentence.[26]

But subsequently, by the provisions of Act 80 of 1973, this power to suspend was taken away from the Courts. Section 2A of this Act provides:

(1) Notwithstanding anything to the contrary in any law contained, no person shall on conviction for a contravention of a provision of section 2(a) or (c) be dealt with under section 352 of the Criminal Procedure Act, 1955 (Act No. 56 of 1955[27]), or the corresponding provision of the Criminal Procedure Ordinance, 1963 (Ordinance No. 34 of 1963), of the territory, if such person was at the time of the commission of that contravention eighteen years of age or older.

(2) The provisions of subsection (1) shall apply in respect of any person who is convicted of a contravention of a provision referred to in subsection (1) on or after the date of commencement of the Abuse of Dependence-producing Substances and Rehabilitation Centres Amendment Act, 1973, irrespective of whether or not the contravention in question was committed before such date.

I have cited the provisions of the legislation dealing with drug abuse in some detail. I have done so because it is a significant indicator of the attitude of the legislature towards the control of anti-social behaviour. It is too early

[24] Ibid., p. 93.

[25] See my reservations on the possible use of rehabilitative centres, below, page 536.

[26] As much of the sentence as all but 4 days could be suspended. See *S.* v. *Shangase* (*supra*) at p. 429.

[27] Sec. 352 *inter alia* confers the power upon the Court to suspend part of a sentence of imprisonment.

to say what effect the legislation will have upon the prevalence of the offence. That it will lead to a significant increase in the South African prison population—both short-term and long-term is beyond question.

When he opened the Victor Verster Prison near Cape Town on 15 March 1968 the Hon. P. C. Pelser, Minister of Justice and Prisons, said the following:

> The past has unquestionably shown that harsh and inhuman prison sentences have not brought about a decrease in crime. In consequence the conviction has arisen, and it is today accepted, that the prisoner should rather be treated positively in an effort to rehabilitate him. This method is being favoured more and more and the prejudices of the past have to a great extent been replaced by such a positive approach. A scientific approach to the problem of crime has thus become essential, and in consequence the concept in respect of the treatment of the prisoner must at least be founded on the results of research and reliable information. In the past too much reliance has been placed on the easy and convenient formula that quick and effective punishment is the only remedy for crime.

Despite this statement and despite protestations from the judiciary and academicians, there has been no perceptible change in the attitude of the legislature towards punishment over the past 25 years. It is true that some of the harsher and more brutal forms of punishment such as whipping are no longer compulsorily prescribed. On the other hand it would seem as if there is still great reliance placed upon punishment in itself and the tendency remains to deal punitively with *ad hoc* problems such as assaults with a 'dangerous weapon' and drug abuse. Although it is true that the legislation dealing with drug abuse provides for rehabilitation centres (to which a committal procedure is prescribed), it seems highly unlikely—bearing in mind the average of 30,000 annual convictions for the use or possession of dagga and the few facilities available for treatment—that any significant number of dagga addicts or users would ever be committed for such treatment. The vast majority will almost certainly be dealt with only through the mainstream of the criminal justice system.

The dangers of this approach could well be described in the following terms:—The process of *criminal justice* is primarily directed at the maintenance of stability in the community which it serves. Its impact is profound. Those responsible for drafting and enacting criminal laws and stipulating the sanctions often have an incomplete appreciation of the effects which statutory provisions of a criminal nature have upon the tone and contentment of the lives of those whose behaviour they seek to control. The draftsman and the legislator are confronted by a social ill. The seriousness and extent of the disease are often measured only by repute. Reaction is sometimes governed significantly by the maturity and proclivity, initially of an individual and ultimately of the group responsible for launching the legislative process. In most societies there is very little attempt to diagnose the causes and to relate control measures, at least in part, to such causes as are capable of ascertainment. Individualization of treatment, bearing in mind the object of the legislative exercise, rarely receives consideration. Over-reaction and a reliance upon fear as the stimulus for conforming conduct are often the major ingredients of the legislative dish.

In the short term such measures may produce results. Moreover, they have the advantage, especially amongst communities unsophisticated and immature, of being politically rewarding. In the long term, because of their broad framework, their net is flung so wide that they tend to enmesh also the innocent and to subjugate the guiltless. They produce discontent and a refusal to participate in the enforcement of legislative provisions. They tend to strengthen power structures not subject to public scrutiny or independent control. Therefore, any community should be on its guard once it recognizes the symptoms of lack of respect and discontent. The recognition of such symptoms should compel a society to re-examine the structure of its criminal law to ensure that it provides the justice and stability it seeks.[28] These comments, despite the many peculiarities and complexities of the South African situation, are in full measure relevant to its problems in the field of punishment.

In so far as the future is concerned it is noteworthy that the Government appointed a Commission of Enquiry into Criminal Procedure and Evidence on 19 June 1970. 'Penal reform and Punishment', the Commissioner[29] said unequivocally,[30] 'clearly does not fall within any of the Commission's specific terms of reference as set out in paragraph (a) to (j)'. He went on to say: 'Neither is it an aspect of "criminal procedure and evidence" within the meaning of that expression in the general mandate to the Commission as set out in paragraph (k) of the terms of reference. It was apparently also so understood by the legal profession and the general public, because no other memoranda or representations were received by the Commission on this difficult matter in regard to which sharp differences of opinion exist especially amongst experts in the field'. The learned Commissioner accordingly concluded: 'In the circumstances I must respectfully decline the invitation to consider the suggestion and make a recommendation thereon.'

The Commissioner was, in addition, requested to recommend that these

[28] This is repeated from an article by the author, entitled 'Crime and its Control', *Acta Juridica*, 1971, p. 167.
[29] The Hon. Mr. Justice D. H. Botha—Judge of the Court of Appeal.
[30] R.P. 78/1971, p. 52. The learned Commissioner was responding to a request that he should also investigate the penal aspects of the South African Criminal Jurisprudence.

aspects of the Criminal Law should also be investigated. He did not do so, despite the fact that he states in the Introduction to his thorough report:[31]

> A fair and just system of criminal procedure is a requisite for any civilized and democratic society. A learned writer once said, and it is generally accepted in the civilized world, that *the level of civilization of a people can be largely measured by the procedure which it prescribes for the maintenance of its substantive criminal law*. Our courts continually refer to the fundamental requirements of our criminal justice *that an accused person is entitled to a fair and just trial in accordance with prescribed legal principles, and that in the adjudication of a criminal case any unfairness or injustice must be avoided* [my italics].

It seems to me that punishment is part of 'the adjudication of a criminal case' and that also in its determination 'any unfairness or injustice must be avoided'. Whilst it is accepted that the Commissioner ruled correctly that penal reform and punishment were not included directly or indirectly within his terms of reference, it is perhaps unfortunate that a recommendation indicating the need for enquiry, review and reform of these aspects of the South African Criminal Law, was not made. It is equally unfortunate that the authorities did not see fit to incorporate any reference to punishment in the Commissioner's mandate.

It seems to the author that when 'the level of civilization' of our people comes to be measured,[32] the yardstick will inevitably be applied in respect of an area—and a vital area—as yet untouched by the reformer's broom. The discussion so far has shown that penal legislation is undoubtedly an area where there are cobwebs and dusty corners. Only through a thorough multidisciplinary enquiry into crime and punishment will the opportunity arise for the concerned academician, practitioner, judicial officer and criminologist to make his voice heard in a forum where positive results are at least a possibility. Only through the recommendations of such a Commission can a sentencing policy be enunciated which can serve as a blueprint for future legislative provisions with a penal content.[33]

(b) The Courts

For those unfamiliar with the structure of the South African courts I quote, in Appendix I to this article, from Hiemstra's outline published in *The Standard Encyclopaedia of South Africa*.

It is of importance to note that Magistrate's Courts and Regional Courts

[31] Ibid., p. 4.

[32] This is a reference to the comment incorporated by reference in the report of the Commissioner cited under footnote 30 above.

[33] Support for this proposal is *inter alia* to be found in the *Annual Survey of South African Law*, 1970, p. 467. This Survey each year contains a most thorough analysis of developments in respect of criminal justice.

are obliged to follow the decisions of the Superior Courts. The Appellate Division and the various divisions of the Supreme Court accordingly fashion penal policy save in so far as their authority has been ousted by the specific injunctions of the legislature, e.g., in respect of offences under the provisions of the Abuse of Dependence-producing Substances and Rehabilitation Centres Act, No. 41 of 1971, referred to above.

The objects which should be served when assessing punishment have been stated on more than one occasion by the Appellate Division.[34] These objects are described in the authoritative work on *South African Criminal Law and Procedure* by Burchell and Hunt as:

> . . . (1) retribution (including the ideas of expiation, atonement, revenge and denunciation); (2) prevention; (3) individual deterrence; (4) general deterrence; and (5) reformation. Some of these, like general deterrence, prevention and most forms of retribution, are concerned solely with the interests of the community. Reformation, on the other hand, views the welfare of the individual and also, since by definition a reformed criminal commits no crime, the community as well.[35]

The learned authors add a further purpose of punishment, viz. 'fairness and consistency'.

These general purposes of punishment are to be served by a consideration of various factors. Most recently in *S. v. Zinn*[36] the Court of Appeal per Rumpff, J.A., said:

> What has to be considered is the triad consisting of the crime, the offender and the interests of society.

In *S. v. Gool*,[37] Miller, J. after citing the above factors adds the following significant statement:

> The result of over-emphasis of any one of the relevant factors is often underestimation or even total disregard of one or more of the other factors. A mind tending to pre-occupation with the desirability of deterring others from committing an offence is apt to give insufficient attention to other factors which in the particular circumstances of the case may be more important for the purposes of assessing a just and proper sentence for the accused then standing in the dock. It is necessary always to be alert to that danger.

---

[34] See R. v. *Swanepoel*, 1945 A.D. 444, (Ellison Kahn, op. cit.—in the author's view correctly—states that the citation of authorities was 'eclectic and limited'); R. v. *Mzwakala*, 1957(4) S.A., 273; R. v. *Karg*, 1961(1) S.A., 231 (A.D.); *S.* v. *Whitehead*, 1970(4) S.A., 424 at p. 439; *S.* v. *Matthee*, 1971(3) S.A., 769 at p. 774, and E. M. Burchell and P. M. A. Hunt, *South African Criminal Law and Procedure*, vol. 1, Cape Town, Juta & Co., 1970, pp. 67–80.

[35] Ibid., p. 67.

[36] 1969(2) S.A., 537 at p. 540.

[37] 1972(1) S.A., 455 at p. 456.

This statement is significant because it is an indication of a new direction in South African penal practice. Sentences are being individualized. In the past the emphasis has fallen almost exclusively upon retribution and deterence; the result was that the offence and not the offender, in the main, received the consideration of the Court. This latter trend, it seems to the author, is now being reversed.[38]

Pre-sentence investigation and reports are being called for. This is particularly so in the case of juveniles; however, with adults attempts are also being made to tailor the punishment so as to fit also the offender.[39] The moral blameworthiness of the offender should be considered as at least equally important if not more important than the prevalence of the offences and the difficulties of its detection.[40] Maisels J. ends his judgement in R. v. *Samson*[41] with a sentence which expresses the concern at the use of retributive and harsh punishments by the Court when he says:

> After all, the days when transportation was considered a proper punishment for petty theft are over.

Reaction against retributive punishment is to be found also in judgements of the Court of Appeal and the ringing phrase 'Justice must be done, but mercy, not a sledge-hammer, is its concomitant' was coined by Holmes J.A.[42] The same Judge expressed enlightened views in respect of punishment when in *S.* v. *V.*,[43] he says:

> Punishment should fit the criminal as well as the crime, be fair to the accused and to society, and be blended with a measure of mercy ... *The element of mercy, a hallmark of civilised and enlightened administration, should not be overlooked, lest the Court be in danger of reducing itself to the plane of the criminal ... True mercy has nothing in common with soft weakness, or maudlin sympathy for the criminal, or permissive tolerance. It is an element of justice itself* [my italics].

The judgement by Jansen J.A. in this case (*S.* v. *V.*) is based, *inter alia*, upon the consideration that there was a real possibility that a substantial

---

[38] See, e.g., *S.* v. *Karg* (*supra*) at p. 236 ('the retributive aspect has tended to yield ground to the aspects of prevention and correction'); *S.* v. *Baptic*, 1963(1) P.H., H. 96(N); *S.* v. *Anderson*, 1964(3) S.A., 494 (A.D.); *S.* v. *Maree*, 1964(4) S.A., 545(0) at p. 560 and the authorities cited under notes 52 and 68, *infra*.

[39] The practice has long been in use in respect of juveniles. See *R.* v. *Du Plessis*, 1957(2) S.A., 13(0); *S.* v. *Yibe*, 1964(3) S.A., 502(E) and see *S.* v. *Adams*, 1971(4) S.A., 125(C) for the practice to be adopted and the format of reports. See also the discussion of recent cases in an article by James Lund, 'An Increase in the use of Pre-sentence Reports', *South African L.J.*, 1972, **89**, p. 158.

[40] R. v. *David and Alfred* (an unreported full-bench decision of the Southern Rhodesian Court, referred to in R. v. *Samson*, 1962(4) S.A., 64).

[41] Ibid., p. 66.

[42] *S.* v. *Harrison*, 1970(3) S.A., 684 (A.D.) at p. 686A.

[43] 1972(3) S.A., 611 at p. 614.

sentence of imprisonment would '. . . damp the fires of irresponsible youth'.[44] This tends to confirm the noteworthy trend away from the approach advanced, for example, in the judgements of the Court *a quo* in R. v. *Roberts*[45] and R. v. *S*[46] that the death penalty had to be imposed because of the risk of the repetition of the crime.

Extra-curial statements by Judges also reflect a growing awareness of the need to individualize punishment. Mr. Justice Hiemstra in a Foreword to the first issue of the Criminological Journal issued by N.I.C.R.O. (National Institute for Crime Prevention and Rehabilitation of Offenders) said the following in this respect:

> Startling developments have occurred throughout the Western world in the criminological field. South Africa's comparative isolation inevitably results in a delayed reaction, especially in areas of a philosophical rather than of a practical character. We are rightly proud of an efficient Prisons Department with its enlightened rehabilitative ideals. Our punishment system still tends, however, to be significantly retributive with insufficient emphasis upon the positive protective impact of the individualised treatment of the offender.
>
> Crime will, unfortunately, always be with us. A sentimental concern for the offender is as destructive as an over-reliance upon punishment as the mainstay of our crimino-legal structure. Constructive forms of punishment tailored to protect the public whilst catering for the requirements of the offender are plain common sense.
>
> For too long have we relied upon prison as providing the panacea for the anti-social ills of our society. Our unbelievably large prison population (short-term in particular) indicates our over-reliance in this respect. Moreover it imposes a grossly disproportionate cost burden on the South African tax-payer. Reform in this area has been too long delayed.

Mr. Justice Harcourt in a paper delivered at the 1972 Law Conference of the Association of Law Societies of the Republic said:

> . . . perhaps it is not too much to ask that, at any rate in cases of serious crime, the courts should, as in many states of America, be assisted by reports from the variety of experts, psychiatrists, psychologists, social welfare workers, and prison officers described above. Then at least it might be possible to have some assurance that our sentencing process is founded on something more than imperfect knowledge, trained intuition and a hope and a prayer.

This new approach towards sentencing by the Superior Courts in South Africa becomes even more obvious when one analyses developments since

---

[44] Ibid., p. 621.
[45] Referred to in 1957(4) S.A., 265 (A.D.) at p. 269.
[46] Referred to in 1958(3) S.A., 102 (A.D.).

1960[47] as evidenced by judgements delivered in respect of the various forms of punishment which can be imposed by the Courts.

(i) *Imprisonment:*

Table 1 illustrates the significant increase in the number of persons detained in South African prisons.

TABLE I

Year	Annual Number of Receptions into Prison	Daily Average Population
1959	311,163	49,886
1960	322,355	52,956
1961	289,969	55,762
1962	346,527	62,769
1963	288,908	66,575
1964	297,237	70,351
1965	284,528	72,627
1966	339,143	74,033
1967	423,464	73,030
1968	486,260	80,534
1969	496,071	88,079
1970	484,661	90,555
1971	474,065	91,108
1972	440,922	91,253

The prison population is in fact growing at a rate nearly three times that of the country's population growth. Even more significant is the incidence of short-term imprisonment in South Africa. Commenting on our prison population in a radio address in 1971 the Chief Justice, the Hon. Mr. Justice N. Ogilvie-Thompson, said the following:

Statistics show that the ratio of our prison population to the total population of the country is strikingly high. Thus in 1969—the last year for which internationally comparative figures are available to me—the number of incarcerated prisoners per 100,000 of our population was no less than 417—a figure nearly six times the corresponding figure for that year in France with a total population just short of 2½ times our own and considerably more than five times the corresponding figure in England with a total population more than double our own. The Report of the Commissioner of Prisons for the year ended 30th June, 1970 shows that more than 55% of all sentenced prisoners (excluding capital cases) for the year ended 30th June, 1970 had been sentenced to imprisonment

---

[47] The author could hardly hope to add to the comprehensive survey done by Ellison Khan for the period 1910–60 in his article: 'Crime and Punishment 1910–1960—Reflections on Changes in the Law of Criminal Punishment and its application', op. cit.

for only one month or less. The total of those who had been sentenced to four months or less actually constituted slightly over 86% of the aggregate of all sentenced prisoners during that year; and of that 86% a substantial proportion were first offenders. These figures are not indicative of any undue leniency on the part of the Courts, but show what a large number of crimes which are in themselves relatively unserious entail a prison sentence, and what a high proportion of all sentenced offenders is comprised by these short-term prisoners. This is in appreciable measure attributable to the composition of our population and the number of infringements of the Criminal Law associated with so-called pass offences and breaches of what are sometimes generically designated 'curfew regulations'.

Nevertheless, the cardinal fact remains that a strikingly high proportion of our prison population is comprised of those serving short-term sentences.

It need hardly be emphasised that such a large proportion of short-term prisoners is inherently undesirable.

Later, in 1973, the Chief Justice in an article published in *Crime, Punishment and Correction*[48] pointed to the fact that no fewer than 256,246 of the 474,065 persons who were committed to jail in the year ending 30 June 1971 were sentenced to terms of one month or less. The author feels he should stress that no less than 91 per cent of the total of those so committed were sentenced to serve terms of imprisonment of 6 months or less and 84 per cent were sentenced to 4 months or less.[49] The prison population is largely non-white, the majority are Bantu (77 per cent) followed by coloureds (13 per cent), whites (3 per cent) and Asiatics (0·55 per cent).[50]

The problem of a large percentage of petty offenders in jail has caused concern since 1910.[51] The Courts have for some time—but recently more firmly—indicated that unnecessary use of short-term imprisonment is unacceptable.[52] A few of these dicta should be mentioned. In *S. v. Butelezi*[53] the Court (*per* Harcourt J., Friedman J. concurring) says:

[48] (The NICRO Criminological Journal), **2**, No. 1, March 1973.

[49] The prison figures for the period ending June, 1972 (Statistical Report of the Commissioner of Prisons of the Republic of South Africa for the period 1.7.71–30.6.72, R.P. 91/1972) reflects admissions of 440,922 of which 238,866 were committed to serve sentences of one month or less. The percentage of those committed to serve periods of 4 months and 6 months imprisonment or less, remained at the rate of 91 per cent and 84 per cent of the total committals respectively.

[50] See R. N. Leon, 'Punishment in South Africa: A Brief Historical Perspective', *Crime, Punishment and Correction*, **2**, No. 3, October 1973, p. 6.

[51] See Ellison Kahn's article, op. cit., at pp. 212–15.

[52] See, e.g., R. v. *Persadh*, 1944 N.P.D., 357 at p. 358; R. v. *Wegkamp*, 1960(2) S.A., 655(T); *S. v. Muller*, 1962(4) S.A., 77(N); *S. v. Butelezi*, 1964(3) S.A., 519(N); *S. v. Shange*, 1967(2) S.A., 81(C); *S. v. Cerkic*, 1968(2) S.A., 541(C); *S. v. Ghoor*, 1969(2) S.A., 555 (A.D.); *S. v. D'Este*, 1971(3) S.A., 107(E); *S. v. Smith*, 1971(4) S.A., 419(T); *S. v. Mafuya*, 1972(4) S.A., 565(o); *S. v. Mantusse*, 1973(3) S.A., 223(T) and *S. v. Moraka*, 1973(3) S.A., 658(C).   [53] See note 52 above, at pp. 521–2.

The crime was, it is true, a serious one of housebreaking, but the evidence shows that the accused did no more than open the door of the complainant's garage. The evidence suggests that it had not been locked and, in any event, the value of the article stolen, namely an umbrella worth R5, was not great. In addition, to this, however, the cases emphasising the desirability of keeping first offenders out of gaol, if such a course is reasonably possible, indicate clearly that this is so even where there has been a substantial infringement of the complainant's rights and thus a deliberate infringement. Thus, in *S. v. Muller* the crime was fraud and in *Persadh* v. R., 1944 N.P.D. 357, the accused, an Indian of 26 years of age was convicted of the theft of 12 dozen eggs and was yet accorded the relief of a suspended sentence.

Furthermore, the magistrate appears to have been over-influenced by the fact that the crime in question was very prevalent in the coal mines in the district in question and that because of the shifting population of such area detection of such crimes is difficult. These are undoubtedly matters which it was proper for the magistrate to take into account but, as has been said, such objective factors must not be taken too far and must not be allowed to obscure the fact that the subjective elements, particularly the moral blameworthiness of the offence, are equally important, if not more important elements to be considered—see R. v. *Samson*, 1962(4) S.A., 64 (S.R.), and the cases cited therein.

In *S. v. Shange*[54] the Court (*per* Steyn J., Watermeyer J. concurring) said:

> I am of the view that it is the duty of the Court to seek, in so far as the nature of the offence, the public interest and the circumstances which are properly to be taken into account when assessing punishment, to impose short-term imprisonment (without the option of a fine) when in fact no other alternative exists. If it is borne in mind that the motivation for the imposition of this form of punishment is its deterrent effect (both for the offender and others), this comment has particularly application in respect of those of our citizens whose living conditions, education and approach is such that a short spell in prison in fact is not the type of punishment likely to fulfil any significant role as a deterrent. In the very nature of things rehabilitation cannot be achieved, and the detrimental effects of imprisonment upon the individual (without its advantages) and the burden upon the State is in a considerable measure the most important consequence of an unconsidered resort to this form of punishment.

This dictum was approved not only in the Cape Court in *S. v. Cerkic*,[55] but also by the Transvaal Court in *S. v. Smith*,[56] the Orange Free State in *S. v. Mafuya*[57] and the Rhodesian Court of Appeal.[58]

Most recently Marais J. (F. S. Steyn concurring) in *S. v. Mantusse*[59] after

[54] See note 49, at p. 82—the judgement is in Afrikaans and the quotation is the author's free translation of this portion of the judgement.

[55] See note 49 above, at p. 542.

[56] See note 49 above, at p. 421.

[57] See note 49 above, at p. 567.

[58] R. v. *Mutizwa*, 1968(4), 278(T) at p. 280. See also *S. v. Ndamase*, 1973(3) S.A., 614(E).

[59] See note 52 above, at p. 224.

detailing the paucity of information before the Court before a sentence of short-term imprisonment was passed on a youthful first offender, said:[60]

> The idea that this sort of crime—stabbing amongst Bantu, especially where alcohol has been used—will be exterminated by, or even in the smallest measure be reduced—by sentences of, e.g. four months' imprisonment, is antiquated and can only help to increase our already large prison population even further.

At the other end of the scale I would point to the fact that inordinately lengthy periods of imprisonment have been frowned upon by the Courts for some time. The sentence of a train-wrecker found guilty of assault with intent to murder was reduced by the Appellate Division from 25 to 15 years.[61] In doing so the Court stated:[62]

> There is no doubt that a sentence of twenty-five years' imprisonment is exceptionally long, according to our practice. Counsel for the Crown referred us to two *Government Notices* (G.N. 1551 of the 8th September, 1911 and G.N. 286 of the 28th February, 1936) in terms of which a sentence of imprisonment for life is deemed for the purposes of remission to be a sentence of imprisonment for twenty years. Whether or not this provision furnishes a useful guide to the longest sentence that should ordinarily be imposed, I see no reason to doubt that a period substantially less than twenty-five years is normally sufficient to meet the deterrent, preventive, reformative and retributive ends of justice to which reference is made in *Rex* v. *Swanepoel, supra* at pp. 454, 455.

In a minority judgement in the same Division[63] Rumpff J.A. said:

> In the Republic of South Africa sentences of 50 or 60 or 70 years' imprisonment, or more, are not imposed, as is done in some other countries, the maximum sentence imposed in the Republic being, in practice, not more than 25 years, and that only in very exceptional cases.

In a subsequent judgement[64] the same Court, *per* Ogilvie-Thompson J.A. said with reference to this limitation:

> Without necessarily concurring in the existence of a maximum as thus suggested, I certainly share the view that a sentence of 25 years will only be appropriate in very exceptional circumstances.

It is, however, clear from what has been stated above that it is the prevalence of short-term imprisonment which causes the most concern. The practical problem facing the South African Courts is that there are many statutory offences which require the imposition of a penalty upon contravention; the impecuniosity of many citizens renders a fine as an alternative

---

[60] The author's translation.
[61] R. v. *Mzwakala*, 1957(4) S.A., 273 A.D.
[62] At p. 278.
[63] S. v. *Tuhadeleni and Others*, 1969(1) S.A., 153 (A.D.) at p. 189.
[64] S. v. *Whitehead*, 1970(4) S.A., 424 (A.D.) at p. 428.

to imprisonment unrealistic and the result only too often is incarceration.[65] Decriminalization seems unlikely to gain favour and fines are often the only practical sanction other than imprisonment. This form of sentence has, as will appear evident, not always been imposed with a sufficient awareness of the need to individualize punishment so as to render it a real alternative.

(ii) *Fines:*

As long ago as 1924 Feetham J. said:[66]

> Where a fine is imposed as an alternative to imprisonment it should, I think, bear some relation to the probable sources and earnings of the person on whom it is imposed and to the number of months' imprisonment which are considered sufficient as an alternative punishment.

Thirty years later in R. v. *Nhlapo*,[67] Ramsbottom J. referred to the fact that the Court ought to inform itself of an accused's ability to pay a fine— that there should at least be an enquiry as to his means. The Court stressed the fact that before fines are imposed on poor people such an enquiry should be made. He went on to say:

> Where the Court decides to impose a fine, the intention being to keep a person out of prison, the Court should not stultify itself by imposing a fine which it has no reason to suppose the accused can pay.

---

[65] It is a problem which the South African Criminal Jurisprudence shares with many other countries. So, for example, the Task Force of the President's Commission on Law Enforcement and Administration of Justice in the United States of America in its report on *The Courts* (Washington, D.C., 1967) says at p. 18:

> Two unfortunate characteristics of sentencing practices in many lower courts are the routine imposition of fines on the great majority of misdemeanants and petty offenders and the routine imprisonment of offenders who default in paying fines. These practices result in unequal punishment of offenders and in the needless imprisonment of many persons because of their financial condition.
>
> Thirty years ago the National Commission on Law Observance and Enforcement called attention to the inordinate number of offenders who were imprisoned for failure to pay fines. A more recent study of the Philadelphia County jail showed that 60 per cent of the inmates had been committed for nonpayment. And in 1960 there were over 26,000 prisoners in New York City jails who had been imprisoned for default in payment of fines.

That the problem in South Africa was even more acute, appears from the Report of the Lansdown Commission (U.G. 47 of 1947, para. 545) which found that on analysis of nine representative gaols in respect of prisoners admitted during the period 1 January 1945, to 30 June 1946, 65 per cent of whites, 87 per cent of coloureds and Indians, and 83 per cent of natives were incarcerated in default of the payment of fines. No more recent representative statistics are available.

[66] See R. v. *Frans*, 1924 T.P.D., 419.

[67] 1954(4) S.A., 56(T) at p. 58.

The dilemma which a Court faces when assessing a fine in respect of impecunious persons who commit serious offences has been raised and discussed in a number of decisions of our Courts.[68] These decisions indicate a lack of uniformity of approach. Some of the judgements question the obligation to make an enquiry as to means as envisaged in *Nhlapo*'s case.[69] In *Manwere*'s case[70] the majority of the Court affirmed the decision in *Nhlapo* and *Frans* and dissented from the decision in R. v. *Motlagomang*. It stated that '... whether a fine is extremely small or extremely heavy can only be judged by reference to the means and resources of the person on whom it is imposed'.[71] However, the minority indicated that fines may be imposed even where the Court knows the accused cannot pay them,[72] and that 'Whilst the question of the ability of an accused to pay is a most important factor to be considered by a Court in deciding upon the quantum of a fine there are cases in which this factor might well be outweighed by other factors'.[73]

There seems to be no reason why the procedure prescribed in R. v. *Taurayi*[74] should not be adopted as a matter of invariable practice in all Courts, irrespective of the offence with which an accused is charged. In that case Lewis J. spelled out the course to be followed, thus:

> If, as in this case, an accused, when invited to say something in regard to sentence, replies that he has nothing to say, I can see nothing difficult or improper in the magistrate saying to the accused: 'The option of a fine exists for this offence; I am considering giving you the option of a fine, and it would assist me in assessing the fine, and it might also be in your own interests, if you would give me some information as to your earnings or other financial resources, although you are not obliged to do so if you do not wish to'. If the accused declines the invitation then, of course, the magistrate has to do the best he can in assessing the fine on an estimate of what the accused's financial resources are likely to be.
>
> If the accused does volunteer information in the form of an unsworn statement, which the Crown does not accept as correct, or which the magistrate himself is not prepared to accept as correct, on account of its improbability, then again I can see no reason why the accused should not be asked whether

---

[68] See, e.g., R. v. *Motlagomang and Others*, 1958(1)(T) 626 at pp. 628–30; R. v. *Kaurikomio and Others*, 1958(1) 699; R. v. *Rice*, 1959(1) S.R., 138; R. v. *Mojafe*, 1958(2) S.A., 116(T); R. v. *Taurayi*, 1963(3) S.A., 109; S. v. *Apollos*, 1971(3) S.A., 265(C); S. v. *Jansen*, 1972(3) S.A., 86(C); S. v. *Manwere*, 1972(4) S.A., 425 and S. v. *Ndamase* (*supra*) (see note 58 above).

[69] R. v. *Kaurikomio and Others* and R. v. *Rice*, cited under 68 above. The overwhelming burden of authority is, however, the other way.

[70] 1972(4), p. 425.

[71] At p. 429.

[72] *per Davies*, A.J.A., at p. 430.

[73] At p. 429.

[74] 1963(3) at p. 114.

he wishes to support this statement by sworn evidence, tested by cross-examination in the usual way, and told that otherwise his unsworn statement is liable to be rejected. In any case, the magistrate is not bound to act on the information whether on oath or not, if he does not believe it.

In the event of the magistrate being satisfied on due enquiry that the accused has no financial resources at all, then it seems to me that his proper course is to assess the fine in some proportion to the average income which a person in the accused's station of life is likely to command, thus enabling the accused to keep out of gaol if he is able to invoke the assistance of friends or relatives in paying the fine.

The consideration which has motivated Courts, to insist upon an enquiry as to means and to relate the fine to an accused's capacity to pay, is the appreciation that the sentence must be individualized in order to ensure a fair and equitable punishment.[75] In *Taurayi*'s case[76] the Court underlined the importance of this consideration thus:

> . . . fines imposed should bear some relation to the means of an accused for otherwise the rich man gets the benefit of the option of a fine, but for a poor man the option may be rendered nugatory.

This statement differs but little from that of Grotius[77] when he said:

> In many instances, the magnitude of a punishment can only be measured by the situation of the person on whom it is to be inflicted. Thus a fine imposed upon the poor would be a heavy sentence, though it would scarcely affect the rich; and a man of high rank would feel the weight of a disgrace, that would but lightly touch an ignoble person.

In the author's experience the aforesaid judgements and comments have failed to have sufficient impact upon sentencing practice especially in the lower courts. As recently as 1971 in *S. v. Apollos*[78] it is recorded that fines for possession of a dangerous weapon (the possession of knives being the most common contravention) were determined by Magistrates—in order to ensure uniformity[79]—in accordance with the length of the blade. Pocket knives with blades of less than $3\frac{1}{2}$ inches—R25 or 50 days; pocket knives or knives with a fixed blade up to 4 inches—R100 or 150 days; with longer blades—5 months' imprisonment and more. Only a rigorous enforcement of the rule of sentencing practice formulated in *Taurayi*'s case is likely to

---

[75] R. v. *Taurayi*, at p. 114 and *S.* v. *Apollos*, at p. 266.

[76] At p. 111.

[77] *De Jure Belli Ac Pacis*, 2:20:33, p. 236 of Campbell's translation.

[78] See note 68 at pp. 265–6.

[79] On consistency in sentencing see the enlightening article by the Hon. Mr. Justice Nicholas, 'The Courts: Disparity in Sentencing; Consistency and Discretion—Are they Reconcilable?', *Crime, Punishment and Correction*, 1, No. 2, November 1972, at p. 22.

eliminate absurdities of this nature and to achieve the equity and fairness so long sought by the Superior Courts.[80]

On the other hand, Courts sometimes tend to be too lenient when assessing the penalty for an offender who has adequate resources to meet a monetary penalty appropriate to his moral guilt and his ability to pay. Scaling punishment upward—within reason—seems to be as just as scaling it downward with reference to income and resources. In *S. v. Bersin*[81] the Court, while pointing to the fact that there is no reported case dealing with this proposition, considered that there seemed to be no logical reason why some upward adjustment should not be justified, although of course 'there are obvious limits to any such adjustment'. In the penultimate paragraph the Court stressed, however, that it should not unduly penalize an accused who discloses that he possesses means well above the average. This was interpreted as laying down the proposition that wealth is not a reason for increasing a fine.[82] But this latter proposition 'although well settled is open to obvious criticism and may not stand the test of time'.[83]

Moreover, the South African Courts seem to have underestimated the importance of substantial fines either as an alternative to imprisonment or in addition thereto. Fines in excess of R1,000 are seldom imposed, even for offences involving dishonesty and committed for pecuniary gain. An illustration of what seems a somewhat unrealistic approach in this respect is apparent when the Court of Appeal[84] describes the imposition of a fine of R5,000 upon two offenders who made substantial profits from a large number of thefts as 'the massive fine'.

Whether a system whereby fines are calculated on a rigid basis (i.e. determined not in a fixed sum, but X times the offender's daily or weekly income) should be introduced, is a matter which could with benefit be considered by the Legislature. It has advantages particularly in a country where both the enactment of criminal sanctions and the administration of justice is at present still almost exclusively in the hands of the privileged and more affluent section of the community and where those who come into conflict with the law are preponderately the underprivileged and the poor.[85]

[80] Administrative machinery has been created and is often implemented, which authorizes fines to be paid in instalments. This does ameliorate some of the hardships which flow from the present practice in lower Courts in terms of which fines are still almost invariably imposed without any reference to an accused's ability to pay.

[81] 1970(1) S.A., 729(R) at p. 731.

[82] *S. v. Manwere, supra* at p. 427.

[83] Ibid. The author seriously questions whether this proposition is 'well settled' in South African Law. There seems to be no authority laying this down as a rule although in practice significant differentiation in fines is seldom encountered.

[84] In *S. v. Sparks and Another*, 1972(3) S.A., 396 (A.D.) at p. 411; see also at p. 410(A).

[85] See in this regard the provisions of the Alternative Draft Model Penal Code proposed

It seems to the author to be imperative that radical improvements should be carried out, whether through legislation or through rules of practice, to bring the system of determining and imposing fines into line with fundamental principles of fairness and equity.

(iii) *Corporal Punishment:*

In his article on 'Crime and Punishment 1910–1960', Prof. Kahn points to the fact that the Republic was at that time—1960—out of step with the rest of the civilized world in respect of the imposition of corporal punishment.[86] In so far as his comments were intended to apply to adult whippings it is encouraging to record that there has been a substantial decrease in the number of persons subjected to this form of punishment.[87] This is due principally to the amendment of the penal code which deleted provisions prescribing whipping for specific offences. Whippings are, however, still commonplace for juvenile offenders.[88]

---

for the Federal Republic of Germany which follows the Scandinavian concept of fines related to the daily income of the offender. It is discussed by Jürgen Baumann in *Law and State*, Vol. 1, Tübingen, Institute for Scientific Cooperation, 1970, p. 53 at pp. 55–8.

[86] Note 5 above, op. cit., at p. 210. See his exhaustive survey from p. 207 onwards.

[87] The Reports of the Department of Prisons show that the following number of whippings were administered. (As juvenile whippings, usually imposed on persons under the age of 18 years, are not administered under the authority of the Prison's Department they are not shown in the Commissioner's returns):

1963/64	16,887
1964/65	15,756
1965/66	8,888
1966/67 } 1967/68 }	11,332
1968/69	5,273
1969/70	5,181
1970/71	5,427
1971/72	4,536

[88] No statistics could be traced in respect of juvenile whippings. On 25 September 1970, the Hon. the Minister of Justice in reply to a written question in the House of Assembly (*Hansard*, Vol. 30 of 1970, Column No. 5025) stated that the number of persons upon whom whippings were imposed during the year 1968/69 was 39,654. The Commissioner of Prison's Report quoted above, shows the administration of 5,273 whippings in prison for this year. Presumably the difference, i.e. 34,381, represents the number of juvenile whippings administered in that year. To what extent this is a reliable indication of the annual incidence of this form of punishment for juvenile offenders, is not known. However, in a study of young offenders dealt with by the juvenile court in the magisterial district of Cape Town in 1958, Dr. James Midgley found that whipping was the most frequently imposed sentence. 'No less than ... 57 per cent of those convicted were whipped. Whippings were imposed for all types of offence, for all age and ethnic categories and irrespective of previous conviction.' It should be noted, though, that the vast majority of offenders came from the 'coloured' population and that in any case 'white children were

The Supreme Court has in general cautioned against the excessive use of whippings as a form of punishment. Thus, for example, Fannin, J. says:[89]

> Within comparatively recent times corporal punishments of quite horrifying severity were inflicted for a great number of offences, and I for one do not believe that the general deterrent effect of such punishments justified the suffering and indignity which were inflicted upon those who were so punished. I am of the opinion that a whipping is a punishment of a particularly severe kind. It is brutal in its nature and constitutes a severe assault upon not only the person of the recipient but upon his dignity as a human being.

Limitations in respect of the age of an offender, the nature of the offence and more general limitations have also been imported by the Superior Courts as a means of curbing the frequency of this form of punishment. Thus, for example, it is only a proper punishment 'in special circumstances';[90] it is only justifiable in exceptional cases where the accused is over 30 years of age;[91] the number of strokes should only in rare cases be six strokes or more[92] and this form of punishment is inappropriate—even for juveniles—where the offence is one of negligent or reckless driving.[93] In *S. v. C.*[94] the Court urged (in the case of a juvenile accused) that resort should not be had 'to such an extreme remedy, unless the Court has at least caused an investigation by a probation officer to be undertaken in order to have some guidance (both by way of factual information and a professional recommendation) as to whether this form of punishment is in fact appropriate'.[95]

Generally caution and restraint are the hallmarks of the judgements of the Supreme Court,[96] although a whipping is considered appropriate and preferable to imprisonment for a youthful offender.[97]

The author's experience in one of the Divisions of the Supreme Court

---

sentenced to whipping less frequently than children from other categories'. 38 per cent of those . . . whipped received 6 strokes while 24 per cent were given 4 and 13 per cent 8 strokes. See J. Midgley, *Sentencing in the Juvenile Court,* mimeo.

[89] In *S. v. Kumalo and Others,* 1965(4) S.A., 565(N) at p. 574.

[90] *per* Cillie, J. P. (Bekker, J. concurring) in *S. v. Zimo,* 1971(3) S.A., 337(T).

[91] *S. v. Masondo,* 1969(1) P.H., H.58(N).

[92] *S. v. Makhating,* 1969(1) P.H., H.108.

[93] *S. v. Risaba,* 1971(2) 339(T); *S. v. Porter,* 1964(2) P.H., H.193(C); cf. however, *S. v. Hatting,* 1972(3) S.A., 847(o) where a whipping was considered not inappropriate when imposed upon a juvenile for driving under the influence of liquor.

[94] 1973(1) S.A., 739(C).

[95] Ibid. at p. 742. The Court added (op. cit.): 'An over-hasty resort to quick and easy remedies can do more harm in the case of a youth than in respect of any other category of offender.' In the same judgement the Court discusses the other forms of disposition of which the Court can avail itself in the case of a juvenile.

[96] See, e.g., *S. v. Zondi,* 1970(1) P.H., H.34(N) and *S. v. Ncobo,* 1965(4) S.A., 589(E).

[97] *S. v. Areto,* 1970(2) P.H., H.145 (Botswana H.C.) and see the comments made by Bekker, J. in his concurring judgement in *S. v. Zimo* cited under note 90 above.

over the past nine years—confirmed by the returns of the Department of Prisons—is that corporal punishment for adults is, despite the high frequency of crimes of violence, imposed only in exceptional cases, and most frequently by less experienced judicial officers. That it is still imposed at all is regrettable; but as long as it remains a permissible form of punishment for adult offenders some judicial officers—especially those for whom retribution has much meaning—will continue to use it despite the fact that it failed to have any effect upon the rising crime rate during the lengthy period in which it was a 'corrective' compulsorily prescribed by Parliament.[98] As Professor Kahn pointed out, 18,543 persons were whipped pursuant to these provisions in the year 1957/58.[99] A further improvement towards the attainment of civilized standards in the treatment of offenders is nevertheless still possible. Whereas in 1940 1,864 non-juvenile persons were whipped, the number was as high as 4,536 in the year 1971/72.

For juveniles a whipping is administered with a light cane and is still very frequently imposed.[100] A major problem for the judicial officer is the absence of a realistic alternative. Probation is in its infancy and black probation officers are as yet a novelty. Family life amongst the urban non-whites is often fractured and community structures are weak. Accordingly, the Court cannot readily enlist the community aids which are essential for the success of a community-orientated form of treatment. This is regrettable because the South African Bantu's normally strong family and community ties would render him particularly amenable to this form of treatment and control. Moreover, the belief and faith judicial officers have in punishment as a necessary antidote for anti-social behaviour leads to the infrequent imposition of non-punitive measures such as probation, postponement of sentence or suspended sentences with compensation or community service as a condition of suspension.[101] The Committee of Enquiry into Criminal Procedure and Evidence,[102] although excluding punishment from the ambit of its enquiry, recommended an amendment of the law in respect of juvenile whippings to reduce the number of strokes which may be imposed upon a convicted juvenile to seven, and to prescribe how he should be clad when he is beaten.[103]

[98] By the Criminal Sentences Amendment Act, No. 33 of 1952, secs. 1, 3, 4 only amended in 1959 and withdrawn by an amendment of the Criminal Procedure and Evidence Act in 1965.

[99] See note 5 above, op. cit., at p. 211.

[100] See note 88 above.

[101] These forms of sentencing are available—see secs. 352 and 357 of the Criminal Procedure Act, No. 56 of 1955, referred to below.

[102] See above page 537.

[103] See p. 19 of the Report—R.P. 78/1971. The Commissioner also emphasized that the Legislature envisaged that this form of punishment should be a moderate correction.

More positive and therapeutic methods of dealing with the large number of young offenders will be delayed for as long as public faith in punishment remains unshaken. The Courts have done much to limit the use of whippings as a punitive measure. Administrative machinery such as a strong probation service has to be created before any real reform, particularly in respect of the juvenile, can be anticipated.

(iv) *Capital Punishment:*
The death penalty—'The uttermost reach of the law's visitation'[104]—remains a much debated, but still much used form of punishment in South Africa. The Reports of the Commissioner of Prisons reflect the following picture for the past six years:

Death Sentences and Executions

Period *1.7.66–30.6.67:*
Sentenced 206
Executed 121

Period *1.7.67–30.6.68:*
Sentenced 181
Executed 99
(Annual Survey 1969, page 467)

Period *1.7.68–30.6.69:*
In prison on 30.6.68 59 ⎫
Admitted during period 107 ⎬ 166
Executed 84
(Annual Survey 1970, page 469)

Period *1.7.69–30.6.70:*
In prison on 30.6.69 65 ⎫
Admitted during period 95 ⎬ 160
Executed 80
(Annual Survey 1971, page 503)

Period *1970–1971:*
In prison on 30.6.70 41 ⎫
Admitted during period 100 ⎬ 141
Executed 80

[104] *per* Holmes, J. A. in *S.* v. *Pietersen,* 1973(1) S.A., 148 (A.D.) at p. 155.

Period *1971–1972*:
In prison on 30.6.71   51 ⎫
Admitted during period   91 ⎬   142
                                          ⎭
Executed   56

(Extracted from the Reports of the Commissioner of Prisons)

Much has been written about it[105] and much will doubtless still be written. As a judicial officer who is obliged by law to impose this penalty and in view of the fact that it has some political sensitivity, the writer prefers not to comment upon this as a form of punishment in the Republic. That the death penalty should be included within the ambit of any enquiry made of the South African punishment scene speaks for itself. In view of the Legislature's approach towards punishment any change in the foreseeable future does not seem likely.[106]

(v) *Other forms of Punishment:*

(a) *Probation*

As indicated above, this form of disposition is seldom used. Even so, the authorities are now providing pre-sentence reports and, especially in the case of juveniles, supervision is sometimes being ordered.[107] No statistics are presently available to gauge the extent to which it is actually being used.

(b) Section 352 of the South African Criminal Code prescribes a number of non-institutionalized treatment methods including a caution or reprimand, postponement of sentence under various conditions, and suspension of fines as well as of imprisonment. This Section is reproduced as Appendix 2.

Save for suspended prison sentences, which are frequently imposed, much of this legislation is a dead letter in practice. There are a number of reasons for this state of affairs. Firstly, the lower Courts have as yet little confidence in these provisions. Secondly, the services available to the Courts from probation officers, who are likely to recommend these sentences, are totally

---

[105] For more recent comments see 'Hanged by the neck until you are Dead', *South African L.J.*, 1970, 60; 'Name not a Rope in his House that Hang'd Himself', Ibid, p. 465; *The Death Penalty in South Africa*, 1970 (33) T.H.R.—H.R.108; House of Assembly Debates, *Hansard*, Vol. 25, Col. 2603 (14 March 1969) and see the *Annual Survey of South African Law*, 1971 at p. 568.

[106] The General Council of the Bar of South Africa most recently (on 20 July 1973) expressed itself in favour of some amendments to the law which deals with the imposition of the death penalty. A right of appeal was suggested for all cases where the death penalty was imposed, save where such appeal is frivolous or vexatious. It was also contended that consideration should be given to Judges being invested with a discretion in all cases where the death penalty is as yet mandatory.

[107] See *S.* v. *Adams*, 1971(4) S.A., 125(C); J. S. Steyn, 'Crime and its Control', *Acta Juridica*, 1971 at p. 189.

inadequate. Thirdly, they are innovations and lawyers have not been trained in their use. Fourthly, they pose administrative problems and impose burdens on those who have to undertake and supervise their execution. These provisions as well as 'binding over'[108] and compensation orders—whether as conditions of suspension or otherwise[109]—are accordingly seldom used in practice.

(c) *Periodical Imprisonment:*

This innovation—so-called week-end imprisonment—was introduced in 1959.[110] It is not often used in practice[111] although its use for offences such as drunken driving has been encouraged by the Superior Courts.[112] The author has some doubt whether the prison authorities really support this form of punishment. It places additional administrative burdens upon them, and in practice one finds that offenders sentenced to this type of punishment are often permitted—with attractive incentives—to serve a sentence of periodical imprisonment as one unbroken sentence. In fairness the author must add that in many centres there are no facilities available. Despite these factors, Courts are not using this method of imprisonment frequently enough. This is regrettable because it is less destructive than short-term imprisonment. Its imposition should in the author's view, not be confined to those convicted of drunken driving but should also be imposed for common law offences not so serious as to merit lengthy imprisonment. (In fact those with drinking problems tend to take out 'insurance' on Friday evenings before reporting for imprisonment thus causing all sorts of mayhem.)

Conclusions

It speaks for itself that this analysis of the punishment scene in the Republic of South Africa has been not only condensed but also somewhat eclectic.

---

[108] See the provisions of Section 384.

[109] See Sections 352 and 357 of the Criminal Code.

[110] Sections 329 and 334 (bis) of the Code.

[111] The Reports of the Commissioner of Prisons reflect the following use of this form of sentence over the past five years:

1.7.66–30.6.67	:	243
1.7.67–30.6.68	:	217
1.7.68–30.6.69	:	201
1.7.69–30.6.70	:	224
1.7.70–30.6.71	:	388
1.7.71–30.6.72	:	388

[112] See, e.g., *S.* v. *Lombard*, 1967(4) S.A., 538 (A.D.) at p. 545 and *S.* v. *Bhadloo*, 1971(1) S.A., 55(N).

Accordingly these 'conclusions' and suggestions reflect the author's assessment of South African priorities and they are not necessarily representative of what is generally considered to be of primary importance in this field.

The law and practice of punishment in South Africa have various unsatisfactory features. This is probably the unavoidable result of an uncoordinated and many-faceted series of legislative developments over the past 25 years.[113] In addition there has been no broad overview of the punishment scene since it was investigated by a Commission of Enquiry under the Chairmanship of Mr. Justice Lansdown in the years 1945 to 1947.[114]

Similarly, even if not to the same extent, the Courts have not been successful in moulding a penal approach which is either sufficiently consistent or clearly defined. This lack of clarity cannot provide reasonably precise guidelines for the lower Courts which deal with more than 90 per cent of those who come into contact with the Criminal Justice System. As will be seen below, administrative measures have been invoked in order to eliminate some of the unsatisfactory features of the South African punishment system. For several, and I think obvious, reasons any significant administrative interference with the processes of Criminal Justice should be avoided. Indeed, administrative action has tended to confuse even further an already confused situation.

Accordingly the greatest need is for an objective review of punishment in South Africa. The author's view is that this should be the task of a Commission of Enquiry under the chairmanship of a Judge of the Supreme Court—preferably of the Court of Appeal—and should include representatives of the various disciplines which have a direct interest in the matters with which the Commission will be concerned. Police, prisons, the psychiatric and social work professions as well as the academic criminologists, should be represented on such a multi-disciplinary Commission of Enquiry. However, this suggestion has been made repeatedly by Judges and academic lawyers without any response from the Government.[115] An alternative suggestion, which has been made, is that the Law Commission, recently established by Act 19 of 1973, could give specific attention to the revision of penal law. The Law Revision Committee (which preceded the Law Commission) recommended that this new Commission should have standing committees to serve the various branches of the law. It is to be hoped that

[113] For example, the Drug legislation referred to above, emanated from the Department of Social Welfare and Pensions. Various Government Departments as well as Provincial Councils put forward proposals for penal sanctions in accordance with the proclivities of various individuals or groups.

[114] UG.47/1947.

[115] See, e.g., *Annual Survey of S.A. Law*, 1968, p. 473, 1969, p. 469 and 1970, pp. 466–77.

one such standing committee will be similar to the English Criminal Law Revision Committee (set up by R. A. Butler, the then Home Secretary, in 1959). Such a committee could then secure a continuous revision and reform of all aspects of criminal law including punishment.

It is, however, possible that despite the efforts of the reformer, no co-ordinated review of punishment will take place in South Africa in the foreseeable future. The problem here, as elsewhere, is that the criminal justice system is not viewed as an entity. Each aspect of the system—detection, apprehension, confrontation, disposition, incarceration and re-socialization—has been permitted to develop in a distinct separate compartment with little interdisciplinary dialogue. Bureaucratic insularity has become a disturbing phenomenon inhibiting growth, development and reform of the system as a whole.

Accordingly it is necessary to have a brief look at the three major influences which will, principally, shape the future developments in the field of punishment in South Africa. These are: Parliament, the Courts and administrative measures.

(a) *Parliament:*

For many reasons it is unlikely that an enlightened penal system will be forged through the parliamentary process. There is little demand from the voter or any group of voters for measures of this kind. In fact, such pressures as emanate from within the South African political framework would tend to consolidate the emphasis upon punishment as the principal means of controlling all anti-social conduct.

Looking at developments over the past twenty-five years therefore, it seems likely that the present situation will be maintained with sporadic out-bursts of 'law and order' measures designed to give effect to the principle that severe forms of punishment are the pre-eminent means whereby anti-social conduct can be combatted. In so far as this legislative framework may produce inequity, administrative methods will occasionally be fashioned to mitigate its impact.[116]

It seems that the only penal reform measure with a real prospect of acceptability is a state system of compensation for victims of crime. Mr. Justice V. G. Hiemstra has, on several occasions, urged that com-pensatory provisions be enacted, and representations have been made for their introduction. This measure is politically palatable because it cannot be categorized as being 'soft on criminals'. Such a scheme would have an important effect in South Africa where a large section of the community tends to view the criminal justice system with some antipathy. Community

[116] See the comments under Administrative Measures below.

participation in and respect for law and order are often wanting. Should those who are in the main the victims of crime succeed in obtaining some compensation for the many crimes of violence prevalent in their communities, their view of criminal justice may, to some extent, be modified.

Real hopes for broad-based legislative reform depend therefore either on the appointment of a Commission of Enquiry or the establishment of a permanent committee of Criminal Law Review. Any spontaneous parliamentary demand for change in the penal field appears unlikely in the present climate of political and public opinion.

(b) *The Courts:*

Summarizing what has been said above about the rôle of the Courts, it is clear that the various Divisions of the Supreme Court have attempted to give enlightened guidance in respect of punishment. So far, however, it would seem as if the impact of their decisions has not been substantial. Short-term imprisonment is still regarded by many as the panacea for anti-social behaviour. No judicial conferences are held and efforts by the Superior Courts through the medium of review judgements[117] seem to have been ineffective as far as punishments are concerned in bringing about any real change in the quality of justice for the overwhelming number of unrepresented accused who appear before our lower Courts.

Most recently the Courts have been proposing that there be procedural safeguards when assessing penalties. Thus, for example, in *S.* v. *Taylor*[118] the Court laid down that where an undefended person qualifies for a compulsory sentence—

> . . . the trial court must—
>
> (a) inform the convicted person that he is entitled to lay before the court evidence of circumstances which if accepted may persuade the court to impose a lighter sentence than the compulsory sentence;
>
> (b) ask the convicted person whether he wishes to lead such evidence, or make submissions, to persuade the court to impose such lighter sentence;
>
> (c) whether the convicted person leads evidence and/or makes submissions or not, *mero motu* consider whether mitigating circumstances exist in the particular case; and where the convicted person does not lead evidence or make submissions, question him in order to elicit whether such circumstances exist;
>
> (d) in all cases, record in the record of proceedings whether or not in its opinion such circumstances exist, and if it finds that they do exist state,

---

[117] A system of automatic review of Magistrate's judgements where sentences which include corporal punishment or exeed three months' imprisonment or a fine of R100 is imposed, is a most valuable innovation of the South African criminal procedure. 1972(2) S.A. 307(C).

what they are. It is not sufficient, in my view, only to enter the circumstances upon the record if and when such circumstances have been found to exist. The court should record that it has considered the matter.

This decision was confirmed in *S.* v. *Maxaku*. In this latter case the Court went further and emphasized that—

Our Courts do consider that the sentencing process is as distinct and vital a factual enquiry as the determination of the guilt of an accused.[119]

and at p. 256 the Court went on to conclude that—

It must be remembered that it is sanctions which ultimately sustain the system of criminal justice. It little avails the court to determine guilt or innocence in accordance with long established principles of fairness and then to leave the assessment of penalty to a hazardous guess based on no or inadequate information. In such event the punishment may be so harsh as to be unjust or so lenient as to undermine the respect which the community should have for the processes which sustain law and order.[120]

Should the superior Courts in future rigorously enforce the various procedural safeguards—and where appropriate enlarge upon them—they could well secure a less retributive and more protective penal system for those they serve.

(c) *Administrative Measures:*

Whilst legislative measures to curb the high incidence of short-term imprisonment have not been enacted, administrative measures have been invoked in an attempt to deal with this disturbing phenomenon. Thus the Commissioner of Prisons Report for the year 1970/71 states—

Of the 401,475 prisoners with sentences of up to and including four months, admitted during the year, 186,679 were released on parole. Although these are reflected in the statistics as admissions, the majority were released within 24 hours after admission.[121]

During the following year—1971/72—181,449 were released in this way. This constituted nearly 50 per cent of those admitted to prison to serve sentences of four months or less.[122]

Other administrative steps have been taken to deal with two categories of crime which make a large contribution to short-term committals. Bantu Aid Centres have been created in an attempt to reduce the number of convictions under the laws designed to curtail the influx of Africans into

[119] 1973(4) S.A. 248(C), at p. 254.
[120] See also *S.* v. *Shirindi*, 1974(1) S.A. 481(T).
[121] R.P. 101/1971 at p. 6.
[122] Committals for up to and including four months' total 370,761—R.P. 91/1972.

urban areas.[123] Detoxification centres, in a somewhat rudimentary form, have been initiated to limit the high incidence of convictions for public drunkenness.[124]

It was encouraging to note that the State President in his address when opening the 1974 session of Parliament announced that it was the intention of the State to investigate a more extensive probation service as a penal reform and crime prevention measure. It is hoped that this will include a programme for the training of volunteers to assist probation officers and an extension of the ambit of the service to cater more extensively both for adults and for racial groups other than whites.

It is also possible that greater use may be made of executive clemency in an attempt to reduce the large number of executions carried out in South Africa every year. The figures given above (under the heading Capital Punishment) indicate that only 56 persons were executed, although 142 were either in prison as at 30.6.1971 and awaiting execution or admitted during the year 1971/72. This is certainly an improvement on the experience of the three previous years. However, figures for one year provide an inadequate basis upon which to draw conclusions about changes in policy.

Parole is used extensively in the Republic. Often the term is applied inappropriately to what is no more than early release for large numbers of short-term prisoners. Many black and coloured prisoners are also released 'on parole' after serving only a part of their sentences without any supervision being exercised over them after release. Moreover, the parole system is riddled with inconsistencies. Offenders are excluded from parole by virtue of the nature of the offence they have committed often without reference to their eligibility as individuals.[125]

---

[123] It should be remembered that approximately 42 per cent of the prisoners who received sentences of up to 4 months' imprisonment for the year 1970/71 are imprisoned because they committed offences under the 'influx control regulations'—House of Assembly debates, Vol. 34, col. 7539 (26 May 1971), quoted in *Annual Survey of South African Law*, 1972, p. 453.

[124] It really is misleading to call such provisions as presently exist detoxification centres. Offenders are locked up, dried out and released—but without going through the courts and prisons. It is, however, hoped that the requisite medical and social services needed to give these measures a meaningful rehabilitative content will be provided as part of what is presently still an experimental procedure.

[125] There are some strange bedfellows in this respect. A list of 'non-parolable' offences reveals that, *inter alia*, the following crimes are grouped together: A contravention of the Provisions of the Suppression of Communism Act; stock theft; foreign Bantu who desert their employment on the mines; rape; offences concerned with wild life conservation; abduction; unlawful possession of uncut diamonds; certain drug offences; driving a vehicle under the influence of liquor.

Other Forces for Change:

There are at least three other major factors which are pre-requisites for change.

First, there is a great need for the establishment of Criminological Institutes or Centres for the Study of Criminal Justice in South Africa. The creation of such an Institute had already been mooted by the Prime Minister when he was Minister of Justice some ten years ago; there are, however, no indications that this may possibly become a reality in the near future. It speaks for itself that an independent institute or centre could make a real contribution, providing those involved in criminal justice with reliable information which could assist in the prevention of crime and the treatment of offenders. Moreover, and perhaps more importantly, an institute could have a profound effect upon the training of the lawyer. Sir Rupert Cross says:

> A criminal lawyer who confines his attention to the criminal law to the exclusion of the theories of punishment and the treatment of offenders is a miserable specimen.[126]

We need to direct the penetrating light which the human sciences such as sociology, criminology and psychology cast also upon our system of legal education. Just as these sciences cannot achieve meaningful reform unless they understand and involve themselves in the discipline of the law, so the law needs the enlightenment and the understanding of mankind which the advances in these human sciences have achieved. This viewpoint is reflected in a significant statement by the Polish Minister of Justice:

> The judge who is a traditionalist in his manner of thinking must become a jurist with an open mind, aware of the general principles of the strategy of crime control. At the current stage of the application of modern methods of social defence, a judge cannot confine himself to hearing a case and passing sentence. He must interest himself, to varying degrees, in the execution of the sentence; he must have a thorough knowledge of correctional problems and relate his decisions to their application. This requires a reform of legal studies so that they may provide jurists with adequate training in criminology, sociology and psychology.
> Statistical research on crime and crime prediction must be improved.
> As the conviction grows that the complex problems of crime cannot be solved by a policy of repression alone, the repressive role of judicial organs will be increasingly limited, yielding to preventive action by the state and society.[127]

In the same way, the South African Minister of Justice in 1968 (see page 536 above) gave a clear indication of his belief that 'a scientific approach to the problem of crime [was] essential' and that 'in the past too much reliance

[126] Rupert Cross: *Punishment, Prison and the Public*, London, Stevens, 1971, preface, p. xiii.

[127] 'Planning Crime Prevention and Control in Poland', *International Review of Criminal Policy*, No. 26, 1968, U.N., by Stanislaw Walczak, Minister of Justice, Poland.

has been placed on the easy and convenient formula that quick and effective punishment is the only remedy for crime'.

The positive leadership reflected in these ministerial statements can do much to change attitudes in the legal profession and also alter public attitudes towards punishment.

This brings me to the second point. The vengeful retributive public attitude towards crime, the criminal and correction, is one of the most significant factors inhibiting progress and reform. Reform will be retarded for as long as the public belief that punishment is the only real and substantial protection against crime is fostered and maintained.

Versele in a recent article[128] puts it well when he says:

> One pre-requisite for reshaping judicial policy towards offenders is to reform and mobilise the public. The latter's view of crime and punishment is still dominated by a ritualistic dramatic approach in which aggressive impulses of self-defence are uppermost . . .
>
> It is essential to convince the public that money spent on the treatment of offenders is not useless expenditure, but a real social investment. It must be demonstrated that the social rehabilitation of offenders is economically profitable and that open treatment is not only cheaper than imprisonment, but also keeps offenders in the production sector and enables them to meet their own needs and provide a livelihood for their families.

Thirdly, reform must be seen as a many-pronged probe of the criminal justice system. It must give attention to prevention and to public participation in crime prevention. Particularly in South Africa it must include greater emphasis on social planning in housing lower income groups. It must seek to improve police protection. An efficient, respected police force will, for a long time to come, be the most effective crime prevention measure, certainly in our community. Thus greater attention must be given to conditions of service and modern technological aids. Enlistment of police (both full-time and a reservist's force) amongst our black people must be dramatically stepped up.

However, in order to achieve the long-term goal of a totally rational and just system it is essential to reach the lawyer who makes and applies the law. Versele, in my opinion with much justification, says that:

> The sociologist who is concerned with the field of law is appalled at the gulf which separates justice as it is administered in day-to-day courtroom practice and justice as it is professed or proclaimed at gatherings of lawyers and, for that matter, in constitutions and laws.[129]

---

[128] Severin Carlos Versele, 'Public Participation in the administration of Criminal Justice', *International Review of Criminal Policy*, No. 27, 1969, U.N.

[129] Op. cit., p. 9.

It is towards the closing of this gap that the reformer must apply his idealism, his zeal and his energies. The law and the lawyer hold the key. It is only through the leadership of the law that processes such as decriminalization, pre-sentence investigation and reports, compensation for victims of crime, probation and meaningful parole systems, to mention but a few advances, can be designed and implemented.

The attainment of the ideal of a criminal justice system which is 'as rational and just as law can be'[130] is within the reach of every society. Its attainment is essential should we wish to achieve long-term contentment and tranquillity. In a society such as ours where the power of law-making and the duty to see to its administration is in the hands of so few of us, the task is an awesome responsibility. Courageous leadership, vigorous objective research, constant critical analysis of research findings, and conscientious application of the necessary techniques to achieve progress and reform, are essential for our very survival, because no people can survive without doing reasonable justice to other peoples.

[130] See footnote 3 above.

APPENDIX I

The South African Court Structure. From Hiemstra, in *The Standard Encyclopaedia of Southern Africa*, Vol. 3, 1st Ed., 1971.

COURTS OF JUSTICE. The central repository of judicial power in the Republic of South Africa is the Supreme Court. It sits in seven territorial divisions, from which an appeal lies to the highest court of the country, namely the Appellate Division of the Supreme Court, with its seat at Bloemfontein. The total of judges in all the divisions together was over 70 in 1970.

To relieve the Supreme Court of less important work, there exists a structure of lower courts. Alongside them are the Bantu courts, where Native law and custom is applied.

The Supreme Court has an overriding jurisdiction in all disputes which are amenable to trial in a court of law, whether civil or criminal. It may therefore try cases for which other courts are specially provided, but will do so only in highly exceptional cases.

The Supreme Court superseded the superior courts existing in the four colonies before Union (1910), and was instituted and governed by sections 95 to 116 of the South Africa Act. In the Republic of South Africa Constitution Act (No. 32 of 1961) the Supreme Court is in section 94 referred to as 'the judicial authority of the Republic'. The details of its composition are now governed by the Supreme Court Act (No. 59 of 1959). The Court is entirely free from political pressure and is the refuge of the citizen who is unlawfully oppressed. Its powers are inherent and are not, as in the case of the magistrate's court, exclusively to be found within the four corners of the establishing Act or other Acts. The Court conforms to the democratic concept of an independent judiciary. Its judges are drawn almost exclusively from the bar, but in a few instances Government law advisers have been appointed. A judge is not allowed to hold any other office of profit.

The Court has four provincial divisions, with their seats in the four provincial capitals. In addition, three divisions have the status of provincial divisions, namely, Eastern Cape (with its seat at Grahamstown), Northern Cape (seat at Kimberley) and South-West Africa (seat at Windhoek). Each of these seven divisions has a judge president. There are two 'local' divisions: Witwatersrand (seat at Johannesburg) and Durban and Coast (seat at Durban). The difference between provincial and local divisions is that the latter have no appellate jurisdiction. They have no separate judge president, but fall under the judge president of the nearest provincial division.

In civil trials and applications by way of petition a judge sits alone. There is provision for a court of two or three judges in civil trials, but this is rarely applied. The Court has appellate jurisdiction in regard to the courts of the magistrate with ordinary jurisdiction, the regional magistrate, the Bantu Commissioner (in criminal cases only) and the Bantu Divorce Court. Appeals are heard by two judges. There is also appellate jurisdiction from one judge in civil applications to three judges of the same division. From there an appeal lies to the Appellate Division. The intermediate appeal to three judges of the same division may, by consent of both parties, be waived, so that the matter goes straight to the Appellate Division. The Supreme Court also holds circuit sessions in country towns, but in criminal matters only. Although a substantial part of the Supreme Court's time (about one-third) is spent on criminal work, it does only a small portion of the volume of criminal work in the country. Before regional courts were established, it dealt with about 0·5% of the total, and since regional courts commenced in 1952, the figure declined to 0·2%. Only serious crime is tried by the Supreme Court.

The number of judges in the various divisions were as follows in 1970: Appellate Division, 11; Transvaal Provincial Division (sitting also in the Witwatersrand Local Division), 23; Cape Provincial Division, 11; Orange Free State Provincial Division, 7; Natal Provincial Division (sitting also in the Durban and Coast Local Division), 11; Eastern Cape Division, 8; South-West African Division, 2; Northern Cape Division, 3; total, 76.

Criminal Jurisdiction. The Court has jurisdiction over all offences, but in practice tries only those which are so serious that the ordinary magistrate's court or the regional court would not be competent to impose a sufficient penalty. Except where minimum or maximum sentences are laid down by law, its punitive jurisdiction is also unlimited and includes the death-sentence and imprisonment for life. All crime may be tried by one judge sitting alone, but in cases where the death-sentence or a very long term of imprisonment seems likely, he usually appoints two assessors, mostly practising advocates. The Court decides by a majority on issues of fact, but on points of law the judge's ruling is binding on the assessors. The sentence is a matter for the judge alone.

Trial by jury existed since the establishment of the Supreme Court in 1828, but became progressively rarer and was abolished in 1969.

The *Appellate Division*, also called the Court of Appeal, is the highest court and ultimately decides appeals from all courts (including Bantu courts and certain tribunals which are not part of the judicial system—*see* below). So as not to burden the Appeal Court with cases in which there is no reasonable prospect of success, leave to appeal must first be given by the court from which the appeal lies (except in civil trials in provincial or local divisions, where there is an appeal as of right). Originally, in criminal cases tried in the Supreme Court, an appeal lay only on points of law, but since 1948 (Act 37 of 1948, section 14) also on fact. The State, however, may appeal only on a point of law in a criminal case. (*See* also Appeal Court.)

The Appellate Division hears appeals from the mandated territory of South-West Africa, and until 1955 (when the Federal Supreme Court of Rhodesia and Nyasaland was established) it also heard appeals from the High Court of Southern Rhodesia. It is not a court of first instance and consequently only takes cognisance of cases first tried in other courts. Until 1950 it was possible to appeal further to the Judicial Committee of the Privy Council, but this right was abolished by Act 16 of 1950, now superseded by section 23 of the Supreme Court Act (No. 59 of 1959). (*See* Privy Council, Judicial Committee of the.)

Special criminal courts may be established, consisting of judges, and these are then neither a provincial nor a local division, but purely courts *ad hoc*. In terms of section 112 of the Criminal Procedure Act (1955), an attorney-general who intends to charge a person with treason, sedition, public violence, or advancing the aims of Communism (or an attempt to commit any of these offences) may apply to the Minister of Justice for the constitution of a special criminal court, which may consist of two or three judges, who need not all be drawn from the same division. For a valid decision such a court must be unanimous; if it is not, the accused may be tried again. Such courts were constituted in 1922 to try participants in the Witwatersrand mining strike, during the Second World War, and again in 1958, to hear a treason case against 31 accused charged with subversive activities. An appeal from such a court lies to five judges of the Appellate Division, whereas in ordinary criminal appeals three are competent to sit.

Courts which are not part of the Supreme Court, but in which a judge presides *ad hoc*, are the Water Court, the Special Court for Income-Tax Appeals, and the Special Court appointed in terms of the Regulation of Monopolistic Conditions Act (1955). The Commissioner of Patents also sat as a judicial officer, but since 1964 his work is also done by a judge of the Supreme Court.

Lower Courts. Of the lower courts the one with the smallest jurisdiction was the court of the special justice of the peace. This court dwindled in importance and was abolished in 1968. It had civil as well as criminal jurisdiction and was meant for trivial cases in thinly populated areas.

Courts of the magistrate with ordinary jurisdiction. These courts handle the great bulk of judicial work. Their powers are defined in Act 32 of 1944 and some other Acts which confer special jurisdiction upon them. There are 253 magisterial districts, each under the control of a magistrate with judicial as well as administrative functions. Where necessary there are additional and assistant magistrates. The total number of magistrates is about 600 . . .

The magistrate may try all crimes except treason, murder and rape. Sentences of a fine not exceeding R200 or 6 months' imprisonment may be imposed, and corporal punishment to a maximum of 10 strokes. (Corporal punishment is in all courts limited to 10 strokes.) A case may be referred back to the magistrate by the Attorney-General, with punitive jurisdiction increased to a fine of R400 or one year's imprisonment. Special powers are granted in some Acts to impose heavier sentences, *inter alia* a R1,000 fine or 5 years for dagga (marijuana) offences,[32] and 5 years for escaping from prison. For a stock theft a R1,000 fine may be imposed, or 3 years' imprisonment. Where corrective training is a compulsory sentence (it varies from 2 to 4 years, in the discretion of the prison authorities) it may also be imposed by the magistrate. These maxima are in respect of each count, and where a person is charged on several counts a magistrate's sentence can also run into many years.

All sentences of magistrates which include corporal punishment or exceed 3 months' imprisonment or a fine of R100 are subject to automatic review by a judge. This system is probably unique in the world. The judge reads the record to satisfy himself that justice was done.

Court of the regional magistrate. This is an intermediate court, established in 1952 in order to relieve the Supreme Court of the great pressure of criminal work. It has criminal jurisdiction only. The system operates over the whole country except the Transkei and certain districts in Natal, which are controlled by the Department of Bantu Administration. Treason and murder are excluded, but rape may be tried unless the accused prefers to be tried by a superior court. Sentences not exceeding R600 or 3 years may be imposed, or corrective training, also where this is not compulsory. Where the indeterminate sentence (minimum 9 years) or imprisonment for the prevention of crime (5 to 8 years) is compulsory, the regional magistrate may impose it. An appeal lies to the provincial division of the Supreme Court and thence, with leave, to the Appellate Division. The number of regional magistrates is about 60.

Bantu courts. Alongside the lower and superior courts is a structure of Bantu courts. They hear civil disputes between Bantu and Bantu, and some have criminal jurisdiction, but only over Bantu. If any of the parties to a civil dispute are other than Bantu, the case must go to the inferior or superior court which has jurisdiction. Whites, Coloureds and Asiatics have equal access to all courts other than Bantu courts.

Until 1927 there was great diversity between the provinces as regards Bantu courts. The Native Administration Act (No. 38 of 1927) regulated the position by establishing the following courts:

Courts of chiefs and headmen. The State President may confer jurisdiction upon these to decide civil disputes which arise from Native law and custom. This excludes suits arising from civil marriages. Appeal lies to the Bantu commissioner, who hears evidence afresh, because the court of the chief or headman keeps no record of its proceedings. Criminal jurisdiction may also be conferred in respect of offences punishable by Native customary law. By section 23 of Act 54 of 1952 jurisdiction over minor common law or statutory offences was conferred on them, subject to appeal to the Bantu commissioner. From there the appeals come to a parting of the ways. Civil appeals go to the Bantu Appeal Court, criminal appeals to the Supreme Court.

Court of the Bantu commissioner. Courts of Bantu commissioners, called 'Native Commissioners' until 1952, are established in terms of section 10(1) of the Native Administration Act 'for the hearing of all civil causes and matters between Native and Native only'. Criminal jurisdiction can also be conferred, and this was increasingly done until in 1957 all Bantu commissioners received the same criminal jurisdiction as ordinary magistrates. There is no limit to the value of the subject-matter in civil disputes, but causes of action are limited. There is no jurisdiction to make declarations affecting the status of a person in regard to his mental capacity, or to decide cases of perpetual silence, provisional sentence, the validity of a will (except by consent or where the estate is worth less than R600), or nullity of marriage, divorce or judicial separation. Such cases have to be tried by either the Bantu Divorce Court or the Supreme Court. Bantu Commissioners are members of the Civil Service who have passed the Civil Service Law examinations. They may summon Bantu assessors in an advisory capacity. The number of Bantu Commissioners is about 400.

APPENDIX 2

Non-Custodial Measures (from S. 352 South African Criminal Code).

Powers of courts to impose suspended sentences or a caution or reprimand.—
(1) Whenever a person is convicted before any court of any offence other than an offence specified in the Fourth Schedule or an offence in respect of which the imposition of a prescribed punishment on the person convicted thereof is compulsory, it may in its discretion—
    (a) postpone for a period not exceeding three years the passing of sentence and release the person convicted on one or more conditions (whether as to compensation, the rendering to the person aggrieved of some specific benefit or service in lieu of compensation for damage or pecuniary loss, submission to instruction or treatment or to the supervision or control (including control over the earnings or other income of the person convicted) of a probation officer as defined in the Children's Act, 1960 (Act No. 33 of 1960), compulsory attendance at some specified centre for a specified purpose, good conduct or otherwise) which the court may order to be inserted in recognizances to appear at the expiration of that period; or
    (a)*bis* postpone the passing of sentence, release the person convicted and order that, within a period not exceeding three years specified by the court, he may be called upon by any magistrate to appear before him; or

    (b) pass sentence, but order the operation of the whole or any part of the sentence to be suspended for a period not exceeding three years on such conditions as aforesaid as the court may specify in the order; or

    (c) impose a fine but suspend the enforcement thereof until the expiration of such period not exceeding three years as the court may fix for payment, in instalments or otherwise of the amount of the fine, the amounts of any instalments and the dates of payment thereof being fixed by order of the court; or

    (d) discharge the person convicted with a caution or reprimand.

(2) (a) Whenever a person is convicted of an offence specified in the Fourth Schedule or an offence in respect of which the imposition of a prescribed punishment (other than a punishment prescribed by section three hundred and thirty-four *ter*, three hundred and thirty-four *quat*, or three hundred and thirty-five) on the person convicted thereof is compulsory, the court may in its discretion—

    (i) pass sentence, but order the operation of a part of the sentence to be suspended on conditions as provided in paragraph (b) of sub-section (1); or

    (ii) if the person convicted is sentenced to both whipping and imprisonment, order the whole of either the one or the other such sentence to be suspended as aforesaid.

(3) (a) Any court which has sentenced a convicted person to a term of imprisonment as an alternative to a fine, may where the fine has not been paid, at any stage before the termination of the imprisonment suspend the operation of such sentence and order the release of the person convicted on conditions relating to the payment of the fine or such portion thereof as may still be due in terms of sub-section (5) of section three hundred and thirty-seven (whether as to the entering by the accused into his own recognizances, with or without sureties, in the amount of such fine or such portion, for the payment of that amount or as to the taking up of a specified employment and payment of the fine in instalments by the accused, or his employer, or otherwise) which may be satisfactory to the court.

    (b) Any court which has suspended a sentence in terms of paragraph (a) may for good cause at any time during the period of suspension cancel the order of suspension and recommit the person convicted to serve the balance of the sentence subject to the provisions of sub-section (5) aforesaid, or further suspend the operation of the sentence on one or more conditions as the court may deem fit.

    (c) If the conditions upon which any recognizance under paragraph (a) has been given are not observed by the person who gave it, the court may declare the recognizance to be forfeited and such declaration of forfeiture shall have the effect of a judgement in a civil action in that court: Provided that the provisions of this paragraph shall not apply in the event of any condition upon which a recognizance has been given, not having been observed by reason of the death of the person who gave it.

(4) If at the end of the period for which the passing of sentence has been postponed under paragraph (a) of sub-section (1) the court is satisfied that the person convicted has observed all the conditions of the recognizances, the court may discharge him without passing any sentence, and such discharge shall have the effect of an acquittal, except for the purpose of Chapter XVI.

(4)*bis* If the convicted person has, at the end of the period within which he may in terms of an order under paragraph (a)*bis* of sub-section (1) be called upon to appear, not been so called upon, he shall be deemed to have been discharged with a caution under paragraph (d) of sub-section (1).

(5) If the operation of a sentence or any portion of a sentence has been suspended in terms of paragraph (b) of sub-section (1) or in terms of sub-section (2) and the person convicted has observed all the conditions specified in the order throughout the period of suspension, such sentence or portion thereof shall not be enforced.

(6) (a) If the conditions of any order made or recognizance entered into under this section be not fulfilled, the person convicted may, upon the order of a magistrate be arrested without warrant, and such magistrate may then commit the person convicted to undergo the sentence which has been or may then be lawfully imposed, or may, in his discretion, grant the person convicted an extension of time (where this is possible) for the purpose of carrying out such conditions, or may, if no sentence has been imposed and the person convicted is then under the age of twenty-one years, make in respect of him any order which can be made in terms of section three hundred and forty-two upon the conviction of a person of his age.

(a)*bis* A convicted person who has been called upon to appear before a magistrate in terms of an order under paragraph (a)*bis* of sub-section (1), may be arrested without warrant upon the order of a magistrate, and the magistrate before whom he appears may pass sentence upon him in respect of the offence of which he has been convicted.

(b) The Court which has suspended the operation of a sentence under paragraph (b) or (c) of sub-section (1) or under sub-section (2) or (3) or any other court of equal or superior jurisdiction, may, if satisfied that the person convicted has through circumstances beyond his control been unable to perform any condition of such suspension, or for any other good and sufficient reason, grant an order further suspending the operation of the sentence subject to such conditions as might have been imposed at the time of the passing or suspension of the sentence.

(7) If a convicted person has been discharged with a caution or reprimand under paragraph (d) of sub-section (1), the discharge shall have the effect of an acquittal, except for the purpose of Chapter XVI.

(8) Any court which has under this section postponed the passing of sentence or suspended the operation of any sentence on condition that the person convicted shall submit himself to instruction or treatment or to the supervision or control of a probation officer, or shall attend at some specified

centre for a specified purpose, may for good cause at any time during the period of postponement or suspension amend such condition.

APPENDIX 3

Murder in South Africa

	No. of persons charged with murder	No. of persons convicted of murder—without *and* with extenuating circumstances
1962	3,621	845
1.7.63 to 30.6.64	3,120	929
1.7.64 to 30.6.65	3,640	1,075
1.7.65 to 30.6.66	4,494	1,440
1.7.66 to 30.6.67	4,968	1,653

(These are the latest available *overall* figures obtainable from the Department of Statistics.)

Note:
The Annual Average Figures for the Two Periods 1935–1946 and 1963–1967 are:

Years	Total convictions for murder	Murder	Extenuating circumstances	Reprieves	Executions
1935–1946	1,507 (± 125 p.a.)	510	997 (66%)	297 (58%)	213 (± 18 p.a.)
1963–1967	5,942 (± 1,188 p.a.)	659	5,283 (89%)	184 (28%)	475 (± 95 p.a.)

(The population of South Africa was 11¼ million in 1946 and 18 million in 1967.)

SOVIET CRIMINOLOGY—ITS DEMISE AND REBIRTH, 1928-1963*

Peter H. Solomon, Jr.

To the Western observer one of the most unusual features of Soviet criminology in the 1960s and the early 1970s was its marked practical orientation. More than in most other countries criminologists in the U.S.S.R. directed their research towards such practical aims as making legal institutions more effective or reducing the frequency of particular types of crime. Even more striking was the degree of Soviet criminologists' personal involvement in extra-research activities which facilitated the utilization of criminology. These activities included: preparation of special internal reports on current research for interested government agencies; helping the judicial organs through the preparation of methodological aids, through instruction of their staff, and through service on their advisory councils; and participation in decision-making on current penal policy, including membership on the *ad hoc* commissions of the Praesidium of the Supreme Soviet which recommended and prepared new legislation.[1]

The utilitarian cast of Soviet criminology in the post-Stalin period did not appear accidentally; it was the product of criminology's troubled and interrupted history in the U.S.S.R. After a strong period in the decade of the 1920s, Soviet criminological research was cut off entirely in the 1930s, to revive again only in the late 1950s. The outline of this story is already familiar to Western criminologists, but the details of these dramatic events,

* This article is one of the products of a larger research project on criminologists and criminal policy in the Soviet Union. At an early stage the Institute of Criminology of Cambridge, England, graciously received me for a three-month stay. Much of the research for this project followed later during a year at Moscow University under the auspices of the Inter-University Committee on Travel Grants and with the financial support of an NDEA-related Fulbright Hays Award. The Russian Institute of Columbia University and the Research Office of the University of Toronto have also supported work on this project. To all of these institutions the author expresses his gratitude.

[1] For more detail on the practical and political activities of Soviet criminologists during the 1960s, see Peter H. Solomon, Jr., 'Specialists in Soviet Policy-Making: Criminologists and Criminal Policy in the 1960s' (Unpublished Ph.D. Dissertation, Columbia University, 1973).

the reasons for criminology's demise and the circumstances of its revival, have yet to be fully explored.[2]

One must look at the details of the story of criminology's 'fall and rise' to account for the practical bias in the criminology of the period which followed. For at each stage of criminology's development in the U.S.S.R. after 1928 the perceptions of its utility on the part of politicians and of scholars played a significant rôle. How these perceptions changed and what impact these changes had upon criminology forms the subject of this essay.

Demise

Even in Tsarist times Russian lawyers and doctors had begun studying crime, but it was after the Revolution that criminology in Russia experienced its major expansion. By the end of the 1920s there were more than a dozen institutes, centres, laboratories, and clinics studying crime and the criminal, most of which benefited from governmental support. Research spanned a wide range, from biopsychological studies of individual offenders to sociological-statistical analyses of crime as a whole.[3]

Political conditions in the 1920s contributed to this expansion of criminology. To begin with, the Soviet régime did not regard criminologists as subversive, as had the Tsarist government in its last years.[4] Secondly, the prevailing philosophy of criminal law, influenced by Italian positivism and by Marxism, viewed crime as a social rather than a legal problem, thus encouraging criminology.[5] Thirdly, the régime's approach to scholarship as a whole was primarily one of *laissez faire*.[6]

[2] Leon Radzinowicz, *In Search of Criminology*, London, Heinemann Educational Books, 1961, pp. 169–70; Walter Connor, *Deviance in Soviet Society*, New York, Columbia Univ. Press and London, 1972, pp. 27–34.

[3] S. S. Ostroumov, *Prestupnost' i ee prichiny v dorevolyutsionnoy Rossii*, Moscow, M.G.U., 1960; Yu. P. Kasatkin, 'Ocherk istorii izucheniy prestupnosti v SSSR', *Problemy iskoreneniya prestupnosti*, ed. V. N. Kudryavtsev, Moscow, Iur. lit., 1965.

[4] With good reason Tsarist officials suspected the young criminologists. Not only did they write highly critical studies of Tsarist administration of justice, but some of them were also politically active. For example, M. N. Gernet, later a leading Soviet criminologist, used to frequent Marxist circles with some of his colleagues. In 1911 Gernet flagrantly denounced capital punishment and in the same year resigned his post at Moscow University in protest against the restrictive measures imposed by Kasso, the Minister of Education. Ostroumov, op. cit., pp. 321–36; A. A. Gertsenzon, 'M. N. Gernet—ego zhizn', obshchestvennaya i nauchnaya deyatelnost'; in Vol. I of M. N. Gernet, *Istoriya tsarskoy tyurmy*, 3rd ed., 5 vols.; Moscow, Gosiurizdat, 1960.

[5] Harold Berman, *Justice in the USSR*, rev. ed., N.Y., 1963, p. 35.

[6] The leading centre of natural science, the U.S.S.R. Academy of Sciences, remained aloof from politics until 1928. Although the party did create a Marxist centre for the

The principal benefactor of these conditions was the largest criminology centre, the State Institute for the Study of Crime and the Criminal, founded in 1925. Although it was a government institute, supported by state funds and under the joint patronage of four R.S.F.S.R. commissariats (Internal Affairs, Justice, Health, and Education), its work was not politicized.[7] Few of the Institute's staff were Bolshevik party members; and most did not bother to explore the political or the ideological implications of their work.[8]

Scholars of the State Institute contributed frequently to the practice of the administration of justice, but in their own way and according to their own definition of utility. The Institute's relations with the commissariats which sponsored it were based upon personal and professional ties between scholars and administrators, rather than upon institutional pressures. These ties were closest with the R.S.F.S.R. Commissariat of Internal Affairs, where the Institute's director E. G. Shirvindt was also the chief of the prison system. This link led to mutually advantageous and practically significant research, including, for example, clinical studies of difficult prisoners and a larger survey project on hooligans in prison.[9]

Towards the end of the decade the political conditions which had favoured the development of criminology changed. The intense atmosphere fostered by the adoption of the First Five-Year plan supplied the momentum for the establishment of an orthodox line in most fields of study. Just as in other social sciences,[10] scholarship in criminology became politicized; and estab-

---

social sciences, the Communist Academy, it allowed other social science institutes, such as the RANION group, to continue unmolested until the late 1920s. See Loren Graham, *The Soviet Academy of Sciences and the Communist Party, 1927–1932,* Princeton Univ. Press, 1967, pp. 28–31.

[7] Kasatkin, loc. cit.; B. S. Utevskiy and B. Osherovich, *Dvadtsat' let vsesoyuznogo instituta iuridicheskikh nauk,* Moscow, Iurizdat, 1946.

[8] 'Disput k voprosu ob izuchenii prestupnosti v SSSR', *Revolyutsiya prava,* 1929, No. 3, p. 67.

It was left to the leading communist at the Institute, its director E. G. Shirvindt, to square the Institute's work with Marxism. According to him, Marxists had been wrong to pay so little attention to crime, 'just because it was going to disappear'; the thorough study of crime was the only rational basis for Soviet criminal policy 'in the transitional period'. Moreover, this study had to embrace clinical as well as socio-economic analysis; because 'Marxists too need to understand the mechanisms of the influence of social factors . . .', E. G. Shirvindt, 'O problemakh prestupnosti (Tseli i zadachi Gosudarstven-nogo Instituta)', *Problemy prestupnosti,* I, Moscow–Leningrad, 1926, pp. 3–13.

[9] See Peter H. Solomon, Jr., 'A Selected Bibliography of Soviet Criminology', (University of Cambridge, Institute of Criminology, Bibliographic Series, No. 4, 1969), reprinted in the *Journal of Criminal Law, Criminology and Police Science,* Vol. 61, No. 3, 1970, pp. 393–432, items C2 and C5.

[10] Raymond Bauer, *The New Man in Soviet Psychology,* Cambridge, Mass., Harvard U.P., 1959; Susan Gross Solomon, 'Controversy in Social Science: Soviet Rural Studies in the 1920s' (Unpublished Ph.D. Dissertation, Columbia University, 1973).

lished scholars became vulnerable to attack because of their imputed ideological persuasion.

The Party's instrument for harnessing social sciences became the Communist Academy. Having begun in 1918 as a society of Marxian scholars
centred around a library, the Academy expanded in the middle 1920s into a
network of loosely organized sectors for Marxian scholarship in the social
sciences.[11] Near the end of the decade many of these sectors of the Academy
accepted from the Party the political assignment of establishing the hegemony
of Marxist scholarship over colleagues working outside the Academy.

Prominent in the Communist Academy's legal sector were E. B. Pashukanis and his close associate N. V. Krylenko, a leading prosecutor for the
R.S.F.S.R. Commissariat of Justice, and later (from 1931) its Commissar.
As representatives of a 'nihilistic orientation', Pashukanis and Krylenko
were urging that law and legal institutions start to disappear with the construction of socialism and that the remaining law become elastic and responsive to political needs. They were naturally hostile to criminology, a field
committed to improving the existing legal and social institutions for dealing
with criminals.[12] It was these persons who undertook the assignment in
1929, 'to elaborate the methodology for the study of crime and the criminal,
thereby accomplishing ideological leadership of the corresponding institutions for research on crime'.[13]

In preparation for imposing ideological leadership on the State Institute,
Pashukanis and Krylenko staged a dramatic event in March 1929—a debate
in the Communist Academy 'On the question of the study of crime'. The
aim of the 'debate' was to make the methodological direction of the State
Institute's work by the Communist Academy appear legitimate and necessary,
through a demonstration of the criminologists' 'theoretical errors'. Although
billed as a comradely discussion of methodological questions in crime study,
the 'debate' resembled a judicial inquest. Even in their invitation to the

[11] M. N. Pokrovski, 'O rabote Kommunisticheskoy Akademii', *Vestnik Kommunisticheskoy Akademii*, 1929, No. 32.

[12] Berman, op. cit., ch. 1., summarizes the philosophy and politics of the legal nihilists.
Translations of some of their works are found in *Soviet Legal Philosophy*, (ed. Hazard and
Babb, Cambridge, 1951). For a detailed study of Pashukanis' jurisprudence, see Robert
Sharlett, 'Pashukanis and the Commodity Exchange Theory of Law, 1924–1930', (Unpublished Ph.D. Dissertation, Indiana University 1968). N. V. Krylenko is best known in
the West as the prosecutor in the trials of the specialists, 1928–31; these trials are well
portrayed by Roy Medvedev in *Let History Judge*, New York, 1972. For details on Krylenko's life, see B. Osherovich, 'Tov. Krylenko kak borets za Marksistsko-lenin-skuyu
teoriyu ugolovnogo prava (k 50-letiyu so dnya rozhdeniya)', *Sovetskaya iustitsiya*, 1935,
No. 17, p. 3.

[13] 'Direktivy po sostavleniyu plana Kommunisticheskoy Akademii na 1929–1930 gody',
Vestnik Kommunisticheskoy Akademii, 1929, No. 33, p. 279.

participating criminologists, Pashukanis listed the 'charges' which he would level against them.[14]

According to Pashukanis and his colleagues, the theoretical errors of the criminologists consisted of two 'deviations', Lombrosianism and positivism.[15] The accusations focused particularly upon the incompatibility of psychiatric (or biopsychological) study of criminals and Marxist assumptions about the social nature of crime. All physicians who performed clinical studies of criminals and attempted to generalize about either physical or psychological traits were guilty of 'Lombrosianism'.[16] Nor did the sociological and legal studies by scholars at the State Institute escape censure. Because their authors generally wrote not as committed Marxists but as representatives of 'objective social science', they were guilty of the second heresy, 'positivism'.[17]

The criminologists at the 'debate' found it difficult to answer the charge that their research was ideologically unsound. One reason was that, although the attackers claimed to recognize what kind of criminology *was not* Marxian, neither they nor the criminologists could be sure just what type of criminology *was* Marxist! This cognitive problem was complicated by the fact that the criminologists under attack were far from united in their attitudes or in their responses to the demand for ideological rectitude. Some of them believed that a broad requirement of Marxian scholarship was appropriate in the Soviet state, while others denied this vociferously.[18] Moreover, there

[14] 'Disput', loc. cit.

[15] For purposes of analysis we have summarized the charges against the criminologists, which were presented in a series of speeches. At the meeting the tone of criminology's critics varied considerably. The older Marxist scholar A. Ia. Estrin spoke softly but firmly about the 'mistakes' of the criminologists. However, S. Ya. Bulatov and B. S. Mankovskiy, two aspirants at the Institute of Soviet Law, attacked their colleagues from the State Institute with crude and often meaningless epithets. For example, Mankovskiy referred to M. N. Gernet as a 'representative of the petty-bourgeois wing of the Russian school'.

[16] In Soviet parlance the epithets 'Lombrosian' and 'neo-Lombrosian' became terms of abuse. Although the only un-Marxian ingredient in biopsychological study was the notion of inherited criminal characteristics, Soviet critics applied the term indiscriminately to all practitioners of the clinical study of criminals, regardless of the fact that the overwhelming majority of them totally rejected the idea of inherited characteristics.

[17] In Soviet usage, positivism became a pejorative term, describing any non-Marxian social science.

[18] Those who accepted the norm of a Marxian scholarship included E. G. Shirvindt, A. A. Gertsenzon, and a psychiatrist, T. E. Segalov. Shirvindt went on to argue that the State Institute's work *was* Marxist and that the good reviews of its publications in the Communist Academy's legal journal proved it. For his part Segalov not only accepted the norm but also the definition of Marxian scholarship implied in the critics' words. He proceeded to defend the Moscow Office for the Study of the Criminal and Crime on the grounds that it had recently reduced the proportion of biopsychological research.

On the other side, V. A. Vnukov, a psychiatrist from the State Institute, rejected the

were also among the criminologists some (both believers and opportunists) who were willing to concede that the whole psychiatric or clinical side of criminology was tainted *if* they could thereby save sociological and statistical research from this stigma.[19]

But criminologists of all methodological and political profiles agreed on one point, that *their criminology could be justified in terms of its utility.* The psychiatrists pointed out that their clinical studies helped the prisons;[20] the sociologists emphasized the practical uses of statistical studies in the administration of justice.[21] The utility of criminology became the main defence of the State Institute scholars against their attackers.

In effect, the criminologists were proposing that utility replace ideological rectitude as the standard for judging criminology. This position had legitimacy, because of the strong Marxian penchant for practical scholarship expressed in the slogan 'unity of theory and practice'. The argument had added potency, since at the time academic politicians were condemning natural science for its separation from practice; and the need to make a practical contribution was becoming a prescribed norm for all scholarship in the U.S.S.R.[22]

The State Institute's director E. G. Shirvindt tried to use the practical nature of criminology as a way of discrediting the entire 'inquest'. Since criminology was mainly an applied field, he argued, what right had the Communist Academy, a centre for social theory, to judge criminology? The responsibility for the Institute's political guidance belonged to the Collegium of the R.S.F.S.R. Commissariat of Internal Affairs, the commissariat with which the Institute had 'practical ties'.[23]

Pashukanis answered this challenge directly.

---

application to scholarship of any political criteria, and he mocked both Shirvindt and Segalov for having accepted the premises of the attackers. Vnukov defended the psychiatric and the biological research as scientifically advanced, 'the latest word from German scholarship'!

[19] An aspirant at the Institute of Soviet Law and student of A. Ya. Estrin, A. A. Gertsenzon joined the attack on the clinical study of criminals, while defending sociological-legal studies of crime on grounds of utility. Also, E. G. Shirvindt implicitly conceded the same point, when in defending the Institute's work he referred primarily to the social-legal study.

[20] Segalov and Vnukov agreed on this point despite their differences about the ideological requirements for criminology.

[21] Besides A. A. Gertsenzon, N. A. Cherlyunchakevich from the R.S.F.S.R. Commissariat of Internal Affairs and S. Motylev from Gosplan defended sociological-statistical study.

[22] Graham, op. cit.

[23] 'Disput', loc. cit., pp. 54–7.

Now he [Shirvindt] insists that this institute is a practical one: we work together with the N.K.V.D., he says; only before its Collegium are we accountable, and we recognize no other leadership, etc. But when one poses the question, what have you managed to produce on behalf of practice, he says: please, one cannot demand immediate practical results from a scientific research institute.

One way or the other: either you are a practical institution, then show us something practical, something this institute has produced which has been applied, or you are a scientific institution, of a theoretical profile, and then from the hegemony of the Communist Academy you cannot escape in any way, comrades, because the centre for Marxist thought is the Communist Academy![24]

The irony was that although criminologists had urged the criterion of practice as an alternative to that of ideological rectitude, their opponents limited its effectiveness as a defence of criminology by not allowing the criminologists to be the judges of its utility. Only the Communist Party, or its spokesmen, could decide what was practical and what not in the period of socialist construction. From 1929, until after Stalin's death, the meaning of 'practical' in criminology became a matter of political definition.

In summarizing the discussions at the Communist Academy, Pashukanis claimed that the dispute had 'proved conclusively' that the State Institute for the Study of Crime and the Criminal needed methodological leadership from the Communist Academy.[25] Nevertheless, it took a full two years for the Academy group to establish its control, largely because the Institute had high-level patronage in the R.S.F.S.R. Commissariat of Internal Affairs.

In December 1929 the Communist Academy succeeded in placing some Marxist legal scholars on the council of the Institute (Krylenko, Kuzmin, Estrin) and in prompting the formation of party group in the institute. The new party group in turn decided to examine the work of each of the Institute's sectors, 'in preparation for reorganization'.[26] But that reorganization did not take place right away. During 1930 the Institute not only continued research as usual, but it entered into another dispute with the Krylenko-Pashukanis group. Under Shirvindt's guidance Institute scholars opposed N. V. Krylenko's draft criminal code which anticipated the 'withering away of law and the state' by eliminating specific crimes and punishments and by empowering judges to apply 'general principles of law'.[27]

[24] Ibid., p. 67.
[25] Ibid.
[26] 'Min' [P. Kuzmin], 'O Gosudarstvennom institute po izucheniyu prestupnosti i prestupnika', *Sovetskoe gosudarstvo i revolyutsiya prava*, 1930, No. 3, pp. 154–8.
[27] According to Berman, op. cit., pp. 45–6, Krylenko proposed a new code annually from 1929 to 1935 which, although never promulgated, influenced penal practice. Shirvindt's opposition to Krylenko's first draft code included a draft code of his own, which the Institute prepared during 1930 and a collection of essays criticizing Krylenko's plans. For the latter, see *Klassovaya bor'ba i prestupnost'*, ed. E. G. Shirvindt, Moscow, 1930.

Shirvindt successfully resisted the attempts of the Communists on the Institute's Council to obstruct the Institute's operations but only because the R.S.F.S.R. Commissariat of Internal Affairs supported his opposition to the Communist Academy's plans for the Institute. One indication of the Commissariat's support was the publication of a defence of the State Institute in the Commissariat's journal even after a Krylenko supporter had denounced the Institute in the legal journal of the Communist Academy.[28]

Finally, when the R.S.F.S.R. Commissariat of Internal Affairs was established on 1 January 1931, and the prison administration was transferred to the R.S.F.S.R. Commissariat of Justice, Shirvindt's patronage collapsed.[29] After this Shirvindt could no longer prevent the reorganization of his institute. Later that month, the Institute's Council met to formally criticize Shirvindt and to plan the Institute's reorganization; in February Shirvindt resigned as director.[30]

In the spring of 1931 the 'reorganization' of the State Institute took place. Three quarters of the Institute's staff 'turned over' as the biopsychological and police science sections were closed down entirely; at the same time, the provincial branches were terminated. Moreover, the 'reformers' of the Institute insisted that the profile of the remaining two sections ('social-economic' and 'penitentiary') be drastically changed.[31] Because the criminologists had proved themselves ideologically incompetent, Krylenko and his associates declared that 'all theoretical philosophizing should be expelled from the Institute'. Henceforth, only the Marxist scholars at the Communist

---

[28] This exchange of articles took place under pseudonyms. Kuzmin, recently appointed to the Council of the Institute, wrote as 'Min', while B. S. Utevskiy, a Shirvindt protégé and specialist on penology and corrective-labour law, answered Kuzmin under the *nom de plume* 'Kuz'. See 'Min', loc. cit. and 'Kuz' [B. S. Utevskii], 'Ob odnoy kritike Gosudarstvenogo instituta po izucheniyu prestupnosti i prestupnika', *Administrativny vestnik*, 1930, No. 5, pp. 64–9.

[29] *Ezhegodnik sovetskogo stroitelstva i prava na 1931 god*, Moscow, Iurizdat, 1931, p. 449, note.

[30] N.L., 'Na perelome' (zasedanie Gosudarstvennogo instituta po izucheniyu prestupnosti, 24 ianvariya i 2 fevraliya 1931 g.), *Sovetskaia iustitsiya*, 1931, No. 4, pp. 8–13.

After his resignation from the directorship of the State Institute, Shirvindt found work in the Commissariat of Water Transport. With the establishment of the U.S.S.R. Procuracy in 1933, Shirvindt became a Senior Assistant for the supervision of places of confinement. In 1936, he was arrested, and he remained in the camps until his release in 1955. See B. S. Utevskiy, 'Vidnyy deyatel ispravitelnotrudovoy sistemi', *K novoi zhizne*, 1966, No. 5; 'Evsei Gustavovich Shirvindt', *Sovetskoe gosudarstvo i pravo* [hereafter SGIP], (1958, No. 12), p. 130.

[31] In addition, the names of the remaining sectors changed. The social-economic sector became the sector for criminal policy; and the penitentiary sector became the sector for corrective-labour policy. A new criminal procedure sector was also added. Utevskiy and Osherovich, op. cit.

Academy's Institute of Soviet Construction would concern themselves with social or legal theory. For its part, the State Institute, now renamed the Institute of Criminal Policy, would become 'a factory for the theoretical processing of [legal] practice according to our political line'. Ironically, in the name of ideological purity, Krylenko was promoting the separation of theory and practice, a most un-Marxian notion![32]

The practical consequence of the expulsion of 'theoretical philosophizing' from the State Institute was the curtailment of sociological criminology; under Krylenko's hegemony the Institute of Criminal Policy virtually ceased studying crime, its causes and the administration of justice. Instead, criminologists performed such 'practical tasks' as: simplifying the system of criminal statistics;[33] preparing a propagandist book on the prison system; and studying foreign legislation. The 'old criminologists', who were declared incompetent to 'assimilate the Marxist-Leninist method', worked at the reorganized Institute's Bureau of Foreign Information.[34] Thus, Krylenko transformed the State Institute from a research centre into a service bureau for the R.S.F.S.R. Commissariat of Justice!

Although criminology's emasculation was perpetrated in the name of ideological purity, there were also other reasons why criminology's utility might have appeared limited during the early 1930s. The official acceptance of Krylenko and Pashukanis's 'nihilistic jurisprudence' was the most important reason.[35] Because the postulates of this theory included the belief that both legal institutions and crime in the U.S.S.R. were actually in the process of disappearing, research on crime might have seemed to the regime both inappropriate and potentially embarrassing. For, if crime were rapidly disappearing, there was little need for its study; by the same token, if crime studies were carried out, they might show that crime was in fact not disappearing.

Another reason why criminology's utility may have been perceived as limited during the early 1930s was its irrelevance to the principal crime problem of those years—the repression of the so-called 'class enemies' who threatened the success of the collectivization and the industrialization

---

[32] N.L., loc. cit., pp. 7–9.

[33] Simplification of the criminal statistics was needed to relieve the burden which had fallen to the police and the courts, after the Moral Statistics Department of the Central Statistics Administration (TsSU) closed in 1931. The Department had collected data not only on crime but also on suicide and on prostitution. For references to its published collections of statistics, see Solomon, 'A Selected Bibliography', G1, G2, G3.

[34] Utevskii and Osherovich, op. cit. See also, 'Vsesoyuznoe statisticheskoe soveshchanie', *Sotsialisticheskaya zakonnost'* (hereafter *SZ*), 1934, No. 8, pp. 26–7; and *Ot tyurem k vospitatelnym uchrezhdeniyam*, ed. A. Ia. Vyshinskii, Moscow, Iurizdat, 1934.

[35] Berman, op. cit., pp. 41–5.

drives.[36] Criminologists were hardly needed to chronicle the growing application of terror to 'kulaks' and to supposed industrial saboteurs; ideologists rather than criminologists were best qualified to explain the appearance of these new threats to the regime's plans.

But criminologists were not to remain settled for long even in this condition. In 1936 an abrupt and fundamental change occurred in Soviet legal policy, which affected criminologists' assignments once again. As the terror increased, Stalin decided to put a new face of legality upon his government and its policies. There followed the promulgation of the 1936 Constitution, and with it the references to 'unlimited repression of class enemies' and of the 'withering away of law' ceased.[37] The 'stability of law' became the new slogan, but the terror went on; and legalism came to serve as a façade for it.

Two consequences of the new emphasis on legality affected criminologists and the Institute of Criminal Policy. One was the downfall of Krylenko and Pashukanis and their replacement by Vyshinskiy as the new *doyen* of Soviet criminal law.[38] The second was a new political definition of the rôle of legal scholars, provided by Vyshinskiy himself.

Both of these developments were heralded by another reorganization of the former State Institute. In December 1936, two sectors from Pashukanis's Institute of Soviet Construction and Law were transferred to the Institute of Criminal Policy, whose name had now changed to All-Union Institute of Juridical Sciences.

The new name reflected the fact that this was no longer an institute for criminal law, but a general legal institute. Along with the addition of scholars from Pashukanis's Institute went a shuffle of the administrative positions at the Institute, in which the Krylenko–Pashukanis group was demoted.[39] Within a few months, a Vyshinskiy representative at the Institute,

[36] See Merle Fainsod, *Smolenskunder Soviet Rule*, Cambridge, Mass., Harvard Univ. Press, 1958, pp. 195–264.

[37] Berman, op. cit., pp. 46–58.

[38] A. Ya. Vyshinskiy, R.S.F.S.R. Deputy Assistant Procurator under Krylenko in the 1902s, Procurator-General of the U.S.S.R. from 1933, became the 'little Stalin' of Soviet law in 1937. The same year Vyshinskiy also made his fame abroad as the prosecutor at the Great Purge Trials. In spite of his appointment as U.S.S.R. Minister of Foreign Affairs in 1941, and as Minister of Foreign Affairs in 1949, Vyshinskiy remained a leading figure in legal policy. See Donald Barry, 'The Soviet Legal Profession: An Analyais of Biographical Data and Career Patterns', *Canadian–American Slavic Studies*, Vol. 6, No. 1 (Spring, 1972).

[39] The Institute's director, A. S. Shlyapochnikov, a Krylenko protégé, was demoted to deputy director (one of two), and G. I. Volkov, a Marxist not as closely associated with Krylenko, became the new director. Krylenko himself was on the staff as head of the criminal law sector. For more details, see A. S. Shlyapochnikov, 'Na novye rel'sy', *SZ*, 1936, No. 12.

B. Mankovskiy began attacking the Pashukanis group and their 'incorrect theories', and soon the members of that group were arrested.[40]

In 1938 Vyshinskiy assigned to the remaining legal scholars, including former criminologists, a part in restoring the *appearance* of a normal legal system. Their specific tasks included: reviving and improving legal education, partly by preparing new textbooks;[41] preparing legislation which would reverse the 'anarchic measures' introduced by Pashukanis and Krylenko; and emphasizing in their scholarship the continuities between Soviet legality and bourgeois jurisprudence, through studies on the history of Russian and Western law.[42]

Vyshinskiy's new conception of the rôle of the legal scholar made the revival of criminological research unlikely. Now the scholar who would attempt to study crime would run the double risk of hinting at the reality of mass repression and of deviating from his assigned task of promoting the legal institutions which masked it. Moreover, Stalin and Vyshinskiy did not reject the ideological approach to *crime* which had gained acceptance under Krylenko and Pashukanis. Although legal institutions were fully restored, the assumption that crime was disappearing in Soviet socialist society was never denied. The consequent refusal by Soviet politicians to recognize the existence of a crime problem also inhibited the revival of criminology.[43]

[40] B. S. Mankovskiy, 'Protiv antimarksistskikh teoriy v ugolovnom prave', *SZ*, 1937, Nos. 5, 6, 7. By the end of 1937, Pashukanis, Krylenko, Estrin, and Shlyapochnikov had been arrested; and of these only Shlyapochnikov survived. Interview. (The interviews with Soviet criminologists cited in this article were conducted by the author during his stay in Moscow from August, 1968 through May, 1969. For a list of the individuals interviewed and other pertinent information, see Solomon, 'Specialists in Soviet Policy-making', op. cit., pp. 344–6).

[41] The reform of legal education also had beneficial substantive effects. It allowed for the training of a new generation of lawyers well versed in legal principles and distinctions. If the weak legal education of the Krylenko and Pashukanis years had continued, the reform of the legal system after Stalin's death would have been more difficult to implement. See Berman, op. cit., pp. 45–6.

[42] Utevskiy and Osherovich, op. cit.
Not all of the historical studies were scholastic, as some later critics have maintained. For examples of solid scholarship see Gernet's history of Tsarist prisons, Gertsenzon's studies on Jean Paul Marat, and Utevskiy's exploration of the history of the principle, *'nullem crimen sine lege'*. For these and others, see *Sovetskoe ugolovnoe pravo. Bibliografiia 1917–1960*, compiled by F. M. Asknaziy and N. V. Marshalova; Moscow, Gosiurizdat, 1961, pp. 162–90.

[43] Naturally officials in the judicial ministries were forced to recognize the existence of crimes which they were prosecuting. However, between 1938 and 1954 the officials rarely engaged in 'frank and businesslike' discussions of the struggle against crime on the pages of Soviet legal journals. Scanning the relevant sections of the principal bibliography on Soviet criminal law reveals the extreme paucity of such discussions during those years. Ibid., *passim*.

Despite great obstacles former criminologists did try once during Stalin's lifetime to revive their field. The attempt occurred during the last years of World War II (1944–6), when the political atmosphere in the U.S.S.R. was more relaxed than it had been during the 1930s or would become shortly thereafter. With some support from the judicial agencies, the All-Union Institute of Juridical Sciences organized a three-day conference on the study of crime, which was attended by representatives of the judicial agencies and legal research institutes.[44]

Three former criminologists presented reports. M. N. Gernet, speaking on the history of criminological study in the U.S.S.R., eulogized the 1920s. The second speaker, B. N. Khlebnikov, described the sorry state of Soviet criminal statistics since 1931, and called for reforms. Finally A. A. Gertsenzon spoke directly on the question of establishing a new criminology institute and a series of special bureaux to study crime locally.[45] All of the speakers noted that the present 'abnormal' situation in criminology and criminal statistics was due to the 'false theories' of the now purged and disgraced Krylenko and Pashukanis. But, their main argument in favour of the revival was that criminology would serve what they thought to be *practical* needs of the administration of justice.

The conference reports were published in 1945, and a few other articles and a book also appeared in which the authors continued the case for criminology.[46] But their pleas fell upon deaf ears. Whatever relaxation of terror and ideological vigilance had made the revival of criminology seem possible soon ended. From 1948 until 1954 there were no further discussions of the revival of criminology; there were only harsh denunciations of criminology as a bourgeois monstrosity.[47] The revival of criminology had to wait until after the death of Stalin.

[44] The Chairman of the U.S.S.R. Supreme Court, I. T. Golyakov, edited the published version of the three reports, and in the preface he argued for the elimination of the shortcomings in criminal law which the authors discussed. *Problemy izucheniya prestupnosti. Sbornik statey*, ed. I. T. Golyakov, Moscow, Iurizdat, 1945.

[45] Gertsenzon, 'Zadachi izucheniy prestupnosti', Gernet, 'Izuchenie prestupnosti v SSSR (Istoricheskiy ocherk)', Khlebnikov, 'Sovremennoe sostoyanie i zadachi sovetskoy ugolovnoy statistiki v oblasti izucheniya prestupnosti', ibid.

[46] Ibid., A. A. Gertsenzon, 'Blizhayshchie zadachi izucheniya prestupnosti', *SZ*, 1944, No. 1; Utevskii and Osherovich, op. cit.

[47] For example, see B. S. Nikiforov, 'Reaktsionnaya amerikanskaya biokriminologiya', *Trudy instituta prava*, 1951, Vyp. 1.

Rebirth

In the years immediately following Stalin's death in March 1953 terror was curtailed, political prisoners were released, and reforms were initiated in criminal law and procedure.[48] As the administration of justice was gradually normalized, a more contemporary and a more empirical legal scholarship became feasible once again. During 1954 and 1955 some legal scholars alluded in print to the desirability of crime study.[49] The legal journal, *Sovetskoe gosudarstvo i pravo*, in a 1955 editorial, also supported criminological study.[50] Moreover, within the walls of the U.S.S.R. Ministry of Internal Affairs, actual criminological research began once again. The initiator of this first research was none other than E. G. Shirvindt, the former director of the State Institute, who immediately upon release from a labour camp returned to become a Senior Scientific Worker in the Main Administration of Corrective-Labour Institutions.[51]

However, it was Khrushchev's public denunciation of Stalin and his cult of personality at the 20th Congress of the C.P.S.U. in 1956, which created the opportunity for an open discussion of the possible revival of criminology. The revelation of 'Stalin's crimes' and the 'consequences of the cult of personality' shattered the restraints which had made legal scholars cautious in their advocacy. When in 1956 an editorial in the party journal *Kommunist* referred specifically to the need for crime study, many scholars were ready to write supporting briefs.[52]

Fortunately for criminology, some former criminologists had outlived Stalin and were ready to take part in its revival. Among these were the above-mentioned E. G. Shirvindt, Prof. M. D. Shargorodskiy of Leningrad

---

[48] Berman, op. cit., ch. 1.

[49] M. D. Shargorodskiy and N. S. Alekseev, 'Aktualnye problemy ugolovnogo prava', *Uchenye zapiski LGU*, No. 182, Seriya iuridicheskikh nauk, 1954, vyp. 5, pp. 154–296; M. D. Shargorodskiy, 'Nekotorye zadachi sovetskoy pravovoy nauki v nastoyashchee vremya', loc. cit., 1955, No. 187, pp. 3–30; V. N. Kudryavtsev, 'Razvivat' nauku sovetskogo ugolovnogo prava', *SZ*, 1956, No. 1.

[50] 'O sostoyanii i zadachakh nauki sovetskogo ugolovnogo prava', *SGiP*, 1955, No. 2, pp. 3–12.

[51] E. G. Shirvindt remained with the U.S.S.R. Ministry of Internal Affairs until his death in 1958. Interview.

[52] 'Ukreplenie sotsialisticheskoy zakonnosti i iuridicheskoy nauki', *Kommunist*, 1956, No. 11; B. S. Utevskiy, 'XX s'ezd KPSS i zadachi nauki ugolovnogo prava', *SZ*, 1956, No. 9; S. S. Ostroumov, 'O sudebnoy statistike', *SGiP*, 1957, No. 1; Yu. P. Kasatkin, 'K izucheniyu konkretnykh prichin vyzyvayushchikh prestupleniya', *Uchenye zapiski Tadzhikskogo gos. Universiteta*, 1956, Vyp. 4, No. 11.

University,[53] his former protégé Prof. B. S. Utevskiy,[54] Prof. A. A. Gertsenzon, and A. S. Shlyapochnikov.[55]

In 1956 Shirvindt and Utevskiy were the main initiators. Within the U.S.S.R. Ministry of Internal Affairs they succeeded in organizing a penological research section and at the same time in establishing a corrective-labour sector in the Ministry's Higher School.[56] Especially important for the morale of scholars outside the Ministry of Internal Affairs was the conference on corrective-labour law which Utevskiy and Shirvindt organized

[53] Professor of criminal law at Leningrad University, Mikhail Davidovich Shargorodskiy, began his scholarly career at the Kharov criminology centre, just two years before it closed in 1931. After Stalin's death, Prof. Shargorodskiy became a leading advocate of a reformed penal system. His liberal penal philosophy is reflected in his two-volume history of punishment in Russia, *Nakazanie po ugolovnomu pravu ekspluatatorskogo obshchestva*, Moscow, Gosiurizdat, 1957, and *Nakazanie po sovetskomu ugolovnomu pravu*, Moscow, Gosiurizdat, 1958. Shargorodskiy was also one of the first to call for the revival of criminology (see note 50, *supra*), and he remained one of its most outspoken supporters. At a conference in Leningrad in 1963 Shargorodskiy spoke with unusual candour about the need to overcome conservative and ideological restraints upon the emerging field. See *Nauchnaia konferentsiya 'Problemy sovetskogo ugolovnogo prava v periode razvyornutogo stroitelstva kommunizma', (14-17 maia 1963 g.)'*, Leningrad, L.G.U., 1963, pp. 68 ff.

[54] Boris Samoylovich Utevskiy, a leading penologist in the 1920s, co-author of three textbooks on corrective-labour law with E. G. Shirvindt (1927, 1931, 1957), spent the Stalinist years at the All-Union Institute of Juridicial Sciences. In 1956, Utevskiy became head of the new corrective-labour kafedra at the Ministry of Higher Internal Affairs School. After an illness in 1958 he relinquished the post, but remained a member of the kafedra despite his seventy years. Up to his eighty-third birthday in 1970, Utevskiy remained an active and independent-minded scholar. Interviews.

[55] Upon returning from eighteen years in the camps in 1955, the former director of the Institute of Criminal Policy, A. S. Shlyapochnikov worked at the All-Union Institute of Juridical Sciences, the continuation of his old institute. In 1963 he moved to the Procuracy Institute where he joined Prof. A. A. Gertsenzon's sector. In 1966 as a form of academic rehabilitation Shlyapochnikov was awarded a doctoral degree without dissertation on the basis of his accumulated writings. See Shlyapochnikov, *Nekotorye aktualnye problemy sovetskogo ugolovnogo prava i kriminologii. (Doklad o opublikovannykh na etu temu rabotakh predstavlennykh na soiskanie uchenoy stepeni doktora iuridicheskikh nauk)*, Moscow, 1966.

[56] The research section for corrective-labour institutions in the R.S.F.S.R. Ministry of Internal Affairs operated from 1956 to 1958 during which time it published a periodical, for internal use only, entitled *Ispravitel'no-trudovye uchrezhdeniya*. When the research section closed, the periodical was superseded by the Ministry's journal *K novoy zhiznei*. Among the staff of the research section were A. M. Yakovlev, I. V. Shmarov, and E. V. Boldyrev.

The Ministry's Higher School was established in 1953, before which time there was no higher educational training for police or prison officials. Its corrective-labour *kafedra*, founded in 1956, became the main research and teaching centre in penology until the founding of the All-Union Institute for the Defence of the Social Order in 1965. During the late 1950s it studied methods of reforming the prison system. B. S. Utevskiy, 'Razvitie sovetskoy ispravitel'noy-trudovoy nauki', *Trudy vysshey shkoly*, Vyp. 16, Moscow, 1967, pp. 114–27.

in the spring of 1957. The conference was a 'happening', the first official discussion either of penology or of the study of crime, since Stalin's death. Appearances by the Minister of Internal Affairs N. P. Dudorov and by R.S.F.S.R. Supreme Court Justice G. V. Anashkin indicated that penology and criminology had high-level patronage.[57]

The conference's principal speaker on crime study was Prof. A. A. Gertsenzon who had been a long-standing proponent of criminology. As the youngest and most active of the returning criminologists, Prof. Gertsenzon became a focal figure in criminology's revival.[58]

Late in 1957, Gertsenzon succeeded in establishing a sector for criminal law at the All-Union Research Institute of Police Science, where, under his direction, criminological research was carried out. In 1960, Gertsenzon's sector moved from the U.S.S.R. Procuracy's police science centre to the Institute of State and Law of the Academy of Sciences, where as the 'sector for the study and prevention of crime', it became the country's leading criminology centre until 1963.[59]

Between 1957 and 1963 scholars and practical workers tried their hands at criminological research in a number of institutions, both in Moscow and in the provinces.[60] However, the main burden for the leading representatives

[57] V. N. Roshchin and V. N. Kalinin, 'Nauchnaia konferentsiya po sovetskomu ispravitel'no-trudovomu pravu', *SGiP*, 1957, No. 12; N. I. Zagorodnikov, and I. V. Shmarov, 'Konferentsiya po voprosam sovetskogo ispravitel'no-trudovogo prava', *Sovetskaya iustitsiya*, 1957, No. 8 and Interviews.

[58] The career of Aleksey Adolfovich Gertsenzon had three phases. A promising young criminologist in the 1920s, by the end of that decade Gertsenzon was the author of two books, including a study of alcoholism and crime in the R.S.F.S.R. When the Moscow Criminological Centre closed in 1931, Gertsenzon moved to the Institute of Criminal Policy (the reorganized State Institute), where the second phase of his career began. At the new post Gertsenzon served as criminal statistics specialist; between 1933 and 1947 he wrote four textbooks on the subject. Always anticipating the revival of criminology, Gertsenzon included sections on crime study in each of these texts; and, as we have seen above, took part in the 1944–45 attempt to revive the field. In addition, Gertsenzon contributed to the history of criminal law with a study of the 'revolutionary democrat' Jean Paul Marat. After 1956 Gertsenzon's career entered its final stage, as Aleksey Adolfovich returned again to criminology. As head of the leading criminology research sector (after 1963 located within the All-Union Institute for the Study and Prevention of Crime) from 1957 until his death in 1970, Gertsenzon gave both moral and intellectual encouragement to aspiring young criminologists. He was the leading methodologist of Soviet crime study and the teacher of a new generation of criminologists. During these years Gertsenzon served as the chairman of two legislative commissions—one which prepared the R.S.F.S.R. criminal code in 1959 and one which drafted a major statute on alcoholism prevention in 1965 (see ch. III). 'Shest'desyatletie A. A. Gertsenzon', *SGiP*, 1962, No. 4, p. 170; A. S. Shlyapochnikov, 'Pamyati vydayushchego sovetskogo kriminologa', *Voprosy bor'by s prestupnostiyu*, 1971, Vyp. 13, pp. 178–88. Interview.

[59] Kasatkin, loc. cit.; *Kriminologiia*, Moscow, Iur. lit., 1968, p. 82.

[60] Criminological studies revived *circa* 1960 at Moscow University (S. S. Ostroumov,

of the new field was to establish its legitimacy and institutional expression. As a victim of Stalinism, criminology had every opportunity to take advantage of the 'undoing of the consequences of the cult of personality'. But criminologists themselves realized that they had to convince the authorities that criminology would be a worthwhile and not a dangerous enterprise.[61] In making a case for criminology, scholars returned to both of the issues which had dominated the politics of criminology's demise, the ideological acceptability and the practical utility of the field. To a degree this flashback represented a conscious appeal to history, as in Shirvindt's attempt to prove that criminology had been an innocent victim of Stalinism.[62] But the criminologists' arguments also signified their recognition of the continued significance of these same issues.

Although the criteria for assessing criminology's legitimacy were ostensibly the same as they had been in the 1930s, in the post-Stalin period they acquired new meanings. As of 1956 the implications of the canons 'ideological acceptability' and 'practical utility' were not yet clear; they were to become evident only gradually during the years of criminology's revival. By 1960 criminologists and politicians seemed to have reached agreement on what made criminology ideologically acceptable; but the question of just how criminology should contribute to practice took even longer to resolve.

During the late 1950s there emerged two distinct requirements for an ideologically acceptable criminology: the theories and methods of the field had to be compatible with Marxian assumptions about crime; and the study of crime had to support, rather than embarrass, the Soviet regime.

The definition of a Marxian criminology required special elaboration in the post-Stalin period no less than it had earlier. Proceeding cautiously, some criminologists revived the arguments of the 1920s and rejected biological, psychiatric, and even psychological research on criminals, as if in shunning 'neo-Lombrosianism' the new Soviet criminology could gain sanction. Soviet criminologists also contrasted their work with Western

---

N. F. Kuznetsova), at Leningrad University (M. D. Shargorodskiy, N. P. Grabovskaya), and at Riga University (L. A. Klyuchinskaya). Criminological research was also begun in the 1960s at the Kharikov Juridical Institute, at Voronezh University, and at the Ukrainian Police Academy in Kiev. Interviews.

[61] There was considerable resistance to criminology in some circles. According to A. A. Gertsenzon, the opponents of criminology fell into three groups. There were persons who feared the return of biocriminology; and there were those who worried lest criminology became divorced from criminal law; but the largest group had no concrete objections at all—'they were simply afraid of innovations'. A. A. Gertsenzon, *Predmet, metod, i sistema sovetskoy kriminologii*, Moscow, Gosiurizdat, 1962, p. 10.

[62] E. G. Shirvindt, 'K istorii voprosa ob izuchenii prestupnosti i mer bor'by s ney', *SGiP*, 1958, No. 5.

'bourgeois' criminology, which they claimed was imbued both with Lombrosianism and with positivism.[63]

In a more constructive vein, criminologists devoted considerable attention to the elaboration of a theory of crime causation which could be related to historical materialism. They not only examined a variety of social and psychological factors which seemed to influence crime, but also constructed social-psychological models of crime causation which had considerable explanatory power.[64] Their theories remain compatible with Marxism, because they accepted the premise that all causes of crime, social or psychological, were 'remnants of the past' which could and would be conquered on the road to communism.[65]

Soviet political leaders, however, seemed even more concerned that the study of crime should present to the public positive and optimistic conclusions about Soviet experience. Conscious of this concern, criminologists carefully reported not only the problems but also the achievements of the U.S.S.R. in fighting crime.[66] Moreover, through critical studies of crime and its causes in bourgeois countries, they succeeded in making the Soviet situation look good by comparison.[67] Convincing the authorities that criminology would not threaten the Soviet regime, either by embarrassing it or by diluting the purity of historical materialism, was only a part of criminologists' justification of their field's revival. They were also obliged to prove that criminology would be useful.

Practicality had served as the main argument in criminology's defence in 1929–30 and as the grounds for reviving the field in the pleas of criminology's proponents in the 1940s. Once again, utility was the obvious basis for supporting criminology in the 1950s, but criminology's proponents had further

[63] Ibid., F. M. Reshetnikov, 'O nekotorykh kharakternykh chertakh sovremennoy amerikanskoy kriminologii', *SGiP*, 1958, No. 10; A. A. Gertsenzon, 'Sovremennaya burzhuaznaya kriminologiya', *SGiP*, 1963, No. 3.

[64] A. B. Sakharov, *O lichnosti prestupnika i prichinakh prestupnosti v SSSR*, Moscow, 1961, and review article by R. Beerman, 'Study of the Soviet Criminal', *Soviet Studies*, Vol. 14, No. 1, July, 1962. For Soviet literature on crime causation theory see Solomon, 'A Selected Bibliography', section D.

[65] See Robert Osborn, 'Crime and the Environment: the New Soviet Debate', *Slavic Review*, **XXVII**, No. 3, Sept. 1968, pp. 393–410.

[66] Full accounts of these achievements are found in V. N. Kudryavtsev, 'Osnovnye napravleniya kriminologicheskikh issledovaniy', *Problemy nauchnogo kommunizma*, vyp. 2, Moscow, 1968, and in G. M. Minkovskiy, 'Ob issledovaniy prestupnosti nesovershen-noletnikh', loc cit.

[67] For example, see *Prestupnost v kapitalisticheskom mire posle vtoroy mirovoy voyny*, Moscow, Nauka, 1963, and Solomon, 'A Selected Bibliography', section Ma. Despite the caution and responsibility shown by Soviet criminologists, the politicians insisted that criminal statistics remain unpublished and secret, in order to prevent ideological and political embarrassment. Interviews. *Kriminologiya*, op. cit., p. 96.

reason to emphasize criminology's practical potential. The 1956 *Kommunist* editorial which had sanctioned the revival of crime study did so in the name of restoring the proper relationship between theory and practice in the law, which Stalin's lieutenant Vyshinskiy had allegedly destroyed![68] Whereas under Vyshinskiy legal scholars had engaged in highly theoretical and historical studies in order to promote the image of Soviet legality, legal scholars were now called upon to contribute once again to the actual administration of justice. Just what forms of assistance legal science in general, or criminology in particular, could provide, the journal did not specify.

Not surprisingly, the proponents of criminology responded to this cue, by attempting to demonstrate that criminology's revival would help bridge the now infamous gap between theory and practice in legal science. In their appearances in the press and at conferences, they publicized the contributions which criminology had made in Tsarist times and in the 1920s and asserted that a revived criminology would prove even better.[69] But they too were ambiguous about precisely what the criminologists' practical rôle should be.

Meanwhile, as the new criminologists began to conduct research, the rudiments of a practical rôle took shape. Most of the research carried out between 1957 and 1961 consisted of crime studies in particular districts, which the researchers used to offer suggestions to local officials on ways of improving their operations.[70] Political leaders quickly recognized the utility of 'local studies'. In 1961 the head of the Communist Party's Department of Administrative Organs N. R. Mironov wrote 'the most important practical significance of the study of crime in the U.S.S.R. falls within the limits of particular localities, where the results of study can be used to determine correctly the means which state and social agencies will exploit in the struggle against violations of the law'.[71]

In addition to their research efforts, criminologists also became involved during the late 1950s and early 1960s in specifically practical activities. At conferences and in private meetings, they began to meet officials from the

[68] 'Ukreplenie sotsialisticheskoy zakonnosti', loc. cit.

[69] Utevskiy, 'XX s'ezd KPSS', loc. cit.; Ostroumov, 'O sudebnoy statistike', loc. cit.; Shirvindt, 'K istorii voprosa', loc. cit.; S. S. Ostroumov, *Prestupnost i eyo prichiny v dorevolyutsionnoy Rossii*, op. cit.

[70] For example, see the full report of the Perm oblast study, *Gosudarstvennye i obshchestvennye mery preduprezhdeniya prestupnosti*, Moscow, Gosiurizdat, 1963. Also, in Solomon, 'A Selected Bibliography', items E21, E22, E23, E26, E27.

[71] N. R. Mironov, 'O nekotorykh voprosakh preduprezhdeniya prestupnosti i drugikh antiobshchestvennykh yavleniy i borby s nimi v sovremennykh uslovyiakh', *SGiP*, 1961, No. 51, p. 9.

central judicial ministries to discuss problems in the administration of justice and crime prevention.[72] One mutual concern was the need to improve the collection and the utilization of criminal statistics.[73] The criminologists in Gertsenzon's sector at the Institute of State and Law contributed towards this goal by preparing a series of manuals on criminal statistics and crime study especially for the use of the 'practical workers'.[74]

Another type of practical work carried out by criminologists and criminal law scholars was preparation of new legislation. Scholars participated in the work of the commissions which prepared the main instruments of the post-Stalin criminal law reforms—the Fundamental Principles of Criminal Legislation of the U.S.S.R. and Union Republics (1958) and the R.S.F.S.R. Criminal Code (1960), and the Code of Criminal Procedure (1960).[75]

A consequence of the various practical activities of Soviet criminologists during the late 1950s and the early 1960s was increasingly close relations with the judicial agencies, the Procuracy, Courts, and M.V.D. The effects of these relations upon criminology became an issue of controversy among scholars of criminal law. To B. S. Utevskiy, one of the original criminologists who remained from the 1920s, the development was an unhappy one. Utevskiy reasoned that the more crime study became tied to the legal system, the more criminology would develop into a legal science rather than a field of social enquiry. Consequently, Utevskiy sought the disengagement of criminology from law and its establishment as an independent social science.[76] A. A. Gertsenzon, on the other hand, opposed the separation of criminology from law precisely because he approved criminology's practical ties with the administration of justice.[77]

The final determination of the shape of criminology's practical rôle in the 1960s was a consequence of changes in political leadership attitudes towards the utility of social research in general. Proponents of empirical social research in post-Stalin Russia had fought an uphill fight to gain acceptance of their work. Despite the formation of the Soviet Sociological Association in 1958, the new sociologists were much hampered by the restrictions which

[72] Interviews. For references to papers or reports from nine conferences held between 1960 and 1962, see Solomon, 'A Selected Bibliography', L 1–9.

[73] Ostroumov, loc. cit.; E. G. Boldyrev, 'Nekotorye voprosy ugolovnogo uchyota i statisticheskoy otchetnosti', *Sovetskaya kriminalistika na sluzhbe sledstviya*, No. 9, 1958.

[74] Solomon, 'A Selected Bibliography', F9, F12, F13.

[75] Donald Barry and Harold Berman, 'The Jurists', *Interest Groups in Soviet Politics*, ed. H. Gordon Skilling and Franklyn Griffiths; Princeton Univ. Press, 1971, pp. 321–3.

[76] B. S. Utevskiy, 'Sotsiologicheskie issledovaniya i kriminologiya', *Voprosy filosofii*, 1963, No. 2. For the views of other scholars on the independence of criminology, see Solomon, 'A Selected Bibliography', C25, C31, C34.

[77] A. A. Gertsenzon, *Vvedenie v sovetskuyu kriminologiyu*, Moscow, Iur. lit., 1965, pp. 35–41. For a picture of the disagreement in retrospect, see *Kriminologiya*, op. cit., pp. 7–25.

philosophers and ideologists imposed upon them.[78] However, just before the 22nd Congress of the C.P.S.U., *Kommunist* sanctioned the expansion of a practically-oriented sociology, and the Congress added its approval.[79] In the autumn of 1962, Khrushchev's ideological deputy, L. Ilichev, told a special meeting of the U.S.S.R. Academy of Sciences that the party had decided to lend its backing to the expansion of empirical social research.[80] But Ilichev warned that in giving sociology moral support, the party was also insisting that it become more instrumental.

In another speech, a party spokesman for the social sciences, P. N. Fedoseev, said that the 'social assignment' [*sotsialnyy zakaz*] of researchers would be 'to produce results from which they would make practical suggestions, which would then be realized'.[81] Since the realization of practical suggestions would often require decisions by politicians, Fedoseev and Ilichev were thus including in their notion of the social scientists' practical rôle a contribution to policy formation.

This broader conception of the utility of social science could be applied to legal research no less than to sociology. Six months later the Soviet leadership did just that, when it decided to reorganize the legal research institutes.[82] The immediate pretext for the reorganization was an administrative reshuffling in the judicial agencies which resulted in the abolition of the R.S.F.S.R. Ministry of Justice in April 1963. Overburdened with new responsibilities, the remaining judicial agencies needed whatever help legal scholars might provide.[83]

[78] Alex. Simirenko, 'An Outline History of Soviet Sociology', *Soviet Sociology: Historical Antecedents and Current Approaches*, Chicago, Quadrangle, 1966, p. 23.

[79] 'Povysit' rol obshchestvennykh nauk v stroitel'stve kommunizma', *Kommunist*, 1961, No. 10.

[80] L. I. Ilichev, 'Nauchnaya osnova rukovodstva razvitiem obshchestva, Nekotorye problemy razvitiya obshchestvennykh nauk', *Stroitelstvo kommunizma i obshchestvennye nauk. Materialy sessii obshchego sobraniy Akademii Nauk SSSR. 19–20 oktiabriya, 1962*, Moscow, Nauka, 1962. For the official 'conclusions' of the conference, see 'Postanovlenie obshchego sobraniya Akademii Nauk SSSR', *Vestnik Akademii Nauk*, 1962, No. 12.

[81] *Stroitel'stvo kommunizma*, op. cit., p. 120. As of 1961 P. N. Fedoseev was the director of the Institute of Philosophy of the Academy of Sciences and the Academic Secretary of the Academy's section for Economic, Philosophical, and Legal Sciences. In 1962, he became a Vice-president of the Academy and shortly thereafter a full member of the party's Central Committee. For further bibliographical details see *Deputaty verkhovnogo soveta SSSR, Sedmoy sozyv*, Moscow, Izbestiia, 1966, p. 458.

[82] 'Iuridicheskaya nauka v usloviyakh kommunisticheskogo stroitel'stva', *Kommunist*, 1963, No. 16, pp. 27–35.

[83] In the name of eliminating wasteful 'parallelism', it was decided to abolish the eight-hundred-man R.S.F.S.R. Ministry of Justice. Its functions were assigned to the Supreme Court apparat (supervision of the court system and selection of judges) and to the new seventy-man Judicial Commission of the R.S.F.S.R. Council of Ministers (supervision of the *advokatura* and the *notariat*, legal advice and legislative reference for govern-

The guiding purpose behind the reorganization of legal research institutes was, however, the achievement of a broad practical contribution such as Ilichev and Fedoseev had endorsed. The party journal *Kommunist* echoed Fedoseev's words, when it explained editorially, '*It must be arranged that the conclusions and generalizations of scholars will not lie on the shelves of the archives but will find the shortest route to those agencies which are occupied with law-making and with the application of legal norms*' [italics in original].[84] Just as social researchers in general were to contribute to decision-making by providing suggestions 'which would then be realized', so legal researchers were expected to make a similar contribution by dispatching their conclusions to the 'agencies occupied with law-making'.

Kommunist's editors emphasized that these contributions to 'law-making' by legal scholars needed to be regularized. The scholars' participation in the preparation of the Fundamental Principles of Criminal Legislation had been exemplary, but the infrequency of such engagements was to be deplored.[85] Moreover, *Kommunist* continued, it was especially important that those legal scholars who performed sociological research (like criminologists) participate fully in 'law-making'.

> Concrete sociological research must play an important role not only in evaluating existing legal norms, but also in the process of preparing new legal acts . . . In issuing a law, the legislator [*sic*] is obliged to predict its social effect, in what direction it will guide the given social process . . . To answer these questions we are calling upon the legal research institutes and upon legal science.[86]

Significantly, *Kommunist*'s enumeration of the law-making tasks of the legal scholar included more than technical work related to the form of legislation. Both 'evaluation of existing legal norms' and the 'prediction of the effects of proposed changes' seemed to bear directly upon the content of decisions in legal policy.

Thus, *Kommunist* recorded a major change in the definition of criminology's practical rôle. As of 1963 criminology's utility was no longer viewed either as making narrow contributions to the operations of the judicial agencies (the Krylenko view), or as maintaining the trappings of legalism in the face of an apparatus of terror (Vyshinskiy's definition), or as aiding local law enforcement (Mironov's image). Criminology's practical rôle now included

---

ment agencies, systematization of legalization). See 'O uprazdenenii ministerstva institutsiy R.S.F.S.R. i obrazovanie iuridicheskoy komissii soveta ministrov R.S.F.S.R.', *Sovetskaya iustitsiya*, 1963, No. 10, p. 4.

[84] 'Iuridicheskaya nauka', loc. cit., p. 33.
[85] Ibid., p. 27.
[86] Ibid., p. 34.

a range of practical contributions—to the operational efficiency of the central ministries, to local law enforcement, and also to decision-making in criminal policy.

To facilitate the new practical rôle for legal scholarship as a whole, Soviet leaders chose a familiar organizational model, the attachment of research institutes to government agencies. Just two years before, in a major reform of natural science, they had affirmed the principle that applied research institutes should be joined to the ministries which most benefited from their work.[87] Adopting this same principle for legal science, the political leaders decided to affiliate legal research institutes with the U.S.S.R. Procuracy, the U.S.S.R. Supreme Court, the R.S.F.S.R. Ministry for the Defence of the Social Order and the new Juridical Commission of the U.S.S.R. Council of Ministers. Such affiliation, they believed, would improve the communication of research results, and would give the understaffed judicial agencies the opportunity to use the institutes to perform research and staff work for them.[88]

As a result of the reorganization there emerged three new legal research institutes, each of which was attached to one or more judicial agency. The institute most relevant to criminology was the All-Union Institute for the Study and Prevention of Crime. Formed in 1963 and placed under the sponsorship of the U.S.S.R. Procuracy and the U.S.S.R. Supreme Court, the All-Union institute drew together the scholars from other institutes who were studying criminal law and procedure, criminology, and police science.[89]

The concentration of criminological studies in this new research institute had profound effects upon the development of Soviet criminology as a scholarly discipline and as a practical enterprise. To begin with, the establishment of the institute resolved, at least temporarily, the debate over criminology's status among the sciences; the close link to the two judicial agencies meant that, however sociological its research methods became, criminology in the U.S.S.R. would remain a part of legal scholarship.

At the same time, the new All-Union institute also provided a framework for the realization of the new broad conception of criminology's practical

[87] Loren Graham, 'Reorganization of the USSR Academy of Sciences', *Soviet Policy Making*, ed. Peter Juviler and Henry Morton, New York, 1967, ch. 8.

[88] 'Iuridicheskaya nauka', loc. cit.

[89] V. N. Kudryavtsev, 'Ukreplyat' svyaz nauki s praktikoy', *Byulleten verkhovnogo suda SSSR*, 1963, No. 6. The other two new legal research institutes which resulted from the reorganization were the All-Union Institute of Soviet Legislation (1963) and the All-Union Institute for the Defence of the Social Order (1965). See 'O zadachakh instituta sovetskogo zakonodatelstva', *Uchenye zapiski VNIISZ*, Vyp. 2 (1964); and S. Borodin, 'Vsesoyuznyy nauchno-issledovatelskiy institut okhrany obshchestvennogo poryadka', *SZ*, 1965, No. 2.

rôle. The institute's statute listed among the responsibilities of its researchers the whole gamut of practical activities which Soviet criminologists came to perform in the 1960s, including the application of research to current policy problems, assistance to the judicial agencies, and participation in the formulation of new legislation.[90] Moreover, the performance of these tasks was encouraged by the U.S.S.R. Procuracy and the U.S.S.R. Supreme Court's sponsorship of the institute, for judicial officials would be less likely to disdain the criminologists' assistance when it had been sanctioned by their superiors. At the same time, the criminologists would not shirk their practical responsibilities when their plans and reports were to be reviewed by the highest judicial officials.[91]

In the light of Soviet criminology's history, its practical bias in the contemporary period was to be expected. The suppression of criminological research partly on the grounds that it served no purpose and the subsequent legitimation of the field's rebirth on the grounds of its utility made some kind of practical contribution by criminologists *sine qua non*. The nature of the revived criminology's practical cast, however, remained to be determined gradually through the years of its revival.

A further question of interest is how through their various practical and political activities criminologists affected penal policy and practice in the U.S.S.R. I have argued elsewhere that, along with judicial officials, criminologists exerted a considerable influence upon most of the decisions taken in penal policy which related to their expertise. At the same time, it appeared that their advocacy was successful only when it did not conflict with the main lines of penal policy then in operation; when it did conflict, criminologists had difficulty gaining a hearing from the decision-makers.[92] Whether the impact of Soviet criminologists will in the future become even more distinctive must depend not upon the extent of their practical effort, but upon the receptivity of politicians to a broader range of options.

[90] Ibid.
[91] See Solomon, 'Specialists in Soviet Policy-making', loc. cit., pp. 85–110.
[92] Ibid., especially chapters five and six.

AN ITALIAN ENQUIRY
CONCERNING THE MAFIA

Giuliano Vassalli

Reports of the Italian Parliamentary Commission of Enquiry on the Mafia in Sicily (1971–1972)

In the summer of 1973 the Italian Writers Federation completed the commercial publication of the records of the Parliamentary Commission of Enquiry on the phenomenon of the Mafia in Sicily, which had been submitted when the Fifth Legislature was dissolved prematurely in the spring of 1972. This publication has made the material, gathered by the impressive efforts of the Commission over several years, available to a much wider group of readers. Although the findings of the Enquiry are still incomplete, the materials presented in this publication are of interest not only to the wider group of politicians, scholars and curiosity-seekers but also to criminologists. In fact, although this complex investigation was carried out by politicians, who did not always follow a precise scientific methodology, it provides an excellent introduction to the in-depth study of an important criminal phenomenon. It was an attempt to explore in depth the many ethnic, historical psychological, social and political factors underlying the Mafia, the key personalities and a large number of the minor actors involved, specific and significant aspects of some of its most obvious manifestations and to outline possible solutions to it.

The 'Parliamentary Commission of Enquiry on the Phenomenon of the Mafia in Sicily' was established by the Law of 20 December 1962 n. 1720, adopted by Parliament at the close of the Third Legislature (1958–63) when the resurgence of the Mafia had again been marked by a succession of terrible crimes. The commission was composed of thirty members of parliament (fifteen deputies and fifteen senators). It started its work during the Fourth Legislature (1963–8), but within that period (during which it was necessary to establish a structure, organize the work, define criteria and overcome various difficulties) it was only possible to publish (7 August 1963) a First Report, which was of a general nature accompanied by a series of proposals for administrative and legislative action, and some minor reports. Among these was the report (of 17 November 1965) on an enquiry conducted by two commissioners at judicial offices in Sicily, 'on the frequency of dismissals for insufficient evidence in trials of Mafia-connected offences', as well as another of the same year on the correlation between criminality and the behaviour of public administrators, with special reference to construction and the purchase of building lots in the city of Palermo.

The Government and Parliament responded to the proposals of 7 August 1963, but in so far as they related to the material concerning the prevention and suppression of Mafia activities, by enacting the Law of 31 May 1965 n. 575, entitled 'Measures against the Mafia'. This law established some specific regulations aimed at rendering the existing general preventive measures more efficient or rigorous for those suspected of belonging to organizations. These general measures—established by the law of 27 December 1956 n. 1423 for all persons 'dangerous to safety and public morals'—included warnings to alter behaviour, compulsory repatriations, special surveillance, prohibition to stay in one or more towns or in one or more provinces, and compulsory stay in a specified town distant from the places of normal residence.

The importance of the results of the Commission's investigations during the Fourth Legislature (especially in the field of illicit enrichment of Mafia members with construction interests and the hidden conspiracies of which these illicit and parasitical crimelinked activities were the fruit) and the certainty that a tenacious investigation would have produced results at least as worthy of attention and action led to the renewal of the same Commission in the succeeding legislature, which having begun in 1968 should have lasted until 1973. It was in fact the early dissolution of the Fifth Legislature that forced the Commission to abandon the preparation of the final report expected by Parliament, the published outline of which promised a complex of data, analysis and proposals of unprecedented scope and thoroughness. Even so the Commission thought it worthwhile to publish a 'Report on work completed and on the state of the phenomenon of the Mafia at the conclusion of the Fifth Legislature' immediately after the dissolution of the Chamber and before the new Parliament sat in May 1972. This report contains the collected data on the functioning of the Commission, the method and procedures followed, its various actions both in relation to general and specific problems and in relation to those individual episodes to which its immediate attention had been drawn because of their seriousness or probable significance, as well as the first results gathered in the various areas of investigation.

Appendices to the same volume contain an important historical study designed by the Commission to Professor Francesco Brancato, 'The Mafia in Public Opinion and in Enquiries from the Unification of Italy to Fascism'[1] and the text of all the evidence from witnesses gathered by the Commission in the courses of its investigations. The evidence was obtained from the head of the police, the prefects and provincial police chiefs of the four Sicilian provinces being studied (Palermo, Trapani, Agrigento, Caltanissetta), the Commanding General and other officers of the carabinieri, the chairman of the Sicilian Regional Assembly and the chairmen of the various parliamentary groups in the assembly, the mayors of the capital cities and the presidents (of the provincial councils) of the four above-mentioned provinces, the highest-ranking magistrates, both of the prosecutor's offices and of the courts and tribunals, the representatives of the local bar, and political party and trade union leaders.

The great majority of these statements were given in response to lists of questions that the Commission had prepared, directed at eliciting the following information: (1) the general situation locally regarding Mafia activities, in particular crimes; (2) the development of the phenomenon in recent years, relations with the administrative and political life of the island and links with North American Mafia groups; (3) the attitude of the people; (4) any local action needed to discover more about the phenomenon and the requirements for combating it; (5) behaviour of public officials and of professionals in comparison with Mafia behaviour; (6) cases of sudden or unjustifiable enrichment; (7) results of preventive measures; (8) efficacy of control efforts and the outcome of criminal trials; (9) factual basis of rumours concerning relations between the Mafia and influential persons of the island; (10) the desirability or otherwise of more frequent transfers in the public administration. The responses of the witnesses were always followed by a debate which was often lively, between them and the Commission members.

Besides this principal report and its appendices, the Commission published other volumes in 1971 and 1972, giving a preview of the results of its labours on particular topics on which the investigation could be said to have been completed. In chronological order volumes appeared containing: the 'report on the investigation conducted on the events connected with the untraceability of Luciano Leggio' (nicknamed Liggio)—one of the most fearsome Mafia leaders, who disappeared near the end of 1969 from a Rome clinic at the time when he was supposed to be under arrest and transferred to a place of obligatory residence; the biographies of over ten of the leading Mafia personalities of the postwar period (Genco, Russo, Navarra, Di Carlo,

[1] Another important study, of a sociological character, was conducted for the first Commission by Professor Franco Ferrarotti, Professor of Sociology at the University of Rome.

Leggio, Zizzo, the Grecos, the La Barberas, Buscetta and Mancino); the report (already completed by the previous commission) on the municipality of Palermo; the 'report on the investigation concerning the education system in Sicily'; the 'report on the wholesale markets' (again with particular reference to the case of Palermo); and finally an imposing volume on the 'relations between the Mafia and banditry in Sicily'. In this the mysterious events of the 'Giuliano gang' (1944–50) and of the trial conducted after the death of the famous gang-leader are gone over again, through the questioning both of the police who took part in the struggle against banditry and of the surviving bandits, some of whom are still serving the heavy sentences meted out to them more than twenty years ago. It is a truly impressive historical, judicial and human document.

This diverse collection of documents merits attention (even though it is incomplete), not only because of the authenticity of an investigation accomplished, with very broad powers and authority, through direct interrogation of a large number of the main characters but also because of the broad front on which the Commission sought to proceed in its work. Suffice it to say that the Commission itself, at the beginning of the Fifth Legislature (1968), divided into 12 committees, devoted respectively to sociological and historical investigation, the drug traffic and the connection between the Mafia phenomenon and American gangsterism, judicial matters and examination of the vicissitudes of Mafia criminal trials, investigation of the educational system, rural institution, credit institutions, industrial development, local government (i.e., the Region of Sicily, the provinces and the municipalities), the conduct of the civil service and so forth.

At the commencement of the Sixth Legislature (1972) the Commission was re-established, but of course with new members and a different chairman because of the composition of the parliamentary parties. But due to various difficulties, some inherent in the composition of the Commission, it has barely functioned and has not published any conclusive document up to the present. In fact some members resigned in October 1973, announcing that they considered the Commission to have become useless with no prospects of productive work. On the other hand, it has begun to work intensively again in 1974 and has announced publication of new reports. In reality it is difficult to choose between the opposing arguments for and against the continuation of the Commission. Those in favour agree that the Commission (conventionally known by now as the 'anti-Mafia Commission') still represents a certain restraining influence on the Mafia because it must make them aware of the existence of public interest and political action beyond that exercised by all other state bodies, central or local. The opposition argue that merely being alive without producing concrete results is harmful and that the Commission will end as another symbol of the impotence of the state before the Mafia. The truth is that in order to act effectively all parliamentary commissions would have to consist only of members absolutely independent of party interests and gifted with a superior objectivity—an ideal difficult to achieve given the present level of political battle.

From the Parliamentary Enquiries of the Last Century to the Rebirth of the Sicilian Mafia (1943)

The enquiry on the Sicilian Mafia approved by the Italian Parliament in 1962 and still underway is not the first in Italian history. As early as 1867, only six years after unification and seven after the expulsion of the Bourbons by Garibaldi, the Chamber of Deputies of the Kingdom of Italy felt the need to concern itself with this social scourge which flawed the life of a large part of one of the main regions of the country and cast its baleful shadow over the rest. Yet the enquiry of 1867 (in which the Mafia figured neither as a principal nor a specific subject of investigation and which owed its origins to an insurrection that took place in Palermo) did not squarely face the problem. It considered the events it examined as the product partly of common criminality in a population not yet accustomed to liberal institutions and partly of the underdeveloped economic and social institutions of the island. This resulted in a few laws, limited to the provision of public works and to a few social services and to the postponement of some existing proposals which had included harsher measures for vagrant criminals, whose dangerous activity was already sufficiently apparent.

The second parliamentary enquiry, 'on the social economic conditions of Sicily' came closer to the problems of Mafia activities. It was established under the law of 3 July 1875, which also contained the exceptional measures of public safety aimed at combating what was called 'manutengolismo'— in other words, the abetting of crime through a conspiracy of silence (omertà) which both supported the Mafia crimes and protected the criminals. This enquiry occurred, in fact, following the years in which Mafia activities had reached a peak with an impressive series of property and personal crimes, not to mention the enormous and incomprehensible enrichment of a few persons in a country weighed down by centuries of extreme poverty. The Commission worked admirably from the point of view of the material collected and the large number of persons questioned.[2] But it allowed its

[2] The reports and documents concerning the work of the 1875 commission have recently been published: Archivio centrale dello Stato, L'inchiesta sulle condizioni

conclusions to be influenced by those who saw in the Mafia phenomenon a 'moral disease' for which no other remedy was recognized than to inspire 'a salutary terror' through repressive and police measures. And these measures were indeed applied on a broad scale in the immediately succeeding years, arousing protests and resentment in many quarters. The measures were often applied indiscriminately to people who did not deserve punishment or police action (including very young children). They were also utilized against socialists and revolutionaries not having any connection with the Mafia and they represented discrimination against a single region of the country, considered almost as the natural headquarters of illegality and immorality in social life. On the other hand, the Mafia continued to dominate and prosper as usual, which explains the observation of Renè Alby, French Vice-Consul at Cirgentil, in a dispatch of 6 January 1878 to his ministry concerning an attack on two French citizens that had gone unpunished: 'La Mafia, comme l'hydre antique, argumente une nouvelle force des mutilations mêmes qu'elle subit'.[3]

After numerous other studies and reports in which, for approximately thirty years, the Mafia was examined in the greatest variety of circumstances, a third parliamentary enquiry should be mentioned: 'On the conditions of the peasants in the southern provinces and Sicily', approved in 1907 and carried out until 1910 by an outside expert, Professor Giovanni Lorenzoni.[4] As even the title indicates, this enquiry placed the Sicilian problem in the wider context of the 'southern question', and appropriately revolved around the conditions of the peasants, in whose ground the parasitical and exploitative activities of the Mafia took root. Lorenzoni above all exposed the defects of the rest of Italy in its lack of understanding of the problems of Sicily, the insufficiency of government activity and the ineffectiveness of a policy of pure repression based on the use of special laws.

Nonetheless it was precisely by the use of special laws and the pitiless repression carried out under the direction of the famous prefect Mori that fascism, beginning its decisive action along these lines in 1925, succeeded in crushing Mafia activities in the course of a few years. The islands used as jails and prisons filled beyond imagination and undoubtedly crime decreased

---

sociali ed economiche della Sicilia (1875–76). The inquiry into the social and economic conditions of Sicily (1875–76), edited by Salvatore Carbone and Renato Crispo, with an ntroduction by L. Sandri (Bologna, Cappelli, 1969) (2 vols.).

[3] The dispatch is published in: *Archivio du Ministère des Affaires Etrangères*, Paris, Correspondence politique Italie, Vol. 6, pp. 72–6, quoted in Brancato, op. cit.

[4] This was published beginning in 1910: *Inchiesta parlamentare sulle condizioni dei contadini nelle provincie meridionali e nella Sicilia*, Vol. VI, 'Sicilia', ('Parliamentary inquiry into the conditions of the peasants in the southern provinces and Sicily') Tomo I (parte I and II), Relazione del delegato tecnico Professor Giovanni Lorenzoni, Rome, 1910.

significantly. Repression was accompanied and supported by a patriotic campaign aimed at exalting the virtues of the Sicilian people and contrasting them to the 'noxious weed' of the Mafia. Laws were also passed aimed at agricultural reclamation and colonization of the large estates. But even though inspired by the idea of transforming the environment in which the Mafia had been created and developed, through splitting up the large estates, these efforts stopped at the surface. They were not accompanied by a genuine transformation of rural life, were not supported by the necessary public works (in particular irrigation and roads), and in the end were abandoned because of the Ethiopian venture and the Second World War. Moreover even in 1937 there was a new increase in crime, in which it would probably not have been impossible to recognize the characteristics of the Mafia.

In any case, the historians agree that fascism succeeded only in temporarily weakening the Mafia without eradicating it. This is because the social and economic conditions that gave rise to it remained unchanged, because it was mainly the brigands that infested the rural parishes and the countryside that had been affected and not the 'powerful friends' in the cities, because a great and deep resentment had been created in all those, and their families, who felt themselves unjustly caught in the great repression. So the Mafia was able, for two decades of fascism, to keep the idea of a re-emergence still smouldering under the ashes. Unfortunately—and it is most painful to say it —the moment for this re-emergence came with the landing of the Allies on the island in 1943. Even without making hypotheses about the prior existence during the war of links between Mafia members on the island and United States intelligence services, it is a fact that the allied military government entrusted ninety per cent of the local administration in Sicily to separatists. And Sicilian separatism coincided for the most part with support of the old feudal equilibrium and the maintenance of the old agrarian structure in which the Mafia was supremely interested. In those days even the relations between the Mafia and organized banditry resumed under the common banner of separatism.

Furthermore, once on its feet again, the Sicilian Mafia was able to develop and prosper in the succeeding decades. It would seek from time to time to use political ties according to its interests and become part of different social and economic contexts from those of its native soil. The years immediately following 1943 only mark one of the occasions of the Mafia's periodic rebirth and reassertion of authority. The connection between the Sicilian Mafia and the North American one, notwithstanding the mystery that still surrounds it, is something much more enduring and profound than the events of the 1939–45 war, into which it entered at one point.

Definitions and Essential Characteristics of the Mafia. The Mafia as a Mentality, as an Individual Attitude, as an Association, as an Economic Organization, and as a Power

A definition of the Mafia still seems extremely difficult. The etymological attempts, dominated by the greatest uncertainty when not by downright fantasy, are no help. As a matter of fact they go from the Tuscan 'maffia' meaning poverty, to the French 'maufé' or 'meffier' meaning distrust, to an Arabic word that is said to mean 'protection', to other origins all equally uncertain. It is certain on the other hand that the word came into prominence and spread in Sicily around the middle of the last century with a double meaning: that of one who attracts attention for excellence, enterprise, capability, skill, superiority over others, boastfulness, arrogance and even beauty: and that of occult power, governed by its own secret laws, capable of taking situations in hand and also of righting wrongs, in general a mysterious and powerful association.[5]

In any event, after 1860 when the Mafia began to operate extensively and to show itself through a series of unambiguous signs as a real force, the term developed to mean a 'combination of associations governed by laws contrary to those of the State and of the rest of society, inclined to act for their own purposes with every means (especially including crime), in which the dominant principles of conduct are domination, revenge and above all omertà and silence'. This meaning is so commonly accepted by now that Italian legislators can use the terms 'Mafia' and 'Mafia association' without further definition or specification. Yet, in every instance it is a very complex phenomenon, as is universally recognized, even if some of its manifestations seem elementary and typical in their recurrent cunning and brutality. The complexity not only derives from the multiplicity of its causes which are, as has been said, psychological, ethnic, historical, and social, but is inherent in the wide range of points of view from which one may legitimately speak of the 'Mafia'.

The Mafia is in fact first of all a *mentality*. Because of this it has come to consider social and political organization as something foreign in which one does not take part. Consequently it either ignores such organization completely where this is possible (e.g., in the isolated countryside in the past, where the Mafia member placed himself in the rôle of exclusive determiner

[5] Cf., inter alia, Giuseppe Pitrè, *Usi, costumi, credenze, e pregiudizi del popolo siciliano* (Uses, Customs, Beliefs and Prejudices of the Sicilian People), Palermo 1899, Vol. II, pp. 287 et seq.; Brancato, op. cit. and sources there cited.

of the relationship between landlords and peasants); or bends it to particular ends of economic conquest, exploitation and power (as happens almost always nowadays by means of the multiple connections that the Mafia has established with the holders of administrative power, and, sometimes, with the actual holders of political and judicial power). According to this mentality, national and local powers are external, pre-existent realities it is necessary to reckon with—but only in the sense of making oneself a friend through deception, favours, bribery, and also infiltrating one's own people into the positions and offices of power. It is, therefore, a profoundly anti-democratic and substantially antisocial mentality, as has been pointed out before.

But Mafia mentality believes in pride also, in the sense that it is considered unseemly to turn to the police or the judge to solve one's own or others' problems and to satisfy one's interests. Thus omertà is conceived as a law of honour, in that omertà is specifically concerned with preserving respect for these forms of 'private justice' and guaranteeing them the possibility of future enforcement. Notwithstanding that some claim to recognize morally positive elements in this aspect of the Mafia mentality (which may account also for the popularity of certain well-known literature) and despite the limitations and defects of official justice of which each of us is aware, it cannot be denied that this outlook also indicates a markedly antidemocratic and antisocial mentality.

The Mafia is also an *individual attitude*. Because of this, on individualisticly conceived impulses the Mafia member tends to make arrogant displays of his own power, although availing himself of methods which must remain secret. It is a power that can obviously manifest itself in occasional good works for the 'protected ones', but in its fundamentally egoistic and dis-honest impulse it is almost always directed towards evil. Whoever does not yield to the will of the mafioso must be destroyed, not just to remove an obstacle to Mafia operations, but as a punitive-vindictive and exemplary requirement—a universal warning. In this barbarous attitude the mafioso finds his own moral justification, since he does not recognize the validity of the laws of the state and society. He is accustomed to see their manifesta-tions as forms of injustice and repression, or at least as the invasion of an area which should naturally be reserved for the individual and those associations which the individual considers it proper to create for his own purposes.

The Mafia is also necessarily an *association* or as it has been called, a com-bination of associations governed by similar laws, sometimes mutually allied, sometimes in competition and rivalry with each other. The term 'cosca' was developed in the last century in Sicily for these minor groups;

and so as to designate more precisely the aggregate of associations, the term 'cosche mafiose' was frequently used. In Calabria, where the Mafia is becoming increasingly common the term is 'ndrine'. Another designation is 'family', one that has been commonly used in literature since the end of the last century.

The Mafia has all the essential characteristics of an association—the permanence of the affiliation, division of functions, organization, methods and also the existence of 'chiefs'. Moreover, in some situations in the past (e.g. in the province of Agrigento) swearing in of new members was carried out following a special form dictated by the 'chief of discipline' or by the 'chief of the family' and even linked with a holy image.

A typical characteristic of Mafia associations, at least so it seems, is that of being rather small and restricted in order to facilitate the maintenance of secrecy. This implies a mode of action whereby the Mafia association makes use of a series of outsiders for the prosecution of its ends. So the 'hit men' that the Mafia uses are not always members; and the bandits (members for their part of that other criminal association, the 'gang') were certainly not members. The Mafia repeatedly made use of them in the past, particularly during the time of the bandite Salvatore Giuliano, but it was then quick to disentangle itself when Giuliano had become too flashy and distinctive a phenomenon. Similarly, those administrators or politicians which the Mafia has frequently succeeded in using, even without the former being conscious of it, are not members of the Mafia or even necessarily permanently linked to it. The Mafia, again, is an *economic organization*, in the essential goals that it sets itself. And it is an economic organization of an exquisitely parasitical type, because it produces neither wealth nor work, but occupies all those ganglia of economic life where it is possible to extract a profit. Through mediation imposed with threats or violence it usurps the rôle of trade unions and magistrates in labour relations; through protection of property and persons it usurps the rôle of the police; through overbearingness and bribery it corners land for property speculation; by the same means it obtains monopoly positions in the distribution and sale of products. The economic goals of the Mafia are virtually limitless. Its mentality, its mode of being and its rules render it potentially fit for every type of illicit business and every manner of interference.

Finally, the Mafia is a *power*. The parliamentary 'anti-Mafia' Commission (spring 1972) was forced to this painful conclusion, for it was brought out so many times during the enquiry: 'With its extraordinary adaptability', the conclusions read, 'the Mafia has always known how to survive and prosper even in settings different from that in which it originated; and it has been able to do this to the extent that it has continually represented itself as an exercise of autonomous, extra legal, power and has sought a close connection with all forms of power and in particular with public power, in order to draw near to it, utilize it for Mafia purposes, or interpenetrate its very structures.'

Unfortunately as everyone knows, this extra-legal power, which the Mafia operates, avails itself not only of timely and opportunely acquired 'friendships', not only of bribery and penetration into the nerve centres of the administration, but also of bloodshed and fear. Sometimes it is enough for the Mafia just to have trusted people who are in the lowest positions, but nevertheless useful as observers and for operational purposes. The terror that the Mafia is able to arouse, the fear that many have of becoming victims of this mysterious organization, the widely known difficulty of timely and definitive action by the legal authorities, are in fact the principal and most dynamic sources of the Mafia's power. Professor Ferrarotti (in the study cited above) went to the extent of speaking of an 'acceptance of the Mafia in the average conscience of social groups in which it operates, acceptance that has determined the Mafia's institutionalization'. And in fact it is certainly possible to perceive the characteristics of a 'criminal legal organization' in this system of 'agreements among friends'. Agreements which must, however, be fulfilled on pain of warnings, persecution and even death.

The Mafia and Political Life. The Mafia and Administrative Corruption. The Mafia and Crime

This approach to a definition of the Mafia permits us to have a better understanding of the relations between the Mafia and the collateral phenomena in which it takes root, prospers and lives: for example the relations between the Mafia and politics, between the Mafia and corruption, between the Mafia and crime.

Naturally the parliamentary commission, composed of politicians of all parties from the right to the extreme left, was occupied again and again with the relations between *the Mafia and political life*.[6] Indeed, several times it had to deal through special investigations with accusations against noted Sicilian politicians, even members of parliament, of collusion with individual members of the Mafia, of protection accorded to these, of votes requested, accepted and obtained.

On the whole, even when specific accusations did not prove sufficiently

[6] In 1958–59, at the initiative of the Regional Assembly of Sicily an inquiry into Mafia interference in the political life of the island was conducted by a Commission under the chairmanship of an eminent magistrate.

well grounded, it was widely recognized that the Mafia has always needed to seek out political support, even if discreetly, and that one of the most typical and obvious methods with which it has sought such support has been the promise of votes at election time. Regrettably, it must be recognized that in a multi-party, parliamentary democracy such as Italy where there are many lists of candidates presented at every election, and in addition a so-called 'preferential vote' within the various lists, all forces that are in a position to promise votes are able to rely on the acquisition of political friendships and protection which may be of use to them in the future. Among these forces there may well have been, and there still may be in some cases, the Mafia.

Certainly in a totalitarian regime, whether of left or right, in which the representatives of the people are pre-selected from above or included on the slate of the only party, for which everyone has to vote, a collusion between the Mafia and politics would not only be inconceivable, but the Mafia itself would hardly be able to survive. In this sense the Mafia is also the sad and humiliating price that Italy pays to the democratic principle by which it is governed and intends to continue being governed.

The phenomenon in the administrative field is in any case more serious. Here also, because of elections for regional councillors, provincial councillors and town councillors, the system is analogous to that of the political elections at national level, and presents the same dangers. But the greatest danger is the Mafia's desire to connect itself with the holders of local administrative power, for it is mainly their decisions to which Mafia economic ambitions are tied. One only has to consider the modification of town plans, building permits, licences for markets and so on. The 'anti-Mafia' Commission's attention has rightly focused—and must continue to focus—on this area, the cause of shameful abuses and source of scandalous enrichment.

Even so, it does not appear that the Mafia has sought to enter political or administrative life directly, participating in elections with its own members (except for an almost isolated attempt immediately after the war, in the Genco Russo case). It aims at economic power, and all the other powers only interest it to the extent that they assure attainment of that goal. Here too the Mafia occupies a position of independent power. Many of the political party spokesmen questioned by the Commission of enquiry were in agreement in pointing out that the 'Mafia cannot and will not identify with any political force'. In fact, it is 'a power in itself, an independent secret organization, a fact that involves interests having a logic and dimension apart from the operations, the arrangements and the alignments of politics. The Mafia is a power that searches out contacts with the other powers wherever they are found.'

The relationship between the *Mafia and administrative corruption or opportunism* is also quite clear. The Parliamentary Commission often found itself
asking if certain abuses, certain irregularities, a certain unscrupulous mode
of conduct on the part of public administrators from whom Mafia members
had drawn profits, were the product of Mafia pressure or collusion, or if
they were merely a sign of that decline in administrative morality from which
a large part of Italy suffers in many local administrations. The Commission
asked itself if, in other words, those same favours could not also have been
obtained by non-members of the Mafia and without any characteristic Mafia
methods. Unfortunately a definite response could not usually be given. The
sad reality is that, with the spread of corruption and in general with the
relaxing of certain restraints of caution and decorum the Mafia, to the
extent that it is an organization devoted to economic gain, has open to it an
easier passage to the fulfilment of its ends.

The same could be said for forms of misgovernment other than corruption
in the narrow sense. Italy is swarming with minor public agencies of every
kind. The region of Sicily has been a field especially fertile for their experiments. These agencies have been created at every turn to solve the most
varied problems. And when, instead of solving them they have created new
ones or simply showed themselves useless, they are left to go on just the
same, adding yet more agencies to those established in the past, which likewise are rarely abolished. Here also it is difficult to see if the meddling of
speculators, *arrivistes* and profiteers from public funds is linked to the Mafia
or is an autonomous form in common with general opportunism and laxity.
In this respect it is not out of place to note that the Mafia is a phenomenon
characteristic of and exclusive to capitalist society, or that society which at
least in certain sectors preserves the principles or institutions of the so-called
mixed economy and of capitalist economy. It is clear, in fact, that in a state
with an exclusively socialist economy, in which land has been collectivized,
in which it is not possible for real property to exist beyond certain minimal
limits, in which production, distribution and the market are entrusted
exclusively to the state, a Mafia organization would not even have the
opportunity of birth and in any case would soon be discovered and exposed.
The Mafia is one of those purely parasitical forms of life that, as far as is
known, have no chance of success in countries with a rigidly communist
economic structure.

Finally the relations between *the Mafia and crime* were also sufficiently
clarified by the Commission. It could not fail to establish that wherever the
Mafia operates, one encounters crime for that reason alone. The illicit acts
committed by these illicit associations are serious by nature, and in any case
contemporary penal laws in the countries of continental Europe embrace

such a number of specific criminal acts as not to leave room outside of criminal law for serious illicit activities: the only case in Italy is monetary fraud which is punished only by an administrative fine. Cases of forged documents is an exception to this.

The Mafia needs every kind of crime in order to operate; crimes against the person, from threats to kidnapping to murder; property crimes, from cattle theft to robbery and extortion; crimes against public safety such as intentional fires; crimes against the public economy and public health, such as clandestine butchering and other infractions of this type; crimes against the public administration, such as the omission of official acts, abuse of office, betrayal of official secrets, tampering with bidding and bribery; crimes against the administration of justice, such as perjury or refusal to testify and tampering with witnesses. Most of the time the mafioso does not commit these crimes directly himself, but he is the instigator and organizer, and as such is liable under Italian criminal law as the principal participant. At the same time this justifies the definition of Mafia associations as 'criminal conspiracies'.

But the problem is not one of establishing the mafioso's criminal *liability*, but of identifying and discovering him. This is sometimes extremely difficult because the 'law of silence' holds sway, whether by virtue of an old custom that is very difficult to eradicate or because of fear. Because of this the failures to indict and the frequent acquittals, even if accompanied by the qualification 'for insufficient evidence', have provoked many protests. This has also made it necessary for the state to act not according to the provisions of the criminal law, but according to those of the preventive measures authorized by the previously cited laws of 1956 and 1965, based on rumour, notoriety and well-grounded suspicion of engaging in antisocial activities which do not require proof of a crime.

A particular form of criminality connected with the Mafia is 'banditry', extinguished in Italy around 1950 with the killing (in his sleep by another bandit working for the police) of the famous Salvatore Giuliano. As I have already indicated, the Italian Parliamentary Commission dedicated particular attention and a special study to this sector. Although the phenomenon is no longer recent, its seriousness was sufficient to justify attention for its own sake: Giuliano had held the forces of the state in check for over five years and was responsible for 430 homicides. But above all the interest of the Commission was legitimate because of the obvious connections between the Giuliano gang and the Mafia. The conclusion of the investigation, difficult to deny, can be found in the words of the original police officers and men who participated in numerous operations against the gang: 'Giuliano was finished when the Mafia decided to abandon him'; and it decided to abandon him 'because he had become a sensational phenomenon which departed from the characteristics of Mafia organization'.

Origin, Causes and Evolution of the Mafia Phenomenon in Sicily

The search for remedies against Mafia activity, the most important assignment of the Parliamentary Commission of Enquiry, obviously presupposes an identification of its causes: a difficult subject, because even if (despite recurrent arguments) it is easy to single out these causes within a complex of ethnic, psychological and historical factors and social and cultural backwardness, it remains difficult to reach an equally convincing analysis.

There is a most interesting and significant point which merits immediate attention: the Sicilian Mafia never extended all over the island. It began and it developed in the provinces of Western Sicily (Palermo, Agrigento, Trapani e Caltanissetta), just touching the province of Messina in the part closest to Palermo, but leaving the provinces of Eastern Sicily (Messina, Catania, Enna, Siracusa and Ragusa) for a long time unmarked, at least until recently when the Mafia spread its tentacles throughout Italy. Obvious these latter provinces have experienced various forms of crime, including violent crime (it is enough to recall the very sad present condition in this respect of the city of Catania), but the forms themselves are not clearly traceable, at least up to now, to authentic Mafia associations. It is not difficult to grasp the reasons for this localization. In the western part of Sicily, when the Mafia began to make a name for itself round the middle of the last century (in a highly visible form from 1860 onwards) large estates were very common and the population was concentrated in relatively few cities and towns. These consisted of agglomerations that were either difficult to get to or situated in the midst of broad expanses of uninhabited land crossed by mule tracks that were impassable for most of the year. In this situation the dominant figure was the feudal owner, the greatest holder of wealth in the village and the only possible dispenser of a part of this wealth to the miserable labourers in the fields. There was almost a complete lack of a middle class to act as a balancing force between the two extremes and to prevent as Brancato has well put it, 'The lowest class being brutalized and the highest's feeding an unrestrained ambition to predominate'. Every form of intermediate task (which were admittedly necessary) were taken on by the Mafia with its administrators, renters and overseers. This was especially so when the owner of the large estate was away and needed someone to make sure of the work of the badly payed labourers, to take care of collecting revenues and to defend his ownership.

The Mafia profited from this situation to the extent of supplanting the landowner in the exercise of his rights and blackmailing him, imposing absolute freedom of action for the Mafia as the price for its presence and services. Its domain extended to a monopoly of irrigation water, mills, storage facilities, small agricultural credit, and retail commerce in agricultural products. In Eastern Sicily, on the other hand, especially along the coast, centres of habitation were much more frequent, communications were better, and small and medium sized landholdings had long since developed.

It is clear therefore how this detailed consideration of the two different situations leads to the recognition of a primary economic and social cause of the Mafia. Next to this should be placed more narrow historical and political causes. It has been stated that the beginning of a genuinely dangerous Mafia organization may be assigned to the year 1860, that is to the end of Bourbon rule and the integration of Sicily into an Italy united at that time. This transition from almost absolute monarchy to constitutional monarchy in a country relatively lacking in liberal traditions faced the large estate owners, and those they had always used, with the necessity of organizing their own defence against feared social upheavals. But since these not only did not occur, and there was not even a renewal of the economic and social structures of the country, there was time and opportunity to become organized for stridently conservative purposes.

In this way, especially in the defence of ownership and the struggle against the feared innovations seen in the new royal and parliamentary power, an agricultural Mafia (Mafia of the pastures and Mafia of the gardens) was established, an enemy of every outside interference. This gradually developed into opposition towards all official forms of state power. To this must be added the consideration that in the last decades of the last century and the first decades of this, the acquisition of vast agricultural properties and the expansion of lands already owned were typical aspirations of many Sicilians (and not only Sicilians) because, among other reasons, of the greater 'dignity' that was associated with such holdings. A rich agricultural middle class thus came into land ownership alongside the aristocracy and frequently it had to pay tribute to the Mafia, which was, within certain limits, sometimes able to present itself as the guardian of the interests of the peasants. Furthermore, the expansion of agricultural holdings led to the strengthening of those Mafia means of defence that had proved useful. The first agricultural fortunes of several mafiosi were created in this period.

We leave the succinct description of the results of this situation to the report of the Parliamentary Commission of Enquiry:

The environment is that of a vast territory relatively near the capital of the island geographically, but in reality an unknown and isolated hinterland in which peasants, small-holders, sharecroppers and renters, shepherds and labourers live. Notables and nobles remain in Palermo and entrust the estates to administrators and large renters. The overseers see to the rest, guaranteeing respect for the law and customs and maintaining the social and political order which is easily disturbed by the fundamental agricultural question. The Mafia is naturally ranged in support of the conservation of existing social structures. It is indeed in a position to defend the feudal arrangement, but does so in order to exploit it for its own purposes, sometimes against the landowners, always against the peasants' movement.

And in fact, there are significant increases in wealth which permit all the Mafia large-scale renters, for example from the Corleonese, to pass in time from the status of have-nots to that of owners of more or less vast expanses of land situated in the very estates previously administered by themselves.

Rural social conflicts, which as we know have constituted one of the fundamental bottlenecks in the development of our country, assume particular forms in Sicily because the Mafia acts as defender of social immobility, using violence and other illegal means.

Nevertheless, despite the opposition of the Mafia, the large estate was abolished and the lands distributed to the peasants; but the Mafia has not disappeared because it has been able to extend its activities towards other sectors, gradually transplanting itself from the archaic structures of the country-side to the new ones of the city and industrial society.

For the sake of completeness, it is important to add to this brief review of the economic, historical and social causes of the Mafia phenomenon, the fact that contemporary scholars are much less inclined to recognize ethnic origins based on differences between the Sicilians, or of a part of them (or of the inhabitants of Calabria, where forms of the Mafia are also certainly established), and the rest of the population of Italy, where as a matter of fact neither poverty nor isolation have ever led to phenomena similar to the Mafia. The Commission of Enquiry itself generally shrank from accepting suggestions of this type. Even so one must consider that, at least from the psychological point of view, a certain position not absolutely contrary to some elements connected with the idea of the Mafia can be observed in the attitudes of some Sicilians of the greatest variety of social background. For example, not a few of those questioned by the Commission tended either to diminish the importance of the Mafia phenomenon or not to accept that one must speak of 'Mafia' in referring to episodes that the witnesses tended to consider episodes of 'common criminality'. Perhaps some may fear that there is a risk of confusing 'Sicilianism', understood as veneration of friendship and regional solidarity, with Mafia characteristics. One almost has the impression of a desire to eliminate every discriminatory theory about Sicily,

if not in fact to condone those expressions which can be positively interpreted as affirmations of individuality and even of greater justice.

It is certain in any case that the economic and social cause, in itself the
most valid as far as the origins of the phenomenon go, is also the most
useful for explaining the survival of the Mafia in contemporary times in spite
of intervening changes in the society. With the collapse of the agricultural
economy that occurred in Italy following the Second World War, the Mafia
maintained to the full its aim of parasitical exploitation of situations and
went on to apply methods of domination and bribery in the new forms of
economic activity into which it moved. Basic among these activities were
construction, acquisition of development property, wholesale markets, water
supply, public works, and sometimes bank credit, funerals, and cemeteries.
The Parliamentary Commission of Enquiry properly concentrated its efforts
particularly on these aspects of the Mafia phenomenon. It has not yet been
possible to complete some of these particular investigations, but those that
have been completed have produced impressive results concerning the
importance of Mafia infiltration and the resulting riches and power obtained
by the mafiosi.

Suffice it to recall what was discovered about property speculation in
Palermo and about the wholesale markets in the same city. In Palermo under
growing Mafia pressure, even if the individuals are not always identifiable,
gradual modifications of the town plan have been accomplished that in the
end have resulted in an increase of maximum permissible building density
from 7 cubic metres per square metre of land to 21 metres per metre, which
is one of the highest permissible densities in Italy. (A national law of August
1967, for that matter, set the maximum permissible density for urban construction at 3·5 metres.) Unusual variations, going beyond even the absurd
limits of the plan modifications, have been authorized through illegitimate
licences. Official eyes have been closed to other violations. From this
monstrous property speculation, permitted by the municipal administrators
on the greatest variety of pretexts, the simultaneous ruination of the city
and the fortunes of several Mafia chiefs have resulted.

The studies and investigations carried out on the wholesale markets (produce, meat, fish) have produced information of even greater value to
criminologists. In these markets the situation is dominated by a criminal
environment: a high incidence of convicted criminals among the traders;
the presence of rival gangs; not uncommon outbreaks of bloodshed; serious,
unrelenting intimidation of the most important users of the products such
as hotels and institutions. In the produce market alone there are 18 persons
who have been both convicted of crimes and reported for criminal conspiracy, 64 producers, dealers and retailers placed under special preventive

measures, 38 commission agents (out of 139) with serious records of offences from assault to robbery. The situation is similar in the meat market, where ten years ago (on the occasion of the first local administrative enquiries) no fewer than 51 butchers were found to be under preventive measures.

These people have helped to establish a generally criminal atmosphere and a system that many authorities prior to the Parliamentary Commission had been forced to define as 'made up of pushing, grabbing and illegality'. This included, among other things, unauthorized entry to and occupation of the market without either the required licence or the payment of market fees; arbitrary exclusion of individual producers and co-operatives; impossibility of ascertaining the name of the seller in cases of complaints about the quality or health conditions of the merchandise sold; absence of all possibilities of either statistical or price supervision. On top of all this, there are enormous profits made at the expense of the collectivity and to the advantage of many traders in the market, who nevertheless reported derisory incomes when it came to paying taxes, or else did not report at all. Despite the praiseworthy efforts of a few, the Municipality of Palermo and the managements of the markets turned out to be largely responsible for this situation: for not having expeditiously attended to the carrying out of the plans for building a new market; for not having improved the existing markets and completed their facilities; for not having enforced the regulations on licences, stalls and charges; for not having amended the regulations themselves in response to the serious situation discovered; for not mounting an adequate information and surveillance campaign aimed at getting rid of the persons with the worst records. In a word, at the conclusion of the investigations the Commission had to point out that 'the wholesale market sector in Palermo is permeated with the Mafia phenomenon and it is dominated by pressure groups concentrated in a few families and in genuine gangs'; and that 'the presence of the public administration in this sector has been characterized by failings and favouritism from which the Mafia of the markets has benefited greatly'.

The Commission also made efforts to extend its investigations to other fields of activity of the 'new Mafia': cigarette smuggling and drug trafficking. The completed researches (mostly concerning individual figures in the Mafia and particularly vicious homicides) demonstrate convincingly the rôle played by the Sicilian Mafia in the drug field in 1945–62. It was not possible to get reliable and unambiguous information on the succeeding periods. But the opinions gathered by the investigators generally suggest that the Mafia still plays a primary rôle in the drug trade. In the field of smuggling, on the other hand, although it was not able to complete its investigations, the Commission was of the opinion that:

Without any shadow of doubt the phenomenon in Sicily is not disassociated from that of the Mafia, under cover of which it lives and prospers. Naturally the Sicilian smuggling organizations are not identical in every case with the Mafia gangs, but at the same time there is no lack among the smugglers of true Mafia elements, who tend to monopolize the organization, direction and high-level financing of this activity. The evidence indicates a particularly interesting close connection between the zones of influence of specified Mafia gangs and zones of operation of certain smuggling organizations, as well as between episodes of fighting that occur simultaneously in the Mafia world and in the world of smuggling.

All in all, as the concluding report of the Commission points out:

Criminal activity (with specific reference to smuggling and the drug traffic) is no longer an instrument for maintaining positions of prestige already gained, nor the indirect means of obtaining large and illicit profits; but it is in itself a source of gain. The efficiency and the strictness of Mafia organization, the Sicilian underworld's international connections, and the considerable margins of profit in drug trafficking explain the ease with which the Mafia has been able to move into the field and achieve important positions.

Through these positions, connected with large-scale urban speculation or the international traffic itself, the Mafia has conquered new and more solid economic positions and is presumably now even better prepared and more powerful. Atrocious crimes, inexplicable in terms of specific motive or reason but certainly committed by the Mafia, have occurred in the last few years while the Commission was at work and in spite of the fact that many mafiosi were in prison or compulsory residence outside of Sicily. Mafia assassination activities have even reached high-ranking magistrates, something almost unheard of before. The head prosecutor in Palermo (one of the leading witnesses question by the Commission) was assassinated along with his chauffeur in broad daylight in a street in Palermo on 5 May 1971. The case is still shrouded in mystery.

Even if in its progress and modernization, the Mafia has shown that it counts most of all on the utilization of connections and friendships established with the wielders of public power, it still maintains its own soldiers, according to the needs of the moment, ready to act against anyone. In fact it strikes with iron and fire against rivals with whom it has not reached agreement; in situations where the agreements have not been respected; against anyone whom it feels has betrayed it or could betray it in the future; and against investigators who are too bothersome or who come too close to the discovery of some of the mysteries. The disappearance of a journalist who closely investigates Mafia criminal organizations is one of the most worrying and repugnant facts of recent years.

Remedies Against the Mafia and Ways to Combat it

A close examination of the whole of the enquiry papers shows that the Parliamentary Commission perceived the remedies against the Mafia in four categories: cultural, educational and civil measures; economic, political and administrative measures; criminal justice measures; police preventive measures. One can practically say that this is a classic plan of action, reflecting all the theories usually invoked in the fight against crime.

At the educational, cultural and civil level the Commission particularly dwelt on the 'investigation regarding the educational system in Sicily', dealing thoroughly with the problem on every level: elementary schools, auxiliary schools, professional schools, private schools, and University. While it found an active Mafia presence in school construction, in preserving unnecessary schools, in the utilization of state grants, in the failure to acquire properties planned for schools, it found in contrast a school atmosphere not very conscious and not very active in the face of Mafia penetration. Many Mafia influences are intertwined and confused with a well-rooted system of 'clientelism' and personal influence, unfortunately characteristic of Sicilian society in general, and not only of Sicilian society. The Commission concluded that a basic educational campaign has yet to be undertaken, and that the problem of Mafia power 'must be confronted as a national problem, the solution to which must constitute an integral part of the more general problem of the South; and it is this above all that must be confronted with the commitment of the entire nation . . . It requires all the commitment of the professors and students, making use of inter-disciplinary methods and research groups, in order to provide a critical knowledge of the Mafia phenomenon . . . The school can counter authoritarian power, overbearingness and the Mafia tradition with democratic participation, the new generation's craving for progress and social justice.'

The suggestions for administrative remedies in the educational sector, as in other important sectors, are more precise. Proposals for the school include: the sharp reduction in the discretionary powers of the regional education commissioner, a stricter delimitation of national and regional areas of competence, the issuing of norms to effectuate the regional statute, more oversight, effective fulfilment by the schools of their obligations to children in the more remote areas, modernization, up-grading and definition of the legal status of teaching personnel hired by the region, abolition of schools that have become unnecessary, stimulation of school building with the help of a simplification of procedures, and so on.

In the grave area of the wholesale markets the Commission (as several local commissions in the preceding decades had already done in vain) also indicated the need for a whole series of legislative, social and administrative actions: reform of the law to provide a way to prevent persons accustomed to domination and parasitical profits from moving into the markets, and to eliminate them from the business of trader; expansion and transfer of some markets to permit sufficient selling spaces so as to ensure competitiveness; strict standards in the revision and granting of licences and in the reconstitution of market commissions; encouragement of producer associations and the exposure of pseudo-co-operatives; installation of facilities for conservation of the products; and so on.

More generally in the field of local administration, beginning with the region, the Commission recommended stricter controls, less discretionary power, and strict reporting of abuses. At this point the problem emerges with that of crime suppression; the measures for which must fall as heavily on administrators unfaithful to their duties as on genuine Mafia crimes.

While it is still too soon to have an accurate overview of the suppression of crimes attributable to administrators, it has on the other hand been possible to devote various studies and observations to Mafia crimes. These are very serious common crimes varying from extortion to kidnapping and homicide. Thus there are no problems of reform of the criminal law needed in this area. However, grave practical problems of enforcing criminal justice do exist. First of all, trials of Mafia members collide with a traditional wall of silence, because of this one can never get worthwhile testimony concerning some episodes. Rarest of the rare are the people who 'have seen' or who 'have recognized'. This can well be attributed to several causes: the simple advantage of not getting involved in dangerous and certainly anxiety-provoking affairs; 'omertà', that is a mentality that accepts or even approves the system of not aiding the authorities in the solution of cases involving private 'settlements of accounts', a mentality that considers it downright dishonourable to turn to the police; and finally the genuine fear that these consortia of pitiless criminals evoke. This silence is in any case a big factor in the criminal process. It makes investigation difficult by forcing the authorities to rely on circumstantial evidence and suspicions, but most important, it makes convictions difficult.

However, the high number of acquittals of Mafia members also depends on other factors. The investigations conducted in 1965, when police interrogation of suspects still existed in Italy (it was abolished by the Law of 5 December 1969), revealed a systematic judicial distrust of all confessions made to the police. This was carried to the point in judicial opinions where all declarations made to the police were called mere 'extra-judicial disclosures', while those made to magistrates were called 'judicial declarations'.

These were regarded completely differently from the 'disclosures', in terms of their recognized probative value. A certain conflict between the police and magistrates in Sicily has always existed. Even in 1868, at the time of the first campaigns against the mafiosi, police authorities complained of the attitude of the magistracy, always zealous in punishing police offences against prisoners.

Of course the problem of judicial attitudes towards 'police evidence' do not just concern Sicily. Sensational acquittals of mafiosi accused of serious violent crimes have also been handed down by mainland courts, to which the cases had been transferred by the Court of Cassation because of 'legitimate suspicion' of the local atmosphere. The magistrates justify themselves by arguing that the standards of proof are the same for everybody and that it is not possible to use a different standard for suspected members of the Mafia from that used for other defendants. But even here, especially as regards the jurors in the courts of assize, the effectiveness of intimidation cannot be excluded. In the Leggio trial at Bari in 1969, the jurors, the presiding judge, and the prosecuting attorney all received this letter:

> You people of Bari have not understood or rather you do not want to understand what Corleone signifies and what the Men of Corleone are capable of doing. You in particular are judging honest gentlemen of Corleone, whom the carabinieri and police have accused out of whimsy. We only want to warn you that if a gentleman from Corleone is convicted, you will be blown up, you will be destroyed, you will be slaughtered, and the same will happen to your families. We believe we have made ourselves clear.
>
> 'NO ONE MUST BE CONVICTED OTHERWISE YOU AND YOUR FAMILIES WILL BE CONDEMNED TO DEATH. A SICILIAN PROVERB SAYS: A MAN WARNED IS HALF SAVED. ALL YOU HAVE TO DO NOW IS BE JUDICIOUS.'

The prosecutor still demanded that Leggio be sentenced to life imprisonment, but the court set him free. What hidden weight might those threats have had on this decision?

The difficult situation in bringing mafiosi to justice, especially the major obstacle created by omertà and silence, some time ago led Italian legislators to favour a system of police measures, now called 'preventive measures' (to emphasize that their application is no longer assigned to police administrative commissions but to the courts, and at the same time to indicate their difference from the 'security measures' of the penal code). These preventive measures are less restrictive than custodial penalties (the most serious is the obligatory residence in a place, at one time called 'compulsory domicile' and 'house-arrest') and do not require proof that the person subject to them has committed a crime. An appraisal of the conduct, style of life, activities and financial resources is enough, and it is enough if common opinion or the police single out the subject as inclined to crime, notoriously involved in illicit traffic, or dangerous to public safety or morality. One school of Italian constitutional thought considers these measures unconstitutional, but this has not been the opinion of the Constitutional Court since the application of the most serious of the measures was entrusted to the courts with rights of appeal and review in Cassation.

The police generally consider that very extensive application of these measures has given, and can continue to give, satisfactory results in the fight against the Mafia. However, they recommend parallel supporting provisions, such as a series of auxiliary prohibitions and property measures. They also demand a strict registration of all recognized Mafia figures, and they go so far as to request the same for relatives, given that it has been shown to be a common practice to employ relatives in the civil service or other important offices. Most recently it has had to be recognized that compulsory residence has produced the undesirable side-effect of introducing Mafia methods into parts of Italy, including the North, which had previously been free of them. The mafioso brings his family and other friends arrive taking advantage of the unconditional freedom of movement in Italy. New headquarters for crime are thus created, as has been seen recently in kidnappings for ransom. Many municipalities refuse to accept the mafiosi. Thus the entire execution of these measures of prevention needs to be re-examined.

Finally the police demand that special surveillance of mafiosi who have returned from a compulsory residence be made obligatory. The desirability of eliminating the maximum limits of the special measures now established by law has even been outlined, bringing them closer in this respect to the security measures, for which the law in Italy fixes only a minimum term, leaving the issue of termination to the court's judgement of whether or not the subject is still dangerous. Yet even here one cannot go beyond certain limits. A minimum standard of proof and the necessity of convincing the judge apply equally to these measures. Here also judicial errors are possible, as in criminal trials. There is evidence for these fears in many decisions where preventive measures have not been applied, or where that quality denoting a mafioso is not found in someone whom the police, on the other hand, were convinced of involvement.

The conclusion is as follows: if one cannot give up an intensification of the police and penal measures, one still cannot depend entirely on them. Thorough social reform, reform of the administrative machinery and a reform in habits are indispensable.

Difficulties and Complexities of the Struggle Against the Mafia

We have already used the expression 'new Mafia'. In reality it is the result, as Brancato has shown, of an evolution of the forms and modes of Mafia activity, but not of its essential nature—which has always remained the same. But as Brancato also recognized, this evolution has made the fight against the Mafia even more difficult than in the past, because of the levels of power and criminal unscrupulousness it has reached and because of the capacity it has demonstrated for penetrating and influencing the public and private bodies on which the life of the people depends. Beyond all else, the Sicilian Mafia has lately shown a tendency to create its own points of reference and support outside the island, in the rest of Italy. It has enlarged the field of its operations beyond the European continent of North America, where it boasts of the greatest possibilities for mutual relations and understanding and whence it receives influences and stimuli that have probably helped it to modify its methods and activities.

Regarding Mafia territorial expansion in Italy in recent years, it is sufficient to recall that demands have been made in Parliament for the extension of the Commission's powers to Calabria and, most recently, the enactment of an 'anti-Mafia law' for Naples. As usual the Mafia succeeds in confusing itself in the public mind with the established underworld in Naples and other cities, thus concealing its precise outlines.

The complexity of the phenomenon of the Mafia has been matched by the increasing complexities of investigating it, of identifying the phenomenon against which one must and can react with some hope of success, of implementing the all-out war that a modern, civilized state must wage against this pack. This worried passage from the conclusions of the Parliamentary Commission of Enquiry in the spring of 1972 helps to indicate the complexity of the task:

> The Mafia of today is no longer the Mafia of yesterday; over time the phenomenon has shown itself to adapt to social, economic and political transformations. With its extraordinary adaptability, the Mafia has always known how to survive and prosper even in settings different from that in which it originated; and it has been able to do this to the extent that it has continually represented itself as an exercise of autonomous, extra-legal power and has sought a close connection with all forms of power and in particular with public power, in order to draw near to it, utilise it for Mafia purposes, or interpenetrate its very structures.
>
> This search for connections represents the element peculiar to the Mafia in comparison with other forms of extra-legal power and naturally it also appears

in current manifestations of the phenomenon. Indeed, in most recent times, the greater and frequently tumultuous speed of social and institutional change has accentuated the need for the Mafia constantly to find or create new forms of relationship with the social and public structures. Similarly, the natural tendency of the Mafia to adapt itself to the environment in which it operates leads it, in a society undergoing transformation (like the present one in contrast to the former agricultural one) to modernise its operational norms with equal frequency, to modify them radically where necessary and to select according to circumstance the paths that appear most favourable. The Mafia of today, therefore, is not only different from that of the past; it appears constantly different from itself, in a tangle of heterogeneous and even contradictory manifestations. Thus the Commission, born to study a phenomenon considered relatively circumscribed in its territorial dimensions and operational articulations, has found itself faced with a subject of investigation that manifests vague and frequently new outlines, such as to pose further research obligations every time that a conclusion was thought to have been reached. The Mafia, in other words, has never lent itself to being photographed in a stationary pose, but has appeared, especially in recent times, as a phenomenon in continuous motion, difficult to grasp, but one that it was still necessary to follow if one wanted to understand the innermost essence.

In conclusion, it seems to me that from the criminological and politico-penal point of view the complexity of the struggle against the Mafia merits three considerations of a general order.

The first has to do with the rather limited importance in this field of the disappearance of the social and economic circumstances that historically were at the root of the phenomenon. According to many of the enquiries conducted in the second half of the last century and in the first years of the present one, in order to eliminate the Mafia phenomenon it would have been enough to provide—again quoting Brancato—

> for the construction of housing and roads and means of communications which, rendering the countryside less arid and harsh and favouring human as well as commercial relations among the population of the rural centres, would have improved customs and therefore driven off the spirit of the Mafia. But as the history of these last years demonstrates, the Mafia in the course of its evolution has instead greatly strengthened itself as it has moved away from the rural centres and the area of large estates to assault the centres of greater and more modern economic and productive activities.

This seems to me a point truly worthy of consideration by the criminologist. Even if it can be shown that at the root of a criminal phenomenon there is an ascertainable cause, this does not mean that elimination of that cause can suffice to eliminate the phenomenon once this has developed into habitual behaviour and given birth to a particular psychology. The criminality of the same or similar social groups can move on to different areas and interests.

On the other hand, some of the characteristic methods of Mafia activity have lamentably been adopted on a broad scale in many areas of southern Italy (Calabria, Apulia and most importantly Campania). I am referring to the explicit and implicit extortions, enterprises and other economic activities, which are given no chance to work or develop except upon payment of premiums and tolls to local blackmailers.

Following these findings regarding, on one hand, the evolution of the Mafia towards different interests from its original ones and, on the other hand, the imitators that certain Mafia methods have unfortunately found in other parts of Italy, one could perhaps doubt the prevailing theory of the etiology to the Mafia phenomenon, generally ascribed as we have seen to the large estate and to economic characteristics of certain parts of Sicily. But historical investigation and at least the original locale of all the most typical elements of the true Mafia phenomenon support the dominant etiological interpretation.

The second consideration concerns the difficulty of isolating the struggle against the current manifestations of the Mafia from the context of the struggle to achieve on a general plane a system that is more civilized, more democratic, more independent of the sway of wealth and power. As we have seen, the Mafia of today profits from the economic and moral weakness of the elements it enters into contact with. It injects itself into the elementary necessities of a lot of people's lives, and into the chronic difficulty of jobs. When it assures work to someone, it makes him a 'friend' and binds him to it for the future. It injects itself into the electoral ambitions of politicians and seeks to bind them with the promise and the guarantee of votes. It injects itself into others' craving for money, and gains by bribery what it cannot gain by other means. But the need for jobs, electoral ambitions and craving for wealth are not isolated phenomenon of the soil that gave root to the Mafia. In fact political and administrative corruption, hiring motivated by hopes for votes and aspirations for power, dishonesty, laxity in the management of local governments and bribery infect not only the entire region of Sicily but contemporary Italian life in every region, as well as life in many other countries, in Europe and elsewhere.[7]

How then can one expect success in prosecuting the battle against the Mafia if the evil plant of corruption is not eradicated from the entire country? The Mafia basically does nothing but take advantage of the moral defects

[7] A courageous and precise analysis of these vices is found in the report that Senator Giuseppe Alessi (President of the Region of Sicily in the optimistic years after the war) made to the Commission during the Fourth Legislature: *Mafia ed enti locali: il Comune, la Provincia, la Regione* ('The Mafia and Local Governments: the Municipality, the Province, the Region').

of a system in a more unscrupulous and menacing manner than other speculators eager for wealth. Only if these defects are eliminated from the framework of the entire national life can the problem of the fight against the Mafia be isolated and reduced to a fight against intimidating and violent methods.

The criminological lesson one draws from this consideration is very simple: the battle against determined forms of criminality can never ignore the general context of the life of a country and can never succeed if this is not surrounded by an authentic moral firmness, capable of liberating the society in general from those faults on which criminality feeds.

The third consideration concerns the demonstrated need for a high level of technical capability in the planning and execution of social welfare programmes and administrative actions directed at removing the causes of, or opportunities for, criminal conduct. We have seen that amongst the preventive measures against the Mafia rightly recommended by the Parliamentary Commission of Enquiry, a series of legislative and administrative provisions were designed both to bring about more healthy economic progress and development in Sicily and to impose and enforce order in certain activities, with the aim of removing them from the domain of the Mafia. The suggestions on the reorganization of the markets are an example of this. It still needs to be said that no measure can succeed if it is not conceived, adopted and put into effect through the collaboration of truly competent and able minds with the will not to rest at the surface, nor to be content with action for the sake of mere appearance. In the postwar period the Italian state has spent huge amounts on the creation of agencies for the improvement of conditions in Sicily or for public works of various kinds, sometimes with specific reference to sectors where the Mafia had shown itself, such as forests or mining. But some of these agencies have merely consumed public funds, if not even become new channels for the enrichment of the Mafia. Indeed many works have been carried out in name only in order to justify the expenditure of the money: a prime example, as the enquiry has shown, was the reforestation of great expanses of land and the modernization of the sulphur mines. An effective intervention must deal with the basic issues of the situation and it must be supported by controls over the utilization of funds, by technical competence and by a genuine will to work for the public good.

So let the all-out, ceaseless war continue against the most noticeable criminal activities characteristic of the Mafia. However, it must be born in mind that a complete extermination of the Mafia phenomenon can only be pursued with a hope of success in the context of a real moral and social transformation of the whole of Italian life.

AN ANNOTATED BIBLIOGRAPHY OF THE WRITINGS OF LEON RADZINOWICZ

Keith O. Hawkins

In this bibliography I have attempted to gather together references to the books, essays, public lectures and newspaper articles written by Leon Radzinowicz, and by means of brief annotations to give some idea of the substance and scope of their contents.

In three respects, however, I have been selective. First, with one exception, I have not included book reviews. Secondly, while the bibliography is intended to give a clear picture of Leon Radzinowicz's own writings, it is not intended to give more than a general view of his other contribution to publications in criminology in his capacity as editor of the works of others. This contribution has been very substantial. Leon Radzinowicz was joint editor (with J. W. C. Turner) of *The Journal of Criminal Science* (2 vols.) and the pamphlet series of *English Studies in Criminal Science*. He also edited volumes 1–7 of the *English Studies in Criminal Science* with J. W. C. Turner, and was sole editor of volumes 8–10. With volume 11, the series became known as the *Cambridge Studies in Criminology*, with Leon Radzinowicz as general editor. The most recently published of the Cambridge Studies, 'Who Becomes Delinquent' by D. J. West and D. P. Farrington, is the thirty-fourth volume to appear. When acting as editor, Leon Radzinowicz has supplied introductory remarks in the form of Editorial Notes, Prefaces, Forewords, etc. I have not given references to these, except where he has in effect written what amounts to an essay on the general subject. Thirdly, Leon Radzinowicz has, of course, published books and articles in Polish, French, Italian and other languages. I have, however, begun the bibliography with his earliest work in English.

A few of the shorter articles which bear titles sufficient to give an indication of their contents have not been annotated. I have arranged the references chronologically by date of publication and alphabetically within years.

A. BOOKS

—— *A history of English criminal law and its administration from 1750* (London: Stevens, 1948—)

Vol. 1: *The movement for reform* (1948)

'The studies of which Dr. Radzinowicz in this volume gives us the first fruits,' wrote Lord Macmillan in his Foreword to volume 1, 'mark a new departure in research. Hitherto the history of our criminal law has been expounded mainly from the juristic standpoint of statutes, decided cases and text-writers; the important and copious sources of information to be found in the national collections of State Papers have not been utilised adequately or at all. The dominant purpose of the present treatise is to set out the results of the investigations which Dr. Radzinowicz has undertaken in this largely unexplored field, in order to display the gradual growth of public opinion which has led to the reforms brought about by modern criminal legislation. With the help of the material thus gathered he has been able to exhibit in the most vivid form the process of law in the making.'

This volume surveys the place of capital punishment in the eighteenth-century criminal law and illustrates penal policy by reference to developments in the law of larceny. It goes on to consider the administration of capital punishment in eighteenth-century penal practice, including the application of capital statutes by the courts, the commutation of sentences of death by the Royal Prerogative, and the process of execution. It analyses eighteenth-century penal philosophy, emphasizing the contributions of reformers like Eden, Romilly and Bentham, and the various beginnings of the movement for reform of the criminal law. This latter theme is developed further with accounts of Romilly's campaign, the Committee of 1819, and the part played by Sir Robert Peel.

Extensive appendixes to the volume include a survey of capital statutes of the eighteenth century, the interpretation of certain capital statutes by the courts, the views of foreign observers, and some leading petitions for the reform of the criminal law.

Vol. 2: *The clash between private initiative and public interest in the enforcement of the law* (1956)

'The theme of this volume is the enforcement of the criminal law, as distinct from the reform of its substance, during the eighteenth and early nineteenth centuries. From a study of documents—proclamations, advertisements, offers of reward, Home Office correspondence—there emerges a system by which men hoped that the public peace might be preserved and offenders brought to justice, a system which was as ingenious as it was perplexing. It was largely inspired by the creed of *laissez-faire* and to an appreciable extent was worked by private initiative, principles which were so natural to the Englishman's way of life and thought. It was devised to appeal to the common motives "that govern the actions of mankind", whether honest citizen or rogue.'

Against a background of the climate of opinion about the law and its administration at the turn of the seventeenth century, Radzinowicz considers 'the various benefits which accrued to private individuals from the discovery and conviction of offences' which the state employed as its main weapon against public disorder and crime, particularly impunity for accomplices and a variety of rewards. He then discusses the centres of regular and incidental police. The many weaknesses in police services and new departures in the rôle and administration of police forces are described.

Ten appendixes offer extensive supporting illustrations and evidence.

Vol. 3: *Cross-currents in the movement for the reform of the police* (1956)

By the middle of the eighteenth century, says Radzinowicz in the Preface to this volume, 'there was already a growing realisation that the traditional arrangements for keeping the peace had become inadequate; but it was a further seventy-five years before a radical break was effected and a modern police established. Even then the reform was confined to London; and another quarter of a century had to pass before similar forces were operating over the whole kingdom. The recasting of the ancient civil power was not just a matter of the appointment of more and better constables but was regarded as potentially a grave constitutional issue likely to lead to exorbitance in the powers of the Crown and its ministers, with jeopardy to the chartered liberties of the subject.

In this volume the movement for reform is traced through a labyrinth of trial and error, advances and regressions, theoretical anticipations, curious alternative stratagems, and alarms which created a momentary readiness for change, only to give way suddenly to apathy and even hostility.'

The foundations of police reform, including the contributions of Henry and John Fielding and early legislation are described, together with the subsequent waning interest in the matter. Radzinowicz then discusses the movement for the reformation of manners, a cross-current in which the movement for reform of the police was caught up. The work of Patrick Colquhoun and his proposed measures for the control of crime are examined and an account is given of the changing pressures for reform, from the public concern which was stimulated by the celebrated Ratcliffe murders to the contrasting disinterest which followed. The views of Blackstone, Adam Smith, Paley, Beccaria, and von Humboldt are compared with those of Bentham and his doctrine of police. Finally, an account is given of Chadwick's conception of a preventive police force.

Eight appendixes provide further extensive supporting materials.

Vol. 4: *Grappling for control* (1968)

'The present volume follows through to their culminating points two protracted campaigns, on one side for the reform of the capital laws, on the other for the establishment of regular police.

At the end of the eighteenth century the capital code overshadowed the whole of criminal law. By 1861, for all practical purposes, the only offence to carry the death penalty was murder. At the end of the eighteenth century the enforcement of the law still depended upon the unpaid parish constable and the offer of rewards, and the quelling of riots upon the intervention of the armed forces. By 1861 the country was covered by a network of professional police charged with the prevention of crime, the detection of offenders and the maintenance of order. Systematic enforcement of the law had replaced suspended terror as the accepted basis of control.

Earlier volumes have already shown that the movement towards this conclusion was neither swift nor smooth. Tradition, inertia, local jealousies, class distrust, fear of expense and fear of tyranny all contributed to evasions and delays. Yet the poor might engulf the country in a tide of disorder and crime, so the search continued for more acceptable expedients. Charity and relief could be used not merely to placate but to coerce the poor; the army and the yeomanry could be called in to keep them down; undesirables could be spirited out of the country by impressment. Of all such expedients the most far-reaching was transportation. So much has been written about it of late that it has not been examined in detail here. What does emerge is that its existence made it easier to relinquish reliance on the death penalty and its withdrawal clinched the argument for a general system of police.'

—— *In search of criminology* (London: Heinemann Educational Books, 1961).

A critical survey of the evolution of thought, ideas, education and research in criminology in Western Europe and the United States. The discussion focuses on the major figures and the leading centres of study in Italy, Austria, Germany, France, Belgium, Holland, Denmark, Norway and the U.S.A. Radzinowicz concludes with a summary of trends and a series of propositions about criminological research and teaching. (Translated into Italian, French and Spanish.)

—— *The need for criminology* (London: Heinemann Educational Books, 1965).

'Its central purpose is to make a survey and to suggest how the City of New York "could marshal its resources to provide new knowledge, and a better mechanism for continuing improvements in criminal justice".' Included are surveys of past and present work in criminology in the United States, particularly in New York, a debate on the ways of stimulating criminological study and research in New York, and a description of the organisation and workings of the Cambrian Institute of Criminology.

—— *Ideology and crime* (London: Heinemann Educational Books, 1966).

A broad perspective on changing attitudes to crime, criminal law and procedure, and penal practice over the last two centuries. The liberal humanist thinkers are contrasted with their nineteenth-century successors, the determinists. The developments of twentieth-century criminology are analysed in an attempt to achieve a more pragmatic approach in establishing first 'who are the criminals and what makes them so' and secondly 'ways of dealing with them'. (Translated into Italian.)

—— and Wolfgang, M. E. (eds.), *Crime and justice* (New York: Basic Books, 1971), 3 vols.
A large-scale collection of extracts and essays in three volumes:

Vol. 1: *The criminal in society* '. . . sets the scene. It raises questions about the nature of deviance, of which crime is often regarded as only one aspect; about the proper scope of the criminal law; about the true shape and trends of crime; about social disharmonies that may be responsible for crime in general and for juvenile delinquency in particular.'
Vol 2: *The criminal in the arms of the law* '. . . looks at the enforcement of criminal justice. It weighs the evidence relative to how far the actual performance of the police or of the courts defeats their stated ends, how far they discriminate against certain classes, how far they threaten the liberties they are designed to protect, and how far they themselves are in need of fundamental re-appraisal.'
Vol. 3: *The criminal in confinement* '. . . explores the correctional system not in terms of its official objectives but of its actual effects and effectiveness. It analyses, for example, the unintended consequences of imprisonment. It challenges over-simplified assumptions about the results of probation or parole supervision. It examines critically some of the outstanding correctional experiments of recent years. And it also examines critically the experimental methods and statistical tools of criminology itself.'

B. ESSAYS, PUBLIC LECTURES, EDITORIAL NOTES AND NEWSPAPER ARTICLES

—— 'A note on methods of establishing the connexion between economic conditions and crime', *The Sociological Review*, 1939, vol. 31, no. 3.

A discussion of difficulties involved in establishing workable concepts of 'economic situation' and 'criminality' which preface Radzinowicz's study of economic conditions and crime in Poland (q.v.).

—— 'The after conduct of convicted offenders in England', *Canadian Bar Review*, 1939, vol. 17, no. 8, pp. 558–78. A rewritten version of this paper will be found under the title 'The after conduct of discharged offenders' in Radzinowicz and Turner (eds.), *The modern approach to criminal law*, pp. 142–61 (volume 4 of the *English Studies in Criminal Science*, 1945).

A follow-up study of adult prisoners and borstal boys.

—— 'The evolution of the modern English prison system', *Modern Law Review*, 1939, vol. 3, no. 2, pp. 121–35. A rewritten version of this paper called 'English prison system', appears in Radzinowicz and Turner (eds.), *The modern approach to criminal law*, pp. 123–41.

The English prison system has developed through three phases, culminating in a reformist approach. Various reasons are given to suggest why a reformative prison system is likely to be adopted successfully in England. The ways in which the prison system of the thirties was being transformed are described, and, in particular, the advances being made in the classification of prisoners are outlined.

—— 'The persistent offender', *Cambridge Law Journal*, 1939, vol. 7, no. 1, pp. 68–79. A rewritten version of this paper is also to be found in Radzinowicz and Turner (eds.), *The modern approach to criminal law*, pp. 162–73.

A critical comparative analysis of the measures adopted in England and other European countries for the control of persistent offenders.

—— 'The present trend of English penal policy', *Law Quarterly Review*, 1939, vol. 55, no. 218, pp. 273–88. A rewritten version of this paper appears as 'The assessment of punishments by English courts' in Radzinowicz and Turner (eds.), *The modern approach to criminal law*, pp. 110–22.

An analysis of changes in penal policy in England during the first part of the present century, with an assessment of their significance.

—— 'English criminal statistics. A critical analysis', *Law Quarterly Review*, 1940, vol. 56, no. 224, pp. 483–503. A slightly amended version of this essay also appears in Radzinowicz and Turner (eds.), *The modern approach to criminal law*, pp. 174–94.

An assessment of 'the real value of English criminal statistics as a source of information', including problems of reporting and recording, the influence of criminal law and procedure, and difficulties in interpreting criminal statistics.

—— and Turner, J. W. C., 'The language of criminal science', *Cambridge Law Journal*, 1940, vol. 7, pp. 224–37. This essay also appears as 'The meaning and scope of criminal science', in Radzinowicz and Turner (eds.), *The modern approach to criminal law*, pp. 12–26.

An analysis of the development and usage of the vocabulary of criminal science, followed by a statement of the tasks and main purpose of criminal science. Three branches of criminal science are identified: criminology, criminal policy and criminal law.

—— 'The influence of economic conditions on crime—I', *The Sociological Review*, 1941, vol. 33, no. 1, pp. 1–36; 'The influence of economic conditions on crime—II', ibid. no. 2, pp. 139–53.

A study of the relationships between indices of criminal behaviour and economic conditions in Poland from 1928 to 1934, a period which covers the peak of prosperity and the trough of depression.

—— and Turner, J. W. C., 'Conviction and probation', *Canadian Bar Review*, 1941, vol. 19, no. 7, pp. 500–7. This essay is reprinted in the English Studies in Criminal Science pamphlet series.

An Introductory Note reviewing the development of probation in England and the arguments for changes in it proposed in the Criminal Justice Bill of 1938.

—— 'International collaboration in criminal science', *Law Quarterly Review*, 1942, vol. 58, no. 229, pp. 110–39. A slightly amended version of this essay also appears in the *University of Toronto Law Journal*, vol. 4, no. 2, pp. 307–37 and in Radzinowicz and Turner (eds.), *The modern approach to criminal law*, pp. 467–97.

The similarities in problems of criminal policy and the principles adopted by different countries are illustrated by reference to England and Poland. The benefits to be obtained by collaboration between researchers lead to a suggestion for the establishment of an International Commission for collaboration in penal reconstruction.

—— and Turner, J. W. C., 'International Commission for penal reconstruction and development', *Canadian Bar Review*, 1942, vol. 20, no. 6, pp. 503–4. Reprinted in the English Studies in Criminal Science pamphlet series.

An Introductory Note.

—— and Turner, J. W. C., 'A study on punishment', *Canadian Bar Review*, 1943, vol. 21, no. 2, pp. 91–101. This essay is reprinted in the English Studies in Criminal Science pamphlet series, and further reprinted under the title 'Punishment; outline of developments since the 18th century' in Radzinowicz and Turner (eds.), *The modern approach to criminal law*, pp. 39–50.

An Introductory Essay outlining the broad development in penal philosophy and policy in England.

—— 'Some sources of modern English criminal legislation', *Cambridge Law Journal*, 1943, vol. 8, no. 2, pp. 180–94.

'A preliminary report on the Blue Books and Parliamentary Debates for the period 1760–1940.'

—— and Turner, J. W. C., Editorial note to *Mental abnormality and crime* (London: Macmillan, 1944), pp. viii–xxiv.

The evolution of *mens rea* and the legal concept of mental abnormality is discussed, followed by a critical assessment of the present law relating to the mental element in criminal responsibility and the means of dealing with mentally abnormal individuals.

—— 'Lombroso', *The Saturday Book* (London: Hutchinson, 1945), pp. 103–8.

A brief discussion of the precursors, work and achievements of Cesare Lombroso.

—— 'Present trends of English criminal policy: an attempt at interpretation', in Radzinowicz and Turner (eds.), *The modern approach to criminal law*, pp. 27–38.

The development of penal policy in England is outlined and an analysis of the outstanding features of English penal legislation and practice is contrasted with the authoritarian conception of criminal policy in force in Nazi Germany.

—— and Turner, J. W. C., 'The social problem group', *Canadian Bar Review*, 1945, vol. 23, no. 3, pp. 177–81. Reprinted in the English Studies in Criminal Science pamphlet series.

An Editorial Note.

—— 'The Waltham Black Act: a study of the legislative attitude towards crime in the eighteenth century', *Cambridge Law Journal*, 1945, vol. 9, no. 1.

An article based on a chapter of Volume 1 of the *History of English criminal law* (q.v.).

—— 'An early stage in the movement for the reform of criminal law', *Law Quarterly Review*, 1947, vol. 63, no. 249, pp. 94–111.

'The Committee of 1770 and an attempt to set up a Commission of Inquiry in 1787.' An article which forms a chapter of Volume 1 of the *History of English criminal law* (q.v.).

—— 'The Criminal Justice Act, 1948', *Studi in memoria di Arturo Rocco* (Milan, Juffre, 1952), vol. 2, pp. 405–18.

The place of the 1948 Act in the development of English penal policy and a brief discussion of its most important provisions.

—— 'First steps towards government control over police before Peel', *Law Quarterly Review*, 1954, vol. 70, no. 277, pp. 88–108.

An article which forms a chapter of Volume 2 of the *History of English criminal law* (q.v.).

—— 'The Ratcliffe murders', *Cambridge Law Journal*, April 1956, vol. 14, pp. 39–66.

An article which forms a chapter of Volume 3 of the *History of English criminal law* (q.v.).

—— Preface to *Sexual offences. A report of the Cambridge Department of Criminal Science* (London: Macmillan, 1957), pp. xiii–xxvii.

A general discussion of some of the problems involved in carrying out research on sexual offences and a description of the major findings of the survey.

—— *Sir James Fitzjames Stephen 1829–1894 and his contribution to the development of criminal law* (London: Bernard Quaritch, 1957). The Selden Society Lecture.

A broad appraisal of character, career, writings and achievements. Stephen is described as a man, a lawyer, an historian of the criminal law and as a judge. An extensive bibliography of Stephen's writings is appended.

—— *Changing attitudes towards crime and the devices used to combat it* (Lecture to the Royal Institution of Great Britain, delivered on 28 February 1958).

A general account of changes in penal philosophy and the differing approaches to penal policy and crime control since the end of the eighteenth century. Radzinowicz traces the emergence of the police, the use of the army as a means of social control, the eras of capital punishment and transportation, the development of the prison system and the contribution of the Gladstone Committee. Contrasts are drawn between the penal system in the fifties and earlier practices.

—— Preface to *The results of probation. A report of the Cambridge Department of Criminal Science* (London: Macmillan, 1958), pp. x–xvi.

The origins and development of the probation system in England are briefly reviewed.

—— 'Changing attitudes towards crime and punishment', *Law Quarterly Review*, 1959, vol. 75, no. 299.

'The substance of a Friday Discourse delivered at the Royal Institution of Great Britain' published as *Changing attitudes towards crime and the devices used to combat it* (q.v.).

—— Ancel, M. and Radzinowicz, L. (eds.), *Introduction au droit criminel de l'Angleterre* (Paris: Les Editions de l'Epargne, 1959), with an Introduction by Leon Radzinowicz (in French).

—— 'Criminal law, criminology and forensic science', *Medicine, Science and the Law*, 1960, vol. 1, no. 1, pp. 7–15.

A brief discourse on the nature, development and scope of the three areas of study.

—— 'Criminological and penological research'. Address to the Second United Nations Congress on Prevention of Crime and Treatment of Offenders (London, 1960).

—— and McClintock, F. H., 'Robbery in London', *The Economist*, 26 November 1960, vol. 197, no. 6118, pp. 860–1.

A brief survey of the extent and trends of robbery in London suggesting that though robberies and attacks by individuals appeared to have stopped rising since 1957, organised gang robberies were still on the increase. Far too many robbers were still escaping punishment, but at the same time commonly held views about the incidence and gravity of robbery were grossly exaggerated.

—— 'New departures in maintaining public order in the face of Chartist disturbances', *Cambridge Law Journal*, April 1961, vol. 18, pp. 51–80.

An article based on a chapter of Volume 4 of the *History of English criminal law* (q.v.).

—— Preface to McClintock, F. H. and Gibson, E., *Robbery in London. An enquiry by the Cambridge Institute of Criminology* (London: Macmillan, 1961), pp. vii–xix.

A general survey which takes in the approach of the study and its main findings.

—— 'Public opinion and crime', *Medicine, Science and the Law*, 1961, vol. 2, no. 1, pp. 24–32.

A survey of 'the national scene, with reference to recent developments in crime and even more to recent changes in that climate of public opinion in which we all work'.

—— 'The study of criminology in Cambridge', *The Medico-Legal Journal*, 1961, vol. 29, pp. 122–33.

An account of 'what has been achieved and of what is being planned for the immediate future, together with some assessment of problems important to the continued development of the Institute'.

—— Introduction to Webb, S. and B., *English prisons under local government* (London: Longmans, new edition published by Cass reprinted in 1963), n.p.

General remarks on the changing place of imprisonment in penal policy.

—— 'Problem of counting criminals', *The Times*, 12 August 1963.

A critique of English criminal statistics written following the appointment of the Departmental Committee on Criminal Statistics.

—— Report on problems of administration and organisation of criminological research, given to the First European Conference of Directors of Criminological Research Institutes, Strasbourg, 9–12 December 1963, pp. 5–13.

A discussion on how best to carry out criminological research, what characteristics a research institute ought to possess, its most suitable teaching and research aims, and the place of an institute of criminology in legal and social studies.

—— 'Cesare Beccaria and the English system of criminal justice: a reciprocal relationship', *Estratto dagli Atti del Convegno Internazionale su Cesare Beccaria* (*Turin*, n.d. [1964]), pp. 57–66. This essay also appears in Italian as 'Cesare Beccaria e il sistema Inglese', *La Scuola Positiva*, 1964, pp. 553–64.

An outline of Beccaria's achievements and his influence on Bentham, Blackstone, and Romilly, and through them on the development of English criminal and penal law.

—— *Criminology and the climate of social responsibility* (Cambridge: Heffer, 1964). An address to the Howard League for Penal Reform, 7 May 1964.

The 'expansion of achievement and ideas' in English penology is discussed, including legislative changes, the development of research in criminology and the announcement of the appointment of the Royal Commission on the Penal System. Radzinowicz concludes by proposing six practical measures to enhance the traditional procedure of the Royal Commission.

—— Report on the work of the Second Conference of Directors of Criminological Research Institutes, Strasbourg, 26–28 November 1964, pp. 139–50.

An historical perspective prefaces critical comments on papers by Houchon, Christie, and Hood.

—— 'Sentencing policy in criminal cases', *The Times*, 30 May 1964.

The development of the interest of the judiciary in sentencing and a suggestion that judicial conferences be organised to counteract the limitations imposed by judicial isolation.

—— 'The criminal in society', *The Journal of the Royal Society of Arts*, 1964, vol. 112, no. 5100, pp. 916–29. The Peter Le Neve Foster Lecture. The Lecture is reprinted in *The Irish Law Times*, vol. 99, nos. 5115–20 and is also reproduced in amended form as 'The criminal in society: hidden challenge and significance of the "dark figure"' in the *Security Gazette*, July 1964, pp. 249, 251.

A discussion of the dimensions of crime and some of the implications of hidden delinquency.

—— 'Ideology and crime: the deterministic position', *Columbia Law Review*, 1965, vol. 65, no. 6, pp. 1047–60.

An abridged version of one of the series of James S. Carpentier Lectures, subsequently published as part of *Ideology and crime* (q.v.). It describes the contributions made by the early positivists, including Quetelet, Guerry, Mayhew, Bonger, Lombroso and Ferri, and concludes with an assessment of their significance.

—— 'Economic pressures' in Radzinowicz and Wolfgang (eds.), *Crime and justice*, vol. 1, *The Criminal in society*, pp. 420–42. This is a reprint of a paper presented to the National Commission on the Causes and Prevention of Violence, with the title 'Economic conditions and crime' (1968).

The discussion treats three approaches to the relationship between economic conditions and crime. First, the view of crime as an inevitable consequence of the capitalist system is considered with an analysis of Bonger's Marxist interpretation. The second approach encompasses efforts to outline 'the extent to which economic factors—much more narrowly defined—can be regarded as among the very many contributory causes of certain types of crime'. Problems relating to indices of crime and economic situations are also discussed. Thirdly, the question of crime as part of the general economic activity in an expanding society is addressed. Finally, some common fallacies in the connection between economic conditions and crime are pointed out.

—— Evidence given before the U.S. Senate Judiciary Committee, Subcommittee on Criminal Laws and Procedures, March 1968 (on capital punishment).

—— 'Impressment into the army and the navy—a rough and ready instrument of preventive police and criminal justice', in Wolfgang, M. E. (ed.) *Crime and culture. Essays in honor of Thorsten Sellin* (New York: Wiley, 1968), pp. 287–313.

Part of Volume 4 of the *History of criminal law* (q.v.).

—— 'The dangerous offender', *Police Journal*, 1968, vol. 41, no. 9, pp. 411–47. The fourth Frank Newsam Memorial Lecture, given at the Police College, Bramshill, 1 August 1968.

A lengthy public lecture which considers the potentially dangerous groups within society and the dangerous types of offender. Radzinowicz then seeks to identify the 'growing points' of danger. The problems of control, detection and conviction are discussed, followed by suggestions as to how the penal system should deal with dangerous offenders.

—— 'Hanging: has abolition worked?' *Sunday Times*, 21 September 1969.

Radzinowicz considers arguments for and against capital punishment, presenting an analysis of murder and manslaughter statistics since 1961, and bringing to light difficulties in their interpretation. He concludes that to test the assumed deterrent effectiveness of capital punishment it would need to be reintroduced on a wider scale. But 'if we are not prepared for the full dosage—and no sensitive society should be— then we would be best advised to forget the whole thing'.

—— 'A foreseeable failure', *Sunday Times*, 24 January 1971.

Radzinowicz argues that the failure of the suspended sentence was 'not altogether surprising'. Its introduction in a country with a highly developed probation system, like Britain, may be retrogressive; secondly, assumptions about its deterrent effectiveness are unproven.

—— 'Some current problems and future prospects of international collaboration in penal matters', in Buhl, J. P., Christensen, B., Christiansen, K. O., von Eyben, W. E., Le Maire, L. & Naaben, K. (eds.), *Liber amicorum in honour of Professor Stephan Hurwitz LL.D.* (København: Juristforbundets Forlag, 1971), pp. 387–406.

The substance of a speech made at the conclusion of the Fourth United Nations Congress on the Prevention of Crime and the Treatment of Offenders, Kyoto, Japan, 1970. Suggestions for the adoption of the Standard Minimum Rules for the treatment of prisoners are followed by critical observations on the participation of the public in crime prevention and control and on criminological research. Radzinowicz then proposes 'the building of genuine links and reliable bridges between social planning and social defence', and concludes with comments on future prospects for research and policy on an international scale. (Also reproduced in the *Revue de science criminelle et de Droit pénal comparé* and *scuola positiva*.)

—— 'The police: is the get-tough school right?', *Sunday Times*, 29 August 1971.

An attack on the 'web of factual misconceptions, misplaced nostalgia and wishful thinking' of those who call for sterner measures in administering the criminal law and penal system.

—— 'The vision of Ramsey Clark', *Virginia Quarterly Review*, 1971, vol. 71, no. 3, pp. 459–64.

An extended review of Clark's book *Crime in America*.

—— 'The criminal law explosion—can it be controlled?' *Columbia Journal of Law and Social Problems*, 1972, vol. 9, no. 1, pp. 88–130.

'Recent years have seen a great increase in crime and lawlessness. This phenomenon, which has affected virtually every aspect of contemporary life, raises major questions regarding the continued capacity of the criminal law and its instrumentalities—the police, the courts, and the correctional agencies to exercise effective controls. It also raises major questions on the functions of our institutions generally, and on the measures that should be taken to improve them. In searching for effective means of asserting greater control there must be some awareness of the danger that some of the measures traditionally recommended may exacerbate rather than alleviate the difficulties we confront.'

A public address on the 'Them and us' theme (q.v.) followed by critical comments from H. S. H. Edgar, P. A. Lacovara and H. R. Uviller, and questions from the audience.

—— 'Them and us', *Cambridge Law Journal*, 1972, vol. 30, no. 2, pp. 260–79. A lecture given under the auspices of The New Bridge at the Mansion House, 26 April 1972.

General observations on trends in the nature and extent of crime throughout the world preface a consideration of social explanations and the importance of opportunity to commit crime and to get away with it. Radzinowicz then assesses deterrence and the conditions in which general deterrence may operate. Brief, critical appraisals of imprisonment and alternatives to imprisonment are made, followed by problems in the administration of justice and a warning against attempts to tamper with the procedural protections of the accused.

See also 'The criminal law explosion—can it be controlled?' (above).

Leon Radzinowicz

Born: 15 August 1906.
Educated: Paris, 1924–5; Licencie en Droit, Geneva, 1927; Doctor of Law (cum maxima laude) and Diploma of the Institute of Criminology, Rome, 1928; Doctor of Law, Cracow, 1929.
Assistant Professor, University of Geneva, 1928–31.
Enquired into and published a report on working of the penal system in Belgium, 1930.
Made Chevalier de l'Ordre de Leopold, 1930.
Assistant Professor, Free University of Warsaw, 1932–6.
Visiting Lecturer, Universities of Paris, Brussels, and Strasbourg.
Came to England in 1937 on behalf of the Polish Ministry of Justice to report on the English penal system.
Assistant Director of Research, University of Cambridge, 1946–9.
Director, Department of Criminal Science, Faculty of Law, University of Cambridge, 1949–59.
M.A., Cantab., 1949; LL.D., Cambridge, 1951.
First Head of Social Defence Section, United Nations, New York, 1947–8.
Publication of Vol. I of the *History of English Criminal Law* (under the auspices of the Pilgrim Trust), 1948.
Fellow of Trinity College, Cambridge, since 1948.
Member of the Royal Commission on Capital Punishment, 1949–53.
James Barr Ames Prize and Medal, Faculty of Harvard Law School, 1950.
Coronation Medal, 1953.
Member Advisory Council on the Treatment of Offenders, Home Office, 1950–63.
First Wolfson Professor of Criminology, University of Cambridge, 1959–73; First Director of the Institute of Criminology, Cambridge, 1960–72.
Studied and reported on the state of criminology in Europe and the United States, 1960–1.
Member of the Royal Commission on the Penal System in England and Wales, 1964–6.
Member Advisory Council on the Penal System, Home Office, 1966–74.
Chairman Sub-Committee on Maximum Security in Prisons, 1967–8.
Walter E. Meyer Research Professor of Law, Yale Law School, 1962–3.
Fellow Silliman College, Yale, since 1966.
First President British Academy of Forensic Sciences, 1960–1.
First Chairman of the Criminological Council of the Council of Europe, Strasbourg, 1963–70.
Enquired into and reported on the research and teaching of criminology in the United States under the auspices of the Ford Foundation and the Bar Association of the City of New York, 1964–5.
Consultant to the President's National Commission on Violence, Washington, 1968–9.
Lionel Cohen Lecturer, University of Jerusalem and other Centres, 1969.
Visiting Lecturer in Consultation with Criminological Centres in Denmark and Norway, 1963; Yugoslavia, 1964; Buenos Aires and Mendoza, 1969–70; South Africa, 1972.
Hon. LL.D. Leicester, 1965.
Carpentier Lecturer, Columbia Law School, 1965.
Adjunct Professor of Criminal Law and Criminology, Columbia Law School, from 1964.
Visiting Professor of the Virginia Law School from 1968.
Distinguished Visiting Professor, Rutgers University, from 1970.
Visiting Professor, Department of Sociology, University of Pennsylvania, 1970–4.
Consultant to the Minister of Justice, N.S.W., and the National Institute of Criminology, Canberra, 1973.
Knighted 1970.
Elected Fellow of British Academy, 1973; Hon. Foreign Member of American Academy of Arts and Sciences, 1973; Hon. Foreign Member of Australian Academy of Forensic Sciences, 1973.
Publications: Selden Society Lecture on Sir James Fitzjames Stephen, 1957; *In Search of Criminology*, 1961; *The Need for Criminology*, 1965; *Ideology and Crime*, 1966; *The Dangerous Offender* (Frank Newsam Memorial Lecture), 1968; publication of Volumes I, II, III and IV of the *History of English Criminal Law* (1948, 1956 and 1968) under the auspices of the Pilgrim Trust and the Rockefeller Foundation; *Crime and Justice* (edited with Professor M. E. Wolfgang), 3 vols., 1971; co-editor and editor, Cambridge Studies in Criminology, 1940–, 33 vols.

INDEX

In this index references will be found to subjects and authors treated in both text and footnotes; purely bibliographical material is not indexed.